The Unauthorized Encyclopedia of
Corgi Toys

4880 Lower Valley Road, Atglen, PA 19310 USA

Bill Manzke

For Maggie

Corgi Toys, Corgi Majors, Corgi Classics, Husky Toys, Corgi
Juniors, Whizzwheels, Corgi Rockets, Cameos, The Original
Omnibus Co., and the names of various features which appear
on the models produced are trademarks of Mettoy Ltd. PLC and/
or its successors Corgi Toys Ltd. and Corgi Classics Ltd., Hot
Wheels, Auto-City, and Holiday Hot Wheels are trademarks of
Mattel Inc. The names and external appearance of the prototypes for the various models produced that appear in this book
are the trademarks of the manufacturers of the original vehicles
as licensed to Mettoy Ltd. PLC, its successors, or Mattel Inc.
Photographs of models appearing in this book which are not part
of the author's collection are used with the permission of the
owners of the models and/or photographers.

Copyright © 1997 by Bill Manzke
Library of Congress Catalog Card Number: 97-67194

Designed by Bonnie M. Hensley

ISBN: 0-7643-0308-2
Printed in China
1 2 3 4

Published by Schiffer Publishing Ltd.
4880 Lower Valley Road
Atglen, PA 19310
Phone: (610) 593-1777; Fax: (610) 593-2002
E-mail: schifferbk@aol.com
Please write for a free catalog.
This book may be purchased from the publisher.
Please include $3.95 for shipping.
Try your bookstore first.

We are interested in hearing from authors
with book ideas on related subjects.

Table of Contents

Acknowledgments

The list of people who helped create this book is indeed large. While I hope that each of you is listed and credited here, there is a chance that I missed someone. If you were missed, my sincere apologies, as my system of note taking can be chaotic!

I would like to thank Dr. Ed Force for his kind permission allowing us to include and expand upon the variation listing first published in his book, *Corgi Toys*. I hope our works are complementary to each other. Thanks also go to Peter Schiffer at Schiffer Publishing Ltd,. who helped guide the initial development of the book.

I would like to thank Colin Hill and Julia Southwick of Corgi Classics Ltd., Susan Pownall of the Corgi Collector Club, Kerstin Chalupa of Reeves International, James Segil of Mattel Inc., and Lucy Coudert of F.A.O. Schwarz for loaning photos and/or providing reference materials for use in the book. I would also like to thank Yvonne Park of Eddie Stobart Ltd. for providing information concerning models produced for that company, and Carole of HSS Hire Service Group PLC and Simon Berry of Berry Bros. & Rudd Ltd., London, for providing examples of the promotional Corgi vehicles made for their firms. Thanks also to Aaron Bryant of Cord Camera for his help with photography techniques and equipment selection.

Many people who contributed information and materials asked to remain anonymous. Sources were contacted in person and via internet correspondence. I would like to thank the following people for their invaluable help: Steve Ryan, Alex Lakhtman, Michael Hylton, Chris Potter, Andy Pena, Munish Madan, Karen Preece, Gary Hirst, Frank Wright, Bob Porcja, Derk Riesthuis, Henk van Brakel, John M. Dean, Dana Johnson, John Eio, Tony Howden, Tom Hammel, Ian Cousins, Wilf Bainbridge, and George Taylor. Thanks also to those of you who responded with information using the *Variation Report Form* in Ed Force's earlier book *Corgi Toys*.

A special note of gratitude is extended to Helen Colborn, who entered mountains of data into the computer, and who has the patience of a saint.

Finally, and most importantly, I wish to truly thank my wife, Maggie, who not only put-up with the rantings of her husband during the creation of this book, but also rolled up her sleeves and pitched in when help was needed. Her help, both in assisting me with this book and in creating a nurturing and loving environment for our family is more valuable than any words could ever say.

Bill Manzke

Foreword

In the early planning stages, I set out to make *The Unauthorized Encyclopedia of Corgi Toys* a book that was different in content and viewpoint than anything else in print on the subject. The other books available are either chronological histories of Corgi's original parent company, Mettoy, model-by-model catalogs of each item produced, or highly focused works in one specific Corgi range. These formats are fine for their purposes, and most are well-done works. However, those formats prevent a more detailed study of what Corgi Toys are really like. That gap is exactly what I hope to fill with this book.

My own involvement with Corgi Toys began in 1964 with a present of three cars from my grandmother. Those three cars are still in my collection, although one is pretty banged-up, along with many brethren. My passion for Corgi Toys continued unbroken into adulthood, although at times it had to be pursued covertly. Society's acceptance of adults who collect toys is a recent phenomenon. I am a collector, not a dealer, of Corgi Toys and Husky Toys. Others may be interested in speculating on the future value of their collections. I'm in the hobby for the joy of it, and would still collect Corgi if their value was negligible.

In researching this book, I tried to make use of any resource available. This includes obtaining data from the Internet. To my knowledge, this is the first book on the subject to do so. The Internet has opened a fabulous new world for collectors. Not only can you find items for sale, you can also converse with collectors halfway around the world. There are active discussions taking place on almost any topic, and diecast toy collecting is one of the more popular subjects. The number of on-line resources grows daily, and the quantity of information available can be staggering.

The models and related items shown in this book are from a number of collections. You will notice that not every model pictured in this book is in pristine "mint-in-mint-box" condition. This stems from a rational philosophy about collecting. Let's face it. Not many collectors have unlimited funds to enlarge their collection, or unlimited time to seek-out new pieces. (The author definitely falls into this category!). Those collectors fortunate enough to be able to purchase only pristine models have wonderful collections, and have made major investments to obtain them. The competition for available pieces at this level tends to be intense. A mint/boxed item may sell for double of that which a mint duplicate will fetch without a box. Recently, the condition of the box and packaging materials has begun to affect values as well, with phrases like "mint-in-mint-box" coming into usage. This style of collecting is simply beyond the means of the average collector.

A more rational approach for most collectors is to continuously upgrade. It can be summed-up in the statement: "Condition only matters if I already have one." There are many rare items available on the market that are in less than mint condition. They usually sell for a fraction of the cost of a "MIMB" model. Of course, every collector's preference (and budget) are different. Usually the rarest models are still collectible in much worse condition than more common models. In some cases, a rare model may no longer exist except in chipped or well-played-with form. In one case, the author purchased the first piece that could be found of a Corgi produced in 1966, purchasing it in 1996!

The author's first Corgi Toys.

This also brings up the subject of restorations. As an antique car owner, the subject of restoration is a familiar one. However, when it comes to Corgi Toys, it is a topic where honesty is mandatory to prevent abuse. Restored Corgi Toys are only replicas of what they used to be. Unlike restored antique cars, though, it is sometimes difficult to spot a restoration from an original Corgi Toy. The potential for abuse may be too much for some, so let the buyer beware. For example, there are more 1969 Firebird Trans-Am's today than were actually built new!

This book emphasizes features between different but similar models. Where possible, this book presents photos of model variations not shown in other books on the subject. Often, verbal descriptions cannot fully convey the differences in two similar models. The old adage "A picture is worth a thousand words" applies. In this case, there are hundreds of thousands of words expressed by the models pictured in this book.

There may be some surprises, too, since many of you may have undiscovered variations sitting in your own collections. Every variation known from the literature available at press time for this book has been included in the variation listings. If you do find that you have discovered an item not described in the book, *please* use the report form at the back of the book to share your find. If you have access to e-mail, you may send your discovery to me at *manzke.madhouse@mci2000.com*. The tables used in this book are organized on a computer, and will be continuously kept as up-to-date as possible by the author.

So, sit back with *The Encyclopedia of Corgi Toys* and enter the world of the Corgi Toy enthusiast. Whether you collect models or just remember them fondly from your childhood, Corgi Toys are a source of continuing joy to everyone whose lives they touch.

Bill Manzke

A group of post-Mettoy Corgi models.

Section 1: History

1.1—Beginnings

Corgi Toys were launched into a marketplace very different than today's. In the mid-1950s, there were no diecast toy magazines, no limited collectors editions, no collectible toy market at all. Toys were, well, toys. Their sole market was to the children of the era. Adults merely tried to purchase whatever children desired at the time. At that time, the market for diecast toy cars in Britain was dominated by Dinky Toys, though other competitors had begun to appear. In the United States, the force in diecast toy cars was Tootsietoy. Both Dinky and Tootsietoy had long histories in their respective markets, and could count on name recognition from parents when they made purchases for children.

In the early 1950s, Dinky made a concerted run at the American market. Models of American vehicles were actively promoted in better stores. Tootsietoy reacted with a short-lived effort to upgrade some existing models with lithographed tin base plates. These were mainly 6-inch models of contemporary American sedans. Dinky, though, had a superior-quality product and solidified its foothold on the American market. Tootsietoy quickly refocused its product offerings and retreated from the high end. Interestingly, Tootsietoy's lithographed tin bases were superior to Dinky's in some ways, but their inferior body casting details and two-piece die technology could not compete with Dinky's products. The market for diecast toy cars in America was split into premium quality vehicles offered by Dinky in better stores, and budget-priced, simplified vehicles dominated by Tootsietoy. Dinky would remain the leader in its market segment until the explosive appearance of Corgi Toys on the American scene, but I'm getting ahead of the story.

Corgi Toys were the creation of the Mettoy Co. Ltd. in Britain. Mettoy was formed in the depression year of 1933 by Philipp Ullmann, a German immigrant who had gained experience in the toy industry there. For many years, Mettoy developed and manufactured a wide variety of tin lithographed toys including cars, trucks, airplanes, and trains. By the early 1950s, they were a major player in the British tin lithographed toy market. However, the toy market of that time was beginning to move away from stamped tin toys as children became interested in the more detailed diecast toys and low-priced plastic toys became available. Mettoy realized this and set out to obtain the expertise to enter the diecast toy field. Their first efforts, introduced in 1948, were simple, somewhat bulky castings of vehicles based on British prototypes of the era. Many were fitted with friction motors, a holdover from the tin lithographed toys. In the early 1950s, these toys were re-christened Castoys. These toys, as well as Mettoy's tin toys, were not actively marketed in the United States. The Castoys line was offered through 1959, overlapping the production of Corgi Toys by four years. Mettoy also produced some other diecast products of various sizes, although not in an organized series as were Corgi Toys. Most notably, a promotional beverage truck was produced exclusively for CWS Soft Drinks, now considered a direct ancestor of Corgi Toys, as will be seen later.

Mettoy continued producing other toy products after the introduction of Corgi Toys. Some of their many products included tin lithographed doll houses, plastic sports figures, musical toys, and toys for smaller children. Mettoy also represented Fisher-Price in the British market for a time. The effect of these other product lines on the fortunes of Mettoy would lead to the eventual downfall of the company.

A Dinky Toys 1948 Plymouth showing the state of the art in the early 1950s.

This Tootsietoy Packard from the mid-'50s could be had for a time with a tin lithographed base.

This early Mettoy car can be considered an ancestor to the first Corgi Toys. *(Photo By Michael Hylton & Chris Potter)*

Another view of the Mettoy Rolls-Royce. *(Photo By Michael Hylton & Chris Potter)*

Fortunately, no Corgi ever had a wind-up key like this! *(Photo By Michael Hylton & Chris Potter)*

This Mettoy coach is in near-mint condition.

Red seats were included in the coach.

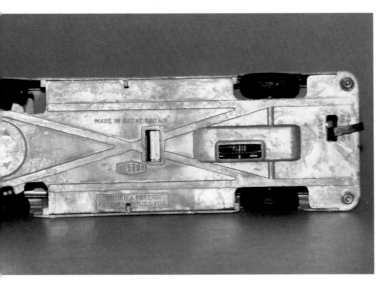

The base of the coach with its steering and motor control.

1.2—The Late Fifties:

The New Kids in Town

Corgi Toys were born, if you will, in 1956. Mettoy, long a player on the British toy market, saw an opportunity in the emerging diecast toy car segment, then dominated by Dinky Toys. Dinky had grown complacent in their market leader position, and lacked the innovation they would soon learn was needed to stay on top. As is common in business, Dinky created the market for high quality diecast toy vehicles only to lose it to a more innovative competitor. Mettoy's Corgi Toys would be Dinky's ultimate undoing.

Corgi Toys burst onto the market in Britain with a media campaign not unlike the toy ads seen today. In a blitz campaign, Mettoy introduced a complete range of diecast cars and trucks all fitted with windows. At that time, windows were a new innovation in diecast toys, and created quite a demand among young boys. The slogan "The Ones with Windows" would be the Corgi Toys catch phrase throughout the late '50s. Market leader Dinky would be slow to react to this challenge, not introducing its first model with windows until 1958. Mettoy had the edge, and sales growth was explosive. Most of the new Corgi Toys were based on British prototypes recognizable to British boys. Some were very similar to models offered by Dinky, such as the Rover or Bedford, while others were of prototypes not modeled by competitors. The occasional head-on head nature of the competition between Corgi Toys and Dinky toys would continue for over a decade.

Mettoy soon realized that just beating Dinky Toys in their home market, Britain, would not be enough to maintain market share. To compete, Corgi Toys would need to expand into the European and American markets. Children in these markets would not recognize British cars for the most part. Models of European and American vehicles would need to be added to the line. The first European car, the 210 Citroen DS19, would be introduced in December 1957. The first American car, the 211 Studebaker Golden Hawk, would arrive in February 1958. A flood of non-British vehicles would follow. A network of importers was also established to serve the expanded markets. In the United States, Reeves International was chosen as the exclusive importer. This relationship has lasted throughout the history of Corgi Toys.

Mettoy continued to expand the Corgi Toys range through the remainder of the '50s. New number series were established as the need arose. Saloon cars (family sedans to Americans) occupied the 200 series. Racing and Formula 1 cars were numbered in the 150s, trailers in the 100s, and sports cars in the 300s. Small vans and commercial vehicles were numbered in the 400s, while large trucks were given the special series name Corgi Majors and numbered in the 1,100s. Gift sets occupied the series of numbers from 1-50. This number series would remain in place throughout the Mettoy years, and continue in modified form for their successor company until the Mattel takeover.

The first Corgi Major, the 1101 Carrimore Car Transporter, was introduced in October 1957. It was a very complex model—the upper deck could be folded down to meet the lower one. The rig was pulled by a Bedford S tractor unit. The Bedford would be used the next year to pull a machinery flatbed trailer as 1104, and on the 1100 Carrimore Low Loader. In 1959, the Bedford S would also appear on the 1110 Mobilgas Tanker, which would later also be produced in Milk and U.S. Army versions.

A number of military Corgi Majors were also released in the late 1950s. Only the largest military models would be called Majors. The first would be the Bristol Bloodhound Missile and Launching Ramp in 1958, which was also part of the larger Gift Set 4. This would be followed in 1959 by the 1106 Decca Mobile Radar Van and 1109 Bristol Bloodhound Missile on Loading Trolley. An unmarked International Troop Carrier was added as 1118, and would also appear in Gift Set 9. A tall model of a Corporal Missile would follow mounted either on a Launching Ramp (1112), or with a truly massive Erector Vehicle (1113). The corporal missile was obviously meant to be thrown by its owner, since it was later fitted with a "Percussion Head" that would hold explosive caps!

One last unique Corgi model would appear in 1958. The 1401 Service Ramp would be the only model in its series. Intended to be used as a lift to repair imaginary problems with Corgi Toys, it was an extremely heavy model. The racheting lifting mechanism was limited in its travel and had trouble staying up. "Corgi Toys" were well advertised on the ramp treads. The model would ultimately have a short life.

201M Austin Cambridge (Mechanical).

200 Ford Consul — the first Corgi Toy.

207M Standard Vanguard (Mechanical).

202M Morris Cowley (Mechanical).

204M Rover 90 (Mechanical).

209 Riley Police Car.

10

302 MGA.

215 Ford Thunderbird Convertible (215S shown).

210 Citroen DS19 (210S with suspension shown).

403M Bedford K.L.G. Plugs Van (Mechanical).

211 Studebaker Golden Hawk (211S shown).

414 Bedford Army Ambulance.

214 Ford Thunderbird Hardtop (214S shown).

412 Bedford Ambulance.

Gift Set 2 Land Rover and Rice Pony Trailer

223 Chevrolet Impala State Patrol Car.

408 Bedford A.A. Van.

102 Rice Pony Trailer.

213S, 208 and 208S Jaguars.

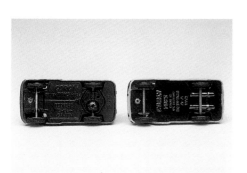

Mechanical (left) and standard (right) baseplates.

1401 Service Ramp (the only model in this number series).

101 Platform Trailer (late version with cast hitch).

406 Land Rover (the first Corgi Land Rover).

222 Renault Floride including very late blue version.

458 E.R.F. Earth Dumper shown with later 494 Bedford TK version.

409 Jeep FC-150 Pick-up shown with later 470 version.

1.3—The Early Sixties:

Phenomenal Growth

The early 1960s were hectic years for Mettoy as Corgi Toys became popular around the world. The innovative models being introduced were superior to anything being offered by competitors. The vast American market had been opened by Reeves International and sales there were expanding rapidly. The size of this market would create strong demand for American vehicles, which would occupy an ever growing percentage of the product line. Even so, Corgi Toys continued to use British vehicles as their mainstay.

The first problem to present itself to Mettoy in the early 1960s was how to maintain the popularity of Corgi Toys as competitors caught up. Plastic windows, the trademark feature of Corgi Toys in the late '50s, were no longer a unique selling point. Dinky Toys had already copied them along with other Corgi features on new models aimed at both the British and American markets. Corgi Toys ended production of mechanical versions in 1960, decreasing the variety of models produced. Mettoy was in need of more solid innovations to keep the sales momentum going.

The first big feature to be introduced in the early '60s was "Glideamatic" spring suspension. Actually, suspension was first introduced on the 222 Renault Floride in October 1959. By 1960, almost every new model would be equipped with the feature, and many existing models would be reworked. Those that could not be refitted with spring suspension would not last long in the line. Suspension was generally accompanied by a vacuum formed interior. While advertised as a new feature itself, the shallow vacuum formed interior part also served the important purpose of hiding the workings of the suspension.

The early '60s also saw the beginning of opening parts on the models. Opening parts had long been a part of Mettoy's tinplate toy line, adding "play value" to toys. The extension of the idea to diecast toys would not be unique either, since some larger diecast toys produced as far back as the 1920s and '30s by other manufacturers had opening parts. However, Corgi's competitors were not manufacturing diecast models with these features at the time. The first car with an opening feature in the

Corgi Toys range was the 218 Aston Martin DB4 released in March, 1960. This model was issued with an opening hood. Engine details were cast into a separate insert in the engine compartment. An opening trunk (boot) first appeared on the 224 Bentley Continental in April, 1961. The floodgates were then opened as numerous other models began to appear with opening parts. The most noteworthy model of this period was the 241 Ghia L6.4, the first model with opening hood, trunk lid and doors. Mettoy used this model to demonstrate how many new features could be designed into one model. It even had a silver foil rear-view mirror on the dash!

A number of other innovations were introduced during this period. Most would be short lived gimmicks applied to only a few models. Trans-o-Lite was a feature which used room light to make headlights or taillights on a model glow. Light was transmitted through plastic tubes from a collection point on the body. The 441 Volkswagen Toblerone Van was the first with this feature, introduced in February, 1963. A cam-actuated flashing bulb first appeared on the 437 Cadillac Superior ambulance in October, 1962. Steering front wheels (operated by pushing down on the front of the car) were only one of the features found on the 224 Bentley Continental of April, 1961. Rhinestone "jeweled" headlights and taillights also first appeared on this model. Jeweled headlights would, unfortunately, become popular for a time and appear on many more models. Possibly the most unique of the early 1960s gimmicks to appear was the working windshield wiper system on the 247 Mercedes-Benz 600 Pullman. Driven by an ingenious cam mechanism (so unique that the designers put a transparent plastic cover on it), disks with painted-on wipers oscillated behind the windshield when the model was pushed. Adding to the effect were simulated areas of raindrops on the unwiped surfaces—a fascinating model.

The first of a long line of Corgi Toys tied into popular characters from films and television appeared in 1965. Character toys had been around for many years by the time the first Corgi character-based models appeared. In the 1930s for example, Tootsietoy issued a series of vehicles based on newspaper comic strips. The tie-in of popular media characters with the popular Corgi Toys range in the early 1960s was a natural pairing. Mettoy's feedback mail from Corgi Model Club members let them gauge the feelings of the customers on this subject. The first character vehicle, the 258 "The Saint's Volvo" P1800, literally fell into Mettoy's lap when the television show chose to use a car identical to an existing Corgi model. Mettoy only needed to change the model's body color and add a "Saint" stick figure to the hood (which the real car did not have).

The next character vehicle would bring Corgi's name to the attention of vast numbers of people worldwide. In October, 1965, Mettoy released the Corgi 261 James Bond Aston Martin DB5. This model, actually based on Corgi's earlier DB4 casting but heavily reworked, was the sensation of the 1965 Christmas season. Like the incredible car from the movie, Corgi's model had pop-out machine guns in front, a pop-up bullet-proof screen in the rear, and an operating ejector seat that would throw its occupant across a room. No other diecast model would even come close to the market appeal or features of the DB5 for quite some time. Mettoy's rush to market created a somewhat inaccurate model, but the sensation caused upon its release was to lead to a rapid sellout of every model that could be produced.

Many models introduced during this period would continue in various forms into the mid 1970s. The 226 Morris Mini Minor, introduced in January, 1960, would be the first of literally millions of Mini's from Corgi. October, 1960, would see the introduction of the 418 Austin London Taxi, a staple in numerous London tourist shops appearing in various Gift Sets well into the Whizzwheels era. The suspension equipped 438 Land Rover of December, 1962, was itself an extension of the earlier (although completely different) 406 version. Land Rovers would be found throughout the range for many years to come based on the 438 casting. The last bow for any of these long lived designs would come with Corgi's mid-1970s scale change from 1:43 to 1:36. (These are average numbers, as Corgi didn't maintain a consistent, exact scale.)

In January, 1964, Mettoy launched an entirely new range within the Corgi Toys line called Corgi Classics. This new range introduced a highly detailed group of antique and vintage cars with much finer, more delicate detail than the standard range. The first models introduced were the 9011 1915 Model 'T' Ford and 9001 1927 Bentley 3 Liter LeMans Winner. Additional models would follow. These models would appeal to older collectors for many years to come, and would ultimately become part of the resurrection of Corgi Toys Ltd. when reissued in the 1980s. The originals from the 1960s have finer details, though, especially on the underside. Younger collectors would find these models highly fragile in the 1960s, leaving the Corgi Classics range with a limited customer base. Adults of the time generally did not collect diecast toy cars, with the exception of one or two favorite pieces to display on a desk or shelf.

It was in the early 1960s that Mettoy was approached by Woolworth to create a private brand of small diecast vehicles to compete with the widely popular Matchbox series produced by Lesney. The range was to be exclusive to Woolworth with its own brand name, be about the same size as contemporary Matchbox vehicles, yet possess the windows and suspension features of Mettoy's Corgi Toys. The result, christened Husky Toys, was an entire range of models that were primarily packaged on blister cards and introduced in Woolworth stores worldwide in 1964. The entire initial range was listed on the back of each card. The early days of the Husky Toys range have not been written about as extensively as Corgi Toys in the past, but they are the direct ancestors of Corgi Juniors. Some of the more uncommon variations on early Husky models are just now coming to light, with more yet to be found.

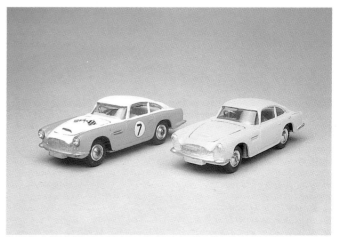

218 Aston Martin DB4 and 309 Competition version.

221 Chevrolet Yellow Cab with later 480 version.

419 Ford Zephyr Police minus the usual decals.

220 Chevrolet Impala with later 248 version.

1121 Circus Crane Truck with both axle types.

1123 Circus Animal Cage.

224 Bentley Continental.

231 Triumph Herald Coupes.

418 Austin London Taxi including Whizzwheel versions.

Kit 601 Batley Leofric Garages.

426 Circus Booking Office.

Gift Set 14 Hydraulic Tower Wagon with later 478 version.

234 Ford Consul Classic.

Three-wheeled 233 Heinkel Bubble Car.

1120 Midland Red Motor Express Coach missing its labels.

232 Fiat 2100 showing blind in rear window.

230 or 253 Mercedes-Benz 220 SE coupe.

420 Ford Thames Airborne Caravans.

228 Volvo P1800 with 258 "The Saint" version.

237 Oldsmobile Sheriff Car.

Many colors of the 238 Jaguar Mk.X Saloon.

430 Ford Thunderbird Bermuda Taxi.

Both versions of 437 Cadillac Superior Ambulance.

Gift Set 19 Circus Land Rover with Elephant Cage and Trailer (labels missing).

Gift Set 2S Land Rover (with suspension) and Pony Trailer.

Gift Set 17 Land Rover and Ferrari Racer on Trailer.

Late cast wheel version of 1130 Circus Horse Transporter.

441 VW Toblerone Van.

428 Mister Softee Ice Cream Van with 359 Field Kitchen Version.

1105 Bedford TK Car Transporter.

Another view showing the Trans-o-Lite feature.

One vanilla cone, please.

434 VW Kombi (Microbus) and 433 VW Van.

239 VW Karmann Ghia.

445 Plymouth Wagon and 443 U.S. Mail version.

436 Citroen ID19 Safari.

310 Chevrolet Corvette Sting Rays demonstrating the headlights.

464 Commer Police vans with 355 Military version.

Gift Set 24 Commer Construction Set.

240 Fiat (600) Jolly.

241 Ghia L 6.4 in blue and green.

The Ghia even had an inside rearview mirror!

9001 (900 first version) Bentley 3-Litre LeMans.

Early and late 245 Buick Riviera models.

Hillman Imp with the rear window open.

431 VW Pick-Up with red canopy.

The Trans-o-Lite feature with one side covered.

9012 (901 second version) Model 'T' Ford in yellow.

466 Commer Milk Float (Co-op version has different wheels).

468 London Transport Routemaster Bus with different advertisements.

1964 Olympics and Corgi Ski Club (both 475) and 1968 Olympics (499) versions of the Citroen ID19, each missing some small parts.

315 vacuum-plated Simca 1000.

236 (RHD) and 255 (LHD) Austin A60 Driving School cars.

503 Circus Giraffe Transporter with the "Daktari" version.

312 vacuum plated Jaguar 'E' Type (similar to earlier 307).

9021 1910 Daimler 38hp in red (the only color issued).

247 Mercedes-Benz 600 Pullman.

1127 Simon Snorkel Fire Engine with Bedford TK cab.

The windshield wipers on 247.

9013 (901 third version) Model 'T' Ford with top up.

1133 International 6 x 6 Troop Transporter.

A variety of 320 Ford Mustang versions.

355 Military Police and 356 U.S. Personnel Carrier.

314 Ferrari Berlinetta showing-off its engine.

The Corgi dog in the package tray.

358 Oldsmobile Army Staff Car.

447 Ford Thames Wall's Ice Cream Truck.

9032 (903 second version) 1910 Renault 12/16.

The four officers found in 358.

Joe's Diner and Potates Frites versions of 471.

Gift Set 38 1965 Monti Carlo Rally.

64 Working conveyor on Forward Control Jeep.

318 Lotus Elan S2 Convertible with later 319 coupe version.

Red and blue versions of 246 Chrysler Imperial Convertible.

The Esso Tiger decal on the trunk lid of the Lotus.

Note the features that would have been on the unreleased 507 Chrysler Bermuda Taxi.

Later version of 1137 Ford Tilt Cab 'H' Series with Trailer.

The sensational 261 James Bond Aston Martin.

Husky 3(A) Mercedes-Benz 220 Saloon.

Husky 14(A) Guy Warrior Tanker in Shell and early Shell-BP versions.

256 VW 1200 East African Safari and 492 VW 1200 Polizei.

Husky 7(A) Buick Electra Sedan and 9(A) Police version.

Husky 19(A) Commer Walk-Thru Van.

Husky Citroen ID19's (the gold version is a later, larger casting).

Husky 8(A) Ford Thunderbird Convertible.

Husky 16(A) Aveling-Barford Dump Truck.

Early 4(A) and later 4(B) Husky Jaguar Mark X Fire Chief Cars.

Husky 10(A) Guy Warrior Coal Truck in 2 colors.

23

This Corgi Commer Van may be a pre-production version of an unissued model (Possibly 461). Note there is no roof light. *(Photo By Michael Hylton & Chris Potter)*

The Trans-o-Lite feature and differently colored windows are easily seen in this view. *(Photo By Michael Hylton & Chris Potter)*

This side view shows the typical Corgi practice of orange taillights on a red model. *(Photo By Michael Hylton & Chris Potter)*

1.4—The Late Sixties: King of the Hill

In the late 1960s, Corgi Toys were the undisputed leaders in the diecast toy vehicle market. The phenomenal growth of the late '50s and early '60s allowed Mettoy the luxury of trying increasingly outlandish gimmicks in the Corgi line. The middle through the end of the decade would prove to be the pinnacle of Corgi Toys popularity. However, two events toward the close of the decade would send the company into a sales dive from which Corgi Toys would never fully recover.

The late 1960s could best be described as the era of the character Corgi. The 261 James Bond Aston Martin would continue to be a strong seller. It was replaced with a slightly larger and more accurate DB5, 270, in 1968. The new car kept all of the existing features, adding extending tire slashers to the rear wheels and revolving number plates. Bond also received a rocket firing Toyota 2000 GT, 336, in 1967. The Man from U.N.C.L.E. got a specially modified 1961 Oldsmobile, 497, with spotlights and a roof telescope that made the occupants pop in and out. The year 1966 saw the introduction of the now famous model of the 267 Batmobile with special bat wheels, front slasher, firing rockets, and rear flame. Gift Set 3(B) arrived in 1967 adding a trailer hitch to the Batmobile to haul the 107 Batboat. The Green Hornet's Black Beauty, 268, was released in 1967 with a flying scanner and front-mounted rocket launcher. The old standard Land Rover grew zebra stripes for Daktari, with a tiger on the hood, also in 1967.

The most phantasmagorical character model arrived in 1968. The 266 Chitty Chitty Bang Bang, from the movie of the same name, wowed the public as much as the real car had in the movie. The model sprouted wings with a flip of the brake lever, with front and rear add-on pieces to complete the effect. The model was made up of many small, detailed pieces which faithfully followed the design of the prototype. The wheels were borrowed from the 9041 Rolls-Royce, but all other parts were unique to the model.

Additional character vehicles arrived in 1969. The 803 Beetles Yellow Submarine followed the design of the cartoon vehicle. The model featured revolving periscopes and figures that pop-up through hatches. Popeye went sailing in the 802 Popeye's Paddle Wagon and Noddy went driving in his 801 Noddy's Car with various friends (the occupants changed over time in order not to offend some customers).

Many new gimmicks were tried in the late 1960s. Firing missiles and scanners have already been mentioned. Many cars would be packaged with loose accessories like golf bags, umbrellas, suitcases, new figures, pylons, animals, and all manner of rally number labels for the owner to apply. Farm Tractors sprouted vibrating spring exhausts. The 109 Pennyburn Workman's Trailer came with tools. A racing cyclist was packaged with the Gift Set 13 "Tour de France" Renault. Even the 302(B) "London to Sydney Marathon" Hillman Hunter came with a kangaroo. Removable tubular chassis could be found on the 319 Lotus Elan Hardtop, 271 Ghia Mangusta, and in Gift Set 37.

Take-off Wheels with Golden Jacks would be the big news in 1968. This unique system would add removable wheels to the list of Corgi features. A cam actuated clamp engaged a flange on the back of each wheel. When the jack pin was lowered, the wheel would be released. The wheels for this system were the best ever done by Mettoy, with some being unique to only one model. The existing Rover 2000TC and Oldsmobile Toronado were refitted with this system. New models would include the 338 Chevrolet Camaro, 341 Mini-Marcos, and 302(B) Hillman Hunter. Two further models would appear briefly in 1970, the 273 Rolls-Royce and 300(B) Chevrolet Corvette, but would soon be replaced by new Whizzwheels versions. Additional models would have had Take-off Wheels had events not interfered.

Many innovative new Corgi Majors were produced in the late 1960s. An entirely new Carrimore Car transporter and Semi Box Tractor-trailer were released with new Ford Tilt-cabs on the front as 1138 and 1137, respectively. The big Ford would also appear as the 1142 Holmes Twin Boom Wrecker. The aging Bedford TK would gain a dump (tipper) body to become 494. A Scammell would eventually replace the big Ford on the car transporter, becoming 1148. Chipperfield's Circus would gain two Scammells in the 1139 Menagerie Transporter and 1144 Circus Crane Truck.. An open-top trailer would be mated to the Scammell to create 1147 Ferrymasters truck with covers, or the 1151(A) Co-op truck without covers. The most unusual Majors model of the time would be the 1145 Mercedes-Benz Unimog with Gooseneck Dumper. This model used real coil springs to simulate the off-road capabilities of the real vehicle.

The Corgi Classics line of vintage automobiles at first expanded, then faded during the late 1960s. The 9041 1912 Rolls-Royce Silver Ghost would be added in 1966 as the last new Classics model. Additional models were planned, and appeared in the catalogs, but were never released. The market was saturated at the time due to the mainly adult interest in the range. By 1970, Corgi Classics were no longer offered. Some would suffer horrible fates, being resurrected for character cars. Others would never appear again in the Mettoy era.

The Husky Toys range was greatly expanded as Woolworth and Mettoy went after the market dominated by Lesney's Matchbox series. An increase in size would gradually occur, following Lesney's lead. The larger size allowed more room for new features. Some models would get diecast base plates to hide the suspension spring. Opening parts would appear on some models. Character cars, many of them smaller versions of Corgi models, would be grouped in a special Extras series. Larger trucks would also appear in a new Husky Majors series. At the end of the decade, Woolworth's exclusive contract would run out. Mettoy would quickly drop the name Husky Toys and re-label the range Corgi Juniors. Base text would be hastily wiped clean and a temporary Corgi Juniors label applied.

Tragedy hit Mettoy on March 10, 1969, when a major fire destroyed the warehouse at the factory in Swansea. While the production facility went mostly undamaged, the contents of the warehouse were lost. Records for the year's production were also lost. Somewhere in a dump near Swansea must lie the charred remains of many rare 1969 Corgi Toys. Shortages soon occurred with many sales lost to the competition. The Northampton facility picked-up whatever it could, but some 1969 Corgi Toys are among the most scarce.

The diecast toy market changed almost overnight at the end of the late 1960s when American toy maker Mattel Inc. introduced their Hot Wheels line of diecast cars with low-friction wheels. The Lesney "Matchbox" series, and Mettoy's Husky Toys would take an immediate sales hit. Corgi Toys sales would also take a dive, even though they were a much larger scale and did not directly compete with Hot Wheels. A crash conversion program would take Mettoy into the beginning of the next decade.

A new range of modified Husky cars with low friction wheels was launched called Corgi Rockets. Rockets would last only two years due to their overly complicated design. Corgi Toys era as king of the hill was at an end.

440 and 491 Ford Cortina Estate in three colors.

328 Monti Carlo Hillman Imp and 340 Monti Carlo Sunbeam Imp.

Early and late 324 Marcos 1800 GT.

259 Citroen Le Dandy.

263 Rambler Marlin and its Gift Set 10 variant.

The Le Dandy in two colors.

1138 Carrimore Car Transporter with Ford Tilt Cab.

The promotional Hammonds Commer Van and its plain box.

490 VW Breakdown Truck.

264 and 276 Oldsmobile Toronado versions.

The swinging booms in action.

The TV screen in the limo with one of the scenes provided.

322 International Rally Rover 2000.

330 Porsche Carrera 6 including Gift Set version.

332 Lancia Fulvia Sport Zagato.

327 MGB GT with blue seats.

319 Lotus Elan Coupe removed from its chassis.

9041 1912 Rolls-Royce Silver Ghost with 1980s reissue version.

1142 Holmes Twin Boom Wrecker.

262 Lincoln Continental Executive Limousine with the notorious flaking plating.

479 Commer Mobile Camera Van and 508 Holiday Camp Special.

Husky 32(A) VW Conveyor Truck.

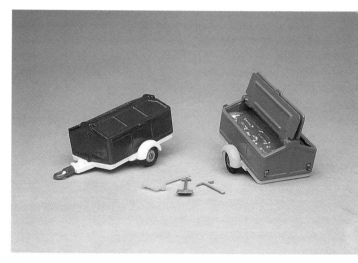

109 Pennyburn Workmen's Trailer and Gift Set 10 version.

270 New James Bond Aston Martin D.B.5 with added features.

341 Mini-Marcos GT 850 with Take-off Wheels.

Husky version of the James Bond Aston Martin.

The Rover 2000 in many of its forms.

506 Sunbeam Imp Panda Police car..

The Camaro's hiding headlamps.

Early and late 1143 American LaFrance Aerial Rescue Truck.

348 Flower Power Mustang.

Gift Set 8(B) Lions of Longleat with later Whizzwheels.

277 The Monkee's Monkeemobile.

335 Jaguar 'E'-type 2+2 with later 374 version.

Gift Set 13 Renault R16 Tour de France.

Gift Set 12 with earlier style racers.

338 Chevrolet Camaro SS 350 with Take-

1139 Circus Menagerie Transporter.

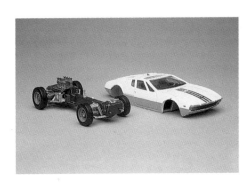

271 Mangusta de Thomaso and its chassis.

345 MGC GT Competition Model.

148 Carrimore Mk.IV Car Transporter with Scammell Cab.

260 Renault 16 with Whizzwheel variant 202(B).

1144 Circus Crane Truck minus its cage.

159 Cooper-Maserati with driver-operated steering..

302(B) Hillman Hunter Rally with factory supplied decals applied.

347 Chevrolet Astro I show car (The real car was red).

Husky 24(A) Ford Zephyr Estate.

Husky 25(A) Refuse Wagon (Garbage Truck).

1145 Mercedes-Benz Unimog Articulated Dumper.

Husky 21(B) Jaguar E-Type 2+2.

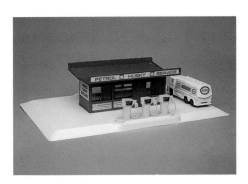

Husky 3006 Service Station minus some of its vehicles.

1147 Scammell Ferrymasters Truck.

Husky 40(A) Ford Transit Caravan.

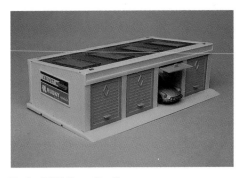

Husky 2001 Four-Car Garage.

Husky 23(A) Guy U.S. Army Tanker.

Husky 29(A) ERF Cement Truck.

Early plastic and later diecast Husky Baseplates.

Various Husky and later Corgi Junior 22(B) Aston Martin DB6.

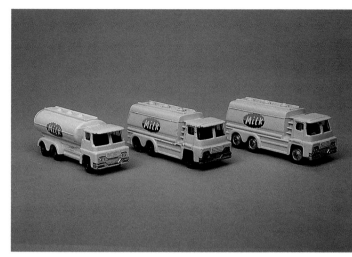
Husky 17(A) and 17(B) Guy Milk Tankers.

Husky 36(A) Simon Snorkel Fire Engine with Bedford TK cab.

Husky 14(B) Guy Shell and Esso Petrol Tankers.

Husky 39(A) Jaguar XJ6 (Also found as Husky 89).

Husky 38(A) Horse Trailer.

Corgi Rockets 906 and Corgi Juniors 46(A) Jensen Interceptors.

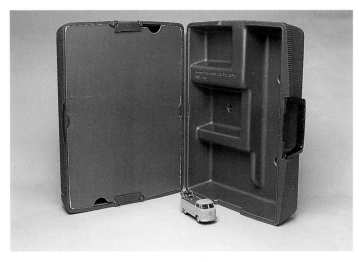

The blow-molded case has an integral hinge.

Husky 28(A) Ford F-350 Wrecker.

The cardboard divider removed to show what holds the Corgi cars in place.

Reeves International 400(X) Corgi Carry Case.

The Corgi logo appears on the latch.

1.5—The Early Seventies: Turmoil and Chaos

The early 1970s were a disastrous time for Corgi Toys sales. The 1969 factory warehouse fire at Mettoy had earlier interrupted the flow of new models onto the market. Mattel's Hot Wheels were grabbing an ever-larger market share, especially in the lucrative American market, with their innovative new products. Corgi Toys were no longer seen as the market leader in cool innovations and sales figures took a tumble. All of the major diecast toy manufacturers were scrambling to meet the Hot Wheels challenge, and Mettoy was no exception.

Design and development of new Corgi products took a back seat for a couple of years as much of the existing product line was refitted with what would be called Whizzwheels. The swift conversion to low-friction Nylon wheels on thin axles was technically simple, though it eliminated any possibility for steering or the short lived Take-Off-Wheels designs. However, the marketing of the reworked models would be tricky, since stores still had ample supplies of the older product. The Whizzwheel conversions had to come onto the market quietly so that sales of existing stock would not be killed-off completely. Only a few new products with no pre-Whizzwheels variants could be marketed aggressively. This Catch-22 situation only worsened the sales situation.

For today's collectors, the rushed change-over to Whizzwheels in the early 1970s created a bonanza of additional variations that wouldn't have existed otherwise. In many cases, the versions either before or after the change were produced in very low quantities. In some cases, marketing decisions to change colors or decorations on some models didn't occur until production of the Whizzwheel version had already occurred. Add to that the short-lived, early rubber-tired Whizzwheel models and the scarcity of some models produced around the time of the factory fire, and this period must be considered one of the liveliest for collectors.

The early 1970s were not devoid of innovative new models, as one might think from the preceding paragraphs. Many new ranges appeared in the first half of the decade. Dragsters and Funny Cars were introduced in 1971. A new range of Formula 1 cars in a new scale of 1:36 arrived in 1972. Children's TV shows were represented with models for Basil Brush and the Magic Roundabout in the same year. Mettoy would also import diecast aircraft under the Corgi name from Hong Kong. A range of military tanks and vehicles was introduced in 1973. New Corgi cars began appearing in the new (and ill advised) 1:36 scale that same year. Corgi outdid themselves in 1974, introducing two Formula 1 racers in the then-huge 1:18 scale. (How times change!) All in all, it was a hectic, transitional time for Corgi Toys.

Focusing on smaller vehicles, the Husky line of smaller diecast cars become Corgi Juniors in 1970. The exclusive contract Mettoy made with Woolworth expired, and still the Husky name had not gained the visibility the company wanted. The existing products would be altered by removing all Husky logos and references. Early reworked models received small "Corgi Juniors" stickers on their base plates, due to the crash-program nature of the changeover. These would give way to base plates with engraved text when time was found for tooling modifications in the following years. Some models were renumbered in the transition from Husky to Corgi Juniors. Individual models received new numbers 50 lower than their Husky number in some cases, and the Extras line was renumbered from the 1,200-1,400s to the 1,000s.

The new Juniors would bear the brunt of the Hot Wheels attack on the marketplace. Mettoy had first met the Hot Wheels challenge by creating a new line separate from Husky called Corgi Rockets. These somewhat over-complicated vehicles incorporated the low friction wheel concept into a removable sub-chassis. Existing Husky models were refitted with the new base plates to create much of the new line, although many new castings were also used. Track systems were also offered, until Mattel threatened to file suit for violation of patent rights. Mettoy then decided to fit the low friction Whizzwheels to the Corgi Junior line, and Rockets vehicles and track systems were quickly phased-out.

By renaming the Husky line, Mettoy incorporated the name recognition enjoyed by the standard Corgi range for its smaller vehicles. In the USA, this increased visibility was enhanced by a promotion at Citgo service stations. Many of the new Corgi Juniors were offered to customers who filled-up at the pump. While complete details about which models were offered have not been determined, some have been identified. Corgi Juniors would subsequently enjoy a growing share of overall Corgi sales through the decade. This would be especially true in the USA, where similarly sized Hot Wheels and Matchbox vehicles were also highly popular. This increased popularity would help offset declining sales in the standard Corgi Toys line.

343 Pontiac Firebird with early Whizzwheels.

Chipperfield's Performing Poodles Chevrolet.

303(B) Roger Clark's Ford Capri with decal application instructions.

311(B) Ford Capri 3-litre V6 with later 331 version.

342 Lamborghini P400 GT Miura with later 319(B) version.

273 Rolls-Royce Silver Shadow, its replacement wheels, and 280 Whizzwheels version.

300(B) Chevrolet Corvette with Take-off Wheels, the last with this feature.

510 Citroen ID21 Tour de France Team Manager's Car.

375 Toyota 2000 with Whizzwheels but no James Bond features.

377 Marcos Volvo 3-litre with Whizzwheels.

509 Porsche 911S Targa Polizei.

Various 383 and 384 Volkswagens.

The last non-Whizzwheel car, 513 Citroen ID19 Alpine Rescue.

Police and PTT versions of 373 VW 1200 Police.

Three versions of 280 Rolls-Royce Silver Shadow with Whizzwheels.

An uncommon German issue of 373 with the earlier 492 for comparison.

1146 Carrimore Tri-deck Mark V Transporter with Scammell Handyman Mk.III Tractor.

313(B) Graham Hill Ford Cortina GXL.

Corgi, Juniors and Rockets GP Beach Buggy models.

382 Porsche 911S Targa in green.

1150 Mercedes-Benz Unimog 406 Snow Plow.

Whizzwheel version of 418 Austin London Taxi.

388 Mercedes-Benz C111 with gullwing doors.

163 Ford Capri Santa Pod Gloworm Dragster.

389 Reliant Bond Bug 700 ES.

The Chassis of 163.

386 Bertone Barchetta.

Two colors of 284 Citroen SM.

312(B) Marcos Mantis.

Mack Tanker in 1152 Esso and 1151 Exxon versions.

304(B) Chevrolet Camaro.

461 Police "Vigilant" Range Rover.

391 James Bond Ford Mustang Mach 1 and later 329(B).

393 Mercedes-Benz 350 SL coupe.

1106(B) Mack Container Truck.

402 Ford Cortina GXL Police.

151(B) Yardley McLaren.

1103(B) Chubb Pathfinder Airport Crash Truck.

Gift Set 19(B) Corgi Flying Club, the last version of the 1:43 Land Rover.

1104(B) Newmarket Race Horse Transporter with Bedford TK Cab.

700 Motorway Service Ambulance.

394 (Red) and 396 Datsun 240-Z.

The Mack Tank Transporter portion of Gift Set 10(B).

Juniors 45(A) Mercedes-Benz 280 SL.

1154 Mack Priestman Crane Truck.

Gift Set 11(B) London Set.

Juniors 20(B) Volkswagen 1300.

The sticker found on many Juniors that had previously been Husky Toys.

Juniors 26(B) and 26(C) ERF Fire Engines.

Super Juniors 2006 Mack Esso Tanker. Note the Corgi style Whizzwheels.

Juniors 37(A) NSU Ro-80.

Juniors 11(B) Austin Healey LeMans.

Juniors 64(A) Morgan Plus 8.

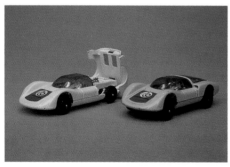

Rockets 904 (Yellow) and Juniors 41(A) versions of the Porsche Carrera 6.

Juniors 6(C) DeTomaso Mangusta.

Juniors 47(A) Scammell Cement Truck.

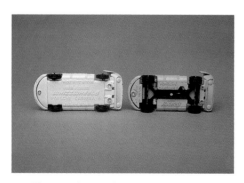

The complex Rockets base versus the same car's Juniors base.

Super Juniors 2002 Hoynor Car Transporter with Ford Tractor.

Juniors 16(B) Land Rover Pick-up and the Army 79(A) version minus its rear cover.

A very late version of Juniors 31(B) Land Rover Wrecker.

Mettoy, Corgi Toys Ltd., and Mattel Auto-City versions of Juniors 29(D) ERF Simon Snorkel.

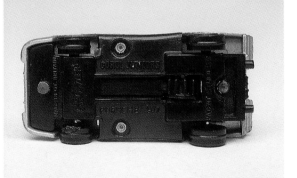

A transitional 1984 version of Juniors 54(A) Ford Multi-bucket Truck, made without windows to use-up existing parts.

Juniors 9(C) Range Rover Police.

Juniors 94(A) Porsche 917, similar to 51(A) but with added Growlers feature.

Juniors 32(B) Lotus Europa.

The Growlers mechanism as found on some Juniors of the period.

Juniors Growlers 82(A) Can-Am Racer and the later non-growling 20(D) Penguinmobile version.

Mettoy and Mattel Auto-City versions of Juniors 15(C) Mercedes-Benz Bus.

1.6—The Late Seventies: A Larger Scale for Smaller Kids

Corgi Toys enjoyed a brief resurgence of popularity in the late 1970s. The turmoil caused by the introduction of Mattel's Hot Wheels had died down, and Corgi was back to making interesting and innovative products popular with older children. This was also a time of unique market opportunities. The Queen's Silver Jubilee occurred during this period, and all of Britain celebrated. Many companies would produce special commemorative items, and Mettoy was no exception. Corgi produced a beautiful rendition of the Queen's horse-drawn coach, the only horse-drawn item in the full-size Corgi range. (Other horse-drawn Wild West items were to be found in the Juniors range.) In addition to the coach, Corgi's Routemaster was issued in several commemorative silver versions with special silver packaging.

Corgi's larger 1:36 scale was now firmly established, with even the popular Mini-Cooper and Land Rover reintroduced in the larger size. Most older collectors hated the new size, but they sold well to the pre-teen market. Character toys were alive and well with many new models. The ever-popular James Bond got his under-water equipped Lotus Esprit and a space shuttle in both the Corgi and "Juniors" ranges, though the word "Juniors" was dropped from packaging during this period. A larger 1:36 scale DB5 was introduced, including the regular special features that had made the smaller model so popular. Two sizes of Buick were made available for Kojak, from the popular American TV series. The Muppets drove away in four fanciful vehicles unlike anything else in the line, although Miss Piggy had trouble deciding which color dress to wear. Tarzan went ape with a large gift set that included the new size Land Rover with trailer, figures, a boat, and open-out packaging that created a diorama for added play value.

A wide variety of character vehicles were created following a licensing agreement with DC Comics. Often, both 1:36 scale and "Juniors" size vehicles were made from the same design. Kojak's Buick gained roof lights to become a Metropolis Police Car. Superman gained a SuperVan and fist throwing Supermobile in two sizes, plus a "Juniors" Newspaper Delivery Van. Spiderman got a Jeep and a motorcycle, along with one of the strangest looking helicopters ever made. Other superheroes were less fortunate, only receiving repainted versions of existing Corgi models. The Hulk was so mad that he broke out of his cage in the back of his Mazda Pick-up.

A new group of circus models appeared in 1978 in Gift Set 48(C), decorated for the Jean Richard Circus. The set included plastic stands and a cardboard backdrop. The vehicles from the set were also available separately. These were Corgi's first Circus models since the Chipperfield's Circus set of vehicles was discontinued in 1972.

New models appeared in the Formula 1 and Military ranges, further expanding their variety. Customized Chevrolet Vans were released in two sizes in a rainbow of colors, including versions for the super heroes. Many of the larger semi (or artic) Majors received new-style tractor units in the new scale, retaining the existing trailers in new finishes. The last 1:43 models to be offered by Corgi under Mettoy would be the C384 Volkswagen 1200 (Beetle) Rally and C19 Gift Set with the last version of the old Land Rover pulling a trailer and Nipper airplane.

One final group of models from this time is worth mentioning, although not a part of Corgi's regular offerings. The Marks & Spencer department store chain contracted with Mettoy to produce a group of private brand vehicles for exclusive distribu-

tion in their stores. Labeled "St. Michael" brand, the entire range consisted of then-current Corgi vehicles with the Corgi name removed from the base plate. All of these models were produced in finishes different than that offered in the Corgi product line, with the exception of the Formula 1 cars. These models are rarely seen outside of Britain. Some of the finishes used on them were quite attractive, and may have done well in overseas markets.

Two of the many, many versions of 469 Routemaster Bus.

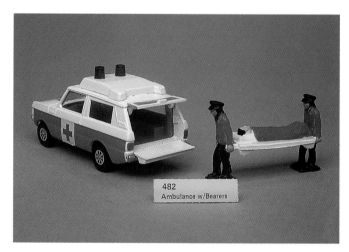

482(B) Range Rover Ambulance with its original display tag.

921 Police Hughes Helicopter.

401 VW 1200 Driving School Car with Traffic Cones.

302(C) VW Polo.

413(B) Mazda Motorway Maintenance Truck with its accessories.

424(B) Security Van, basically a redecorated 700 Motorway Ambulance with bars added to the windows (Should have been 704).

490(B) Caravan Trailer, unlike any other Corgi trailer.

Gift Set 41(B) Silver Jubilee Coach, the only horse-drawn, full-size Corgi Toy.

1158 Ford Exxon Tanker for the United States. The European market 1157 Esso version is similar.

1160 Ford Gulf Tanker showing-off the opening features.

Queen Elizabeth II can be found in either a blue or yellow dress.

471 QEII Silver Jubilee Routemaster Bus.

1126(B) Dennis Simon Snorkel.

Mettoy and Corgi Toys Ltd. versions of 425(A) London Taxi.

The three scales of Corgi London Taxis.

319(C) Jaguar XJS with 320(B) The Saint's Jaguar.

The Saint's Jaguar from another angle.

436(B) Chevrolet Spider-Van with its highly decorated interior.

Juniors E60(B) James Bond Lotus Esprit and transition-period street version, which still shares the same windows.

Juniors E70(B) Mercury Cougar XR7 Fire Chief Car.

Super Juniors E2011(A) Mack U.S. Army Tanker.

A transition-period version of Juniors E30(D) Ford Cement Truck.

Juniors E14(C) Guy Warrior Esso Tanker and E97(A) Exxon Tanker.

Juniors E20(C) Cement Mixer.

Juniors E87(B) and 95(A) Leyland Coca-Cola Delivery Trucks.

Juniors E52(B) Mercedes-Benz 240D Taxi with a transition-period E59(C) sedan in a similar color.

Juniors Leyland Delivery Trucks E74(B) Ryder and E87(B) Pepsi.

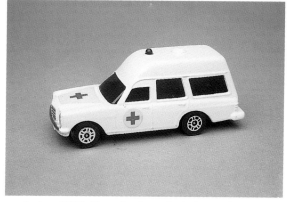

Juniors E1(E) Mercedes-Benz Ambulance.

Various Juniors E81(A) Daimler Fleetline London Buses.

Juniors E28(C) Police and E28(D) Sheriff versions of Buick Regal sedan.

The two known color combinations of Juniors E17(D) Buick Regal City of Metropolis Police Car.

Juniors E42(C) Rescue Team Range Rover with a similar Corgi Toys Ltd. version.

Juniors E45(B) Starsky & Hutch Ford Torino and later E70(C) Ford Torino Fire Chief.

Juniors E97 Texaco and BP Oil Leyland Tankers.

Juniors E98(B) Mobile Grocery Shop.

Juniors E55(B) Refuse (Garbage) Truck with much later Iveco model.

Later Corgi Toys Ltd version of Juniors E86(A) Fiat X1/9.

Juniors E10(C) Triumph TR7.

1.7—The Early Eighties: The End for Mettoy

The early 1980s were a sad time for Mettoy and their Corgi Toys. The company had invested heavily in their new Dragon computer, a product in a market segment entirely outside of their normal business. The early days of home computers were a time when many companies tried entering the market only to quickly fail. Mettoy would be a part of that shake-out.

The Corgi Toys product line continued with some new and innovative models. Increasingly, however, existing castings would be reissued with new model numbers and more outlandish paint and graphics. Corgi Toys were, after all, still considered children's toys. Decorations were targeted at the pre-teen market, which had largely abandoned toy cars for video games and action figures. Increasingly, marketing gimmicks like packaged sets were used to try to stimulate sales.

Many excellent new castings were issued in the Corgi and "Juniors" lines in the years just prior to Mettoy's closure. Many would continue in production beyond the end of the decade for Mettoy's successors. Cars such as the Rover 3500, Ford Escort, Ford Sierra, and Peugeot 505 would later go on to find new life as police vehicles and fire service cars. The Citroen 2CV, released as a James Bond movie tie-in in yellow during this period, would continue in other colors as a standard "Deux Cheveau." Corgi even released a Allis-Chalmers Fork Lift Truck during this period.

One product line was ahead of its time: the Corgitronics range. There would eventually be nine different models in the range, with multiple sub-variations on some. Each model had some type of "electronic" feature, from a beeping horn to clicker-controlled motion. One, C1006, packaged a working radio into a van body. These models mostly used existing castings modified to fit the new equipment. Only the C1001 HGB-Angus Firestreak and the C1009 MG Meastro were entirely new castings, although the compressor portion of the C1007 Road Repair Unit had not been seen before. None of the Corgitronics would survive into the Corgi Toys Ltd. era except for the MG Maestro. The Compressor would appear briefly without the Land Rover as C799, but this may have been to use-up existing castings. The Maestro would later become the only Corgitronic model to be substantially modified, with the lighting system being replaced by a sound chip.

During the early 1980's, Corgi and Reeves International, the American importer, made a major marketing push with the "E" range (replacing the term "Juniors"). Cartoon character vehicles with drivers American children would recognize were plentiful. Tie-ins to live action TV shows, such as Simon & Simon, allowed Corgi to reuse existing castings alongside new ones. The latest Pontiac Firebird and Chevrolet Corvette received special packaging to play off the popularity of the real cars. Production of many of these models was moved to Singapore, and these vehicles were packaged on special blister cards with graphics unique to the American market. It is possible many were shipped directly from Singapore to the USA, never passing through Britain.

The Firebird and Corvette, along with the Ford Mustang, were used for special tie-ins to American professional sports teams. In perhaps the most extensive reuse ever of the same castings, The Ford Mustang and the Pontiac Firebird were issued in 1982 and 1983, respectively, decorated for each of the Major League Baseball teams. The Corvette was issued in 1983 decorated for each NFL football team. An additional series decorated for NHL Hockey teams was issued using various other castings from the line. Production numbers for these sports-oriented vehicles were quite high, although hometown teams almost always sold out in their home markets. During this time, "E" series Corgi's were as plentiful as Matchbox and Hot Wheels vehicles on American toy shelves. The entire "E" range was heavily overproduced, however, and the models glutted stores. Many could still be found on store shelves five or more years later.

The heavy investment by Mettoy in the ill-fated Dragon computer, combined with the worldwide decline of diecast toy sales caused by the popularity of new computer games and action figures finally spelled the end for Mettoy on October 31, 1983. The firm could no longer sustain the heavy losses it was incurring, and court appointed receivers were charged with disposing of the remaining inventory and assets of the company. Unlike other brands, however, this would not be the end for Corgi Toys. A new company, Corgi Toys Ltd., would be formed from the wreckage of the old to continue the Corgi story.

Introduced as 2029, the Mack Fire Engine would later carry the number 1185.

1117(B) Faun Streetsweeper minus the operator.

A later version of 339(B) Rover 3500 Police Car.

806(B) 1956 Mercedes-Benz 300 SC with top up, part of the Corgi Classics range revival.

The side of the Rover you never want to see.

1365 London Bus & Taxi, now using a Juniors-size taxi as part of the Little/Large series.

Corgitronics 1004 Beep Beep London Bus with Hamley's side panels for sale in that store.

Gift Set 25(C) Talbot Matra Rancho with two Motorcycles on Trailer.

326(A) Chevrolet Caprice Police Car and Corgitronics 1008 Fire Chief Car.

Juniors E114(A) Stage Coach, part of a series of Wild West vehicles.

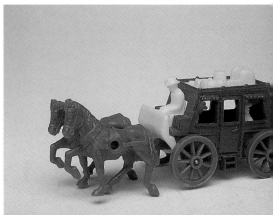

Left: Juniors E102(A) Renault Turbo.

Right: Juniors E131(A) Magnum Ferrari or identical E136(A) Ferrari 308GTS.

Left: Juniors E137(A) VW Turbo, a racing version of E92(A) VW Polo.

Right: A transitional-period version of E136(A) Ferrari 308GTS.

Left: Either E139(A) or E205(A) Porsche 911 Turbo (uncertain as to which).

Right: E74(B) Jaguar XJS from the transitional period.

Left: Juniors E156(A) 1957 Chevy Convertible, a real grease machine.

Right: Various Juniors Matra Rancho's including E223(A) Safari Park Matra Rancho on card.

Left: Juniors 1982 Baseball Cars, in this case E400(A) Baltimore Orioles and E421(A) Philadelphia Phillies.

Right: An assortment of Mettoy Era, transitional, and Corgi Toys Ltd. Juniors E180(A) Pontiac Firebirds.

Enough of these rare mismatched Firebirds were made to fill the shelves of the store where this example was purchased.

Juniors E184(A) Range Rover with open top.

Juniors E175(A) Pipe Truck did not follow any specific prototype.

Later version of Mettoy era ERF Fire Engine with Corgi Toys Ltd. version.

Juniors E182(A) 4x4 Renegade Jeep.

Juniors E125(A)Ford Transit Dropside Truck in both Wimpey and BTS versions.

Left: Later Opel version of the Juniors E170(A) Vauxhall Nova.

Right: Special España '82 issues E116(A) Mercedes-Benz Bus and E117(A) Chevrolet Van.

Left: Two versions of Juniors E124(A) Mercedes-Benz 350 SL.

Right: E3111(A) Wild West Railroad Set first issued in 1982.

Left: Resin Prototypes of a series of Tom & Jerry cars that were never produced.

Right: E3112(A) Wild West Frontier Set contained a non-standard, open flat wagon.

Left: The interior of one of the prototypes showing the mount for the figure.

Right: The 275(B) Royal Wedding Mini Metro from happier times for the British royal family.

Left: The 1983 series E500(A) Baltimore Orioles baseball Pontiac Firebird & E600(A) Baltimore Colts football Chevrolet Corvette.

Right: E140(A) Ford Mustang Cobra, a popular model of a popular American car.

1.8—Corgi Toys Ltd.: The New Company

The death of Mettoy was not the end of the Corgi Toys story, but rather a time for rebirth. Much like Dr. Who in the BBC science fiction series, Corgi Toys Ltd. was formed from the remnants of the old company—but with a very different face—on March 29, 1984. The non-Corgi Toy activities were either sold-off or abandoned, so that the company could focus on its core business. There were many challenges for the new company. Business relationships needed to be rebuilt. Left-over Mettoy stocks needed to be sold. New customers in new market segments needed to be cultivated. The list of tasks was daunting.

The first task for the new company was to define who their customers were and who they wanted them to be. Except for the "Juniors" line, children and teens had lost interest in diecast toys. The emergence of home video games caused a revolution in the toy market. Soon, other toys such as "Transformers" would further distance diecast vehicles from the toy market. Complicating matters, Mettoy had heavily overproduced the "Juniors" line toward the end, causing a glutted market, especially in the United States. "Juniors" would be heavily discounted at stores in order to move existing stock.

For Corgi Toys Ltd. to survive, the company had to refocus its efforts away from the children's toy market. Corgi's best hope was to recapture its customers from the 1960s; adults who had fond memories of diecast toys from their childhood. Solido and Vitesse were both proving that a nostalgic adult collector market existed. Corgi's task was to capture it. However, there were still buyers of traditional Corgi Toys, and the "Juniors" line still held a noticeable share of the market. Revenue from these lines would need to continue during the transitional period for the company to survive.

Within the first year, Corgi Toys Ltd. set out to distinguish itself from its predecessor, Mettoy. A new and very different "Traffic" logo was developed, and for the first time the Corgi dog disappeared. Packaging was changed to a dark blue with the new logo and various traffic symbols. The expanding Classics range received a silver/gray version of the design to strongly distinguish it from the standard and "Juniors" lines. Limited edition and promotional items, especially in the Classics range, began to be issued soon afterward. The American market had mostly been lost at the time of Mettoy's failure, so product offerings were refocussed on the domestic British market.

In an effort to recapture adults who were former Corgi collectors, the original 1960s Corgi Classics models were reissued in special presentation boxes. These reissues proved to be popular enough that additional versions were produced in new paint schemes. Numbering these new versions soon became a problem. With the volume of new promotional versions of the same castings increasing, and the company's decision to issue a new model number for each new livery (a nod to collectors), Corgi soon found itself outgrowing the inherited Mettoy numbering scheme. The "Juniors" line had gone through a general renumbering in 1984 in order to bring some rationality to the range. At that time, the "Juniors" prefix was changed from E to J. The standard and Classics product lines (prefix C) needed something similar, but without breaking the all-important historical connection. Corgi chose to use a new suffix number, "/1" and higher, adding it to whatever existing product numbers were in use at the time. The new suffix number was added to all models produced from January 1987 onward. In some cases, it was added without any change to the model. In other cases, the paint scheme

was changed at the same time. Gift sets were slow to have the suffix applied, since they seldom changed, but most appeared with the "/1" by 1989.

Another distinction was implemented during this time period. In January, 1989, the Classics range was numerically differentiated from the Standard range by changing its prefix to D from the standard C (i.e.: C859/X to D859/Y). This provided a quick distinction for the Classics range when only looking at the number. An additional prefix, Q, came into use across all product ranges in July, 1989. This signified a model that was a special premium item for an outside firm, and not generally available. This numbering system lasted into the first year of Mattel ownership, after which Corgi vehicles were numbered using Mattel's scheme.

In the United States, distribution of Corgi Toys would remain exclusively with Reeves International as before during the Mettoy era, with one notable exception during the transitional period in 1984. In that year Hartoy Inc., an import and distribution company founded by an ex-Lesney executive and importer of the then-new Lledo Days Gone line to the U.S., marketed various Corgi products decorated in either "Coca-Cola" or "Hershey's" schemes. Various sets were issued briefly, but Hartoy soon replaced the Corgi products with vehicles from cheaper Asian manufacturers. Packaging for the Hartoy imported, Corgi based products is distinctive from the remainder of the Corgi product line, with minimal references to the Corgi brand.

Many significant models were introduced during the independent years of Corgi Toys Ltd. The Thorneycroft Van was introduced in 1984, and could be considered the model that saved Corgi. A massive number of variations, including a large number of promotional versions, were issued by the company. This model, along with the Standard series Routemaster and Ford Escort Van castings, were used extensively by the company to expand sales without incurring additional tooling costs. The Thorneycroft was also transformed into a Renault for the French market, and a Mack for the American market, by a simple exchange of cab castings. Letters to the editor of Corgi Collector magazine may have complained about the many reuses of the same castings, but this economizing helped the company regain its financial footing and rebuild the product line for the future.

Some other significant models introduced during this period include the Bedford Pantechnicon and OB Coach, Morris 1000 and J Vans, and Bedford CA Van (the latter in a larger scale than the original 1950s version). For American collectors, a 1957 Chevrolet was introduced to accompany the Mettoy Era 1957 Thunderbird, and the American LaFrance Aerial Ladder Truck was reintroduced minus the extending ladder feature. The Model T Ford from the old Classics range gained van and tanker body versions, making it the oldest hybrid model in the line. A new line of modern cars in racing liveries was launched in 1985 as the Turbos series, spawning many police and fire versions for specific international markets. New models were continuously introduced into the standard Corgi and "Juniors" ranges also, although not as well publicized as the popular Classics range.

In November, 1988, Corgi Toys Ltd. launched a new series within the Classics range of vintage sports and saloon cars of the 1950s and 1960s. Based mostly on British prototypes, the series was highly detailed and widely popular among collectors. Paint finishes were restricted to actual prototype colors, and racing variants were representative of actual past racing cars. Even the factory terminology for the paint colors was used. This fidelity to actual prototypes was also found in the decoration of the light commercial and transport vehicles in the Classics range, as collectors tastes and expectations refined. Corgi still released models at times with existing castings "standing-in" for the actual prototype, but for the most part actual vehicles were modeled whenever possible.

The new marketing strategy pursued by Corgi Classics Ltd. resulted in a resurgence of the company. Growth was steady, and former export markets were reentered. The market position and strength of the company proved attractive to former competitor Mattel Inc., whose purchase of the company in December 18, 1989, would start a new chapter in Corgi's history.

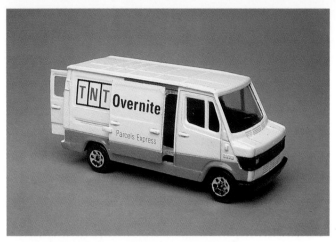

C576/09 Mercedes-Benz 207D Van, TNT Overnite.

C385 Mercedes-Benz 190.

J3700 Coca-Cola Race Team Car & Transporter showing three wheel types on the Firebird.

C577 Ford Escort Van, Plessey.

J3200H Hershey's Milk Chocolate Turbo Racing Team Set.

C1120 Dennis Aerial Ladder Fire Engine, which uses the earlier Snorkel body mated to the ladder used on the American LaFrance Ladder Truck.

C815 1954 Bentley 'R' Type, Top Up.

C860 (Silver) and C860/02 (Black) 1912 Rolls-Royce Silver Ghost.

C825 1957 Chevrolet Bel Air Hardtop.

C862 (Yellow) and C862/02 (Maroon) 1910 Renault 12/16 with original 1960s issue for comparison.

C863 (Black), C863/02 (Blue), and C863/03 (Red) Model 'T' Ford Phaeton, Top Up.

C880 Model 'T' Ford Tanker, BP.

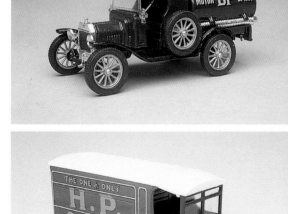

C907 Thorneycroft Box Van, H.P.Sauce.

A comparison of Model 'T' bases from the 1960s and 1980s.

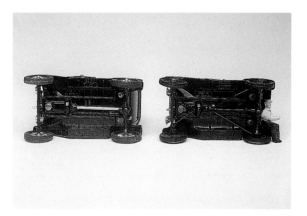

C883 Thorneycroft Open Truck with Barrels, Taunton Cider.

A resin prototype of D730/01, factory prototype MGA with half-tonneau , and pre-production model of the D732 MGA, which was produced with its top up.

A closer look at the prototype MGA with half-tonneau.

The pre-production MGA beside a similar 1950s Corgi Toys MGA.

A prototype Jaguar XK120 in an unfamiliar paint scheme.

The resin prototype next to a production version of the MGA hardtop from Gift Set D53/01.

A resin prototype of a Ferrari 250 GT, which was changed to a Ferrari 250 GTO in production as seen by the model on the right.

A resin prototype of D738 Triumph TR3a.

Another resin, this time the D735 Austin Healey, Top Up.

D708/01 Ford Cortina, also found in Gift Set D53/01.

D949/27 Bedford OB Coach, British Railways 1229W with destinations signs "Relief" and "Medstead".

Another Morris 1000 Van, Q957/20 Guernsey Post Office, showing its humped roofline.

J84 Volvo 760 Saloon (Sedan).

C599 1930 AEC Double Decker Bus in the familiar London Transport colors.

The C957/03 Corgi Collector Club Morris 1000 Van has been found with two different wheel types.

Two colors of the J10 Aston Martin D.B.5 (actually a D.B.6).

Hundreds of versions of Double Decker Bus models have been produced, many of which are quite colorful.

D54/01 National Resources Light Commercial Van Set.

J15(A) Lotus Esprit with the James Bond opaque window molding.

C957/07 MacFisheries and C957/02 Gas versions of the Morris 1000 Van.

C1231/22 Volvo Globetrotter Articulated Truck, Steiff.

J22/01 BMW 325i Racer.

J9/02 Iveco Container Truck, Mars.

J81 Buick Police Car, NYPD.

J12/01 Iveco Tanker BP with later Auto-City Shell version.

J97 Land Rover One Ten, Fire Salvage.

Q55/01 York Fair (Pennsylvania, not Britain) Set Bedford Pantechnicon and OB Coach.

1.9—Corgi Toys Ltd. Division: The Mattel Era

On December 18, 1989, Mattel Inc., the American based maker of Hot Wheels, purchased Corgi Toys Ltd. The announcement was made to Corgi Collector Club members in the January/February 1990 issue of the magazine. Quoting the official press release printed in that issue:

"LOS ANGELES—Mattel Inc. and Corgi Toys Ltd. today announced an agreement by which Mattel will acquire the British maker of miniature diecast models and scale model diecast cars... The Corgi brand, which enjoys a strong consumer awareness and a sizable market share in Europe, particularly in the United Kingdom, will add significantly to Mattel's position in this important market sector."

With that, Corgi Toys Ltd. came under the Mattel banner as an independently run division. The combination would be beneficial to both companies. In addition to the product line, Mattel gained access to Corgi's stronger European distribution network for its own products. Corgi gained access to Mattel's deeper pockets for the development of new products. In the United States, distribution of most Corgi Toys Ltd. products would remain with Reeves International Inc., separate from other Mattel products. Other arrangements would be used in other countries in which the marketing of products would be more unified.

One of the most readily apparent changes made under the Mattel banner was the demise of the old Mettoy style numbering system. Starting with the first Corgi models of 1956, the same numbering system had been used through Corgi's history and modified once with a suffix by Corgi Toys Ltd. due to the shortage of available numbers. In actuality, Mettoy had also outgrown the system, and routinely reused numbers. Mattel's system was adopted in January, 1991, for new products being introduced. Models no longer in production but still on sale did not change numbers. However, some models in continuing production, such as Royal Mail and police vehicles, received new numbers on their next production run. The number system change was also used by Corgi to implement changes in colors and decorations on most of their products.

Another major change was the transfer of production out of Britain to China. Offshore production had actually been done before on a limited basis. Mettoy had produced some "Juniors" for the American market in Singapore prior to its closure, and the Corgi Aircraft line was imported from the Asian Pacific. However, Mattel moved all model production to factories in China where they already had other products being manufactured. The Morris J Van of April, 1990, was the first Classics model with production solely outside of Britain, and production of the remainder of the product line was soon transferred. Transferal of production outside of Britain cannot be placed totally at Mattel's feet, however, since the introduction of the Morris J Van was only four months after the purchase of Corgi by Mattel.

The association with Mattel gave Corgi new freedom in product innovation. A new competitor, Exclusive First Editions, was making waves in the British diecast market by introducing detailed transit vehicle models scaled to match "OO" scale train sets. Growth in the market segment was rapid, with eager buyers from both the collector and model railroader segments. Corgi, under the code name "Project Zulu," quietly developed its own 1:76 scale line of vintage transit vehicles. Released under the Original Omnibus Company banner, this new series was introduced to the public in March 1994. Models have included exclusively British transit vehicles from the World War II era through

the 1960s. These models proved popular and the range steadily grew during the Mattel years.

Another new product line grew at the urging of Corgi's distributor in the USA, Reeves International. Reeves realized that American collectors could not relate to many of the British vehicles produced by Corgi. Only British sports cars would be recognizable to the average American customer. Reeves had already done much to promote American prototypes, especially fire equipment such as the reintroduction of the American LaFrance aerial ladder truck. Corgi traditionally relied heavily on Reeves for marketing decisions for the American market. Seeing the success of vintage bus models in Britain, Reeves convinced Corgi to launch a parallel line of 1:50 scale American coaches. The resulting line of transit buses and inter-city coaches is immediately recognizable to adult American collectors.

One additional new line of American prototype vehicles was created in 1993, still during Mattel's tenure and, surprisingly, for a different American importer. Specialty Diecast Co. and Corgi cooperated in creating a completely new line of racing collectibles for the growing American market for NASCAR and NHRA racing and support vehicles. Racing Champions, a relatively new competitor, experienced explosive growth with their line of diecast racers and support vehicles. Other manufacturers stampeded into the market to capitalize on the frenzied growth of this market sector. Corgi, with the help of Specialty Diecast, joined the fray with a series of high quality 1:64 scale Racing Transporters, followed quickly by accompanying racers where possible. Separate distribution and marketing of these models made sense, since the targeted customers were racing enthusiasts and not traditional diecast toy collectors. Decorations on the models in this special range were all licensed copies of actual vehicles. One particular problem with this market segment is the dynamic nature of the prototypes' decorations. Racing teams and drivers frequently change sponsors, and cars seldom look the same from one year to the next. Complicating matters is the high degree of education prospective customers have as to correct prototype paint schemes. Models in this range, while potentially generating strong sales, risk growing stale on the shelves quickly. Time will judge their continued success.

In the Classics range, many new castings were introduced during the Mattel years. E.R.F., Foden, Scammell, and Bedford commercial vehicles were well represented. Additional 1:50 scale busses and inter-city coaches would appear. A special series was started for British brewery vehicles, another niche market that proved highly popular. New versions of the Morris Traveler and Mini Van were introduced, including a Mini Van for the tenth anniversary of the Collector Club in 1994. This van also signaled the revival of the Corgi dog logo, which recalled the original logo of the 1960s. The Corgi hold on James Bond licensing would continue with special anniversary issues of the famous DB5 in two scales, and a special tie-in to the movie "Goldeneye." The latter, involving a Ferrari 355, was marketed as a Corgi but was actually produced by the firm Detail Car. Corgi Toys Ltd. became the British distributor of Detail Cars in an unusual reversal of roles for the company, and worked closely with them in joint marketing.

By far the biggest collector event to occur during Mattel's watch was the introduction of the new Chipperfield's range. Not a reissue of the original 1960s Chipperfield's models (except for possibly the trailer portion of the horse transporter), this range borrowed heavily upon the then current line of castings. Actual Chipperfield's Circus vehicles were modeled, with twelve vehicles in the set. Aside from being a nostalgic reminder of past models, the range was marketed as a limited edition set, and quickly sold out. Collector demand was insatiable, and most models in the range escalated rapidly in value once issued. Secondary manufacturers provided figures and display cases for the range with Corgi's blessing. In all, it was a bonanza for the company.

One final range must be mentioned, for it ceased to exist after the management buyout that would end Mattel's control over Corgi. The former Juniors range, (the term "Juniors" by then long out of usage) was a marketing problem for Mattel, since the range directly competed with their mainstay Hot Wheels line. When production of Corgi products was moved to China, Mattel began the process of blurring the lines between the two ranges. The term Corgi Auto-City was coined to designate the models formerly in the Juniors and Haulers ranges. Hot Wheels decorations began to appear on models with Corgi base plates, and some limited cross-packaging did occur. At the time the two companies separated, Mattel retained the Auto-City line, simply changing the logo on the packaging. Not initially marketed in the United States, Mattel in effect created a European Hot Wheels line.

97746 Toymaster Bedford CA Van and Corgi Morris J Van Set.

97200 BRS Parcels Services Bedford Box Van and Morris J Van Set.

The resin prototype of 96893 Morris J Van, Royal Mail.

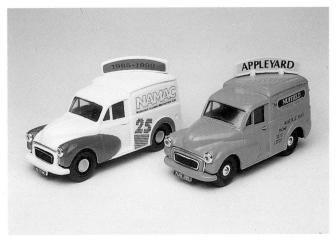

96843 NAMAC (similar to Q957/21) and earlier D957/11 Appleyard Nuffield Morris 1000 Vans.

96890 Morris J Van for Corgi Collector Club 1991.

96965 VW Van Corgi Collector Club 1992 next to a similar Mettoy era model.

Left: 96955 Mini Van Corgi Collector Club 1994 reintroduced the Corgi dog logo.

Right: 97396 1957 Chevy California Highway Patrol. *(Corgi Classics Ltd. photo)*

Left: Some of the Corgi Collector Club 1995 Morris Traveller models can be found without the year on the rear doors.

Right: 97315 Guy Arab Utility Bus, London Transport Wartime. *(Corgi Classics Ltd. photo)*

Left: 93500 Model Brum, a BBC children's television character unfamiliar to Americans.

Right: A collection of models from the various ranges in 1993. *(Corgi Classics Ltd. photo)*

Left: 97342 Burlingham Seagull Coach, West Coast. *(Corgi Classics Ltd. photo)*

Right: An assortment of British Trams. *(Corgi Classics Ltd. photo)*

Left: 96445 30th Anniversary James Bond Aston Martin DB5. *(Corgi Classics Ltd. photo)*

Right: Various models from the Cameos range. *(Corgi Classics Ltd. photo)*

Left: The well detailed resin prototype of 97198 Guy Arab Bus 'Southdown'.

Right: 98529 Race Transporter F.A.O. Schwarz. *(F.A.O. Schwarz photo)*

Left: Another resin prototype showing the more typical opaque windows.

Right: 90560 Auto-City Ferrari 348tb.

Left: 97886 Scammell Highwayman Crane Truck from the Chipperfield's Circus range. *(Corgi Classics Ltd. photo)*

Right: 93179 Mercedes-Benz 190e 2.3 Taxi.

Left: 97327 Atkinson 8 Wheel Rigid Truck 'Eddie Stobart'. *(Corgi Classics Ltd. photo)*

Right: 90472 Jaguar XJ40 Saloon (Sedan).

Left: 97162 Atkinson Elliptical Tanker, Pollack. *(Corgi Classics Ltd. photo)*

Right: 90470 Jaguar XJ40 Police.

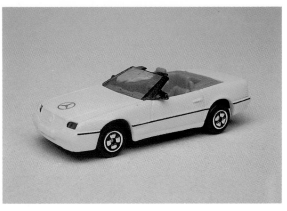

90571 Auto-City Mercedes-Benz 500 SL convertible.

90086 Auto-City London Taxi, Cutty Sark Whisky.
(Model courtesy of Berry Bros. & Rudd Ltd, London)

"Where to, Mac?"

90010(?) Auto-City Ford Transit Van, BP.

90076(?) Auto-City BMW 325i.

Auto-City (Haulers) M.A.N. Truck, Robinsons, part of assortment 93176.

Auto-City (Haulers) Ford Cargo Truck, Dairylea, part of assortment 93176.

Auto-City (Haulers) Kenworth Truck, Ferrari, part of assortment 93176.

Auto-City (Haulers) Kenworth Dump Truck, Wolf, part of assortment 93176.

(Number Unknown) Cameo Morris Open Truck, HSS. *(Model courtesy HSS Hire Services)*

(Number Unknown) Cameo Morris Open Truck with Barrels, Morris Tanker, and Model 'T' Ford Van issued for an Amoco Christmas promotion.

90320 Auto-City Iveco Refuse (garbage) Truck.

The Auto-City Custom Van with "Team Racing" decorations did not carry the Hot Wheels logo when packaged as a Corgi.

91341 Superhaulers Volvo Globetrotter Tanker, BP.

1.10—Corgi Classics Ltd.:
Independent Once More

On August 7, 1995, a management group headed by Chris Guest accomplished a management buyout of Corgi from Mattel Inc. The new company, Corgi Classics Ltd., obtained the rights to the Corgi name and logos, as well as most of the existing product lines. The "Auto-City" lines of former Juniors and Haulers vehicles were retained by Mattel, and soon could be found outside the United States repackaged as Hot Wheels. Mattel had achieved its intended European toy market penetration during its association with Corgi, and a separate Juniors range had become redundant. At the same time, Corgi had refocused its product offerings, and was now competing directly with other companies outside of the child's toy market. Corgi had helped to define the Nostalgia Model Vehicle market with their Classics and Original Omnibus ranges. A separation of the two companies was natural.

Corgi Classics Ltd. has a strong market position. New products, such as in the Original Omnibus Co., Golden Oldies, and Showman's ranges are highly popular with collectors. Many new offerings sell-out quickly and can be found soon afterward selling at a premium. The company continues to market promotional models for companies that request them, but that segment is now a much smaller percentage of Corgi production. Corgi's strength is once again in its standard product line.

The latest news prior to publication was a Corgi announcement on August 2, 1996, about the acquisition of the assets of Bassett Lowke Ltd. by Corgi Classics Ltd. Bassett Lowke is a well known British toy manufacturer first established in 1899. Their line of quality white metal kits and pre-assembled models will compliment Corgi's already strong product line. Manufacturing by Bassett Lowke was suspended prior to the acquisition by Corgi Classics Ltd. Corgi's plans as to how the Bassett Lowke product line will be integrated into Corgi's range of products wasn't finalized at the time of publication.

The future looks bright for the newly independent Corgi Classics Ltd. With a strong product line, good market position, name recognition, and a loyal following of collectors, we can look forward to the introduction of new and interesting Corgi models for many years to come.

45201 MGB Roadster, Top Up, (1:18 Scale). *(Corgi Classics Ltd. photo)*

95100 MGF Hard Top, (1:18 Scale). *(Corgi Classics Ltd. photo)*

02401 Austin Healey, Top Up, and 02501 Austin Healey, Top Down, which have added details versus earlier models . *(Corgi Classics Ltd. photo)*

A selection from the Showman's Range. *(Corgi Classics Ltd. photo)*

42702 Original Omnibus Co. Van Hool Alizee Coach, National Express. *(Corgi Classics Ltd. photo)*

52501 Mack B Series Box Van, New York Central. *(Corgi Classics Ltd. photo)*

52002 Mack CF Series Pumper, Lionel City Fire Co. *(Corgi Classics Ltd. photo)*

51901 American LaFrance Aerial Ladder Truck with Closed Cab, Boston. *(Corgi Classics Ltd. photo)*

53902 Yellow Coach 743 Bus, Lionel Bus Lines. *(Corgi Classics Ltd. photo)*

19601 Bedford S Bottle Truck, Bass Worthington. *(Corgi Classics Ltd. photo)*

GM 5301 New York Bus Service, (number unknown). *(Corgi Classics Ltd. photo)*

16302 Scammell Highwayman & Tanker Trailer, Esso. *(Corgi Classics Ltd. photo)*

27601 Atkinson 8 Wheel Truck & Trailer with Loads, F.B.Atkins. *(Corgi Classics Ltd. photo)*

This Shell Racing Transporter was found at Shell stations as a Christmas promotion in 1996.

Section 2:Focus Topics

2.1—Why the Name Corgi?: Naming the Breed

The Corgi name and the dog logo have become hallmarks of quality diecast toys and models. However, when Mettoy was in the planning stages for a full-out market attack on then king of the hill, Dinky Toys, there was no such awareness of the Corgi name. In order to penetrate the market so firmly controlled by Dinky, Mettoy had to come up with a product name and marketing plan that grabbed and held the attention of potential customers. Rapid market penetration was essential, since once Corgi's innovations were on the market, rivals such as Dinky would be sure to copy them. A catchy name had to be found.

Mettoy hit upon the perfect name with Corgi Toys. Corgi is the name of a breed of small herding dog native to Wales, the same area where Corgi Toys were first produced. The Corgi is a sturdy, short-legged dog favored by British royalty. Its name is short and easy to remember (although often misspelled in the United States where the breed isn't so well known.) The breed's distinctive profile lent itself to brand logos, and the name ends with the same sound as its rival Dinky. Who can estimate how many sales went to Corgi by children asking for "the one with the dog?." Once the initial market foothold was established, Corgi kept up the pressure by constantly introducing unique innovations, redefining state-of-the-art in diecast toys. However it was the Corgi name, coupled with innovations, that gained Corgi its initial market penetration.

In 1964, Mettoy again faced the problem of naming a new product line. Woolworth approached Mettoy to develop an in-house line of small diecast vehicles to compete with the phenomenally popular Matchbox Toys by Lesney. Since these were to be exclusive to Woolworth, the Corgi or Mettoy names were not to be used. The name of the product line needed to be just as appealing to the North American market as to Europe. Mettoy named the new line Husky Toys, another reference to a breed of dog. The name also carried a dual meaning of being a well known working dog and of being strong and sturdy, or husky. The profile of the dog's head was used as a logo, paralleling Corgi. The Husky Toys name and logo would continue until the exclusivity agreement ended between Mettoy and Woolworth in 1970. The small vehicle line was then renamed Corgi Juniors to associate the products with the popular larger line. Husky base plate dies were hurriedly altered by blanking-out the Husky name (and logo where present) so that a small Corgi Juniors label could be attached.

The continuing value of the Corgi name is evident in the company's recent history. When Mettoy closed its doors in 1983, the new company that emerged was named Corgi Toys Ltd., maintaining continuity of product identity. The dog logo was replaced by a non-descript design incorporating the name Corgi with a traffic symbol (often referred to as the skid-mark logo in the United States). The value of the Corgi product name was recognized by Mattel Inc. when it purchased the company in late 1989, so much so that Mattel was slow to put their own logo on Corgi packaging. The original dog logo, not used since 1984, was revived in 1994 during Mattel's ownership. Then in 1995,

Corgi Classics Ltd. was formed when the company became independent once more. The new company caters to the nostalgia market in its marketing approach, and much of the packaging and literature now recalls designs from the Corgi Toys line of the 1960s.

Present logo used by Corgi Classics Ltd. *(Artwork provided by Corgi Classics Ltd.)*

The 40th Anniversary logo. *(Artwork provided by Corgi Classics Ltd.)*

2.2—The Corgi Model Club: Mettoy's Club for Corgi Collectors

The Corgi Model Club was formed soon after the introduction of Corgi Toys by Mettoy as a marketing tool to reach new Corgi collectors (at that time, mostly pre-teenage boys). The club was used by Mettoy to introduce collectors to new Corgi models in order to generate interest and increase sales to repeat customers. Information about the demographics of new members was used by the company to analyze changes in their market. From its founding in late 1956, Bill Baxter served as club secretary. The club's first newsletter appeared in December, 1956. Subsequent newsletters were sent to club members on a regular basis, illustrating Corgi models being introduced that month. Applications for membership could be found packaged in almost every Corgi Toy box. Periodicals read by young boys of the time often contained advertisements for Corgi Toys on which additional membership applications could be found. Club members were able to correspond with the club secretary, the channel through which "By Special Request" models were initiated.

New members to the club received a club packet in the mail. Over time, the contents of this packet changed. Initially, new members received a numbered certificate, a lapel pin with the

Corgi logo, and the current newsletter. Members also received the quarterly "Corgi Model Club Magazine." At some point, the then-current Corgi catalog was added. In the mid 1960s, the quarterly magazine was discontinued in favor of a new feature section in the weekly magazine "TV Century 21." Unfortunately, this magazine was only available to members in Britain.

Beginning in 1967, the club added the "Corgi Model Club Member's Handbook" to mark the tenth anniversary of the club. The handbook contained many interesting articles on Corgi Toys, their features, how to display them, and other tidbits. Many unique illustrations were included in the book, including a view of the Commer Police Van in a "POLICE" version never produced. Around 1967, the format of the numbered certificate was changed. Also, the form of the club pin varied over time, with variations now being reported by collectors.

The American distributor of Corgi Toys, Reeves International Inc., advertised and promoted Corgi Toys and the Corgi Model Club heavily in the 1960s. Ads showing the latest models appeared in boys' magazines, such as "Boy's Life," on a regular basis. In the mid-'60s, Reeves offered a packaged promotion to encourage new members to join the Corgi Model Club. For only one dollar, new members would receive a tube in the mail containing the membership certificate and pin, the latest Corgi catalog, the handbook, *and* a Corgi vehicle. Depending on when the membership application was received, either the Ferrari 250 LM Berlinetta or the Mustang Fastback Competition was included. There must have been many, many Mustangs and Ferraris sent out this way. These models did not have a normal outer box, since they were being sent in the mailer tube. Rumors persist that some of the Mustangs were decorated differently than the normal production, such as blue rather than red stripes, but none of these models have come to the attention of the author.

Sometime in the mid 1970s, the club faded out. Marketing strategies had changed, and the demographics of Corgi Toy buyers became progressively younger. When Bill Baxter passed away, the club was left without a champion. Character Toys came to dominate the product line, and the club format simply became obsolete.

Left: Two versions of the Corgi Model Club pin with an original box.

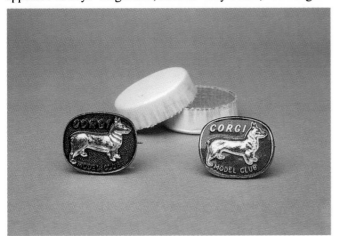

Below: The certificate and welcome letter for new members.

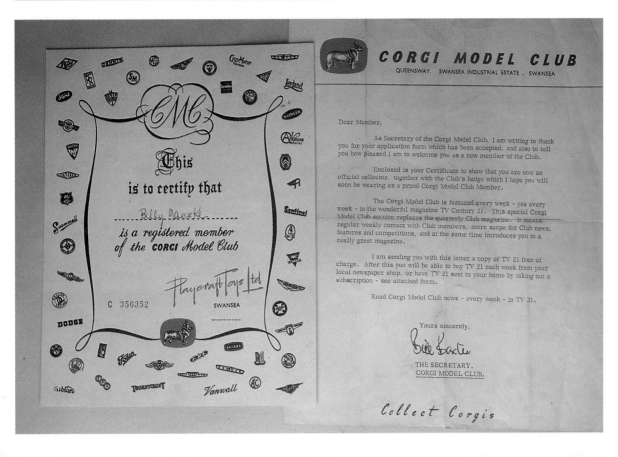

2.3—The Corgi Collector Club: Today's Forum for Collectors

Soon after the formation of Corgi Toys Ltd. in 1984, management realized that they would need a direct link to Corgi Toy collectors and their interests if they were to survive and grow. Toward this end, the Corgi Collector Club was formed. At first, it was a vehicle for the company to announce new offerings to collectors. However, it soon grew to have a life of its own, generating discussion on past Corgi Toys as well as reviewing new offerings.

From the beginning, a bi-monthly magazine was issued to members. At first, the magazine was black and white, but by Issue 9, January 1986, the magazine was produced with a color cover and some color pages. New offerings were displayed to tempt collectors. For Issue 13, September/October 1986, Susan Pownall replaced Mike Broadfield as editor, a position she still holds today. The nineteenth issue of the Corgi Collector magazine, September/October 1987, saw the first of many articles by the enigmatic Dai Caste. His familiar greeting "SH'MAE" at the beginning of each article opened a discussion on inside information, data from collectors, and commentary which was both stimulating and amusing. The magazine slightly revised and refined its format by Issue 41, May/June 1991, and then again with Issue 57, January 1994, when the size was enlarged from the previous A5 format (a metric term roughly equivalent to the American half-page size) to A4 format (roughly full page). The magazine is now published ten times per year with color illustrations throughout.

On the first anniversary of the founding of Corgi Toys Ltd., the Collector Club issued the first in a series of special model vehicles solely for club members. In 1987-88, the issuance of the club model was revised to correspond with the beginning of each calendar year. This creates some confusion among new collectors, since there is no 1987 club model. Instead, the club

Morris Minor Van issued in mid-1987 was decorated with '87 on one side and '88 on the other. All other club models represent only a single year. Club models issued from 1991 through 1993 were shipped in foam containers and do not have decorated outer boxes. In 1995, that year's club model was issued for the first time in a color more like the production vehicle it represented, and not in the bright blue and yellow of previous models, sparking an ongoing, heated debate.

Special models commemorating major company events were issued on two other occasions and are not part of the normal annual club model series. The first, a two-vehicle set, commemorated the move of Corgi from Swansea to Leicester after the Mattel buyout. The other model commemorated the management buyout of Mattel in 1995. These were offered separately to club members through special promotions in the club magazine. Club members also have the opportunity to acquire promotional or private issue models which become available on a limited basis through the club.

Each issue of the Corgi Collector magazine contains fascinating reading. Articles about new offerings, historical data, and member's collections are presented. An editorial section for member's letters and a For Sale/Wanted section round out the magazine. Bargains on scarce older models can be found in the advertisements for those who act quickly. Usually, the club has back issues of the magazine and some previous years' club models available for purchase by new members. Information about joining the Corgi Collector Club can be obtained from:

The Secretary
Corgi Collector Club
P.O. Box 323
Swansea SA1 1BJ   UK

1986 Ford Model 'T' Van club model.

1987-88 Morris 1000 Van club model.

1989 Ford Popular Van club Model.

1992 Volkswagen Van club model.

1990 Bedford CA Van club model.

1993 Double Decker Bus club model.

1991 Morris J Van club model.

1994 Mini-Van club model.

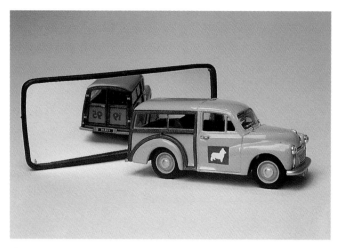

1995 Morris Traveller club model.

Early Corgi Collector Magazine covers.

Prototype of 1996 Land Rover club model without hood logo. *(Corgi Collector Club photo)*

Late 1980s covers including a Christmas issue.

The hood logo on production 1996 Land Rover club models.

A later large format issue with one of the club's many contests.

The special issue of Corgi Collector Magazine issued for the management buy-back of the company from Mattel Inc.

Susan Pownall, Editor of the magazine since soon after the club's formation. . *(Corgi Collector Club photo)*

2.4—The Corgi Heritage Center:
Home for a Factory Collection

During the time Corgi Classics Ltd. was based in Swansea, a museum area was set-up at the factory for visitors. In the museum was a collection of historic Corgi Toys, as well as displays illustrating the history and manufacturing of the products. After the Mattel buyout, however, the corporate offices were moved to Leicester, and much of the production moved offshore to China. The museum collection was placed in storage until a new location could be determined.

Around the time of the management buyout of Mattel in the summer of 1995, an agreement for a new home for the collection was reached. Corgi Classics Ltd. entered into a joint venture with Chris Brierley Models to house the collection at a facility in Lancashire. The new museum was called The Corgi Heritage Center, and is the factory supported Corgi Museum.

At this writing, the author is not aware of any other museums specifically devoted to Corgi Toys, as there are for Matchbox Toys and others. Other museums have displays of Corgi Toys as part of a broader collection, but they will not be listed here. A visit to the Corgi Heritage Center is well worth the trip while in Britain. The address of the museum is:

The Corgi Heritage Center
53 York St.
Heywood
Nr. Rochdale
Lancashire OL10 4NR
Phone: 011 (44) 1706 365812

The museum offers collectors a historical overview of Corgi Toys production, as well as displays of products over the years.

The cover of Corgi Collector Magazine announcing the opening of the Corgi Heritage Centre.

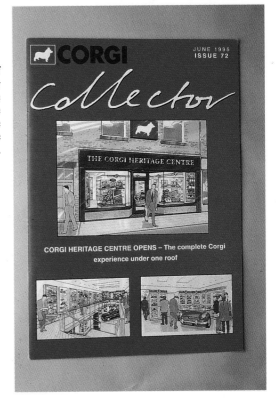

2.5—Catalogs, Ads, and Publications: Temptation in Print

One of the things that is most visible to customers and that generates the most repeat sales, is the catalog. Corgi was a master in creating colorful, pocket catalogs for their products, often showing artists renderings of products in some exciting scene, or illustrating some fabulous new feature. Over the years, since the first fold-out catalog of 1957, these pocket references have taken many forms. Many collectors best remember the many-paged pocket catalogs of the '60s, but other formats have been produced.

The size and style of the catalogs produced by Mettoy and its successors grew and shrank with the product line. Relatively few Corgi Toys were produced in the early years, especially when compared to the peak years of the late 1960s. By the early '60s, the catalog could be found as a quarter-sheet size, multi-page collection of the artwork found on the boxes of the time, with additional artwork to illustrate sets and features. This size catalog was the norm through the 1960s, 1970s, and early 1980s, with exceptions in 1967 and 1970. The catalog for 1967 was long and thin with actual photos of the models. The 1970 catalog was also long and thin, but was a fold-out pamphlet rather than a stapled catalog. Such pamphlets would also appear in the mid '70s. Corgi and Corgi Classics catalogs changed to a full-sheet format in the late 1980s, with different catalogs for the various ranges. There were also very small folded pamphlets similar to the catalog enclosed in the boxes of models beginning in the late '80s.

Husky and Corgi Junior catalogs were less consistent in size. At least two pocket catalogs are known to exist for the Husky Toys and Corgi Rockets ranges. Corgi Juniors were often shown photographed in groups in full-page format pamphlets in the early and mid 1970s. By the late '70s, the Juniors name had been dropped, and the "E" Corgi series (Juniors) would appear in the main Corgi Toy Catalog.

Corgi and its various makers produced much more in print than just pocket catalogs. In addition, the various distributors of Corgi toys around the world also produced promotional materials for their own markets. One need only look into current diecast toy magazines for proof. Dealer catalogs with extensive ordering information, and dealer press releases were produced most years for retailers. Shop signs and displays were also plentiful. Mettoy and their agents around the world were also good about answering letters written to them.

A small sample of the printed materials produced are presented in this section. To date, no complete list exists for these types of support materials.

Corgi Toys Catalog Supplement of June, 1960.

Corgi Toys Catalog Supplement of June, 1962.

1963 Corgi Toys Catalog.

Canadian 1968 Husky Toys Catalog.

1970 Corgi Rockets Catalog.

Corgi Model Club Collectors Handbook from 1966.

1971 Corgi Toys Catalog.

1971 Corgi Juniors Catalog.

1974 Corgi Juniors Catalog Supplement.

1974 Corgi Toys Catalog Supplement.

More catalogs.

1975 & 1976 Corgi Catalogs.

Mettoy's last Corgi Catalog from 1983.

Corgi Toys Catalogs.

Corgi Toys Ltd.'s first Corgi Catalog from 1984.

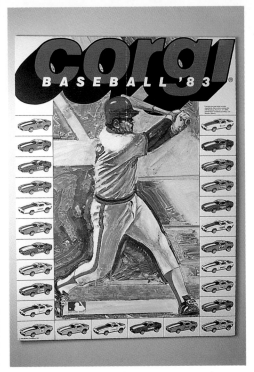

The new image 1985 Corgi Catalog.

1987 Corgi Classics Catalog in the new large format.

The baseball poster offered on the back of the c.1983 Baseball Cars.

The 1995 Catalog for the Original Omnibus Company range of 'OO' Scale public transport vehicles.

Catalogs were misleading sometimes. Four of the cars pictured here were never produced.

Whether all of the Corgi Rockets track accessories were ever produced is not known.

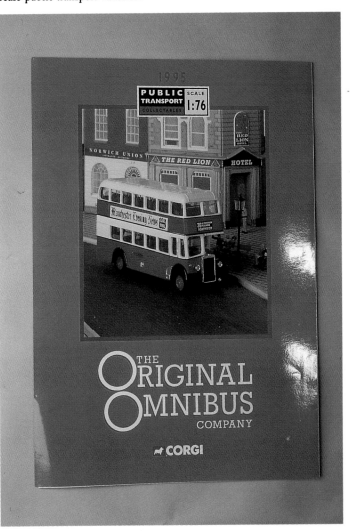

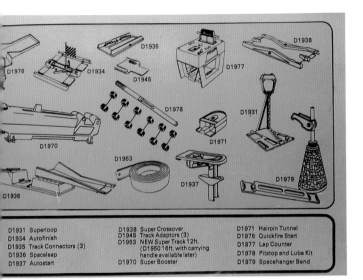

D1931 Superloop	D1938 Super Crossover	D1971 Hairpin Tunnel
D1934 Autofinish	D1945 Track Adaptors (3)	D1976 Quickfire Start
D1935 Track Connectors (3)	D1963 NEW Super Track 12ft.	D1977 Lap Counter
D1936 Spaceleap	(D1950 16ft. with carrying	D1978 Pitstop and Lube Kit
D1937 Autostart	handle available later)	D1979 Spacehanger Bend
	D1970 Super Booster	

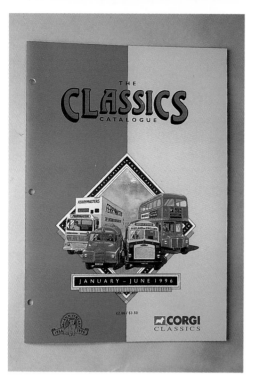

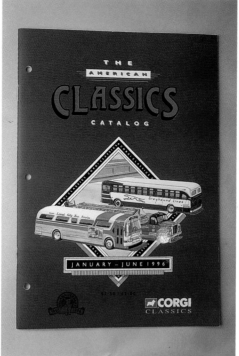

The January-June 1996 Corgi Classics Catalog.

The January-June 1996 Corgi American Classics Catalog.

The 1990s Chipperfield's range also had its own catalog.

Various other items available.

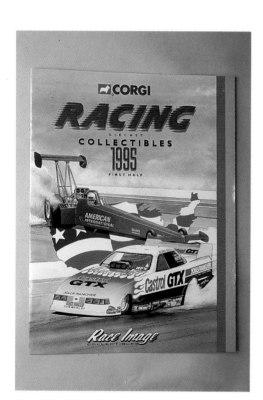

The Racing Collectibles Catalog.

Plastic Corgi Collector Club membership cards with an in-box leaflet.

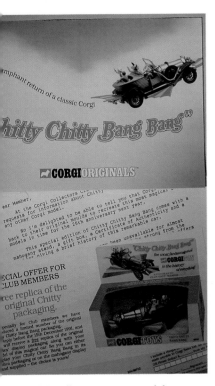

Special mailers were sent to club members for the reissue of Chitty-Chitty-Bang-Bang.

A dealer leaflet introducing the military models in the 1970s.

The back side of the dealer leaflet.

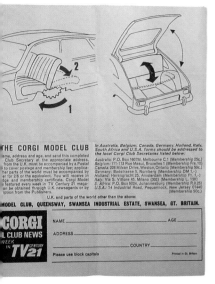

In-box leaflets were often quite detailed.

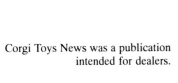

Corgi Toys News was a publication intended for dealers.

The introduction of 'Funny Cars' to dealers.

This ad is one of many that appeared in Boys' Life magazine.

Right: Reply letters written by the Corgi Model Club staff could be quite detailed.

Another ad placed in Boys' Life magazine.

Left: This letter from Mettoy explained the demise of the Corgi Model Club.

Smaller monthly ads showing new models also appeared in magazines.

Right: A letter from the Corgi Collector Club.

2.5—Character Vehicles:

Tuning In to Customers

Corgi found a sales bonanza producing models of popular characters from television and films. It could easily be said that Mettoy was the best in the diecast toy business in their time. The added customer recognition of popular characters associated with Corgi Toys resulted in some very high production numbers. Character toys also have a down side, though, since they are very time and market dependent. Popular characters in one market may be totally unknown in others, and fads come and go quickly. With the exception of characters with long-term popularity, such as Batman or James Bond, character vehicles could often be found in clearance aisles once their popularity had faded.

The first licensed character vehicle for Corgi Toys was 258, The Saint's Volvo, introduced in March, 1965. In essence no more than a redecorated 228 Volvo P1800, it still went on to sell over one million copies for Corgi. Additional sales were made by the smaller Corgi Rockets and Corgi Junior versions. While neither the most popular of Corgi's character vehicles, nor the most laden with features, it was nevertheless one of the few early Corgi castings to last well into the Whizzwheel era. (The Land Rover and London Taxi are two other examples.) With no opening features and a simple vacuum formed interior, it is a true testament to the power of Character marketing.

Mettoy was quick to pick-up on the potential of this market. Their next effort would forever change the nature of the diecast toy scene. In October of 1965, Corgi introduced the 261(A) James Bond Aston Martin DB5. Basically an extensive rework of Corgi's previous 218(A) of 1960, this model was crammed with every gimmick Corgi could fit into the available space in the body. With a working ejector seat, extending machine guns, and a rear bullet-proof shield, the model caused a sensation on both sides of the Atlantic. No other model had ever been marketed with features like these by any diecast manufacturer, and stocks sold out as soon as they could be delivered.

The number of character vehicles grew continuously after that. James Bond continued to be a popular theme, with many varied types of vehicles. Batman also obtained all manner of vehicles, with the Batmobile itself in production from 1966 into the late 1970s. Most comic book superheroes, and some TV shows, became topics for Corgi vehicles, and most models that appeared in the Corgi Toys range had smaller versions produced as Husky Toys or Corgi Juniors. The Saint's Volvo would even appear in the Corgi Rockets line. Character vehicles were very prolific in the Juniors line in the late '70s through the closure of Mettoy. The younger target market for Juniors would drive the creation of models associated with Saturday morning cartoons and professional sports teams. These models were usually produced in high numbers, but the younger age of the owners meant most weren't kept in collectible condition for long.

Character vehicles almost always carry a higher value among collectors. This is partly due to crossover collectors who collect items related to comic book or TV characters. The added competition for available models drives up the price. In addition, Corgi collectors connect character vehicles to their own childhood memories. Even the most over-produced items will eventually increase in value. This section presents only a small sample of the character models produced, which could easily fill a book themselves.

258 Corgi Toys and 905 Corgi Rockets versions of The Saint's Volvo P1800.

The same Corgi Toys Volvo with the later 320(B) Jaguar XJS with the same decoration.

The E32(C) Juniors Jaguar XJS for the Saint, still in its original display card.

261 James Bond Aston Martin DB5 with the earlier 218 Aston Martin DB4.

The DB4-style rear of the 261, correct DB5 style rear on 270, and incorrect DB6 rear on Husky/Juniors versions.

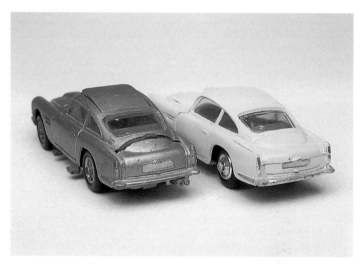

A rear view shows how Mettoy modified the DB4 die set to create the James Bond model.

336 James Bond Toyota 2000.

The corrected and improved 270 James Bond Aston Martin DB5.

The first version of the long-selling 267 Batmobile.

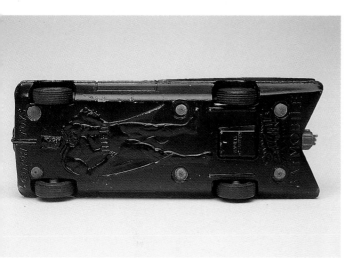

Batman was shown on the base.

497 The Man from U.N.C.L.E. Oldsmobile.

The special bat wheels on early Batmobiles.

1205 Husky or 1005 Corgi Juniors "The Man from U.N.C.L.E." imaginary car.

Various Batman-related Juniors.

This stickered Husky base needs verification and may or may not be authentic.

268 The Green Hornet car, based on a 1965 Chrysler Imperial Sedan, showing its operating features.

Gift Set 7(B) Daktari Land Rover with Figures.

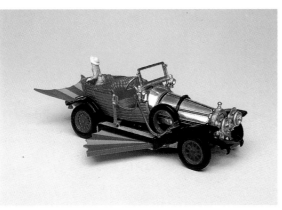

Gift Set 14(B) Giant Daktari Set with specially decorated Giraffe Transporter and Dodge Truck.

266 Chitty-Chitty-Bang-Bang (minus a few loose pieces).

805 Hardy Boys Rolls-Royce. The band could also play on the roof.

277 Monkeemobile, which in reality was a customized 1966 Pontiac GTO.

Here they come...

The base of the Monkeemobile shows a correctly detailed Pontiac chassis.

647 Buck Rogers Starfighter was too far-out for many collectors.

E50(B) The Daily Planet Van delivered news about Superman in two different colors.

E24(C) Shazam's Thunderbolt.

E68(A) Kojak's Buick, a 1973 Buick Regal, was the first of many versions of this casting.

The Carry Case portion of E3114(A) Superheros Set.

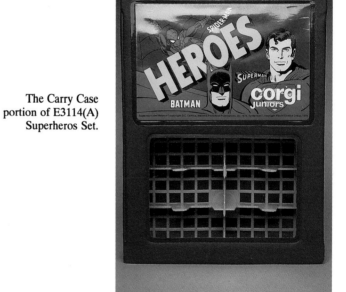

E33(D) Wonder Woman's Car, which must have been a snug fit.

Hey, there, it's E82(B) Yogi Bear's Jellystone Park Jeep.

E2030 Kermit's Kar, with two known color variations.

E2033 Animal's Percussionmobile, just drumming along.

E2032 Miss Piggy's Sports Car, with part of Miss Piggy's wardrobe.

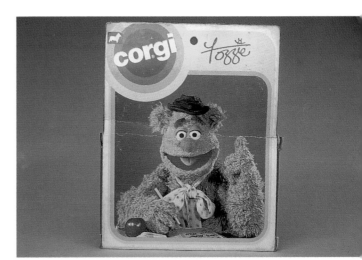

A typical box illustration from the Muppet Series.

Fozzie Bear's Truck out of its box.

2.7—Mini's

The most prolific and varied group of cars produced by Corgi during the Mettoy Era must be the various Mini's. These small, boxy cars were extremely popular in Britain from their introduction in the late '50s. Corgi's model of the car in its various forms were equally popular, and numerous! In *The Great Book Of Corgi,* Marcel Van Cleemput reports an astounding 7.3 million of the original 1/43 models alone (+1969 sales for which records were lost). This doesn't include the updated versions or Cameo issues of the late '80s and early '90s. The later 1/36 models are still in production, with new and interesting versions still being introduced.

Naturally, with such high production totals and varied issues, production variations often occurred. Some changes were evolutionary due to changing production techniques, or modifications made necessary by a new model introduction. Others were due to production haste or error. The Mini's were especially prone to the latter due to their design. To facilitate creating as many different models as possible from as few dies as possible, Corgi fitted the dies with removable inserts. In that way, the same die set could be used to create either an Austin Se7en (Yes, the spelling is correct.) or a Morris Mini Minor, simply by changing the inserts for the grill and base text. However, this also allowed for perfectly fitting but incorrect combinations of die parts to be assembled. Models with mismatch errors were more common than anyone would like to admit, especially in the mid '60s when a number of new versions were introduced each year. Not all mismatches are errors, though. Problems with the dies while in use could occasionally prompt a substitution of a different insert in order to allow production to continue. One such case could be the existence of two different grill types on the green 450 Mini Van.

The first Mini produced by Corgi, the 226 Morris Mini Minor, changed many times throughout its eight-year production life. When first issued, the model had the original "Patent Application" base with holes inboard of each wheel for assembly of the suspension. The holes soon disappeared as assembly methods changed. When the patent was granted, Corgi used the opportunity to redesign the base, moving the text insert away from the edge. The wheels on the first models were smooth and crimped to the axles. These soon were replaced by shaped wheels when they became available. Later, the shaped wheels were made free on the axles which had peened ends. Near the time when the body color was changed from light blue to maroon, the shaped wheels were replaced by cast wheels. In 1972, the 226 Morris Mini Minor was refitted with Whizzwheels and renumbered 204(B).

The Mini's produced by Corgi in the early days tended to have metal flow problems in the dies, evidenced by the sag seen over the rear side windows of some models. This problem was corrected around 1967 by revising the design of the die set. The new die set was phased into production for the higher volume models, while the old die set continued to be used for a time for lower volume models. Mini's produced by the new die set can be identified by their thicker window pillars, a strong forward arch at the bottom of the grill, and a slightly different curvature over the taillights. The changeover in 226 Morris Mini Minor production occurred prior to the color change to maroon, although the light blue version is hard to find. The Austin Se7en was discontinued prior to the introduction of the new die set since the grill insert was no longer usable.

Corgi loved introducing new variations of the Mini into the product line, since the basic die set was already in-place. Jeweled headlights, a popular feature of the time, were fitted to the 227 Mini-Cooper Competition of May 1962, with special paint and racing decals. The application of wicker printed side stickers and a change of color in November 1965 created the popular 249 Mini-Cooper with Wickerwork. In 1967 or 1968, a small number of the 349 Pop-Art Morris Mini's were released to the public prior to a management decision not to proceed with the model. (The author knows of six examples, there are probably more.) Instead, production of the 249 Wickerwork version was continued in a limited manner, mostly to supply models for the GS48 Car Transporter Set. Late 249's are notable in that they use the new die set for the body casting. The final run of the 249 Wickerwork version deleted the red roof to cut costs, making an all-black version.

By far, the most popular Mini's produced by Corgi (and the most expensive today) were the red and white rally versions. Corgi hit upon a gold mine when they began to duplicate winning rally cars soon after the rallies were run. Memories of the competitions were still fresh when Corgi's models would hit the shelves. These models tended to have short production lives, though, as they were rendered stale stock as soon as the next version was introduced. (A similar phenomenon is occurring today with NASCAR collectibles.) Of the red and white rally versions, the 333 R.A.C. Sun Rally version had the lowest production run, while the 339 1967 Monti Carlo Rally version had the highest. Beware, though, since the 339 model has many sub-variations which cannot be quantified for numbers produced. Also, additional detail changes occurred during the production of the Whizzwheel conversion of the 1967 Monti Carlo Mini-Cooper, renumbered 308(B), which was produced in yellow rather than red and white.

Special features were often found on the Rally Mini's, with each new introduction trying to top the last. The 317 Monti Carlo Mini-Cooper of February, 1964, was the first and only Mini with a swiveling spotlight on the roof. However, its introduction caused a permanent change in the window die for all Minis to accommodate the spotlight, which was present from 1964 to 1967 when it was again changed for the 339 Mini-Cooper. This is a good indicator of the age of any more common model of the period. The 321 Monti Carlo Mini-Cooper of February, 1965, saw the creation of a completely different seat mold used on all subsequent Monti Carlo Minis. This vacuum-formed part possessed representations of rally equipment in the back seat area. Careful collectors should be on the watch for incorrect seat moldings in Minis from this period. The base of the 321 was altered to accept a sheet metal sump guard. The 321 of 1965 was the only model that also possessed added small spotlights at the hood edge, which were in addition to the standard five jeweled lights.

The 1966 update to the 321, introduced in January, 1966, (same number, different model) reverted to a more standard Morris grill insert in the die set, using only four jeweled lights. The trick for 1966 was the silk screened autographs printed on the roof. Following soon afterward was the 333 R.A.C. International Rally Mini-Cooper of February, 1967. This short-lived model used the Austin grill die set, which by then was no longer needed for the 225 Austin Se7en. It was fitted with six jeweled lights, as many as could fit on the model. The model was produced with the large black "21" missing from the driver's door decal, although it is present on the opposite door.

The Monti Carlo Mini model with the largest production run was the 339 Monti Carlo Mini-Cooper S of 1967. Introduced in March, 1967, the casting was initially identical to the 333 introduced two months before with only trim changes. Features new to this model were the addition of a vacuum-plated roof rack with two spare tires, a black plastic mud flap and placard molding under the front bumper, and updated Monti Carlo decals. The initial models also had the Austin grill like the 333, although the main headlights were of smaller diameter than normal. The grill reverted to the Morris type when the revised design die set was placed into production, and the headlights returned to their proper larger diameter. When available, cast wheels were fitted to the model followed by treaded "plastic" tires. The final form of the 339 was carried over into the 308(B) Whizzwheel version of February, 1972, which was produced only in yellow. Later versions of the 308(B) could be found with blue rather than red seats, although it is believed that it was always produced with clear windows. Base colors and wheel pattern types are still to be documented.

The final 1:42 scale Mini produced by Corgi was the 204(B) Morris Mini Minor with Whizzwheels of February, 1972. Essentially the final version of the 226 fitted with Whizzwheels, it was mainly used in sets. It was produced in various shades of orange or dark blue, with bases of various colors. The windows on later models were tinted to help hide the archaic vacuum formed seats. Die wear is increasingly evident on later models, since this was in essence the least glamorous model in the range.

The Mini Van and Mini Countryman were also represented by Corgi Models in the '60s. The Mini Countryman was only produced in the 485 version with roof rack, surfer and surfboards. It shared base components with the 450 Mini Van and 448 Police Mini Van, using a similar replaceable insert design in the dies. Wheel and tire type variations, and differences in painted trim are known for these models, but the green Mini Van is the only documented case of an incorrect insert being used for a model, substituting the Countryman grill for the spartan grill design normally used.

One last group of 1:42 scale Mini's were produced by Mettoy. The 334 "Mini Magnifique" was a unique casting in which Mettoy attempted to cram as many features into the model as they could. It was produced concurrently in either metallic blue or metallic green. Known variations involve differences in the pattern in the sunroof and tire types. Producing this model must have been expensive. The Whizzwheel conversion, 282, no longer had the sunroof and used borrowed labels from the 308(B) Monti-Carlo Mini. It was produced in white with a black hood and trunk lid.

In the mid-'70s, the scale of Corgi Toys progressively changed from 1:42 to 1:36. The Mini underwent this change with the introduction of the 200(B) Mini 1000. Actually larger than advertised, the new Mini was somewhat out of proportion in appearance. It featured opening doors and a molded interior. This basic casting would go on to be produced in many, many color schemes under the numbers 200(B), GS38(B), 201(B), as well as various numbers in the Corgi Toys Ltd., Mattel, and Corgi Classics Ltd. numbering schemes. The most interesting variation to-date is the Corgi Classics Ltd. Rally version with added Rally headlights on the hood. The 1:36 Mini has appeared in many boxed sets in a rainbow of paint schemes, and is presently being produced in a wide variety of rally schemes.

The mid-'80s saw the introduction of a more inexpensive line of vehicles by Corgi Toys Ltd. The Cameo series included a Mini very close in size to the original 1:42 models. The Cameo version, however, is a simplified, low cost version in which the seats and base are one integral molding. It had been used in cereal promotions and has been produced in a number of colors. Documentation is hard to come by on the Cameos, however, and the extent of the variations produced cannot be quantified by the author. At a minimum, tan, blue, white, and dark green versions are known to exist, as well as promotionals for Kellogg's, Cadbury's, Filofax, and Safeguard.

Around 1993, Corgi Classics Ltd. introduced a new 1:43 Mini Cooper to capitalize on the growing nostalgia market. While some of the early publicity photos showed models based on the earlier castings from the 1960s, the actual models produced were quite different. Rally headlights were permanently molded into a plated plastic grill. The interior and rally type wheels of the prototype are well represented, with non-removable "child-proof" rubber tires used. Many nostalgic versions of this later mini were made. The Monti-Carlo rally issues of the 1960s were duplicated in a set, with one also appearing individually. The wickerwork Mini also reappeared, though it looked strange with the rally headlights. Numerous other versions in other colors were also produced, including an issue of the Monti-Carlo model with a BMC medallion in the package.

The 10th anniversary of the Corgi Collector Club was celebrated in 1994 with a club model based on a new version of the Mini-Van. This casting is about the same size as the 1960s original, but is in actuality a totally new casting. The new model no longer had the opening rear doors like the original, but made up for it with a highly detailed interior with rearview mirror, chromed bumpers, headlights, and taillights. Proper van-type wheels are modeled. The unfortunate rhinestone headlights of the Mini-Cooper were not reused, as a more scale looking chromed plastic version was affixed instead. Other versions released by Corgi include RAC and AA versions, which echo the Dinky Toys versions of the mid 1960s. These could be considered predecessors to Corgi's Golden Oldies series, which also echo earlier Dinky Toys models. Perhaps in the future a Joseph Mason Paints version may follow which duplicates a rare and sought after Dinky promotional. The Corgi casting has also appeared in various police versions and is still in production as of this writing.

As popular as the Mini was in the Corgi product line, only one version was produced in the smaller Husky/Corgi Junior scale. Possibly, the prototype's diminutive size may not have lent itself well to such a small scale, or regular wheels from the product line may have looked out of proportion on such a model. The sole model to appear was the Juniors E21(C) B.V.R.T. Vita-Mini 1300 Mini-Cooper S. This model was of a "hot rodded" mini which must have been based upon a show car, at least in part. It is possibly a response to the Matchbox Mini of the period which is also an out-of-scale, hot rodded model.

Corgi Mini's from the 1960s through the 1990's.

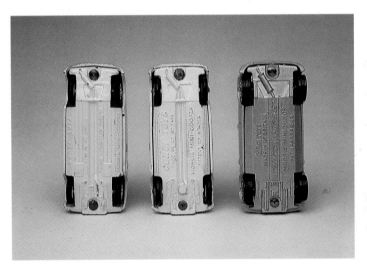

Three different 227 Mini-Cooper Competition.

225 Austin Se7en Mini (red) among four early 226 Morris Mini-Minors.

Patent application, patent number, and Whizzwheels baseplates.

Late (maroon) 226 Morris Mini-Minors with four 204(B) Whizzwheel versions.

All of the red-and-white Monti-Carlo Mini-Cooper S models together in one photograph.

The rarest of the mid-1960s Mini-Coopers, 321 (1965), 321 (1966), and 333 (RAC Rally).

Early and late 339 Monti-Carlo Mini-Coopers.

The seldom-published rear view for comparison purposes.

Early and very late 249 Mini-Cooper with Wickerwork beside 349 Pop-Art Mini.

334 BMC Mini-Cooper Magnifique and the simplified 282 Whizzwheel version.

485 Austin Mini Countryman with Surfer, 448 Austin Police Minivan and 450 Austin Minivan.

The Countryman grill version of the 450 Minivan beside the 1994 Corgi Collector Club Minivan.

One of many Cameo Minis from the 1980s.

The only Juniors Mini, E21(C) B.V.R.T. Vita-Mini 1300 Mini-Cooper S.

2.8—Land Rovers: Corgi's Workhorses

The workhorse of the Corgi line for many years was the Land Rover 109" wheel base pick-up. Produced in a phenomenal number of versions, this 1:43-scale model served as the basis for many, many of Corgi's offerings. The first Land Rover in the Corgi range was the 406 Land Rover 109" wheel base pick-up of 1957. This model was produced in either blue with a white roof, or yellow with a black roof. While it had windows, there was no suspension or interior and the base was a tin stamping. Realizing the versatility of the model, Corgi soon expanded its usage into gift sets and service vehicles. A version for the RAF, 351, was produced which pulled a model rocket on its trailer in GS-3. The R.A.C. variant, 416, possessed an added cast sign board on the cab roof, although very late examples can be found without it. A version with a tin cover over the rear was used to pull a horse trailer in GS-2, and later a circus elephant in a cage on a trailer in GS-19. A planned gift set with a racing car and trailer would not appear until this casting was out of production. The most noteworthy version of the early casting was the 417 Land Rover Wrecker version of 1960. It would be equipped with a half-canopy with spotlight and a working crane operated from a side-mounted spare tire. The 406 Land Rover and its related variations can be found with either smooth or shaped wheels depending on the date produced, although the wheels are always found crimped to the axle pins. The early Land Rover casting would be in production until 1962, when it was replaced in all applications with a totally new version with updated features.

In late 1962, Corgi introduced a totally new casting of an updated Land Rover. The older version was not designed for spring suspension. In redesigning the Land Rover model, Corgi not only fitted spring suspension and a vacuum formed interior, but also updated the appearance of the model to the latest design of the prototype. However, the designers made sure that add-on pieces used to create such models as the wrecker would also fit the new casting. Peened end axles pins with free turning wheels were also a feature. Even though the model casting was entirely new, Corgi maintained their practice of keeping the model number while adding an "S" suffix to indicate suspension was added. An extremely rare version, a 406S yellow pick-up without cover, has recently come to light and was part of a well publicized auction. The standard Land Rover would quickly be modified by Corgi with the addition of a plastic rear cover and renumbered 438. This is the standard model familiar to most collectors. A version without a cover did continue, though, packaged in the GS-5 Agricultural Gift Set produced from 1967 through 1972.

The 438 Land Rover casting, and its wrecker variant, were reused heavily throughout the Corgi product line by Mettoy. The GS-2 Land Rover and Rice's Pony Trailer would be updated with the new casting, being produced in tan and white through 1968. In that year, an expanded horse trailer for two horses was issued and the set number was changed to GS-15(B). This set was in blue and white and would later be converted to Whizzwheels, lasting through 1977. The wrecker variant, 417S, continued in the identical colors and decorationsas its predecessor. The wrecker boom would be filled-in to make it more sturdy. A plastic rear cover would replace the tin one in 1965, changing the model number to 477 (and thereby eliminating the awkward "S" designation). The 417/477 Land Rover Wrecker set the record for longest unchanged paint scheme on a Corgi, remaining basically the same from 1960 through 1977 (beating the London Taxi by three months). The 438 Land Rover and 477 Wrecker would both be fitted with Whizzwheels by 1974. Sometime in the early '70s, Corgi quietly replaced the very worn die set for the Land Rover with a new one. The exact date when this occurred is not clear. There are a few spotting features which distinguish models made from the latter die set from the earlier one. The fastest way to identify later models is through the shape of the front license plate. Other spotting features are the shape of the side windows and wheel openings. Evolutionary changes occurred to Corgi's Land Rover throughout its production life. Wheel types went from shaped to cast to Whizzwheels. Various tire types could also be found. A plastic tow hook replaced the tin version in the late '60s, and the vacuum formed interior lost its separate molded steering wheel in the mid '70s. Also somewhere in the '70s, the plastic rear cover on those models that used it changed shape to a more arched design that no longer followed the roof shape. The last of the 1/43 Land Rovers would be produced in 1977, well into the 1/36 scale era.

Many character and special-use models were issued based on the Land Rover casting. The popular TV show "Daktari" led to the creation of a green and black zebra-stripe Corgi model equipped with a tiger gracing the hood and other figures. Similar stripes can be found on the white Land Rover in the GS-8(B) "Lions of Longleat" set, along with the driver standing through a hatch in the roof and a cage in the rear. Many collectors don't realize that the 487 Chipperfield's Circus Parade Vehicle and the 466 "Vote for Corgi" models are actually based upon the 477 Wrecker with a special rear insert added. While no special uses of the complete wrecker seem to exist, the standard 438 model was used for many "specials" for specific markets. A U.S. Army version was produced in olive drab for the United States. European markets received special "Lepra" and "TS Radio" versions. Others may exist, since Mettoy was not good at keeping clear records of promotional items produced on special order.

The Land Rover was not ignored in the shift to 1/36 scale in the 1970s. The new larger model, however was of a completely different four-door version of the vehicle. This eliminated the possibility of a wrecker version. This model was made in a variety of versions, some with added gear on the roof accessed by a ladder. Tarzan got one of these in a green and tan zebra-stripe scheme. Many law enforcement and rescue versions have appeared. Sets using this casting have also included horse trailers, a circus animal trailer, or a rescue boat and trailer. The most unique versions of the 1/36 Land Rover are the two that appeared as Corgitronics. A "POLICE" version was fitted with a siren and light while a "Roadworks" version towed an air compressor trailer with sound. The Corgitronics models would only last until Mettoy's closure in 1983, but the standard model has continued and is still in production in Corgi Classics Ltd.'s "Toys" line at this writing.

Many versions of the Land Rover appeared in the Juniors line over its history. The earliest was an unusual forward control (cab-over-engine) version introduced into the Husky line in 1965. Painted in olive drab with a plastic cover over the bed, this model only lasted until 1968 and was out of production long before the change-over to Corgi Juniors. The first actual Juniors Land Rover was an updated 109-inch wheel base pick-up introduced in 1971 in the usual (for Corgi) green. This casting was also the basis for a military ambulance version introduced in 1975. A completely different casting was introduced in 1970 as the Land Rover

Wrecker. Both the pick-up and wrecker were based on the then-current Land Rover, with the headlights now located in the outer fenders. This is where the similarity ends, however, since the wrecker casting used an entirely different cab roof and rear shape. Many variations of the wrecker have been produced, and more may appear as Mattel finds uses for a wrecker in the Hot Wheels line. One final "juniors" version of the Land Rover was introduced in the early 1980's by Corgi Toys Ltd. This model is of a closed Land Rover One Ten van body. The front is again different, showing the then current design with the grill pulled flush with the front fenders. Numerous variations of this model were also produced, and it was still in production when the Mattel separation occurred.

A postscript can now be written to the 1:43 scale Land Rover story. In 1996, the Corgi Collector Club model was a Land Rover produced from modified original dies. The model has been extensively upgraded with an injection molded interior, better wheels, and crisper details. The original Whizzwheels era die is still evident, however, in much of the detailing on the body. A second version for Chipperfield's Circus was also to be produced. This model was due for release at the time of this writing, and opens a new chapter for Corgi. These are the first models produced by the new Corgi Classics Ltd. from original (although modified) Mettoy dies. This may signal the opening of a new nostalgia market for Corgi to conquer, since many adult collectors have fond memories of similar Childhood Corgi Toys.

416 and 416S R.A.C. Land Rovers (plastic canopy missing from the rear model).

406 and 438 Land Rover 109" W.B. in the common Green.

357 Land Rover Weapons Carrier minus the antenna on the fender.

A rear view showing metal and plastic tow hooks.

Vote for Corgi in 472, or come to the circus with 487, both based on the Breakdown Truck casting.

First (417) and last (477) Land Rover Breakdown span 18 years with the same red and yellow.

There were many evolutionary changes to the model over time.

A side view to illustrate the differences between early and late models.

The shape of the front license plate is a sure give-away.

Left: The 1996 Corgi Collector Club model, produced from upgraded original dies.

Right: Juniors E16(B) Land Rover Pick-up and E79(A) Army Ambulance (minus its hood).

Left: New castings were always modeled from then-current Land Rover vehicles.

Right: The last Juniors size Land Rover, the One Ten, as used by municipal police and fire services.

2.9—American Cars

One of Corgi's major concerns has always been market penetration outside of Britain. The largest export market for Corgi Toys has always been the United States, which receives the largest share of attention. One of the problems with this market for a British toy car maker is the completely different types of cars and trucks found on American roads. In order to capture and maintain its market share in the United States, Corgi has produced many, many vehicles patterned after American prototypes. Over the years, nearly every type of American vehicle has been produced. Some are common sights on the roads, or were at the time. Others are strictly dream machines.

The first Corgi Toy of an American car was the 211 Studebaker Golden Hawk, introduced in February, 1958. Both a standard and "Mechanical" version were introduced, although the standard version was produced with a diecast rather than a stamped steel base. The choice of a Studebaker may seem strange as a first choice to today's collector, since Studebaker was by far a minority manufacturer in the American market. One must consider the existing market at the time for Corgi Toys to understand the selection. Corgi Toys were mainly a British phenomenon in 1958, having been on the market only two years. The Golden Hawk resembled contemporary European car designs more than any other American make at the time, making it more attractive to the home market. Other American cars of the period were entering the "Big Tail Fin" era, which would have looked very strange to the British market. The Studebaker would be updated with suspension and an interior in May, 1960, as 211S, replacing the former versions. The updated model was first issued in a vacuum-plated, gold finish, which was later changed to metallic gold paint to reduce costs.

The second American car, or pair of cars, were not introduced until March, 1959. The 214 Ford Thunderbird Hardtop came in both standard and mechanical versions. The roof was a separate casting to allow the same body casting to be used for the 215 Ford Thunderbird Convertible, which came in December, 1959. By the time the convertible version was introduced, Mettoy had given-up on the friction motor "Mechanical" models. A convertible version of the "Mechanical" type would not have been possible due to the heavy diecast interior added to the body. The Studebaker and T-bird Hardtop ultimately would be the only American cars with friction motors.

The first American truck introduced in the Corgi Toys line would be the 409 Forward Control Jeep Pick-Up of April 1959. Once again, Mettoy had picked an unusual prototype to model. The Forward Control version of the famous Jeep never sold well in the United States due partly to its small size. Most people today have never seen one of these pick-ups on the road. Mettoy may have felt the model would resemble some Land Rover vehicles enough to be accepted in the British market. The model also lent itself to interesting modifications such as the Tower Truck (with its figure who constantly was reaching for the sky) and the Agricultural Conveyor Truck. The latter is almost never found with its belts intact. If one turns up, *don't turn the crank!* The Forward Control Jeep received a new base with suspension, an interior, and a new cover for the rear under the new item number 470 in March, 1965, making it one of the last suspension conversions done.

The early 1960s saw a sharp increase in the number of American vehicles introduced into the Corgi Toys range. Reeves International, the American importer of Corgi Toys, was heavily promoting Corgi to better department stores. These stores were eager to add the Corgi models to their store shelves due to their superior quality and features. As often happens, one store followed another in picking up Corgi Toys. Increased sales in the States were matched with an increasing number of American car and truck models, creating an upward spiral. Four versions of the Chevrolet Impala were followed by a Corvair and Corvette. The Ford Thunderbird Convertible sprouted a surrey roof to become the Bermuda Taxi, while an Oldsmobile Super 88 could be found in Sheriff, Army, or standard trim. The popular station wagon body type was represented by a Plymouth in either a standard version, or in an extremely accurate rendition of a U.S. Mail car.

Mettoy used many of the American vehicles to introduce new features. The 437 Cadillac Superior Ambulance of October, 1962, incorporated a battery operated roof light which could be made to flash by rolling the car forward. Electrical contact was made through a cam on the rear axle and the light from the bulb was distributed to four corner lenses through plastic light tubes. The model was later upgraded to eliminate the cam on the axle when flashing bulbs became available. Revolving jeweled headlights would appear on the 310 Chevrolet Corvette Sting Ray while the 245 Buick Riviera used Trans-o-Lite plastic light tubes to simulate working headlights and taillights. Turn signals could even be simulated on the Buick with the proper movement of fingers over the proper locations.

The early 1960s also saw the introduction of Husky Toys as a private brand for F.W. Woolworth. From the beginning, American cars were represented in the range, since Woolworth had many stores in the States. The 1959 Buick Electra, with its distinctive slanted headlights, appeared in 1964 as the 9(A) Police Car and 7(A) in civilian form. A 1961 Ford Thunderbird Convertible was modeled as 8(A) from 1964 through 1966, after which it gained a removable hardtop. These models matched the smaller scale then being produced by Lesney. Later Husky Toys would grow in size to keep-up with the changes in "Matchbox" vehicles, their main competitor.

The late 1960s saw an explosion of American vehicles in the Corgi Toys line, with many being created through the licensing of character toys (discussed in another section). In the States, Reeves had successfully generated the same enthusiasm over Corgi Toys that was found in Britain. Many new American vehicles would be introduced, including the first to appear in the Corgi Majors and Corgi Classics ranges. Some of the more noteworthy models of this period are the 267 Batmobile with the 107 Batboat and trailer soon added, the 268 Green Hornet's Car, and the 277 Monkeemobile. These refugees from Hollywood were big sellers then, and highly prized today as well. The Oldsmobile Super 88 from earlier in the decade would be reworked into the 497 "Man from U.N.C.L.E." car, which never really existed in the TV Show. An additional dream car, this time a Chevrolet show car called the Astro 1, would appear in 1969 as one of the first Whizzwheel models. This model copied the prototype with its tip-back roof design to allow entry for the driver and passenger.

Standard American cars, ones that actually could be seen on the streets, were well represented in the late 1960s. The "Pony Car" craze was well represented by the Ford Mustang Hatchback in normal (320) and "competition" (325) forms. A later version (348) sprouted paisley decals as the "Flower Power" version. The Chevrolet Camaro would appear in convertible form with "Take-off Wheels" as the 338, while its kissing cousin, the

343 Pontiac Firebird, would end-up being delayed until 1970 to become one of the first Whizzwheels models. A "Take-off Wheels" version was shown in the 1969 catalog, but never produced. As with the real cars, Corgi's Camaro and Firebird shared some parts, although no top-up Firebirds or top-down Camaros have ever been found.

Larger American cars were represented by the Oldsmobile Toronado with either normal cast wheels (264) or "Take-off Wheels" (276). The Rambler Marlin fastback came in red and black alone as 263, or in Gift Set 10 in blue and white with a roof rack and trailer, two kayaks, and a figure. The 262 Lincoln Continental Executive Limousine was a massive model of a massive car. It came with a simulated TV lit with a hidden bulb. Unfortunately, the limo almost always is found with flaking vacuum plating on the bumpers due to a material incompatibility. The aging 1959 Chevy Impala was reworked in 1965 into a sandwich design to incorporate a central vacuum plated molding that represented the grill, bumpers and side trim. All of the previous versions were renumbered after undergoing this change. This also made the later Kennel Club and Chipperfield's versions much simpler to create. A beautiful Chrysler Imperial convertible was released in red in August, 1965. Everything opened on this model, which included a golf bag in the trunk and two seated figures. While much has been written about the planned Bermuda Taxi version of 1969 that never materialized, the cars that would have become the 507 were in fact built. A last minute change by management converted the production back to standard 246 convertibles. These late, dark blue models have revised body and interior designs that would accept the surrey roof planned for the Bermuda Taxi. In addition, they are without the door window moldings found on earlier versions and have dark blue flocking on the floor and trunk floor. Only the inclusion of the non-existent side labels and surrey roof would have been needed to complete the conversion.

American trucks were not ignored in the late 1960s either. The highly detailed Ford Tilt-cab appeared with both a closed trailer with sliding sides (1137), and with a totally revised car carrier trailer which could now carry six (small) cars (1138). The Ford Tilt-cab also appeared with a highly detailed Holmes Twin-Boom Wrecker body as the 1142. The wrecker booms swung independently and had two separate winches. The other truck of American design was the Dodge Kew Fargo in either a livestock carrier version (484), or as a panel sided "tipper" dump body version (483). This truck was produced by Chrysler Corporation around the world under different nameplates. In the States, it was a Dodge D-series, while Dodge trucks in the past were known as a Fargo in Canada and elsewhere. The livestock version also appeared in the large Agricultural Gift Set 5, and redecorated in the Giant "Daktari" Gift Set 14.

The late 1960s also saw the addition of more American cars to the Husky Toys line, which was still an exclusive line for Woolworth at the time. However, Husky Toys were marketed by Corgi importers in countries where Woolworth did not have stores. This may explain why some late Husky models are found in packaging with item numbers 50 higher than expected. Some beautiful models of American vehicles were produced, which would have also done well in the larger Corgi Toys line if produced. The 31(A) Oldsmobile Starfire, introduced in 1966, and the 9(B) Cadillac Eldorado, introduced in 1968, represented the long and sleek look of American cars of the time. The 15(B) Studebaker Wagonair TV Camera Car, and its civilian equivalent only found in Gift Set 3005, were first produced in 1967.

This was one year after Studebaker left the automobile business entirely. American trucks were represented by the 28(a) Ford F350 Wrecker, introduced in 1966, and the 35(A) Camper from the following year. The year 1968 brought the 5(B) Willys Jeep (although Willys had not been part of the name for quite some time by then). American dream machines would also appear in the Husky Extras range, with the Batmobile of 1967 and the Monkeemobile of 1968 echoing their larger Corgi cousins. No truly American trucks would appear in the Husky Toys line, but this would soon be rectified early in the next decade.

The early 1970s, as stated elsewhere in the book, were a time of sheer chaos at Mettoy. Mattel's Hot Wheels had turned the market on its ear, and Mettoy was scrambling to convert its Corgi Toys and Corgi Juniors to low friction Whizzwheels as quickly as possible. Many of the American cars in the Corgi product line would go out of production, since the emphasis would turn to sporty, more exotic vehicles to emphasize speed. A sedan whizzing down a track just wouldn't look right. The Pontiac Firebird had already been released with Whizzwheels, as was the Astro 1. The Camaro, Corvette, '63 Stingray Stock Car and Batmobile would be converted after existing stocks of the old version had dwindled. The introduction of new American cars slowed, with less accurate racing or hot rod designs appearing more frequently. The year 1971 saw the release of the 166 Ford Mustang "Organ Grinder" dragster, which barely resembled the previous Mustang. A newer 1971 Ford Mustang Mach 1 (391) was introduced the following year, at the last minute having James Bond labels added to the box. Racing labels were added in 1973 and the number changed to 329(B). No other American cars appeared at all until 1976 in the Corgi Toys line, unless the 809 Dick Dastardly racer is included (only the cartoon characters being American).

The early 1970s were somewhat kinder to American trucks in the Corgi Toys range. The current design Mack truck, seen everywhere on American roads even today, was introduced as a replacement for the Ford Tilt-cab with a redecorated box trailer as 1100(B). It would also appear as a fuel tanker in "Esso" markings as 1152. When "Esso" became "Exxon" in the States, models shipped there also changed. A nice container truck version was produced as 1106(B) with two removable containers. Model 1154 paired the Mack with the former Priestman cab, circus crane boom, and Simon Snorkle outriggers to create a reasonable crane truck. By far, the oddest match-up would be in Gift Set 10(B) Tank Transporter with British Centurion MkIII Tank, where the Mack would be paired with the old machinery flatbed trailer that first appeared in 1958 behind a Bedford 'S'. It was equipped with the grill guard that first appeared on the crane truck and painted a dark olive drab (Darker than the 1960s military models). It would have been more accurate hauling the 902 U.S. Army M60A1 Medium Tank, but was probably targeted for the best worldwide appeal.

The early 1970s saw Husky Toys renamed Corgi Juniors. Soon afterward, Whizzwheels would also be applied across the line. Unlike Corgi Toys, the entire product line continued into the Whizzwheel era, with Juniors also picking-up former Corgi Rockets designs. A Corgi Juniors version of the Mack "Esso" tanker was added in the Super Juniors line in 1971, followed soon after by a military version. New models of American cars in the early 1970s included only a police and fire version of a Mercury Cougar, and a dune buggy converted from a Volkswagen. The Cadillac Eldorado lost its hood in 1971, and sprouted a hot rod engine. A nice representation of a G.M.C.

Greyhound Bus was released in 1975, breaking the log-jam a bit. The early 1970s were, after all, the era of gasoline lines and the start of America's love affair with small, foreign economy cars.

The late 1970s saw Corgi go after a younger customer base, and the size of Corgi Toys and Corgi Juniors grew. A model of Kojak's 1973 Buick finally returned a 4-door sedan to the Corgi range as 290 in 1976. As with most sedans, it was soon followed by a police version, the Buick gaining roof lights and a figure as 416(B). A Superman version, 260(B) Metropolis Police Car, followed in 1979 with two sets of roof lights (the two is better than one theory). A special Fire Chief version was also made for the Marks & Spencer Department Store chain, but not otherwise available. Additional American cars in the new larger scale included the 291(A) AMC Pacer in 1977, and its Rescue version 484(B) in the following year. A French version of the 484(B) was also produced, though it isn't clear why. The year 1978 saw the introduction of the Chevy Custom Van, which would appear in many versions. An ambulance version with a reworked roof was also issued as 405(B).Toward the end of the decade, the Corgi line finally got a Jeep, which could also be had in a Spiderman version. No new American trucks would appear, with the Mack giving way to a larger Ford of European design.

Things were busy in the "Juniors" Line in the late 1970s, with the introduction of numerous character related cars. Cartoon and comic book characters would be added to numerous existing vehicles. New American models for the latter 1970s would include "Juniors" versions of the Kojak and Police Buicks, as well as Taxi and Sheriff versions,. The Chevy Van would also appear, having even more versions than the larger Corgi model. The Starsky and Hutch Ford Torino also appeared in both lines, as did the AMC Pacer. No American designs would appear in the Super Juniors range, though.

The early 1980's saw interest for the larger Corgi Toys dying in the United States. Corgi's E-series "Juniors," however, were in their heyday, with most major toy store chains handling them. Mettoy and Reeves International, the U.S. importer, created special models of particular interest to American children. The latest cars, a Dodge Magnum, Ford Mustang, Pontiac Firebird, and Chevrolet Corvette were introduced. Special series cars decorated for American football, baseball, and hockey teams were produced in overwhelming numbers. Character tie-ins were plentiful. Popular older cars, like the 1957 Ford T-bird were introduced. Larger Corgi models of the 1957 T-bird were also produced, at first as a Vega$ character model, then as a part of a revived Corgi Classics line. The full size Corgi line also gained a Chevrolet Caprice sedan, which could be found in civilian, racing, police and Corgitronic fire chief versions. The Ford Torino also gained a version with a horn. In the end, though, nothing could help Mettoy's slide, and the company closed its doors in October 1983.

A new company, Corgi Toys Ltd., emerged from the ashes in April 1984. Along with it came a new philosophy and a new target market: adults. American vehicles produced by the company would change, too. While some of the existing models would continue, new models would be restricted to a 1957 Chevrolet and a Mack AC Bulldog antique truck. The Mack Bulldog would share a number of different body types with Thorneycroft (British) and Renault (French) chassis. The old

1960s vintage Model T Ford Chassis would also be resurrected and would gain a van and tanker bodies. The Mack and Model T would be used heavily for promotional and limited run items. Over time, Corgi models would become increasingly centered on models from Britain and Europe as the company struggled to survive and grow. Most of the sales outlets in the United States would be lost as stocks of the Mettoy era "Juniors" ran out. New Corgi models would end up in mostly specialty and hobby shops, fostered by the new company's emphasis on adult collectors. The American LaFrance ladder truck would reappear late in the decade alongside the Mack pumper, which had been in continuous production.

The Mattel buyout did more to increase the appearance of new American prototypes, though development of a more extensive fire engine and transit bus line was mostly due to the urging of Reeves International. Reeves needed products that would be recognizable to American customers in order to generate sales. A more modern closed cab and extended bumper were developed to give more variety to the American LaFrance models. A transitional piece also was developed to allow the American LaFrance cab to be mounted to the pumper body. A Mack B Series cab and chassis was used in the fire department and promotional lines. Bus collectors were offered vintage Yellow Coach and G.M.C. bus designs, and a modern MCI coach. These would all appear in colorful, but prototypically accurate, paint schemes which would be familiar to many American baby-boomers.

Corgi Classics Ltd. was formed in August, 1995, by a management buyout. Most of the existing product line, including American vehicles, continued in production. The American market for vintage fire-fighting equipment and buses continues to be well supported. The racing transporter has appeared as the Corgi Roadshow Vehicle and as a Christmas promotion at Shell stations. Mattel kept the former Juniors line when Corgi bought back its independence again, merging it slowly into their Hot Wheels line. The American cars still in the Auto-City line would become Hot Wheels Auto-City models, although few had emerged in the United States at the time of publication. What the future will hold for American designs in the new Corgi Classics Ltd. product line only time will tell. Perhaps in time additional nostalgia markets will be found, or new American vehicles will become Corgi models.

Two versions of 229 Chevrolet (Chevy) Corvair (1960 vehicle).

Left: 235 Oldsmobile Super 88 (1961 vehicle) in two color combinations.

Right: 264 Oldsmobile Toronado (1966 vehicle) with and without tow hook.

Left: 439 Fire Chief version of the Chevrolet Impala (1959 vehicle).

Right: Later 276 Oldsmobile Toronados with Take-off Wheels'.

Left: Early and late 310 Chevrolet Corvette Sting-Ray (1963 vehicle) with later 337 Stock Car.

Right: 481 Police, 482 Fire Chief, and 486 Kennel Club versions of the updated Chevy Impala.

Left: 325 Ford Mustang Competition (1965 vehicle) in three wheel types.

Right: Husky 30(A) Ambulance and unnumbered civilian version of the Studebaker Wagonaire (1965 vehicle).

Left: Husky 31(A) Oldsmobile Starfire (1965 vehicle).

Right: Corgi Junior (sticker base) version of 9(B) Cadillac Eldorado (1967 vehicle).

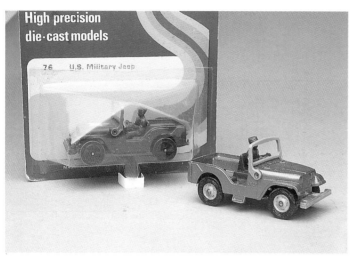

Husky 5(B) Civilian and Juniors E76(B) U.S.Army Jeep CJ5.

Juniors Civilian and Taxi Buick Regal (1973 vehicle).

343 Pontiac Firebird 400 Convertible (1967 vehicle), among the first with Whizzwheels.

Even the Firebird's dashboard and steering wheel are prototypically accurate.

Later Police and Fire Chief Regals.

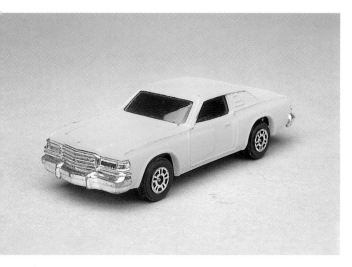

Juniors E93(B) Dodge Magnum (1978 vehicle).

Corgi and Juniors versions of the Mack Esso Tanker.

1100(B) Mack Transcontinental Truck. Mack trucks are among the most common on American roads, even today.

Juniors E62(B) AMC Pacer in red and in dark blue with unplated plastic parts (factory goof).

Juniors E90(A) Fireball Van, one of many versions of this 1970s Chevrolet Van (also resembles the smaller Bedford van).

2.10—Glideamatic Conversions: Suspension is Added

In the endless quest to gain and hold the largest market share possible, Mettoy needed to introduce a continuous stream of "new" features in the Corgi Toys line. Competitors were quick to pick up on each other's new features and copy them, so any market advantage gained was short lived. Some innovations would turn out to be only gimmicks and would appear on only a single or a few models. Others would capture attention and develop into an industry standard. Competitors who couldn't keep up with the changes in buyers' expectations quickly lost out.

One of the lasting Corgi innovations, which would change the marketplace, was Glideamatic spring suspension. The addition of suspension to diecast toy cars was a major step forward, giving Corgi models a completely different feel than the old rigidly supported models. The design of the suspension system was simple. Two spring steel wires were attached at their center to the hidden inner surface of a diecast base plate. These spring wires ran fore and aft along the base with their ends pressing downward on the axle shafts of the model. The mounting holes for the axle shafts were slotted to allow vertical movement. Force applied to the wheels caused the wheel and axle to retract into the body and rebound, as on a real car.

Glideamatic spring suspension was first introduced on the 222 Renault Floride in October, 1959. Most new models from then onward would be released with suspension. In addition, existing models would be retrofitted whenever possible. These retrofitted models would keep the same catalog number with an added "S" on the end. The first of these was the 210S Citroen DS19, released in June, 1960. This car, as well as most others, would be upgraded with a vacuum formed interior at the same time. Customer demand was high for the models with suspension, and Mettoy was happy to oblige them. Soon, existing stocks of models without suspension would prove hard to move, giving urgency to the conversion program. Models which could not be converted would quickly be phased out of the line.

The addition of suspension to an existing model gave it a totally different feel than before. Models that had stamped steel bases would become heavier with the diecast base required by the design. This gave the customer an increased sense of quality and value. In actuality, it would have been as easy or easier to design the suspension system into a stamped base plate. However, Mettoy had learned from experience with the discontinued "Mechanical" versions of Corgi Toys that customers preferred the more massive feeling of a car with a diecast base. A diecast base is also easier to design into strange shapes and can become the lower portion of the visible body of a vehicle if needed. Suspension, besides adding bounce to the vehicle, also allowed models to conform to uneven surfaces and to react to bumps in its path more realistically. Models without suspension often wobbled when placed on any but a flat surface.

When Mettoy was approached by F.W. Woolworth to create a new line of diecast toys to compete with Matchbox for introduction in 1964, suspension was considered a desirable feature. The resulting Husky Toys line was too small to use the spring wire design of their bigger Corgi brothers. Instead, plastic tabs were extended from the center of the base plate to support the axles. The natural springiness of the plastic material was used to create the suspension effect. Much less spring force was necessary due to the very light weight of the models. This system is easily visible on the bottom of most early Husky models. Designers soon learned, however, to hide the plastic spring tabs inside a diecast base plate if the model was large enough to house the parts.

The designers of the Corgi Toys line were aware of the plastic tab suspension design on Husky Toys models. Some Corgi Toys from the mid-1960s attempted to incorporate it into larger models. However, Corgi Toy cars were too heavy for a plastic spring, and many of the cars sagged after a short period of time. Some models, like the 320 Ford Mustang or 251 Hillman Imp, are difficult to find without a sagging suspension. Later versions of the Mustang don't seem to have this problem, though.

Corgi Majors also began appearing with suspension in the early 1960s, although it wasn't as much of a selling point for the bigger models. Tricky variations were tried on various Majors models, such as enclosing the rear axle in a cast-sprung differential and propeller shaft. The Mercedes-Benz Unimog, in its many forms, used a very flexible coil spring arrangement in order to emulate the real vehicle. Other Majors models would continue without suspension with no apparent harm to sales.

Suspension systems became less important with the introduction of Whizzwheels. The small axle rod diameter itself provided some rebound on uneven surfaces. By the time Whizzwheels were introduced, suspension was a non-issue in marketing the line. When Mettoy collapsed and was replaced by Corgi Toys Ltd., new Classics models were introduced without suspension. Corgi had begun its shift from being a high play value toy to a static collectible model.

Corgi Forward Control Jeeps with and without suspension.

These three Land Rovers show the progression from tin baseplate, to suspension, to Whizzwheels.

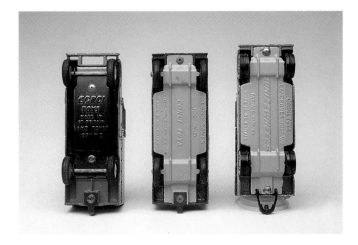

2.11—Wheel and Tire Types

The wheels and tires used for Corgi toys prior to the introduction of Whizzwheels were unique to Corgi Toys. The many types produced were developed in a straightforward, evolutionary process that can be traced back to Mettoy. That these wheels were unique and distinctive to Corgi owes more to the development process at Mettoy than to what the competition was doing.

The initial Corgi Toys of 1956 used a spun aluminum wheel pressed or crimped in place onto a straight rod. To this were mounted rubber tires resembling O-rings with a tread pattern added. The amount of tread present varied with the tire size and mold used. The wheel assembly rotated as one fixed unit. This design is an offshoot of the friction toy line at Mettoy, since the wheels must be fixed to the axle in order for a friction motor to propel the toy. Most of the initial offerings in the Corgi range came in both standard and friction-drive Mechanical versions. Standardization on the fixed-wheel design minimized the differences between these two types of models, reducing the number of different processes needed to assemble the line. Aluminum was used as the wheel material since the wheels could then be made in large quantities, cheaply, on a screw-forming machine. The plain Smooth wheel shape did not require special tooling for the crimping process, and also provided a smooth surface for the application of hub stickers with wheel patterns (used on some of the racers).

Mettoy had hedged their bet on Corgi Toys initially by providing both friction-drive and standard versions of the models. Dinky, as well as other competitors in the diecast toy market, were not marketing friction drive in their models. Mettoy's traditional rivals offered friction-drive toys, but not resembling high quality diecast models. By having their products in both market segments, Mettoy could promote whichever version became popular. When sales of the friction-drive Mechanical models proved weak, they were discontinued. The last Mechanical Corgi Toys were made in 1959.

Without the design constraints of the friction motor, Corgi was free to make changes to the wheel and axle design. Dinky had adopted a spun aluminum wheel on some of its models of the late '50s, copying Corgi. Dinky's wheel had a more attractive, dished shape, however. In response, Mettoy introduced the Shaped wheel type, basically an undercut on the existing wheel easily done on the screw machine. These wheels were phased into production without special mention as they became available starting in 1961. Mettoy also briefly used a heavy looking diecast wheel on some racers and the Aston-Martin DB4, but this wheel was not popular and may have caused assembly problems with the crimping process. It was generally replaced by the Shaped wheel when it became available.

The next wheel assembly change was actually brought about due to another Corgi innovation—"Glideamatic" spring suspension. This system used wires crimped to the inner side of a cast base plate, starting a shift away from stamped steel. These wires press down on the axle shaft to provide the spring load. Unfortunately, they also act as a very effective brake for the axle, preventing it from turning freely. Faced with models that wouldn't roll freely, Mettoy revised its assembly process to allow the wheels to turn freely on the axles. This process, used by most of the competitors, involves using a larger, free-fitting hole in the wheel to allow motion. The wheels are captured in place between the base plate and peened ends on a longer axle shaft. Peening the axle ends is a similar process to crimping wheels in

place and would require minimal machinery changes at assembly.

Mettoy no longer needed to concern themselves with damaging wheels while crimping them onto the axle shaft, and this allowed them to create more detailed and delicate wheels. The first and most attractive of these new wheels was the diecast wire wheel introduced in 1964 on the 245 Buick Riviera and soon applied to others. This masterwork of die making actually gave the appearance of wire wheels and could be seen through if properly made. No other manufacturer had anything that could compare. This wheel would last into the late '60s when worn dies forced it to be retired. A similar family of wheels were made for the Corgi Classics range introduced in the same year using the same technology.

Mettoy's shaped aluminum wheel was beginning to look too toy-like when compared to the new wheels being developed. In 1965 or 1966, Mettoy began producing a diecast wheel with a simple finned design. At first, this wheel was only used on the better cars in the Corgi range. However, it was soon added across the range. This is known as the "Cast Wheel," even though subsequent wheel types were also cast. Versions of this wheel were made in every size to replace the remaining Shaped wheels.

In the mid '60s, Corgi also began to use a new molded tire with better detail on the tread and sidewalls. Mettoy had noted the praise received over the special tires first used on the Batmobile in 1966. The old O-ring tire design (unfortunately known as "Rubber" tires to collectors) was becoming dated. Replacements were designed which were shaped more like a real tire. Tread and side wall detail was simulated, and the name "Corgi" added. These tires were molded in a synthetic rubber material that had a higher gloss than the old style. This type of tire has unfortunately been termed the "Plastic" tire by collectors. The term is inaccurate, but to change it now would cause extreme confusion.

The existing wheel designs were appropriate for normal automobiles. However, racing cars with exposed wheels looked like toys with them. The Batmobile of 1966 had used a wide tire on special wheels which was highly popular. Mettoy decided to put the tire on other models and created a generic cast wheel. This wheel type is known as the "Wide 8-spoke" wheel. It was first used in 1967 on the 156 Cooper-Maserati Formula 1 Racer.

The final wheel type to be introduced on Corgi automobiles prior to the introduction of Whizzwheels was actually a family of designs known as Take-Off-Wheels. Basically a marketing gimmick, wheels on these specially prepared cars possessed an added flange on the inner face. The wheel slid over an axle and was held in place by a retractable clamp. The clamp was operated by a cam on a pivoting peg, or Golden Jack. Some of the most beautiful wheels ever found on Corgi models were produced for this line. Sadly, they were brought to market just before the Hot Wheels invasion that caused the creation of Whizzwheels. Three models originally planned to get Take-Off-Wheels never did. One however, the 342 Lamborghini P400 GT Miura, was able to use-up the stock of wheels specially made for it by using one per model under the hood as a spare.

The number of wheels used on Corgi Majors since their introduction is almost countless. In general, wheel types followed the lead of those on the automobiles. However, a much higher percentage of cast wheels with special patterns were always used, depending on the application. Through the '60s, the same general shift from Smooth to Shaped to Cast wheel types occurred. One extra step was the introduction of Large Diameter Cast

Wheels with thin Plastic tires first seen on the 1138 Car Transporter with Ford Tilt Cab of 1966. The outer diameter of this type was the same as the tire on the largest version of the Shaped wheel, though its appearance was far superior.

The wheel types on the Husky Toys and pre-Whizzwheel Corgi Juniors are generally less varied. A generic dark gray to black, hard plastic wheel was used for early Husky production, at times with a painted silver center. Later Husky models had either vacuum-plated plastic hubs or diecast hubs with hard black plastic tires attached. The earliest Corgi Juniors also used these wheels until the Whizzwheel conversion.

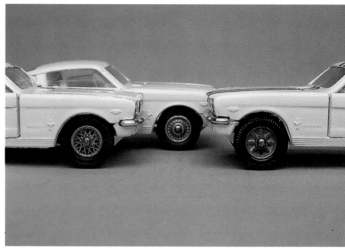

A rare example where wire wheels, cast wheels and wide eight-spoke wheels appear under the same model.

This MGA has smooth wheels crimped on the axles.

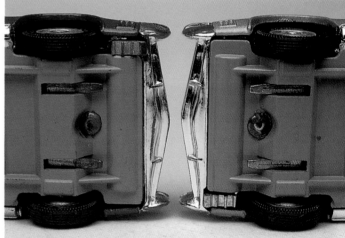

Not all Take-off Wheels had golden jacks, some where silver.

Under this Chevrolet are shaped wheels free spinning on the axles.

The crash program to convert to Whizzwheels caused some Take-off Wheels to only be used as under-hood spares.

Husky models progressed from the plastic wheel at left to a cast metal wheel with plastic tire.

Late Husky and early Corgi Junior plated plastic wheel shown opposite a five-double-spoke (5dblspk) Juniors Whizzwheel.

2.12—"Whizzwheels" Conversions: Follow the Leader

Mattel's Hot Wheels hit the toy market by storm, catching Mettoy and every other toy maker by surprise. Suddenly, Corgi Toys went from being the leading market innovator to being old-fashioned. In nothing less than a stampede, kids abandoned their former favorite makes of toy cars for the faster, loop-de-loop Hot Wheels line. Mattel's marketing of their new line of cars and track sets was masterful in execution. Their aggressive defense of their patents on the track systems ensured that competitors would be all but frozen out of the sales bonanza.

Mettoy and Lesney bore the brunt of lost sales. Lesney's Matchbox series was well established as the market leader at the time in 1:64 and smaller scale diecast. Mettoy basically owned the lion's share of the market in 1:43 scale, and the Husky Toys line had made major inroads into Lesney's territory. Husky Toys, with their plastic spring suspension, had one-upped Lesney's Matchbox Series earlier. Mettoy and Lesney had to react quickly to Hot Wheels, or face mountains of unsold inventory and no sales.

Mettoy at first over-reacted to Hot Wheels by thinking in their typical one-up the competition style. In an effort to protect the large tooling investment in the Husky line, they revamped some of the existing vehicles adding some new ones to create Corgi Rockets. The Corgi name was used in an attempt to borrow product recognition from the larger line. Mettoy missed the mark, though, by overcomplicating the models with a removable chassis. Tooling and assembly costs for this added, and unwanted, feature would put the Rockets at a price disadvantage. Removable parts quickly become missing or broken parts, leaving a negative feeling about the product.

Mettoy also created extensive track sets for the rockets. Many unique options would be created on which the Rockets could zoom along. The fate of the track sets would be even more disastrous. Mattel aggressively protected their patents on the Hot Wheels track sets, and threatened litigation against any company that violated their rights. To avoid a messy situation, track set production for Rockets ended quickly. This left Mettoy with an overcomplicated product that could only be used on the competition's track. Rockets would soon be abandoned.

Although the Corgi product line was in a completely different scale than Hot Wheels, sales took a major hit. Since there was no real competition initially in 1:43 scale, Mettoy initially took a cautious approach. Marketing would coin the phrase Whizzwheels for a new, low-friction wheel design. The new wheel, known as the Red Dot type by collectors, was a variation of the existing wide, eight-spoke wheel with an added red nylon insert against a smaller wire axle. The red color of the insert emphasized its low friction quality. This wheel reused the existing wide soft plastic tires, making an interesting interim hybrid between old and new. Similar designs were adopted by other brands (like Dinky). Mettoy soon realized, though, that the Red Dot design was costly in a time of falling sales, and the rubber tires added friction on the track sets planned for the Corgi line. Only a handful of newly introduced models would end up with the Red Dot wheels, some of which had been scheduled to be additional Take-Off-Wheel models prior to the last-minute change. The planned track sets would materialize only briefly, abandoned for the same reason as the Rockets sets.

After only one year, a new simpler and faster, but more toy-like Whizzwheel design would be introduced. Basically a one-piece design, it could be made cheaply and in large quantities using a simple two-piece mold. Market research had shown that appearance was much less important to boys than speed. The new wheel design would be fast, especially with the mass of a 1:43 Corgi riding on it. The loss of the Corgi-size track sets would have minimal impact, since a Corgi filled a child's hand in size and with momentum could travel over almost any indoor surface for a good distance. The new wheel was a single nylon part, hollow in the back and with a raised narrow ridge for the car to roll on. The thickness of the tire is for appearance and axle support only. The ridge does all of the work. The silver foiled pattern in the new wheel is often called the "Circle of Bubbles" pattern. Early Whizzwheel conversion models can be spotted and dated by this design.

Over time, Mettoy tinkered with the pattern on the wheels to improve their appearance. Initially, only pattern changes were done to the original design so that the silver foiling process could be maintained. These patterns are referred to with names like "4 Crown." However, the desire for a more realistic looking wheel on some premium models in the mid-1970s drove the development of what is known as the Silver Center Whizzwheel design. By that time, the upheaval over Whizzwheel conversion of the product line had receded, and low-friction wheels were the norm in the market rather than the exception. Mettoy developed a more realistic wheel design with a recessed center which more closely resembled an actual car wheel. Recessing the center led to a process change to mask spray painting of the center of the wheel, but the improved appearance more than compensated for the loss of the shiny foiled surface. By the late '70s, the Whizzwheels name fell out of use even though the wheel type continued. By then low-friction wheels were assumed by the marketplace, leaving no advantage in calling attention to them.

The Whizzwheel conversion of the smaller 1:64 scale line immediately followed the conversion of the line from Husky Toys to Corgi Juniors. The Corgi name was necessary for market recognition in the falling sales period following the Hot Wheels invasion. Corgi Rockets, already based on some Husky designs, were proving expensive to produce. Maintaining two separate lines, both with the Corgi name, made no sense. Mettoy decided to apply small versions of the larger Corgi Whizzwheels and eliminate the costly Rockets. The Rockets name would continue briefly referring to the unsold inventory of track sets and accessories. A new Junior-size Whizzwheel would replace the existing wheel designs. The smaller axles easily fit into the existing plastic spring designs of the Husky Juniors with minimal modification. Only marketing requirements for adding the text "Whizzwheels" to base plates complicated the process. The initial Juniors Whizzwheel design was quite thin and undecorated when compared to Hot Wheels and Matchbox models of the time, but it gave Mettoy a complete 1:64 low-friction wheeled product line quickly. The thin wheels did tend to be a little wobbly on the thin axles, so subsequent new products would be designed to accept a thicker design with wider contact with the axle wire. The thicker wheels would be designed with protruding patterns to accept silver paint or foiling.

The Juniors wheel types never appeared to be well controlled once the thicker Whizzwheels were in general usage. This may be due in part to Mettoy's early relocation of some production offshore, or due to lack of interest by the company. Over time, numerous hub patterns were introduced. A sample of the names used by collectors are "five spoke," "four-crown," "four-division," and "eight-division." While new patterns would often see initial high usage, old designs often returned to cause confusion. Often, otherwise identical models could be found coming from the same carton with two or three different wheel types. While mixing on a single model is rare, parallel assembly stations on the production line must have used whatever was easily available. Some of the larger Super Juniors actually used Whizzwheels from the 1:43 Corgi line. There are also a few examples of Juniors-size Whizzwheels used on special Corgi applications where small wheels were required. As with the 1:43 Corgi line, the term Whizzwheels became unnecessary in the late '70s. New models no longer carried the "Whizzwheels" wording from then onward, though no effort was made to remove it from existing models. Some models packaged in the mid-'90s as Hot Wheels Auto-City vehicles still had "Whizzwheels" on their base plate, although Mattel is slowly erasing any references to Corgi on the remaining product line.

The original Whizzwheel with red nylon center and diecast gold wheel.

Circle-of-bubbles (COB) and Silver Center Whizzwheels.

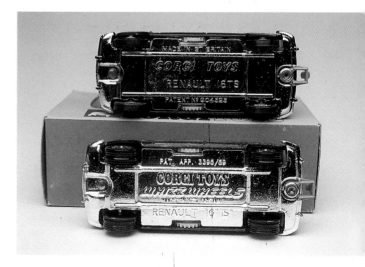

Baseplates of normal wheel and Whizzwheel versions of the Renault 16.

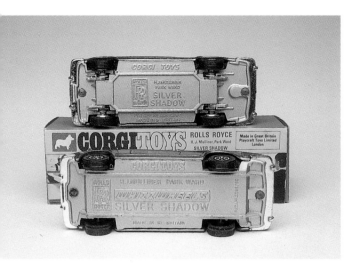

Take-off Wheel and Whizzwheel versions of the Rolls-Royce.

Although no longer called Whizzwheels, this Corgi Toys Ltd. model has the Silver Center type wheel.

This Hot Wheels Auto-City model (formerly Corgi) has the Juniors 4 Division (4div) wheel pattern.

Another Whizzwheel pattern.

2.13—Packaging: Boxes and Cards

A wide variety of packaging types have been used to hold Corgi Toys over their long history. To completely illustrate all of the various types could easily take-up a small book on its own. However, an examination of the highlights of the main types will give the reader a good understanding of the strategies used by Corgi over time. Packaging is always designed purposefully to present products in the most attractive manner to the customer of the time. As the customer base and preferences change, so must the packaging.

Following is a brief overview of the more common Corgi packaging types. Specially decorated packages for specific models are not included except where needed to represent a specific style or configuration. Dates shown are approximate and denote starting dates. Styles often overlapped while older stock was depleted.

c.1956	Corgi vehicles except "Mechanical"	Blue Box	"CORGI TOYS" in black rectangle, model number in black background.
c.1956	Corgi "Mechanical" vehicles	Blue Box	"CORGI TOYS" in black rectangle, model number in red background, "MECHANICAL" in red in description.
c.1959	Corgi vehicles	Blue and Yellow Box	"CORGI TOYS" in blue area, model number in black background.
c.1959	Corgi Major vehicles	Tan Box Bottom w/ Blue and Yellow Lid	"CORGI MAJOR TOYS" in blue area, model number in black background.
c.1962	Corgi vehicles	Blue and Yellow Box	Same as c.1959 with added feature descriptions in blue area.
c.1962	Corgi Major vehicles	Blue and Yellow Box	Similar to c.1962 vehicle box.
c.1962	Corgi vehicles	Blue and Yellow Box	Special variation of standard box w/ "By Special Request" splash replacing blue area on sides with vehicle drawing.
c.1963	Corgi Gift Sets	Foam Molded Bottom w/ Slip-over Lid	Bottom and contents usually clear plastic shrink wrapped.
c.1964	Corgi Classics vehicles	Tan Box Bottom w/ Black Band on Printed Lid	Two vintage cars depicted on top, "CORGI CLASSICS" in black band on top, black ends.
c.1965	Corgi vehicles	Blue and Yellow Box	Similar to c.1962 but off sides split in quarters w/ blue in diagonal corners, some have special feature artwork on one side only.
c.1966	Corgi vehicles	Blue and Yellow Box	Printed gummed label over previous model's box describing revised specifications. (Usually replaced by new properly printed box soon afterward.)
c.1966	Corgi vehicles and Corgi Classics vehicles	Bubble Card	Vacuum formed clear plastic bubble on openable cardboard back and bottom.
c.1967	Corgi vehicles	Blue and Yellow Box	Similar to c.1965 but no blue area on sides w/ vehicle drawing.
c.1968	Corgi vehicles and Corgi Majors	Blue and Yellow Box	New non-italic "CORGITOYS" w/o space between words, words in contrasting colors, sides w/ vehicle drawing yellow, off sides blue, "CORGI" on lower end flaps w/ model number in white rectangle, vehicle side view on upper end flaps.
c.1968	Corgi vehicles and Corgi Majors	Blue and Yellow Box	Window box w/ or w/o upper display flap, end flaps similar to standard c.1968 box.
c.1970	Corgi vehicles	Blue and Yellow Box	Special gummed labels covering over references to "Take-off Wheels" on c.1968 style box for models introduced w/ early Whizzwheels.

c.1970	Corgi vehicles	Red and Yellow Box	Simplified version of earlier window box, large "WHIZZWHEELS" on red top, yellow front face w/ "CORGITOYS WHIZZWHEELS", side view of vehicle low on end flap in yellow, red upper area on end flap with logo and model number.
c.1973	Corgi vehicles and Corgi Majors	Dark Box w/ Canted Racing Stripe	New type larger window box w/ model tipped to viewer if possible. midnight blue w/ three various color stripes along canted left and top edges of window, "CORGI" and description in yellow areas. (Word "TOYS" dropped.)
c.1973	Corgi Military vehicles	Olive and White Box	No window, white sides w/ vehicle side view, olive offside and flaps w/ yellow and red "CORGI" and description.
c.1975	Corgi vehicles and Corgi Majors	Dark Box w/ Straight Racing Stripe	Similar to c.1973 window box except window opening now not canted, three stripes extend around perimeter of window.
c.1978	Corgi vehicles and Corgi Majors	Dark Box w/ Straight Racing Stripe	Similar to c.1975 window box except "corgi" now all lower case.
c.1981	Corgi vehicles, Corgi Classics and Corgi Majors	Black Box w/ Red fade to Yellow	Much larger window box w/ black edges and end flaps, red area on top fades to yellow on box front, "corgi" on front, model number and description on insert inside window, end flaps have cut-outs for bar-code.
c.1981	Corgitronics	Black, Dark Blue and Chrome Box	Very large window box, "corgitronics" on all sides w/ "tronics" in contrasting colors, "chromed" insert visible through window.
c.1982	Corgitronics	Graph Paper Box	Very large window box w/ windows on both sides, illustrations of operation of model, visual clues and arrows.
c.1983	Corgimatics	Yellow Graph Paper Box	Similar to c.1982 Corgitronics box but with different pattern and colors.
c.1983	Corgi Classics	Black See-through Box	Similar to c.1982 Corgitronics box but much smaller with different pattern and colors.
c.1984	Corgi and Corgi Classics	Early Corgi Toys Ltd. Boxes	Continuation of some Mettoy box designs by Corgi Toys Ltd. in 1984 only. New company name appears on box.
c.1985	Corgi except Corgi Classics	Blue Traffic Signs Box	Blue window box w/ new "CORGI" logo, traffic signs and blueprint lines.
c.1985	Corgi Classics	Gray Traffic Signs Box	Gray window box w/ new "CORGI CLASSICS" logo, traffic signs and blueprint lines. "Limited Edition" and other labels when needed.
c.1985	Corgi Collectors' Classics	Silver Collectors' Classics Box	Silver bottom w/ clear plastic slide-off sleeve, silver box lid with logo, silver end label w/ model number and description, flocked vacuum formed insert. (Used only for models made from 1960's dies.)

c.1985	Corgi Classics Sets	Special Lift-off Lid Box	Box graphics unique to model, series or set. (Too numerous to list.)
c.1987	Corgi Classics	Gray Traffic Signs Box	Similar to c.1985 box except larger w/ model presented at an angle.
c.1990	Corgi Classics	Clear Plastic Window Box	Hybrid window box, clear plastic front, top, and end flaps, cardboard back, bottom and support surfaces, "Classic CORGI Models" on front, "D" series number and description seen through end flap.
c.1990	Corgi except Corgi Classics	Clear Plastic Window Box	Similar to Corgi Classics Box except "CORGI" logo and different graphics.
c.1991	Corgi Classics	Clear Plastic Window Box	Same as c.1990 box except model has Mattel 5 digit item number
c.1991	Corgi Classics	Styrofoam Mailer	Plain white shipping box w/ slide-out Styrofoam liner, no printing or identification. (Used for club models and other premiums.)
c.1991	Corgi Classics	Beige Window Box	Similar to c.1987 window box except new light beige graphics.
c.1992	Corgi except Corgi Classics	Blue Traffic Signs Box	Similar to c.1985 box except small Mattel logo added to bottom corner, manufacturer name on bottom changed.
c.1994	Corgi Classics	New Blue and Yellow Box	Close fitting blue and yellow box similar to early 1960's design, new logo w/ corgi dog, photo of model on 3 sides, Mattel UK Ltd. on bottom.
c.1996	Corgi Classics	New Blue and Yellow Box	Similar to c.1994 box except division between blue and yellow now diagonal, end flap color matches adjacent surfaces, manufacturer name on bottom changed.

The original Corgi Toys' all-blue box.

Promotional models were sometimes shipped in unmarked boxes.

Variation on the blue box used on "Mechanical" models.

The slide-off-lid, hard box found on many Corgi Majors.

The first type of blue-and-yellow box.

Accessories and small parts came in less-colorful boxes.

By Special Request.

The Corgi Classics box, which can also be found with a hard slide-off lid.

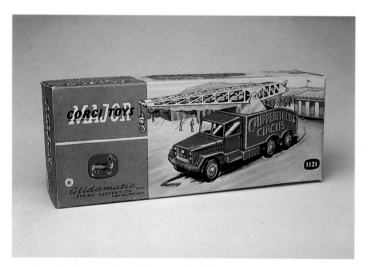

Corgi Majors version of the standard blue-and-yellow box.

The first use of a vacuum-formed display card package.

Trans-o-Lite and other features began to appear on the box.

This type of overlabeling was used when new models were released more quickly than boxes could be printed.

The 1967-style blister pack as used on the Jaguar XKE.

A 1967-style box.

A 1968-style box.

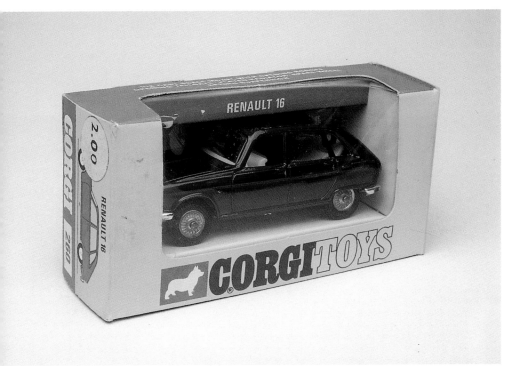

Some 1968-style boxes were the first to have windows.

A typical 1968-style end flap showing a model side view.

A 1970 style Whizzwheels box.

Corgi Majors version of the 1968-style box.

As specifications were changed, labels were added to the boxes.

Early Whizzwheels models used 1968-style boxes with labels describing the new features.

A 1970-style end flap with model side view.

The 1973-style angled-stripe box.

Many character vehicles had special box designs with only a few of the standard style markings.

The color of the stripe varied from model to model.

Special silver 1975-style boxes were used for models issued for the Queen's Silver Jubilee.

Corgi Kits packaging was unique to these models.

A 1978 style box, which is generally similar to the 1975 style except for the lower case 'corgi.'

The oversized 1981 style box as produced by Mettoy.

Corgi Toys Ltd. continued the same style box in 1984, only adding the new company name.

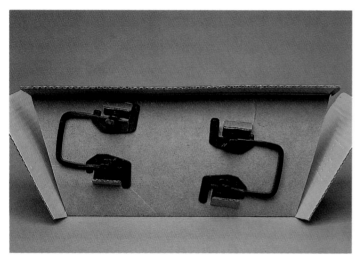

Models were held in place by plastic clips in order to hold them at an angle as viewed through the window.

A 1982 Corgitronics box with see-through windows.

A 1983 Corgi Classics box as issued by Mettoy.

Hartoy Hershey's set blister card from the transitional era around 1984.

A 1985 Corgi Classics range box with 'Limited Edition' label.

Special silver Corgi Collectors' Classics box, this one with goof 'Model T-Bird' label.

Hartoy Coca-Cola set which has no Corgi identification on the box.

Larger 1987 Corgi box, otherwise similar to the 1985 style.

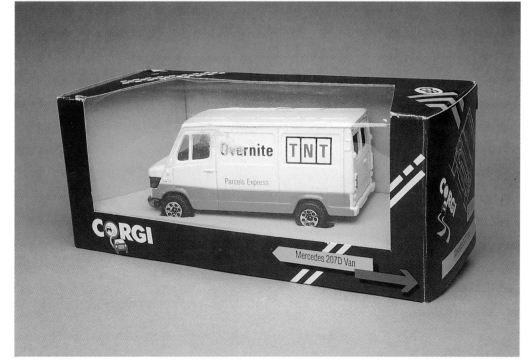

Larger 1987 Corgi Classics box.

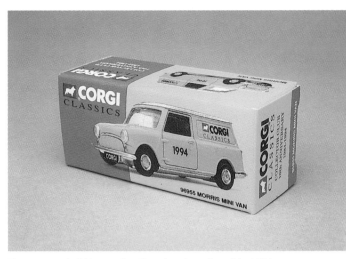

The retro-styled blue-and-yellow box introduced in 1994.

The hybrid plastic and cardboard 1990-style box, also used through 1991 with Mattel model numbers.

A current Corgi Classics Ltd. blue-and-yellow box showing the angled division between colors.

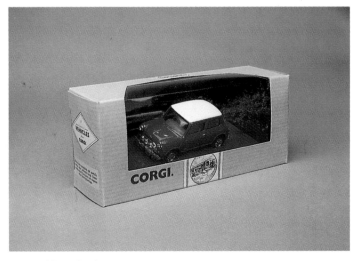

A 1991 Beige box.

The box used for Corgi Cameo models, a separate product line mostly used for promotional models.

2.14—Packaging: Husky & Corgi Juniors

The packaging of Husky and Corgi Junior models evolved along the same lines as their larger Corgi brothers. Initially at Woolworth's request, Husky packaging was decorated so as to be distinct from the Corgi line. However, when the name of the product line was changed to Corgi Juniors, Mettoy was quick to create packaging strongly linked to the contemporary Corgi designs. This remained true until the early 1990s when Mattel began the process of associating the former Juniors more closely with the Hot Wheels line.

The following listing is a representation of Husky and Corgi Junior packaging types at various times. This list is not all-inclusive, since Mettoy, and later Corgi Toys Ltd., frequently created special packaging for specific markets and models. However, it can be generally said that specially packaged models generally followed the appearance cues found on standard packaging. Individually packaged models are not known to have had inserts in any of the packaging styles. Inserts and/or assembly instructions may have been found in larger sets where it was deemed necessary.

(Mid '60s)	Husky Vehicles	Card	Red/White	36 Item Checklist on Back. "Made in Great Britain" Markings Without Company Identification.
(Late '60s)	Husky Vehicles	Card	Yellow/Red/White	Line Drawing Behind Vehicle, Ad on Back
c.1970-72	Corgi Junior Vehicles	Card	Blue/Yellow	Cut-out Collector Card of Model in Card w/Description, Traffic Scene on Back.
c.1970-72	Corgi Junior Gift Sets	Box	Yellow w/Blue Center Area	Drawing Related to Set on Front, Some Sets Have Corgi "Technocrats" or Other Corgi Related Graphics.
c.1973-75	Corgi Junior Vehicles and Gift Sets	Card	Various Background Color w/Contrasting "Swiggle"	"CORGI JUNIORS" Text, Usually Drawings of 12 Other Items in Range on Card Backs. Multi- Colored "Swiggle" Runs Down Right Half of Card. Boxed Sets and "SUPER JUNIORS" Similar w/Design Along Edge of Window Opening. Mettoy-Playcraft Ltd.
c.1976-80	Corgi Junior Vehicles	Card	White Card w/Large Red/Orange/Yellow Target Logo	Bi-Lingual Card Back Usually Showing 12 Items from Range. "CORGI" without Juniors Reference, Character Vehicles Have Smaller Target Logo w/Vehicle Related Graphics. Mettoy Co. Ltd.
c.1976-80	Super Juniors and Gift Sets	Box	Dk. Blue/Yellow Box w/Red/Orange/Yellow Target	"CORGI" or "CORGI SUPER" without Juniors Reference, Vehicle or Set Related Graphics, Mettoy Co. Ltd.
c.1978	Corgi Junior Vehicles	Small Non-Hanging Card	Sm. White Card w/Target Under Vehicle	Card No Larger Than Plastic Bubble, No Provision for Hanging, "CORGI" on Long Edges, Number and Description on Short Edges, Bi-Lingual Card Back.
c.1981	Corgi Junior Vehicles	Card	Plain Yellow w/Logo and Black Edge.	(International Card Outside USA Market) Multi-Lingual Target Logo Still Used on Back, Mettoy Co. Ltd. (May Be From Period Prior To Mettoy Closure.)
c.1981-83	Corgi Junior Vehicles	Card	Small Target Logo w/Other Graphics	Graphics Related to Vehicle When Possible, Short and Long Card Variants, Multi-Lingual Back. Mettoy Co. Ltd. (Less Common in USA Market.)

c.1981-83	Corgi Junior Vehicles	Card	White Card w/Red Diagonal Stripe & Diagonal Text	(USA Market) Vehicles Grouped into Sub-Series Such as "Cool Convertibles", Photo of Real Car or Related Character, Some Models Made in Singapore, "Warranty!" Back w/USA Address (Reeves International), Drawings of 9 Other Vehicles from Line. Mettoy Co. Ltd.
c.1982-83	Corgi Junior Vehicles	Card	Baseball, Football or Hockey (Special)	(USA Market) Special Series of Vehicles Produced for Reeves International Numbered Outside Normal Range, Special Card Graphics w/Poster Offer on Back.
c.1984	Corgi Junior Vehicles & Sets	Card or Box	Coca-Cola or Hershey Graphics	(Hartoy Imports to USA Market Not By Normal USA Distributor. Time Period Immediately Following Mettoy Closure. Hartoy was USA Distributor of Lledo Products.)
c.1984	Sets	Box	Various	1984 Only. Mettoy Era Logo, Box Style, and E-Series Number, but with Corgi Toys Ltd. Manufacturer Name.
c.1984-87	Corgi Junior Vehicles	Card	Dk. Blue w/Traffic Logo	Tall Card w/Afterprinting for Model Description. (Made in GB)
c.1984-87	Corgi Junior Vehicles	Hanging Window Box	Dk. Blue w/Traffic Logo	Window Box w/Card Hanger Back, Glued Closed, Afterprinting for Model Description. (Made in GB)
c.1986-88	Sets	Large Card	Scene on Dk. Blue Card w/Traffic Logo	Large Hanging Card w/Multiple Vehicles in Themed Sets. (Made in GB)
c.1986	Corgi Junior Vehicles	Short Card	Red/Yellow Card w/o Data	(European Market?) Short Hanging Card, No Model Identification, Traffic Logo but Unusual Card Color.
c.1988-92	Corgi Junior Vehicles	Hanging Window Box	Dk. Blue w/Traffic Logo	Same as Earlier Style Except Vehicle Data Preprinted. (Corgi Hong Kong Ltd.)
c.1988-92	Corgi Junior Vehicles	Card	Corgi Freeway Logo	(USA Only?) Freeway Logo Card Not Like Earlier or Later Graphics. (Corgi Hong Kong Ltd.)
c.1988-92	Sets	Box	Dk. Blue w/Traffic Logo	Traffic Logo Graphics Mixed with Earlier Set Name Graphics.
c.1993-95	Corgi Junior Vehicles	Card	Corgi Traffic Logo w/"Auto-City"	New Graphics. (Mattel UK Ltd, Made in China)
c.1995	Corgi Junior Vehicles	Hanging Window Box	Blue/Red/Yellow w/Traffic Logo	Clear Plastic Gummed Labels with Vehicle Data. (Corgi Toys Ltd., div. of Mattel, Made in China)
c.1995-96	Former Corgi Junior Vehicles	Card	Hot Wheels Logo w/Auto-City	(All Markets Except USA) Blue/Yellow Graphics. Vehicles Retained Corgi Baseplate but Card has Hot Wheels Logo. (Transitional Repackaging of Existing Stock)
c.1995-96	Sets	Box	Hot Wheels Logo w/Auto City	Reworked Auto-City Graphics with Hot Wheels Logo where Corgi Traffic Logo Had Been. (Transitional Repackaging of Existing Stock)

An early Husky Toys card.

1970 Corgi Juniors card (left) and 1973 card
(right) with a late '70s character card.

Early Corgi Juniors Crime Busters Gift Set, with packaging similar to the last Husky Toys Gift Sets.

Another early Corgi Juniors set.

Corgi Rockets Action Speed Set box top.

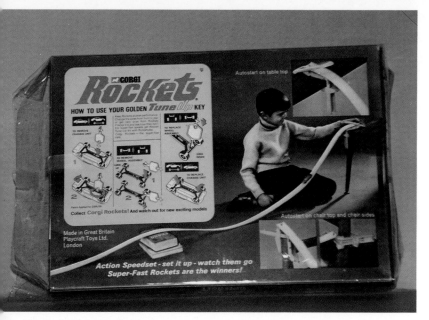

The back of the Rockets set.

Unusual 1973-style window box for E2009 Aerocar.

1973 style Corgi Super Juniors window box.

1976-style Corgi Juniors cards.

1973-style Corgi Juniors Gift Set window box.

1976-style Corgi Super box, the word Juniors having been dropped.

The large, 1976 box-style E4540 Super Hero Dealer Pack, the contents of which were resold separately.

1976 box-style E3051 Filling Station Gift Set.

The back of the box with printed, cut-out buildings.

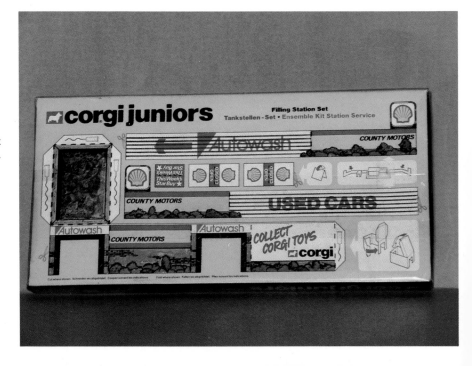

1981-style yellow international card.

1983 Baseball and Football car cards for the American market.

1981-style card for the American market, often with photos of the real vehicle.

Unusual 1984 set with Corgi Toys Ltd. markings but with old E3035 number.

1986 short card, generally not seen on the American market.

Large, 1986-style theme-set card.

1985-style hanging window box.

1988-style Freeway card.

1995-style hanging window box.

1993-style Corgi Auto-City card design as used for the former Juniors.

1993 style Corgi Auto-City card design as used for the former Haulers.

1996 Hot Wheels Auto-City card design. Various models from the line could be found drawn on the card.

1996 Hot Wheels Auto-City Gift Set, in which all vehicles still have Corgi or Corgi Juniors baseplates.

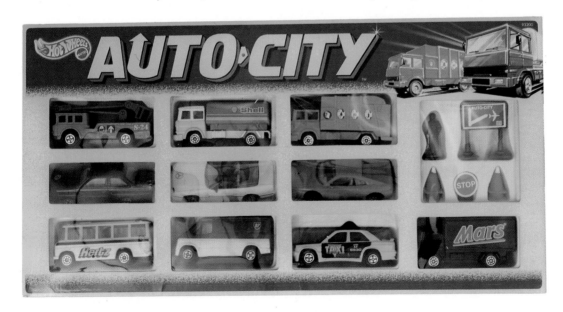

2.15—Copies and Reissues: *Caveat Emptor*

With the sustained popularity of Corgi Toys over the last forty years, it comes as no surprise that other companies would try to cut in on the market. The most reputable manufacturers are often dogged by offshore copy-cat companies. Sometimes, though, these clones are the result of the original company selling-off old dies and molds. Telling the difference between the authorized and unauthorized copy can sometime be difficult. It is up to the individual collector to decide whether such models should be collected or not.

The Routemaster shown could easily be mistaken for a Corgi model. A closer examination, though, reveals it to be a close copy made in Hong Kong. A side-by-side comparison with an actual Corgi 469 Routemaster shows just how exact the copy is to the original. All major dimensions are identical to the point

that parts could be interchanged if they were disassembled. Even the ribs and base text are identical. Only a closer examination shows where the Hong Kong model differs. The grill is rendered without the characteristic tapered sides, and various body panel details are out of proportion. The model appears to have been sold in London souvenir shops where unwary purchasers might easily believe that it was a Corgi product.

Corgi's Oldsmobile Toronado was a model of a very distinctive American car. Corgi's version made its last bow as a Take-Off-Wheel model. However, a remarkably similar Toronado was later offered by Pilan of Spain. This model is so close to the Corgi offering that it could have easily used some of the same dies. Pilan's model is most quickly identified by its opening doors. Pilan produced the standard version of their model in a turquoise very similar to the color used on early Corgi Toronados. They got some additional mileage out of the casting by also producing Police and Fire versions. No real American Police or Fire Departments ever used Toronados to the author's knowledge. The "Fire Brigade" markings on Pilan's red model are particularly

British in origin, making for an amusing hybrid of two cultures.

Milton of India produced many models which were made from old worn Corgi dies, although published descriptions have stated otherwise. Milton's products are of inferior quality and finish, and not easily mistaken for the original Corgi models. They are known to have produced models of the Plymouth Station Wagon, '59 Chevy Impala, Commer Van, and others. Another firm, Kiko in South America, also produced clones of some Corgi and Corgi Junior products. Kiko models were made from surplus Corgi and Juniors dies, but with inferior wheels.

Many, many copies of all levels of quality have been made of models in the Juniors line by companies in the Far East. Normally, these models have inferior detail and quality control. Seldom are these models marked with a manufacturer's name. Complicating matters, production of some of the Juniors line was moved offshore from Britain earlier than the standard Corgi line. Mettoy even produced some Juniors in Singapore prior to their closure. Copy-cat companies have had ample opportunity to develop duplicates. Even the patterns on the wheels, normally a product line identifier, have been copied. The most amusing copies tend to be the knock-offs of imaginary vehicles produced by Corgi. Sadly, the lower quality copies of Juniors models have at times replaced existing Corgi products on store shelves due to their lower price.

The Pilan Toronado was made in a number of versions, including a blue one that is very similar to Corgi's model.

This bus could easily fool an unwary buyer.

2.16—Code 3's:

After Market Reworks

The term "Code 3" is a commonly used term within the hobby which identifies models which have been modified without participation from the original manufacturer. To make things clear to the reader, a quick explanation of the "Code" system developed over the years is in order:

Code 1: Finished products which are entirely manufactured and finished by the original manufacturer or to the original manufacturer's specifications. Promotional and special order products produced for other firms entirely by the original manufacturer fall into this category.

Code 2: Finished products which are entirely manufactured, but only partially finished by the original manufacturer to specifications provided by the original re-seller. Final finishing and decoration is done by the original re-seller or by an outside firm to the original reveler's specifications.

Code 3: Products offered for resale which have been modified from the original manufacturer's specifications without the participation or knowledge of the original manufacturer.

Originally, Code 3 models were created and offered for resale without any knowledge or participation from the original manufacturer. However, changes in the collectibles market have created sufficient demand for specially modified and decorated models that manufacturers, Corgi in this case, now produce various undecorated or "in the white" models. This practice first emerged among model railroaders in the 1970s. It has since spread to the diecast model hobby. Today, Code 3's can even be seen being promoted in Corgi Collector magazine, although they are clearly identified as such. Code 3's should *never* be confused with forgeries. Legitimate Code 3 re-sellers are careful to clearly identify their products as such.

There are many Corgi-based Code 3 models in existence, with more coming onto the market each day. Some are reworked quite beautifully, with plated parts or added details. However, when such a model is resold without supporting documentation, information about the model's origin can be lost. Collectors should always take care to examine unusual models closely to determine their authenticity. Honest dealers will not hide information.

2.17—Restoration:

A Tough Question

Whether any specific model should or can be restored is one of the toughest questions in the hobby today. Ten years ago, it was believed that a Corgi Toy should never be tampered with for any reason, no matter the condition. This is partly responsible for the vast difference in the perceived value of a mint and boxed model compared to an identical blemished un-boxed example. However, the increasing age and rarity of good examples of scarce Corgi models has lead to the emergence of sources for restoration supplies. Many of the supplies are exact duplicates of easily lost or broken parts. Even labels and decals are being reproduced.

A number of factors must be considered when deciding whether to restore a model. First, the availability of parts, paint, and graphics for any model must first be determined. The list of available parts grows daily, so fresh information is critical. Advertisements for restoration parts suppliers can normally be found in commercial hobby magazines. Suppliers can also be found at larger toy shows. Second, the condition of the model must be considered. There should be no physical damage to major diecast body and baseplate parts. The alloy used in diecast cars tends to crack if heavily damaged, rendering the part unusable. Some vehicles damaged beyond restoration can act as parts suppliers for similar models. Finally, the return on invested time and money must be present. It is possible to spend more on the restoration of a model then it would cost to purchase an identical mint example. This determination may change over time with increasing Corgi values, although a restored model will never be worth more than a small fraction of a mint original model. Collectors must decide on the merit of restoration for each model, and if it is more desirable to own the damaged original or a restored model.

There are some models which should *never* be restored. Factory prototypes, extremely rare variations, promotional models, and factory goofs should be left in whatever state they are found. Restoration of these types of models destroys their value and erases any hope of verifying their authenticity. Rare or one-of-a-kind models are a valuable historical link to the past that can provide insight into what was going on at Corgi at the time of their creation.

Aside from the question of whether or not any individual model should be restored, a second question of ethics must also be asked. The suppliers of these excellent restoration parts are providing an honest service for the honest hobbyist. However a dangerous potential for abuse of legitimate restoration parts exists. It is certainly as easy to take a common model and restore it to resemble a more rare Corgi as it would be to recreate its original appearance. So long as the evidence of restoration is obvious, there is no concern. It is when deception is used that ethics are called into play. In some cases, the difference between a common model and a rare one is simply a matter of adding a label or decal. If an otherwise un-restored model is altered in this way, it would be extremely difficult for the average collector to detect. Restored models should always be represented as such. To do otherwise would be fraud. As always, let the buyer beware!

Left: This Ghia is very restorable if the bumper/grill molding can be found.

Below: This Studebaker is beyond restoration, but could supply parts for another model.

126

These two rare Rovers should *never* be considered for restoration.

This original label with the model that needs it may be worth more than if the label were installed.

This fire-damaged Rolls-Royce can't even supply parts, since heat has made the metal parts brittle.

Removal of the non-original decals would help this model, but the damaged front bumper cannot be replaced.

Only the model at left may ethically be restored to the more desirable Chipperfield's version.

2.18—Juniors Postscript: Hot Wheels Auto-City Line

As part of the management buy-out that created Corgi Classics Ltd., the Corgi products once referred to as Juniors and Haulers (Trucks) were separated from the Corgi product line and retained by Mattel. These product lines had been re-christened Corgi Auto-City by Mattel. After the separation, the packaging was changed to replace the Corgi logo with that of Hot Wheels. However, the remainder of the package was largely unchanged. As of this writing, Mattel was continuing to use the same stock numbers for individual items and sets as were used while they were part of the Corgi range. An interesting phenomenon, which is bound to be short lived, is the packaging of existing stocks of vehicles with the Corgi name on their base into Hot Wheels display cards and boxes. Models have begun to appear with altered base plates, however, indicating that new production of these vehicles will no longer carry the Corgi name. There is at least one documented case where the base text on a model was altered incorrectly. The former E85(A) Skip Dumper can be found with amusing "Hot Wheels Juniors" base text. The die for this model may have been altered by a person who did not read English and was simply following instructions to remove the word Corgi.

It is interesting to note that Mattel began intermixing the Corgi Auto-City and Hot Wheels products well before the separation of the two companies occurred. In the early 1990s, the Hot Wheels Thunderstreak racer was redecorated in "Fuji Film 2" markings and packaged as a Corgi for the European market. The 1995 Corgi Toy catalog shows Auto-City (Juniors) 93230 Race Set with the Juniors Jaguar XJR9 Racer and the U.S. Custom Van both decorated for "Hot Wheels Team Racing." There are likely to be more of such cross-over models since documen-tation about the Auto-City line has been generally poor due to weak collector interest.

Tracking the former Corgi models may become more difficult as they evolve. The Auto-City line is not being marketed individually in the United States at this writing, although some vehicles are showing up in sets. By and large, the former Juniors are unpopular among Hot Wheels collectors and are unlikely to be well documented by them. This stems from a basic difference in philosophies. Hot Wheels are fast toys that happen to resemble cars, while the former Juniors are model cars that happen to be fast toys. There is also a difference in scale between the two lines. Eventually the two lines should merge and intermix in sets. The former Juniors are well suited for special promotional decorations, and Mattel is expert in maximizing the use of existing dies. There are few duplications between the product lines, since the majority of the former Corgi products are based on European vehicles.

Whether duplicated vehicles, such as the '82 Firebird, '83 Corvette or '57 Chevy, will reappear is yet to be seen. The former Corgi '57 Thunderbird was already spotted in a regular Hot Wheels (not Auto-City) set. For the 1996 Christmas season, F.A.O. Schwarz has had a 16-vehicle limited edition set produced composed entirely of former Corgi vehicles in a special gold and black scheme. Mattel also produced a limited "Holiday" Hot Wheel set of four cars, two of which were based on the former Juniors Porsche with an added Santa figure at the wheel and Christmas presents on the rear spoiler. Mattel has been known to market some surprising things, and collector demand can be fickle. At least some of the former Corgi Junior castings will probably be around for many years to come.

Larger Hot Wheels Auto-City card designs were used in various sets.

The special Hot Wheels Holiday '96 card design containing a modified version of the former Corgi Porsche.

Section 3
Variation Listings

3.1—The Mettoy Years: 1956—1983 Factory Closure

This section contains the variation listing for models produced from the introduction of Corgi Toys in 1956 through the failure of Mettoy on November 1, 1983. This section originally appeared in Ed Force's book Corgi Toys, and is used with his kind permission. It has been extensively reviewed and updated, not only incorporating the former appendices, but also including new data uncovered since the last publication of the list. In some cases, the order of variations listed for a specific model has been changed in order to properly reflect the order in which each variation was produced. The format of this section of the variation listing has been preserved for ease of use for those familiar with the previous book.

NOTE: Entries marked "???" indicate uncertain or unavailable data. Entries followed by "?" indicate data which requires further authentication of details.

NOTE: Values shown are in U.S. Dollars for mint-in-mint boxed condition as of January 1997. Subtract 35-40 percent for mint unboxed, 50-60 percent for excellent, 60-70 percent for vg/chipped.

Corgi Variations

Gift Sets

1-A   Carrimore Car Transporter and Four Cars   12/1957-1962 $700-800
No. 1101 Car Transporter carrying four cars.
1. 205 Riley, 208S Jaguar, 300 Austin Healey, 305 Triumph; 1957-1960. 2. 214-A Ford Thunderbird hardtop, 215-A Ford Thunderbird convertible, 219-A Plymouth Sport Suburban, 220-A Chevrolet Impala, (Set 1A, 1959 only).
3. 210S Citroen, 219 Plymouth, 226 Mini, 305 Triumph (Set was 1C in 1961 and 1962.)
1-B   Ford Tractor and Beast Carrier   12/1966-1972 $150-160
No. 67 Ford 5000 Tractor & 58 Beast Carrier.
1. Standard colors.
1-C   Peugeot and Caravan   1982-1983 $45-50
Peugeot 505 373-B and Caravan 490-B.
1-D   Ford Sierra and Caravan Trailer   1983-Close $40-45
No. 299 Ford Sierra and 490 Caravan Trailer.
1. Shown in 1983 Corgi catalog with blue Sierra, 2-tone blue & white Caravan.
2-A   Land Rover and Pony Trailer   2/1958-1968 $175-200
First Version: Land Rover based on 406-A with tin cover over rear, horse trailer (102-A) with wire towing arm.
1. Green Land Rover with tan cover, red horse box with black base, both with smooth wheels.
2. Same as 2-A1 except both with shaped wheels crimped on axles.
3. Tan Land Rover with cream cover, tan and cream trailer, (unconfirmed).
Second Version: Land Rover based on 438-A with plastic cover over rear, horse trailer (102-A) with cast towing arm.
4. Tan Land Rover with cream cover, tan and cream horse trailer, both with shaped wheels, axles free on Land Rover but crimped on trailer.
5. Same as 2-A4 except trailer axles free.
2-B   Unimog with Dumper and Priestman Cub Shovel   11/1971-1973 $120-140
No. 1145 Mercedes-Benz Unimog with Dumper and 1128 Priestman Cub Shovel.
1. Standard colors.
2-C   Construction Set   10/1980-1980 $200-225
No. 54 Tractor with Shovel, 440 Mazda Pickup, and Corgi Junior 20 Cement Mixer.
1. Orange Tractor and Mazda with Block Logo.
3-A   R.A.F. Land Rover and Thunderbird Missile   7/1958-1963 $400-425
No. 350 Thunderbird Missile on Trolley and 351 R.A.F. Land Rover.
1. Land Rover without suspension.
2. Land Rover with suspension;Corgi catalog number 351S.

3-B   Batmobile, Batboat and Trailer   6/1967-1981 $200-225
No. 267 Batmobile and 107 Batboat on Trailer.
1. Hubs with red bat emblems on car, big labels covering fin of boat; 1967-1972.
2. Red tires and chrome wheels on car, boat as above; 1973
3. Chrome wheels with black tires on car, boat as above; 1974-1976.
4. Chrome wheels on car, boat with small bat emblem ovals on fin and chain labels on hull, Whizzwheels on trailer; 1977-1981.
4-A   R.A.F. Land Rover, Bloodhound Missile   11/1958-1961 $500-550
No. 351 R.A.F. Land Rover, 1115 Bloodhound Missile, 1116 Ramp and 1117 Trolley.
1. Standard colors.
4-B   Country Farm Set   7/1974-1975 $70-80
No. 50 Massey Ferguson Tractor, red trailer with hay load, figures and fences.
1. Standard tractor.
5-A   British Racing Cars   3/1959-1963 $300-325
No. 150 Vanwall, 151 Lotus XI and 152 B.R.M racing cars.
1. Green 150 Vanwall, dull blue 151 Lotus and dark green 152 B.R.M., all with smooth wheels; 1959 only.
2. Same cars with shaped wheels; 1960-1961.
3. Red 150S Vanwall, bright blue 151A Lotus and light green 152S B.R.M., 1963.
4. Red 150 Vanwall, otherwise 5-A1;1959.
5-B   Agricultural Set   10/1967-1972 $300-350
No. 62 Farm Trailer, 69 Massey Ferguson Tractor, 71 Harrow, 438 Land Rover in non-standard green (various shades) without plastic cover over rear, 484 Farm Truck, 1490 Skip, figures and accessories.
1. Land Rover with shaped wheels, rubber tires, metal tow hook.
2. Land Rover with shaped wheels, plastic tires, plastic tow hook.
3. Land Rover with cast wheels, plastic tires, plastic tow hook.
5-C   Country Farm Set   4/1976-1976 $100-120
No. 50 Massey Ferguson Tractor, red trailer, figures and fence; differs from 4-B in not having hay load.
1. Standard tractor.
6-A   Rocket Age Set   9/1959-1960 $800-1000+
No. 350 Thunderbird Missile on Trolley, 351 R.A.F. Land Rover, 352 R.A.F. Staff Car, 353 Radar Scanner, 1106 Decca Radar Van, 1115 Bloodhound Missile, 1116 Ramp and 1117 Trolley.
1. Standard colors.
6-B   VW Racing Tender and Cooper-Maserati   10/1967-1969 $160-180
No. 490 VW Breakdown Van, red trailer and 156 Cooper-Maserati.
1. White 490 with Racing Club labels, blue 156 Cooper.
7-A   Massey Ferguson Tractor, Tipping Trailer   7/1959-1963 $120-140
No. 50 Massey Ferguson Tractor and 51 Tipping Trailer.
1. Standard colors.
7-B   Daktari Set   11/1967-1975 $130-150
Green and black Land Rover pickup (based on 438) and figures. (Also used in GS14-B).
1. Shaped wheels, rubber tires;1968-1971.
2. Cast wheels, plastic tires;1972-1973.
3. Whizzwheels;1974-1975.
8-A   Combine Harvester, Tractor and Trailer   10/1959-1962 $400-450
No. 50 Massey Ferguson Tractor, 51 Tipping Trailer and 1111 Combine Harvester.
1. Standard colors.
8-B   Lions of Longleat   8/1968-1974 $175-200
White and black Land Rover pickup (based on 438) with yellow cage, lions' den, figures and accessories.
1. Cast wheels, 1969-1973.
2. Whizzwheels; 1974.
8-C   French Construction Set   4/1980-1980 $???
1110-B Crawler, 1156-A Cement Mixer, E20 Mixer.
9-A   Corporal Missile   11/1958-1962 $600-650
No. 1112 Corporal Missile & Ramp, 1113 Erector Vehicle and 1118 Army Truck.
1. Standard colors.
9-B   Tractor with Shovel and Tipping Trailer   12/1968-1973 $175-200
No. 69 Massey Ferguson Tractor and 62 Tipping Trailer.
1. Standard colors.
10-A   Rambler Marlin with Kayak and Trailer   7/1968-1969 $200-225
No. 263 Rambler Marlin, roof rack with kayak, and 109 Pennyburn Trailer.
1. Blue Marlin with white roof, yellow rack, red and white kayak, blue and white trailer with red hitch, cast wheels, plastic tires.
10-B   Centurion Tank and Transporter   10/1973-1978 $130-150
No. 901 Centurion Tank on olive drab Mack low loader.
1. Standard Centurion Tank.
10-C   Jeep and Motorcycle Trailer   3/1982-1983 $40-45
Open Jeep based on 441-B, two-wheel trailer, yellow and blue motorcycles.
1. Red Jeep and trailer.
11-A   ERF Dropside Truck and Trailer   3/1960-1964 $200-225
No. 456 ERF Dropside Truck, 101 Flat Trailer, 1485 and 1488 sack and plank loads.
11-B   London Set   9/1971-1974 $130-150
No. 204 Mini, 418 London Taxi, 468 Routemaster Bus, Policeman figure.
1. Orange Mini, standard taxi and bus.
2. Blue Mini, standard taxi and bus.

11-C **London Set** 3/1980-1982 $50-60
No. 425 London Taxi and 469 Routemaster Bus.
1. Standard colors, plus mounted policeman figure; 1980-1981.
2. Standard colors, without mounted policeman; 1982-1982.

12-A **Circus Crane Truck and Cage Wagon** 7/1961-1965 $250-300
No. 1121 Circus Crane Truck, 1123 Circus Cage Wagon, and figures.
1. Standard colors.

12-B **Grand Prix Racing Set** 7/1968-1972 $400-450
No. 155 Lotus, 156 Cooper-Maserati, 330 or 371 Porsche Carrera 6, 490 VW Breakdown Van, red trailer, figures and accessories.
1. White 490 VW with Racing Club labels, 330 Porsche; 1969.
2. White 490 VW with Racing Club labels, 371 Porsche; 1970-1972.

12-C **Glider Set** 7/1981-Close $75-85
No. 345 Honda Prelude, two-wheel trailer and glider.
1. White Honda with green trim, white trailer with green trim and red #24, red and white glider; 1981-1982.
2. Yellow Honda, yellow trailer with green trim and red #24, red and yellow glider; shown in 1983 Corgi catalog.

13-A **Fordson Tractor and Plough** 3/1964-1966 $130-150
No. 60 Fordson Tractor and 61 Four Furrow Plough.
1. Standard colors.

13-B **Tour De France Set** 8/1968-1972 $150-175
White and black Renault 16 Paramount Film Unit based on 260 with labels, roof sign, tailboard, camera, cameraman and cycle.
1. Black printed roof sign.
2. Red printed roof sign.

13-C **Tour De France Set** 2/1981-1982 $80-90
No. 373 Peugeot 505 with rack, cycles and figures.
1. White Peugeot.

14-A **Tower Wagon and Lamp Standard** 2/1961-1965 $100-120
Jeep Tower Wagon (later no. is 478), 606 Lamp Standard and workman figure.
1. Red Tower Wagon with unpainted arms and yellow basket.

14-B **Giant Daktari Set** 5/1969-1973 $450-500
Green and black Land Rover pickup (based on 438), blue and tan Dodge Kew Fargo Livestock Truck, tan 503 Giraffe Truck and figures.
1. As above; all vehicle colors are nonstandard.

15-A **Silverstone Racing Layout** 12/1963-1966 $2000-2500+
No. 150S Vanwall, 151A Lotus XI, 152S B.R.M., 215S Ford Thunderbird, 304S Mercedes-Benz 300SL, 309 Aston Martin, 417S Land Rover Breakdown Truck, 602 Phone Boxes, 604 Press Box, 605 Club House, two 603 Pits, 1501, 1502 and 1503 figures, playmat.
1. Standard colors.

15-B **Land Rover and Horse Box Trailer** 11/1968-1977 $100-120
Blue and white 438 Land Rover and 112 Horse Box Trailer, two horses.
1. Shaped wheels on Land Rover, cast wheels on trailer, rubber tires on both; 1968-1969.
2. Shaped wheels on Land Rover, cast wheels on trailer, plastic tires on both; 1970-1972.
3. Cast wheels and plastic tires on both Land Rover and trailer; 1973-1974.
4. Whizzwheels on Land Rover, cast wheels and plastic tires on trailer; 1975.
5. Whizzwheels on Land Rover, wider 8-spoke cast wheels with wide plastic tires on trailer; 1976-1977.

16-A **Ecurie Ecosse Transporter and Racing Cars** 10/1961-1966 $450-500
No. 1126 Ecurie Ecosse Transporter, 150S Vanwall, 152S B.R.M. and one other car.
1. Other car is 151A Lotus XI; standard colors; 1961-1964.
2. Other car is 154 Ferrari; standard colors; 1964-1966.

17-A **Land Rover and Ferrari Racing Car** 3/1963-1967 $180-220
Red and tan 438 Land Rover, yellow two-wheel trailer with 154 Ferrari.
1. Standard Ferrari.

17-B **Military Set** 10/1975-1980 $70-80
No. 900 Tiger Tank, 906 Saladin Armored Car and 920 Bell Army Helicopter.
1. Standard colors.

18-A **Fordson Tractor and Plough** 8/1961-1964 $120-130
No. 55 Fordson Tractor and 56 Four Furrow Plough.
1. Standard colors.

18-B **Emergency Set** 8/1975-1977 $80-100
No. 402 Ford Cortina Police Car, 482 Range Rover Ambulance, 921 Police Helicopter, figures and accessories.
1. Standard colors.

19-A **Circus Land Rover and Elephant Cage** 4/1962-1969 $275-300
Red and blue 438 Land Rover and 101 Platform Trailer, with 607 Elephant Cage.
1. As above (nonstandard colors).

19-B **Corgi Flying Club Set** 9/1972-1977 $80-100
Blue and orange 438 Land Rover with Corgi Flying Club labels, blue two-wheel trailer and plastic airplane. Land Rover has red dome light.
1. Orange and yellow airplane.
2. Orange and white airplane.

19-C **Emergency Set** 11/1980-1981 $70-80
No. 339 Rover 3500 Police Car, 931 Police Helicopter, figures and accessories.
1. Standard colors.

20-A **Golden Guinea Set** 11/1961-1963 $250-300
Gold plated 224 Bentley Continental, 229 Chevrolet Corvair and 234 Ford Consul.
1. As above (nonstandard finish).

20-B **Car Transporter and Five Cars** 10/1970-1973 $800-1000+
No. 1146 Scammell Car Transporter, 201 The Saint's Volvo, 311 Ford Capri, 343 Pontiac Firebird, 372 Lancia Fulvia, 377 Marcos 3 Litre and 378 MGC GT.
1. Standard colors.

20-C **Emergency Set** 9/1978-1980 $65-75
No. 429 Jaguar Police Car, 482 Range Rover Ambulance, 921 Police Helicopter, figures and accessories.
1. Standard colors.

21-A **Milk Truck and Trailer** 5/1962-1966 $250-300
Blue and white 456 ERF Dropside Truck and 101 Flat Trailer with 1462 and 1487 Milk Churns.
1. As above (nonstandard colors).

21-B **Circus Crane and Cages** 4/1970-1972 $1600-1800+
No. 1144 Circus Crane Truck, flat trailer with cages and 607 Elephant Cage.
1. Red and blue trailer.

21-C **Superman Set** 9/1979-1981 $200-225
No. 265 Supermobile, 260 Metropolis Police Car and 929 Daily Planet Helicopter.
1. Standard colors.

22-A **Agricultural Set** 5/1962-1966 $400-450
Fordson Tractor, Tipping Trailer, Plough, Trailer with 1487 Milk Churns, 57 Massey Ferguson Tractor with Fork, 438 Land Rover, 1111 Combine and figures.
1. 55 Fordson Tractor, 51 Tipping Trailer, green open 438 Land Rover, yellow 101 Flat Trailer with milk churns, 1962-1964.
2. 60 Fordson Tractor, 62 Tipping Trailer, green open 438 Land Rover, red 100 Dropside Trailer with milk churns.

22-B **James Bond Set** 9/1979-1981 $200-225
No. 269 James Bond Lotus Esprit, 271 James Bond Aston Martin and 649 James Bond Space Shuttle.
1. Standard colors.

23-A **Circus Set** 3/1963-1968
                                   (Booking Office) $900-1000+
                                   (Giraffe Truck) $650-750
Red and blue 438 Land Rover, 1121 Circus Crane Truck, two 1123 Circus Cage Wagons with figures, 101 Platform Trailer with 607 Ele- phant Cage, one other vehicle.
1. Other vehicle is 426 Booking Office; 1963-1965.
2. Other vehicle is 503 Giraffe Truck; 1966-1968.

23-B **Spiderman Set** 11/1980-1981 $200-225
No. 261 Spiderbuggy, 266 Spiderbike and 928 Spidercopter.
1. Standard colors.

24-A **Constructor Set** 8/1963-1968 $150-160
Two Commer chassis-cab units, four different rear body units, milk load, rear seat and milkman figure.
1. One red and one white chassis-cab, red van, yellow pickup, light blue milk float and white ambulance bodies.

24-B **Mercedes-Benz 240D and Caravan Trailer** 7/1975-1981 $35-45
No. 285 Mercedes-Benz 240D and 490 Caravan Trailer.
1. Standard blue Mercedes, white and blue Caravan; 1975-1979.
2. Brown and white Mercedes, tan and brown Caravan; shown in 1980 and 1981 Corgi catalogs.

25-A **Shell or BP Garage** 4/1963-1965 $1600-1800+
No. 603 Service Station, 609 Gas Pumps, three 601 Garages, 602 Phone Booths, 224 Bentley Continental, 225 Austin 7, 229 Chevrolet Corvair, 234 Ford Consul, 419 Ford Police Car, two 606 Lamp Standards, 1505 Figures, Playmat.
1. Shell garage and gas pumps.
2. BP garage and gas pumps.

25-B **VW Racing Tender and Cooper-Maserati** 8/1970-1971 $150-175
No. 490 VW Breakdown Truck with Racing Club labels, red two-wheel trailer with yellow and white 159 Cooper-Maserati. Note: Gift Set 6-B includes the earlier blue 156 Cooper-Maserati.
1. Tan 490 VW Breakdown Truck.
2. White 490 VW Breakdown Truck.

25-C **Matra Rancho and Motorcycle Trailer** 11/1980-1981 $50-60
Red 457 Matra Rancho and two-wheel trailer with yellow and blue motorcycles.
1. As above.

26-A **Beach Buggy and Sailing Boat** 7/1971-1976 $50-60
Open purple 381 Beach Buggy, yellow trailer, red and white sailboat, blue sail.
1. Chrome wheels on Beach Buggy, Whizzwheels on Trailer.

26-B **Matra Rancho and Racing Car** 5/1981-Close $70-80
No. 457 Matra Rancho, two-wheel trailer and 160 Hesketh Racing Car.
1. Yellow and black 457 Matra, yellow Hesketh and Trailer, #17 and Team Corgi labels.

27-A **Priestman Cub Shovel, Machinery Carrier** 8/1963-1972 $180-200
No. 1128 Priestman Cub Shovel on 1131 Low Loader Machinery Carrier.
1. Standard colors.

27-B **French Police Set** 6/1978-1978 $???
Details unknown; issued only in France.

28-A **Car Transporter and Four Cars** 8/1963-1966 $750-800
No. 1105 Car Transporter with four cars.
1. 217 Fiat 1800, 222 Renault Floride, 230 Mercedes-Benz 230SE and 234 Ford Consul; 1963-1965.
2. 228 Volvo P-1800, 229 Chevrolet Corvair, 239 VW Ghia and 252 Rover 2000; 1966.
3. Other combinations of cars are possible.

28-B **Mazda Pickup and Dinghy on Trailer** 8/1975-1978 $50-60
Yellow and red 493 Mazda Pickup, yellow two-wheel trailer, red and yellow dinghy, diver figure. Truck has black toolbox and chrome wheels; Trailer has Whizzwheels.
1. Black and white "Ford" and red and yellow flame labels on truck.
2. Blue and white "Sea Spray" labels on truck.

29-A **Massey Ferguson Tractor, Tipping Trailer** 4/1965-1965 $120-130
No. 50 Massey Ferguson Tractor with driver and 51 Tipping Trailer.
1. Standard colors.

29-B **Ferrari Daytona and Racing Car** 4/1975-1977 $75-85
Blue and yellow 323 Ferrari Daytona and 150 Surtees on yellow two-wheel trailer.
1. As above (nonstandard colors).

29-C **Jeep and Horse Box** 5/1981-1983 $40-45
No. 441 Jeep with Corgi Pony Club labels and tan top, Horse Box Trailer, figures and accessories.
1. Metallic golden orange Jeep and Trailer.

30-A **Grand Prix Set** 7/1973-1973 $275-300
Available initially only by mail order, later through larger chain stores in U.S. market to eliminate stock, some sold with sets broken-up into individual models.
1. 150-B3 (1500) Surtees TS9 (disassembled), 151-B2 (1501) Yardley McLaren M19A (disassembled), 154-B3 (1504) John Player Special (disassembled), 153-B2 Surtees TS9 (assembled).

30-B **Circus Land Rover and Cage Trailer** 7/1978-1981 $120-140
Yellow and red Land Rover (based on 421) with blue loudspeakers, yellow and red cage trailer with figures.
1. Pinder-Jean Richard labels.

31-A **Buick Riviera and Cabin Cruiser** 1/1965-1968 $180-200
No. 245 Buick Riviera, 104 Dolphin Cabin Cruiser or Trailer, and figures.
1. Light blue Buick.
2. Dark metallic blue Buick.
3. Metallic gold Buick.

31-B **Safari Land Rover and Big Game Trailer** 4/1976-1980 $100-120
White and black Land Rover (based on 421) with roof hatch and Game Park labels, white and black cage trailer, figures.
1. Chrome wheels; 1976.
2. Red wheels; 1977-1980.

32-A **Massey Ferguson Tractor with Shovel, Trailer** 5/1965-1966 $150-160
No. 53 Massey Ferguson Tractor with Shovel, driver, and 62 Tipping Trailer.
1. Standard colors.

32-B   **Lotus Racing Set**   7/1976-1979 $100-120
Black and gold 315 Lotus Elite, gold trailer, black and gold 154 Lotus Racing Car.
1. Number 3 and "Team Car" labels on Elite, J.P.S. labels on Racer; 1976.
2. Number 7 labels on Elite, otherwise as Type 1; 1977-1978.
3. Texaco labels on Racer, otherwise as Type 1; 1979-1979.

33-A   **Fordson Tractor and Beast Carrier**   3/1965-1966 $150-160
No. 60 Fordson Tractor, 58 Beast Carrier Trailer and figures.
1. Standard colors.

33-B   **Deutsche Lebensrettungsgesellschaft Set**   4/1980-1982? $???
White and red Land Rover (based on 421) and white two-wheel trailer with white and red lifeboat. Made for sale in Germany.
1. Deutsche Lebensrettungsgesellschaft labels (German Lifesaving Society).

34-A   **David Brown Tractor and Trailer**   9/1976-1979 $70-80
No. 55 David Brown Tractor and 56 Tipping Farm Trailer.
1. Standard colors.

35-A   **London Set**   7/1964-1969 $160-170
No. 418 London Taxi, 468 Routemaster Bus and policeman figure. Note: policeman is standing and directing traffic, similar (but not identical) to the figure in Gift Set 11-B, not mounted as in Set 11-C.
1. Corgi Toys labels on Bus; 1964-1966.
2. Outspan Oranges labels on Bus; 1967-1969.

35-B   **Chopper Squad Surf Rescue Set**   8/1978-1979 $50-60
Blue 419 Chopper Squad Jeep and two-wheel trailer with red and white boat.
1. Chopper Squad labels on Jeep, Surf Rescue labels on boat.

36-A   **Oldsmobile Toronado and Speedboat**   12/1967-1970 $200-225
Blue 264 Oldsmobile Toronado, silver two-wheel trailer with blue and yellow Speedboat, and figures. (Set also rumored to exist with Rambler Marlin.)
1. Swordfish labels on boat.

36-B   **Tarzan Set**   8/1976-1978 $250-275
Light metallic green 421 Land Rover and two-wheel trailer with white cage, brown and tan boat on cream trailer, accessories, figures and panorama.
1. As above.

36-C   **Off Road Set**   1983-Close $40-45
No. 447 Renegade Jeep, white two-wheel trailer with blue Powerboat.
1. #5 and stripe labels on Jeep and boat. Jeep is standard color.

37-A   **Lotus Racing Team Set**   8/1966-1969 $450-500
No. 490 VW Breakdown Van, green and yellow 318 Lotus Elan Convertible, yellow and green 319 Lotus Elan Hardtop, 155 Lotus Racing Car, red two-wheel trailer, extra Lotus Elan chassis and accessories.
1. White 490 VW with Racing Club labels, 319 Lotus with red interior.
2. White 490 VW with Racing Club labels, 319 Lotus with black interior.

37-B   **Fiat X1/9 and Powerboat**   4/1977-1980 $55-65
White and green 314 Fiat, white two-wheel trailer with white and gold Powerboat.
1. Union Jack, Carlsberg and number 15 labels on boat.

38-A   **Monte Carlo Rally Set**   3/1965-1967 $450-500
No. 321 Mini, 322 Rover and 323 Citroen DS19 Rally Cars.
1. Standard colors, including 322-A1 Rover.

38-B   **Mini Camping Set**   2/1977-1978 $100-120
No. 200 British Leyland Mini, red and blue plastic tent, figures and grille.
1. Cream Mini (nonstandard color).

38-C   **Powerboat Team**   3/1980-1981 $60-70
White and red 319 Jaguar and silver trailer with red and white Powerboat
1. Team Corgi Carlsberg labels on car and boat, Union Jack and #1 labels on boat.

39-A   **Royal Wedding State Landau**   6/1981-1981 $40-50
Revision of 41-B State Landau.
GS41-B State Landau repackaged and renumbered without change.

40-A   **The Avengers Set**   1/1966-1969
                                            (Green Bentley) $750-800
                                            (Red Bentley) $550-600
White 318 Lotus Elan, 9001 Bentley, John Steed and Emma Peel figures, umbrellas.
1. Green 9001 Bentley, John Steed driving.
2. Red 9002 Bentley, John Steed driving.

40-B   **Batman Set**   9/1976-1981 $250-300
No. 267 Batmobile, 107 Batboat on Trailer and 925 Batcopter.
1. Batboat with second type labels, Trailer with Whizzwheels.

41-A   **Carrimore Car Transporter and Six Cars**   7/1966-1966 $800-900
Available only by mail-order, 1138-A Car Transporter, 226 Morris Mini-Minor, 249 Mini-Cooper Deluxe, 251 Hillman Imp, 252 Rover 2000, 321 Monte-Carlo Mini-Cooper, 440 Ford Cortina Estate.
1. Standard colors.

41-B   **Silver Jubilee State Landau**   4/1977-1980 $40-50
Landau, four horses, two riders, two footmen, Queen Elizabeth II, Prince Philip and Corgi Dog figures, mounted on plinth.
1. Queen in yellow dress.
2. Queen in blue dress.

42-A   **Agricultural Set**   3/1978-1980 $80-90
No. 55 Tipping Farm Trailer, Silo and Con- veyor Belt as in Gift Set 43-A (see below).
1. Dark yellow conveyor and silo supports, standard tractor and trailer.

43-A   **Silo and Conveyor Belt**   3/1978-1980 $50-60
Clear plastic silo with yellow supports, yellow two-wheel conveyor.
1. Corgi Harvesting Company label on silo.

44-A   **Police Land Rover and Horse Box**   6/1978-1980 $50-60
White 421 Land Rover and Horse Box Trailer, mounted policeman figure.
1. Police labels on Land Rover sides, roof sign and trailer.

45-A   **All Winners Set**   7/1966? $600-800?
Supposed to include 261 James Bond Aston Martin, 310 Corvette, 314 Ferrari, 324 Marcos and 325 Mustang, for export only. Probably not issued (Need confirmation).

45-B   **Royal Canadian Mounted Police Set**   7/1978-1980 $70-80
Blue 421 Land Rover and Horse Box, mounted policeman figure.
1. Police roof sign on Land Rover, RCMP emblem labels on Land Rover and trailer.

46-A   **All Winners Set**   10/1966-1969 $500-700
Includes 312 Jaguar E-type, 314 Ferrari 250LM and three other cars.
1. Silver 310 Corvette, gold 312 Jaguar, red 314 Ferrari, white 324 Marcos and white 325 Mustang; 1966.
2. Others standard colors of 310, 312 or 325 may be possible.
3. 264 Toronado, 312 Jaguar, 314 Ferrari, 327 MGB and 337 Corvette Stock Car, in standard colors.

46-B   **Super Karts**   5/1982-Close $25-35
One orange and one blue go-kart, with pullback action, silver and gold drivers.
1. Front Whizzwheels, rear wide rubber slicks.

47-A   **Ford Tractor and Conveyor**   9/1966-1969 $180-200
No. 67 Ford Tractor, blue-silver-red Conveyor Trailer, figures and accessories.
1. Conveyor is that used on 64-A FC Jeep.

47-B   **Pony Club Set**   8/1978-1980 $50-60
Brown and white 421 Land Rover and Horse Box Trailer, horse and rider figures.
1. Corgi Pony Club labels.

48-A   **Car Transporter and Six Cars**   7/1966-1969 $500-600
No. 1138 Car Transporter, 226 Mini, 249 Mini DeLuxe, 252 Rover, 333 Mini Rally, 340 Sunbeam Imp and 440 Ford Cortina Estate Car.
1. Standard colors.

48-B   **Car Transporter and Six Cars**   1970-1973 $700-800
No. 1148 Scammell Car Transporter, 226 Mini, 249 Mini DeLuxe, 258 The Saint's Volvo, 339 Mini Rally, 340 Sunbeam Imp and 345 MGC GT.
1. Standard colors.

48-C   **Jean Richard Circus Set**   11/1978-1981 $200-250
Yellow and red Circus Land Rover and Cage Trailer, 426-B Booking Office Van, Open Trailer, 1163 Human Cannonball Truck, ring, seats, backdrop and figures.
1. Pinder-Jean Richard labels.

49-A   **Flying Club Set**   6/1978-1980 $50-70
Green and white 419 Jeep, green two-wheel trailer, blue and white airplane.
1. Corgi Flying Club and emblem labels.

Agricultural

50-A   **Massey Ferguson 65 Tractor**   76mm 5/1959-1966 $90-100
Red engine cover, silver grille, seat and steering wheel, detailed chassis including fenders and axle mountings, red plastic wheels, black rubber tires.
1. Cream chassis.
2. Gray chassis.

50-B   **Massey Ferguson 50B Tractor**   100mm 6/1973-1977 $50-60
Dark yellow body and chassis castings, black plastic interior, engine, grille and exhaust, black painted roof panel, red plastic wheels, black plastic tires.
1. Dark yellow body, red wheels, black roof, " 50B" label on left rear fender.
2. White body and wheels, black roof, (St. Michael set 8403).

51-A   **Massey Ferguson 30cwt. Tipping Trailer**   90mm 5/1959-1965 $20-30
Tipper, tailgate and chassis castings, unpainted hydraulic cylinder, red plastic wheels, black rubber tires; tipper tips and tailgate opens.
1. Dark yellow tipper and tailgate, red chassis.
2. Gray tipper and tailgate, red chassis.

53-A   **Massey Ferguson 65 Tractor with Shovel**   122mm 4/1960-1966 $100-120
Details as on 50-A plus red diecast shovel arm mounts, diecast shovel arms same color as chassis, silver diecast shovel, unpainted sheet metal shovel controls.
1. Cream chassis and shovel arms.
2. Gray chassis and shovel arms.

54-A   **Fordson Power Major Tractor with Halftracks**   88mm 3/1962-1964 $150-160
Blue body and chassis castings, silver grille, headlights, seat, steering gear and vibrating exhaust stack, orange wheels and halftrack hubs, black rubber tires, rubber treads, maroon and white Fordson Power Major decals.
1. Light orange diecast wheels, headlights outside radiator, gray treads.
2. Dark orange plastic wheels, headlights outside radiator, ? treads.
3. New casting with headlights set in grille, dark orange plastic wheels, black treads.

54-B   **Massey Ferguson 50B Tractor with Shovel**   150mm 5/1974-1981 $50-60
Main color body, chassis, shovel arm mount and shovel castings, second color shovel arm castings, two silver shovel control castings, black hydraulic cylinders, interior, engine, grille and exhaust, red plastic wheels, black tires.
1. Dark yellow first and red second colors, 50B label on left rear fender; black painted roof panel; 1974-1979.
2. Red-orange first and white second colors, black roof with Block label; 4/1980-1981.
3. Red body and scoop, white wheels and arms, black roof, (St. Michael set 8802).
4. Same as 54-B2 except red roof.

55-A   **Fordson Power Major Tractor**   82mm 5/1961-1963 $90-100
Blue body and chassis castings, silver seat, steering wheel, vibrating exhaust stack, grille and headlights, wire and sheet metal steering gear, black diecast and yellow plastic hitch apparatus, orange wheels, black rubber tires, maroon and white Fordson Power Major decals.
1. Light orange diecast wheels.
2. Dark orange diecast wheels.
3. Dark orange plastic wheels.

55-B   **David Brown Tractor**   105mm 1/1977-1982 $50-60
Body, chassis, unpainted hitch and red rear wheel castings, red plastic engine block, interior and front wheels, black plastic roof, stacks, hitch parts, steering wheel, seat and tires, black and white David Brown and #1412 labels.
1. White body, red chassis.

56-A   **Four Furrow Plough**   90mm 5/1961-1963 $20-30
Single frame casting with yellow plastic parts.
1. Red frame.

56-B   **Tipping Farm Trailer**   130mm 1/1977-1980 $20-30
Chassis and opening tailgate castings, red plastic tipper and wheels, black hydraulic cylinder and tires.
1. Dark yellow chassis, silver tailgate; 1977-1978.
2. White chassis and tailgate; 1979-1980.

57-A   **Massey Ferguson 65 Tractor with Fork**   124mm 5/1963-1967 $100-120
Red body and shovel arm mount castings, cream chassis casting, silver seat, steering wheel, fork arms and fork castings, silver painted grille, sheet metal fork controls, red plastic wheels, black rubber tires.
1. Massey Ferguson 65 decals.

58-A   **Beast Carrier Trailer**   113mm 11/1965-1971 $40-50
Body, tailgate and chassis castings, red plastic wheels, black rubber tires, green rubber webbing, four plastic calf figures, cardboard floor cover.
1. Dark yellow body and lowering tailgate, red chassis.

60-A   **Fordson Power Major Tractor**   88mm 7/1964-1966 $90-100
Blue body, chassis and steering wheel castings, silver seat, hitch, hitch control, steering arms and vibrating exhaust stack castings, silver painted grille including headlights, red plastic wheels, black rubber tires, driver.
1. Fordson Power Major decals.

61-A Four Furrow Plough 94mm 7/1964-1970 $20-30
Single frame casting with chromed plastic parts.
1. Blue frame.
62-A Tipping Farm Trailer 108mm 2/1965-1972 $20-30
Tipper, tailgate, two raves (stakes) and chassis castings, black hydraulic cylinder and tires, red plastic wheels; tipper tips, tailgate opens.
1. Red tipper and tailgate, yellow chassis and raves.
64-A Jeep FC-150 Pickup with Conveyor Belt 186mm 6/1965-1969 $120-140
Single body casting, unpainted mounting and parts, three yellow conveyor castings, clear windows, yellow interior, gray SW, silver headlights and front bumper, crank and gears, orange grille, two rubber belts, gray diecast base, shaped wheels.
1. Red body, rubber tires.
2. Red body, plastic tires.
66-A Massey Ferguson 165 Tractor 75mm 7/1966-1973 $70-80
Red engine cover and two fender castings, gray engine-dash-seat and chassis castings, white grille, silver headlights and exhaust stack, black plastic SW, red diecast wheels, black plastic tires.
1. Black and white Massey Ferguson 165 decals.
67-A Ford 5000 Super Major Tractor 94mm 1/1967-1973 $90-100
Blue body and chassis castings, two gray fender castings, unpainted front axle and mounting, rear hitch and hitch control castings, chrome plastic SW, exhaust stack and parts, gray plastic front and diecast rear wheels, black plastic tires, driver figure, jewel headlights.
1. Ford Super Major 5000 decals.
69-A Massey Ferguson 165 Tractor with Shovel 130mm 3/1967-1973 $100-110
Details as on 66-A plus red shovel arms, unpainted shovel and hydraulic cylinder castings, sheet metal shovel controls.
1. Black and white Massey Ferguson 165 decals.
71-A Tandem Disc Harrow 92mm 7/1967-1972 $20-30
Yellow main frame, red upper frame, axle and two wheel castings, unpainted control, linkage and disc castings, red plastic hitch, black plastic tires.
1. Control and linkage raise and lower wheels.
72-A Ford 5000 Tractor with Rear Trencher 150mm 12/1970-1974 $100-110
Details as on 67-A plus yellow trencher arm, mounting and control castings, three black hydraulic cylinders, chromed trencher, black control lines.
1. Ford Super Major 5000 decals.
73-A Massey Ferguson 165 Tractor with Saw 90mm 3/1970-1973 $100-110
Details as on 66-A plus yellow arm, mounting, control and rear box castings, chromed circular saw, housing and grid.
1. Massey Ferguson 165 decals.
74-A Ford 5000 Tractor with Side Scoop 80mm 9/1969-1972 $110-120
Details as on 67-A plus yellow scoop arm, mounting and control castings, three hydraulic cylinders, chromed scoop, black control lines.
1. Ford Super Major 5000 decals.

Trailers

100-A Dropside Trailer 110mm 6/1957-1965 $20-30
Single body casting, front and rear chassis castings, rubber or (later) plastic tires; front chassis swivels.
1. Cream body, red chassis, smooth wheels, wire hitch; 1957-1961.
2. Cream body, red chassis, shaped wheels, hitch part of front chassis; 1962-1965.
3. White body, cream chassis, other details unknown.
4. White body, blue chassis, other details unknown.
5. Silver gray body, blue chassis, other details unknown.
101-A Platform Trailer 110mm 1/1958-1964 $20-30
Single body casting, front and rear chassis castings, rubber tires; front chassis swivels.
1. Silver gray body, metallic blue chassis, wire hitch, smooth wheels.
2. Silver gray body, metallic blue chassis, cast hitch, shaped wheels.
3. Metallic blue body, yellow chassis, wire hitch, smooth wheels.
4. Silver gray body, yellow chassis, wire hitch, smooth wheels.
5. Silver gray body, yellow chassis, cast hitch, shaped wheels.
6. Yellow body and chassis, cast hitch, shaped wheels.
7. Blue body, red chassis, other details not known.
8. Red body, light blue chassis, cast hitch, shaped wheels;GS19-A.
9. White body, light blue chassis, cast hitch, shaped wheels;GS21-A.
102-A Rice Pony Trailer 86mm 1/1958-1965 $20-30
Body, chassis and tailgate castings, lowering tailgate, horse figure, four wheels and tires.
1. Red body and tailgate, black chassis, wire hitch, smooth wheels crimped on axles;1958-1961.
2. Red body and tailgate, black chassis including hitch, shaped wheels crimped on axles;1962.
3. Ivory body, red chassis, other details unknown.
4. Tan body and tailgate, cream roof, silver chassis including hitch, shaped wheels crimped to axles;1963.
5. Tan body and tailgate, cream roof, silver chassis including hitch, shaped wheels free on axles;1964-1965.
104-A Dolphin Cabin Cruiser 133mm 7/1965-1968 $30-40
Plastic boat with blue deck and superstructure, white hull, two-tone blue motor with gray propeller and white painted motor cover, clear windows, gray wheel, red and white stripe labels, and figure, on die-cast trailer.
1. Red trailer, smooth wheels, rubber tires.
2. Red trailer, cast wheels, plastic tires.
107-A Batboat 130mm 11/1967-72, 8/1976-80
(Early) $125-150
(Late) $90-100
Black plastic boat with red seats, fin and jet, chrome dash, gold wheel, blue windshield, Batman and Robin figures, on gold diecast trailer.
1. Black-yellow-silver labels covering most of fin, red-yellow-white labels on hull, cast wheels, plastic tires; 1967-1972.
2. Small black-yellow oval bat emblems on fin, red-yellow-black chain labels on hull, Whizzwheels; 1976-1980.
109-A Pennyburn Workmen's Trailer 77mm 1/1968-1969 $50-60
Diecast body & chassis with two opening covers, red platic tow hook, cast wheels, plastic tires.
1. Medium blue body, yellow chassis, red plastic interior with chromed tools, loose plastic tools, (available separately only as 109-A).
2. Dark metallic blue body, white chassis, no interior or tools, (available in GS10-A only).
112-A Rice Beaufort Double Horse Box 100mm 2/1969-1972 $30-40
Body, chassis and two gate castings, light brown plastic interior, felt gate linings, two horse figures, red plastic hitch.
1. Blue body and tailgate, white roof, silver gray chassis, cast wheels, rubber tires;1969.
2. Same as 112-A1 except cast wheels, plastic tires;1970-1972, through 1975 in GS15-B.
3. Same 112-A1 except wide 8-spoke cast wheels in modified base, wide plastic tires;1976-1977 in GS15-B only.

Racing Cars

150-A Vanwall Racing Car 94mm 7/1957-1965
(Regular Issue) $80-100
(Plated Trophy Model) $250-300
Upper body, lower body-base and seat castings, clear windshield, unpainted steering wheel and dash, silver exhaust pipes, name and racing number decals, smooth wheels, rubber tires.
1. Medium green body, yellow seat, #1 or #3; 1957-1960.
2. Same as 150-A1 except "BRITISH MADE" base.
3. Same as 150-A1 except heavy spoked wheels.
4. Red body, unpainted seat, #1.
5. Red body, blue and white trim decal, including racing number 25, silver nose, driver figure, suspension; numbered 150S in Corgi catalogs; 1961-1965. Later issues had adhesive wheel-spoke discs.
6. Green body, smooth wheels, cream seat, number "20" decal, no suspension, " BRITISH MADE" on base with Vandervell Products Ltd. promotional decal.
7. Same as 150-A4 except shaped wheels, silver seat, suspension, " MADE IN GT. BRITAIN" base.
8. Plated gold body, red seat, heavy cast spoked wheels, black display base, (St. Michael Trophy model).
150-B Surtees TS9 Racing Car 116mm 6/1972-1974 $40-50
Body, chassis and wing castings, black upper engine, air scoop and mirrors, chromed diecast lower engine, exhaust pipes and suspension, driver figure, Brooke Bond Oxo-Rob Walker and #16 labels, chrome wheels.
1. Metallic blue body, white chassis and stripes.
2. Metallic purplish body, white chassis and stripes.
3. Same as 150-B1 except disassembled, Corgi model number 1500;GS30-A only.
151-A Lotus Eleven 54mm 7/1958-1964
(Regular Issue) $80-100
(Red with Yellow Seat) $600-800
Single casting, clear windshield, unpainted SW, clear plastic headlights, racing number decal, sheet metal base, smooth wheels, rubber tires.
1. Silver gray body, red seats, grille and exhaust pipes, 1958-1960.
2. Dull blue body, red seats and grille, silver exhaust pipes; 1958-1960.
3. Dull turquoise body, red seats and grille, silver exhaust pipes; 1958-1960?
4. Red body, cream seats, silver grille and exhaust pipes; 1958-1960?
5. Yellow body?
6. Pewter gray body?
7. Red body, Yellow seat, other details not known.
8. Bright blue body, stripes and racing number decal, red seats, driver figure, silver grille and exhaust pipes; Corgi catalog number 151A, 1961-1964.
151-B McLaren-Ford M19A Racing Car 116mm 12/1972-1977 $35-45
Single body casting, chrome engine-exhaust-rear suspension casting, black front suspension casting, black mirrors and parts, driver figure, unpainted diecast base, chrome wheels, Yardley McLaren and #55 labels.
1. White body with orange stripes.
2. Same as 151-B1 except disassembled, Corgi model number 1501;GS30-A only.
152-A B.R.M. Racing Car 90mm 12/1958-1965 $80-90
Upper body and lower body-base castings, silver diecast seat, dash and SW, clear windshield, silver exhaust pipes, racing number decal, smooth wheels, rubber tires.
1. Dark green body, #1, #3 or #7; 1958-1960.
2. Light green body, no driver, no suspension?
3. Light green body, Union Jack decal, driver figure, #1, #3, or #7, suspension; Corgi catalog number 152S, 1961-1965. Later issues had adhesive wheel-spoke discs.
4. Plated gold body, red seats, heavy cast spoked wheels, black display base, (St. Michael Trophy model).
152-B Ferrari 312 B2 Racing Car 100mm 3/1973-1975 $30-40
Body, chassis-exhaust, gold engine and chrome suspension castings, black plastic engine parts, chrome mirrors, driver figure, chrome wheels, white diecast base including exhaust pipes and suspension members, labels including Ferrari emblems and racing number 5.
1. Red body with white fin.
153-A Campbell Bluebird 128mm 9/1960-1965 $125-135
Body and base castings, clear windshield, driver, flag decal, red exhaust grooves.
1. Blue body and base, black plastic wheels; 1960.
2. Blue body and base, metal wheels, rubber tires; Corgi catalog number 153A, 1961-1965.
153-B Surtees TS9B Racing Car 112mm 9/1972-1974 $40-50
Body casting with straight front and sidepods, white wing and green base castings, chrome suspension castings (rear includes exhaust pipes, upper engine and roll bar), black plastic engine and air scoop, driver figure, chrome wheels.
1. Red body with white stripes and wing, Ceramica Pagnossin and number 26 labels.
2. Blue/white body, " Norris 34" labels;GS30-A only.
154-A Ferrari Racing Car 90mm 1/1963-1972 $45-55
Single body casting, chrome plastic engine, roll bar, dash and SW, clear windshield, driver figure, silver diecast base with exhaust pipes, Ferrari emblem and racing number 36 decals, suspension.
1. Red body, shaped wheels, rubber tires.
2. Red body, cast wheels, plastic tires.
154-B Lotus Racing Car 130mm 3/1973-1982 $40-50
Black diecast body and base, gold diecast engine, roll bar, exhaust pipes, suspension, mirrors, dash and SW, driver figure, gold cast wheels.
1. Black and gold John Player Special labels; 1973-1978.
2. Black and gold Texaco labels (John Player name still cast on base) ; 1979-1982. Model still used in Gift Set 32 in 1983, but no longer offered separately.
3. Same as 154-B1 except disassembled, Corgi model number 1504;GS30-A only.
155-A Lotus-Climax Racing Car 90mm 12/1964-1969 $55-65
Green body and base castings, unpainted engine and suspension castings, chrome plastic exhaust pipes, mirrors, SW and suspension members, driver figure, suspension, shaped wheels, rubber tires.
1. Black and white racing number 1 and yellow stripe decals.
155-B Shadow-Ford DN1-1A Racing Car 130mm 6/1974-1976 $40-50
Black body and base castings, chrome suspension and exhaust pipe castings, black plastic cockpit, driver figure, chrome wheels.
1. White and black number 17, UOP and American flag labels.
2. Red/orange/yellow labels on front wings, otherwise 155-B1, (may be preproduction model).
156-A Cooper-Maserati Racing Car 88mm 5/1967-1969 $45-55
Dark blue body and chassis castings, unpainted engine, gearbox and suspension castings, chrome plastic SW, roll bar, mirrors, exhaust pipes and suspension members, driver figure, suspension, cast eight-spoke

wheels, plastic tires.
1. Red-white-blue Maserati emblem and number 7 decals.

156-B   Shadow-Ford DN1-1A Racing Car   130mm 6/1974-1977 $40-50
White body and base castings, red stripe over air intake, other details as on 155-A.
1. Embassy Racing, Graham Hill, Esso and number 12 labels.
2. Labels without Embassy name.

158-A   Lotus-Climax Racing Car   90mm 7/1969-1972 $50-60
Orange and white body and white base castings, body casting includes front wings, unpainted cast rear wing, driver tilts to steer car, cast eight-spoke wheels, other details as on 155-A.
1. Black and white stripe and number 8 labels.

158-B   Tyrrell-Ford 006/2 Racing Car   115mm 9/1974-1978 $40-50
Dark blue body casting, chrome suspension, exhaust pipes and coolers, SW and mirrors, driver figure, black plastic engine, chrome wheels.
1. Blue-black-white Elf and number 1 labels.

159-A   Cooper-Maserati Racing Car   88mm 3/1969-1972 $45-55
Yellow and white body and white base castings, body includes front wings, unpainted diecast rear wing, driver tilts to steer front wheels, other details as on 156-A.
1. Yellow-black-white stripe and number 3 labels.

159-B   STP Patrick Eagle Racing Car   130mm 7/1974-1977 $40-50
Red body casting, chrome engine and suspension castings, black plastic base and upper engine, clear windshield, driver figure, chrome wheels.
1. Red-white-black STP and number 20 labels.

160-A   Hesketh-Ford 308 Racing Car   130mm 10/1975-1978 $40-50
White body and wing castings, chrome suspension, exhaust pipes, coolers, roll bar, mirrors and SW, driver figure, black plastic base, chrome wheels.
1. Red-white-blue Hesketh name, stripe and number 24 labels. Model has been reissued for Gift Set use but not sold individually.

161-A   Commuter Dragster   122mm 6/1971-1973 $40-50
Maroon body and base castings, silver engine casting, chrome plastic front suspension and exhaust pipes, clear windshield, driver, two types of spoked wheels.
1. Ford Commuter, Union Jack and number 2 labels.

161-B   Tyrrell P34 Racing Car   112mm 7/1977-1977 $40-50
Dark blue body and wing castings, gold SW, chrome plastic engine and exhaust pipes, driver figure, black plastic base, four small and two large chrome wheels. Same casting as 162-B, which is blue with white labels.
1. Yellow number 4 and stripes, white Elf and Union Jack labels.

162-A   Quartermaster Dragster   145mm 4/1971-1973 $35-45
Dark metallic green upper and pale green lower body castings, silver and gold engine and scoop castings, silver plastic front wing and exhaust pipes, driver, two types of spoked wheels. Casting also used for 170-A.
1. Green-yellow-black Quartermaster and number 5 labels.

162-B   Tyrrell P34 Racing Car   112mm 1/1978-1979 $40-50
Same castings and details as 161-B, but no yellow trim.
1. White and blue First National City, number 4 and Elf labels.

163-A   Ford Capri Santa Pod Gloworm   113mm 7/1971-1976 $35-45
White and blue body and red chassis castings, amber windows, unpainted diecast latch and rack to raise body, black engine with gold base, air scoop, exhaust pipes, gold front suspension and SW, two types of wheels; modified 303-B casting.
1. Red-white-blue lettering, flag and trim labels.

164-A   Wild Honey Dragster   75mm 12/971-1973 $35-45
Yellow body casting, unpainted engine, front suspension and base castings, green windows and roof, chrome and black plastic suspension, black grille, driver figure, Whizzwheels.
1. Red and yellow Wild Honey and Jaguar Powered labels.

165-A   Adams Drag-Star   112mm 3/1972-1974 $35-45
Upper body, lower body-base and four gold engine castings, unpainted bumper castings, chrome exhaust pipes, front hood panels and strips between upper and lower body, black catwalk, amber windshield, driver, two types of spoked wheels.
1. Light orange body with red nose and trim.

166-A   Mustang Organ Grinder Dragster   100mm 10/1971-1974 $35-45
Yellow body, silver air scoop and gold engine castings, green windshield, red interior, roll cage and bumpers, driver figure, chrome exhaust pipes, black diecast base suspension, two types of spoked wheels.
1. Green and yellow name, stripe and number 39 labels.

167-A   U.S. Racing Buggy   94mm 12/1972-1974 $30-40
White body, red base, silver air scoop and gold engine castings, red plastic body panels and interior, black exhaust pipes and roof rack with spare wheel, driver and riding mechanic figures, suspension, chrome eight-spoke wheels. Casting later used for 259-B Penguinmobile.
1. Red-white-blue star, stripe and USA 7 labels.

169-A   Silver Streak Jet Dragster   160mm 2/1973-1976 $45-55
Metallic blue body and base, silver engine and gold side tank castings, orange plastic nose and jet, clear windshield, driver figure, black Firestone lettering on nose, chrome wheels. Casting later used for 263-B Captain America Jetmobile.
1. Flag labels on left and sponsor labels on right side tank.

170-A   Radio Luxembourg Dragster   145mm 10/1972-1976 $45-55
Blue upper and lower body, silver engine and gold air scoop castings, chrome plastic front wing and exhaust pipes, clear windshield, driver figure, two types of spoked wheels. Same casting as 162-A Quartermaster, including base lettering.
1. Blue-yellow-white John Woolfe Racing and Radio Luxembourg label, #5 rear label.

Motorcycles

171-A   Red Wheelie Motorcycle   112mm 1982-Close $20-40
Red plastic body and front fender, black handlebars, stand, dash and seat, chrome wheels, engine and exhaust pipes, flywheel-powered rear wheel, black rubber tires.
1. Yellow-black-white trim labels.

172-A   White Wheelie Motorcycle   112mm 1982-Close $20-40
White plastic body and front fender, other details as 171-A.
1. Black and white Police labels.

173-A   Cafe Racer Wheelie Motorcycle   112mm 1982-Close $20-40
Black plastic body and front fender, silver racing wind guard and seat, other details as 171-A.
1. "750 CLASS" and "26" labels.

Scale Racers

190-A   J.P.S. Lotus Racing Car   265mm 7/1974-1977 $55-65
Black body, air scoop and rear wing castings, gold front suspension and exhaust pipes, chrome engine and

roll bar, amber windshield, driver figure, gold metal wheels, gold trim, Union Jack labels; 1:18 scale.
1. Gold number 1, John Player Special and Texaco labels.

191-A   McLaren M23 Racing Car   258mm 9/1975-1980 $55-65
Red and white body and wing and white engine cover castings, chrome exhaust pipes, suspension, SW and mirrors, black engine, amber windshield, red plastic base and wheels; 1:18 scale.
1. Red-white-black Texaco-Marlboro, other lettering and number 5 labels.

Automobiles

200-A   Ford Consul   92mm 7/1956-1961 $110-120
Single casting, clear windows, sheet metal base, silver bumpers, headlights and grirlle, smooth wheels, rubber tires.
1. Cream body.
2. Light tan body.
3. Dark tan body.
4. Gray body.
5. Two-tone green body.
6. Cream and green body.
7. Gray and green body.

200M-A   Ford Consul (Mechanical)   92mm 7/1956-1959 $140-160
Same details as 200-A except black diecast base, flywheel motor.
1. Bright blue body.
2. Green body.

200-B   British Leyland Mini 1000   84mm 2/1976-1978 $40-50
Main body and two opening door castings, clear windows, black SW, silver bumpers, grille and headlights, red taillights, black diecast base, suspension, Whizzwheels, Union Jack stripe label on roof. Same casting as 201-C.
1. Metallic blue body, white interior.
2. Metallic blue body, red interior.
3. Metallic blue body, red interior, tow hook.

201-A   Austin Cambridge   90mm 7/1956-1961 $150-160
Single casting, clear windows, sheet metal base, silver bumpers, grille and headlights, smooth wheels, rubber tires.
1. Turquoise body.
2. Gray body.
3. Silver and green body.
4. Two-tone green body.

201M-A   Austin Cambridge (Mechanical)   90mm 7/1956-1959 $200-220
Same details as 201-A except black diecast base, flywheel motor.
1. Cream body.
2. Orange body.
3. Light gray body.
4. Medium gray body.

201-B   The Saint's Volvo P-1800   92mm 6/1970-1972 $160-180
Single body casting, clear windows, driver figure, jewel headlights, silver grille and bumpers, gray diecast base, suspension, Whizzwheels, red hood label with white Saint stick figure covers entire hood. Same casting as 228-A and 258-A.
1. White body, black interior, circle of bubbles pattern Whizzwheels.
2. White body, yellow interior, circle of bubbles pattern Whizzwheels.
3. Same as 201-B1 except different wheel pattern with chromed thin outer ring.

201-C   British Leyland Mini 1000   84mm 9/1978-Close $30-40
Red interior, chrome bumpers, grille and headlights, other details as 200-B.
1. Silver body, no labels.
2. Silver body, no labels, tow hook.
3. Silver body, " 8" and "Team Corgi" labels, no tow hook.
4. Same as 201-C3 plus tow hook.
5. Same as 201-C4 without "Team Corgi" label.
6. Same as 201-C4 plus white "Team Corgi" on windshield.
7. Same as 201-C3 except orange body.
8. Same as 201-C3 except dark blue body without "Team Corgi" label.
9. Same as 201-C8 except "3," "Michelin" and "ESSO" labels.

202-A   Morris Cowley   93mm 7/1956-1960 $125-135
Single casting, clear windows, silver bumpers, grille and headlights, sheet metal base, smooth wheels, rubber tires.
1. Light gray body.
2. Blue body.
3. Green body.
4. Blue and greenish tinted off-white body.
5. Blue and gray body.

202M-A   Morris Cowley (Mechanical)   93mm 7/1956-1959 $150-160
Same details as 202-A except black diecast base, flywheel motor.
1. Greenish off-white body.
2. Medium green body.

202-B   Renault 16TS   98mm 5/1970-1972 $40-50
Main body, opening hood and hatch castings, detailed engine, clear windows, dark yellow interior, lifting hatch cover, gears on base adjust front seat backs, chrome plastic base, grille and bumpers, gray tow hook, suspension, Whizzwheels, Renault decal on hatch. Same castings as 260-A.
1. Metallic dark blue body, circle-of-bubbles pattern Whizzwheels.

203-A   Vauxhall Velox   95mm 7/1956-1960 $150-160
Single casting, clear windows, silver bumpers, grille and headlights, sheet metal base, smooth wheels, rubber tires.
1. Cream body.
2. Yellow body.
3. Red body.
4. Yellow and red body.

203M-A   Vauxhall Velox (Mechanical)   95mm 7/1956-1959 $200-220
Same details as 203-A except black diecast base, flywheel motor.
1. Red body.
2. Orange body.

203-B   De Tomaso Mangusta   97mm 9/1970-1973 $35-45
Main upper body and lower body-base castings, clear front window, cream interior, gold SW and engine, amber windows, gray antenna, black grille, amber headlights, orange taillights, spare wheel, suspension, Whizzwheels, three gold stripes and black emblem on hood. Same body as 271-A, revised base with no separate chassis.
1. Metallic dark green upper body, silver lower body and base.

204-A   Rover 90   98mm 7/1956-1960 $160-180

Single casting, clear windows, silver bumpers, grille and headlights, sheet metal base, smooth wheels, rubber tires.
1. Off-white body.
2. Light gray body.
3. Dark gray body.
4. Maroon and gray body.
5. Metallic bronze and red body.
6. Metallic red and white body.

204M-A   Rover 90 (Mechanical)   98mm 7/1956-1959 $200-220

Same as 204-A except black diecast base, flywheel motor.
1. Red body.
2. Green body.
3. Metallic green body.
4. Gray body.

204-B   Morris Mini Minor   72mm 1/1972-1973

                                (Orange) $90-100
                                (Blue) $200-250

Single body casting, plastic interior and SW, silver grille, bumpers and headlights, red taillights, diecast base, suspension, Whizzwheels. Same castings as 308-A.
1. Orange body, yellow interior, clear windows, silver gray base.
2. Orange body, yellow interior, green tinted windows, black base.
3. Orange body, yellow interior, blue tinted windows, ? base.
4. Medium non-metallic blue body, yellow interior, clear windows, ? base.
5. Dark metallic blue body, red interior, blue tinted windows, black base.
6. Dark metallic blue body, cream interior, blue tinted windows, black base.
7. Dark metallic blue body, yellow interior, clear windows, black base.

205-A   Riley Pathfinder   100mm 7/1956-1961 $125-135

Single casting, clear windows, silver bumpers, grille and headlights, sheet metal base, smooth wheels, rubber tires. Casting also used for 209-A.
1. Red body.
2. Dark blue body.

205M-A   Riley Pathfinder (Mechanical)   100mm 7/1956-1959 $170-180

Same details as 205-A except black diecast base, flywheel motor.
1. Red body.
2. Blue body.

206-A   Hillman Husky   87mm 7/1956-1960 $125-135

Single casting, clear windows, silver bumpers, grille and headlights, sheet metal base, smooth wheels, rubber tires.
1. Tan body.
2. Metallic blue and silver body.

206M-A   Hillman Husky (Mechanical)   87mm 8/1956-1959 $145-155

Same details as 206-A except black diecast base, flywheel motor.
1. Cream body.
2. Gray body.
3. Dark blue body.

207-A   Standard Vanguard   93mm 2/1957-1961 $125-135

Single casting, clear windows, silver bumpers, grille and headlights, diecast base, smooth wheels, rubber tires.
1. Red and white body, black base.
2. Red and greenish off-white body, black base.
3. Red and greenish off-white body, gray base.
4. Red and gray body.

207M-A   Standard Vanguard (Mechanical)   93mm 2/1957-1959 $160-170

Same details as 207-A except different black diecast base, flywheel motor.
1. Yellow body.
2. Red and greenish off-white body.

208-A   Jaguar 2.4 Litre   96mm 3/1957-1963
                             (No Suspension) $120-130
                             (Suspension) $140-150

Single casting, clear windows, silver bumpers, grille and headlights, rubber tires. Casting also used for 213-A.
1. White body, sheet metal base, no interior or suspension, smooth wheels crimped on axles;1957-1959.
2. Light yellow body, red interior, gray SW, suspension, gray diecast base, smooth wheels crimped on axles;Corgi catalog number 208S:9/1960-1962.
3. Same as 208-A2 except shaped wheels crimped on axles;1963.

208M-A   Jaguar 2.4 Litre (Mechanical)   96mm 3/1957-1959 $160-170

Same details as 208-A except different black diecast base, flywheel motor.
1. Metallic blue body.

209-A   Riley Pathfinder Police Car   100mm 6/1958-1961 $110-120

Modified 205-A casting with unpainted diecast roof sign, gray antenna, white and blue Police lettering.
1. Black body, smooth wheels.

210-A   Citroen DS19   100mm 12/1957-1965 $90-100

Single body casting, clear windows, silver bumpers, grille and headlights, gray diecast base, rubber tires. Casting also used for 323-A.
1. Dark cream body, red roof, smooth wheels;1957-1959.
2. Metallic green body, black roof, smooth wheels;1957-1959.
3. Yellow body, black roof, smooth wheels;1957-1959.
4. Red body, yellow interior, gray SW, suspension, smooth wheels;Corgi catalog number 210S, 1960-1963.
5. Yellow body, ? interior, gray SW, suspension, smooth wheels;Corgi catalog number 210S, 1960-1963.
6. Red body, yellow interior, gray SW, shaped wheels;Corgi catalog number 210S, 1964-1965.

211-A   Studebaker Golden Hawk   105mm 12/1958-1966
                             (No Suspension) $140-150
                   (Suspension, Plated) $100-110
                  (Suspension, Painted) $150-160

Single body casting, clear windows, silver bumpers, grille and headlights, gray diecast base, rubber tires.
1. Light blue body, gold trim, base with rear axle bulge, no suspension or interior, smooth wheels crimped on axles;1958-1960.
2. Plated gold body, white trim, red interior, suspension, base without bulge, smooth wheels crimped on axles, gray SW;Corgi catalog number 211S, 9/1960-1963.
3. Same as 211-A2 except shaped wheels crimped on axles;1963 only?
4. Same as 211-A3 except body now painted gold;1964-1966?
5. May exist as 211-A4 except shaped wheels free on axles.

211M-A   Studebaker Golden Hawk (Mechanical)   105mm 12/1958-1959 $160-170

Gray diecast base with rear axle bulge, flywheel motor, otherwise as 211-A.
1. White body, gold trim.

212-A   Road Rover   NOT PRODUCED   N/A

Never produced. Prototype models exist.

213-A   Jaguar 2.4 Litre Fire Chief's Car   96mm 1/1959-1961
                             (No Suspension) $150-160
                             (Suspension) $200-210

Single body casting, unpainted roof sign-siren-bell casting with red and white Fire labels, gray antenna, shield decals on doors, otherwise as 208-A.
1. Red body, no interior or suspension; 1959-1960.
2. Red body, yellow interior, suspension; Corgi catalog number 213S, 9/1961.

214-A   Ford Thunderbird Hardtop   102mm 3/1959-1965
                             (No Suspension) $120-130
                             (Suspension) $100-110

Main body with seperate hardtop casting, clear windows, silver bumpers, grille and headlights, red taillights, gray diecast base, rubber tires.
1. Light green body, cream top, smooth wheels, base with rear axle bulge; 1959-1961.
2. Charcoal body, red top, yellow interior, gray SW, suspension, shaped wheels, no bulge on base; Corgi catalog number 214S, 6/1962-1965.

214M-A   Ford Thunderbird Hardtop (Mechanical)   102mm 3/1959-1959 $275-300

Gray diecast base with rear axle bulge, flywheel motor, otherwise as 214-A.
1. Pink body, black hardtop.
2. Light green body, white hardtop.

215-A   Ford Thunderbird Roadster   102mm 12/1959-1965
                             (No Suspension) $120-130
                             (Suspension) $100-110

Same body casting as 214-A, clear windshield, SW, silver seats, bumpers, grille and headlights, red taillights, gray diecast base, rubber tires; casting also used for 430-A Bermuda Taxi.
1. White body, blue interior, unpainted metal SW, smooth wheels, rear axle bulge on base; 1959-1960?
2. White body, blue interior, unpainted metal SW, shaped wheels, rear axle bulge on base; 1961.
3. Red body, light orange interior, gray plastic SW, driver figure, shaped wheels, suspension, no bulge on base; Corgi catalog number 215S, 6/1962-1965.
4. Dark metallic blue body, yellow interior, other details not known although existence confirmed.

216-A   Austin A40   87mm 6/1959-1962 $120-130

Single casting, clear windows, silver bumpers, grille and headlights, red taillights, sheet metal base, smooth wheels, rubber tires.
1. Light blue body, dark blue roof.
2. Red body, black roof.

216M-A   Austin A40 (Mechanical)   87mm 6/1959-1960 $275-300

Gray diecast base, flywheel motor, otherwise as 216-A.
1. Red body, black roof.

217-A   Fiat 1800   96mm 5/1960-1963 $65-75

Single body casting, clear windows, plastic interior, SW, silver bumpers, grille and headlights, red taillights, suspension, gray diecast base, smooth wheels, rubber tires. Casting later used for 232-A Fiat 2100.
1. Light blue body, bright yellow interior. (More than one shade of light blue may exist.)
2. Mustard tan body, ? interior.
3. Cream body, brown roof, ? interior.
4. Light blue body, dark blue roof, light yellow interior.

218-A   Aston Martin DB4   96mm 3/1960-1965 $100-120

Main body and opening hood castings, detailed engine, clear windows, plastic interior, silver bumpers, license plates, grille and headlights, red upper taillights, suspension, gray diecast base, rubber tires; early issues had open hood scoop. Casting also used for 309-A.
1. Yellow body, red seats, open hood scoop, heavy cast spoke wheels crimped on axles.
2. Same as 218-A1 except closed hood scoop.
3. Yellow body, red seats, Closed hood scoop, smooth wheels crimped on axles with "wire look" printing or labels.
4. Yellow body, red seats, Closed hood scoop, smooth wheels crimped on axles.
5. Same as 218-A4 except red body, yellow seats.
6. Yellow or Red versions with shaped wheels crimped on axles may exist.
7. Same as 218-A4 except shaped wheels free on axles.
8. Same as 218-A5 except shaped wheels free on axles.
9. Red versions of 218-A1, -A2, or -A3 may also exist.

219-A   Plymouth Sports Suburban   107mm 7/1959-1963 $90-100

Single body casting, clear windows, red interior, gray SW, silver bumpers, grille and trim, gray diecast base with rear axle bulge, rubber tires. Casting also used for 443-A and 445-A.
1. Dark cream body, tan roof, smooth wheels.
2. Dark cream body, tan roof, shaped wheels.

220-A   Chevrolet Impala   105mm 1/1960-1965 $60-80

Single body casting, clear windows, plastic interior, gray SW, silver bumpers, grille, headlights and trim, suspension, gray diecast base (two types), rubber tires; casting also used for 221-A, 223-A and 439-A.
1. Pink body, yellow interior, base with hexagonal panel under rear axle, smooth wheels.
2. Grayish tan body?, other details not known.
3. Light blue body, yellow interior, other details not known.
4. Light blue body, red interior, shaped wheels, base with two raised lines.
5. Red body, yellow interior, shaped wheels free on axles, base with raised lines.

221-A   Chevrolet Impala Taxi   105mm 6/1960-1965 $100-120

Modified 220-A casting with white taxi sign, red lettering and decals, gray antenna, red interior, otherwise as 220-A.
1. Light orange body, smooth wheels, base with hexagonal panel under rear axle.
2. Light orange body, shaped wheels, base with two raised lines.

222-A   Renault Floride   91mm 10/1959-1965 $80-100

Single body casting, clear windows, plastic interior, gray SW, silver bumpers, headlights, rear grille and license plates, gray diecast base (two types) rubber tires.
1. Maroon body, cream interior, smooth wheels, base with holes under axles.
2. Maroon body, cream interior, smooth wheels, suspension, base with holes.
3. Metallic blue body, red interior, smooth wheels, base with holes.
4. Metallic blue body, red interior, smooth wheels, suspension, base with holes.
5. Metallic blue body, red interior, shaped wheels, suspension, base with raised lines.
6. Light olive body, red interior, smooth wheels, suspension, base with holes.
7. There may be a light olive version with suspension and base with lines.
8. Metallic blue body, yellow interior, shaped wheels free on axles, suspension, base with raised lines.

223-A   Chevrolet Impala State Patrol   12/1959-1965 $110-130

Modified 220-A casting with white State Patrol decals or labels, yellow interior, gray antenna, otherwise as 220-A.

1. Black body, State Patrol decals, smooth wheels, base with hexagonal panel.
2. Black body, State Patrol labels, smooth wheels, base with hexagonal panel.
3. Black body, State Patrol labels, shaped wheels crimped on axles, base with raised lines.
4. Black body, State Patrol labels, shaped wheels free on axles, base with raised lines.

224-A Bentley Continental 110mm 4/1961-1966 $100-120
Main body and opening trunk castings, clear windows, red interior, gray SW, chrome grille and bumpers, jewel headlights, red jewel taillights, luggage and spare wheel in truck, suspension, gray diecast base, shaped wheels, gray rubber tires.
1. Greenish off-white upper body, light olive green sides.
2. White upper body, light olive green sides.
3. Black upper body, silver gray sides.
4. Plated gold body; from GS20-A Golden Guinea Gift Set.

225-A Austin Se7en Mini 72mm 1/1961-1967
(Red) $100-120
(Yellow) $250-300
Main body and lower body-base castings, clear windows, gray SW, silver bumpers, grille and headlights, orange taillights, suspension, rubber tires. Grille and hood emblem differ from 226-A and 227-A.
1. Light yellow body, red interior, smooth wheels, patent application base.
2. Red body, yellow interior, smooth wheels, patent application base.
3. Red body, yellow interior, shaped wheels crimped on axles, ? base.
4. Red body, yellow interior, shaped wheels free on axles, patent no. base.

226-A Morris Mini-Minor 72mm 2/1960-1971
(Blue) $100-120
(Maroon) $80-90
(White, Mauve or Yellow) $250-350
Main body and lower body-base castings, clear windows, plastic interior, SW, silver bumpers, grille and headlights, red taillights, suspension. Body color on light blue versions varies from powder blue through medium blue.
1. Light blue body and base, yellow interior, smooth wheels crimped on axles, rubber tires, 4 holes in base at axles, patent application on base.
2. Same as 226-A1 except red seats.
3. Same as 226-A2 except no holes in base.
4. Same as 226-A3 except shaped wheels crimped on axles.
5. Same as 226-A4 except shaped wheels free on axles.
6. Same as 226-A5 except patent no. base.
7. Same as 226-A6 except cast wheels.
8. Same as 226-A7 except plastic tires.
9. Same as 226-A8 except, " East African Safari" or "Monte-Carlo" label on hood, cheap looking number label on door, new type body casting with strong arch at base of grill, hole in center of base, (used by secondary manufacturer for board game).
10. Dark metallic maroon body and base, yellow interior, new type body casting with strong arch at base of grill, cast wheels, rubber tires, patent no. base.
11. Same as 226-A10 plus "Monte-Carlo" label on hood, hole in center of base, (used by secondary manufacturer for board game).
12. Same as 226-A10 except plastic tires.
13. Same as 226-A10 except yellow body, base & interior, "MUSTARD MANIA" Sticker on Roof, "Colman's Mustard" Stickers on Doors (Promotional model).
14. Mauve body, other details unknown.
14. White body, other details unknown, (quantity used by Mettoy for cover photo on Club magazine in Union Jack pattern, may not have been released to public sale).

227-A Morris Mini-Cooper 72mm 5/1962-1965 $200-225
Jeweled headlights, red taillights, shaped wheels, rubber tires, flags and racing number 1, 3, or 7 decals, otherwise as 226-A. Casting used for 317-A, 321-A, 333-A and 339-A rally versions, and 249-A Deluxe Mini.
1. Yellow body and base, white roof and hood, patent application base, red interior, shaped wheels crimped on axles.
2. May exist like 227-A1 but with shaped wheels free on axles, patent application base, ? hood color.
3. Yellow body and base, white roof only, patent no. base, shaped wheels free on axles.
4. Blue body and base, white roof and hood, patent application base, yellow interior, shaped wheels crimped on axles.
5. Same as 227-A4 except red interior.
6. May exist like 227-A4 but with shaped wheels free on axles, patent application base, ? hood color.
7. Blue body and base, white roof only, patent no. base, shaped wheels free on axles, yellow interior.
8. Same as 227-A7 except Austin 7 base, (known factory casting mix-up).
9. Same as 227-A7 except red interior.
10. Pale green body, white hood and roof, patent appl. base, red interior, shaped wheels, rubber tires, flag decals on hood, #3 decals on doors.

228-A Volvo P-1800 88mm 7/1962-1965 $70-80
Single body casting, clear windows, plastic interior, gray SW, silver bumpers, grille and trim, jeweled headlights, suspension, gray diecast base, shaped wheels, rubber tires. Casting also used for 258-A and 201-B.
1. Tan body, red interior and taillights.
2. Tan body, yellow interior, red taillights.
3. Dark red body, yellow interior, orange taillights.
4. Dark orange body, yellow interior, red taillights.
5. Pink body, yellow interior, red taillights.
6. White body, red interior and taillights (possibly altered 258-A, needs verification).

229-A Chevrolet Corvair 96mm 6/1961-1966 $60-70
Main body and opening rear hood castings, detailed engine, clear windows, interior, gray SW, silver bumpers, headlights and trim, white rear window blind, suspension, gray diecast base, rubber tires.
1. Light blue body, light yellow interior, red taillights, smooth wheels crimped on axles.
2. Same as 229-A1 except body color taillights.
3. Plated gold body, red interior, smooth wheels crimped on axles;Golden Guinea Gift Set.
4. Light blue body, light yellow interior, red taillights, shaped wheels crimped on axles.
5. Medium blue body, bright yellow interior, red taillights, shaped wheels crimped on axles.
6. Medium blue body, bright yellow interior, red taillights, shaped wheels free on axles.

230-A Mercedes-Benz 220SE Coupe 101mm 2/1962-1964
(Red) $70-80
(Black) $120-130
Main body and opening trunk castings, clear windows, plastic interior, gray SW, silver bumpers, grille, headlights and license plates, red taillights, spare wheel, suspension, self-centering steering, gray diecast base, shaped wheels, rubber tires; model reissued as 253-A without steering.
1. Cream body, red interior.
2. Cream body, yellow interior?
3. Dark red body, yellow interior.
4. Black body, yellow interior.

231-A Triumph Herald Coupe 87mm 11/1961-1966 $100-110
Main body, lower body-base and opening front body castings, detailed engine, clear windows, red interior, gray SW, silver bumpers, grille, headlights and license plates, suspension, rubber tires.
1. Gold lower body, base and roof, white upper body, smooth wheels crimped to axles.
2. Gold lower body, base and roof, white upper body, shaped wheels free on axles.
3. Light blue lower body, base and roof, white upper body, shaped wheels free on axles.
4. Yellow lower body, base and roof, white upper body, (may be pre-production model).

232-A Fiat 2100 95mm 8/1961-1964 $70-80
Single body casting, clear windows, yellow interior, gray SW, rear window blind, jewel headlights, silver grille, bumpers and license plates, red taillights, suspension, gray diecast base, shaped wheels, rubber tires; modified 217-A casting.
1. Light mauve body, purple roof.

233-A Trojan Heinkel 63mm 1/1962-1972 $70-80
Single body casting, clear windows, plastic interior, gray SW, silver bumpers and headlights, suspension, gray diecast base.
1. Light mauve body, red interior, red taillights, smooth wheels, rubber tires.
2. Pink body, red interior, orange taillights, smooth wheels, rubber tires.
3. Red body, yellow interior, orange taillights, smooth wheels, rubber tires.
4. Dark blue body, yellow interior, orange taillights, smooth wheels, rubber tires.
5. Orange body, yellow interior, red taillights, smooth wheels, rubber tires.
6. Orange body, yellow interior, red taillights, cast wheels, rubber tires.
7. Orange body, yellow interior, red taillights, cast wheels, plastic tires.
8. Dark orange body?.

234-A Ford Consul Classic 94mm 7/1961-1965 $80-90
Main body, lower body-base and opening hood castings, detailed engine, clear windows, gray SW, silver bumpers, grille and headlights, red taillights, suspension, shaped wheels, rubber tires.
1. Cream body and base, pink roof, yellow interior, shaped wheels crimped on axles.
2. May exist as 234-A1 except shaped wheels free on axles. (Need confirmation)
3. Plated gold body, red interior, shaped wheels crimped on axles;from GS20-A.

235-A Oldsmobile Super 88 106mm 12/1962-1966 $75-85
Single body casting, clear windows, red interior, gray SW, silver bumpers, grille and headlights, red taillights, suspension, gray diecast base, shaped wheels, rubber tires. Casting also used for 237-A, 358-A, and modified for 497-A.
1. Light blue body with white stripes.
2. Light metallic blue body with white stripes.
3. Dark metallic blue body.

236-A Austin A60 Motor School Car 95mm 6/1964-1968 $80-90
Single body casting, clear windows, red interior including right hand drive SW, two figures, red plastic roof sign which steers front wheels, silver bumpers, grille, headlights and trim, red taillights, L plate decals, suspension, gray diecast base, shaped wheels, rubber tires; same casting as 255-A.
1. Light blue body with silver trim.

237-A Oldsmobile Super 88 Sheriff's Car 106mm 6/1962-1966 $100-110
Modified 235-A casting with red dome light, County Sheriff labels on doors, otherwise as 235-A.
1. Black upper body, white sides.

238-A Jaguar Mark X Saloon 105mm 9/1962-1967
(Lt. Blue) $90-100
(Metallic Red, Metallic Blue) $110-120
(Silver) $140-150
(Metallic Green) $190-200
Main body, opening hood and trunk castings, detailed engine, luggage in trunk, clear windows, plastic interior, gray SW, silver grille and bumpers, jewel headlights, suspension, silver diecast base, shaped wheels, rubber tires.
1. Metallic red body, yellow interior, orange taillights.
2. Metallic blue body, yellow interior, red taillights.
3. Dark blue body, red interior, red taillights.
4. Turquosie green body, red interior, red taillights.
5. Light blue body, red interior, red taillights.
6. Metallic green body, red interior, red taillights.
7. Silver body, red interior, red taillights.
8. Metallic red body, red interior, orange taillights.

239-A VW 1500 Karmann-Ghia 90mm 2/1963-1968 $70-80
Main body, opening front and rear hood castings, detailed engine, spare wheel, luggage, clear windows, plastic interior, silver bumpers and headlights, suspension, silver diecast base, shaped wheels, rubber tires.
1. Cream body, red interior including SW, red taillights.
2. Light red body, yellow interior including SW, orange taillights.
3. Gold body, yellow interior including SW, red taillights.
4. Gold body, red interior including SW, red taillights.

240-A Ghia-Fiat 600 Jolly 79mm 7/1963-1965 $130-140
Single body casting, clear windshield, chrome dash, floor, SW and railings, red seats, two figures, red and silver canopy, silver bumpers and headlights, red taillights, suspension, gray diecast base, shaped wheels, rubber tires. Casting also used for 242-A, without canopy.
1. Light blue body.
2. Dark blue body.

241-A Ghia L6.4 Chrysler V8 106mm 11/1963-1969 $65-75
Main body, opening hood, trunk and two door castings, detailed engine, clear windows, plastic interior including steering wheel, Corgi dog figure, chrome grille and bumpers, jewel headlights, suspension, gray diecast base, rubber tires.
1. Metallic dark olive body, cream interior, shaped wheels, taillights not painted red.
2. Metallic blue body, cream interior, shaped wheels, red taillights.
3. Metallic blue body, red interior, shaped wheels, red taillights.
4. Metallic silver blue body, other details not known.
5. Metallic cooper body, other details not known.
6. Metallic lime gold body, yellow interior, cast wheels, red taillights, darker gray base.

242-A Ghia-Fiat 600 Jolly 79mm 7/1965-1966 $160-170
Single body casting, clear windshield, chrome dash, floor, SW and railings, red seats, two human figures and Corgi dog, silver bumpers and headlights, red taillights, suspension, gray diecast base, shaped wheels, rubber tires; same casting as 240-A, which has plastic canopy.
1. Dark yellow body.

245-A Buick Riviera 111mm 6/1964-1968 $90-100
Single body casting, clear windows, red interior, gray SW, chrome bumpers and grille, Trans-o-lite headlights and taillights, suspension, gray diecast base, gray tow hooks, (also used in GS31-A).
1. Metallic gold body, spoked wheels, rubber tires.
2. Pale blue body, spoked wheels, rubber tires.

3. Medium metallic blue body, spoked wheels, rubber tires.
4. Medium metallic blue body, cast wheels, plastic tires.

246-A Chrysler Imperial Convertible **106mm 8/1965-1968**
(Red) $110-120
(Blue) $225-250

Main body, opening hood, trunk and two door castings, detailed engine, golf bag in trunk, clear windshield, aqua interior, black SW, two figures, chrome bumpers, grille, headlights and trim, red taillights, suspension, gray diecast base, rubber tires.
1. Red body, dark gray base, shaped wheels, aqua interior.
2. Darker red body, dark gray base, cast wheels, aqua interior.
3. Same as 246-A2 except tan interior.
4. Metallic dark blue body, light gray base, cast wheels, dark blue flocking on floor of aqua interior and trunk, modified body and seat castings to accept surrey roof intended for 507-A, (NOTE: This is probably the released version of what was originally intended to ba 507-A Chrysler Bermuda Taxi which was never produced. The marketing decision to continue with 246-A was probably made after the dies had already been modified).

247-A Mercedes-Benz 600 Pullman **119mm 11/1964-1969 $65-80**

Single body casting, clear windows, working wipers, cream interior including SW, chrome grille, bumpers and trim, silver headlights, silver and orange taillights, suspension, gray diecast base, wiper switch and gears, shaped wheels, rubber tires.
1. Metallic maroon body.
2. Dark red body (lighter than maroon).

248-A Chevrolet Impala **105mm 8/1965-1967 $75-85**

Upper body and lower body-base castings, clear windows, cream interior, gray SW, chrome bumpers, grille, headlights and stripe between castings, red taillights, suspension, shaped wheels, rubber tires. Casting also used for 480-A, 481-A and 482-A. (Completely different casting from earlier Chevrolet Impala).
1. Tan body and base, light cream roof.

249-A Morris Mini-Cooper Deluxe **72mm 11/1965-1968 $120-130**

Main body and lower body-base castings, clear windows, yellow interior, gray SW, silver bumpers and grille, jewel headlights, red tailligths, yellow and black wicker work decals on sides and rear, suspension. Same casting as 227-A.
1. Black body and base, red roof, shaped wheels, rubber tires.
2. Black body and base, red roof, cast wheels, rubber tires.
3. Same as 249-A2 except new type Morris body casting (identified by strong arch in base of grill).
4. Same as 249-A3 except plastic tires.
5. Same as 249-A3 except black roof;GS48-B, 1970-1973.

251-A Hillman Imp **82mm 12/1963-1967 $85-95**

Single body casting, clear windows, yellow interior and SW, silver bumpers, headlights and trim, red taillights, opening rear window, folding rear seat, luggage, suspension, gray diecast base, shaped wheels, rubber tires. Casting also used for 328-A and 340-A.
1. Metallic copper body with white trim.
2. Metallic blue body.
3. Metallic dark blue body.
4. Metallic copper body without white trim;GS41-A.
5. Light blue body, "Jensens" decals on doors, bright yellow interior.

252-A Rover 2000 **98mm 10/1963-1966**
(Metallic Blue) $80-90
(Metallic Maroon) $150-175

Single body casting, clear windows, plastic interior, gray SW, Trans-o-lite headlights, red taillights, silver bumpers, grille and license plates, suspension, gray diecast base, shaped wheels, rubber tires. Casting also used for 322-A rally car.
1. Metallic steel blue body, red interior.
2. Metallic kingfisher (medium) blue body, red interior.
3. Metallic maroon body, yellow interior.
4. Metallic maroon body, red interior.

253-A Mercedes-Benz 220SE Coupe **102mm 9/1964-1968 $80-100**

Main body and opening trunk castings, clear windows, plastic interior, gray SW, silver bumpers, grille, headlights and license plates, orange taillights, spare wheel and luggage in trunk, suspension, gray diecast base, shaped wheels, rubber tires. Same castings as 230-A but without self-centering steering; base modified.
1. Metallic maroon body, yellow interior, light gray base; 1964-1966.
2. Metallic dark blue body, cream interior, medium gray base; 1967-1968.

255-A Austin A60 Motor School Car **95mm 9/1964-1968 $200-220**

Left hand drive steering wheel, otherwise as 236-A, which is right hand drive and is painted a lighter shade of blue.
1. Medium blue body with silver trim.

256-A Volkswagen 1200 East African Safari Car **93mm 12/1965-1969 $200-225**

Main body, opening front and rear hood castings, detailed engine, clear windows, brown interior and SW, spare wheel on roof which steers front wheels, jeweled headlights, East African Safari label on hood, Nairobi label on rear window, number 18 decals on doors, white plastic mud flaps, suspension, unpainted base and bumpers, shaped wheels, rubber tires, rhinoceros figure. Casting also used for 492-A police car, with dome light in place of spare wheel.
1. Light red body.

258-A The Saint's Volvo P-1800 **95mm 3/1965-1969**
(White Hood) $150-160
(Red Hood) $200-225

Driver figure, Saint figure decal on hood, otherwise as 228-A. Casting also used for 201-B, which has large red hood label and Whizzwheels.
1. White body, black Saint stick figure decal on hood, shaped wheels, rubber tires.
2. White body, red decal covering hood with white Saint stick figure, shaped wheels, rubber tires.
3. White body, red decal covering hood with white Saint stick figure, cast wheels, plastic tires;GS48-B.
4. White body, blue decal covering hood with white Saint stick figure, other details not known.

259-A Citroen Le Dandy Coupe **103mm 4/1966-1969**
(Maroon) $95-105
(Blue and White) $150-165

Main body, lower body-base, opening trunk and two door castings, clear windows, plastic interior including SW, folding seat backs, chrome grille and bumpers, jeweled headlights, red taillights, suspension, spoked wheels, rubber tires.
1. Metallic maroon body and base, yellow interior; 1966.
2. Metallic dark blue hood, sides and base, white roof and trunk lid, aqua interior; 1967-1969.

259-B Penguinmobile **98mm 8/1979-1980 $50-60**

White frame and black base casting, gold body panels, seats and air scoop, chrome engine, yellow exhaust pipes, driver figure, yellow and orange parasol, gold four-spoke wheels, Pengiun labels. Casting based on 167-A.
1. Black and white lettering on orange-yellow-blue labels.

260-A Renault 16 **99mm 3/1969-1969 $50-60**

Main body, lower body-base-grille-bumpers and openings rear hatch castings, clear windows, dark yellow interior and SW, cargo cover, orange taillights, Renault decal on hatch, adjusting seat backs controlled by plastic gears, gray tow hook, suspension, cast wheels, plastic tires. Same casting as 202-B, which has Whizzwheels. Casting also used for 13-B without rear hatch.
1. Metallic maroon body, chrome base-grille-bumpers casting.

260-B City of Metropolis Police Car **150mm 1/1979-1981 $50-60**

Main body and two opening door castings, clear windows, off-white interior, black SW, chrome bumpers, grille and headlights, orange taillights, chrome and red roof bars and lights, shield label on hood, Police and stripe labels on sides, suspension, black plastic base, chrome wheels. Same Buick Regal casting as 290-A and 416-B.
1. Metallic blue body, white roof and stripes.
2. Red body, " Fire Chief" and "City Fire Department" trim, (St. Michael 8803).

261-A James Bond Aston Martin DB5 **97mm 10/1965-1968 $225-250**

Main body and opening roof hatch castings, clear windows, red interior and SW, two figures, left seat raises to eject passenger, rear bullet shield raises, front rams and guns emerge, unpainted levers, silver grille, bumpers and headlights, red taillights, suspension, gray diecast base, spoked wheels, rubber tires. First and smallest of three versions.
1. Metallic gold body.

261-B Spiderbuggy **130mm 8/1979-1981 $70-80**

Main body and hood castings, clear windshield, dark blue dash, seat and crane, black SW, chrome base with bumper and steps, silver headlights, chrome wheels, plastic bag, Spiderman and Green Goblin figures. Casting based on 419-B Jeep.
1. Red body, blue hood.

262-A Lincoln Continental Lehmann Peterson Limousine **146mm 9/1967-1969**
(Gold) $90-100
(Blue) $155-165

Main body, opening hood, trunk and four door castings, clear windows, plastic interior including SW, purplish-blue carpets, lighted TV screen that accepts various scenes, chrome dash, grille and bumpers, jewel headlights, red taillights, white emblem decals, suspension, gray diecast base with plastic battery cover and two levers, shaped wheels, plastic tires.
1. Metallic gold body, black roof, maroon interior.
2. Dusty blue body, tan roof, bright blue interior.

262-B Captain Marvel Porsche **120mm 7/1979-1980 $50-60**

Main body casting, gold parts, red seat with driver, red-yellow-blue Captain Marvel labels, black plastic base, gold wheels. Same casting as 397-A Porsche.
1. White body.

263-A Rambler Marlin Fastback **105mm 6/1966-1969 $80-90**

Main body and two opening door castings, clear windows, cream interior, folding seat backs, chrome bumpers, grille and headlights, orange taillights, gray tow hook, suspension, gray diecast base, cast wheels.
1. Red body, black roof and window trim, rubber tires.
2. Same as 263-A except plastic tires.
3. Metallic dark blue body, white roof and window trim, plastic tires, yellow roof rack for red and white kayak;GS10-A only.
4. Same as 263-A3 except without white window trim;GS10-A only.

263-B Captain America Jetmobile **152mm 7/1979-1980 $40-50**

Body and chassis castings, black nose cone, red shield and jet, red-white-blue Captain America labels, light blue seat and driver, chrome wheels, shaped tires. Casting based on 169-A dragster.
1. White body, metallic blue chassis.

264-A Oldsmobile Toronado **105mm 1/1967-1968 $80-100**

Single body casting, clear windows, cream interior, chrome SW, bumpers, grille, headlight covers and trim, raising jewel headlights, suspension, gray diecast base, cast wheels, rubber tires. Casting also used for 276-A, with Golden Jacks.
1. Metallic peacock blue body.
2. Same as 264-A1 plus plastic tow hook. (GS36-A1 only).

264-B The Incredible Hulk's Mazda Pickup **126mm 7/1979-Close $55-65**

Single body casting, clear windows, black interior, chrome rack and tailgate, plastic cage, green and red figure, black grille, base and tow hook, silver headlights and license plate, Incredible Hulk label on hood, chrome wheels. Same casting as 493 Mazda Pickup and its derivatives.
1. Metallic light brown body, gray cage; 1979-1980.
2. Metallic light brown body, red cage; 1981-Close.

265-A Supermobile **142mm 9/1979-1981 $60-70**

Upper body and lower body-base castings, clear canopy, red interior with driver, chrome arms with moveable "striking fists," chrome rear panel and exhaust pipes, red and yellow labels, three wheels. One fist moves forward when other is pushed back.
1. Blue body, red fists.
2. Blue body, chromed diecast fists, (factory prototypes for trade show).

266-A Chitty Chitty Bang Bang **160mm 11/1968-1972 $350-375**

Body and chassis castings, silver hood, headlights, dash and SW, gold radiator, windshield frame and exhaust pipes, black grille and hood strap, dark red interior, four figures, red and orange wings (side wings retract), silver horn, brake and taillights, silver diecast base, dark red spoked wheels, black plastic tires and spare. Hand brake operates wings.
1. Metallic copper body, black chassis with silver running boards.

266-B Spiderbike **112mm 9/1979-Close $60-70**

Single body casting, dark blue plastic front body and seat, amber windshield, red handlebars, spiderwebs and wheel mountings, gold engine and exhaust pipes, black plastic five-spoke wheels, chrome and black stand, blue and red figure.
1. Medium blue body, black wheels.
2. Medium blue body, white wheels.

267-A Batmobile **125mm 10/1966-Close**
(Bat Hubs) $350-400
(Red Whizzwheels) $450-500
(Black Whizzwheels) $100-110

Black upper body and lower body-base castings, blue tinted canopy with chrome support, interior parts and rocket launchers, maroon interior, gold headlights, light red bat emblems on doors, light red exhaust from gray pipe, front chain cutter controlled by gold cross on hood, red dome light, gold rocket control gear, plastic rockets.
1. Matte black body, gold hubs with red bat emblems, wide black rubber tires, no tow hook.
2. Gloss black body, gold hubs with red bat emblems, wide black rubber tires, no tow hook.
3. Same as 2 plus gold tow hook. (Originally only in GS3-B, later alone).
4. Gloss black body, red Whizzwheels with chrome center, gold tow hook.
5. Gloss black body, black Whizzwheels with 8-spoke chrome center, gold tow hook, light red interior.

268-A The Green Hornet's Black Beauty 125mm 11/1967-1972 $300-350
Main body and opening trunk castings, green windows and interior, silver SW, two figures, opening chrome grille and panels with weapons behind them, green headlights, red taillights, radar scanner in trunk, two levers, Green Hornet decal on roof, suspension, black diecast base, shaped wheels, plastic tires.
1. Black body.

268-B Batbike 110mm 12/1978-Close $50-60
Single body casting, black and red plastic parts, gold engine and exhaust pipes, clear windshield, chrome stand, black plastic five-spoke wheels, Batman figure and labels.
1. Black body.

269-A DAF City Car NOT ISSUED N/A
Not issued as such; issued in 1970 as number 283.

269-B James Bond Lotus Esprit 120mm 7/1977-Close $100-110
Upper body and lower body-base castings, black windows, grilles and hood panel, black grill on hood triggers white fins and tail, white plastic periscope fires rockets, red 007 label, multicolored head-and taillight labels, black Whizzwheels.
1. While body and base.

270-A James Bond Aston Martin 101mm 2/1968-1977
(Tire Slashers) $250-275
(Whizzwheels) $115-125
Main body and opening roof hatch castings, clear windows, red interior, two figures, passenger seat raises to eject passenger, raising bullet shield, emerging rams and guns, two levers, gold bumpers and grille, suspension, gray diecast base, red plastic rear hubcaps. Model is larger than 261-A, smaller than 271-B.
1. Metallic silver body, gray base, spoked wheels, plastic tires, extending red spinners from rear axles.
2. Metallic silver body, modified base (color?), black Whizzwheels with silver centers, no wheel spinners.

271-A DeTomaso Mangusta Ghia 5000 97mm 1/1969-1969 $70-80
Main body and lower body-base castings, clear windows, black interior, gold SW, silver engine, exhaust pipes and gearshift, gray antenna, black grille, amber headlights, red taillights, spare wheel, gold stripes and black emblem decal on hood, suspension, removable metallic gray chassis, spoked wheels, plastic tires. Same body casting as 203-B, which does not have separate chassis.
1. White upper body, light blue lower body and base.

271-B James Bond Aston Martin 126mm 5/1978-Close $90-100
Silver diecast base, chrome four-spoke Whizzwheels, black SW, no red rear hubcaps, otherwise as 270-A, which is a smaller casting.
1. Metallic silver body and base.

272-A James Bond Citroen 2 CV6 107mm 6/1981-1982 $45-55
Body and hood castings, clear windows, red interior, black SW, chrome headlights, black plastic grille, silver bumpers, red taillights, suspension, black plastic base, chrome wheels. Same casting as 346-A.
1. Dark yellow body and hood.

273-A Rolls-Royce Silver Shadow 122mm 3/1970-1970 $90-100
Main body, opening hood, trunk and two door castings, clear windows, bright blue interior, folding seat backs, gold SW, detailed engine, spare wheel, chrome bumpers and grille, jeweled headlights, red taillights, suspension, silver diecast base, Golden Jacks, silver wheels, plastic tires. Casting revised as 280-A, with Whizzwheels.
1. Metallic white upper body, dusty blue lower body.
2. Metallic silver upper body, metallic blue lower body, (colors identical to 280-A1 except for blue interior and wheel type).

273-B Honda Ballade Driving School Car 120mm 6/1982-1983 $40-50
Main body and lower body-base castings, clear windows, tan interior, black SW, tow hook, mirrors, bumpers, vents and large steering wheel on roof, which steers front wheels, chrome grille and headlights, red taillights, Corgi Motor School labels, chrome wheels.
1. Red body and base.

274-A Bentley T Series 118mm 11/1970-1973 $75-85
Main body, opening hood, trunk and two door castings, clear windows, cream interior, folding seat backs, gold SW, detailed engine, chrome bumpers and grille, jewel headlights, orange taillights, black stripe on each side, suspension, silver diecast base, Whizzwheels. Same body casting as 273-A and 280-A, different grille.
1. Rose red body.

275-A Rover 2000TC 97mm 4/1968-1970
(Green) $70-80
(White) $150-160
Single body casting, amber windows and roof panel, chrome bumpers and grille, jeweled headlights, red taillights, black plastic spare wheel cover on trunk lid, suspension, gray diecast base, Golden Jacks, cast wheels, plastic tires. Casting revised in 1971 as 281-A, with Whizzwheels.
1. Metallic olive green body, light brown interior.
2. Metallic maroon body, other details not known.
3. White body, red interior.

275-B Austin Mini Metro 91mm 1/1981-Close $20-30
Main body, opening rear hatch and two door castings, clear window, plastic interior, folding seat backs, black SW, chrome headlights, orange taillights, black plastic base, grille and bumpers, Whizzwheels.
1. Purple body, light cream interior, silver Royal Wedding logo; 1981 only; 6/1981.
2. Red body, light cream interior.
3. Bright blue body, red interior.

276-A Oldsmobile Toronado 111mm 6/1968-1970
(Metallic Red) $70-80
(Gold) $150-160
Golden Jacks, cast wheels, plastic tires, gray tow hook, otherwise as 264-A.
1. Metallic red body, cream seats, orange taillights, gold jack pegs.
2. Metallic gold body, red seats, red taillights, gold jack pegs.
3. Metallic gold body, red seats, red taillights, silver jack pegs.

276-B Triumph Acclaim HLS 120mm 1981-1983 $20-30
Main body and lower body-base castings, clear windows, light brown interior, black SW, mirrors, tow hook, bumpers and vents, chrome grille and headlights, red taillights, chrome center wheels, front wheels steer; casting also used for 277-B and 278-B driving school cars.
1. Metallic peacock blue body and base, black trim.

277-A Monkeemobile 122mm 12/1968-1970 $250-300
Main body and lower body-base castings, clear windshield, yellow interior, gold SW, four figures, chrome engine, grille and headlights, orange taillights, suspension, eight-spoke cast wheels, wide plastic tires, yellow Monkees logo.
1. Red body and base, white roof.

277-B Triumph Acclaim Driving School Car 120mm 4/1982-1983 $20-30
Black roof-mounted steering wheel steers front wheels, otherwise as 276-B.
1. Shown in 1982 Corgi catalog with dark yellow body and black trim.

278-A Dan Dare Car NOT ISSUED N/A
Announced in 1981 Corgi catalog, not issued.

278-B Triumph Acclaim Driving School Car 120mm 4/1982-Close $20-30
Details as 277-B, Corgi Motor School labels.
1. Yellow body and base.
2. Red body and base.

279-A Rolls-Royce Corniche 141mm 7/1979-Close $30-40
Main body, lower body-base, opening hood, trunk and two door castings, clear windows, light brown interior, folding seat backs, black SW, detailed engine, chrome bumpers, grille and headlights, chrome wheels.
1. Metallic dark red body and base, orange taillights.
2. Metallic bronze body?
3. Metallic white body and base, red taillights.
4. Metallic dark blue body and base, red tailights.

280-A Rolls-Royce Silver Shadow 120mm 9/1970-1978
(Except Silver) $45-55
(Silver) $75-85
Whizzwheels, light brown interior, no spare wheel, otherwise as 273-A.
1. Metallic silver upper and metallic blue lower body, hole in trunk for spare tire mounting; 1970.
2. Metallic silver upper and metallic blue lower body, no hole in trunk; 1971-1973.
3. Metallic blue body, no trunk hole, vent windows in doors.
4. Metallic blue body, no trunk hole, modified doors without vent windows.
5. Metallic silver body, gold bumpers and grill, no trunk hole, no vent windows in doors, Whizzwheels with gold centers, (all other versions have silver trimmed 4 crown pattern Whizzwheels) ;1978?

281-A Rover 2000TC 97mm 9/1971-1973 $60-80
Single body casting, amber window, light orange interior, black grille, chrome bumpers and headlights, orange taillights, suspension, gray diecast base, Whizzwheels. Same casting as 275-A, which has Golden Jacks.
1. Metallic purple body.

281-B Austin Mini Metro Datapost 91mm 1/1982-Close $15-25
Red interior, Datapost, Hepolite and number 77 labels, otherwise as 275-B.
1. White body, blue roof, hood and trim.

282-A BMC Mini-Cooper 76mm 2/1971-1974 $90-100
Main body, opening hood, trunk and two door castings, clear windows, red interior, folding seat backs, silver SW, detailed engine, chrome bumpers, grille and trim, jewel headlights, red taillights, orange and black stripe and black and white number 177 labels, suspension, black diecast base, Whizzwheels. Modified 334-A casting without roof hatch.
1. White main body, black hood, trunk and doors.

283-A OSI DAF City Car 71mm 5/1971-1974 $30-40
Main body, sliding left door, opening hood, hatch and two right doors, and textured black roof castings, light cream interior, folding seats, gold SW, amber headlights, red taillights, suspension, black diecast base, Whizzwheels.
1. Orange-red body, black roof.

284-A Citroen SM 110mm 6/1971-1975 $45-55
Main body, lower body-base, opening rear hatch and two door castings, pale blue interior and lifting hatch cover, black SW, chrome inner doors and window frames, bumpers and grille, amber headlights, red taillights, black and white Citroen emblem and rear license plate, suspension.
1. Metallic lime gold body and base, chrome wheels.
2. Metallic mauve body and base, spoked wheels.

284-B Mercedes-Benz Fire Chief's Car 127mm 7/1982-Close $25-35
Blue dome light, white "Notruf 112" labels, tan interior, red taillights, no tow hook, otherwise as 285-A.
1. Light red body, black base.

285-A Mercedes-Benz 240D 131mm 3/1975-1981 $25-35
Main body, lower body-base, opening trunk and two door castings, clear windows, plastic interior, black SW and tow hook, chrome bumpers, grille and headlights, orange taillights, suspension, chrome wheels. Casting also used for 284-B, 291-B, 411-B and 412-B.
1. Metallic silver body and base, light blue interior.
2. Metallic light blue body and base, tan interior.
3. Metallic bright blue body and base, tan interior.

286-A Jaguar XJ12C 136mm 12/1974-1979 $40-50
Main body, lower body-base, opening hood and two door castings, clear windows, black SW and tow hook, detailed engine, chrome bumpers, grille and headlights, suspension, chrome wheels. Same casting used for 414-B and 429-A.
1. Metallic dark blue body and base, black roof, orange taillights, cream interior.
2. Metallic red body and base, black roof, orange taillights, cream interior.
3. Metallic golden orange body and base, black roof, red taillights, cream interior.
4. Metallic golden orange body and base, black roof, red tailights, brown interior.
5. Metallic red body, base and roof, orange taillights, brown interior.

287-A Citroen Dyane 114mm 12/1974-1978 $25-35
Main body and opening rear hatch castings, clear windows, black interior, base and tow bar, silver bumpers, grille and headlights, red taillights, marching duck and French flag label, suspension, chrome wheels.
1. Metallic yellow body, black roof.
2. Green body, black roof.

288-A Minissima 61mm 5/1975-1979 $20-30
Upper and lower body and opening rear door castings, black interior, stripes and base, clear windows and headlights, Whizzwheels.
1. Cream upper body and door, metallic lime green lower body, black stripe between.

289-A VW Polo 96mm 8/1976-1979
(Standard Issues) $25-30
(2894-A DBP, 2895-A PTT) $40-50
Main body, opening hatch and two door castings, off-white interior, black dash, SW and base, clear windows, silver bumpers, grille and headlight label, red taillights, suspension, Whizzwheels. Casting also used for 302-C, 309-B and 489-A.
1. Apple green body.
2. Bright yellow body, black DBP and posthorn (German Post Office) labels; Corgi catalog number 2894, 9/1976-1980; made for sale in Germany.
3. Yellow Body, black PTT (Swiss Post Office), Corgi catalog number 2895, other details not known.

290-A Kojak's Buick Regal 149mm 7/1976-1981
(with Hat) $70-80
(without Hat) $120-130
Main body and two opening door castings, clear windows, off-white interior, black SW, chrome bumpers, grille and headlights, red taillights and roof light, gunshot mechanism gear, two figures, suspension, chrome wheels, black plastic base.
1. Metallic bronze brown body, Kojak with hat.
2. Metallic bronze brown body, Kojak without hat.

291-A AMC Pacer 122mm 7/1977-1978 $20-30
Main body and opening hatch castings, clear windows, light yellow interior, black SW, chrome grille and headlights, black plastic grille and tow hook, suspension, chrome wheels. Casting also used for 484-B.
1. Metallic dark red body, white Pacer X labels.

291-B Mercedes-Benz 240D Rally 128mm 7/1982-Close $30-40
Black radiator guard and roof rack, chrome equipment, spare wheel on trunk lid, red interior, black diecast base, Euro Rally label, painted lettering, number 5 and trim, otherwise as 285-A.
1. Cream body, black, red and blue lettering and dirt.
2. Tan body, black, red and blue lettering and dirt.

292-A Starsky and Hutch Ford Gran Torino 146mm 10/1977-1981 $80-90
Single body casting, clear windows, light yellow interior, black SW, chrome bumpers, grille and headlights, orange taillights, white trim label, black plastic base, chrome wheels, three figures.
1. Red body, white trim.

293-A Renault 5 TS 95mm 12/1976-1981 $15-25
Main body, opening hatch and two door castings, clear windows, plastic interior, black SW, gray base and bumpers, black grille, clear headlights, red taillights, suspension, Whizzwheels. Casting also used for 294-A, 295-A, and 428-B.
1. Metallic golden orange body, black trim, tan interior; 1977-1980.
2. Light blue body, dark blue roof, dome light and S.O.S. Medecins lettering, red interior; Corgi catalog number 2932, 4/1980-1981.
3. Same as 293-A2 except black base and bumpers.
4. Yellow body, tan interior, black side trim, (St. Michael sets 8102, 8402).

294-A Renault Alpine 5 TS 95mm 6/1980-Close $15-25
Red and chrome trim labels, chrome six-spoke wheels, otherwise as 293-A.
1. Dark blue body, off-white interior.
2. Black body, red interior.

295-A Renault 5 TS Fire Chief's Car 95mm 7/1982-Close $15-25
Black and white Sapeurs Pompiers labels, blue dome lights, tan interior, amber headlights, gray antenna, otherwise as 193-A. Made for sale in France.
1. Red body.

297-A Ford Escort Police Car 111mm 2/1982-Close $15-25
Blue dome light, red Police labels, tan interior, otherwise as 334-B.
1. Blue body and base, white doors.

298-A Ferrari 308GTS Magnum 118m 2/1982-Close $45-55
Identical to red 378-B except for:
1. Chrome wheels. (378-B1 has four-spoke wheels.)

299-A Ford Sierra 128mm 6/1982-Close $20-30
Main body, opening hatch and two door castings, clear windows, plastic interior, folding seat backs, black SW, lifting hatch cover, plastic base and bumpers, black tow hook and trim, chrome headlights, red taillights, mirrors, chrome wheels. Casting also used for 451-A.
1. Metallic pale brown body, dark brown interior, dark gray base.
2. Metallic pale brown body, white interior, dark gray base.
3. Metallic pale brown body, tan interior, light gray base.
4. Metallic pale brown body, dark brown interior, light gray base.
5. Metallic light blue body, white interior, light gray base.
6. Metallic blue body, tan interior, dark gray base.
7. Red body, white interior, dark gray base.
8. Red body, tan interior, dark gray base.
9. Red body, tan interior, light gray base.
10. Light yellow body, white interior, dark gray base.
11. Dark yellow body, tan interior, light gray base.
12. (There are probably other combinations.)

Sports Cars

300-A Austin-Healey 86mm 7/1956-1963
(Blue) $275-300
(Red or Cream) $140-160
Single body casting, clear windshield, sheet metal base, silver grille, headlights, bumpers and SW, smooth wheels, rubber tires.
1. Cream body, red seats.
2. Red body, cream seats.
3. Blue body, ? seats, other details not known.
4. Plated gold body, red seats and grill, heavy cast spoked wheels, black display base, (St. Michael Trophy model 1961).

300-B Corvette Sting Ray 101mm 4/1970-1972 $90-100
Main body and black opening hood castings, detailed engine, opening headlights, clear windshield, amber roof panel, yellow interior, gold dash and SW, chrome grille and bumpers, flag decals, gray diecast base, Golden Jacks, cast wheels, plastic tires. Same casting as 387-A, which has Whizzwheels.
1. Metallic green body.
2. Metallic red body.

300-C Ferrari Daytona 128mm 3/1979-Close $20-30
Red-yellow-silver-black Daytona, number 5 and other racing labels, black tow hook, otherwise as 323-B.
1. Apple green body.

301-A Triumph TR2 86mm 7/1956-1959 $140-160
Single body casting, clear windshield, silver grille, headlights, bumpers and SW, sheet metal base, smooth wheels, rubber tires.
1. Cream body, red seats.
2. Light green body, white seats.
3. Light green body, cream seats.
4. Dark green body, cream seats.
5. Plated gold body, red seats and grill, heavy cast spoked wheels, black display base, (St. Michael Trophy model 1961).

301-B ISO Grifo 7 Litre 102mm 7/1970-1973 $55-65
Main body, two opening doors and black opening hood castings, detailed engine, clear windows, black dash, gold SW, light blue interior, folding seat backs, chrome bumpers and stripe over roof, jewel headlights, red taillights, suspension, black diecast base, Whizzwheels.
1. Metallic blue body, black hood.

301-C Lotus Elite 120mm 3/1979-1981 $20-30
Red-chrome-white-black stripes, lettering and number 7 labels, otherwise as 315-C.
1. Dark yellow body.

302-A MGA 90mm 5/1957-1965 $140-150
Single body casting, clear windshield, silver grille, headlights, bumpers and SW, sheet metal base, rubber tires.

1. Green body, cream seats, smooth wheels.
2. White body, red seats, smooth wheels.
3. Red body, cream seats, smooth wheels.
4. Red body, cream seats, shaped wheels.
5. Plated gold body, red seats and grill, heavy cast spoked wheels, black display base, (St. Michael Trophy model 1961).

302-B Hillman Hunter 106mm 7/1969-1972 $120-130
Body and two spotlight castings, clear windows, gray interior, gold SW, red radiator screen, black equipment box and spare wheels on roof, jewel headlights, red and jewel taillights, silver grille, number 75 and London-Sydney labels, gray diecast base, Golden Jacks, cast wheels, plastic tires, kangaroo figure.
1. Blue body, black hood, white roof, unpainted spotlights, labels on car.

302-C VW Polo 98mm 3/1979-1981 $15-25
Number 4 and other racing labels, otherwise as 289-A.
1. Metallic light brown body.

303-A Mercedes-Benz 300SL Roadster 96mm 8/1958-1966 $100-120
Single body casting, clear windshield, plastic interior, gray SW, sheet metal base, rubber tires; 303 versions (1958-1960) have smooth wheels, no suspension, 303S versions (7/1961-1966) have shaped or cast wheels, suspension, racing stripes and number, and driver figure.
1. White body, blue interior, smooth wheels.
2. Light blue body, white interior, smooth wheels.
3. Light blue body, yellow interior, smooth wheels.
4. Gold body, ? interior, shaped wheels, suspension, driver (303S).
5. Light blue body, yellow interior, shaped wheels, suspension, driver (303S).
6. White body, yellow interior, shaped wheels, suspension, driver (303S).
7. Cream body, yellow interior, shaped wheels, suspension, driver (303S).
8. Chrome plated body over yellow paint, yellow and brown interior, cast wheels, suspension, driver (303S).
9. Same as 303-A6 except no racing stripes/number decal. May not be authentic.

303-B Roger Clark's Ford Capri 101mm 1/1970-1972
(Red Dot wheels) $200-225
(plastic Whizzwheels) $75-85
Main body and two opening door castings, clear windows, black interior, gold SW, folding seats, chrome bumpers, black grille, clear headlights, red taillights, number 73 labels, white diecast base, suspension. Same casting as 311-A and 331-A.
1. White body, black hood, gold wheels with red hubs, wide plastic tires.
2. White body, black hood, Circle-of-Bubbles pattern Whizzwheels.

303-C Porsche 924 117mm 2/1980-1981 $20-30
Multicolored stripes, lettering and number 2 labels, swiveling roof spotlight, four chrome headlights, red plastic base, otherwise as 321-B.
1. Bright orange body.

304-A Mercedes-Benz 300SL Coupe 96mm 4/1959-1965
(Yellow Body and Roof) $400-450
(Others) $100-120
Main body and hardtop castings, clear windows, rubber tires, 304 versions (1959-1960) had smooth wheels and no suspension. Later versions catalogued by Corgi as 304S (2/1961-1965) have suspension, racing stripes and number, smooth or (in 1965) spoked wheels or shaped wheels.
1. Yellow body and top, smooth wheels.
2. Yellow body, red top, smooth wheels.
3. White body, red top, smooth wheels, suspension (304S).
4. Chrome body, red top, smooth wheels, suspension (304S).
5. Chrome body, red top, spoked wheels, suspension (304S, 1965).
6. Chrome body, red top, shaped wheels, suspension (304S).

304-B Chevrolet Camaro SS 100mm 3/1972-1973 $60-70
Main body and two opening door castings, white plastic top, clear windows, cream interior, folding seat backs, gold SW, silver air intakes, gold grille and headlights, red taillights, suspension, white diecast base, Whizzwheels. Same casting as 338-A, which has Golden Jacks.
1. Medium blue body with white nose stripe.
2. Turquoise blue body with white nose stripe.

305-A Triumph TR3 58mm 3/1960-1962 $140-160
Single body casting, clear windshield, silver SW, grille, bumpers and headlights, sheet metal base, rubber tires.
1. Metallic olive body, red seats, smooth wheels crimped on axles.
2. Same as 305-A1 except shaped wheels crimped on axles.
3. Cream body, other details unknown.

305-B Mini Marcos GT 850 56mm 3/1972-1973 $65-75
Red-white-blue racing stripe and number 7 labels, clear headlights, gold SW, Whizzwheels, otherwise as 341-A.
1. White body.

306-A Morris Marina 1.8 Coupe 95mm 5/1971-1973 $50-60
Main body, opening hood and two door castings, detailed engine, cream interior, black SW, clear windows, chrome grille and bumpers, jewel headlights, red taillights, suspension, black diecast base, Whizzwheels.
1. Metallic dark red body.
2. Metallic lime green body.

306-B Fiat X1/9 117mm 2/1980-1981 $30-40
White Fiat and number 3, multi-colored lettering and stripe labels, otherwise as 314-B.
1. Metallic blue body and base.

307-A Jaguar E Type Coupe 95mm 3/1962-1964 $120-140
Upper body and lower body-base castings, red and clear plastic removable hardtop, clear windshield, tan interior, lighter tan (painted) folded top, unpainted gearbox-shift-drive train, silver grille and bumpers, clear headlights, suspension, shaped wheels, rubber tires. Same casting used without hardtop as 312-A.
1. Maroon body.
2. Metallic dark gray body.

307-B Renault 5 Turbo 98mm 4/1981-1982 $15-25
Main body, opening hatch and two door castings, clear windows, red plastic interior, grille, bumpers and lower sides, black dash, SW, upper grille and base, chrome rear engine, number 8 and lettering labels, suspension, chrome wheels. Casting also used for 381-B.
1. Bright yellow body, black roof and hood.

308-A BMC Mini-Cooper S 74mm 1/1972-1976 $110-120
Chrome plastic roof rack with two spare wheels, number 177 and Monte Carlo Rally labels, six jeweled headlights, otherwise as 204-B.
1. Bright yellow body, red interior, 4 crown pattern Whizzwheels.
2. Same as 308-A1 except blue interior.
3. Same as 308-A1 except different pattern on Whizzwheels.

308-B BMW M1 125mm 4/1981-Close
(Yellow versions) $20-30
Main body and opening rear hatch castings, black plastic base, rear panel and interior, white seats, clear windows, multicolored stripes, lettering and number 25 labels, black grille and headlights, red taillights, 4-spoke wheels. Casting also used for 382-B.
1. Yellow body, labels on hood, roof, and doors.
1. Yellow body, labels on hood only (Produced near time of Mettoy closure).
2. Plated gold body (Mettoy promotional use).

309-A Aston Martin DB4 95mm 4/1962-1965
(Heavy Spoke Wheels) $160-180
(Other Wheel Types) $100-120
Racing number 1, 3 or 7 and flag decals, jeweled headlights, yellow interior, otherwise as 218-A.
1. White top and aqua green sides of body, heavy spoked wheels crimped on axles.
2. White top and aqua green sides of body, shaped wheels free on axles.
3. White top and aqua green sides of body, wire wheels free on axles.

309-B VW Polo Turbo 98mm 3/1982-Close $20-30
Main body, opening hatch and two door castings, clear windows, red interior, black plastic dash, SW and base, black grille, silver headlights, red and orange trim, number 14, suspension, six-spoke wheels. Casting based on 289-A.
1. Cream body with red and orange trim.

310-A Chevrolet Corvette Sting Ray 96mm 8/1963-1968
(Copper) $140-160
(Other Colors) $65-75
Main body, lower body-base and two opening headlight castings, clear windows, silver hood panels, four jeweled headlights, chrome bumpers, suspension, rubber tires.
1. Metallic maroon body, shaped wheels free on axles, yellow interior.
2. Metallic maroon body, wire wheels, yellow interior.
3. Metallic copper body, wire wheels, yellow interior.
4. Metallic silver body, wire wheels, yellow interior.
5. Metallic silver body, wire wheels, red interior.

310-B Porsche 924 Turbo 117mm 1/1982-Close $20-30
Gold trim, yellow interior, four chrome headlights, otherwise as 321-B.
1. Black body with gold trim.

311-A Ford Capri 3 Litre G.T. 101mm 1/1970-1972
(Red Dot wheels) $200-225
(plastic Whizzwheels) $70-80
Main body and two opening door castings, clear windows, black interior, folding seat backs, gold SW, clear headlights, black grilles, silver bumpers, diecast base. Casting also used for 303-B and 331-A.
1. Bright orange (almost glowing) body and base, gold wheels with red hubs, wide tires (early Whizzwheels).
2. Same as 311-A1 except all plastic Whizzwheels, (circle of bubbles pattern).
3. Dark red body, black hood and base, Whizzwheels, (possibly more than one pattern).

312-A Jaguar E Type Competition 95mm 9/1964-1968 $100-110
Blue and white stripes and black number 2 decals, black interior, no top, spoked wheels, driver figure, otherwise as 307-A.
1. Gold plated body.
2. Chrome plated body.

312-B Marcos Mantis 110mm 9/1971-1973 $45-55
Main body, silver gray lower body-base-bumpers-hood panel and two opening door castings, clear windows, cream interior and headlights, folding seat backs, gold SW, orange taillights, suspension, spoked chrome wheels.
1. Metallic red body and doors.

312-C Ford Capri S 120mm 6/1982-Close $25-35
Number 6 and other racing labels, red interior, chrome wheels, otherwise as 343-B.
1. White body, red lower body and base.

313-A Ford Cortina GXL 103mm 10/1970-1973
(Yellow) $250-300
(Other colors) $100-120
Main body and two opening door castings, black painted roof, clear windows, plastic interior, folding seat backs, gold SW, black grille, jewel headlights, red taillights, chrome bumpers, suspension, Whizzwheels, Graham Hill figure. Casting also used for 402-A police car.
1. Tan body and base, black roof and stripes, red interior.
2. Metallic silver blue body, black roof and base, cream interior.
3. Metallic copper body, black base, flat black roof, cream interior.
4. Yellow body, other details not known.
5. Blue body, other details not known.

314-A Ferrari Berlinetta 250LM 96mm 2/1965-1972 $55-65
Upper body, lower body-base and opening rear body castings, detailed engine, spare wheel, blue windows, chrome interior, grille and exhaust pipes, number 4, Ferrari emblem and yellow stripe decals, suspension, spoked wheels.
1. Red body with yellow stripe, rubber tires.
2. Red body with yellow stripe, plastic tires.

314-B Fiat X1/9 117mm 8/1975-1979 $35-45
Main body, lower body-base and two opening door castings, black roof, trim, interior, rear panel, grille, bumpers and tow hook, detailed engine, suspension, chrome wheels. Casting also used for 306-B.
1. Metallic light green body with black roof and trim.
2. Metallic silver body with black roof and trim.
3. Dark metallic blue body, black roof and trim, (St. Michael sets 8002 and 8402).
4. Same as 314-B1 except with "Racing Team" hood trim, (St. Michael sets 8100, 8400).

314-C Jaguar XJS-HE Supercat 135mm 6/1982-1983 $25-35
Silver trim, red interior, dark red taillights, light gray antenna, no tow hook, chrome wheels, otherwise as 319-C.
1. Black body with silver stripes.

315-A Simca 1000 88mm 4/1964-1966
(Blue) $160-180
(Plated) $55-65
Single body casting, clear windows, red interior, gray SW, gray diecast base, suspension, shaped wheels, rubber tires.
1. Chrome plated body, number 8 and red-white-blue stripe decals.
2. Dark blue body, number 6 and red-white-blue stripe decals.

315-B Ford Cortina 103mm 10/1970-1970 $???
Presumably based on 313-A, for export. Details unknown.

315-C Lotus Elite 130mm 1/1976-1978 $40-50
Main body and two opening door castings, clear windows, white interior, black SW, dash, hood panel, grille, bumpers, base and tow hook, light and license plate labels, suspension, four-spoke chrome wheels. Casting also used for 301-C and 382-B.
1. Red body.
2. Metallic green body, " Wings Flying Club" trim, (St. Michael sets 8001, 8401).

316-A NSU Sport Prinz 85mm 12/1963-1966 $80-90
Single body casting, clear windows, yellow interior, gray SW, silver bumpers, headlights and trim, suspension, gray diecast base, shaped wheels, rubber tires.
1. Metallic maroon body.
2. Metallic burgundy body.

316-B Ford GT 70 92mm 5/1972-1973 $45-55
Main body and two opening door castings, clear windows, cream interior, black opening engine cover, detailed engine, chrome exhaust pipes, silver headlights and grille, red jewel taillights, number 32 and flag labels, suspension, black diecast base, eight-spoke wheels.
1. Metallic lime green body.

317-A Morris Mini-Cooper 73mm 2/1964-1965 $175-200
Number 37 and Monte Carlo Rally decals, chrome roof spotlight yellow interior, otherwise as 227-A.
1. Red body and base, white roof.

318-A Lotus Elan S2 Roadster 88mm 7/1965-1966
(White or Copper) $300-350
(Blue) $100-120
Main body, lower body-base and opening hood castings, clear windshield, plastic interior and SW, folding seats, tan dash, silver grille, suspension, shaped wheels, rubber tires. Also used in GS 40-A; lower casting modified to take separate chassis and used in GS 37-A and for 319-A.
1. Metallic light blue body, white number on black disc, white trunk lid decal with ESSO tiger advertisment, black interior.
2. White body, black interior; used in GS 40-A.
3. White body, black interior, white trunk lid decal with ESSO tiger advertisment. (needs verification).
4. Dark green body, yellow stripe, black interior, separate chrome chassis; used in GS 37-A.
5. Same as 318-A4 except red interior; used in GS 37-A.
6. Same as 318-A5 except cast wheels; used in GS37-A.
7. Copper body, other details not known.

318-B Jaguar XJS 145mm 1983-Close $20-30
Red and white trim with number 4 and Motul lettering, dark red taillights, no tow hook, light gray antenna, chrome wheels; otherwise as 319-C.
1. Black body, red and white trim.

319-A Lotus Elan S2 Hardtop 58mm 6/1967-1968
(Green & Yellow) $130-150
(Red or Blue) $75-85
Main body, lower body-base, hardtop and opening hood castings, clear windshield, cream interior, folding seats, tan dash, silver grille, separate chrome diecast chassis, rubber tires. Same upper casting as 318-A; lower casting as 318-A3 and A4.
1. Medium blue body, white hardtop, shaped wheels.
2. Medium blue body, white hardtop, cast wheels, thicker tires.
3. Orange-red body, white hardtop, cast wheels, thicker tires.
4. Yellow body, dark green hardtop and stripes, shaped wheels; used in GS 37-A.
5. Green body, yellow roof and stripes, shaped wheels.

319-B Lamborghini Miura P400 GT 95mm 2/1973-1974 $25-35
Black interior, black diecast base, number 7 and stripe labels, otherwise as 342-A.
1. Metallic silver gray body, purple and yellow stripes.

319-C Jaguar XJS 145mm 11/1978-1981 $25-35
Main body, lower body-base and two opening door castings, clear windows, tan interior, black SW, grille, bumpers and tow hook, chrome headlights, orange-red taillights, four-spoke chrome wheels. Casting also used for 314-C, 318-B and 320-B.
1. Metallic maroon body.

320-A Ford Mustang Fastback 99mm 4/1965-1966 $75-85
Main body and two opening door castings, clear windows, folding seat backs, brown Corgi dog, jeweled headlights, red taillights, chrome grille and bumpers, diecast base same color as body, suspension, rubber tires. Casting also used for 325-A and 348-A.
1. Pale green body and base, cream interior, spoked wheels.
2. Metallic lilac body and base, cream interior, spoked wheels.
3. Dark metallic blue body and base, cream interior, spoked wheels.
4. Dark metallic blue body and base, cream interior, cast wheels.
5. Metallic silver gray body and base, red interior, spoked wheels.
6. Metallic silver gray body and base, red interior, cast wheels.
7. Metallic silver gray body and base, red and white stripes, other details not known.

320-B The Saint's Jaguar XJS 135mm 10/1978-1981 $80-90
Red interior, black trim and Saint figure hood label, antenna, otherwise as 319-C.
1. White body.

321-A BMC Mini-Cooper S Rally Car 73mm 2/1965-1966
(1965 #52) $250-300
(1966 #2 with Signatures) $500-550
Red diecast base, five jeweled headlights, number and Monte Carlo Rally decals, sheet metal sump guard, new type interior with rally equipment in rear, otherwise as 227-A.
1. Red body and base, white roof, number 52; 1965
2. Red body and base, white roof, number 2, autographs on roof; 1966.
3. A version with no racing number may have been used in GS 38-1 for a time.

321-B Porsche 924 125mm 11/1978-1981 $30-50
Main body and two opening door castings, clear windows, dark red interior, black SW, chrome headlights, taillights-license plate label, black plastic grille, base and tow hook, rear window opens, suspension, eight spoke wheels. Casting also used for 303-C, 310-B and 430-B.
1. Metallic light brown body.
2. Red body.

322-A Rover 2000 Rally Car 97mm 3/1965-1966
(Monte-Carlo Rally) $140-160
(RAC Rally) $200-225
Red plastic interior, Trans-o-lite plus two jeweled headlights, decals, otherwise as 252-A.
1. Metallic dark red body, white roof, shaped wheels, rubber tires, number 136 and Monte Carlo Rally decals.
2. White body, black hood, red and black "21" decals, cast wheels, rubber tires.
3. Same as 322-A2 except plastic tires.

323-A Citroen DS19 Rally Car 100mm 3/1965-1966 $130-140
Number 75 and Monte Carlo Rally decals, yellow interior, four jewel headlights, shaped wheels, otherwise as 210S form of 210-A.
1. Light blue body, white roof with gray antenna.

323-B Ferrari Daytona 122mm 6/1973-1978 $25-35
Main body and two opening door castings, amber windows and headlights, black plastic interior and base, number 81, name, emblem and stripe labels. Casting also used for 300-C and 324-B.

1. White body, red roof area, four spoke chrome Whizzwheels, blue "V" on hood.
2. Same as 323-B1 except eight spoke chrome Whizzwheels.
324-A Marcos Volvo 1800 GT 92mm 2/1966-1969 $60-70
Main body, two opening doors and hood castings, clear windows, plastic interior, gray SW, driver figure, red taillights, suspension, diecast base, spoked wheels, self-adhesive racing number labels packaged separately in box.
1. White body, two green stripes, red interior, gray base, rubber tires.
2. Same as 324-A1 except two blue stripes.
3. Medium blue body and base, two white stripes, pale blue interior, rubber tires.
4. Same as 324-A2 except plastic tires.
324-B Ferrari Daytona 122mm 6/1973-1974 $30-40
Corgi, JCB, number 33, lettering and stripe labels, eight-spoke chrome wheels, otherwise as 323-B.
1. Light orange body.
2. Yellow body, black interior, yellow windows, " Team Spindrift Power Boat" trim, (St. Michael sets 8003, 8403).
325-A Ford Mustang Fastback 99mm 12/1965-1969 $75-85
White body and base, two red stripes, pale blue interior, self-adhesive racing number labels packaged separately in box, no Corgi dog, otherwise as 320-A.
1. Spoked wheels, rubber tires.
2. Cast wheels, rubber tires.
3. Cast wheels, plastic tires.
4. Wide gold eight-spoke wheels, wide plastic tires, modified interior and base to accept new wheels;1969, production concurrent with 348-A.
325-B Chevrolet Caprice Classic 149mm 1979-1981 $60-70
Main body, two opening doors and trunk castings, clear windows, plastic interior, black SW, chrome grille and bumpers, red taillights, black diecast base, chrome wheels, whitewall tires. Casting also used for 326-A, 327-B and 341-B.
1. Metallic light green body, dark green interior.
2. Metallic silver upper and navy blue lower body, brown interior; 1983 Reissue?
326-A Chevrolet Caprice Police Car 149mm 11/1980-1981 $40-50
Police labels, silver roof bar with two red lights, red interior, otherwise as 325-B.
1. Black body, white roof, doors and trunk lid.
327-A MGB GT 88mm 3/1967-1968 $120-130
Main body, opening hatch and two door castings, clear windows, silver SW, jeweled headlights, chrome grille and bumpers, orange taillights, luggage, suspension, gray diecast base, spoked wheels, rubber tires. Casting modified for use as 345-A and 378-A MGC.
1. Dark red body, light blue interior.
2. Dark red body, yellow interior.
327-B Chevrolet Caprice Taxi 149mm 12/1979-1981 $40-50
Taxi and TWA labels, white roof sign, gray antenna, red interior, no whitewalls, otherwise as 325-B.
1. Light orange body.
328-A Hillman IMP Rally Car 82mm 1/1966-1966 $115-125
Number 107 and Monte Carlo Rally decals, two jeweled headlights, cream interior, otherwise as 251-A.
1. Dark blue body.
329-A Ford Mustang Mach I 111mm 10/1973-1976 $40-50
Upper body, lower body-base and two opening door castings, amber windows, cream interior, folding seat backs, gold SW, chrome headlights and rear bumper, orange taillights, number 69 and stripe labels, suspension, chrome wheels. Casting also used for 391-A.
1. Green upper body, white lower body and base.
329-B Opel Senator 142mm 12/1979-1983 $30-50
Upper body, lower body-base and two opening door castings, clear windows, plastic interior, black SW, chrome grille and bumpers, red lights, black tow hook. Casting also used for 332-B and 452-B.
1. Cream body?
2. Metallic golden brown body and base, red interior, chrome wheels.
3. Metallic golden brown body and base, red interior, four-spoke chrome wheels.
4. Metallic dark blue body and base, white interior, chrome wheels, no tow hook.
330-A Porsche Carrera 6 98mm 5/1967-1969
(White/Blue) $100-120
(White/Red) $55-65
Upper body, lower body-base and opening rear castings, clear windshield and canopy, tinted engine cover, black interior, gray SW, driver, clear headlights, red jeweled taillights, silver mirrors, number 60 and lettering decals, suspension, cast eight-spoke wheels, plastic tires. Same casting as 371-A, which has Whizzwheels.
1. White body, red trim, blue tinted engine cover.
2. White body, blue trim, amber tinted engine cover.
3. Same as 330-A1 except racing number 1;GS12-B.
331-A Ford Capri 3 Litre GT 101mm 7/1973-1976 $70-80
Number 5, Texaco and stripe labels, white diecast base, chrome headlights and bumpers, orange taillights, otherwise as 311-A.
1. White body and base, black hood and trunk lid, Whizzwheels.
332-A Lancia Fulvia Sport Zagato 92mm 9/1967-1969
(Yellow) $120-130
(Green or Blue) $60-70
Main body, lower body-base, opening hood and two door castings, detailed engine, clear windows, light blue interior, folding seats, gold SW, chrome bumpers and grille, amber headlights, red taillights, suspension, cast wheels, plastic tires. Casting also used for 372-A, which has Whizzwheels.
1. Metallic blue body and base.
2. Metallic green body and base.
3. Yellow and black body?
4. Bronze body and base?
332-B Opel Senator Doctor's Car 142mm 5/1980-1981 $35-45
Chrome roof bar with sirens, red cross and Notarzt labels, clear windows, red interior, four-spoke chrome wheels, otherwise as 329-B.
1. White body and base, red-white-black labels.
333-A BMC Mini Cooper S Rally Car 72mm 2/1967-1967 $350-450
Red body, white roof, orange-white-blue decals, unpainted sump guard, six jeweled headlights, no. 21 and RAC Rally decals, interior with rally equipment in rear, otherwise as 227-A.
1. Shaped wheels, Austin 7 body.
334-A BMC Mini Cooper Magnifique 74mm 12/1968-1970 $70-80
Main body, lower body-base, opening hood, trunk and two door castings, clear windows and roof hatch, red and white striped roof hatch panel, cream interior, folding seats, gold SW, chrome grille, bumpers and trim, jeweled headlights, red taillights, suspension, cast wheels. Casting modified as 282-A.
1. Metallic green body and base, 7 red stripes in sun roof, rubber tires.
2. Same as 334-A1 except plastic tires.
3. Same as 334-A2 except 4 wider red stripes in sunroof.
4. Metallic dark blue body, 7 red stripes in sunroof, plastic tires.
5. Same as 334-A4 except 4 wider red stripes in sunroof.
334-B Ford Escort 1.3 GL 110mm 10/1980-Close $20-30
Main body, lower body-base and two opening door castings, clear windows, black grille and bumpers, chrome and light red headlights, red taillights, chrome wheels. Casting also used for 297-A police car.
1. Metallic pale blue body and base, black interior; 1980-1982.
2. Yellow body and base, black LH drive interior; 1983-Close.
3. Yellow body and base, tan RH drive interior; 1983-Close.
4. Silver body and base, ? interior.
5. Turquoise body and base, ? interior.
6. Red Body, black interior, " AVIS CAR LEASING" on Roof. (promotional issue).
335-A Jaguar E Type 2+2 106mm 6/1968-1969 $120-140
Main body, lower body-base, opening front body, hatch and 2 door castings, clear windows, black interior, folding seat backs, gold SW, silver dash, headlights, bumpers and mirrors, copper exhaust pipes, suspension, detailed engine, spoked wheels, plastic tires. Casting also used for 374-A.
1. Metallic dark red body and base.
2. Metallic dark blue body and base.
3. Orange body and base, black roof. (Preproduction model?)
336-A James Bond Toyota 2000 GT 100mm 10/1967-1969 $350-375
Main body, lower body-base and opening trunk castings, clear windshield, black interior, gray SW, chrome grille and bumper, jewel head- and taillights, red pennant, two figures, lever opens trunk, weapon rack raises, red 007 disc on base, suspension, spoked wheels, plastic tires. Same casting as 375-A.
1. White body and base.
337-A Chevrolet Corvette Sting Ray 96mm 7/1967-1969 $50-65
Main body and lower body-base castings, clear windows, red interior, chrome bumpers, air intakes and exhaust pipes, number 13 and other decals, suspension, cast eight-spoke wheels, wide plastic tires. Revised 310-A casting, also used for 376-A.
1. Dark yellow body and base.
338-A Chevrolet Camaro SS 100mm 8/1968-1970 $70-80
Main body, lower body-base and two opening door castings, clear windows, black plastic top, red interior, gold SW, chrome hood panels and bumpers, black grille, red taillights, suspension, Golden Jacks, cast wheels, plastic tires. Same casting as 304-B, which has Whizzwheels.
1. Metallic lime gold body and base, black hood strope and top.
338-B Rover 3500 136mm 12/1979-Close $20-30
Main body, opening hood, hatch and two door castings, detailed engine, clear windows, plastic interior, lifting hatch cover, black SW, chrome bumpers and headlights, orange taillights, black diecast base and grille, chrome wheels. Casting also used for 339-B and 340-B.
1. Metallic blue body, light brown interior, flat black painted base, black tow hook.
2. Red body, black roof, tan interior, gloss black painted base, no tow hook.
3. Metallic golden brown body, chocolate roof, tan interior, flat black painted base, no tow hook.
339-A BMC Mini-Cooper S Rally Car 74mm 3/1967-1972 $120-160
Number 177 and Monte Carlo Rally decals, six jewel headlights, sheet metal sump guard, chrome roof rack with two spare wheels, interior with rally equipment in rear, red body and base, white roof, red interior, otherwise as 227-A.
1. Shaped wheels, rubber tires, small diameter headlights, Austin 7 body casting.
2. Same as 339-A1 except cast wheels.
3. Cast wheels, rubber tires, large diameter headlights, newer Morris body casting, (strong arch at base of grill).
4. Same as 339-A3 except plastic tires.
5. Same as 339-A4 except Monte-Carlo rear placard now label, (all previous versions have decal).
339-B Rover 3500 Police Car 136mm 6/1980-Close $20-30
White plastic roof sign, blue dome light, red and blue Police and badge labels, light red interior, red taillights, otherwise as 338-B.
1. White body, red stripes.
340-A Sunbeam IMP Rally 84mm 3/1967-1968 $120-130
Number 77 and Monte Carlo Rally decals, six jeweled headlights, cast wheels, modified badges on casting, casting (also used for 506-A), otherwise as 328-A, which is darker blue.
1. Metallic blue body, white stripes, no lines in windshield, rubber tires.
2. Same as 340-A1 except 2 horizontal lines in windshield.
3. Same as 340-A2 except plastic tires.
340-B Rover 3500 Triplex 136mm 1/1981-Close $20-30
Red-white-black number 1, Triplex and other racing labels, red interior and trim, four-spoke chrome wheels, otherwise as 338-B.
1. White sides and hatch, blue roof and hood, red trim.
341-A Mini Marcos GT850 86mm 3/1968-1970 $60-70
Main body, opening hood and two door castings, detailed engine, clear windows, cream interior, gray SW, clear headlights, gray diecast base, Golden Jacks, cast wheels, plastic tires. Casting also used for 305-B.
1. Metallic maroon body, white name and trim decals.
341-B Chevrolet Caprice Classic 150mm 4/1981-1982 $20-30
Number 43 and other racing labels, tan interior, chrome wheels, no whitewalls, otherwise as 325-B.
1. White upper body, red sides, red-white-blue stripes.
342-A Lamborghini Miura P400 95mm 1/1970-1972 $60-70
Main body, lower body-base and opening front body, rear body and trunk castings, clear windows, plastic interior, gold SW, detailed engine, spare wheel, jewel headlights, black grille, hood panels and rear windows, silver mirrors, suspension, Whizzwheels, bull figure. Same casting as 319-B.
1. Red body, silver base, white interior.
2. Bright yellow body, silver base, red interior.
342-B The Professionals' Ford Capri 129mm 2/1980-1981
(with Chrome Bumpers) $90-110
(with out Chrome Bumpers) $75-85
Blue windows, red interior, chrome wheels, three figures, otherwise as 343-B.
1. Metallic silver body and base, black spoiler and trim.
2. Metallic silver body and base, black spoiler and trim, chromed bumpers.
343-A Pontiac Firebird Convertible 103mm 12/1969-1972
(Red Dot Wheels) $100-110
(plastic Whizzwheels) $55-65
Main body, lower body-base and two opening door castings, clear windshield, red interior, folding seats, gold SW, chrome bumpers, grille, scoops and shifter, jeweled headlights, red taillights, suspension.
1. Metallic silver body and base, black hood, stripes and folded top, gold wheels with red hubs, plastic tires.
2. Metallic silver body and base, black hood, stripes and folded top, Circle-of-Bubbles pattern Whizzwheels.
343-B Ford Capri 3.0S 129mm 5/1980-1981 $35-45
Main body, lower body-base, opening hood and hatch and black spoiler castings, detailed engine, clear windows, black interior, bumpers, grille and tow hook, chrome headlights, red taillights, chrome four-

spoke wheels. Casting also used for 312-C and 343-B.

344-A   Ferrari 206 Dino   105mm 9/1969-1973 $70-80
Upper body and lower body-base castings, clear windows, blue front and rear wings and interior, plastic opening doors, gold SW, detailed engine, spare wheel, unpainted mirrors, clear headlights, red jeweled taillights, suspension.
1. Red body and base, white doors, number 30, gold wheels with red hubs, plastic tires.
2. Circle-of-Bubbles pattern Whizzwheels, otherwise as type 1.
3. Yellow body and base, black doors, racing number 23, gold wheels with red hubs, plastic tires.
4. Circle-of-Bubbles pattern Whizzwheels, otherwise as type 3.

345-A   MGC GT   88mm 1/1969-1969
                              (Orange) $275-300
                              (Yellow & Black) $100-120
Main body, lower body-base, opening hatch and two door castings, clear windows, black interior, folding seat backs, luggage, gold SW, jeweled headlights, red taillights, chrome grille and bumpers, suspension, spoked wheels, rubber tires. Modified 327-A casting; same casting used for 378-A.
1. Bright yellow body and base, black hood and hatch, self-adhesive racing number labels supplied separately in box.
2. Orange body, base, hood and hatch, no labels;GS48-B only.

345-B   Honda Prelude   120mm 1/1981-1982 $20-30
Main body, lower body-base and two opening door castings, clear windows, tan interior, folding seat backs, black SW, grille, bumpers, tow hook and trim, chrome headlights, red taillights, chrome wheels, roof hatch.
1. Metallic dark blue body and base.

346-A   Citroen 2CV Charleston   105mm 1981-Close $15-20
Chrome bumpers, plastic interior, otherwise as 272-A.
1. Yellow and black body, ? interior.
2. Maroon and black body, tan interior, white trim; 1983.

347-A   Chevrolet Astro 1   103mm 10/1969-1974
                              (Red Dot Wheels) $100-110
                              (plastic Whizzwheels) $55-65
Front and opening rear body castings, gold triangular body panel and mirrors, clear windshield, cream interior with two figures, black controls, red taillights, black diecast base, suspension. Seats are lifted when rear body is raised.
1. Metallic dark greenish blue body, gold wheels with red hubs, plastic tires.
2. Metallic dark greenish blue body, Circle-of-Bubbles pattern Whizzwheels.

348-A   Psychedelic Ford Mustang   97mm 6/1968-1968 $110-130
Red-orange-yellow number 20 and flower design decals, aqua interior, interior and base modified to fit wider wheels and tires, cast eight-spoke wheels, plastic tires, otherwise as 320-A.
1. Light blue body and base.

348-B   Vega$ Ford Thunderbird   135mm 9/1980-1981 $85-95
Main body, opening hood and trunk castings, amber windshield, black interior and grille, white seats, driver figure, detailed engine, gray antenna, chrome bumpers and spare wheel cover, suspension, black diecast base, chrome wheels, whitewall tires. Casting later used for 801-B and 810-A.
1. Orange-red body and base.

349-A   Pop Art Mini-Mostest   72mm 1969-1969 $1600-2000+
Yellow-blue-purple pop art and "Mostest" decals, yellow interior, jeweled headlights, orange taillights, cast wheels, plastic tires, diecast base of second type 226-A, otherwise as 226-A.
1. Light red body and base.

Military

350-A   Thunderbird Missile on Trolley   136mm 5/1958-1962 $100-120
Missile, trolley, steering front and rear axle castings, red rubber nose cone, plastic tow bar and wire clips, black plastic wheels.
1. Ice blue missile, RAF blue trolley.
2. Silver missile, RAF blue trolley.

351-A   R.A.F. Land Rover   95mm 5/1958-1962 $75-100
RAF blue body and canopy, RAF rondel decal.
1. No interior or suspension, casting based on 406-A, tin canopy.
2. Yellow interior, suspension, casting based on 438-A, plastic canopy;351S, 1962.

352-A   Standard Vanguard R.A.F. Staff Car   95mm 10/1958-1962 $90-100
RAF decals, gray diecast base with rear axle bulge, otherwise as 207-A.
1. RAF blue body.

353-A   Decca 424 Radar Scanner   81mm 9/1959-1960 $50-65
Scanner and RAF blue base casting, silver scanner surface, silver gray plastic arm, gear on base turns scanner.
1. Orange scanner framework.
2. Yellow-brown scanner framework.

354-A   Commer 3/4 ton Military Ambulance   90mm 2/1964-1966 $100-120
Red cross labels, lettering decals, blue rear windows and dome light, driver figure, otherwise as 463-A.
1. Olive drab body.

355-A   Commer 3/4 ton Military Police Van   90mm 2/1964-1965 $100-120
Blue dome light and barred rear windows, driver figure, white decals, otherwise as 464-A.
1. Olive drab body.

356-A   Volkswagen Military Personnel Carrier   90mm 2/1964-1966 $110-130
White decals, driver figure, otherwise as 434-A.
1. Olive drab body.

357-A   Land Rover Weapons Carrier   95mm 2/1964-1966 $150-160
White star decals, gray antenna, yellow interior, otherwise as 438-A.
1. Olive drab body and rear cover.

358-A   Oldsmobile 88 HQ Staff Car   105mm 2/1964-1966 $120-130
White decals, gray antenna, four figures, otherwise as 235-A.
1. Olive drab body.

359-A   Karrier Army Field Kitchen   91mm 2/1964-1966 $140-150
White decals, different cook figure, otherwise as 428-A ice cream truck.
1. Olive drab body.

Sports Cars

370-A   Ford Cobra Mustang   132mm 2/1982-Close $20-30
Main body, opening hood and hatch castings, clear windows, red interior, black SW, detailed engine, chrome headlights, red taillights, black plastic lower body, base, bumpers, tow hook, grille and vents, chrome wheels.
1. Dark yellow upper body, red and green trim.

2. White upper body, red and blue trim.

371-A   Porsche Carrera 6   97mm 5/1970-1973 $35-45
Whizzwheels, purple rear window, new base pattern without Porsche emblem, otherwise as 330-A, which has cast eight-spoke wheels.
1. White upper body, red front hood, doors, upper fins and entire base.

372-A   Lancia Fulvia Sport Zagato   91mm 9/1970-1972 $45-55
Black plastic hood and interior, black diecast base, Whizzwheels, otherwise as 332-A, which has cast wheels.
1. Bright orange body, black opening hood.

373-A   Volkswagen 1200 Police Car   90mm 9/1970-1976
                              (Polizei or Politi) $140-160
                              (Police) $55-65
Single body casting, clear windows, red interior, blue dome light, silver headlights, red taillights, suspension, diecast base, Whizzwheels. Modified 383-A casting.
1. White body, black front and rear hood panels, unpainted base and bumpers, blue and white Police labels on doors (white letters, blue background).
2. Police labels (black letters, white background), otherwise as type 1.
3. White body, unpainted base and bumpers, blue and white Politie labels and emblem decals; for sale in the Netherlands.
4. Green body, white roof, fenders, bumpers and base, white-on-black Polizei and black-on-white number 18 labels; for sale in Germany, replaced by:
5. White body, green lower sides, labels as on type 4; for sale in Germany.
6. Same as 373-A1 plus two passengers, 6 point star pattern Whizzwheels.
7. Same as 373-A2 plus two passengers.
8. Paint and decals as 492-A1, chrome base, no passengers.

373-B   Peugeot 505 STI   130mm 3/1981-1982 $20-30
Main body, lower body-base and two opening door castings, clear windows, tan interior, black SW, grille, bumpers, tow hook, vents and trim, chrome headlights, red taillights, chrome wheels. Casting also used for 450-B taxi.
1. Red body and base, black trim.

374-A   Jaguar E Type 2+2   104mm 6/1970-1976 $80-100
First version: Whizzwheels, doors do not open, black dash and exhaust pipes, otherwise as 335-A.
1. Red body and base, black interior; 1970-1972.
2. Yellow body and base, black interior; 1970-1972.
Second version: new V12 engine block, black diecast base including exhaust pipes, no mirrors, brown interior, no decal on hatch, new grille without horizontal bar.
3. Yellow body, brown interior, second version castings; 1972-1973.
4. Metallic yellow body, brown interior, second version casting; 1974-1975?
5. Metallic yellow body, brown interior, second version casting with new "V12" rear hatch casting; 1975?-1976.

375-A   Toyota 2000 GT   100mm 5/1970-1972 $80-100
Single body casting, clear windshield, cream interior, gold SW, red gear-shift and antenna, chrome bumpers and grille, jeweled headlights and (two red, two amber) taillights, suspension, black diecast base, 'Whizzwheels. Casting also used for 336-A.
1. Metallic dark blue body.
2. Metallic dark purple body.

376-A   Chevrolet Corvette Sting Ray   93mm 9/1970-1973 $40-50
Whizzwheels, new base casting, otherwise as 337-A.
1. Metallic gray body, black hood and base.

377-A   Marcos 3 Litre   88mm 6/1970-1973
                              (White & Gray) $100-110
                              (Yellow or Blue) $60-70
Main body and opening hood castings, clear windows, black interior, gold SW, detailed engine, red taillights, suspension, gray diecast base, Whizzwheels, Marcos emblem label; generally similar to 324-A.
1. Orange-yellow body, black hood stripe.
2. Metallic bluish-green body.
3. White & Gray body, other details not known.
4. Metallic ivory body, other details not known.

378-A   MGC GT   86mm 9/1970-1973 $140-150
Modified base casting, Whizzwheels, orange taillights, otherwise as 345-A.
1. Red body, black hook and base.

378-B   Ferrari 308 GTS   118mm 5/1982-Close $15-25
Main body and opening rear hood castings, clear windshield, black interior, rear vents, bumpers, grille, tow hook and base, tan seats, detailed engine, raising chrome headlights on diecast blocks same color as body, same color lever, chrome wheels. Casting also used for 298-A.
1. Red body, headlight mountings and lever, four-spoke chrome wheels.
2. Black body, headlight mountings and lever, Ferreri emblem, solid chrome wheels.

380-A   Alfa Romeo P33 Pininfarina   94mm 5/1970-1974 $40-50
Upper body and lower body-base castings, clear windshield, black interior, gold SW, light red seats and engine intakes, black bumper, fins and rear grille, clear headlight bar, red taillights, suspension, Whizzwheels.
1. Gold diecast aerofoil.
2. Black plastic? aerofoil.

380-B   BMW M1 BASF   123mm 1983-Close $20-30
Black and white BASF logo, number 80 and trim, chrome wheels, otherwise as 308-B.
1. Red body, black and white trim.

381-A   G.P. Beach Buggy   66mm 9/1970-1976 $40-50
Single body casting, clear windshield, black interior, gold SW, wire roll bar, white plastic top with two maroon surfboards, flower label, unpainted base-engine casting, suspension, Whizzwheels. Purple version of model used in GS26-A, casting modified for use as 395-A.
1. Metallic blue body.
2. Orange-red body.

381-B   Renault 5 Turbo   99mm 1983-Close $15-25
Number 5, lettering and trim tampo printed, blue and white label on windshield, otherwise as 307-B.
1. White body, red roof, red and blue trim.
2. Red lower body and bumpers, otherwise type 1.
3. Dark blue body, white interior, " ELF" trim.

382-A   Porsche Targa 911S   93mm 12/1970-1975 $50-60
Main body, lower body-base, opening rear hood and two door castings, clear windows, orange interior, gold SW, chrome engine and bumpers, jeweled headlights, light red parking lights, taillights and engine fan, suspension, Whizzwheels. Casting also modified for use as 509-A.
1. Metallic silver blue body and base, black roof with gold stripe.
2. Metallic olive green body and base, black roof with gold stripe.
3. Metallic olive green body and base, black roof, no gold stripe.

382-B Lotus Elite 2.2   120mm 1983-Close $20-30
Silver trim, no tow hook, otherwise as 315-C.
1. Dark blue body, silver trim.

383-A Volkswagen 1200   89mm 9/1970-1976

	(Red or Orange)	$50-60
	(Flowers)	$110-120
	(PTT)	$125-135
	(ADAC)	$160-180

Single body casting, clear windows, plastic interior, including SW, silver headlights, red taillights, diecast base and bumpers, Whizzwheels. Casting also used for 373-A and 384-B.
1. Red body, green base and bumpers, flower labels, white interior.
2. Red body, green base and bumpers, white interior.
3. Orange body, white base and bumpers, tan interior.
4. Orange body, black base and bumpers, tan interior.
5. Orange body, silver (or unpainted?) base and bumpers, tan interior.
6. Dark yellow body, tan interior, black base and bumpers, red-white-black PTT labels; for sale in Switzerland.
7. Dark yellow body, white roof, red dome light and interior, unpainted base and bumpers, black and white ADAC Strassenwacht and no. 1341 labels; for sale in Germany.
8. Dark yellow body, white interior, black base and bumpers, red-white-black PTT labels, 4 crown pattern Whizzwheels;for sale in Switzerland.

384-A Adams Probe 16   93mm 11/1970-1973 $50-60
Single body casting, blue canopy with sliding top, white interior, black SW, silver vents, red jeweled taillights, suspension, black diecast base, Whizzwheels.
1. Metallic maroon body.
2. Metallic lime gold body.
3. Metallic lime gold body, black-orange-white stripes.

384-B Volkswagen 1200 Rally Car   89mm 1976-1977 $60-70
White diecast base and bumpers, off-white interior, otherwise as 383-A.
1. Light blue body, red-white-black number 5 and trim labels.
2. Light blue body, "Caledonian Autominiologists 1938-1978" labels; promotional.

384-C Renault 11 GTL   108mm 1983-Close

	(Maroon)	$30-40
	(Light Tan)	$15-25

Upper body, base, two opening doors and rear hatch castings, clear windows, red interior, lifting hatch cover, folding seats, black SW, grille, lower body and lower doors, chrome headlights, red taillights, chrome wheels.
1. Light tan upper body and base.
2. Maroon upper body and base.

385-A Porsche 917   109mm 9/1970-1976 $25-35
Main body and opening rear hood castings, tinted windows and headlights, chrome engine, parts and interior, diecast base, suspension, Whizzwheels, name and number labels.
1. Red body, black base, blue tinted windows and headlights.
2. Blue body, gray base, amber tinted windows and headlights.

386-A Bertone Barchetta Runabout   81mm 2/1971-1973 $40-60
Upper body, lower body-base and rear body-airofoil castings, amber windshield, black interior, silver SW, amber headlights, red jewel taillights, red and yellow Runabouot labels, suspension, Whizzwheels.
1. Yellow body.

387-A Chevrolet Corvette Sting Ray   99mm 6/1972-1973 $80-90
Whizzwheels, black diecast base, chrome dash, emblem decal, black interior, otherwise as 300-B, which has Golden Jacks.
1. Metallic dark blue body, black hood.
2. Metallic rose red body, black hood.

388-A Mercedes-Benz C111   102mm 1/1971-1974 $40-50
Main body, lower body-base and two opening gullwing door castings, clear windows, silver SW, black interior, vents, front and rear grilles, silver headlights, red taillights, Mercedes emblem label, suspension, Whizzwheels.
1. Orange main body, black lower body and base.

389-A Reliant Bond Bug 700 E.S.   64mm 4/1971-1974

	(Lime Green)	$100-120
	(Orange)	$55-65

Main body and raising upper body castings, clear windows, off-white seats, black SW and trim, silver headlights, red taillights, orange and black name labels, black diecast base, suspension, chrome top latch and lever, three Whizzwheels.
1. Bright orange body.
2. Lime green body.

391-A James Bond Ford Mustang Mach 1   110mm 3/1972-1973 $210-230
Black hood and grille, otherwise as 329-A.
1. Red body, black hood, white lower body and base.

392-A Bertone 'Shake' Buggy   88mm 7/1972-1974 $40-50
Upper body and lower body-base castings, clear windshield, green interior, chrome dash, SW, handrails, roll bar, lights and bumpers, gold engine, hood and side labels, suspension, knobby tires.
1. Yellow upper body, white lower body and base, spoked chrome wheels.
2. Solid chrome wheels, otherwise as type 1.
3. Metallic rose red upper body, white lower body and base, spoked chrome wheels.
4. Solid chrome wheels, otherwise as type 3.

393-A Mercedes-Benz 350SL   99mm 1/1972-1979

	(Green)	$100-110
	(White)	$70-80
	(Blue)	$45-55

Main body, opening hood and two door castings, clear windows with chrome frames, pale blue interior, folding seats, gold SW, detailed engine, chrome grille, bumpers and exhaust pipes, amber and orange lights, black diecast base, suspension, chrome wheels (two types).
1. White body, spoked Whizzwheels.
2. Metallic dark blue body, spoked Whizzwheels.
3. Metallic dark blue body, Whizzwheels with solid silver center.
4. Metallic green body, Whizzwheels (type?).

394-A Datsun 240Z   92mm 10/1972-1976 $45-55
Main body and two opening door castings, clear windows, white interior, gold SW, orange roll bar and spare tire rack, chrome bumpers, jeweled headlights, orange taillights, suspension, black diecast base, chrome spoked wheels. Casting also used for 396-A.
1. Red body, number 11, Japan and Castrol labels.
2. Red body, number 11, Japan, Castrol and East Africa Rally labels.
3. Same as 394-A1 except with four lights on front bumper as on 396-A, (known factory mix-up of parts).

395-A Fire Bug   79mm 1/1972-1973 $40-50
Single body casting, clear windshield, black interior, gold SW, chrome roll bar with blue dome lights, yellow ladders, gray tow hook, unpainted diecast engine and base, flame and name labels, suspension, Whizzwheels. Same casting as 381-A.
1. Orange body.

396-A Datsun 240Z   92mm 5/1973-1976 $45-55
Chrome bumper with four lights, white diecast base, number 46, lettering and trim labels, otherwise as 394-A.
1. White body, red hood and roof.
2. Same as 396-A1 except without four lights on front bumper as on 394-A, (known factory mix-up of parts).

397-A Porsche Audi 917   123mm 9/1973-1978 $25-35
Single body casting, gold interior, black dash and SW, driver figure, gold parts and wheels, black plastic base, number 6 and other labels. Casting also used for 262-B.
White body, red and black number 6, L & M, Porsche Audi and stripe labels.
1. Orange body, orange-two tone green-white number 6, Corgi and stripe labels.

Carry Case

400-X Corgi Carry Case   1967-1969 $???
Blue blow molded carry case about the size of a briefcase, blue cardboard divider, black plastic handles. Offered only in U.S. market by importer of Corgi Toys, Reeves International Inc.

Light Commercial

400-A Volkswagen 1200 Driving School Car   89mm 4/1974-1975

	(Red)	$120-130
	(Blue)	$55-65
	(German)	$150-160

Single body casting, clear windows, yellow interior, gold roof-mounted steering wheel steers front wheels, silver headlights, red taillights, unpainted diecast base, bumpers and L plated with decals, gold eight-spoke cast wheels, plastic tires. Modified body and interior of 383-A, different base casting. Same casting used for 401-A. Model does not have traffic cones.
1. Metallic red body, "Motor School" labels.
2. Metallic blue body, "Motor School" labels.
3. Metallic blue body, "Fahr-Schule" labels, (for German market).

401-A Volkswagen 1200 Driving School Car   89mm 7/1975-1977

	(Blue)	$55-65
	(German)	$150-160

Exactly as 400-A with addition of twenty-four traffic cones in box.
1. Metallic blue body, " Motor School" labels.
2. Metallic blue body, " Fahr-Schule" labels, (for German market).

402-A Ford Cortina GXL Police Car   102mm 8/1972-1976

	(Polizei)	$140-160
	(Police)	$50-60

Main body, roof sign and two opening door castings, clear windows, red interior, folding seats, gold SW, blue dome light, chrome bumpers, black grille, jeweled headlights, red taillights, suspension, black diecast base with siren, Whizzwheels. Modified 313-A casting.
1. White body, red and black stripe labels. "POLICE."
2. White body, pink and black stripe labels, "POLICE."
3. White body, ? stripe labels, "POLIZEI."

403-A Bedford 12 CWT Van   81mm 7/1956-1959 $130-140
Single body casting, clear windows, silver grille and headlights, sheet metal base, smooth wheels, rubber tires, logo decals. First type casting with divided windshield, also used for 403M-A and early 408-A.
1. Dark blue body, white Daily Express newspaper logo decals.

403M-A Bedford 12 CWT Van (Mechanical)   81mm 7/1956-1959 $220-240
Black diecast base, flywheel motor, otherwise as 403-A.
1. Dark blue body, white Daily Express newspaper logo decals.
2. Bright red body, black and yellow K.L.G. Spark Plugs logo decals.

403-B Thwaites Tusker Skip Dumper   80mm 7/1974-1979 $40-50
Body, chassis and tipper castings, black plastic engine and SW, driver and seat, hydraulic cylinder, red wheels, black tires (two sizes), name labels.
1. Yellow body, chassis and tipper.
2. Model may at first have had a green engine.

404-A Bedford Dormobile   81mm 8/1956-1962

	(Yellow or Blue/Blue)	$200-220
	(Blue/Yellow)	$125-135
	(other colors)	$95-105

Single body casting, clear windows, silver grille and headlights, sheet metal base, rubber tires. First (divided windshield) or second (single windshield) casting also used for 404M-A, 405-A, 405M-A, 412-A, 414-A and 423-A.
1. Metallic maroon body, divided windshield, smooth wheels; 1956-1959.
2. Cream body, divided windshield, smooth wheels.
3. Turquoise green body, divided windshield, smooth wheels.
4. Medium gray-blue body, divided windshield, smooth wheels.
5. Light yellow body, light blue roof, single windshield, smooth wheels: 1960-1961.
6. Light yellow body, light blue roof, single windshield, shaped wheels; 1962.
7. Two-tone blue body, other details not known.
8. Yellow body, other details not known.

404M-A Bedford Dormobile (Mechanical)   81mm 7/1956-1959 $150-170
Black diecast base, flywheel motor, otherwise as 404-A.
1. Turquoise body.
2. Metallic dark red body.

405-A Bedford Fire Tender   81mm 7/1956-1961

	(Green)	$150-170
	(Red)	$200-220

Dormobile casting with divided windshield, roof rack with two ladders and logo decals, otherwise as 404-A. Replaced by 423-A, with second type casting.
1. Green body, red AFS shield decals.
2. Red body, gold and black "Fire Dept" and small shield decals.
3. Black body, red AFS shield decals, (possibly pre-production model).

405M-A Bedford Fire Tender (Mechanical)   81mm 8/1956-1959 $220-240
Black diecast base, flywheel motor, otherwise as 405-A.
1. Red body, gold and black "Fire Dept" and small shield decals.

405-B Chevrolet-Superior 61 Ambulance   120mm 7/1978-1980 $30-40
Main body, roof and two opening rear door castings, clear windows, red interior, black SW, chrome and

red roof lights, silver bumpers, grille and headlights, orange taillights, red cross and lettering labels, black plastic base, chrome four-spoke wheels, patient on stretcher and attendant figures.
1. White body, orange roof, hood and stripes.

405-C Ford Transit Milk Float 141mm 1/1982-Close $20-30

Single front body casting, clear windows, tan interior, black SW, white plastic rear body, opening compartment door and milk cases, black grille, white and orange lights, black diecast base and bumper, chrome wheels, blue and white labels.
1. White body, blue roof and hood.

406-A Land Rover Pickup 96mm 8/1957-1962
(Without Suspension) $70-80
(Yellow with Suspension) $500++

Single body casting clear windows, silver bumper, grille and headlights, spare wheel on hood, sheet metal base and tow hook, rubber tires. Earlier casting, with front bumper attached by four struts; widely used, replaced by 438-A (new casting) with plastic rear cover.
1. Yellow body, black roof, smooth wheels crimped on axles, thin rubber tires.
2. Metallic dark blue body, cream roof, smooth wheels crimped on axles, thin rubber tires.
3. Same as 406-A2 except thicker rubber tires.
4. Same as 406-A3 except shaped wheels crimped on axles;1962.
5. Medium green body, tan tin cover over rear, smooth wheels crimped on axles, thin rubber tires;GS2-A.
6. Same as 406-A5 except thicker rubber tires;GS2-A.
7. Same as 406-A7 except shaped wheels crimped on axles;GS2-A, 1962.
8. (406S) Newer Casting with Suspension, Yellow Body including roof, Red Seats with Silver Steering Wheel, Shaped Wheels, Rubber Tires, No Canopy, 406S box with illustration as described.

406-B Mercedes-Benz Unimog 406 90mm/95mm 7/1970-1976 $50-60

First version: body, front fenders-bumper and chassis castings, clear windows, red interior, gray SW, black plastic mirrors, plastic rear cover, gray tow hook, unpainted axles and drive trains., red diecast wheels, black plastic tires, suspension, spare wheel: 90mm long.
1. Yellow body, red front fenders and bumper, metallic charcoal gray chassis, olive rear cover; 1970-1973.
2. Tan rear cover, otherwise as type 1; 1974-1975.
Second version: body and chassis castings, white SW, no mirrors, tan plastic rear cover, black plastic base and tow hook, otherwise as first version.
3. Metallic olive body, yellow chassis, tan rear cover; 7/1975-1976.

406-C Mercedes-Benz Bonna Ambulance 145mm 10/1980-1981 $20-30

Main body, lower body-base, opening rear door and two door castings, blue windows and dome lights, white interior, black SW, chrome bumpers, grille and headlights, chrome wheels (two types), labels, patient on stretcher and two attendants.
1. White body and base, red stripes and taillights, red cross and black and white Ambulance labels, four-spoke wheels.
2. White and red body, white base, solid wheels, red and white Falck labels; made for sale in Denmark.
3. Yellow body and base, red cross and stripe, black and white lettering: Corgi catalog number 4061, 1983
4. Same as 406-C1 except solid wheels.

407-A Karrier Mobile Grocery 92mm 9/1957-1961 $140-160

Single body casting, clear windows, grocery store decor inside, red and white decals, silver bumpers and headlights, gray diecast base with rear axle bulge, smooth wheels, rubber tires. Casting also used for 413-A, 426-A, and modified for 359-A and 428-A.
1. Pale green body, Home Services and Hygienic Mobile Shop decals.

407-B Mercedes-Benz Bonna Ambulance 145mm 5/1981-1981 $20-30

Same castings and details as 406-C; no figures.
1. Colors as 406-C1.

408-A Bedford A.A. Road Service Van 91mm 6/1957-1962 $110-140

Main body and roof sign castings, clear windows, A.A. Road Service decals, silver bumper and headlights, sheet metal base, rubber tires. Two casting types, modified first and second type 403-A/421-A castings.
1. Dark yellow body, black roof and nose, divided windshield, smooth wheels; 1957-1959.
2. Dark yellow body, black roof and nose, single windshield, smooth wheels; 1960-1962.

409-A Jeep FC-150 Pickup 90mm 4/1959-1965 $40-50

Body and base castings, clear windows, dark red grille, silver headlights and bumper, sheet metal tow hook, rubber tires. Casting also used for 470-A and 478-A.
1. Light blue body and base, smooth wheels.
2. Light blue body and base, shaped wheels.

409-B Mercedes-Benz Unimog 406 94mm 9/1971-1973 $45-55
Dump Truck 100mm 2/1976-1977 $45-55

First version: cab, tipper, front fenders-bumper and chassis castings, clear windows, red interior, gray SW, black mirrors, gray tow hook, unpainted hydraulic cylinder, axles and drive train castings; red diecast wheels, black plastic tires, spare wheel, suspension; 94mm.
1. Blue cab, yellow tipper, fenders and bumper, metallic charcoal gray chassis; 1971-1973.
Second version: Cab, chassis, rear frame and tipper castings, silver headlights and emblem, white SW, no mirrors, black plastic base and tow hook, unpainted cast wheels, otherwise as first version; 100mm.
2. Yellow cab, chassis and rear frame, blue tipper; 1976-1977.
3. Yellow cab and rear frame, blue tipper and chassis?

409-C Allis-Chalmers ACF 60 Fork Lift 112mm 5/1981-Close $25-35

Body, base and engine cover castings, black SW and foot pedals, driver and seat, yellow fork and roll cage, red gear, plastic wheels (two sizes), large wheels have red painted hubs, red and black AC and stripe labels, tan pallets, light red containers. Made in Singapore.
1. Dark yellow body and base, white engine cover.
2. Details not known, numbered 4091. Made in Hong Kong?

411-A Karrier Bantam Lucozade Van 102mm 8/1958-1962 $150-160

Single body casting, clear windows, gray overhead door, Lucozade labels, silver bumper and headlights, black diecast base, rubber tires. Casting also used for 435-A.
1. Yellow body, smooth wheels.
2. Yellow body, shaped wheels.

411-B Mercedes-Benz 240D Taxi 125mm 8/1975-1980 $35-45

Black roof sign with red and white Taxi labels, black Taxi labels on doors, brown interior, no tow hook, otherwise as 285-A.
1. Bright orange body and base, black roof.
2. No. 4111 German issue; Cream body and base, black "TAXI" on doors.
3. No. 4113 Scandinavian issue; Black body and base, white "TAXI" on doors.

412-A Bedford Utilecon Ambulance 81mm 11/1957-1960
(Type 1, Split Windshield) $120-130
(Type 2, 1 pc. Windshield) $225-250

Clear front and gray rear windows, Ambulance decals, otherwise as 404-A.
1. Cream body, red-white-navy blue decals, divided windshield first casting, smooth wheels.
2. Same as 412-A1 except second casting with single windshield, smooth wheels.

412-B Mercedes-Benz 240D Police Car 125mm 7/1975-1980
(Police) $45-55
(Polizei) $30-40

Blue dome light, brown interior, lettering labels, otherwise as 285-A.
1. White body, green hood, trunk and doors, white Polizei lettering.
2. White body, black hood, trunk and doors, white Police lettering; Corgi catalog number 4123.
3. White body, black hood, trunk and doors, white Polizei lettering; Corgi catalog number 4124.

413-A Karrier Mobile Butcher Shop 92mm 4/1960-1964
(No Suspension) $130-140
(Suspension) $190-200

Butcher shop decor inside, otherwise as 407-A.
1. White body, light blue roof, Home Services and Hygienic Mobile Shop decals, smooth wheels crimped on axles.
2. Suspension, wheel type uncertain, otherwise as type 1; Corgi catalog number 413S, 1963-1964.

413-B Mazda B1600 Motorway Maint. Truck 155mm 1/1976-1978 $45-55

Main body, rack, tailgate, swiveling base and two arm castings, clear windows, black interior, grille, bumper, tow hook, hydraulic cylinder and base, yellow basket with figure, silver headlights, black stripe and lettering labels, chrome wheels. Modified 493-A casting.
1. Dark yellow body, red base and unpainted arms of elevating platform.

414-A Bedford Dormobile Military Ambulance 81mm 1/1961-1964 $80-110

Clear front and white rear windows, red cross decals, second type body casting, otherwise as 412-A.
1. Olive drab body, no suspension, smooth wheels.
2. Olive drab body, no suspension, smooth wheels.
3. Olive drab body, suspension, shaped wheels.

414-B Coast Guard Jaguar XJ12C 136mm 12/1975-1977 $40-50

Chrome roof bar with blue dome light, red-white-blue Coast Guard lettering labels, tan interior, otherwise as 286-A.
1. White body and base, blue stripe on each side of car.

415-A Mazda B1600 Pickup with Camper 138mm 6/1976-1978 $40-50

White camper casting, red interior and opening door, black folding supports, camper locks onto pickup which has no tailgate, otherwise as 493-A.
1. Red truck, white camper.

416-A R.A.C. Land Rover 96mm 8/1959-1964
(R.A.C. Land Rover No Suspension)
$100-110
(TS Radio Land Rover No Suspension)
$400-420
(R.A.C. Land Rover with Suspension)
$110-120
(TS Radio Land Rover with Suspension)
$420-440

First version: sheet metal rear cover, gray antenna, white RAC and Radio Rescue decals, otherwise as 406-A; 1959-1961.
1. Blue body without suspension, cast sign on cab roof "RADIO RESCUE," R.A.C. logo on rear cover, smooth wheels crimped on axles.
2. Blue body without suspension, no cab roof sign, "RADIO (R.A.C. logo) RESCUE" on rear cover, shaped wheels crimped on axles.
3. Same as 416-A2 except shaped wheels free on axles.
4. Yellow body, olive rear cover, open bumper, no suspension, TS Radio decals; made for sale in Belgium.
Second version: white RAC and Radio Rescue decals, gray antenna, yellow interior, gray SW, otherwise as 438-A; 1962-1964.
5. Blue body and plastic rear cover, solid bumper, Corgi catalog number 416S.
6. Yellow body, olive rear cover, solid bumper, suspension, TS Radio decals; made for sale in Belgium.

416-B Buick Police Car 150mm 4/1977-1978 $35-45

Chrome roof bar with red dome lights, white Police and stripe labels, orange taillights, chrome four-spoke wheels, otherwise as 290-A.
1. Metallic blue body, white stripes.

417-A Land Rover Breakdown Truck 110m 7/1960-1965
(No Suspension) $100-120
(Suspension) $80-90

Main body and towing boom castings, clear windows, sheet metal rear canopy, silver revolving spotlight, hook, bumper, grille and headlights, Breakdown Service decals, rubber tires, spare tire turns winch. Two casting types.
First casting type based on 406-A:
1. Red body, silver boom casting open in center, no interior, four strut front bumper, no suspension, smooth wheels crimped on axles, small rubber tires, yellow canopy with silver spotlight.
2. Same as 417-A1 except smooth wheels crimped on axles, large rubber tires.
3. Same as 417-A1 except shaped wheels crimped on axles, large rubber tires.
Second casting type based on 438-A:
4. Red body, silver boom casting solid in center, yellow interior, solid front bumper, suspension, shaped wheels free on axles, large rubber tires, yellow canopy with silver spotlight;Corgi catalog number 417S, 1962-1965. (Note. Replaced by nearly identical 477-A which has plastic canopy.)

418-A Austin London Taxi 97mm 10/1960-1963, 6/1971-1974
available in GS35-A: 7/1964-1969
available in GS11-B: 9/1971-1974
(Smooth, shaped wheels) $85-100
(Whizzwheels) $40-50

Single body casting used throughout production life without change, vacuum formed interior, gray diecast base, suspension.
1. Black body, yellow interior, gray SW, clear windows, no driver, smooth wheels crimped on axles, rubber tires.
2. Black body, yellow interior, gray SW, clear windows, no driver, shaped wheels crimped on axles, rubber tires.
3. Black body, yellow interior, gray SW, clear windows, " young" driver, shaped wheels free on axles, rubber tires;GS35-A.
4. Same as 418-A3 except "old" driver.
5. Black body, revised base casting to accept Whizzwheels, yellow seats, ? SW, no driver, Whizzwheels (4 crown pattern), clear windows.
6. Same as 418-A5 except black SW, blue tinted windows, red seats;GS11-B.
7. Metallic dark maroon body, red seats, modified Whizzwheel type base, gray SW, no driver, clear windows, Whizzwheels (4 crown pattern).
8. May exist like 418-A7 but with yellow seats.

419-A Ford Zephyr Motorway Patrol Car 95mm 8/1960-1965
(Police) $90-100
(Politie) $275-300
(Rijkspolitie) $325-350
Blue dome light, dark blue police decals, gray antenna, otherwise as 424-A.
1. White body, " Police" decals, smooth wheels crimped on axles.
2. White body, " Police" decals, shaped wheels crimped on axles.
3. White body, " Police" decals, shaped wheels free on axles.
4. Cream body, " Police" decals, ? wheels.
5. White body, " Rijkspolitie" decals, ? wheels, (for sale in the Netherlands).
6. White body, " Politie" decals, ? wheels, (for sale in the Netherlands).

419-B Jeep CJ-5 99mm 12/1977-1979 $30-40
Single body casting, removable white plastic top, clear windshield, black dash, SW, seat, tow hook, bumper and base, white plastic wheels, black tires, spare wheel. Reissued as 441-B, used in numerous gift sets.
1. Metallic dark green body, white top.

420-A Ford Thames Airborne Caravan 95mm 2/1962-1967 $85-95
Main body and two opening door castings, clear windows, white blinds, plastic interior with table, silver bumpers, grille and headlights, gray SW, suspension, gray diecast base, all versions except 420-A1 have shaped wheels free on axles, rubber tires.
1. Greenish off-white upper and olive green lower body, tan interior, yellow table and rear floor, shaped wheels crimped on axles.
2. Pale lilac upper and dark plum lower body, yellow interior, tan table and floor.
3. Bluish off-white upper and dark blue lower body, yellow interior, tan table and floor.
4. Same as 420-A3 except ivory interior with red table.
5. Light gray upper and blue lower body?
6. Yellow-green entire body?

421-A Bedford Evening Standard Van 81mm 5/1960-1962 $180-220
Single body casting, clear windows, single windshield, silver bumper, grille and headlights, sheet metal base, smooth wheels, rubber tires. Second Bedford casting.
1. Black body, silver roof, red-white-black Evening Standard newspaper decals and labels.
2. Black lower body, silver roof and upper body, labels and decals as on type 1.
3. May exist with shaped wheels crimped on axles.

421-B Land Rover 109WB 132mm 6/1977-1979 $30-40
Main body and opening rear door castings, clear windows, tan interior, black SW, plastic roof rack and ladder, black diecast base and bumper, black plastic tow hook, silver grille and headlights, spare wheel on hood, suspension, chrome wheels. Used in many gift sets; shown in catalog in Alpine Tours livery but not so issued.
1. Orange body, black roof rack and ladder, no labels; 1977.
2. Red body, white roof rack and ladder, Forest Fire Warden labels; 1978-1979.
3. White body, red roof, black ladder and rack, " Formula 1 Racing Team" trim, (St. Michael sets 8100, 8400).
4. Silver body, black ladder and rack, " Wings Flying Club" trim, (St. Michael sets 8101, 8401).
5. White body, orange roof, black ladder and rack, " Police Accident Unit" trim, (St. Michael set 8402).

422-A Bedford Corgi Toys Van 81mm 6/1960-1962
(Yellow with Blue Roof) $180-200
(Blue with Yellow Roof) $300-350
Second Bedford casting, "Corgi Toys" decals on sides, other details as 421-A.
1. Yellow upper & blue lower body, smooth wheels crimped on axles.
2. Blue body, yellow roof, smooth wheels crimped on axles.
3. Yellow body, blue roof, smooth wheels crimped on axles.
4. Yellow body, blue roof, shaped wheels crimped on axles.

422-B Riot Police Quad Tractor 96mm 9/1977-1980 $40-50
Main body, chassis and two-piece water cannon castings, clear windows, brown interior, black SW, gold water cannons, gold spotlight with amber lens, black headlights, white roof panel, red labels, red plastic wheels, plastic tires. Same casting as gun tractor of 909-A.
1. White body and chassis, red roof.

423-A Bedford Fire Tender 81mm 5/1960-1962 $40-50
Second type Dormobile casting with single windshield, other details as 405-A.
1. Red body, gold and black Fire Dept. and shield decals, smooth wheels, black ladders.
2. Red body, gold and black Fire Dept. and shield decals, shaped wheels, black ladders.
3. Red body, gold and black Fire Dept. and shield decals, shaped wheels, unpainted ladders.

423-B Chevrolet Rough Rider Van 118mm 12/1977-1978 $40-50
Main body and two opening rear door castings, amber windows, cream interior, black SW, cardboard furnishings, silver bumpers, grille and headlights, red taillights, Rough Rider labels, black plastic base, four-spoke chrome wheels. Casting used or modified for numerous other Chevrolet van models.
1. Bright yellow body.
2. Details not known, (St. Michael set 8800).

424-A Ford Zephyr Estate Car 97mm 1/1961-1965 $75-85
Single body casting, clear windows, red interior, gray SW, silver bumpers, grille and headlights, red taillights, suspension, gray diecast base, rubber tires. Casting also used for 419-A.
1. Light blue body, dark blue hood and stripe, red interior, smooth wheels crimped on axles.
2. Same as 424-A1 except shaped wheels crimped on axles.
3. Same as 424-A2 except yellow seats.
4. A version with shaped wheels free on axles may exist.

424-B Security Van 100mm 12/1976-1979 $25-35
Single body casting, blue windows and dome lights, white bars and bumper, yellow diecast base and bumpers, yellow and black Security labels, Whizzwheels. Adapted from 700-A Motorway Ambulance.
1. Black body.

425-A Austin London Taxi 118mm 2/1978-Close $20-30
Main body and two opening door castings, clear windows, light brown interior, black SW, chrome grille and bumpers, silver headlights, orange taillights, yellow roof light, silver diecast base, chrome wheels. Larger scale than 418-A.
1. Black body.

426-A Karrier Circus Booking Office 92mm 1/1962-1964 $250-300+
Single body casting, clear windows, circus decals and posters, silver bumpers and headlights, gray diecast base, suspension, shaped wheels, rubber tires. Same casting as 407-A and 413-A.
1. Red body, light blue roof.

426-B Chevrolet Circus Booking Office 118mm 9/1978-1981 $40-50
Main body and red roof rack castings, clear windows, brown interior, black SW, blue loudspeakers, red opening rear door, lowering stairs and box office, chrome bumpers, grille and headlights, orange taillights, black plastic base, chrome wheels, Pinder-Jean Richard labels. Modified 423-B casting.
1. Yellow body, red roof and rear.

428-A Karrier Ice Cream Truck 91mm 3/1963-1966 $200-225
Single body casting, clear windows, pale blue interior, rotating figure turned by knob on base, sliding side windows, silver bumpers, grille and refrigerator panels, Mister Softee decals, red cone at front, suspension, gray diecast base, shaped wheels, rubber tires. Casting also used for 359-A.
1. Cream upper and light blue lower body.

428-B Renault 5 Police Car 97mm 2/1978-1979 $20-30
Blue dome light, white Police labels on door, red interior, orange taillights, six-spoke chrome wheels, otherwise as 293-A.
1. White body, black hood, hatch and doors.

429-A Jaguar XJ12C Police Car 130mm 2/1978-1980 $35-45
Roof bar casting with blue dome light, pink and light blue stripes, Police labels, gray antenna, tan interior, orange taillights, chrome four-spoke wheels, otherwise as 286-A.
1. White body, pink and light blue stripes.
2. White body, orange side stripe with black "POLICE," yellow and black hood trim, (St. Michael sets 8002, 8102, 8402).

430-A Ford Thunderbird Bermuda Taxi 102mm 7/1962-1965
(White or Cream) $100-120
Plastic canopy, yellow and black labels, yellow interior, driver figure, otherwise as 215-A.
1. White body, blue canopy with red fringe.
2. Cream body, blue canopy with red fringe.
3. Cream body, yellow canopy with red fringe.
4. Cream body, green canopy with red fringe.
4. Metallic blue body (?), other details not known.

430-B Porsche 924 Police Car 116mm 11/1978-1980 $25-35
Blue and chrome dome light, chrome four-spoke wheels, otherwise as 321-B.
1. White body, light green hood and doors, Polizei lettering in white on green panels.
2. White body, black hood and doors, Police labels in white on black panels; Corgi catalog number 4303.

431-A Volkswagen Pickup 90mm 3/1964-1966
(Yellow with Red Cover) $90-100
(Others) $300++
Single body casting, clear windows, red interior, gray SW, plastic rear cover, silver bumpers and headlights, red VW emblem, suspension, gray diecast base, shaped wheels, rubber tires.
1. Dark yellow body, red cover.
2. Dark yellow body, dark olive cover.
2. Gold body (?), other details not known.

431-B Chevrolet Vanatic Custom Van 116mm 12/1977-1980 $25-35
Vanatic labels, otherwise as 423-B.
1. Off-white body.

432-A Chevrolet Vantastic Custom Van 116mm 12/1977-1980 $25-35
Vantastic labels, otherwise as 423-B.
1. Black body.

433-A Volkswagen Delivery Van 87mm 12/1962-1964 $90-100
Single body casting, clear windows, plastic interior, gray SW, silver bumpers and headlights, red VW emblem, suspension, gray diecast base, shaped wheels, rubber tires.
1. White upper and red lower body, red interior.
2. White upper and red lower body, yellow interior.
3. Gray body, ? interior, Vroom and Dreesmann logo; Netherlands promotional.

433-B Chevrolet Van-ishing Point NOT ISSUED N/A
Listed in 1978 Corgi catalog; Never issued.

434-A Volkswagen Kombi Bus 98mm 12/1962-1966 $90-100
Single body casting, clear windows, red interior, gray SW, silver bumpers and headlights, red VW emblem, suspension, gray diecast base, shaped wheels, rubber tires. Casting also used for 356-A.
1. Greenish off-white upper and olive green lower body.

434-B Chevrolet Charlie's Angels Van 116mm 12/1977-1980 $55-65
Charlie's Angels logo, otherwise as 423-B.
1. Pinkish lilac body, solid chrome wheels.
2. Pinkish lilac body, four-spoke chrome wheels.

435-A Karrier Dairy Produce Van 102mm 5/1962-1964 $120-140
Yellow plastic overhead door, "Drive safely on milk" decals, otherwise as 411-A.
1. Light blue body, white roof, no interior or suspension, smooth wheels crimped on axles.
2. Same as 435-A1 except shaped wheels crimped on axles.
3. Light blue body, white roof, red interior, suspension, shaped wheels crimped on axles.

435-B Supervan 116mm 7/1978-1981 $45-55
Super Van labels with picture of Superman, otherwise as 423-B.
1. Silver body.

436-A Citroen ID19 Safari 101mm 4/1963-1965 $95-105
Main body, opening rear hatch and unpainted tailgate castings, clear windows, light brown and light green interior, two figures, adjustable rear seat back, silver bumper, grille and headlights, plastic luggage on roof rack, Wildlife Preservation decal, brown seat adjusting gear, suspension, gray diecast base, shaped wheels, rubber tires.
1. Orange body, red and light green luggage, red luggage to the back.
2. Orange body, red and light brown luggage, red luggage to the front.
(Other luggage variations may well be possible.)

436-B Chevrolet Spider-Van 116mm 6/1978-1980 $50-60
Spider-Van labels, otherwise as 423-B.
1. Dark blue body, solid wheels.
2. Dark blue body, four-spoke wheels.

437-A Cadillac Superior Ambulance 112mm 9/1962-1968 $90-100
Single body casting, clear front and blue rear windows, brown interior, red dome light, silver bumpers, grille and headlights, suspension, gray diecast base with red plastic battery cover.
First type casting:
Steady burning bulb flashes by actuation of cam on rear axle when rolling, ON/OFF switch on red battery housing.
1. Red lower and cream upper body, orange taillights, " Ambulance" decals on rear side windows, amber bullet shaped corner lamp lenses, shaped wheels crimped on axles, rubber tires;1962-1963.
2. Same as 437-A1 except clear beveled corner lamp lenses;1964-1965.
Second type casting:
Flashing bulb mounted higher in body, base modified to eliminate cam. different ON/OFF switch on modified battery housing.
3. White lower and light blue upper body, red taillights, larger "Ambulance" decals on body sides, red cross decal on hood, beveled corner lamp lenses, shaped wheels free on axles, rubber tires;1966.
4. Same as 437-A3 except cast wheels, rubber tires;1967-1968.
5. Same as 437-A3 except cast wheels, plastic tires;1968-1969.
6, Metallic silver lower and dark metallic red upper body, otherwise as 437-A5;1969.

437-B Chevrolet Coca-Cola Van 116mm 6/1978-1980 $40-50
Red and white Coca-Cola logo, otherwise as 423-B.
1. Red body, white trim.

438-A 109" Land Rover with Canopy 96mm 4/1963-1977
(Shaped Wheels) $100-110
(Whizzwheels) $55-65
(Lepra) $350-375

Single body casting, clear windows, plastic interior, gray SW except where noted, plastic rear cover, silver bumper, grille, and headlights, spare wheel on hood, suspension, gray diecast base, sheet metal or plastic tow hook; second Land Rover casting with solid bumper.
1. Dark green body, gray cover, shaped wheels, rubber tires, yellow interior.
2. Dark green body, light tan cover, shaped wheels, rubber tires, yellow interior.
3. Dark tan body, light tan cover, shaped wheels, rubber tires, red interior. (from GS2-A).
4. Metallic green body, gray cover, shaped wheels, rubber tires, yellow interior.
5. Red body, tan cover, shaped wheels, rubber tires, yellow interior. (from GS17-A).
6. Metallic green, dark olive cover, other details not known.
7. Metallic green body, light olive cover, yellow interior, plastic tow hook, shaped wheels, plastic tires.
8. Metallic green body, olive cover, chrome wheels, plastic tow hook.
9. Metallic green body, olive canopy, Whizzwheels, plastic tow hook.
10. Same as 438-A9 except SW now part of revised yellow interior.
11. Metallic green body, orange canopy, Whizzwheels, plastic tow hook.
12. Metallic green body, tan canopy with red "LEPRA" on sides, yellow seats with silver SW, shaped wheels, rubber tires.
13. Dark non-metallic green, no rear cover, yellow interior, metal tow hook, shaped wheels, rubber tires; (from GS22-A).
14. Dark metallic green, no rear cover, yellow interior, plastic tow hook, cast wheels, plastic tires; (from GS5-B).
15. Red body, light blue cover, yellow interior, metal tow hook, shaped wheels, rubber tires; (from GS19-A).
16. Tan body, gray rear cover, yellow interior, Whizzwheels.
(Other variations may exist.)

439-A Chevrolet Impala Fire Chief's Car 104mm 1/1963-1965 $100-120
Dome light, gray antenna, white Fire Chief decal on hood, yellow interior, shaped wheels, two figures, otherwise as 220-A.
1. Red body, four white doors, round shield labels.
2. Red body, white labels cover two doors.
3. Red body, round shield labels on red doors.

440-A Ford Consul Cortina Estate Car 92mm 1/1966-1968 $130-140
Main body, lower body-base and opening hatch castings, clear windows, cream interior, cream and brown plastic body inserts, chrome bumpers and grille, jeweled headlights, red taillights, suspension, diecast base, shaped wheels, rubber tires, figures of golfer and caddy, golf bag on wheels. Casting also used for 491-A.
1. Metallic dark blue body and base, brown and cream panels simulate wood.

440-B Mazda B1600 Custom Pickup 123mm 6/1979-1980 $25-35
Same casting and details as 493-A.
1. Orange body, unpainted rack, red roof and strip of rear bed.

441-A Volkswagen Tobler Van 90mm 2/1963-1967 $100-125
Trans-o-lite headlights and roof panel, "Chocolat Tobler" decals, yellow interior, white VW emblem, otherwise as 433-A. Casting modified to take Trans-o-lite.
1. Light blue body.

441-B Golden Eagle Jeep 97mm 6/1979-1982 $20-30
Tan plastic top, chrome plastic base, bumpers and steps, chrome wheels, otherwise as 419-B. Also used in numerous gift sets in various colors.
1. Metallic golden orange body, red taillights, no label on roof.
2. Metallic brown body, Golden Eagle label on roof, orange taillights.
3. Metallic copper body, Golden Eagle label on roof, headlights and taillights same color as body.
4. Same as 441-B2 except wheel centers white.
(Note: the ROOF label says "Golden Eagle." ALL versions have an eagle figure label on the HOOD.)

443-A Plymouth Suburban U.S. Mail Car 105mm 8/1963-1966 $110-120
Red trim, U.S.Mail and other decals, Zip Code ad label on doors, gray diecast base, suspension, shaped wheels, otherwise as 219-A.
1. White upper and blue lower body, red stripes.

445-A Plymouth Sports Suburban 105mm 4/1963-1965 $90-100
Yellow interior, suspension, gray diecast base, shaped wheels, otherwise as 219-A.
1. Pale blue body, red roof, silver trim.

447-A Ford Thames Wall's Ice Cream Van 86mm 3/1965-1967 $250-300
Main body and rear pillar castings, clear windows, white interior, plastic rear canopy and sliding windows, advertising figure on roof, silver bumpers, grille and headlights, red taillights, Wall's Ice Cream decals, suspension, gray diecast base, shaped wheels, rubber tires. Casting modified and re-issued as 474-A.
1. Light blue body, dark cream pillars, striped canopy, two figures.

447-B Renegade Jeep 99mm 1983 -Close $15-25
White interior, base and bumper, no top, white plastic wheels and rear-mounted spare, Renegade, number 5 and stripe labels, otherwise as 441-B.
1. Dark blue body.

448-A Austin Police Minivan 80mm 10/1964-1969 $150-160
Main body and two opening door castings, clear windows, red interior, silver front bumper, gray antenna, jeweled headlights, red taillights, white Police decals, suspension, gray diecast base. Same casting as 450-A except bars added in rear door windows, navy blue body, policeman and dog figures.
1. Shaped wheels, rubber tires.
2. Cast wheels, rubber tires.
3. Cast wheels, plastic tires.
4. Same as 448-A1 except countryman base casting (known factory mix-up).

448-B Renegade Jeep with Hood 99mm 1983-Close $15-25
Red interior, base, bumper and removable top, white plastic wheels and sidemounted spare, Renegade, number 8 and stripe labels, otherwise as 441-B.
1. Yellow body.

450-A Austin Minivan 80mm 12/1964-1967
(Body Color Police Van Grill) $150-160
(Others) $200++

Like 448-A except no bars in rear door window, no antenna, no decals or figures.
1. Metallic olive green body, body color police van type grill, shaped wheels, rubber tires.
2. Metallic olive green body, body color countryman type grill, shaped wheels, rubber tires.
3. Metallic olive green body, silver police van type grill (?), shaped wheels, rubber tires.

450-B Peugeot 505 Taxi 123mm 1983-Close $20-30
Taxi sign casting, blue-red-white Taxi labels, red interior, otherwise as 373-B.
1. Cream body and base.

451-A Ford Sierra Taxi 128mm 1983(?)-Close $???
Probably not issued before factory closure.

452-A Commer Five Ton Dropside Truck 118mm 8/1956-1962 $120-140
Chassis-cab and rear body castings, clear windows, silver bumper, grille and headlights, sheet metal front base and tow hook, spare wheel, smooth wheels, rubber tires. Same chassis-cab casting as 453-A and 454-A.
1. Red chassis-cab, cream rear body.
2. Blue chassis-cab, cream rear body.

452-B Opel Senator Police Car 130mm 1983(?)-Close $???
Probably not issued before factory closure.

453-A Commer Refrigerator Van 118mm 8/1956-1960 $160-180
Red-white-blue Wall's Ice Cream decals on rear box body, otherwise as 452-A.
1. Medium blue chassis-cab, cream rear body.
2. Dark metallic blue chassis-cab, cream rear body.

454-A Commer Five Ton Platform Truck 118mm 4/1957-1962 $120-130
Flatbed rear body casting, otherwise as 452-A.
1. Yellow chassis-cab, silver gray rear body.
2. Metallic blue chassis-cab, silver gray rear body.

455-A Karrier Bantam Two Ton Van 101mm 1/1957-1960
(Blue) $110-120
(Red CWS) $200-300

Main body and chassis-rear bed castings, clear windows, silver headlights and bumper, smooth wheels, rubber tires.
1. Blue body, red chassis and rear bed.
2. Red body, black chassis and rear bed, non-standard wheels, " CWS" decal on rear, (pre-Corgi Mettoy promotional model c.1955, not considered part of the Corgi Toys range).

456-A E.R.F. 44G Dropside Truck 118mm 1/1961-1964 $110-120
Chassis-cab and rear body castings, clear windows, silver bumper, grille and headlights, sheet metal front base and tow hook, spare wheel, shaped wheels, rubber tires. Chassis-cab casting also used for 457-A and 459-A.
1. Yellow chassis-cab, dark blue rear body, shaped wheels crimped on axles;also used in GS11-A.
2. Light blue chassis-cab, white rear body, shaped wheels crimped on axles;GS21-A only.

457-A E.R.F. 44G Platform Truck 118mm 3/1958-1964 $100-110
Flatbed rear body casting, otherwise as 456-A.
1. Light blue chassis-cab, dark blue rear body, smooth wheels crimped on axles.
2. Light blue chassis-cab, white rear body, ? wheels.

457-B Talbot-Matra Rancho 120mm 2/1981-Close $20-50
Main body, lower body-base and opening tailgate castings, clear windows, plastic interior and body parts, black SW, bumpers, grille and tow hook, silver headlights, opening rear hatch, chrome wheels. Model used in several gift sets in varying colors.
1. Bright green and black body, tan interior, red taillights, four-spoke wheels.
2. Bright red and black body, tan interior, orange taillights, four-spoke wheels.
3. Bright yellow and black body, tan interior, orange taillights, solid wheels.
4. White and dark blue body, white interior, body-color taillights, solid wheels.
5. White and black body, cream interior, body-color taillights, solid wheels.
(Note: base is same color as first (metal) body color; second body color is that of plastic body parts.)

458-A E.R.F. 64G Earth Dumper 100mm 6/1958-1967 $80-90
Chassis-cab, tipper and unpainted hydraulic cylinder castings, clear windows, sheet metal front base, silver bumper, grille and headlights, spare wheel, rubber tires. Chassis-cab casting, shorter than 44G type, also used for 460-A.
1. Red chassis-cab, yellow tipper, smooth wheels.
2. Same as 458-A1 except shaped wheels crimped on axles.
3. Same as 458-A1 except shaped wheels free on axles.

459-A E.R.F. 44G Moorhouse Van 118mm 3/1958-1960 $300-350
Rear box body casting, Moorhouse Lemon Cheese labels, otherwise as 456-A.
1. Yellow chassis-cab, red rear body.

459-B Raygo Rascal 400 Roller 122mm 5/1973-1978 $30-40
Main body, chassis, roller mounting and roller castings, clear windows, green interior and engine, chrome parts, two orange cast wheels and plastic tires, Road Maker label.
1. Dark yellow body, base and mounting, orange and silver roller.

460-A E.R.F. 64G-Neville Cement Tipper 96mm 9/1959-1966 $80-90
Silver gray tipper, cover and tailgate and unpainted hydraulic cylinder castings, cement decal, two plastic filler caps, otherwise as 458-A.
1. Yellow chassis-cab, smooth wheels, silver plastic caps.
2. Yellow chassis-cab, smooth wheels, red plastic caps.
3. Yellow chassis-cab, shaped wheels, red plastic caps.

461-A Police "Vigilant" Range Rover 100mm 1/1972-1979
(Police) $30-40
(Politie) $65-75

Main body, raised roof and opening upper and lower rear door castings, clear windows, red interior, black shutters, blue dome light, two chrome and amber spotlights, black grille, silver headlights, red taillights, red and blue stripe and lettering labels, suspension, silver diecast base and bumpers, eight-spoke wheels. Casting also used for 482-B.
1. White body, blue and white Police labels.
2. White body, blue and white Politie labels; for sale in The Netherlands.

462-A Commer 3/4 Ton Van 89mm 1963-69, 1970-71
(Co-Op) $120-140
(Hammonds) $140-160

Chassis-cab and rear body castings, clear windows, red interior, gray SW, silver bumpers, grille and headlights, suspension, gray diecast base.
1. White chassis-cab, light blue cab roof and rear body, red taillights, cast wheels, plastic tires, CO-OP labels; 1970 promotional.
2. Dark blue body, white upper rear, light green roof, cast wheels, plastic tires, Hammonds labels; 1971 promotional.
3. Red chassis-cab, removable red rear body, trans-o-lite headlights, shaped wheels, rubber tires;GS24-A only, 1963-1969.
4. White chassis-cab, removable red rear body, not equipped with trans-o-lite headlights, shaped wheels, rubber tires;GS24-A only, 1963-1969.

463-A Commer 3/4 Ton Ambulance 89mm 2/1964-1966 $90-100
Chassis-cab and rear body castings, clear front and blue rear windows, blue dome light, red interior, gray SW, silver bumpers, grille and headlights, red taillights, red Ambulance decals, suspension, gray diecast base, shaped wheels, rubber tires. Casting also used for 354-A; chassis-cab casting used for other Commer 3/4 ton models.
1. White body.
2. Cream body.

3. White body, rear body area removable;GS24-A only, 1963-1969.
4. Red chassis-cab with trans-o-lite feature, removable white rear body;GS24-A only, 1963-1969.
5. Red chassis-cab with Trans-o-Lite feature, removable red rear body NOT fitted with dome light on roof, blue windows in cab, clear windows in sides and rear. (Possibly a prototype for an unreleased version of the (461?) Commer.)

464-A Commer 3/4 Ton Police Bus **89mm 7/1963-1968**
(County Police) $100-120
(City Police) $300++
(Rijkspolitie) $300++
(Blue with raised "POLICE") $100-120
(Green with raised "POLICE") $500++

Working roof lamp, battery compartment inside removable rear body.First type casting also used for 355-A.

First Type Casting: (1963-1966)
Steady burning roof lamp centered on middle rib in rear body casting with barred windows, opaque light blue rear windows, cam on front axle to flash lamp when rolling, composite ON/OFF lever on front axle, slotted rotating latch.
1. Metallic dark blue body, red roof lamp, " CITY POLICE" decals with shield.
2. Blue roof lamp, otherwise 464-A1.
3. Metallic dark blue body, blue roof lamp, " COUNTY POLICE" decals with shield.
4. Metallic dark blue body, blue roof lamp, " POLICE" decals (dark letters on light background, possibly a pre-production model).
5. Metallic dark blue body, blue roof lamp, " RIJKSPOLITIE" decals with star, (for sale in the Netherlands).
6. Same as 464-A5 except non-metallic royal blue body, (for sale in the Netherlands).

Second Type Casting: (1967-1968)
Blinking roof lamp between middle and forward rib in rear body casting, no bars on rear body windows, translucent vertically scribed aqua rear windows, base modified to eliminate cam, plastic rotary ON/OFF switch behind slotted rotating latch, white raised "POLICE" surrounded by rectangle cast into rear body sides.
7. Non-metallic navy blue body, blue lamp.
8. Green body, otherwise 464-A7, (for sale in Germany).

465-A Commer 3/4 Ton Pickup Truck **89mm 7/1963-1966** **$55-65**
Open rear body canopy casting, yellow interior, Trans-o-lite headlights, otherwise as 462-A.
1. Red chassis-cab, yellow-orange canopy.
2. Yellow chassis-cab, red canopy.
3. Red chassis-cab, removable dark yellow rear body with separate brown bench;GS24-A only, 1963-1969.
4. White chassis-cab without trans-o-lite feature, removable dark yellow rear body with separate brown bench;GS24-A only, 1963-1969.

466-A Commer 3/4 Ton Milk Float **89mm 4/1964-1965, 1970**
(Co-Op) $150-175
(Standard) $60-70
Covered rear body casting with open sides, white plastic load of milk cases, otherwise as 462-A.
1. White chassis-cab, light blue rear body, shaped wheels, rubber tires; 1964-1965.
2. White chassis-cab, slightly darker blue rear body, cast wheels, plastic tires, CO-OP labels; 1970 promotional.
3. Same as 466-A1 except rear body removable;GS24-A only, 1963-1969.
4. Red chassis-cab with trans-o-lite feature, otherwise 466-A3;GS24-A only, 1963-1969.

467-A Routemaster Bus **122mm 5/1977-1977** **$70-80**
Castings and details as 469-A. Logo details and colors not known.
1. Selfridges promotional.
2. Say Leeds promotional.
3. Hamleys promotional.

468-A London Transport Routemaster Bus **114mm 6/1964-1975**
(Common Versions) $50-60
Upper and lower body castings, clear windows, cream interior and stripe between castings, driver and conductor figures, silver grille, London Transport and other decals, suspension, gray diecast base. Replaced by larger 469-A casting in 1975.
1. Red body, jeweled headlights, Corgi Toys decals, shaped wheels, rubber tires.
2. Light green, cream and brown body, Corgi Toys decals, shaped wheels, rubber tires; Australian issue, 1964.
3. Light green, cream and brown body, Outspan decals, shaped wheels, rubber tires; Australian issue, 1967.
4. Red body, jeweled headlights, Outspan decals, shaped wheels, rubber tires; 1967-1970.
5. Red body, jeweled headlights, Outspan decals, cast wheels, rubber tires;1970-1972.
6. Red body, silver headlights, Outspan decals, cast wheels, plastic tires; 1973-1974.
7. Red body, silver headlights, Outspan decals, Whizzwheels; 1975.
8. Red body, jeweled headlights, Gamages decals, shaped wheels, rubber tires; 1968 promotional.
9. Red body, jeweled headlights, Church's Shoes decals, shaped wheels, rubber tires; 1969 promotional.
10. Red body, jeweled headlights, Madame Tussaud's decals, cast wheels, plastic tires; 1970 promotional.
11. Red body, silver headlights, Design Centre logo, other details not known; 1975 promotional.

469-A London Transport Routemaster Bus **122mm 4/1975-Close**
(Common Versions) $30-40
Upper and lower body castings, clear windows, cream interior and stripe between castings (promotionals have other colors), silver grille and headlights, black plastic base, Whizzwheels or (later) chrome wheels, London Transport and other labels; early types have driver and conductor figures. Larger than 468-A.
1. Red body, BTA Welcome to Britian labels; 1975-
2. Red body, Design Centre labels; 1976 promotional.
3. Orange body, Cadbury's Double Decker labels; 2/1979 promotional listed by Corgi as 469/01.
4. Red body, London Transport Bus labels, 2/1979 promotional listed as 469/02.
5. Red body?, Debenham's labels, 2/1979 promotional listed as 469/03.
6. Red body?, Hamleys labels; 2/1979 promotional listed as 469/04.
7. Light cream body, red interior and stripe, no figures, Aero Unforgettabubble labels; 1982 promotional. This and following variations have six-spoke chrome wheels.
8. Green body, white interior and stripe, no figures, Rowntrees Lion Bar labels; 1982 promotional.
9. Light cream upper and dark blue lower body, red interior and stripe, no figures, TDK Tape Cassettes labels; 1982 promotional.
10. Orange-red body, white interior and stripe, no figures, Oxo labels; 1982 promotional.
11. Light cream upper and orange-red lower body, red interior and stripe, no figures, Oxo labels; 1983 promotional.
12. Yellow upper and green lower body, white interior and stripes, no figures, "Buy before you fly" labels; 1983 promotional.
13. Green body, white interior and stripe, no figures, Pentel labels and white London Country lettering; 1983 promotional.
14. Dark cream body, brown roof and trim, white interior and stripe, no figures, World Airways labels; 1983 promotional.
15. Medium blue upper and dark blue lower body, white interior and stripe, no figures, Barratt labels; 1983 promotional.
16. Red body, cream interior and stripe, no figures, BTA Welcome to Britian labels.
17. Selfridges and Route 11 labels.
18. Selfridges and Route 12 labels.
19. Shillibeers labels.
20. Cream body, Oxo labels.
21. Metallic blue and cream body, Oxo labels.
22. Blue and white body, TDK labels.
23. Red body, Rowntrees Lion Bar labels.
24. Tan and cream body.
25. Tan and cream body, Esso labels (not factory issue).
26. Green body, Esso labels (not factory issue).
27. Black body, John Gay labels.
28. Red body, Manchester United labels, white interior, open top.
29. Red body, Army and Navy labels, white interior.
30. Green and yellow body, Say 'The Leeds' labels, red interior.
(Note: A continuously updated list of bus variations is maintained by Mr.John Gay, 7Horsham Lane, Upchurch, Sittingbourne, Kent, ME97AL (U.K.).)

470-A Jeep FC-150 Covered Truck **92mm 3/1965-1972** **$50-60**
Gray plastic rear cover and tow hook, gray diecast base, suspension, otherwise as 409-A.
1. Mustard tan body, red interior, shaped wheels, rubber tires; 1965-1967.
2. Medium blue body, yellow interior, shaped wheels, rubber tires; 1965-1967.
3. Mustard tan body, red interior, shaped wheels, plastic tires; 1968-1972.
4. Medium blue body, yellow interior, shaped wheels, plastic tires; 1968-1972.
5. Same as 470-A4 except cast wheels.

470-B Open Top Bus **122mm 7/1977-1978, 1983** **$35-45**
Open-top upper body casting, no figures; otherwise as 469-A.
1. Yellow body, red interior and stripe, Disneyland labels, 8-spoke wheels; 1977-1978.
2. Orange body, white interior and stripe, Old Holborn labels, six-spoke wheels; 1983 promotional, sold in box number 469.

470-C Green Line Bus **122mm 1983-Close** **$15-25**
Castings and details as 1982-1983 469-A issues.
1. Green body, white interior and stripe, six-spoke wheels, TDK labels, no figures.

471-A Karrier Mobile Canteen **92mm 3/1965-1966**
(Joe's Diner) $125-150
(Potates Frites) $250-300
Single body casting, clear front and amber rear windows, white interior with rotating figure, gray SW, rotator knob on roof panel, white diecast side panel drops to form counter, label on outside of panel, silver bumpers, grille and headlights, suspension, gray diecast base, shaped wheels, rubber tires. Modified 407-A castings.
1. Medium blue body, " Joe's Diner" label on white side panel, " Snack Bar" decal over driver's compartment.
2. Same as 471-A1 except "Potates Frites" label (for sale in Belgium).

471-B London Transport Silver Jubilee Bus **122mm 4/1977-1977** **$40-50**
Metallic silver body including grille and headlights, red interior and stripe, no figures, eight spoke wheels, "The Queen's Silver Jubilee" lower labels, otherwise as 469-A.
1. Red band, "See More London" side panels.
2. White band, "See More London" side panels.
3. Red band, " Woolworth welcomes the world" side panels.
4. White band, " Woolworth welcomes the world" side panels.

472-A Public Address Land Rover **90mm 10/1964-1966** **$140-160**
Single body casting, clear windows, red interior, gray SW, silver bumper, grille and headlights, yellow plastic rear body and loudspeakers, rotating man with microphone and separate woman with pamphlets, Vote for Corgi decals, suspension, gray diecast base, shaped wheels, rubber tires. Casting also used for 487-A.
1. Green body, yellow rear.

474-A Ford Thames Wall's Ice Cream Van **100mm 10/1965-1968** **$140-160**
Chimes, crank at rear to operate them, chrome bumpers and grille, no separate figures, otherwise as 447-A.
1. Light blue body, cream pillars.

475-A Citroen Safari Winter Sports **101mm 1/1964-1967** **$130-150**
Roof rack with skis and poles, skier figure, hood decal; otherwise as 436-A;
1. White body, 1964 Olympic Winter Sports decal, red roof rack with yellow skis.
2. White body, Corgi Ski Club decals, red roof rack with yellow skis.
3. White body, Corgi Ski Club decal, yellow roof rack with red skis.
(Two green and tan interior combinations are possible; the dash and SW, rear seat and adjusting gear will be one color, the front seat and rear floor the other.)

476-A Mini Surf **NOT PRODUCED** **N/A**
Model apparently announced by Corgi; year not known, Never issued.

477-A Land Rover Breakdown Truck **111mm 10/1965-1977**
(Shaped or Cast Wheels) $85-95
(Whizzwheels) $55-65
Red body, yellow plastic canopy with chrome rotating spotlight, yellow interior, suspension, otherwise as 417-A. (417-A has sheet metal canopy).
1. Shaped wheels, rubber tires including crank, separate silver SW, " Breakdown Service" labels;1965-1969.
2. Shaped wheels, plastic tires including crank, separate silver SW, " Breakdown Service" labels;1970.
3. Cast wheels, plastic tires including crank, separate silver SW, " Breakdown Service" labels;1971-1973.
4. Whizzwheels, large diameter silver painted crank knob, separate silver SW, " Breakdown Service" labels;1974.
5. Whizzwheels, small diameter plated crank knob, separate silver SW, " Breakdown Service" labels;1975.
6. Whizzwheels, small diameter plated crank knob, separate silver SW, revised labels with arched "Breakdown" ;1976.
7. Whizzwheels, small diameter plated crank knob, new interior with molded-in SW, labels with arched "Breakdown" ;1977.

478-A Jeep FC-150 Tower Wagon **118mm 4/1965-1969** **$100-110**
Main body and unpainted pillar and arm castings, clear windows, yellow interior, gray SW, yellow plastic basket, electrician figure, red grille, silver bumper and headlights, rear stripe label, suspension, gray diecast base, shaped wheels. Same castings as used in GS14-A; uses 409-A/470-A castings.
Metallic green body, rubber tires.
1. Metallic green body, plastic tires.

479-A Commer Mobile Camera Van 89mm 12/1967-1972 $120-140
Main body, roof rack, black camera, gold tripod, gray base and two opening rear door castings, clear windows, light blue interior, gray SW, silver bumpers, grille and headlights, red taillights, cameraman figure, Samuelson labels, suspension, gray diecast base, shaped wheels, plastic tires. Casting also used for 508-A.
1. Metallic blue lower body and roof rack, white upper body.

480-A Chevrolet Impala Yellow Cab 102mm 6/1965-1967 $80-90
Red interior, driver, white roof sign, gray antenna, red decals, otherwise as 248-A.
1. Red lower body and roof, dark yellow upper body.

481-A Chevrolet Impala Police Car 102mm 8/1965-1969 $80-90
Yellow interior, driver, red dome light, gray antenna, Police decal on hood, Police Patrol labels on doors, otherwise as 248-A.
1. Black lower body and roof, white upper body, shaped wheels, rubber tires.
2. Same as 481-A1 except cast wheels, plastic tires.

482-A Chevrolet Impala Fire Chief's Car 102mm 6/1965-1969 $80-90
Yellow interior, driver, blue dome light, gray antenna, Fire Chief decal on hood, shield labels on doors, otherwise as 248-A.
1. White lower body and base, red upper body, shaped wheels, rubber tires.
2. Same as 482-A1 except cast wheels, plastic tires.
3. All red body and base, other details not known.

482-B Range Rover "Vigilant" Ambulance 100mm 5/1975-1977 $40-50
Ambulance and red cross labels, otherwise as 461-A.
1. Orange-red lower body sides, white upper body, hatch and tailgate.
2. White body with dark blue stripe, Ambulance lettering, and small red cross label on each side.

483-A Dodge Kew Fargo Tipper Truck 132mm 12/1967-1972 $50-60
Cab, opening hood, tipper, tailgate, charcoal chassis and unpainted drive train castings, clear windows, red interior, gray SW, black hydraulic cylinders, silver headlights, chrome grille and engine, suspension, cast wheels, plastic tires. Body and chassis castings also used for 484-A.
1. White cab and hood; blue tipper and tailgate.

483-B Belgian Police Land Rover 100mm 5/1975-1977 $75-85
Roof casting like 482-B, white body, red seats, red stripe, shield logo on door, (sometimes listed as 463-B).
1. Belgian police labels.

484-A Dodge Kew Fargo Livestock Truck 138mm 4/1967-1972 $55-65
Rear stake body and lowering tailgate-ramp castings, five pigs set in cardboard base, otherwise as 483-A.
1. Tan cab and hood, green rear body and tailgate, 5 pigs set in cardboard base, shaped wheels (also in GS5-B).
2. Tan cab and hood, green rear body and tailgate, 5 pigs set in cardboard base, cast wheels (also in GS5-B).
3. Blue cab and hood, tan rear body and tailgate, " Wamaru Sub-District" decorations, 2 elephants, cast wheels (GS14-B, 1969-1973).

484-B AMC Pacer Rescue Car 123mm 5/1978-1980
(RESCUE) $25-35
(SECOURS) $50-60
Chrome roof bar casting, red roof lights, otherwise as 291-A.
1. White front and orange rear body and hatch, black hood, number 35 and Rescue labels.
2. Secours labels, otherwise as type 1; numbered 4841 by Corgi; French issue.

485-A Austin Mini Countryman Super 79mm 3/1965-1969
(Silver Grill) $115-125
(Body Color Grill) $200-225
Main body and two opening rear door castings, clear windows, yellow interior, chrome roof rack with maroon surfboards, gray antenna, silver bumper and grille, jewel headlights, red taillights, surfer figure, suspension, gray diecast base, rubber tires.
1. Turquoise green body, tan trim, shaped wheels.
2. Turquoise green body, tan trim, aluminum painted parts, shaped wheels.
3. Turquoise green body, tan trim, cast wheels.

486-A Chevrolet Kennel Club Van 102mm 3/1967-1969 $100-110
Upper body, lower body-base and opening tailgate castings, clear windows, pale green interior with dog figures, gray SW, chrome bumpers, grille, headlights and stripe between castings, red taillights, sliding rear side windows, dachshund picture on panel above cab, kennel club labels, suspension, cast wheels. Same base as 248-A; model reissued as Chipperfields's 511-A.
1. White upper body, red lower body and base, rubber tires.
2. White upper body, red lower body and base, plastic tires.

487-A Land Rover Circus Parade Vehicle 90mm 9/1965-1969 $160-180
Yellow interior, blue plastic rear body and loudspeakers, rotating clown and removable, chimpanzee figures. Chipperfieldss Circus and "The Circus is here" labels, otherwise as 472-A.
1. Red body, blue rear, metal tow hook.
2. Red body, blue rear, no tow hook.

489-A VW Polo Police Car 92mm 8/1976-1980 $25-35
Blue dome light, white Polizei labels, otherwise as 289-A.
1. White body, green hood and doors.

4894-A VW Polo German Auto Club Car 92mm 1979-1979 $30-50
Yellow dome light, ADAC Strassenwacht and number 1341 labels, otherwise as 289-A.
1. Yellow body, white roof.

490-A Volkswagen Breakdown Van 99mm 12/1966-1972 $90-100
Main body and unpainted left and right winch castings, red interior and equipment boxes, clear windows, gray SW, chrome tools, spare wheels, red VW emblem, silver bumpers and headlights, unpainted hook on line, red and yellow stripe label, gray plastic tow hook, suspension, gray diecast base.
1. Tan body, no labels, shaped wheels, rubber tires.
2. Same 490-A1 except with "Breakdown" labels.
3. White body, "Breakdown" labels, shaped wheels, rubber tires.
4. White body, " racing Club" labels, shaped wheels, rubber tires (used in GS6-B, GS12-B, GS25-B).
5. Same as 490-A4 except cast wheels, plastic tires (same GS usages).
6. Mustard green body, no labels, shaped wheels, rubber tires.

490-B Touring Caravan 119mm 5/1975-1979 $20-30
Single body casting, white plastic roof and opening door, plastic hitch, red awning, white stripes, clear windows, pale blue interior, flowerpot, blue trim, blue label with license plate, taillights etc., two Whizzwheels.
1. White body with blue trim, red hitch.
2. White body with blue trim and hitch.

491-A Ford Consul Cortina Estate Car 94mm 9/1966-1969 $85-100
Shaped wheels, rubber tires, no golfing figures, otherwise as 440-A.
1. Red body and base.
2. Metallic charcoal gray body and base.
3. Non-metallic medium blue body and base.

492-A Volkswagen 1200 Police Car 91mm 5/1966-1969
(POLIZEI) $75-85
(POLITIE) $200-225
Blue dome light in chrome collar that steers front wheels, two figures in car, police lables, otherwise as 256-A.
1. Dark green body, white fenders, Polizei labels; for sale in Germany.
2. Chromed base, otherwise as type 1, which has unpainted base.
3. White body, Politie lables and emblem decals; for sale in The Netherlands.
4. White body, Polizei labels, for sale in Switzerland.

493-A Mazda B1600 Pickup Truck 125mm 2/1975-1978 $30-40
Main body, rack and opening tailgate castings, clear windows, black interior, tow hook, bumper, grille and base, silver headlights, chrome wheels. Casting also used for 264-B, 413-B, 415-A, 440-B, 495-A and in gift sets.
1. Blue upper and silver lower body.
2. Blue upper and white lower body.

494-A Bedford TK Tipper Truck 105mm 12/1968-1972
(Red & Yellow) $75-85
(Red & Silver) $150-175
Chassis-cab, tipper and unpainted frame castings, clear windows, yellow interior, gray SW, black mirrors, gray hydraulic cylinders, silver grille, bumper and headlights, suspension, gray diecast base, large diameter cast wheels, thin plastic tires.
1. Red chassis-cab, dark yellow tipper.
2. Red chassis-cab, gray or silver tipper.
3. Yellow chassis-cab, blue tipper.
4. Blue chassis-cab, yellow tipper.

495-A Mazda 4x4 Open Back Truck 123mm 1983-Close $20-30
Single body casting, black windows, no interior, black rack, grille, bumper, tow hook and base, silver headlights, white plastic six-spoke wheels, red-white-blue-yellow lettering; same basic casting as 493-A.
1. Blue body, white roof.

497-A The Man from U.N.C.L.E. Oldsmobile 105mm 8/1966-1969
(Dk. Blue) $225-250
(White) $600++
Main body and two turning spotlight castings, blue windows, plastic interior, two figures operated by chrome roof scope, hood label, silver bumpers, grille and headlights, red taillights, gray diecast base, cast wheels, Modified 235-A casting.
1. Light cream to white body, cream interior, unplated spotlights, rubber tires.
2. Metallic dark blue body, dark yellow interior, unplated spotlights, rubber tires.
3. Same as 497-A2 except plastic tires.
4. Same as 497-A3 except plated spotlights.
(Shown decorated identically to late 235-A in some ads, but never produced as such.)

498-A Austin Mini Countryman NOT PRODUCED N/A
Announced in 1967-68 Corgi catalog but not issued; was to be same model as 485-A without roof rack etc.

499-A Citroen Safari Winter Olympics Car 103mm 10/1967-1969 $180-200
Light blue interior, gold diecast bobsled with figure, skier figure, Grenoble Olympiad 1968 hood label, otherwise as 436-A.
1. White body, blue roof and hatch, red roof rack, yellow skis and poles.
2. White body, blue roof and hatch, yellow roof rack, red skis and poles.

500-A U.S. Army Land Rover 95mm 12/1963-1963 $???
Model was identical to 357-A. (for export only).
1. Olive drab body, yellow interior, other details not known.

503-A Bedford Circus Giraffe Transporter 6/1964-1971 $120-140
Single chassis-cab casting, clear windows, yellow interior, gray SW, silver bumper, grille and headlights, three giraffe figures, black mirrors, suspension, gray diecast base, same chassis-cab castings as 494-A.
1. Red cab casting, light blue plastic rear body and lowering tailgate ramp, Chipperfieldss Circus labels, two giraffe figures, shaped wheels, rubber tires.
2. Same as 503-A1 except same diameter cast wheels.
3. Same as 503-A1 except large diameter cast wheels, thin plastic tires, giraffe box now turquoise, lighter blue in Chipperfields's labels.
4. Tan cab casting, tan and brown plastic rear body, Wamaru Sub-District labels, two giraffe figures, shaped wheels;GS14-B, 1969-1973.
5. Same as 503-A4 except cast wheels.
6. Same as 503-A4 except large diameter cast wheels, thin plastic tires.

506-A Sunbeam Imp Police Car 83mm 5/1968-1972 $120-130
Tan interior, driver figure, blue dome light, base includes front plate for Police label, cast wheels, two horizontal lines engraved into windshield, plastic tires, otherwise as 340-A.
1. White body, black hood and lower door panel, white decal with red "Police" letters on doors.
2. Lt. blue body, white band from doors extending over roof, phosphorescent white label on doors with black "Police" letters.
3. Same as 506-A2 except white only on lower doors (unconfirmed).
4. White body, black roof, same labels as 506-A2.

507-A Chrysler Bermuda Taxi NOT PRODUCED N/A
Announced in 1969 Corgi catalog but not issued; was to have been based on 246-A. Modified castings reused for 246-A3, but without surrey roof or labels as shown in 1969 catalog.

508-A Commer 2500 Holiday Camp Minibus 90mm 7/1968-1969 $100-120
Main body, roof rack and two opening rear door castings, clear windows, white interior, gray SW, silver bumpers, grille and headlights, Holiday Camp Special and Union Jack decals, luggage and tarpaulin on roof rack, suspension, gray diecast base, shaped wheels, plastic tires; same casting as 479-A.
1. White upper body, orange lower body, rear doors and roof rack.

509-A Porsche Targa Police Car 92mm 6/1970-1975
(POLIZEI) $80-90
(RIJKSPOLITIE) $150-160
Main body, lower body-base, engine-bumper, siren, opening rear hood and two door castings, clear windows, plastic interior, folding seat backs, gold SW; blue dome light on chrome bracket, jeweled headlights, orange lights and fan, labels, suspension, Whizzwheels; modified 382-A casting.
1. White body and base, red doors and hoods, black roof and interior, unpainted siren, engine and bumpers, orange and white Polizei labels.
2. Orange interior, otherwise as type 1.
3. ? interior, Rijkspolitie labels, otherwise as type 1; for sale in the Netherlands.
4. ? interior, Police labels, otherwise as type 1; for sale in France.

510-A Citroen Tour De France Car 105mm 4/1970-1972 $110-130
Main body, gray lower body-base and four spoked wheel castings, clear windows, black SW, driver figure, gray antenna, black plastic rack with four bicycle wheels, swiveling team manager figure with megaphone in back of car, clear headlights, chrome front bumper, Paramount and Tour de France decals, Whizzwheels. Casting also used for 807-A.

1. Red body, yellow interior and rear bed.

511-A   Chevrolet Circus Performing Poodles Truck   103mm 12/1970-1972 $450-500
Chipperfieldss labels, pale blue interior with poodle figures in back, plastic tires, ring of poodles and trainer figure, otherwise as 486-A.
1. Blue upper body and tailgate, red lower body and base.

513-A   Citroen Safari Alpine Rescue Car   103mm 9/1970-1972 $275-300
Light blue interior, yellow roof rack and skis, gold diecast bobsled, man and dog figures, Alpine Rescue labels, otherwise as 436-A.
1. White body, red roof and hatch, red roof rack, yellow skis, cast wheels, plastic tires.
2. Same as 513-A1 except yellow roof rack, red skis.
3. Same as 513-A1 except both skis and roof rack are yellow.

Corgi Cubs

Metal and plastic toy (not scale model) vehicles introduced 1976-1977:

500   Police Car   120mm $15-30
White diecast body, blue stripes, black Police lettering, red plastic interior and base.
501   Jeep   95mm $15-30
Metallic green diecast body, light orange plastic interior and base.
502   Express Van   98mm $15-30
Orange diecast body, orange-white-blue Express labels, white plastic interior and base.
503   MG TD   105mm $15-30
Metallic blue diecast body, white plastic interior and base.
504   Pickup Truck   98mm $15-30
Yellow diecast body, red plastic interior and base.
505   Fire Chief   108mm $15-30
Red diecast station wagon body, Fire Chief labels, white plastic interior and base.
506   Helicopter   110mm $15-30
Yellow diecast body, red plastic interior, base and rotors.
507   Shell Tanker   112mm $15-30
Yellow diecast body, black plastic tank top, red plastic interior and base, Shell tanker labels.
508   Racer   116mm $15-30
Yellow diecast body, chrome interior, base and parts, Racer and checker labels.
509   Dump Truck   106mm $15-30
Blue diecast body, dark yellow plastic interior and base.
510   Fire Truck   100mm $15-30
Red diecast body, Fire Dept. labels, white plastic interior, rear bed with equipment and base.
511   Ambulance   98mm $15-30
White diecast body, Ambulance labels, red plastic interior and base; same casting and plastic as 502.
512   Milk Truck   98mm $15-30
Blue diecast body, Milk labels, white plastic interior and base; same casting and plastic as 502 and 511.
600   Corgi Cubs Set $50-60
500, 505, 510 and 511.
Each model, with the exceptions of 506 (rotors) and 507 (top of tank), consists of a single casting and one plastic piece; the axles attach to the latter and hold six-spoke chrome fast wheels.

Corgi Kits

601	Batley Garage	5/1961-1969	$70-80
602	AA and RAC Telephone Boxes	6/1961-1966	$30-50
603	Silverstone Racing Pits	11/1961-1966	$70-80
604	Silverstone Press Box	11/1961-1966	$70-80
605	Silverstone Club House, Timekeeper's Box	12/1961-1967	$70-80
606	Lamp Standards	6/1961-1966	$30-50
607	Elephant and Cage	3/1963-1967	$30-50
608	Shell/BP Service Station	2/1963-1966	$150-250
609	Forecourt Accessories	2/1963-1966	
610	Police Box and Telephone Kiosk	2/1963-1966	$30-50
611	Motel Chalet	4/1963-1966	$70-80

Aircraft and Space Ships

647-A   Buck Rogers Starfighter   165mm 8/1980-1983 $60-70
Upper and lower body castings, unpainted parts and interior casting, amber windows, yellow plastic wings, blue plastic jets and nose skid, three small black wheels, two figures.
1. White body, multicolored labels.

648-A   NASA Space Shuttle   150mm 1980-Close $35-45
Main body and two opening hatch castings, black plastic interior, jets and base, unpainted retracting running gear castings, black plastic wheels, United States and flag labels, red and gold plastic satellite with folding arms; satellite fits inside shuttle. Casting also used for 649-A.
1. White body.

649-A   James Bond Space Shuttle   150mm 8/1979-1981 $75-85
Black and yellow Moonraker labels, otherwise as 648-A.
1. White body.

650-A   Concorde — BOAC   190mm 5/1969-1972 $50-60
Upper and lower body castings, white plastic tilting nose, black plastic wheels and nose rest, airline name, stripe and window labels, black diecast standard.
1. White body, dark blue and gold labels.

650-B   Concorde — British Airways   190mm 8/1976-Close $20-30
Upper and lower body castings, white plastic tilting nose, black plastic wheels and nose rest, airline name, stripe and window labels, black diecast standard.
1. White body, red and blue labels.

651-A   Concorde — Air France   190mm 5/1969-1971 $50-60
Upper and lower body castings, white plastic tilting nose, black plastic wheels and nose rest, airline name, stripe and window labels, black diecast standard.
1. White body, blue and red labels.

651-B   Concorde — Air France   190mm 1978-1980 $20-30
Upper and lower body castings, white plastic tilting nose, black plastic wheels and nose rest, airline name, stripe and window labels, black diecast standard.
1. White body, red and blue labels.

652-A   Concorde — Japan Air Lines   190mm 1970? $350-450
Upper and lower body castings, white plastic tilting nose, black plastic wheels and nose rest, airline name, stripe and window labels, black diecast standard.
1. White body, ? labels.

653-A   Concorde — Air Canada   190mm 1970? $250-350
Upper and lower body castings, white plastic tilting nose, black plastic wheels and nose rest, airline name, stripe and window labels, black diecast standard.
1. White body, ? labels.

Stunt Cycles

681-A   Stunt Motorcycle   75mm 11/1971-1972 $180-220
Gold diecast cycle, clear windshield, unpainted spoked diecast wheels, plastic tires, driver figure, cycle stands on red plastic sled with four red Whizzwheels and unpainted diecast baseplate. Made to run on Corgi Rockets track.
1. Driver with blue suit, yellow helmet and black gloves.

High Speed

700-A   Motorway Ambulance   98mm 12/1973-1979 $20-30
Single body casting, dark blue windows and dome lights, dark blue interior, red-white-black labels, red diecast base and bumpers, suspension, Whizzwheels. Casting later modified for 424-B.
1. White body, clear headlights.

701-A   Inter-City Mini-Bus   106mm 12/1973-1978 $20-30
Single body casting, clear windows, brown interior, yellow-green-black labels, silver grille and headlights, red taillights, unpainted diecast base, Whizzwheels.
1. Bright orange body.

702-A   Breakdown Truck   98mm 4/1975-1979 $20-30
Single body casting, black plastic boom with gold diecast hook, amber windows and dome lights, yellow interior, yellow and black labels, black plastic base, Whizzwheels.
1. Red body.

703-A   Fire Engine   115mm 12/1975-1978 $20-30
Single body casting, dark yellow two-piece plastic ladder on unpainted swinging diecast base, blue windows and dome lights, yellow interior, grille and hose, yellow and dark blue stripe labels, black plastic base, Whizzwheels.
1. Light red body.

Character Vehicles

801-A   Noddy's Car   94mm 7/1969-1973
    (Black Face Golly) $1000+
    (Others) $400-450+
Yellow main body, red fenders and base, chrome grille and bumpers castings, clear windshield, black SW and grille, chrome headlights, spare wheel, suspension, cast eight-spoke wheels, plastic tires, two figures in seats and one in open rumble seat; one is Golliwog (804A-1 has Chubby instead, 804A-2 has Noddy alone).
1. As above, with three figures, Golliwog has black face.
1. As above, with three figures, Golliwog has other than black face.

802-A   Popeye's Paddle Wagon   126mm 12/1969-1972 $500-600
Diecast body, chassis, fenders, stacks and other pieces, white plastic deck, davit and rear wheels, blue lifeboat with Swee'Pea figure, Olive holding unpainted diecast wheel, Popeye with telescope (both figures move from side to side), heads of Wimpy and Bluto mounted on metal rods (they bob up and down), chrome and black grille, white front suspension, jewel headlights, unpainted cast front wheels, black plastic tires, gears to make figures roll as vehicle rolls.
1. Yellow body, red chassis, blue rear fenders, bronze and yellow stacks, yellow rear wheels.
2. Yellow body, red chassis, blue rear fenders, bronze and yellow stacks, white rear wheels.

803-A   The Beatles' Yellow Submarine   28mm 2/1969-1970
    (White & Yellow Hatches) $550-600
    (Red Hatches) $450-500
Upper and lower body and two opening hatch castings, yellow lower body, white upper body, unpainted levers, two figures in each hatch, red rail and four yellow pipes in conning tower, black propeller, multicolored painted and decal trim, three cast wheels and plastic tires, rear roller. Turning of wheels makes periscopes turn.
1. Red divider stripe, white forward hatch, yellow rear hatch.
2. No divider stripe, both hatches red.

804-A   Noddy's Car   94mm 1970 $250-300
    88mm 8/1975-1977
1970 issue same casting and details as 801-A with one different figure. 1975 issue hasClosed trunk with spare tire, and only Noddy in the car, plus red interior, (shorter length because ofClosed trunk).
1. Yellow body, red chassis, Chubby instead of Golliwog: 1970.
2. Yellow body, red chassis, Closed trunk, Noddy alone; 1975-1977.

805-A   The Hardy Boys' 1912 Rolls-Royce   116mm 6/1970-1970 $250-300
Yellow hood and blue chassis castings, red plastic main body, yellow roof and window frames, clear windows, brown interior, chrome SW, lamps and radiator shell, black grille, jeweled headlights in gold mounting, gold crank, boxes and wheels, black rear ladders, light gray exhaust, black plastic tires, band figures on roof, gold disk wheels, otherwise 9041-A.
1. Band figures are mounted on green base which can be removed from roof rack.

806-A   Lunar Bug   128mm 10/1970-1972 $100-120
Main body, lower body-base, lowering ramp and four wheel strut castings, clear and amber windows, blue plastic interior and folding wings, chrome and red roof jets, unpainted wheels and struts, plastic tires, Lunar Bug labels.
1. White body, red roof, dark red base and ramp.

807-A   Dougal's Magic Roundabout Car   115mm 11/1971-1974 $225-250
Single body casting, clear windows, red interior, silve headlights, chrome front bumper, rabbit, dog and snail figures, suspension, gray diecast base, red wheels with gold trim. Body casting is same as 510-A Citroen.
1. Yellow body, Magic Roundabout and flower labels.

808-A   Basil Brush's Car   93mm 12/1971-1973 $225-250
Body, chassis, gold lamps and dash casting, clear windshield, Basil Brush figure, blue interior and folded top, red plastic wheels, plastic tires, Laugh Tapes. Body and chassis are based on 9031-9032 1910 Renault models.
1. Red body, dark yellow chassis.

809-A   Dick Dastardly's Racing Car   127mm 7/1973-1975 $125-150
Body and chassis castings, chrome engine, red wings, Dick and Muttley figures, red plastic wheels.
1. Dark blue body, yellow chassis.

811-A   James Bond Moon Buggy   113mm 5/1972-1973 $450-500
Three white body, two blue chassis and three unpainted parts castings, red plastic radar scanner, upper arms, jaws and headlights, amber canopy, yellow tanks and wheels, flag and number 1 label, black plastic base. Radar scanner revolves as model moves.
1. White body, blue chassis.

Classics (1980s Production)

801-B   1957 Ford Thunderbird   132mm 1/1982-1982 $25-35
Main body, opening hood and trunk castings, amber windows, black interior, white seats, detailed engine, chrome bumpers, headlights and spare wheel cover, black grille, orange taillights, black diecast base, chrome wheels, whitewall tires, plastic hardtop. Reissued in 1983 as 810-A.
1. Cream body, dark brown hardtop.
2. Cream body, black hardtop.
3. Cream body, orange hardtop.
4. Cream body, orange hardtop and interior?

802-B   1954 Mercedes-Benz 300SL   125mm 1/1982-1982 $20-30
Main body, lower body-base, opening hood and two gullwing door castings, clear windows, tan interior, black dash and SW, detailed engine, chrome bumpers, grille and headlights, dark red taillights, chrome wheels. Reissued as 811-B in 1983.
1. Red body and base.

803-B   1952 Jaguar XK120 Hard top   120mm 1983-Close $20-30
Main body, opening hood and trunk castings, clear windshield, chrome frame, dash, grille, headlights and bumpers, black hardtop and SW, light cream interior, detailed engine, black plastic base, chrome wheels.
1. Red body, black hardtop.

804-B   1952 Jaguar XK120 Rally   120mm 1983-Close $50-60
Red interior, black folded top, seat cover, rack, floorboards and bonnet strap, number 414 and Rally des Alpes labels, otherwise as 803-B.
1. Cream body.
2. 1983 catalog shows model with number 56.

805-B   1956 Mercedes-Benz 300SC, Top Up   127mm 1983-Close $20-30
Main body, opening hood and trunk castings, clear windows, tan interior, tan folding seat backs, tan top with chrome side irons, detailed engine, chrome grille, lights, bumpers and trim, suspension, black plastic base, chrome wheels.
1. Maroon body, tan top.

806-B   1956 Mercedes-Benz 300SC, Top Down   127mm 1983-Close $20-30
Black folded top, white interior, otherwise as 805-B.
1. Black body.

810-A   1957 Ford Thunderbird   132mm 1983-Close $20-30
White body, otherwise as 801-B.
1. White body, black hardtop.

811-B   1954 Mercedes-Benz 300SL   125mm 1983-Close $20-30
Silver body, otherwise as 802-B.
1. Silver body.

Magic Roundabout

851   Magic Roundabout Train   1973 $300-400
Three piece train with figures hanging out of windows.

852   Musical Carousel   1973 $700-750+
Red and yellow carousel set into medium blue base.

853   Playground (including 851, 852, figures and acc.)   1973 $1000-1200+
Large light blue plastic playground base with crank chain track for 851, 852 inset in base, various figures and accessories.

859-A   Mr. McHenry's Trike and Zebedee- Box   118mm 10/1972-1974 $200-250
Tricycle, hitch, box and base castings, yellow plastic handlebars, front wheel, two box wheels and control wheel, two red trike wheels, yellow and red box cover, figures of Mr. McHenry on trike and Zebedee in box; Zebedee pops up or down when control wheel is turned.
1. Red trike and box.

860   Dougal (sheep dog)   1973 $75-150
Figure in clear dome container.

861   Florence (girl)   1973 $75-150
Figure in clear dome container.

862   Zebedee   1973 $75-150
Figure in clear dome container.

863   Mr. Rusty (beared man in high hat)   1973 $75-150
Figure in clear dome container.

864   Brian (snail)   1973 $75-150
Figure in clear dome container.

865   Basil (boy)   1973 $75-150
Figure in clear dome container.

866   Ermintrude (cow)   1973 $75-150
Figure in clear dome container.

868   Dylan (rabbit with guitar)   1973 $75-150
Figure in clear dome container.

The Magic Roundabout toys were based on a British children's TV series and sold only in Britian.

Military (900 Series)

900-A   Tiger Mark 1 Tank   150mm 11/1973-1978 $45-55
Main body, lower body-base, swiveling turret and raising barrel castings, black plastic barrel end, antenna, cables and treads, olive plastic rollers and turret interior, labels.
1. Tan and green camouflage finish, German emblem, number 144.

901-A   Centurion Mark III Tank   135mm 11/1973-1978 $45-55
Main body, lower body-base, swiveling turret and raising barrel castings, black plastic barrel end, antenna, cables and treads, olive plastic rollers, labels.
1. Tan and brown camouflage finish, Union Jack labels.
2. Olive drab body, Union Jack labels.

902-A   M60 A1 Medium Tank   120mm 7/1974-1980 $45-55
Main body, lower body-base, swiveling turret, small turret and raising barrel castings, black plastic barrel end, antenna and treads, olive plastic rollers and turret interior, labels.
1. Gray-tan-green camouflage finish, white star and number labels.

903-A   Chieftain Medium Tank   146mm 6/1974-1980 $45-55
Main body, lower body-base, swiveling turret and raising barrel castings, black plastic barrel end and treads, olive plastic rollers, red light, labels.
1. Olive drab body, Union Jack and number labels.

904-A   King Tiger Heavy Tank   155mm 12/1974-1978 $45-55
Main body, lower body-base, swiveling turret and raising barrel castings, black plastic barrel end and treads, tan plastic rollers, red lever, labels.
1. Tan and red-brown body, German emblems and B-34 labels.

905-A   SU-100 Medium Tank   142mm 9/1974-1977 $45-55
Main body and lower body-base castings, gray plastic tanks, opening hatch, raising barrel and rollers, black barrel end and treads, red lever, labels.
1. Cream and gray camouflage finish on upper body, gray lower body, red star and number 103 labels.

906-A   Saladin Armored Car   85mm 9/1974-1977 $45-55
Main body, lower body-base, swiveling turret and raising barrel castings, black plastic barrel end and tires, olive cast wheels, red and white labels.
1. Olive drab body.

907-A   Hanomag 251/1 Halftrack Rocket   165mm 7/1975-1980 $60-80
        Launcher and Trailer
Main body, lower body-base, two rocket launchers and single trailer castings, gray plastic roll cage, man with machine gun, front wheels and hubs, black plastic treads, red rockets, trailer with gray plastic opening top and wheels, label.
1. Gray halftrack and trailer, German emblem and number labels.

908-A   AMX 30D Recovery Tank   175mm 10/1976-1980 $45-55
Main body, lower body-base, crane, swiveling base, lowering blade and unpainted hook castings, black plastic turret top with gun, hydraulic cylinder, cables and treads, olive plastic hubs, jewel light, sawhorses, spare cannon barrel, cable, tools and three figures.
1. Olive drab body, Tricolor and number labels.

909-A   Quad Tractor, Ammunition Trailer and Field Gun 277mm 10/1976-1980 $50-60
Tractor body and chassis, trailer body, base and opening doors, gun chassis and raising barrel castings, brown plastic interior and parts, black plastic barrel end and tires, tan cast wheels, unpainted lever, labels. Tractor casting also used for 422-B.
1. Tan tractor, trailer and gun, number and emblem labels.

Helicopters

920-A   Bell Army Helicopter   132mm 3/1975-1980 $20-30
Diecast two-piece body, clear canopy, olive plastic rotors, red plastic parts, labels.
1. Olive and tan camouflage finish, U.S. Army labels.

921-A   Hughes Police Helicopter   140mm 8/1975-1980 $20-30
Diecast two-piece body, clear canopy, red plastic interior and gears, dark blue plastic rotors, winch, line and hook, labels.
1. White body, Police and blue and red trim labels.
2. White body, Politie labels; Corgi catalog number 9212, for sale in The Netherlands.
3. White body, Polizei labels; Corgi catalog number 9921 (9213?), for sale in Germany.
4. Dark yellow body, ADAC labels; Corgi catalog number 9214; for sale in Germany.
5. Swiss Air Rescue Helicopter, details unknown; Corgi catalog number 9216, for sale in Switzerland.

922-A   Sikorsky Skycrane Casualty Helicopter   155mm 10/1975-1978 $20-30
Diecast two-piece body, orange plastic pipes, black plastic rotors and wheels, white plastic lower body with opening rear hatch, red plastic gear, labels.
1. Red diecast and white plastic body, red cross and number labels.

923-A   Sikorsky Skycrane Army Casualty Helicopter 140mm 9/1975-1978 $20-30
Olive lower body, red pipes, otherwise as 922-A.
1. Olive drab and yellow upper body, olive drab lower body, red cross and army labels.

924-A   Bell 205 Rescue Helicopter   145mm 12/1976-1980 $20-30
Two-piece body and two opening door castings, yellow plastic floats, clear windshield, red plastic interior and gear, black plastic rotors, labels.
1. Blue body, red-yellow-black lettering and stripe and white N428 labels.

925-A   Batcopter   140mm 6/1976-1981 $60-80
Red rotors, black trim on large rotors, Batman figure, otherwise as 921-A.
1. Black body, red-yellow-black Batman labels.

926-A   Stromberg Jet Ranger Helicopter   150mm 6/1978-1979 $70-90
Main body and lower body-skids castings, clear windows, yellow interior, trim and stripe between castings, black plastic rotors and fins, unpainted lever, labels.
1. Black body, yellow trim, blue and white emblem labels.

927-A   Chopper Squad Surf Rescue Helicopter 150mm 8/1978-1979 $40-50
Main body and lower body-strut castings, amber windows, silver plastic interior and stripe between castings, white plastic rotors, fins, floats and gear, winch line and hook, labels. Same casting as 926-A.
1. Blue and white body, orange and black Chopper Squad and blue and white Surf Rescue labels.
2. Black and yellow body, yellow pontoons, rotor and blades, Spindrift "S" logo, (St. Michael 8801, also used in St. Michael Gift Set 8403).

928-A   Spidercopter   144mm 10/1979-1981 $60-80
Upper and lower body castings, black windows and rotor, white plastic parts, red plastic tongue, tail rotor and legs, labels.
1. Blue body, Spiderman labels.

929-A   Daily Planet Jet Helicopter   150mm 6/1979-1981 $60-80
Amber windows, silver interior and stripe between castings, white plastic rotors and fins, otherwise as 926-A.
1. Red and white body, red Daily Planet lettering labels.

930-A   Drax Airlines Jet Helicopter   150mm 8/1979-1981 $60-80
Yellow rotors and fins, otherwise as 926-A.
1. White body, black and yellow Drax Airlines labels.

931-A   Jet Ranger Police Helicopter   150mm 6/1980-1980 $30-50
Amber windows, chrome interior and stripe, red floats, rotors and fins, otherwise as 926-A.
1. White body, police labels.

Classics (1960s Production)

9001-9002-9003-9004-A 1927 Bentley   100mm 2/1964-1969
                                    (9004-A) $120-140
                                    (Others) $60-70
Body, chassis and radiator-headlights castings, clear windshield, brown interior, silver SW, tan plastic boxes, black horn, black raised or folded top, driver figure, spoked wheels, plastic tires, copper exhaust pipe, steel muffler, hand brake, cast-in bonnet straps.
1. (9001-A1) Green body and tops of fenders, metallic charcoal chassis and bottoms of fenders, unpainted cast spoked wheels, top up, racing driver, number 8 on radiator, 3/1964-1969.
2. (9002-A1) Red body, black fenders and chassis, red plastic spoked wheels, top up, civilian driver; 2/1964-1969.
3. (9003-A1) Light gray body, gray chassis, top up, other details unkown, never in Corgi catalog; 1965-1967?
4. (9004-A1) "World of Wooster," green body, metallic charcoal chassis including fenders, folded top, dark red interior, unpainted cast spoked wheels, figures of Jeeves driving and Bertie Wooster standing; 2/1967-1969.
5. (9004-A2) "World of Wooster," red body, otherwise as 9004-A1; 2/1967-1969.

9011-9012-9013-A 1915 Model T Ford 85mm 1/1964-1969 $70-80
Body, chassis and radiator-headlights castings, clear windshield, black plastic interior, SW, grille, spare wheel, rack and raised or folded top, one or more figures, spoked plastic wheels, black plastic suspension, gold lamps.
1. (9011-A1) Black body, chassis and wheels, chrome radiator and headlights, folded top, two seated figures; 1/1964-1969.
2. (9011-A2) Chrome plated body, two holes in base, other details unknown.
3. (9012-A1) Yellow body and wheels, black chassis, chrome radiator and headlights, folded top, two seated figures; 1/1964-1969.
4. (9013-A1) Blue body, black chassis and raised top, yellow wheels, figure of man cranking car; 11/1964-1969.
(Note: 9014 Lyons Tea Van, shown in 1967-1968 Corgi catalog, was never issued.)
9021-A 1910 Daimler 38 106mm 7/1964-1969 $70-80
Body-fenders, chassis, radiator-headlights and dashboard-lights castings, black plastic interior, SW, folded top, grille, exhaust pipe and trunk rack, clear windshield, yellow plastic spoked wheels, black plastic tires, four figures (man and woman in back, chauffeur and girl in front).
1. Orange-red body, yellow and gray chassis, gold lamps, chrome radiator shell.
(Note: 9022 blue Daimler with top up, shown in 1967-1968 Corgi catalog was never issued.)
9031-9032-A 1910 Renault 12/16 100mm 4/1965-1969
(Light Purple) $70-80
(Light Yellow) $80-90
Body, charcoal chassis, gold lights and unpainted drive train castings, black plastic top, gray plastic interior, SW and exhaust pipe, cast spoked wheels same color as body, black plastic tires.
1. (9031-A1) Metallic light purple body and wheels.
2. (9032-A1) Light yellow body and wheels.
9041-A 1912 Rolls-Royce Silver Ghost 115mm 5/1966-1970 $50-70
Main body and hood, chassis, gold lights, box and tank castings, clear windows, bronze interior, chrome SW, dash lights and radiator, black plastic grille, jeweled headlights, silver plastic roof rack with spare tire, black plastic tires. Casting also used for 805-A.
1. Silver body and hood, charcoal and silver chassis, silver wheels.
2. Same as 9041-A1 except gold wheels.

Corgitronics

1001-A HGB-Angus Firestreak 158mm 7/1980-Close $75-85
Body, chrome or unpainted bumper, grille-headlights, hatch and fittings castings, chrome plastic ladders, rear box and spotlight, black plastic hose reel and connections, yellow plastic ladder, white water cannon, two red dome lights, Rescue and number 3 labels, chrome wheels, electric siren and lights.
1. Clear windows, yellow interior, figures and accessories.
2. Opaque black windows, interior only at rear, no figures or accessories.
1002-A BL Roadtrain and Trailers 228mm 8/1981-Close $50-60
Cab, cab chassis and semi-trailer chassis castings, amber windows, black grille frame and tanks, orange airscreen, white semi-trailer interior with battery space and controls, freighter and tanker semi-trailer bodies, four-spoked chrome wheels, accessories. Truck goes forward, stops and backs up.
1. White cab body, orange cab and semi chassis, dark blue freighter semi body with Yorkie Chocolate logo and tanker semi body with Gulf logo, playmat.
2. No playmat, otherwise as type 1; 2/1982-Close.
3. Shown in 1981 Corgi catalog with Shell oil freighter and BP tanker bodies; was it ever issued in this form?
1003-A Ford Torino Road Hog 146mm 8/1981-Close $35-45
Single body casting, chrome windows, yellow antennas, chrome bumpers, grille, headlights and trim, red taillights, black plastic base, yellow and silver eagle and trim labels, chrome wheels. Body casting from 292-A. Working horn.
1. Black body.
1004-A Beep Beep London Bus 122mm 8/1981-Close $35-45
Red upper and lower body castings, white plastic stripe between castings, opaque black windows, silver grille and headlights, black plastic base with battery hatch, six-spoke chrome wheels. Horn blows. 469-A casting.
1. BTA side panels.
2. Hamleys side panels, otherwise as 1004-A1.
3. Aero side panels, otherwise as 1004-A1.
1005-A Police Land Rover 126mm 8/1981-Close $35-45
Main body and opening rear door castings, opaque black windows, blue dome light, silver grille and headlights, Police and stripe labels, black diecast base and plastic tow hook, chrome wheels. Working roof light and siren. 421-B casting.
1. White body, red and blue stripes, black lettering.
1006-A Radio Roadshow Van 120mm 5/1982-Close $45-55
Main body and two opening hood castings, opaque black windows, black plastic base with battery hatch, radio control knob inside rear door, chrome four-spoke wheels. Working radio.
1. Yellow body, white plastic roof and rear interior, red plastic loudspeakers, "Radio west 605" side labels (need confirmation).
2. White body, red plastic roof and rear interior, gray plastic loudspeakers, "Radio Tele Luxembourg RTL 209" side labels.
1007-A Road Repair Unit 254mm 7/1982-Close $45-55
Land Rover body and opening rear door, trailer body and base castings, clear windows, brown interior, black SW, red plastic trailer interior and opening panels, chrome trailer tank with switch, black plastic hitches, black diecast Land Rover base with battery hatch, chrome wheels, labels, figure with air hammer. Model makes sound of air hammer.
1. Dark yellow Land Rover and trailer, red" Roadworks" markings with white background behind triangle, yellow exhaust pipe and side panels on trailer.
2. Same as 1007-A1 except red side and roof panel on trailer, silver exhaust pipe, yellow background behind triangle markings.
1008-A Chevrolet Caprice Fire Chief Car 149mm 6/1982-Close $35-45
Body and chrome roof bar castings, opaque black windows, red roof light, chrome bumpers, grille and headlights, orange taillights, Fire Department and Fire Chief labels, black plastic base with battery hatch, chrome wheels. Working siren and roof light. Same body casting as 325-B without opening features.
1. Red body, red-white-orange labels.
1009-A MG Maestro Saloon Car 116mm 3/1983-Close $30-40
Main body and lower body-base castings, opaque black windows, black plastic grille, bumpers, spoiler, trim and battery hatch, clear headlights, red taillights, suspension, chrome wheels. Working headlights.
1. Yellow body, black trim.

Corgi Majors

1100-A Bedford Carrimore Low Loader 225mm 4/1958-1962
(Yellow Cab) $225-250
(Red Cab) $140-160
Cab, semi-trailer, two-piece tailgate and silver winch castings, clear windows, silver bumper, grille and headlights, winch crank, line and two black plastic jaws, rubber tires, Corgi dog decal on tailgate. First Bedford cab type; semi with sides.
1. Yellow cab, metallic blue semi-trailer and tailgate, smooth wheels.
2. Yellow cab, metallic blue semi-trailer and tailgate, shaped wheels.
3. Red cab, metallic blue semi-trailer and tailgate.
1100-B Mack Trans Continental Semi-Trailer 255mm 11/1971-1973 $90-100
Cab, opening hood and silver base, semi-body, chassis, fenders, unpainted trailer rests and two black opening rear door castings, clear windows, red interior, silver SW, red hood latch, black cab chassis, engine, stacks and grille and semi-hatch, sliding doors, silver headlights, light orange Trans Continental logo, two black plastic trailer rest wheels, chrome cast wheels, plastic tires.
1. Orange cab body and semi chassis and fenders, metallic light blue semi body.
1101-A Bedford Carrimore Car Transporter 258mm 10/1957-1962 $130-150
Cab, upper and lower semi-trailer, lowering tailgate, unpainted hydraulic cylinders and hinge bar castings, clear windows, silver bumper, grille, headlights and wheel channels, "Corgi Car Transporter" and dog decals, rubber tires, black diecast cab base. Same cab as 1100-A, same semi-trailer as 1105-A.
1. Blue cab, yellow semi-trailer, blue lettering, smooth wheels.
2. Red cab, pale green upper and blue lower semi-trailer, white lettering, smooth wheels.
3. Same as 1101-A2 except shaped wheels.
1101-B Warner & Swasey 4418 Hydraulic Crane 220mm 9/1975-1981 $50-60
Chassis, cab, crane base, boom, silver knob and gold hook castings, red interior, engine and base, black SW, exhaust and hydraulic cylinders, yellow braces, middle and upper boom sections, yellow cast wheels, black plastic tires, lettering labels.
1. Yellow crane and body, blue chassis, blue and yellow stripe labels.
1102-A Euclid TC-12 Bulldozer 156mm 11/1958-1962
(Yellow) $200-225
(Green) $150-160
Body, chassis, blade, four rollers and two unpainted hydraulic cylinder castings, gray plastic seat, controls and stacks, blue painted engine sides, silver grille and lights, sheet metal base, rubber treads, Euclid decals. Revised as 1107-A.
1. Yellow body, black treads, silver blade surface.
2. Lime green body, black treads, silver blade surface.
3. Lime green body, white treads, silver blade surface.
1102-B Berliet Fruehauf Dumper 282mm 5/1974-1976 $60-70
Cab body and chassis, semi chassis, rear fenders, two-piece opening dumper and unpainted trailer rest castings, clear windows, driver, black interior, stack, dumper knob and semi hitch, two black plastic trailer rest wheels, plastic dumper body, chrome headlights with amber lenses, black grille label, "Road Maker Construction" labels, chrome wheels, black tires.
1. Yellow cab, fenders and dumper, black cab and semi chassis, orange dumper body.
2. Darker orange dumper body, otherwise as 1102-B1.
1103-A Euclid TC-12 Caterpillar Tractor 108mm 5/1960-1964 $140-150
Body, chassis and four roller castings, gray plastic seat, controls and stacks, driver figure, silver grille and lights, blue painted engine sides, rubber treads, Euclid decals. Same body casting as 1102-A; no dozer blade.
1. Lime green body, black treads.
2. Lime green body, white treads.
1103-B Chubb Pathfinder Airport Crash Truck 238mm 9/1974-1980 $85-95
Upper and lower body, gold water cannon and sirens, and unpainted cannon mounting castings, clear windows, yellow interior, black SW, cannon mount and hook, chrome plastic deck, silver lights, cast wheels, plastic tires, yellow battery hatch, gray water hose, light red bulb, labels. Model squirts water.
1. Red body, "Airport Fire Brigade" labels.
2. Same as 1103-B1 except orange bulb, yellow tube.
3. Red body, "New York Airport" labels.
1104-A Bedford Machinery Carrier 235mm 9/1958-1962 $125-140
Cab, semi-trailer, winch, removable black rear fenders and two silver folding ramp castings, clear windows, silver bumper, grille and headlights, black diecast cab chassis, winch crank with line and two black plastic jaws, wire rear axle clip, smooth wheels, rubber tires. First type Bedford cab, semi-trailer without sides.
1. Red cab. silver semi-trailer.
2. Blue cab, silver semi-trailer.
1104-B Bedford TK Articulated Horse Box 255mm 9/1973-1976 $100-120
Cab, lower trailer body and three lowering ramp castings, plastic upper trailer body, clear windows, yellow interior, silver bumper, grille and headlights. red taillights, gray diecast cab base, cardboard trailer interior, horse figures, cast wheels, plastic tires, Newmarket Racing Stables labels.
1. Dark metallic green cab and lower trailer, yellow upper trailer.
2. Medium green cab and lower trailer, yellow upper trailer.
3. Medium green cab and lower trailer, orange upper trailer.
1105-A Bedford Carrimore Car Transporter 270mm 11/1962-1966 $130-150
Cab, upper and lower semi, lowering ramp, unpainted hydraulic cylinders and hinge bar castings, clear windows, yellow interior, silver bumper, grille, headlights and wheel channels, gray diecast cab base, black plastic mirrors, white lettering and Corgi dog decals, suspension, shaped wheels, rubber tires. New cab, 1101-A semi.
1. Red cab, blue lower and pale green upper semi-trailer.
1105-B Berliet Articulated Horse Box 275mm 6/1976-1980 $60-70
Cab body and chassis, lower trailer body and three lowering ramp castings, clear windows, black interior and stack, chrome headlights, amber lenses, cardboard trailer interior, red taillights, horse figures, chrome wheels, white plastic upper semi-body, National Racing Stables labels.
1. Bronze cab body and lower trailer body, cream cab chassis, white upper trailer body.
1106-A Decca Airfield Radar Van 132mm 1/1959-1960 $160-180
Chassis-cab, rear body and scanner castings, clear windows, silver bumper and headlights, gray plastic antenna and scanner rod, gear to turn scanner, sheet metal front and inner rear base, smooth wheels, rubber tires, lettering decals.
1. Cream body, orange vertical stripes, orange scanner with silver surface.
1106-B Mack Container Truck 290mm 7/1972-1978
(Promotional versions) $500-600+
(Silver Trailer) $150-160
(Others) $90-100
Cab, opening hood, black chassis, red bumper-base, semi flatbed, white fenders and unpainted trailer rest castings, clear windows, red interior and hood latch, silver SW, black plastic engine, grille and pipes, silver headlights, red roof lights, two red containers, white ACL labels, two black rest wheels, red

suspension, unpainted cast wheels, plastic tires, black hitch lever.
1. Yellow cab and semi-trailer flatbed, red containers.
1. Yellow cab and semi-trailer flatbed, red containers, promotional labels on containers and top of hood.
2. Yellow cab, silver gray flatbed, red container.
3. Promotional for 3M, special paint and packaging, non-standard load.

1107-A Euclid TC-12 Bulldozer **157mm 4/1963-1966**
(Red) $360-380
(Orange) $280-320
(Green) $140-160
Driver figure, metal control lever, tow hook, black rubber treads, otherwise as 1102-A.
1. Lime green body.
2. Red body.
3. Orange body.

1107-B Berliet Container Truck **288mm 9/1978-1978 $60-70**
Cab, cab chassis, semi flatbed, fenders and unpainted trailer rest castings, clear windows, black interior, stack, trailer hitch lever and rest wheels, chrome headlights, amber lens, chrome wheels, two gray containers, United States Line labels.
1. Blue cab and semi fenders, white cab chassis and semi flatbed.

1108-A Bloodhound Missile on Launching Platform **204mm 10/1958-1960 $120-130**
White missile, four yellow fins and unpainted jet castings, red rubber nose cone, RAF rondel decals; platform with five olive, two unpainted, and cream and silver base castings, hydraulic cylinder; platform rotates and raises. Missile issued alone as 1115-A, platform as 1116-A.
1. As above.

1108-B Ford Michelin Container Truck **285mm 7/1981-Close $35-45**
Tiltcab, chassis, semi-trailer flatbed, fenders, two tanks and unpainted trailer rest castings, clear windows, black plastic interior and hitch lever, white Michelin man figure, gray engine, two yellow containers with blue and white Michelin logo, stripe labels on cab, chrome wheels, two Whizzwheels on trailer rest.
1. Blue cab and semi flatbed, white cab chassis and fenders, yellow containers.

1109-A Bloodhound Missile on Trolley **210mm 2/1959-1961 $120-130**
White, yellow and red missile as in 1108-A, ten olive and two gold trolley castings, two cranks to raise cradle and supports, swiveling front suspension, lifting hitch, spare wheel, smooth wheels, rubber tires, Missile issued alone as 1115-A, trolley as 1117-A.
1. As above.

1109-B Ford Covered Semi-trailer Truck **228mm 8/1979-1980 $50-60**
Tiltcab, chassis, two tanks, low-side semi-trailer, fenders and unpainted trailer rest castings, clear windows, black interior, hitch lever and two rest wheels, gray engine, white Michelin man figure, silver headlights, two yellow plastic covers with blue and white Michelin logo, chrome wheels, black tires. Same cab casting as 1108-B.
1. Blue cab and semi, black cab chassis and semi fenders, yellow covers.

1110-A Bedford Mobilgas Tanker **192mm 4/1959-1965**
(Mobilgas) $250-275
(Shell Chemicals) $1500-2000+
Cab and tanker semi-trailer castings, clear windows, silver bumper, grille, headlights and tanker catwalk and caps, Mobil and Mobilgas decals, rubber tires, gray diecast cab base, sheet metal trailer base.
1. Red cab and semi trailer, blue and white "Mobilgas" decals, smooth wheels crimped on axles.
2. Same as 1110-A1 except shaped wheels crimped on axles.
3. Blue cab and lower semi-trailer, white upper semi-trailer, shaped wheels crimped on axles, " Shell" and "Benzeen-Tolueen-Xyleen" decals, packaged in special box with promotional literature, (Dutch promotional).
4. Same as 1110A3 except only Shell Logo with out other wording.

1110-B JCB 110B Crawler Loader **165mm 6/1976-1980 $50-60**
Main body, chassis, cab, arms, shovel and three control castings, clear windows, red interior, control knob and hubs, driver, black treads, hydraulic cylinder and stack, JCB labels; knob raises arms, control bars operate shovel.
1. White cab, red shovel, rest of body and chassis yellow.
2. White cab and shovel, rest of body orange, Block labels; 1980.

1111-A Massey Ferguson Combine Harvester **165mm 8/1959-1963 $180-200**
Numerous diecast body and component pieces, yellow plastic steering and control wheels and parts, yellow metal blades with unpainted tines, other parts of blade assembly unpainted, silver grid, white and black decals, orange wheels, rubber tires. (Note that blades and tines are diecast).
1. Red body.

1111-B Massey Ferguson Combine Harvester **165mm 7/1968-1973 $125-150**
Body and components basically as 1111-A, but with yellow plastic blades and tines, grid and several other parts, red wheels, plastic tires, driver figure on plastic seat.
1. Red body.

1112-A Corporal Guided Missile on Mobile Launcher **325mm high 6/1959-1962 $140-160**
White and red diecast missile, red rubber and unpainted metal nose cone, olive upper and lower launcher and four each unpainted supports, brace arms, brace screws and black brace pad castings, black plastic hitch, two shaped wheels, rubber tires.
1. As above with rubber nose cone.
2. As above with added percussion head feature in nose cone.

1112-B David Brown-JF Combine Harvester **220mm 3/1978-1979 $90-100**
Diecast scoop and chassis, red plastic parts, yellow plastic blades, frame-work and linkage to 55-B David Brown Tractor.
1. Red and yellow combine, white JF labels, standard 55-B tractor.

1113-A Corporal Missile and Erector Vehicle **295mm 10/1959-1962 $325-350**
Olive cab, chassis, mounting arms, cradle and arms, olive and unpainted gears and knobs, silver headlights, red taillights, clear windows, silver cast wheels, rubber tires, unpainted muffler and exhaust pipe; front wheels steer. Vehicle carries Corporal missile as used in 1112-A.
1. As above.

1113-B Hyster 800 Stacatruck **216mm 10/1977-Close**
(Sealink) $120-140
(Others) $50-60
Body, cab and upright bar castings, clear windows, driver figure, black plastic interior, base, ladders, exhaust stacks, inner upright, gear, knob and lifting brackets, cast wheels, plastic tires, plastic container, Hyster labels.
1. Yellow diecast parts, red plastic forks holding lifting brackets, gray and red United States Line container.
2. Blue body, white cab and upright, white plastic forks, yellow and white Michelin container; 7/1981.
3. Sealink, other details not known.

1115-A Bloodhound Guided Missile **180mm 3/1959-1960 $90-110**
Diecast missile, four fins and unpainted jets, red rubber nose cone, as used in 1108-A and 1109-A.
1. White missile with yellow fins.
2. White missile and fins.

1116-A Launching Ramp for Bloodhound Missile **123mm 3/1959-1960 $80-90**
Details as in 1108-A, except for:
Unpainted diecast bracket at upper end of launching arm.
Standard colors.

1116-B Shelvoke and Drewry Revopak Garbage Truck **150mm 4/1979-Close $25-35**
Chassis-cab, body and raising rear body castings, clear windows, black interior, grille, front base and bumpers, silver headlights, red taillights, brown plastic rear parts, City Sanitation labels.
1. Orange chassis-cab, silver rear body.

1117-A Loading Trolley for Bloodhound Missile **182mm 3/1959-1960 $60-70**
Details as in 1109-A.
1. Standard colors.

1117-B Mercedes-Faun Street Sweeper **125mm 5/1980-Close $25-35**
Cab, rear body, black chassis and unpainted brush housing and arm castings, clear windows, red interior, black SW, grille and hose, white grille trim, chrome headlights and parts, red taillights, amber dome light, black and white Faun and red and white stripe labels, chrome wheels; figure of man holds end of hose.
1. Orange body, light orange figure.
2. Orange body, brown figure.
3. Red body, ? figure.
4. Yellow body, brown figure

1118-A International 6x6 Army Truck **140mm 5/1959-1963**
(Dutch Army) $280-320
(Green Unmarked) $130-140
Chassis-cab, base and rear body castings, sheet metal cover, clear windows, silver headlights, tow hook, red and blue decals, six cast olive wheels, rubber tires. Model later reissued with U.S. Army decals as 1133-A.
1. Olive drab body and base, no suspension.
2. Olive drab body and base, suspension.
3. Dutch Army, other details not known.

1118-B Chubb Pathfinder Airport Crash Tender **238mm 3/1981-1982 $70-80**
Yellow water hose and bulb, no battery hatch, new labels, otherwise as 1103-B.
1. Red body, white stripe and "Emergency Unit 5" label, "Airport Fire Service" and shield label.

1119-A H.D.L. Hovercraft SR-N1 **120mm 6/1960-1962 $80-100**
Superstructure, deck and base castings, clear canopy, white plastic fan housing, red seats, yellow and checkered flaps, three sprung ball bearing landing gear units, yellow decals.
1. Blue superstructure, silver gray deck and base, yellow SR-N1 decals.

1119-B Mercedes-Benz Loadlugger Truck **6/1983-Close $25-35**
"Corgimatic," operating tipping action, yellow cab/chassis, black front bumper, red container, black "Corgi" label on cab, white label on container.
1. Yellow cab, black chassis, red container.

1120-A Midland Red Express Coach **138mm 3/1961-1962 $160-180**
Single body casting, clear windows, yellow interior, gray SW, silver grille and headlights, silver diecast base and bumpers, suspension, rubber tires. gold decals.
1. Red body, black roof, smooth wheels.
2. Red body, black roof, shaped wheels.

1121-A International Circus Crane Truck **200mm 10/1960-1968 $200-225**
Chassis-cab, base, rear body, yellow crane base and winch housing castings, clear windows, silver grille and headlights, silver sheet metal boom and hook, winch crank, line and silver diecast hook, light blue cast-in "Chipperfieldss Circus" lettering, light blue cast wheels, rubber tires, suspension.
1. Red body and base, wheels crimped to axles.
2. Same as 1121-A1 except wheels free on axles.

1121-B Ford Transit Tipper **135mm 1983-Close $45-55**
Cab, rear chassis and black bumper-base castings, black windows, tan roof light (push button), tipper and tailgate, black grille, chrome headlights, black Corgi labels, chrome wheels, tipping action when dome light is pushed.
1. Orange cab and chassis, tan tipper with orange stripe labels.

1123-A Circus Animal Cage Wagon **130mm 1/1961-1968 $130-150**
Main body, four opening panels, unpainted bars, yellow chassis and turning front suspension castings, red plastic tow hook, light blue plastic divider and sheet metal sliding doors, amber skylights, light blue cast-in "Chipperfieldss Circus" lettering and trim, suspension, rubber tires.
1. Red body with blue trim, yellow chassis, smooth wheels crimped on axles.
2. Red body with blue trim, yellow chassis, shaped wheels crimped on axles.
3. Red body with blue trim, yellow chassis, shaped wheels free on axles.

1124-A Launcher for Corporal Missile **107mm 3/1960-1961 $70-80**
Details as in 1112-A.
1. Standard colors.

1126-A Ecurie Ecosse Racing Car Transporter **196mm 10/1961-1965 $180-200**
Main body, lowering upper deck, lowering tailgate and sliding door castings, clear windows, yellow interior, silver bumper, grille and headlights, red taillights, cast-in lettering, gray diecast base, suspension, shaped wheels, rubber tires.
1. Dark blue body, light blue lettering.
2. Dark blue body, yellow lettering.
3. Medium blue body, yellow lettering.
4. Medium blue body, red lettering.

1126-B Simon Snorkel Fire Engine **265mm 6/1977-1981 $55-65**
Main body, gold sirens and unpainted snorkel parts castings, blue windows and dome lights, yellow interior, braces and baskets, chrome rear deck and fittings, black hose reels, hydraulic cylinders, base and fireman figure, silver bumper, grille and headlights, white snorkel arms, black name labels, chrome wheels. (Note: not a revision of 1127-A, but a different model with longer cab and snorkel arms.)
1. Red body, shield labels on doors.

1127-A Simon Snorkel Fire Engine **250mm 9/1964-1976 $100-120**
Main body, rotating base, two snorkel arms, two-piece lower erector, unpainted two-piece upper erector, two rods and linkage, two control knobs, four braces and gold nozzle castings, clear windows, yellow interior, gray SW and basket, five fireman in cab and one in snorkel basket, white cast-in lettering on upper snorkel arm, gray diecast base, suspension.
1. Red body, silver decks, shaped wheels, rubber tires.
2. Red body, silver decks, cast wheels, rubber tires.
3. Red body, silver decks, cast wheels, plastic tires.
4. Red body, silver decks, large diameter cast wheels, thin plastic tires, (same wheels and tires as 1104-B).

1128-A Priestman Cub Power Shovel **157mm 5/1963-1976 $100-120**
Main body, pulley panel, lower body, chassis, lock rod, gray boom, control rod and shovel, unpainted knob and four hub castings, clear windows, gray controls, driver, lines, pulleys, Priestman decals, black treads; body swivels, shovel and boom raise and lower.
1. Orange upper body and panel, yellow lower body, lock rod and chassis, rubber treads.
2. Plastic treads, otherwise as type 1.

1129-A Bedford Milk Tanker **190mm 5/1962-1965** **$250-300**
Cab and tanker semi-trailer castings, clear windows, silver bumper, grille and headlights, two-tone blue and white decals, gray diecast base, shaped wheels, rubber tires. Same casting as 1110-A.
1. Light blue cab and lower tanker semi, white upper tank, Milk logo.
1129-B Mercedes-Benz Semi-trailer Van **206mm 1/1983-1983** **$25-35**
Cab, cab chassis and semi-trailer chassis castings, plastic semi-trailer body, airscreen, opening rear doors, black plastic cab base, amber windows, grille and headlight label, six-spoke chrome wheels. Reissued as 1146-B.
1. Black cab and semi body, white chassis and airscreen, red doors, red-blue and yellow stripes, white Corgi lettering.
1130-A Bedford Circus Horse Transporter **255mm 10/1962-1972** **$250-275**
Cab, lower semi-trailer and three lowering ramp castings, light blue plastic upper semi body, clear windows, yellow interior, gray SW, black mirrors, silver bumper, grille and headlights, red taillights, Chipperfieldss Circus label, horse figures, suspension, gray diecast cab base, rubber tires. (same casting used for 1104-B)
1. Red cab and lower trailer, lt. blue upper trailer, shaped wheels, rubber tires.
2. Same as 1130-A1 except same diameter cast wheels.
3. Same as 1130-A1 except large diameter cast wheels, thin plastic tires.
1130-B Mercedes-Benz Tanker Semi-trailer **190mm 1/1983-1983** **$20-30**
Cab, cab chassis and semi-trailer chassis castings, plastic tank with chrome catwalk, amber windows, labels, black plastic cab base, six-spoke chrome wheels, grille and headlight labels. Reissued as 1167-A.
1. Red cab, black cab and semi chassis, white tank, Corgi Chemco labels.
1131-A Bedford Carrimore Machinery Carrier **240mm 5/1963-1966** **$125-135**
Cab, semi-trailer, removable black axle-fender unit, two folding ramps and yellow spare wheel base castings, clear windows, yellow interior, gray SW, black mirrors, two spare wheels, suspension, gray diecast base, shaped wheels, rubber tires. New type cab unit with mirrors, revised 1104-A semi-trailer with spare wheels, no winch.
1. Blue cab, silver gray semi-trailer and ramps, shaped wheels, rubber tires.
2. Blue cab, silver gray semi-trailer and ramps, same diameter cast wheels, rubber tires.
1131-B Mercedes-Benz Refrigerator Semi-trailer **206mm 1/1983?-Close** **$20-30**
See 1146-B for details. Model may not have been reissed as 1131.
1132-A Bedford Carrimore Low Loader **240mm 5/1963-1965** **$240-260**
Cab, semi-trailer, two-piece lowering tailgate and yellow spare wheel base castings, clear windows, red interior, gray SW, black mirrors, silver bumper, grille and headlights, two spare wheels, suspension, gray diecast cab base, shaped wheels, rubber tires. New type cab unit with mirrors, revised 1100-A semi-trailer with spare wheels, no winch.
1. Yellow cab and tailgate, red semi-trailer.
1132-B Scania Container Truck **140mm 1/1983-Close** **$20-30**
See 1147-B for details. Model may not have been reissued as 1132. If it exists, it has:
1. Danzas logo, yellow chassis-cab, black airscreen, yellow and black container.
1133-A International U.S. Army Troop Transporter **140mm 9/1964-1965** **$225-250**
White U.S. Army decals, otherwise as 1118-A.
1. Olive body and base.
1133-B Scania Tipper Truck **145mm 1/1983-Close** **$15-25**
See 1152-B for details. Model may not have been reissued as 1133. If it exists it has:
1. Green chassis-cab, silver tipper.
1134-A Bedford U.S. Army Tanker **188mm 9/1964-1965** **$400-450+**
U.S. Army decals, otherwise as 1110-A and 1129-A.
1. Olive drab cab and tanker trailer.
1134-B Scania Bulk Carrier **144mm 1/1983-Close** **$15-25**
See 1150-A for details. Model may not have been reissued as 1134. If it exists, it has:
1. Kohler logo, red chassis-cab, white airscreen, red and white silos.
1135-A Bedford U.S. Army Equipment Transporter **240mm 9/1964-1965** **$400-450+**
White U.S. Army decals, otherwise as 1131-A.
1. Olive drab cab and semi-trailer.
1137-A Ford Express Service Semi-Trailer Truck **234mm 3/1965-1970** **$120-140**
Blue and silver Tiltcab, silver grille, gold horns, gray chassis and base, blue semi-trailer body, red chassis and fenders, unpainted trailer rest castings, clear windows, yellow interior, silver SW, trim and ladders, gray mirrors and exhaust stack, chrome sliding doors with red "Express Service" logo, two black plastic trailer rest wheels, suspension.
1. Shaped wheels, thick rubber tires.
2. Large diameter cast wheels, thin plastic tires.
1138-A Ford Carrimore Car Transporter **268mm 4/1966-1969** **$140-160**
Tiltcab, silver grille, gray chassis and base, upper and lower semi-trailer, unpainted hydraulic cylinders, bars and trailer rest castings, clear windows, yellow interior, silver horns, trim and ladders, gray mirrors and ladders, chrome logo panels, red blocks and trim, black and yellow stripe labels, two black plastic trailer rest wheels, suspension, large diameter cast wheels, thin plastic tires.
1. Red and silver cab, pale green upper and blue lower semi-trailer, red Corgi logo.
1139-A Scammell Circus Menagerie Transporter **230mm 10/1968-1972** **$250-300+**
Cab, cab chassis, gray bumper-base, red power train, semi-trailer flatbed, fenders and unpainted trailer rest castings, clear windows, red interior, silver SW, jeweled headlights, three clear plastic cages with animal figures and red lifting eyes, spare wheels, two black plastic trailer rest wheels, Chipperfieldss logo, suspension, cast wheels, plastic tires.
1. Red upper and light blue lower cab, light blue semi-trailer, red fenders.
1140-A Bedford Mobilgas Tanker **198mm 3/1965-1966** **$250-275**
Cab and tanker semi-trailer castings, clear windows, yellow interior, gray SW, black mirrors, silver bumper, grille, headlights and tanker catwalk, Mobilgas decals, suspension, sheet metal tanker base, gray diecast cab base, shaped wheels, rubber tires. Second type Bedford cab unit with 1110-A semi-trailer.
1. Red cab and tanker, blue-white-red Mobilgas decals.
1140-B Ford Transit Wrecker **150mm 3/1981-Close** **$20-30**
Cab, rear body, white boom support, unpainted roof bar, two winch knobs and hook castings, clear windows, black interior and grille, white headlights, amber roof lights, red boom, black diecast bumpers and base, chrome wheels, "24 hour service," taillights and stripe labels.
1. White cab and rear, red roof and trim, silver rear bed.
1141-A Bedford Milk Tanker **198mm 12/1965-1967** **$300-400+**
Two-tone blue and white "Milk" labels, otherwise as 1140-A. Second type Bedford cab with 1129-A semi-trailer.
1. Light blue cab and lower tanker semi, white upper tank.
1142-A Ford Holmes Wrecker **120mm 5/1967-1974** **$130-150**
Tiltcab, lower cab, grille, gray chassis and base, gold horns and booms, rear body, red and unpainted boom frames, unpainted tank, two ladders, winch gears, pulley housings and hook castings, clear windows, red interior, silver SW, silver upper grille, black mirrors, exhaust stack, engine and bumper, two spare wheels, red roof light, Holmes Wrecker decals, taillights and stripe label, cast wheels, plastic tires.
1. White cab, black roof, red rear body, lower cab and grille, gold booms.
2. White cab, black roof, red rear body, lower cab and grille, silver booms.
3. Gold cab & wrecker body, red booms & supports, black cab roof. (Known preproduction model, 3 made)

1143-A American LaFrance Aerial Ladder Truck **282mm 10/1968-Close**
(Red Wheels) $140-150
(Unpainted Wheels) $120-130
(Whizzwheels) $90-100
Red open cab, semi-trailer, ladder rack and tiller seat, chrome or white cab chassis, semi chassis and three decks, gold raising gear, knobs, braces and fitting castings, clear windshield, chrome windshield frame, antenna and lights, jeweled headlights and red lights, black interior, tiller seat, steering wheel and hydraulic cylinders, yellow diecast and plastic ladders, six fireman figures, supsension, cast wheels, plastic tires, shield decals.
1. Red and chrome body, white American LaFrance decals, red wheels.
2. Red and white body, white American LaFrance decals, unpainted wheels.
3. Red and white body, shield labels, modified casting without seperate engine top cover, no antenna, Whizzwheels with silver centers.
1144-A Scammell Circus Crane Truck **202mm 3/1969-1972** **$550-650+**
Upper and lower cab, silver rear bed, light blue crane base and winch housing, red drive train, unpainted hook, rear boom hook and winch crank castings, clear windows, red interior, silver SW, jeweled headlights, red tow hook, sheet metal boom with yellow plastic tip, spare wheel, gray diecast base and bumpers, cast wheels, plastic tires, circus labels, clear plastic cage, red lifting eye, cardboard inner base, rhinoceros figure.
1. Red upper cab and rear body, light blue lower cab, crane base and winch housing.
1144-B Berliet Holmes Wrecker **125mm 3/1975-1978** **$65-75**
Cab, bumper-chassis, rear body, rear bed and framework, two gold booms and hooks, and winch center castings, clear windows, yellow dome light, black interior and exhaust stack, driver, grille label, chrome headlights, amber lenses, white rear framework, light red winch knobs and spools, red-white-blue stripe labels, chrome wheels. Rear body and booms slightly simplified from 1142-A.
1. Red cab, rear bed and framework, blue rear body, white chassis.
2. Orange cab, framework and rear body, white chassis and rear deck, " Rescue Breakdown Services" trim, (St. Michael Gift Sets 8102, 8402).
1144-C Mercedes-Benz Semi-trailer Van **206mm 1/1983-Close** **$20-30**
Cab, cab chassis and semi-trailer chassis castings, clear windows, grille-headlight label, red plastic semi body with two opening doors, black cab chassis plate, yellow Royal Mail labels, six-spoke Whizzwheels.
1. Red cab and semi with black chassis, airscreen.
2. Red cab and semi with black chassis, no airscreen.
1145-A Mercedes-Benz Unimog and Goose Dumper **170mm 10/1969-1976** **$45-55**
Cab, bumper-fenders, cab chassis, tipper, tipper chassis and two unpainted drive train castings, clear windows, red interior, gray SW, black hydraulic cylinders, spare wheel, suspension, red cast wheels, plastic tires.
1. Yellow cab and tipper, red fenders and tipper chassis, charcoal gray cab chassis, black plastic mirrors.
2. No mirrors, otherwise as type 1.
3. Blue cab fenders and tipper chassis, yellow cab and tipper, no mirrors.
1145-B Mercedes-Benz Semi-trailer Van **206mm 1/1983-Close** **$20-30**
Most components as 1144-C, plastic airscreen, red rear doors, yellow-red-black Yorkie Milk Chocolate labels.
1. Yellow cab, blue semi, both with red chassis, red airscreen, four-spoke wheels.
2. Refrigerator box, orange airscreen, six-spoke wheels, otherwise as type 1.
1146-A Scammell Carrimore Tri-deck Car Transporter **282mm 9/1970-1973** **$180-200**
Cab, cab chassis, white drive train, gray bumper-base, three semi-trailer decks, white rear plate, unpainted bars and brace and two gray base castings, clear windows, red interior, silver SW, black hydraulic cylinders and blocks, spare wheel, suspension, cast wheels, plastic tires.
1. Orange cab chassis and lower deck, white cab and middle deck, blue top deck.
1146-B Mercedes-Benz Refrigerator Van **206mm 1/1983-Close** **$20-30**
Most components as 1144-C and 1145-B, white airscreen, red rear doors, six-spoke wheels.
1. White cab with blue chassis, black semi with white chassis, red-yellow-blue stripes and white Corgi lettering labels, black refrigerator box.
2. White cab, semi and refrigerator box, blue cab and semi chassis, red-white-blue-black Christian Salvesen labels.
3. White cab and semi, both with black chassis, orange-yellow-black-white Dunlop logo.
1147-A Scammell Ferrymasters Covered Semi-trailer **235mm 12/1969-1972** **$125-135**
Cab, cab chassis, semi-trailer, fenders, gray cab base-bumper and unpainted hitch lever and trailer rest castings, clear windows, red interior, silver SW, jeweled headlights, two yellow plastic rear covers with black Ferrymasters logo, spare wheel, two black plastic trailer rest wheels, name label on cab, suspension, cast wheels, plastic tires.
1. White cab, yellow cab chassis, semi-trailer and covers, black fenders.
1147-B Scania Container Truck **140mm 1/1983-Close** **$15-25**
Chassis-cab casting, clear windows, orange airscreen, black plastic exhaust stack and cab base, grille label, plastic rear bed and container with red rear doors, six-spoke Whizzwheels.
1. Yellow truck and container, Ryder Truck Rental labels.
1148-A Scammell Carrimore Car Transporter **269mm 5/1969-1969** **$150-170**
Cab, cab chassis, upper and lower semi-trailer decks, rear base, tailgate, unpainted hinge bars and hydraulic cylinder castings, clear windows, red interior, gray SW, yellow plastic blocks, unpainted cast wheels, plastic tires.
1. Red cab chassis and lower deck, rear base and tailgate, white cab and upper deck.
1148-B Scania Container Truck **140mm 1/1983-Close** **$15-25**
Amber windows, white airscreen, light blue and white container with rear doors, white rear deck, other details as 1147-B.
1. Medium blue chassis-cab, Securicor Parcels labels, red rear doors.
2. Medium blue chassis-cab, Securicor Parcels labels, white rear doors.
1149-A Scania Container Truck **140mm 1/1983-Close** **$15-25**
Blue windows, red airscreen, rear bed, roof and rear doors of white container, otherwise as 1147-B.
1. White chassis-cab, BRS Truck Rental labels.
1150-A Mercedes-Benz Unimog with Snowplow **150mm 1/1971-1976** **$55-65**
Cab, rear body, fenders-plow mounting, lower chassis, charcoal upper chassis-rear fenders and two unpainted drive train castings, plastic rear cover, clear windows, red interior, gray SW, black hydraulic cylinder, red flags, gray tow hook, spare wheel, suspension, dark red cast wheels, plastic tires.
1. Green cab and rear body, orange chassis and plow, silver blade,, black mirrors, olive rear cover; 1971-1974.
2. Tan rear cover, otherwise as type 1.
3. Tan rear cover, no mirrors, otherwise as type 1; 1975-1976.
4. Yellow cab and rear body, red chassis and plow, tan canopy, no mirrors.
1150-B Scania Bulk Carrier **144mm 1/1983-Close** **$15-25**
Chassis-cab casting, amber windows, grille label, blue airscreen, blue and white bulk silos, ladders, catwalk and mounting, black cab chassis, six-spoke Whizzwheels.
1. White chassis-cab, blue British Sugar labels.
1151-A Scammell Co-Op Semi-trailer Truck **230mm 1970-1970** **$200-250+**
Cab, cab chassis, semi-trailer, fenders, gray bumper-base and unpainted trailer rest castings, clear

windows, red interior, silver SW, jeweled headlights, black hitch lever, spare wheel, no trailer covers, CO-OP labels, suspension, cast wheels, plastic tires.
1. White cab, light blue trailer.

1151-B   Mack Exxon Tank Truck   275mm 1974-1975 $140-150
Cab, hood, engine-chassis, silver bumper-base, red tanker chassis and fenders, and unpainted trailer rest castings, clear windows, red interior and hood latch, black SW, stacks, grille, hitch lever, hose, front and back tanker brackets and rest wheels, white tanker body, chrome catwalk, red roof lights, silver headlights, yellow taillights, Exxon labels, cast wheels, plastic tires. Also used for 1152-A.
1. White cab and tank, red tank chassis and fenders, black cab chassis.

1151-C   Scania Bulk Carrier   144mm 1/1983-Close $15-25
Clear windows, orange airscreen, orange and white silos and fittings, otherwise as 1150-B.
1. White chassis-cab, black and orange Spillers Flour labels.

1152-A   Mack Esso Tank Truck   275mm 10/1971-1975 $80-90
Esso labels, otherwise as 1151-B.
1. White cab and tank, red tank chassis and fenders, black cab chassis.

1152-B   Scania Dump Truck   145mm 1/1983-Close $15-25
Chassis-cab castings, amber windows, grille label, black exhaust stack, hydraulic cylinders and cab base, light green tipper, six-spoke Whizzwheels.
1. White chassis-cab, green and black Barratt labels.

1153-A   Priestman Cub Boom Crane   230mm 6/1972-1974 $80-90
Body, base, winch, chassis, two-piece bucket and unpainted bucket arms, lower boom, knobs, gears and drum castings, clear windows, driver, gray controls, red plastic parts, yellow hubs, black treads, orange and black Hi Grab and stripe labels.
1. Orange body, red chassis and bucket.

1153-B   Scania Dump Truck   145mm 1/1983-Close $15-25
Yellow tipper, otherwise as 1152-B.
1. Yellow truck, black Wimpey labels, clear windows.
2. Yellow truck, black Wimpey labels, green windows.

1154-A   Mack-Priestman Crane Truck   230mm 10/1972-1976 $120-130
Cab, hood, rear body, cabin, cabin base, winch, black engine-chassis and grille guard, silver bumper-base, unpainted braces, lower boom, knobs, gears, drum and gold hook castings, clear windows, red interior and hood latch, silver SW, black exhaust stacks, silver headlights, sheet metal upper boom with red plastic tip, cast wheels, plastic tires, stripe, name and "Long Vehicle" labels.
1. Red truck, yellow cabin, Hi Lift labels.
2. Red truck, yellow cabin, Hi Grab labels.

1154-B   Giant Tower Crane   354mm high 6/1981-1983 $75-85
Similar to 1155-A1 with additional hinged tower section.
1. White body, orange chassis, cab and booms.

1155-A   Skyscraper Tower Crane   230mm high 8/1975-1979 $60-70
Body, chassis, vertical and horizontal booms, gold hook and unpainted winch drum castings, two light gray boxes and load of blocks, red plastic platform, winch crank and line, black treads, black and white Skyscraper labels.
1. Red body, yellow chassis and booms.

1156-A   Volvo BM 860 S-Rapier Concrete Mixer   210mm 1/1977-1981 $50-60
Cab, cab chassis, rear chassis, chrome chute and unpainted hitch castings, red plastic mixer, orange parts, black stack, ladders, lever and gears, green windows, orange cast wheels, plastic tires, name, stripe and grille labels.
1. Yellow cab and rear chassis, red mixer with yellow and black stripes; 1977-1979.
2. Orange cab and rear chassis, white mixer with yellow and black stripes; 1980-1981.

1157-A   Ford Esso Tank Truck   270mm 4/1976-1981 $50-60
Tiltcab, black cab chassis-bumper, two tanks, red tanker chassis, fenders, and unpainted trailer rest castings, clear windows, red interior, black SW, tank caps, front and rear tank brackets, hose, and rest wheels, gray engine, white tanker body, chrome catwalk, chrome wheels.
1. White cab and tank, red tanker chassis and fenders, black cab chassis, Esso labels.

1158-A   Ford Exxon Tank Truck   270mm 6/1976-1981? $50-60
Castings, details and colors as 1157-A.
1. Exxon labels (for USA market).

1159-A   Ford Car Transporter   352mm 10/1976-1979 $90-100
Tiltcab, cab chassis-bumper, two tanks, semi-trailer, upper deck, lowering ramp and unpainted trailer rest castings, clear windows, red interior, black SW, blocks and parts, silver headlights, white plastic lower deck, black plastic rest wheels and rear base, chrome wheels.
1. Metallic lime green cab and semi, cream cab chassis, upper deck and ramp.
2. Metallic blue cab and semi, cream cab chassis, upper deck and ramp.

1160-A   Ford Gulf Tank Truck   270mm 4/1976-1978 $50-60
Castings and details as 1157-A and 1158-A.
1. White cab, orange chassis, blue tanker body, orange-blue-white Gulf labels.

1161-A   Ford Aral Tank Truck   270mm 7/1977-1980 $80-90
Castings and details as 1157-A, 1158-A and 1160-A.
1. Light blue cab and chassis, white tanker body, blue and white Aral labels.

1163-A   Circus Human Cannonball Truck   150mm 9/1978-1981 $65-75
Berliet cab, silver bumper-chassis and unpainted cannon mounting and trigger castings, clear windows, black interior, exhaust stack and tow hook, dark yellow rear body, light blue cannon, chrome female figure and headlights, amber lenses, yellow roof light and logo labels, chrome wheels.
1. Red cab, dark yellow rear body, blue cannon, silver chassis, "Le Great Marvo" labels.

1164-A   Berliet Dolphinarium Truck   250mm 4/1980-Close $130-150
Cab, cab chassis-bumper, semi-trailer, fenders and unpainted trailer rest castings, clear windows, black interior, exhaust stack, hitch lever and rest wheels, red roof light and pool apparatus, chrome headlights, amber lenses, blue tinted pool sides, yellow female figure, gray dolphins, red-white-blue logo, chrome wheels.
1. Blue cab and semi-trailer.
2. Yellow cab and semi-trailer, blue cab chassis and semi fenders.

1166-A   Mercedes-Benz Tanker   182mm 1/1983-Close $20-30
Cab, cab chassis and semi-trailer chassis castings, clear windows, grille headlight label, plastic tank body and catwalk, black cab chassis plate, six-spoke wheels.
1. Tan cab and tanker, both with black chassis, black and red Guinness labels, chrome catwalk.
2. Tan cab and tanker, both with black chassis, black and red Guinness labels, black catwalk.

1167-A   Mercedes-Benz Tanker   182mm 1/1983-Close $20-30
Castings and details as 1166-A except:
1. White cab and tank, both with green chassis, chrome catwalk, red-white-green 7-up labels.
2. White cab and tank, both with black chassis, black catwalk, red and black Corgi Chemco labels.
3. Black catwalk, otherwise as type 1.
4. Yellow cab and tank, both with blue chassis, black catwalk, blue-yellow-white Duckhams logo.

1168-A   National Express Bus   68mm 1/1983-Close $20-30
Single body casting, clear windows, white interior, black plastic base, 6-spoke Whizzwheels.
1. White body, yellow-brown-red Motorway Express logo.

1169-A   Ford Guinness Tanker   270mm 3/1982-Close $100-120
Castings and details as 1157-A, 1158-A, 1160-A and 1161-A except:
1. Tan, orange and black cab, tan tanker body and black chassis and fenders, Guinness logo.

1170-A   Ford Car Transporter   352mm 5/1982-Close $80-90
Castings and details as 1159-A except:
1. White cab, red chassis and semi-trailer, white decks and ramp.

????   Corgi Tourist Carry Case   (Late 1960's?) $???
Vinyl carry case with storage pockets for 20 cars, center divider with parking space markings, service station forecourt in lid, correct number not known, c.late-'60s.

Airplanes

The following airplane models were made by Lintoy of Hong Kong and sold by Corgi:

1301	**Piper Cherokee**	1972-1973	$40-50
1302	**Piper Navajo**	1972-1974	$40-50
1303	**Lockheed Starfighter**	1972-1974	$40-50
Luftwaffe colors.			
1304	**MIG 21**	1972-1974	$40-50
U.S.S.R Air Force colors.			
1305	**Grumman Tiger**	1972-1974	$40-50
U.S. Navy colors.			
1306	**Mustang**	1972-1973	$50-60
U.S. Navy colors.			
1307	**SAAB Draken**	1972-1974	$40-50
Swedish Air Force colors.			
1308	**BAC-Sepecat Jaguar**	1972-1973	$40-50
R.A.F colors.			
1309	**Concorde**	1974	$40-50
Air France colors.			
1310	**Boeing 707**	1973-1974	$40-50
Air France colors.			
1311	**Messerschmitt ME410**	1973-1974	$40-50
Luftwaffe colors.			
1312	**Boeing 727**	1973-1974	$40-50
TWA colors.			
1313	**Mitsubishi Zero**	1973-1974	$40-50
Imperial Japan colors.			
1315	**Boeing 747**	1974	$40-50
Pan Am colors, reissued as:			
1315	**Boeing 747**	1978-1979	$40-50
British Airways colors.			
1316	**Phantom Jet**	1973-1974	$40-50
1317	**Lockheed Tri-Star**	197?	$40-50
Years not known, Air Canada colors.			
1317	**Spitfire**	197?	$50-60
Years not known. Number may be incorrect.			
1320	**Vickers VC10**	1978-1979	$40-50
British Airways colors.			
1322	**Boeing 747**	197?	$40-50
Years not known, Canadian Pacific Air colors.			
1323	**Boeing 747**	197?	$40-50
Years not known, Wardair colors.			
1325	**Douglas DC10**	1978-1979	$40-50
Swissair colors.			

Corgi Accessories

752	**Whizztrack and connector**	circa 1972	$20-30
761	**Power Blaster and Crashstop**	circa 1972	$20-30
762	**Windicator**	circa 1972	$20-30
771	**Power Blaster Speedset**	circa 1972	$20-30
772	**Drag Strip Special**	circa 1972	$20-30
1341	**Wheels for 344**	1968	$15-25
1342	**Wheels for 300**	1968	$15-25
1351	**Wheels for 275**	1968	$15-25
1352	**Wheels for 276 and 338**	1968	$15-25
1353	**Wheels for 302 and 342**	1968	$15-25
1354	**Wheels for 273**	1968	$15-25
1361	**Wheels for 341**	1968	$15-25
1401	**Service Ramp**	1958-1960	$40-60
1. Metallic blue base.			
2. Non-metallic blue base.			
1440	**Red bulb for 437**	1962	$5-15
1441	**Blue bulb for 464**	1964	$5-15
1443	**Red flashing bulb for 437**	1967	$5-15
1444	**Blue flashing bulb for 464**	1967	$5-15
1445	**Blub for TX in 262**	1967	5-15
1449	**15mm tires**	1970	$15-25
1450	**15mm tires**	1958	$15-25
1451	**17mm tires**	1961	$15-25
1452	**19mm tires**	1961	$15-25
1453	**13mm tires**	1965	$15-25
1454	**Tractor rear tires**	1969	$15-25
1455	**Tractor front tires**	1969	$15-25
1456	**Racing rear tires**	1969	$15-25
1457	**Racing front tires**	1969	$15-25
1458	**24mm truck tires**	1969	15-25
1459	**19mm truck tires**	1969	$15-25
1460	**Adhesive Pack A**	1959-1966	$20-30
1461	**Adhesive Pack B**	1961-1966	$20-30
1462	**Adhesive Pack C**	1961-1966	20-30
1463	**Adhesive Pack D**	1961-1966	$20-30
1464	**Adhesive Pack E**	1961-1966	$20-30
1466	**Tires for 1150**	1970	$15-25

1480	Percussion head for Corporal Missile	1959	$20-30
1485	Planks load	1960-1964	$20-30
1486	Bricks load	1960-1964	$20-30
1487	Milk churns load	1960-1964	$20-30
1488	Cement sacks load	1960-1964	$20-30
1490	Tip with three milk churns	1960-1964	$20-30
1495	Corporal Missile crew	1960?	$15-25
1496	Racing drivers	1960?	$15-25
1497	Two bandits and "007"	1967	$15-25
1498	Rockets for 356	1967	$15-25
1499	Spare missiles and scanner for 268	1967	$15-25
1501	Racing drivers and mechanics	1963-1970	$15-25
1502	Spectators	1963-1970	$15-25
1503	Race track officials	1963-1970	$15-25
1504	Press officals	1963-1970	$15-25
1505	Garage attendants	1963-1970	$15-25

Little/large Gift Sets

Models were first put on the market in 1982, with one exception (1365 Routemaster Bus and London Taxi, in 1983) have not been shown in Corgi catalogs. Sets contained standard Corgi model plus matching (if possible) Corgi Jr. model. Models were current at the time of release in standard production trim. All were introduced 1982 unless noted, and continued until factory close.

1352	Renault 5 Turbo 307-B and 102-A	1982-Close	$25-40
1353	Austin Metro 275-B and 107-A	1982-Close	$25-40
1354	Texaco Special Racers (?) and 53-B	1982-Close	$25-40
1355	Talbot Rancho 457-B and 76-C	1982-Close	$25-40
1356	Fiat X1/9 314-B and 86-A	1982-Close	$25-40
1357	Jeep Golden Eagle 441-B and (?)	1982-Close	$25-40
1358	Citroen 2CV 346-B and 115-A	1982-Close	$25-40
1359	Ford Escort 334-B and 105-A	1982-Close	$25-40
1360	Batmobile 267-A and 69-A	1982-Close	$40-80
1361	James Bond Aston Martin 271-B and 40-C	1982-Close	$40-80
1362	James Bond Lotus Esprit 269-B and 60-B	1982-Close	$40-80
1363	Buck Rogers 647-A and 13-C	1982-Close	$40-80
1364	NASA Space Shuttle 648-A and 5-C	1982-Close	$25-40
1365	London Bus 469-A and London Taxi 71-A	1983-Close	$25-40
1371	VW Turbo 309-B and 137-A	1982-Close	$25-40
1372	Jaguar XJS (?) and (?)	1982-Close	$25-40
1373	Ford Capri 312-C and 61-C	1982-Close	$25-40
1376	Starsky and Hutch Ford Torino 292-A, 45-B	1982-Close	$40-80
1378	Porsche 924 303-C and (?)	1982-Close	$25-40
1380	Mercedes 240 285-A and 59-C	1982-Close	$25-40
1382	Ford Mustang 370-A and 104-A	1982-Close	$25-40
1383	Mack Fire Pumper 2029-A and (?)	1982-Close	$25-40
1384	Ford Thunderbird 810-A and 96-B	1982-Close	$25-40
	1. Cream, red.		
	2. Cream, black.		
1385	Datapost Austin Metro 281-B and 135-A	1982-Close	$25-40
1389	Ford Sierra 299-A and 129-A	1982-Close	$25-40
1390	Porsche 924 (black) 310-B and (?)	1982-Close	$25-40
1393	Jeep (open) 447-B and 182-A	1982-Close	$25-40
1394	Jeep (with hood) 448-B and 183-A	1982-Close	$25-40
1395	Mazda Pick-up 495-A, Range Rover 184-A	1982-Close	$25-40
1396	Space Shuttles (May be identical to 1364)	1982-Close	$25-40
1397	BMW M1 380-B and Mercedes 124-A	1982-Close	$25-40
1401	Lotus Elite 382-B and Triumph TR7 10-C	1982-Close	$25-40
1402	Giant Tipper (?) and Skip Truck 85-A	1982-Close	$25-40
	(After normal production had stopped)		
1403	Mercedes Tanker (?) and Custom Van 185-A	1982-Close	$25-40
1405	Jaguar (?) and (?)	1982-Close	$25-40

Other "Little and Large" combinations may exist. Please report others found using the form presented at the end of this book. "Little and Large" data above obtained from *The Great Book of Corgi* by Marcel R. VanCleemput.

Husky and Corgi Junior

Models produced between 1964 and 1969 were called Husky; in 1970 the name of the series was changed to Corgi Junior. Models are listed under their Corgi Junior number where different from Husky number if known.

1-A Jaguar Mark X   66mm 1964-1967 $15-25
Small casting, yellow interior, clear windows, chrome plastic base, gray plastic wheels.
1. Dark blue body.
2. Metallic blue body.

1-B Jaguar Mark X   71mm 1967-1969 $15-25
Larger casting, yellow interior, clear windows, unpainted diecast base.
1. Dark blue body, gray plastic wheels.
2. Dark blue body, metal wheels with tires.
3. Metallic blue body, metal wheels with tires.

1-C Reliant TW9 Pickup   66mm 1970-1972 $12-15
No interior, green windows, unpainted diecast base, three wheels.
1. Light tan body, black Whizzwheels.
2. Orange body, black Whizzwheels.
3. Orange body, chrome Whizzwheels.

1-D Grand Prix Racer   75mm 1973-1976 $10-12
White interior, black diecast base, Whizzwheels, number 32 label.
1. Metallic green and white body.

1-E Mercedes-Benz 220D Ambulance   76mm 1977-Close $8-10
No interior, black plastic base, Whizzwheels.
1. All white body, purple windows, red cross labels on hood and doors.
2. Off-white body with red roof, blue windows, red cross labels on doors.

2-A Citroen Safari   64mm 1964-1967 $15-25
Small casting, yellow interior, clear windows, chrome plastic base, gray plastic wheels, tan plastic boat on roof.
1. Light yellow body.

2-B Citroen Safari   70mm 1967-69, 1970-73 $15-25
Larger casting, yellow interior, clear windows, unpainted metal base, boat on roof.
1. Lime gold body, tan boat, gray plastic wheels; 1967-1968
2. Lime gold body, blue boat, gray plastic wheels. Husky base; 1969-1969
3. Dark blue body, white boat, metal wheels with tires, Corgi Junior label; 1970.
4. Yellow body, white boat, black Whizzwheels, Corgi Junior base.
5. Yellow body, white boat, chrome Whizzwheels, Corgi Junior base.
6. Metallic purple body, white boat, chrome Whizzwheels, Corgi Junior base.
7. Blue body, white boat, chrome Whizzwheels?, Corgi Junior base.

2-C Blakes 7 Liberator   74mm 1980-1981 $20-30
Spacecraft, no interior, green windows, white diecast base, no wheels.
1. White and gold body.

3-A Mercedes-Benz 220 Sedan   64mm 1964-1968 $15-25
Opening trunk, yellow interior, clear windows, chrome plastic base, gray plastic wheels.
1. Light blue body.

3-B Volkswagen 1200 Police Car   66mm 1968-69, 1970-74 $12-15
Modified 20-B casting, red interior, clear windows, blue dome light, unpainted diecast base, Police labels.
1. White and black body, metal wheels with tires, Husky base; 1968-1969
2. White and black body, metal wheels with tires, Corgi Jr. base; 1970-1971
3. All white body, black Whizzwheels; 1972-1974.

3-C Volkswagen 1300 Police Car   68mm 1975-1976 $10-12
Modified 17-C casting, yellow interior, blue widows and dome light, unpainted diecast base, Whizzwheels, Police labels.
1. White body.

3-D Stromberg's Jet Ranger Helicopter   75mm 1977-1979 $20-30
Yellow plastic interior, base, skids and rotors, clear windows, no wheels, fish emblem.
1. Black and yellow body.

4-A Jaguar Mark X Fire Chief's Car   66mm 1964-1967 $15-25
Modified 1-A casting, yellow interior, clear windows, chrome plastic base, gray plastic wheels, red and white Fire decals, turning chrome siren on roof.
1. Red body.

4-B Jaguar Mark X Fire Chief's Car   71mm 1967-1969 $15-25
Modified 1-B casting, yellow interior, clear windows, unpainted diecast base, red and white Fire labels, turning chrome siren on roof.
1. Dark red body, gray plastic wheels.
2. Dark red body, metal wheels with tires.

4-C Zetor 5511 Farm Tractor   56mm 1970-1979 $10-12
Diecast base includes body parts, black plastic interior, no windows, black plastic wheels of two sizes.
1. Orange main body, red base.
2. Metallic green main body, white base.

5-A Lancia Flaminia   63mm 1964-1968 $15-25
Yellow interior, clear windows, chrome plastic base, gray plastic wheels, opening hood.
1. Light blue body.

5-B Willys Jeeps   62mm 1968-69, 1970-73 $12-15
Brown interior, no windows, unpainted diecast base, folding plastic windshield frame.
1. Metallic green body, yellow windshield, metal wheels with tires; 1968.
2. Metallic green body, gray windshield, metal wheels with tires; 1969.
3. Light tan body, gray windshield, metal wheels with tires, Corgi Junior label; 1970.
4. Light tan body, gray windshield, black Whizzwheels, Corgi Junior base.
5. Orange body, gray windshield, black Whizzwheels; Corgi Junior base.
6. Orange body, gray windshield, chrome Whizzwheels, Corgi Junior base.
7. Bright tan body, gray windshield, chrome Whizzwheels, Corgi Junior base.
8. Red body, gray windshield, chrome Whizzwheels, Corgi Junior base.

5-C NASA Space Shuttle   70mm 1980-Close $8-10
Opening hatches, gold interior, no windows, black diecast base, plastic wheels.
1. White upper and black lower body.

6-A Citroen Safari Ambulance   64mm 1964-1967 $15-25
Modified 2-A casting, blue interior, roof light and rear windows, clear front windows, chrome plastic base, gray plastic wheels, red cross decal on hood.
1. White body.
2. Off-white body.

6-B Ferrari Berlinetta 250GT   59mm 1967-1969 $15-25
Red interior, clear windows, chrome engine, diecast lower body-base same color as upper body, metal wheels with tires.
1. Red body and base.
2. Maroon body and base.

6-C DeTomaso Mangusta   70mm 1970-1973 $12-15
Chrome interior and grilles, diecast lower body-base same color as upper body.
1. Yellow-green body and base, green tinted windows, black Whizzwheels.
2. Metallic purple body, amber windows, black Whizzwheels.
3. Metallic purple body, amber windows, chrome Whizzwheels.

6-D Daily Planet Helicopter   75mm 1979-1980 $20-30
White plastic interior, base, skids and rotors, clear windows, red and white labels.
1. Red main body.

7-A Buick Electra Sedan   69mm 1964-1968 $15-25
Yellow interior, clear windows, chrome plastic base, gray plastic wheels.
1. Orange-red body.

7-B Duple Vista 25 Coach   76mm 1968-69, 1970-73 $12-15
Yellow interior, green windows, white plastic upper body, diecast base same color as lower body, unpainted diecast grille and bumpers.
1. Turquoise lower body, gray plastic wheels; 1968.
2. Turquoise lower body, metal wheels with tires; 1969.
3. Dark red lower body, metal wheels with tires, Corgi Junior base label; 1970.
4. Yellow lower body, black Whizzwheels, modified base.
5. Light purple lower body, black Whizzwheels; modified base.
6. Light purple lower body, chrome Whizzwheels. modified base.
7. Orange lower body, chrome Whizzwheels, modified base.

7-C Dumper Truck   74mm 1976-Close $10-12
Plastic base and operating tipper (same colors), no interior, grille label.
1. Red chassis-cab, yellow tipper and base, clear windows, black plastic wheels.
2. Blue chassis-cab, yellow tipper and base, clear windows, black plastic wheels.

3. Yellow chassis-cab, black tipper and base, no windows, Whizzwheels; 1980-1982.
4. Yellow chassis-cab, red tipper and base, no windows, Whizzwheels; 1983-

8-A   Ford Thunderbird Convertible   66mm 1964-1966 $15-25
Yellow interior, clear windshield, chrome plastic base and grille, gray plastic wheels.
1. Light red body.

8-B   Ford Thunderbird Hardtop   66mm 1966-1968 $15-25
Blue tinted plastic detachable hardtop, otherwise as 8-A.
1. Yellow body.

8-C   Tipping Farm Trailer   69mm 1968-1969, 1970-? $12-15
Diecast tipper and chassis, black plastic hydraulic cylinder, metal wheels with tires.
1. Red tipper, yellow chassis, Husky name cast in.
2. Orange tipper, blue chassis, Corgi Junior label.
3. Probably a later version with Corgi Junior name cast in.

8-D   Rover 3500 Sedan   77mm 1979-Close $8-10
Clear windows, black plastic base, Whizzwheels, opening rear hatch.
1. Metallic blue body, yellow interior; 1979-
2. Bright yellow body, red interior; 1982?
3. White body, red interior; 1983?

9-A   Buick Electra Police Car   69mm 1964-1968 $15-25
Modified 7-A casting, yellow interior, clear windows, red dome light, red and white Police decals, chrome plastic base and grille, gray plastic wheels.
1. Dark blue body.

9-B   Cadillac Eldorado   78mm 1968-69, 1970-71 $12-15
Red interior, clear windows, unpainted diecast base, opening hood, detailed engine, tow hook.
1. Bright blue body, metal wheels with tires, Husky base; 1968-1969.
2. Metallic green body, metal wheels with tires, Corgi Junior label on base; 1970.
3. Metallic green body, black Whizzwheels, modified base, no tow hook.
4. White and black body, black Whizzwheels, modified base, no tow hook.
5. White and black body, chrome Whizzwheels, modified base, no tow hook.

9-C   Police Range Rover   69mm 1973-1980 $10-12
Dome lights, Whizzwheels, Police labels.
1. White body, yellow interior, blue windows, chrome plastic base, labels with crown.
2. White body, white interior, blue windows, black plastic base, simple labels with red background.
3. White body, red interior, smoked windows, black plastic base, labels as on type 2.

10-A   Guy Warrior Coal Truck   70mm 1964-1969, 1970-? $15-25
Blue windows, no interior, chrome plastic base, black plastic coal load.
1. Red body, gray plastic wheels, Husky base.
2. Red body, metal wheels with black plastic tires, Husky base.
3. Red-orange body, gray plastic wheels, Husky base.
4. Red-orange body, metal wheels with black tires, Husky base.
5. Red-orange body, metal wheels with black tires, Corgi Junior label base.
6. Bright orange body, metal wheels with black tires, Corgi Junior label base. May have black plastic base.

10-B   Ford GT 70   73mm 1973-1975 $10-12
Chrome interior and detailed engine, clear windows, unpainted opening rear hatch, unpainted diecast base, Whizzwheels.
1. Bright orange body.

10-C   Triumph TR7   77mm 1977-Close $8-10
Yellow interior, blue windows, black plastic base, Whizzwheels, tow hook.
1. White and blue body, number 3 and TR7 label on hood.
2. Silver and red body, number 3 and TR7 label on hood.
3. Red, blue and white body, number 7 and British Airways label.
4. Orange body, no labels.

11-A   Forward Control Land Rover   66mm 1964-1969 $15-25
Removable tan plastic rear cover, blue windows, no interior, gray plastic wheels.
1. Green body including base, small rear corner windows in cab.
2. Green body, gray plastic base, no corner windows.
3. Green body, black plastic base, no corner windows.

11-B   Austin Healey LeMans Sprite   68mm 1970-1974 $12-15
Amber windows and headlights, diecast base, number 50 labels.
1. Red body, light blue interior, black Whizzwheels, charcoal gray base.
2. Red body, yellow interior, black Whizzwheels, charcoal gray base.
3. Red body, yellow interior, chrome Whizzwheels, black base.

11-C   Supermobile   76mm 1979-Close $20-30
Silver painted sleeves with chrome plastic striking fists, clear canopy, red interior and jet, red and yellow S emblem labels, three small black plastic wheels.
1. Light blue upper and lower body-base castings.

12-A   Volkswagen Tower Truck   60mm 1964-1967 $15-25
Red plastic telescopic tower, blue windows, no interior, chrome plastic base, gray plastic wheels.
1. Yellow body.

12-B   Ford F350-Tower Truck   71mm 1968-1969 $15-25
Red plastic telescopic tower, blue windows, no interior, chrome plastic base.
1. Yellow body, gray plastic wheels.
2. White body, gray plastic wheels.
3. White body, metal wheels with tires.

12-C   Reliant-Ogle Scimitar   73mm 1970-1973 $12-15
Yellow interior, amber windows, unpainted metal base.
1. White body, black Whizzwheels.
2. Metallic blue body, black Whizzwheels.
3. Metallic blue body, chrome Whizzwheels.

12-D   Ford GT 70   73mm 1975-1976 $10-12
Modified 10-B casting, Growler, unpainted diecast opening rear hatch, chrome interior, blue windows, black plastic base, Whizzwheels.
1. Metallic green body.

12-E   Golden Eagle Jeep   68mm 1979-1981 $8-10
Yellow interior, clear windshield, detachable plastic top, silver diecast base, Whizzwheels.
1. Metallic brown body, white top.
2. Metallic brown body, tan top, eagle label on hood.

13-A   Guy Warrior Sand Truck   70mm 1964-69, 1970-72 $12-15
Same castings as 10-A, blue windows, no interior, tan plastic sand load.
1. Bright yellow body, gray plastic wheels, chrome plastic Husky base.
2. Blue body, gray plastic wheels, chrome plastic Husky base.
3. Blue body, metal wheels with tires, chrome plastic Husky base.
4. Blue body, metal wheels with tires, chrome plastic base with Corgi Junior label?
5. Red body, Whizzwheels, black plastic Corgi Junior base.

13-B   Rough Terrain Truck   68mm 1976-1978 $10-12
Main body-base and white cab castings, plastic interior-grille-stripe, plastic tow hook, clear windows, black plastic wheels.
1. Red main body and base, black interior. Used in 3022 set.
2. Blue main body and base, black interior.
3. Blue main body and base, red interior.

13-C   Buck Rogers Starfighter   72mm 1980-Close $20-30
Blue interior and jets, yellow retracting wings, stripe labels, no wheels.
1. White body and base.

14-A   Guy Warrior Tanker   70mm 1964-1966 $15-25
Rounded tank, separate casting forms rear of tank, blue windows, no interior, chrome plastic base and grille, white decals with red and yellow Shell emblems, gray plastic wheels.
1. Yellow body, "Shell-BP" decals form white panels on tank.
2. Yellow body, "Shell" decals form white panels on tank.

14-B   Guy Warrior Tanker   73mm 1966-1969 $15-25
                                        1970-1974 $12-15
Larger casting, squarish tank, no separate rear casting, blue windows, no interior, unpainted diecast base and grille.
1. Yellow body, Shell decals as on 14-A, Husky base, gray plastic wheels.
2. White body, Esso decals, Husky base, gray plastic wheels.
3. White body, Esso decals, Husky base, metal wheels with tires.
4. White body, Ijsselstreek N.V. labels, Husky base, gray plastic wheels; Netherlands promotional.
5. White body, Esso labels, Corgi Junior label on base, metal wheels with tires; 1970.
6. White body, Esso labels, white modified diecast base, Whizzwheels.

14-C   Guy Warrior Esso Tanker   73mm 1975-1976 $10-12
Black plastic base including headlights, blue windows, no interior, red-white-blue Esso labels, Whizzwheels.
1. White body, plastic plastic base.

14-D   Buick Regal Taxi   70mm 1977-1980 $10-12
Chrome interior, amber windows and roof sign, white and black Taxi labels, chrome grille and bumpers, black plastic base, Whizzwheels.
1. Orange body.

15-A   Volkswagen Pickup Truck   60mm 1965-1967 $15-25
Removable tan plastic rear top, blue windows, no interior, chrome plastic base, gray plastic wheels.
1. Turquoise green body.

15-B   Studebaker Wagonaire TV Camera Car   76mm 1967-69, 1970-71 $15-25
Clear front and purple rear windows, turning TV camera and man in rear hatch.
1. Dark yellow body, chrome plastic base-grille, gray plastic wheels.
2. Dark yellow body, chrome plastic base-grille, gray plastic wheels.
3. Dark blue body, chrome plastic base-grille, metal wheels with tires.
4. Light yellow body, chrome plastic base-grille, metal wheels with tires.
5. Metallic turquoise body, unpainted diecast base, metal wheels with tires.
6. Bright yellow body, unpainted die cast Corgi Junior base, black Whizzwheels.
7. Metallic lime body, unpainted diecast Corgi Junior base, black Whizzwheels.
8. Metallic lime body, unpainted diecast Corgi Junior base, chrome Whizzwheels.

15-C   Mercedes-Benz Bus   74mm 1973-Close $8-10
Black plastic base, and grille, Whizzwheels.
1. Metallic blue body, "School Bus" and stripe labels, yellow interior, amber windows.
2. Dark yellow body, new "School Bus" labels, yellow interior, amber windows.
3. Light yellow body, otherwise as type 2.
4. Light yellow body, no interior, faces at windows, no labels; 1982.
5. Light yellow body, no interior, opaque black windows, no labels; 1983.
6. Bright red body, no interior, opaque black windows, no labels; 1983-.

16-A   Aveling-Barford Dump Truck   79mm 1965-1969 $15-25
Chrome plastic snowplow, and base, no windows, or interior, gray plastic wheels.
1. Yellow chassis-cab, red tipper.
2. Red chassis-cab, gray tipper.

16-B   Land Rover Pickup Truck   71mm 1971-1976 $12-15
Amber windows, no interior, black plastic base and tow hook, Whizzwheels.
1. Metallic olive body.

16-C   Rover 3500 Police Car   77mm 1980-1982 $8-10
Modified 8-D casting, yellow interior, clear windows; blue roof bar, opening rear hatch, Police labels, black plastic base and tow hook, Whizzwheels.
1. White body.

17-A   Guy Warrior Milk Tanker   70mm 1965-1968 $15-25
Same castings as 14-A, rounded tank with Milk decals, blue windows, no interior, chrome plastic base and grille, gray plastic wheels.
1. White body.

17-B   Guy Warrior Milk Tanker   73mm 1968-1969 $15-25
Same casting as 14-B, squarish tank with Milk decals, blue windows, no interior, unpainted diecast base and grille.
1. White body, gray plastic wheels.
2. Cream body, gray plastic wheels.
3. Cream body, metal wheels with tires.

17-C   Volkswagen 1300   68mm 1970-1977 $12-15
Clear windows, unpainted metal base, Whizzwheels, flower labels.
1. Metallic olive body, yellow interior.
2. Metallic olive body, red interior.

17-D   Buick City of Metropolis Police Car   70mm 1979-Close $20-30
Chrome interior, bumpers and grille, amber windows, light red roof light, labels, black plastic base, Whizzwheels.
1. Metallic dark blue body, white roof.
2. Same as 17-D1 except non-metallic medium blue, white roof

18-A   Jaguar Mark X   66mm 1965-1967 $15-25
Same casting as 1-A, yellow interior, clear windows, chrome plastic base, gray plastic windows.
1. Light gold plated body.

18-B   Jaguar Mark X   71mm 1967-1969 $15-25
Same castings as 1-B, yellow interior, clear windows, unpainted metal base.
1. Light gold plated body, gray plastic wheels.
2. Darker gold plated body, gray plastic wheels.
3. Darker gold plated body, metal wheels with tires.

18-C   Wigwam Camper Van   77mm 1973-1975 $10-12
Yellow interior, amber windows, black plastic base, Whizzwheels.
1. Metallic magenta body.
2. Blue body.

18-D Snowmobile (1977?) $???
Probably never issued.

19-A Commer "Walk-Thru" Van 64mm 1965-1969 $15-25
No interior, blue windows, sliding side door, diecast base, gray plastic wheels.
1. Lime green body, red sliding door, light gray base.
2. Lime green body, red sliding door, unpainted base.
3. Lime green body, red sliding door, unpainted base. Goodyear Labels. (Second Example Required for Authentication.)
4. Lime green body, red sliding door, Combopost logo, other details not known, Netherlands promotional.
5. Red body and sliding door, unpainted base.

19-B Sport Boat on Trailer 5mm 1969-70, 1970-73 $12-15
Cream deck, red hull, blue windshield, blue outboard motor, diecast trailer.
1. Gold trailer, metal wheels with tires, "Husky" lettering on hull; 1969.
2. Blue trailer, metal wheels with tires, no lettering on hull, Corgi Junior label on trailer; 1970.
3. Gold trailer, black Whizzwheels, "Corgi Junior" lettering on hull.
4. Blue trailer, black Whizzwheels, "Corgi Junior" lettering on hull.
5. Blue trailer, light blue motor, chrome Whizzwheels, "Corgi Junior" lettering on hull.
6. Metallic blue trailer, chrome Whizzwheels, "Corgi Junior" lettering on hull.

19-C Pink Pather Motorcycle 68mm 1980-1982 $20-30
Pink Pather figure, black spoked plastic wheels.
1. Unpainted metal and red plastic motorcycle.

20-A Ford Thames Van 61mm 1965-1969 $15-25
Yellow interior, antenna and ladder, opening rear doors, clear windows, chrome plastic base and grille, gray plastic windows.
1. Red body, including plastic opening doors, gray plastic wheels.

20-B Volkswagen 1300 66mm 1968-69, 1970-71 $12-15
Clear windows, unpainted diecast base, plastic luggage on roof, metal wheels with tires.
1. Blue body, black luggage, yellow interior, Husky base; 1968-1969.
2. Yellow body, brown luggage, red interior, Corgi Junior label on base; 1970.
3. Red body, black luggage, yellow interior, modified base; 1971.

20-C Cement Mixer Trailer 45mm 1976-1977 $10-12
Amber plastic cover raises, gold engine, red plastic barrel, wheel and tow bar, black plastic wheels.
1. Unpainted diecast body.

20-D Penguinmobile 73mm 1979-1981 $20-30
Same castings as 82-A, driver, blue engine, black plastic base, Whizzwheels.
1. White body, "Penguin" and umbrella labels.

21-A Military Land Rover 66mm 1965-1968 $15-25
Blue windows, no interior, olive plastic removable rear cover, white star decal, gray plastic wheels.
1. Olive drab body including integral base, rear cab corner windows.
2. Olive drab body, gray plastic base, rear cab corner windows.
3. Olive drab body, black plastic base, no corner windows.

21-B Jaguar E Type 2+2 69mm 1968-1969 $15-25
Yellow interior, clear windows, cast spoke metals wheels with tires, diecast Husky lower body-base.
1. Metallic maroon body and base.

21-C B.V.R.T Vita-Mini 1300 Mini-Cooper S 55mm 1970-1974 $12-15
Chrome interior and engine, blue windows, unpainted diecast base and grille, Whizzwheels, number 73 and other racing labels.
1. Metallic purple body.

21-D Chevrolet Charlie's Angels Van 68mm 1977-1980 $20-30
Blue windows, no interior, black plastic base, Whizzwheels, pictorial labels.
1. Pink body, "Chevrolet Van" lettering on base.
2. Pink body, "U.S. Van" lettering on base.

22-A Citroen Safari Military Ambulance 64mm 1965-1968 $15-25
Modified 2-A casting, blue interior, rear windows and dome light, clear front windows, red cross decal on hood, chrome plastic base, gray plastic wheels.
1. Olive drab body.

22-B Aston Martin DB6 73mm 1968-1969, 1970 $15-25
Yellow interior, chrome plastic base and grille.
1. Metallic bronze body, clear windows, gray plastic wheels; 1968.
2. Metallic purple body, blue windows, metal wheels with tires; 1969.
3. Lighter purple body, blue windows, metal wheels with tires; 1969.
4. Same as 22-B3 except clear windows.
5. Metallic olive body, blue windows, metal wheels with tires; 1970.

22-C Formula 1 Racer 74mm 1973-1978 $10-12
Gold diecast engine, roll bar and windshield, white driver, unpainted diecast base, Whizzwheels.
1. Dark yellow body, Union Jack and number 3 labels.
2. Dark yellow body, Weetabix labels; promotional model.

22-D Paramedic Emergency Unit 68mm 1981-1982 $8-10
Chevrolet van casting, no interior, blue windows, red and black labels, black plastic base, Whizzwheels.
1. White body.

23-A Guy Warrior U.S. Army Tanker 70mm 1965-1967 $15-25
Same castings as 14-A and 17-A, blue windows, no interior, chrome plastic base and grille, white star and U.S. Army decals, gray plastic wheels.
1. Olive drab body.

23-B Loadmaster Shovel 78mm 1967-1969, 1970-1974 $12-15
Green windows, no interior, working shovel, black plastic wheels.
1. Orange body, chrome plastic shovel and Husky base; 1967-1968.
2. Yellow body, chrome plastic shovel and Husky base; 1968-1969.
3. Yellow body, unpainted diecast shovel and Corgi Junior base; 1970-1974.

23-C Batbike 68mm 1979-Close $20-30
Batman figure, black and yellow bat label, black plastic five-spoke wheels.
1. Unpainted diecast and black plastic motorcycle.

24-A Ford Zephyr Estate Car 61mm 1966-1969 $15-25
Yellow interior, clear windows, chrome plastic base and grille, gray plastic wheels, opening hatch.
1. Metallic blue body.
2. Metallic maroon body.

24-B Aston Martin DBS 73mm 1971-1973 $12-15
White interior, clear windows, unpainted diecast base and grille, opening black hood, detailed engine, Whizzwheels.
1. Light green body, black hood.

24-C Shazam Thunderbolt 77mm 1979-1980 $20-30
Same casting as 28-B, amber windshield, driver, chrome plastic engine and exhaust pipes, red-yellow-black labels, white diecast base, Whizzwheels.
1. Yellow body.

25-A S. & D. Refuse Wagon 69mm 1966-69, 1970-72 $15-25
Blue windows, no interior, chrome plastic base and tipping rear body.
1. Light blue chassis-cab, gray plastic wheels.
2. Red chassis-cab, gray plastic wheels.
3. Red chassis-cab, metal wheels with tires.
4. Orange chassis-cab, metal wheels with tires, Corgi Junior base label; 1970-1972.

25-B Captain America's Porsche 917 72mm 1979-1980 $20-30
Same casting as 51-A and 94-A, no interior, red windows, chrome engine, black plastic base, Whizzwheels, red-white-blue Captain America labels.
1. Metallic dark blue body.

26-A Sunbeam Alpine 61mm 1966-1969 $15-25
Blue plastic top, clear windows, yellow interior, chrome plastic base.
1. Metallic cooper body, gray plastic wheels.
2. Red body, gray plastic windows.
3. Red body, metal wheels with trim.

26-B ERF Fire Tender 76mm 1970-1974 $12-15
Yellow ladder, blue windows and dome lights, no interior, silver diecast base, grille and body panels, Whizzwheels.
1. Red body.

26-C ERF Fire Tender 76mm 1975-1980, 1982-Close $8-10
Yellow ladder, blue windows and dome light, no interior, black plastic base, headlights and rear panel. Grille is now part of body casting. Whizzwheels.
1. Red body.

27-A Bedford TK 7-Ton Lorry 72mm 1966-1969, 1970-1971 $12-15
No interior or windows, diecast bucket and swinging arms, chrome plastic base.
1. Maroon body, unpainted bucket and arms, gray plastic wheels.
2. Orange body, silver bucket and arms, gray plastic wheels.
3. Orange body, silver bucket and arms, metal wheels with tires.
4. Orange-red body, silver bucket and arms, metal wheels with tires, Corgi Junior label on base; 1970-1971.

27-B Formula 5000 Racing Car 74mm 1973-1981 $10-12
Gold engine and windshield, plastic driver, diecast base, Whizzwheels.
1. Black body, white driver, gold radiators, number 4 and blue and white stripe labels, white base.
2. Red body, yellow driver, number 8 and yellow and silver stripe labels, unpainted base. Casting changed to eliminate radiators.

28-A Ford F350 Wrecker 78mm 1966-69, 1970-71 $12-15
Blue windows, no interior, chrome plastic boom, mounting and base-grille.
1. Light blue body, gray plastic wheels, Husky base; 1966-196-
Medium blue body, metal wheels with tires, Husky base; 196—1969.
2. Dark blue body, metal wheels with tires, base with Corgi Junior label; 1970.
3. Dark blue body, black Whizzwheels, Corgi Junior base; 1970.
4. Turquoise green body, black Whizzwheels, Corgi Junior base; 1971.

28-B Hot Rodder 77mm 1973-1976 $10-12
Chrome plastic interior, engine and exhaust pipes, amber windshield, white diecast base, red and blue stripe labels with white stars, Whizzwheels.
1. Yellow body.

28-C Buick Regal Police Car 76mm 1977-1979 $10-12
Chrome interior, bumpers and grille, amber windows, red roof light, black plastic base, Whizzwheels, white and black Police labels.
1. White body, black roof, red taillights.
2. White body, black roof, white taillights.

28-D Buick Regal Sheriff's Car 76mm 1980-1980 $10-12
Same casting and details as 28-C except for black and white Sheriff labels.
1. Black body, white roof.

29-A ERF Cement Mixer Truck 70mm 1966-1969 $15-25
Green windows, no interior, red plastic barrel, turning chute, chrome plastic base.
1. Yellow body, unpainted diecast chute, gray plastic wheels.
2. Yellow body, chrome plastic chute, gray plastic wheels.
3. Yellow body, chrome plastic chute, metal wheels with tires.

29-B ERF Simon Snorkel Fire Engine 79mm 1970-1971 $12-15
Same casting as 36-A, no interior or windows, chrome plastic upper and lower snorkel arms, basket, mounting and baseplate.
1. Dark red body, metal wheels with tires, Corgi Junior label on base; 1970.
2. Dark red body, black Whizzwheels, Corgi Junior base.

29-C ERF Simon Snorkel Fire Engine 76mm 1972-1973 $10-12
New casting with longer cab, blue windows, no interior, yellow plastic upper and lower snorkel arms, basket and mounting, unpainted diecast base, Whizzwheels.
1. Dark red body, deep basket.

29-D ERF Simon Snorkel Fire Engine 76mm 1974-Close $8-10
Same body casting as 29-C, blue windows, no interior, new type snorkel with shallow basket and other changes, yellow plastic base, Whizzwheels.
1. Dark red body.

30-A Studebaker Wagonaire Ambulance 75mm 1966-69, 1970-72 $12-15
White interior, blue windows, sliding rear roof panel, removable stretcher, opening tailgate.
1. White body, red cross decal on hood, chrome plastic base, gray plastic wheels.
2. White body, red cross decal on hood, chrome plastic base, metal wheels with tires.
3. White body, red cross label on hood, diecast Corgi Junior base, metal wheels with tires; 1970.
4. Cream body, white seats, blue windows, white tailgate, cast wheels, plastic tires, Husky base. (May have different Husky Number, used only in 3005-A/B Holiday/Leisure Time Gift Set)

30-B Studebaker Wagonaire Ambulance 75mm 1971-1972 $12-15
Modified casting with cast-in tailgate and braces, ridged blue rear windows and roof panel permanently half open, white interior with stretcher, diecast base, black Whizzwheels, red cross label on hood.
1. White body.

30-C Studebaker Wagonaire Ambulance 75mm 1973? $12-15
Modified casting with two sirens on roof, blue dome light, modified base with smaller 'Whizzwheels" lettering and "Pat App" at rear axle, otherwise as 30-B.
1. White body.

30-D Mobile Cement Mixer 73mm 1976-80, 1982-Close $8-10
Plastic rotating barrel and base including barrel support, no interior, Whizzwheels.
1. Metallic olive green body, yellow barrel and base, amber windows; 1976-1979.
2. Red body, silver barrel, black base, tinted windows? 1980?
3. Orange body, black barrel and base, clear windows; 1982.
4. Blue body, white barrel and base, black windows; 1983.

31-A Oldsmobile Starfire 76mm 1966-1969 $15-25
Yellow interior, clear windows, opening trunk, chrome plastic base-grille.

1. Metallic blue body, gray plastic wheels.
2. Olive green body, gray plastic wheels.
3. Olive green body, metal wheels with tires.

31-B   Land Rover Wrecker   73mm 1970-1980 $12-15
Amber windows and dome light, gold diecast hook, black plastic base, Whizzwheels.
1. Metallic purple body, "Wrecker Truck" labels.
2. Red body, "Wrecker Truck" labels.
3. Metallic blue body, "24 hour service" labels, black Whizzwheels.
4. Metallic blue body, "24 hour service" labels.
5. Metallic dark blue body, "24 hour service" labels.
6. Red body, black plastic base, red windows, no labels, shorter silver hook. (May be from after Mettoy closure.)

32-A   Volkswagen Luggage Elevator Truck   78mm 1966-1969 $15-25
Same casting as 12-A, blue windows, no interior, light blue conveyor frame and ramp, rubber conveyor belt turned by unpainted diecast knob, gray plastic wheels, chrome plastic base.
1. White body, yellow conveyor belt.
2. White body, red conveyor belt.
3. Red body, red conveyor belt.

32-B   Lotus Europa   71mm 1970-1974 $12-15
Yellow interior and opening rear hatch, clear windows, silver diecast lower body-base, Whizzwheels, Union Jack labels.
1. Metallic green body.

32-C   The Saint's Jaguar XJ-S   76mm 1978-1981 $20-30
Same casting as 72-B, red interior, clear windows, black plastic base, Whizzwheels.
1. White body, black Saint figure label on hood.

33-A   Farm Livestock Trailer   69mm 1967-1969, 1970-1970 $12-15
Opening diecast tailgate, four tan plastic calves and base, yellow plastic wheels with tires, bottom of body casting forms base.
1. Olive green body and tailgate, Husky name on base.
2. Turquoise body and tailgate, Husky name on base.
3. Orange body and tailgate, Corgi Junior name on base.

33-B   Jaguar E-Type 2+2   71mm 1970-1975 $12-15
Raising hood, detailed engine, clear windows, silver diecast base, Whizzwheels.
1. Yellow body, red interior.
2. Yellow body, yellow interior.
3. Blue body, red interior.
4. Blue body, yellow interior.
5. Blue body, white interior.

33-C   Chevrolet Ambulance Van   (1977?) $???
Probably not issued.

33-D   Wonder Woman's Wonder Car   62mm 1979-1980 $20-30
Same castings as 74-A, amber windshield, black interior with driver, interior forms black stripe around model's front and sides, white diecast base, Whizzwheels.
1. Orange upper body, Wonder Woman hood label.

34-A   Volvo 400 Farm Tractor   54mm 1967-1969, 1970-1974 $12-15
Diecast base same color as body, yellow plastic wheels with black tires, silver grille.
1. Red body and base, black exhaust stack, Husky base.
2. Red body and base including stack, Husky base.
3. Red body and base including stack, Corgi Junior label on base.

34-B   Sting Army Helicopter   70mm 1975-1978 $10-12
Black plastic interior, parts, skids and rotors, clear canopy, white "Army" labels.
1. Olive drab body.

34-C   Chevrolet Hertz Rental Van   68mm 1980-Close $8-10
Amber windows, no interior, black plastic base, Hertz Truck Rental labels, Whizzwheels.
1. Yellow body, Chevrolet van base.
2. Yellow body, U.S. van base.

35-A   Ford F350 Camper   78mm 1967-69, 1970-72 $15-25
Plastic camper with interior, diecast pickup with windows but no interior, plastic base-grille.
1. Dark yellow pickup, chrome camper, yellow interior, blue windows, chrome Husky base, gray plastic wheels.
2. Dark blue pickup, chrome camper, yellow interior, blue windows, chrome Husky base, gray plastic wheels.
3. Dark blue pickup, chrome camper, yellow interior, blue windows, chrome Husky base, metal wheels with tires.
4. Turquoise pickup, chrome camper, yellow interior, green windows, chrome base with Corgi Junior label, metal wheels with tires; 1970.
5. Turquoise pickup, chrome camper, yellow interior, green windows, unpainted diecast base, black Whizzwheels, modified wheel wells of pickup.
6. Red pickup, white camper and interior, green windows, silver diecast base, black Whizzwheels, casting modified as in type 5.
7. Red pickup, white camper and interior, green windows, silver diecast base, chrome Whizzwheels, casting modified as in type 5.

35-B   Air Bus Helicopter   70mm 1975-1979 $10-12
Left and right body castings, black plastic rotors and base with landing gear, base also forms interior, clear windows, orange-white-black labels.
1. Orange body.
2. Said to exist in blue.

35-C   Tipper Truck   71mm 1983-Close $8-10
Same casting and tipper as 49-B, clear windows, no interior, black plastic base, Whizzwheels, unpainted tailgate.
1. Silver body, blue tipper?
2. Red body, tan tipper.

36-A   Simon Snorkel Fire Engine   79mm 1967-1969 $15-25
No windows or interior, chrome plastic upper and lower snorkel arms, basket, mounting and base.
1. Dark red body, gray plastic wheels.
2. Dark red body, metal wheels with tires.

36-B   Healer Wheeler   76mm 1973-1977 $10-12
Blue interior and dome light, clear windows, black plastic base, Whizzwheels.
1. White body, round red cross labels on doors, black-white-red hood triangle label.
2. White body, side labels with black "Ambulance" and red cross, otherwise as type 1.

36-C   Chevrolet Coca-Cola Van   68mm 1979-1980 $10-12
Blue windows, no interior, black plastic U.S. Van base, Whizzwheels.
1. Red body, red and white Coca-Cola logo labels.

37-A   NSU RO 80   70mm 1969-70, 70-1973 $12-15
Opening hood, chrome plastic engine, interior, bumpers and grille.

1. Metallic blue body, clear windows, blue diecast Husky base, metal wheels with tires; 1969.
2. Metallic dark blue body, blue windows, dark blue diecast base with Corgi Junior label, metal wheels with tires; 1970.
3. Metallic purple body and diecast Corgi Junior base, black Whizzwheels; 1971.
4. Magenta body and Corgi Junior base, black hood, Whizzwheels; 1972.
5. Metallic bronze body and Corgi Junior base, black hood, Whizzwheels; 1973.

37-B   Porsche Carrera Police Car   74mm 1976-1980 $10-12
Blue windows and dome lights, black plastic base, Whizzwheels, Police labels.
1. White body, maroon interior, big lettering on labels.
2. White body, yellow interior, small lettering on labels.
3. White and green body, Polizei labels, other details not known, German issue.

38-A   Rice Beaufort Horse Box Trailer   69mm 1968-69, 1970-71 $12-15
Diecast opening tailgate, horse figure, body casting includes base.
1. Turquoise body, metal wheels with tires, Husky base; 1968-1969.
2. Metallic green body, metal wheels with tires, Corgi Junior base.
3. Red body, metal wheels with tires, Corgi Junior base.
4. Red body, black Whizzwheels, Corgi Junior base, unpainted tailgate.
5. Metallic copper body, chrome Whizzwheels, Corgi Junior base, unpainted tailgate.

38-B   Jerry's Banger   75mm 1980-Close $15-20
Green plastic cannon, red cannonballs, brown figure, chrome engine and exhaust pipes, chrome plastic grille, Whizzwheels.
1. Orange body.

39-A   Jaguar XJ6 4.2   75mm 1968-1969, 1970-1973 $12-15
Opening trunk, clear windows, unpainted diecast base, plastic interior and tow hook.
1. Bright yellow body, red interior, metal wheels with tires, Husky base; 1968-1969.
2. Bright yellow body, red interior, metal wheels with tires, Corgi Junior label on base.
3. Metallic silver body, red interior, black Whizzwheels, Corgi Junior base.
4. Metallic silver body, red interior, chrome Whizzwheels, Corgi Junior base.
5. Metallic maroon body, yellow interior, chrome Whizzwheels, Corgi Junior base.

39-B   Jaguar E Type 2+2   71mm 1975-1977 $10-12
Growler, same casting as 33-B modified with noise maker, opening hood, detailed engine, chrome interior, clear windows, black plastic base, Whizzwheels.
1. Light red body.
2. Purple body.

39-C   Chevrolet Pepsi-Cola Van   68mm 1979-1980 $10-12
Blue windows, no interior, black plastic base, Whizzwheels.
1. White body, red-white-light and dark blue Pepsi-Cola labels, U.S. Van base.
2. Chevrolet Van base, otherwise as type 1.

40-A   Ford Transit Martin Walter Caravan   65mm 1968-69, 1970-71 $15-25
Diecast opening rear door, diecast unpainted base, first base type fits inside body.
1. Light red body, white door and interior, clear windows, Husky base, metal wheels with tires.
2. Lime green body, white body and interior, clear windows, Husky base, metal wheels with tires.
3. Yellow body, unpainted door, blue interior, clear windows, Corgi Junior label on base, metal wheels with tires.
4. Yellow body, unpainted door, white interior, clear windows, Corgi Junior base below bottom of body, black Whizzwheels.
5. Blue body, unpainted door, white interior, clear windows, Corgi Junior base as on type 4, black Whizzwheels.
6. Metallic light blue body, unpainted door, white interior, amber windows, Corgi Junior base as on type 4, chrome Whizzwheels.
7. Metallic gray body, unpainted door, white interior, black Whizzwheels, other details not known.

40-B   Army Red Cross Helicopter   70mm 1977-1978 $10-12
Same casting and parts as 35-B.
1. Olive drab body, Army and red cross labels.

40-C   James Bond Aston Martin   72mm 1979-Close $20-30
Red interior and figures, opening roof hatch, Whizzwheels.
1. Metallic silver gray body, unpainted diecast base-grille, large Whizzwheels, blue windows.
2. Metallic silver body, chrome plastic base-grille, small Whizzwheels, clear windows.

41-A   Porsche Carrera 6   69mm 1969?, 1970-1973 $12-15
Opening rear hood, chrome interior and engine, red front hood, white diecast lower body-base, number 19.
1. There may be a Husky version, and/or one with a Corgi Junior label.
2. White body, hood-number decal, blue windows, Corgi Junior base, metal wheels with tires.
3. White body, hood-number label, purple windows, Corgi Junior base, black Whizzwheels.
4. White body, hood-number label, purple windows, Corgi Junior base, chrome Whizzwheels.

41-B   James Bond Space Shuttle   70mm 1979-1981 $20-30
Same castings as 5-C.
1. White body, black base, number 6 labels.

42-A   Euclid 35 Ton Rear Dump Truck   70mm 1970-1971 $12-15
Body, tipper and metallic charcoal gray base castings, no interior or windows.
1. Dark yellow cab-chassis, red tipper, black plastic wheels, Corgi Junior label on base.
2. Dark yellow cab-chassis, red tipper, black Whizzwheels, Corgi Junior base.

42-B   Terex R35 Rear Dump Truck   70mm 1972-1975? $10-12
Diecast charcoal gray base with new lettering, Whizzwheels (chrome unless noted), otherwise as 42-A.
1. Red chassis-cab, dark yellow tipper, black Whizzwheels.
2. Red chassis-cab, dark yellow tipper, unpainted base.
3. Blue chassis-cab, yellow plastic tipper.
4. Blue chassis-cab, silver tipper?
5. Blue chassis-cab, dull beige plastic tipper.

42-C   Rescue Range Rover   69mm 1977-1980 $10-12
Blue windows and dome lights, yellow interior, yellow stripe labels with "Rescue team" lettering, black plastic base, Whizzwheels.
1. Orange-red body.

43-A   Massey Ferguson 3303 Tractor with Blade   74mm 1970-1980 $10-12
Plastic interior and exhaust stack, lifting diecast blade and arms, black plastic wheels, unpainted diecast base.
1. Yellow body and blade, red interior, Corgi Junior label on base.
2. Yellow body, red blade and interior, Corgi Junior base.
3. Lighter yellow body?
4. Orange body, black blade, yellow interior; 1980.

44-A   Raygo Rascal 600 Road Roller   74mm 1970-1978 $10-12
Body, roller housing and base castings, gray plastic roller, seat and engine, two black plastic wheels. Roller housing pivots on body.
1. Blue body, orange housing and base, Corgi Junior label on base.

2. Corgi Junior base, otherwise as type 1.

44-B   Starship Liberator   75mm 1979-1980 $20-30
Same casting as 2-C, yellow plastic parts, green windows, white turbine.
1. Metallic light blue body, gold diecast collar.

45-A   Mercedes-Benz 280SL   70mm 1970-1974 $12-15
Opening doors, clear windows, diecast base-grille.
1. Metallic silver body, red interior, unpainted base, metal wheels with tires.
2. Metallic light blue body, red interior, unpainted base, black Whizzwheels.
3. Yellow body, red interior, white base, black Whizzwheels.
4. Metallic red body, white interior, unpainted base, black Whizzwheels.
5. Metallic red body, white interior, unpainted base, chrome Whizzwheels.
6. Blue body, yellow interior, chrome base, chrome Whizzwheels.

45-B   Starsky and Hutch Ford Gran Torino   75mm 1977-Close $20-30
Opaque black windows, no interior, red roof light, chrome plastic base-grille, Whizzwheels.
1. Red body, white trim label.

46-A   Jensen Interceptor   73mm 1970-1973 $12-15
Opening doors, yellow interior, green windows, unpainted diecast base-grille.
1. Metallic maroon body, lable on base, metal wheels with tires.
2. Metallic maroon body, black Whizzwheels.
3. Orange body, chrome Whizzwheels.
4. Metallic green body, chrome Whizzwheels.

46-B   Police Helicopter   75mm 1976-79, 1983-Close $8-10
Clear canopy, plastic interior-base-skids and rotors, dashboard and Police labels.
1. White body, blue interior and rotors, Police and stripe labels.
2. White body, red interior and rotors, Police and stripe labels.
3. Metallic blue body, white interior and rotors, City of New York labels.
4. Blue body, red interior and rotors, no labels? 1983.

47-A   Scammell Concrete Mixer   72mm 1971-1976 $12-15
Upper and lower body-base castings, red plastic barrel, amber windows, no interior, Whizzwheels.
1. White upper and blue lower body.

47-B   Chevrolet Super Van   68mm 1978-Close $20-30
Amber windows, Superman figure and lettering labels, black plastic base, Whizzwheels.
1. Silver body, Chevrolet Van base lettering.
2. Silver body, U.S. Van base lettering.

48-A   ERF Tipper Truck   75mm 1970-1973 $12-15
Cab, tipper, tailgate and chassis castings, amber windows, no interior, Whizzwheels.
1. Red cab, silver tipper and tailgate, metallic charcoal gray chassis.
2. Blue cab, yellow tipper and tailgate, unpainted chassis.

48-B   Shovel Loader   78mm 1975-1979 $10-12
Yellow plastic interior, engine, stack, base and working shovel, clear windows, black Growler gear, black plastic wheels.
1. Light red body.

49-A   Pininfarina Modulo   72mm 1971-1973 $12-15
Maroon interior and stripe between upper and lower body castings, clear windows, Whizzwheels, red and black rear hood label.
1. Yellow upper and lower body.

49-B   Tipping Lorry   73mm 1977-1979 $10-12
Blue windows, no interior, light blue plastic tipper, unpainted diecast tailgate, black plastic base, Whizzwheels.
1. Silver chassis-cab, light blue tipper.

49-C   Woody Woodpecker's Car   70mm 1981-Close $15-20
Modified 78-A casting, red interior with figure, red and white stripe labels, navy blue diecast base, Whizzwheels.
1. Yellow body.

50-A   Ferrari 512 S   71mm 1971-1974 $12-15
Clear windows, number 6 label, silver diecast base, Whizzwheels.
1. Metallic maroon body, cream interior and engine cover.
2. Metallic maroon body, white interior, silver engine cover.

50-B   Leyland Daily Planet Van   73mm 1979-1980 $20-30
Daily Planet labels, no interior, black plastic base, Whizzwheels.
1. Red body, opaque black windows.
2. Silver body, opaque black windows.
3. Silver body, transparent blue windows.

51-A   Porsche 917   72mm 1971-1973 $12-15
Chrome interior and engine, clear windows, Whizzwheels, number 23 label.
1. Gold upper body, red lower body-base.

51-B   Volvo 245DL Estate Car   76mm 1976-Close $8-10
Opening rear hatch, black plastic base-grille, Whizzwheels.
1. Metallic green body, yellow interior, amber windows.
2. There may be an orange or a purple variety.
3. Off-white body, yellow interior, clear windows.
4. Off-white body, orange interior, clear windows.
5. Light blue body, yellow interior, amber windows.

52-A   Adams Probe 16   72mm 1971-1973 $12-15
Blue windows, cream interior, black plastic base, Whizzwheels.
1. Metallic purple body.

52-B   Mercedes-Benz 240D Taxi   76mm 1976-1979 $10-12
Amber windows and roof sign, yellow interior, black plastic base, Whizzwheels.
1. Cream body, black and white Taxi labels.
2. Black body?

52-C   Scooby Doo Mystery Ghost Catcher   69mm 1982-Close $15-20
Dark green diecast lower body-base, black Whizzwheels, tan dog figure, hood label.
1. Medium green upper body.

53-A   Fire Launch   74mm 1977-1979 $10-12
Plastic hull, three black wheels, chrome diecast spotlight bar, chrome plastic interior and water cannon, red-white-blue Fire and stripe labels.
1. Red diecast superstructure, light blue hull.

53-B   Formula 1 Racer   73mm 1980-Close $8-10
Same casting as 22-C, gold engine and windshield, plastic driver, black and gold Corgi Special labels, unpainted diecast base, Whizzwheels.
1. Black body, yellow driver.
2. Black body, white driver.

54-A   Ford D1000 Container Truck   73mm 1972-1978 $12-15
Plastic bucket and base, unpainted diecast swinging arms, green windows, Whizzwheels.
1. Red cab-chassis, dark yellow bucket and base.

2. Orange cab-chassis, dark yellow bucket and base.
3. Green cab chassis, white or silver bucket?

55-A   Daimler Fleetline Doubledecker Bus   77mm 1971-1973 $12-15
Yellow interior, no windows, red and blue Esso Uniflo Motor Oil labels on white stripes, red diecast base, Whizzwheels.
1. Red body.

55-B   Refuse Truck   71mm 1976-80, 1982-Close $8-10
Working two-piece dumper, black plastic base, Whizzwheels, no interior.
1. Blue cab, yellow dumper, faintly blue windows.
2. Gold cab, blue dumper, green windows.
3. Green cab, white dumper, clear windows.

56-A   Ford Capri Fire Chief's Car   75mm 1971-1974 $12-15
Blue windows and dome light, white diecast base, Whizzwheels.
1. Red body, white hood, white interior, black "Fire Chief" lettering on white labels.
2. Red body, white hood, white interior, red "Fire" lettering on white labels.
3. Red body including hood, yellow interior, red "Fire" lettering on white labels.

56-B   Chevrolet Spider Van   68mm 1978-1980 $20-30
Blue windows, no interior, black plastic base, Whizzwheels, Spider Van labels.
1. Metallic navy blue body.
2. Metallic dark blue body.
3. Medium blue body.

57-A   Cadillac Eldorado Hot Rod   77mm 1971-1973 $12-15
Modified 9-B casting, silver plastic engine, red interior, clear windows, unpainted diecast base-grille, Whizzwheels, "Caddy Hot Rodder" label.
1. Metallic purplish pink body.

57-B   Ferrari 512S   71mm 1975-1977 $10-12
Same casting as 50-A, Growler, chrome interior and engine cover, clear windows, number 6 label, black plastic base, Whizzwheels.
1. Light blue body.

57-C   Spiderbike   74mm 1979-Close $20-30
Red and blue Spiderman figure, black five-spoke plastic wheels.
1. Unpainted diecast and red plastic motorcycle.

58-A   GP Beach Buggy   61mm 1971-1977 $10-12
Clear windshield, chrome diecast base, Whizzwheels.
1. Metallic dark red body, off-white interior.
2. Metallic copper body, off-white interior.
3. Metallic dark red body, yellow interior.

58-B   Tom's Go-Cart   69mm 1980-Close $15-20
Red plastic exhaust pipe, steering wheel and headrest, gray figure, Whizzwheels.
1. Yellow chassis-fenders, chrome engine cover with label on front.

59-A   The Futura   75mm 1971-1973 $12-15
Blue windows, no interior, black diecast base, Whizzwheels, Futura labels.
1. Orange body.

59-B   Mercedes-Benz 240D Police Car   76mm 1977-1980 $10-12
Blue windows and dome lights, yellow interior, black plastic base, Whizzwheels.
1. White body, green and white Polizei labels.

59-C   Mercedes-Benz 240D   76mm 1982-Close $8-10
Clear windows, black plastic base, Whizzwheels.
1. Dark blue body, tan interior.
2. White body, brown interior.
3. Red body, white interior?

60-A   VW Double Trouble Hot Rod   74mm 1971-1973 $12-15
Chrome interior and engines, green windows, black diecast base, Whizzwheels.
1. Pinkish orange body.
2. Metallic purple body.

60-B   James Bond Lotus Esprit   75mm 1977-Close $20-30
Opaque black windows, no interior, black plastic base, black Whizzwheels.
1. White body, red 007 label.

61-A   Mercury Cougar XR7 Sheriff's Car   75mm 1971-1975 $12-15
Blue windows and dome lights, unpainted diecast base, Whizzwheels, Sheriff labels.
1. White body, black top, yellow interior.
2. White body, black top, white interior.
3. White body, black top, red interior.

61-B   Buick Regal Sheriff's Car   76mm 1979-Close $8-10
Casting and details as 28-D.
1. White and black body.

61-C   Ford Capri 3.0 S   76mm 1980-1981 $8-10
Yellow interior, blue windows, black plastic base-grille, Whizzwheels.
1. Red body, black trim.

62-A   Volvo P-1800   71mm 1971-1973 $12-15
Blue interior, clear windows, unpainted diecast base-grille, Whizzwheels.
1. Red body, black hood.

62-B   AMC Pacer   74mm 1976-1980 $10-12
Chrome interior and bumpers, black plastic base, Whizzwheels.
1. Metallic blue body, blue windows.
2. Metallic maroon body, blue windows.
3. Metallic red body, amber windows.

63-A   Ford Escort Rallye   69mm 1971-1975 $12-15
Red interior, clear windows, unpainted diecast base-grille, Whizzwheels.
1. Metallic blue body, red and black stripes and number 32 labels.

63-B   Surf Rescue Helicopter   75mm 1977-1979 $10-12
White interior, base, pontoons and rotors, blue and white Surf Rescue labels, clear windows.
1. Metallic dark blue body.

64-A   Morgan Plus 8   67mm 1971-1973 $12-15
Black interior, clear windshield, unpainted diecast base-grille, Whizzwheels.
1. Yellow body.
2. Red body.

64-B   The Professionals' Ford Capri   76mm 1980-Close $20-30
Same casting as 61-C, chrome interior, blue windows, black plastic base-grille, Whizzwheels.
1. Metallic silver body, black trim.

65-A   Bertone Carabo   75mm 1971-1973 $12-15
Amber windows, light green lower body-base casting, Whizzwheels.
1. Metallic purple upper body, cream interior and grilles.
2. Metallic purple upper body, red interior and grilles.

65-B   **Caravan Trailer**   75mm 1976-1980 $10-12
Light blue interior, base and opening door, clear windows, black hitch, Whizzwheels.
1. White body.

66-A   **Centurion Tank**   68mm 1976-1978 $10-12
Black plastic base, rotating turret and raising gun barrel, three black wheels.
1. Olive drab body.

66-B   **Ice Cream Van**   (1980?) $???
Probably not issued. (May be Kiko Corgi model from Brazil.)

67-A   **Ford Capri Dragster**   73mm 1971-1973 $12-15
Same casting as 56-A, red and silver interior with engine, roll bars and rear seat, white diecast base, Whizzwheels, Union Jack and "Hot Pants" labels.
1. Yellow body.

67-B   **Road Roller**   68mm 1976-1978 $10-12
Black plastic rollers, body panels and steering wheel; body casting includes base.
1. Orange body.
2. Orange body, gray plastic parts.

67-C   **Popeye's Tugboat**   77mm 1980-Close $20-30
Plastic hull, yellow deck, red superstructure and hull, Popeye figure, Spinach can label.
1. Three black wheels.
2. 3 bumps on bottom (No wheels).

68-A   **Kojak's Buick Regal**   76mm 1977-1980 $20-30
Amber windows, chrome interior, bumpers and grille, red roof light, black plastic base, Whizzwheels.
1. Metallic copper body.

69-A   **Batmobile**   75mm 1976-Close $20-30
Blue canopy, red interior, driver, bat label, black plastic base, Whizzwheels.
1. Black body.

70-A   **U.S. Racing Buggy**   73mm 1971? $12-15
White interior with driver, chrome plastic engine and exhaust pipes, white diecast base, Whizzwheels, red-white-blue stars and stripes labels.
1. Light blue body.

70-B   **Mercury Cougar XR7 Fire Chief's Car**   75mm 1975-1977 $10-12
Same casting as 61-A, blue windows and dome lights, yellow interior, unpainted diecast base-grille, Whizzwheels, red and yellow Fire Dept. Chief labels.
1. Red body.

70-C   **Ford Gran Torino Fire Chief's Car**   75mm 1977-1982 $10-12
Same casting as 45-B, opaque black windows, no interior, red roof lights, chrome plastic base-grille, Fire Dept. Chief labels.
1. Red body.

70-D   **Ford Gran Torino**   75mm 1983-Close $8-10
Same casting as 70-C, blue dome light, gray plastic base-grille, otherwise as 70-C.
1. Blue body.

71-A   **Marcos XP**   69mm 1971-1975 $12-15
Gold interior, amber windows, black diecast base, Whizzwheels.
1. Orange body.

71-B   **Austin London Taxi**   72mm 1980-Close $8-10
Yellow interior, clear windows, unpainted diecast base-grille, Whizzwheels.
1. Black body.

72-A   **Mercedes-Benz C111**   74mm 1972-1977 $12-15
Chrome interior, blue windows, black plastic lower body-base, Whizzwheels.
1. Red body.
2. May exist with blue body and white base.

72-B   **Jaguar XJ-S**   76mm 1979-80, 1982-Close $8-10
Plastic base, Whizzwheels.
1. Navy blue body, white interior, clear windows, chrome base.
2. Navy blue body, white interior, clear windows, black base.
3. Medium blue body, opaque black windows, no interior, black base;
4. Red body, opaque black windows, black base, white Motor Show lettering; 1982.
5. Red body, opaque black windows, black base; 1983.

73-A   **Pininfarina Alfa Romeo P33**   73mm 1971-1973 $12-15
White plastic wing and seats, black interior, clear windshield, white diecast base, Whizzwheels.
1. Blue body.

73-B   **Drax Airlines Helicopter**   75mm 1979-1979 $20-30
Yellow plastic interior, base, skids and rotors, amber windows, Drax Airlines labels.
1. White body.

74-A   **Bertone Barchetta Runabout**   62mm 1972-1975 $12-15
White diecast lower body-base, plastic interior and stripe between castings, clear windshield, Whizzwheels.
1. Orange upper body, black interior and stripe.
2. Orange upper body, red interior and stripe.

74-A   **Leyland Ryder Rental Truck**   73mm 1977-1980 $10-12
Blue windows, no interior, black plastic base, Whizzwheels.
1. Yellow body, Ryder Truck Rental logo labels.

75-A   **Super Stock Car**   69mm 1973-1975 $10-12
Red interior, diecast base, Whizzwheels, Union Jack label.
1. Silver body, yellow base.
2. Silver body, blue base.

75-B   **Spidercopter**   74mm 1977-1982 $20-30
Light red interior, parts and legs, clear canopy, spider labels, black rotor.
1. Metallic blue body.

76-A   **Chevrolet Astro 1**   73mm 1971? $???
Was it issued?

76-B   **U.S. Army Jeep**   62mm 1974-1978 $10-12
Silver gray plastic folding windshield, brown interior and driver, white star label, olive diecast base, black Whizzwheels.
1. Olive drab body and base.

76-C   **Matra Rancho**   73mm 1980-Close $8-10
White interior, clear windows, opening hatch and tailgate, black plastic base-grille, Whizzwheels.
1. Metallic light brown body.
2. Light green body.

77-A   **Ital Design Bizzarini Manta**   72mm 1971-1973 $12-15
Cream interior, clear windows, black diecast base, Whizzwheels.
1. Hot pink body.
2. Blue body?

77-B   **Excavator**   73mm 1977-1980 $10-12
Light red plastic interior, arm and shovel, diecast chassis-base, black plastic wheels.

1. White turning body, metallic blue chassis-base.

78-A   **Ole Macdonald's Truck**   63mm 1971? $12-15
Unpainted diecast base-grille-engine, tan interior and rear body, Whizzwheels.
1. Red cab.

78-B   **Batcopter**   76mm 1978-1981 $20-25
Red plastic interior, skids, base and rotors, blue canopy, Batman labels.
1. Black body.

79-A   **Land Rover Military Ambulance**   71mm 1975-1976 $10-12
Amber windows, no interior, black plastic base, black Whizzwheels, olive rear cover.
1. Olive drab body and rear cover, red cross labels.

79-B   **Olive Oyl's Aeroplane**   68mm 1980-Close $15-20
Red propeller, chrome parts, black seat with figure, black plastic base, two Whizzwheels, wing labels.
1. Yellow body.

80-A   **Porsche Carrera**   74mm 1974-1975 $10-12
Clear windows, black plastic base, Whizzwheels, number 4 and red-white-blue stripe labels.
1. White body, yellow interior.
2. White body, red interior.

80-B   **Fiat X1/9**   73mm 1978-1978 $10-12
Same castings as 86-A, black plastic base and interior, chrome engine, clear windows, number 4 and red-white-blue labels, Whizzwheels.
1. White body.

80-C   **Leyland Marvel Comics Van**   73mm 1979-1980 $15-20
Green windows, no interior, black plastic base, Whizzwheels.
1. Dark green body, Marvel Comics logo labels.

81-A   **Daimler Fleetline Doubledeck Bus**   76mm 1974-Close $10-12
Black plastic base, Whizzwheels (chrome unless noted), no interior.
1. Red body, faces in windows, "Visit Britain—Visit London" labels.
2. Red body, faces in windows, "Coca-Cola" labels.
3. Red body, faces in windows, "See more London" labels.
4. Red body, black windows, "See more London" labels, black Whizzwheels; 1982.
5. Red body, black windows, "See more London" labels; 1982.
6. Green body, black windows, interchangeable labels; 1982.
7. Cream body, black windows, interchangeable labels; 1982.
8. Dark blue body, black windows, interchangeable labels; 1982

82-A   **Can-Am Racer**   73mm 1974-1978 $10-12
Growler, white driver and engine, number 9 and stripe labels, black plastic base, Whizzwheels.
1. Metallic blue body.
2. Purple body.

82-B   **Yogi Bear's Jeep**   61mm 1981-Close $15-20
Green interior with figure, diecast base same color as body, Whizzwheels.
1. Dark yellow body and base, "Jellystone Park" hood label.

83-A   **Commando V100 Armored Car**   73mm 1974-1977 $10-12
Black plastic rotating turret, white labels, black plastic wheels, diecast lower body-base same color as upper body.
1. Olive drab body and base.

83-B   **Goodyear Blimp**   77mm 1980-1981 $8-10
Red and blue plastic fins, blue gondola, red engines and parts.
1. Chrome finish, Goodyear and Corgi labels.

84-A   **Daimler Scout Car**   62mm 1974-1978 $10-12
Brown figure with gun moves sideways, black plastic base and wheels.
1. Olive drab body, red-white-olive rear label.

84-B   **Bugs Bunny Buggy**   70mm 1980-Close $15-20
Red plastic dash and engine, gray figure, carrot label on hood, unpainted diecast base with grille and headlights, Whizzwheels.
1. Orange body.

85-A   **Skip Dumper**   58mm 1974-78, 1980-Close $8-10
Plastic tipper, black plastic seat and steering wheel, black plastic wheels.
1. Yellow body, red tipper.
2. Metallic green body, yellow tipper.

86-A   **Fiat X1/9**   73mm 1974-78, 1980-Close $8-10
Black plastic interior, engine cover, bumpers and base, chrome engine, clear windows, Whizzwheels.
1. Apple green body, no labels.
2. White body, no labels.
3. Gold body, number 4 and stripe labels; 1980.
4. Gold body, number 9 labels.
5. Gold body, number 4, Fiat and stripe labels; 1981.
6. Gold body, number 9 and Fiat labels; 1981.
7. Orange body, number 9 and Fiat labels; red interior; 1981.
8. Apple green body, no labels, red interior; 1983.

87-A   **Mercedes-Benz Coca-Cola Truck**   (1974?) $???
Probably not issued.

87-B   **Leyland Terrier Delivery Van**   73mm 1975-1980 $10-12
No interior, black plastic base, Whizzwheels.
1. Red body, white roofs, red and white Coca-Cola labels, blue windows; 1975-1976.
2. White body, clear windows, red and blue Pepsi-Cola logo; 1975-1980.
3. White body, black opaque windows, red & blue Pepsi-Cola labels (1980?)
4. Dark yellow body, blue windows, Weetabix labels; 1979 promotional.
5. Orange body, opaque black windows, W. H. Smith logo; 1980 promotional.

88-A   **Mobile Crane**   68mm 1975-1980 $10-12
Yellow plastic upper and lower crane booms, mounting and base, amber windows and dome lights, no interior, black plastic wheels and hook.
1. Light red body.

89-A   **Citroen Dyane**   76mm 1975-1982 $10-12
Opening hatch, clear windows, black plastic base, Whizzwheels.
1. Yellow gold body, red interior.
2. Gold body, black roof, red interior.
3. Metallic purple body, yellow interior.

90-A   **Chevrolet Fire Ball Custom Van**   68mm 1977-1979 $10-12
Amber windows, no interior, black plastic base, Whizzwheels.
1. Black body, Fire Ball logo labels.

91-A   **Chevrolet Golden Eagle Van**   68mm 1977-1979 $10-12
Amber windows, no interior, black plastic base, Whizzwheels.
1. Orange body, "Chevrolet Van" base, detailed mountain lake scene, with eagle about to land, dark colors.
2. Orange body, "U.S. Van" base, simpler, lighter-colored scene with eagle in different position.

91-B   Vantastic Custom Van   69mm 1980-1981 $8-10
New body casting with raised rear roof, blue windows, no interior, unpainted diecast base with exhaust pipes and "Hot Rod Custom Van" lettering, Whizzwheels.
1. Black body, yellow and orange Vantastic labels.

92-A   VW Polo   73mm 1977-1981 $8-10
Opening doors, amber windows, black plastic base, Whizzwheels.
1. Metallic lime green body, yellow interior.
2. Metallic medium green body, orange interior.

93-A   Tug Boat   75mm 1977-1979 $10-12
Orange plastic superstructure, yellow plastic hull, three black plastic wheels.
1. Metallic dark green deck.

93-B   Dodge Magnum   72mm 1980-1981 $8-10
Opaque black windows, no interior, unpainted diecast base, Whizzwheels, opening hood, chrome plastic engine, grille and bumpers.
1. Yellow body.

94-A   Porsche 917   72mm 1974-1977 $10-12
Chrome interior and engine, amber windows, black plastic base with Growler gear, Whizzwheels; same casting as 51-A.
1. Metallic silver body.

94-B   Chevrolet Adidas Van   68mm 1978-1981 $10-12
Blue windows, no interior, black plastic base, Whizzwheels, white Adidas labels.
1. Medium blue body, "Chevrolet Van' base.
2. Medium blue body, "U.S. Van" base.

95-A   Leyland Coca-Cola Van   73mm 1977-1982 $10-12
Same casting as 87-B, blue windows, black plastic base, Whizzwheels.
1. All red body, red and white Coca-Cola logo. (87-B1 has white roofs.)

96-A   Field Gun and Soldiers   80mm 1975-1978 $10-12
Chassis and raising gun barrel castings, two black plastic wheels, brown plastic accessory piece with two soldiers.
1. Olive drab gun, white star and "U.S. Army" label.

96-B   1957 Ford Thunderbird   72mm 1980-Close $8-10
Opening hood, detailed engine, clear windshield, black interior, chrome grille, bumpers and spare wheel cover, unpainted diecast base, Whizzwheels.
1. Red body; Vegas$ car; 1980-1981.
2. Cream body; 1982-1983.
3. Light green body? 1983.

97-A   Guy Exxon Tanker   73mm 1975-1976 $10-12
Same casting as 14-C, no interior, black plastic base and headlights, Whizzwheels, red-white-blue Exxon labels.
1. White body, blue windows.
2. White body, purple windows.

97-B   Petrol Tanker   75mm 1977-Close $8-10
No interior, black plastic lower body-base, Whizzwheels.
1. Metallic silver body, red-orange-white Shell labels, opaque black windows.
2. Light red body, red-white-black Texaco logo, amber windows.
3. Exxon logo, other details not known.
4. White body, red and green BP labels with shield to rear, amber windows, black Whizzwheels; 1981.
5. Labels with shield to left, chrome Whizzwheels, otherwise as type 4; 1981-.
6. White body, Total labels, other details not known; 1982?

98-A   Marcos X   71mm 1975-1977 $10-12
Growler, 71-A casting, chrome interior and engine, black plastic base, Whizzwheels.
1. Golden orange body.

98-B   Mercedes-Benz Mobile Shop   72mm 1977-1979 $10-12
Clear windows, yellow front interior, grocery store rear interior, black plastic base, Whizzwheels.
1. Blue body.

98-C   Police Helicopter   77mm 1980-1980 $10-12
Red interior, base, pontoons and rotors, clear windows, Police labels.
1. White body.

99-A   Jokermobile   76mm 1979-1981 $15-20
Same casting as 36-B, blue windows and dome light, no interior, black plastic base, Whizzwheels, Joker labels.
1. White body.

100-A   Hulkcycle   63mm 1981-Close $15-20
Green plastic seat with Incredible Hulk figure, three red plastic wheels.
1. Black body.

101-A   Leyland Punch and Judy Show Van   73mm 1983-Close $20-30
Blue windows, no interior, black plastic base, Whizzwheels.
1. Red body, colorful "Kasperl-Theater" labels; German issue.

102-A   Renault 5 Turbo   70mm 1981-Close $8-10
Red interior, grille, bumpers and lower body stripe, clear windows, chrome mirrors, plastic base, Whizzwheels.
1. Yellow body, black roof, black and white labels, black base.
2. Yellow body, black roof, black and white labels, red base.

103-A   Ford Transit Wrecker   72mm 1981-Close $8-10
Blue windows, no interior, red plastic boom and roof bar, black plastic base and hook, red-white-black "24 hour service" labels, Whizzwheels.
1. White body.

104-A   Ford Mustang Cobra   74mm 1981-Close $8-10
Opening hatch, yellow interior, amber windows, black plastic base and grille, Whizzwheels.
1. Orange body.
2. Yellow body?
3. Red body.

105-A   Ford Escort   75mm 1981-Close $8-10
Opening doors, light brown interior, clear windows, black plastic base and grille, Whizzwheels.
1. Metallic green body.
2. Metallic light blue body.

107-A   Austin Mini Metro   75mm 1981-Close $8-10
Opening doors, clear windows, black plastic base and grille, Whizzwheels.
1. Metallic dark blue body, light tan interior.
2. Bright blue body, red interior.

108-A   Railroad Locomotive   76mm 1981-Close $8-10
Black plastic boiler, yellow cowcatcher, base and parts, unpainted diecast smokestack top and headlight, black plastic railroad wheels.
1. Red cab and chassis.

111-A   Railroad Passenger Coach   75mm 1981-Close $8-10
Yellow plastic body, Union Pacific labels, black plastic railroad wheels.
1. Red chassis.

112-A   Railroad Goods Wagon   75mm 1981-Close $8-10
Green plastic body, red sliding door, black plastic railroad wheels.
1. Red chassis, "Buffalo Bill's Circus" labels.
2. Red chassis, "Wild West Show" labels.

113-A   Paddle Steamer   75mm 1982-Close $8-10
White plastic lower superstructure, stacks, sternwheel and front roller.
1. Yellow upper superstructure, blue hull, "St. Louis Queen" labels.

114-A   Stage Coach   80mm 1981-Close $8-10
Light brown horses, tongue and spoked wheels, yellow interior, driver and roof.
1. Red body.

115-A   James Bond Citroen 2CV6   74mm 1981-Close $20-30
Opening doors, red interior, clear windows, black plastic base, Whizzwheels.
1. Dark yellow body, black grille.

116-A   Mercedes-Benz España '82 Team Bus   74mm 1981-Close $20-30
Amber windows with faces, soccer team labels, black plastic base and grille, Whizzwheels.
1. Red body, white label panels.

117-A   Chevrolet España '82 Team Van   68mm 1981-Close $20-30
Blue windows, no interior, black plastic base, Whizzwheels.
1. White body, soccer team labels.

118-A   Mercedes-Benz Airport Bus   74mm 1983-Close $20-30
Opaque black windows, black plastic base and grille, Whizzwheels.
1. Orange body, black stripes, white "Flughafenbus" labels. German issue.

119-A   Chubb Airport Crash Tender   74mm 1983-Close $20-30
Same casting as 123-A, clear windows, yellow interior, roof panels and nozzle, black plastic base, six Whizzwheels.
1. Red body, number 9 and "Flughafen-Feuerwehr" labels. German issue.

120-A   Dan Dare Car   (1981)   N/A
Not issued.

120-B   Leyland Ice Cream Truck   73mm 1983-Close $20-30
Blue? windows, no interior, black plastic base, Whizzwheels.
1. White body, "Frohliche Eiszeit" labels, German issue.

121-A   Chevrolet Technical Service Van   68mm 1983-Close $20-30
Amber windows, no interior, black plastic base, Whizzwheels.
1. Blue body, white "Technischer Kundendienst" labels. German issue.

122-A   Covered Wagon   75mm 1982-Close $8-10
Light brown horses, tongue and spoked wheels, yellow figures and front base.
1. Green body, removable white plastic top.

123-A   Chubb Airport Crash Tender   74mm 1982-Close $8-10
Clear windows, yellow interior, roof panels and nozzle, black plastic base, six Whizzwheels.
1. Red body, black and white "Airport Rescue" and number 8 labels.

124-A   Mercedes-Benz 500 SL   75mm 1982-Close $8-10
Clear windows, tan interior, black plastic base and tow hook, Whizzwheels.
1. Metallic light green body, silver grille.
2. Red body.

125-A   Ford Transit Dropside Truck   72mm 1982-Close $8-10
Opaque black windows, no interior, black plastic base, Whizzwheels.
1. Yellow body, black Wimpey label; identical to 146-A.
2. Light green body?

126-A   Ford Transit Wrecker   72mm 1983-Close $20-30
Same casting as 103-A, opaque black windows, red plastic boom and roof bar, black plastic base and hook, Whizzwheels.
1. Bright yellow body, "Abschleppdienst hilft Tag und Nacht" labels. German issue.

127-A   Ford Escort ADAC Road Service Car   75mm 1983-Close $20-30
Tan interior, clear windows, black plastic base, Whizzwheels.
1. Golden yellow body, black "ADAC-Strassenwacht" labels. German issue.

128-A   Fred Flintstone's Flyer   69mm 1982-Close $15-20
Fred Flintstone figure, tan plastic front wheels and rear log roller.
1. Orange body.

129-A   Ford Sierra 2.3 Ghia   75mm 1983-Close $8-10
Opening doors, clear windows, plastic lower body-base, Whizzwheels.
1. Yellow body, red interior and taillights, light brown lower body-base.
2. Metallic silver brown body, brown interior, reddish taillights, brownish gray lower body-base.
3. Blue body, other details not known.

131-A   Magnum PI Ferrari 308 GTS   75mm 1982-Close $15-20
Identical to 136-A, clear windshield, white seats, black interior, grille, vents and base, Whizzwheels.
1. Red body.

133-A   Magnum PI Buick Regal Police Car   75mm 1982-Close $8-10
Identical to 150-A, amber windows, chrome interior, grille and bumpers, red roof light, black Police labels, black plastic base, Whizzwheels.
1. Black front and rear, white center of body.

134-A   Barney's Buggy   69mm 1982-Close $15-20
Tan interior, grille and base, Flintstones character driver, black plastic wheels.
1. Red body with brown wheel markings.

135-A   Austin Metro Datapost   70mm 1982-Close $8-10
Same casting as 107-A, opening doors, clear windows, red interior, black plastic base and tow hook, Whizzwheels.
1. White body, blue roof and hood, number 77 and Datapost labels.

136-A   Ferrari 308 GTS   75mm 1982-Close $8-10
Casting and details as 131-A.
1. Red body.
2. Black body.

137-A   VW Polo Turbo   73mm 1982-Close $8-10
Same castings as 92-A, opening doors, amber windows, red interior, black plastic base and tow hook, Whizzwheels.
1. Cream body, red and orange trim and number 6 painted on.

138-A   Rover 3500 Triplex   75mm 1982-Close $8-10
Same casting as 8-D, clear windows, red interior, opening hatch, black plastic base and tow hook, Whizzwheels.
1. White body, blue roof and hood, number 12 and Triplex labels.

139-A   Porsche Carrera Turbo   74mm 1982-Close $8-10
Same casting as 80-A, clear windows, yellow interior, black plastic base, Whizzwheels.
1. Black body, gold name and stripe labels.

160

140-A Ford Mustang Cobra 73mm 1982-Close $8-10
Same casting as 104-A, amber windows, red interior, black plastic grille-lower body-base with tow hook, Whizzwheels.
1. Bright yellow body, name and stripe labels.
141-A Ford Capri 3.0 S 75mm 1982-Close $8-10
Same casting as 61-C, opening hood, red engine, interior, bumpers, grille and base, clear windows, Whizzwheels.
1. White body, green and red number 8, Alitalia name and stripes painted on.
143-A Leyland Royal Mail Van 73mm 1983-Close $8-10
Clear windows, no interior, plastic base, Whizzwheels.
1. Bright red body, yellow Royal Mail labels, black base.
2. Bright red body, yellow Royal Mail labels, yellow base.
144-A Chevrolet British Gas Van 68mm 1983-Close $8-10
Opaque black windows, no interior, black plastic base, Whizzwheels.
1. White body, blue roof, two-tone blue stripes and British Gas lettering labels.
145-A Chevrolet British Telecom Van 68mm 1983-Close $8-10
Blue windows, no interior, black plastic base, Whizzwheels.
1. Dark yellow body, blue British Telecom logo painted on.
146-A Ford Transit Dropside Truck 72mm 1983-Close $8-10
Same casting as 125-A, blue windows, black plastic base, Whizzwheels.
1. Dark yellow body, black Wimpey labels (identical to 125-A1).
147-A Leyland Roadline Van 73mm 1983-Close $8-10
Green windows, no interior, plastic base, Whizzwheels.
1. Bright green body, Roadline logo on white labels, black base.
2. Bright green body, Roadline logo on white labels, gray base.
148-A USS Enterprise 70mm 1982-Close $20-30
Star Trek spacecraft, diecast and plastic body, black NCC-1701 label.
1. White body.
149-A Klingon Warship 75mm 1982-Close $20-30
Star Trek spacecraft, single casting plus white cabin.
1. Metallic dark blue body, yellow and black K labels.
150-A Simon and Simon Buick Regal Police Car 75mm 1982-Close $8-10
Identical to 133-A.
1. Black front and rear, white center of body.
151-A Wilma's Coupe 70mm 1982-Close $15-20
Tan plastic base and rear panel, Wilma Flintstone figure, black Whizzwheels.
1. Yellow body.
152-A Simon and Simon 1957 Chevrolet Convertible 74mm 1982-Close $8-10
Clear windshield, red interior, chrome grille and bumpers, black plastic base, Whizzwheels.
1. Black body, white trim.
153-A DeLorean DMC 12 (1982) N/A
Probably not issued.
156-A 1957 Chevrolet Convertible 74mm 1982-Close $8-10
Same casting as 152-A, clear windshield, red interior, chrome grille and bumpers, black plastic base, Whizzwheels.
1. White body, red and yellow flame trim.
2. Black body, white trim? (identical to 152-A1) ; 1983.
157-A Army Jeep 68mm 1983-Close $8-10
Same casting as 76-B, clear windshield, yellow interior, black diecast base, Whizzwheels.
1. Olive drab body, white star label.
158-A Centurion Army Tank 70mm 1983-Close $8-10
Same casting as 66-A, turning black plastic turret with raising gun barrel, black plastic base, three black plastic wheels.
1. Olive drab body.
159-A Commando V100 Armored Car 72mm 1983-Close $8-10
Same casting as 83-A, turning black plastic turret, black plastic wheels.
1. Olive drab upper and lower body, white star and lettering labels.
160-A VW Hot Rod 73mm 1982-Close $8-10
Same casting as 60-A, chrome engines and interior, clear windows, black diecast base, Whizzwheels.
1. Orange body.
161-A Opel Corsa 1.3SR ?mm 1983-Close $8-10
Opaque black windows, black plastic base and grille, Whizzwheels.
1. Golden yellow body?
170-A Vauxhall Nova Hatchback 71mm 1983-Close $8-10
Clear windows, white interior, opening hatch, black plastic lower body-base-grille, Whizzwheels.
1. Red body.
174-A Quarry Truck 74mm 1983-Close $8-10
Plastic tipper, chrome grille, exhaust stacks and windows, black plastic base, six Whizzwheels.
1. Light yellow chassis-cab, red tipper.
2. Dark yellow chassis-cab, orange tipper.
175-A Pipe Truck 74mm 1983-Close $8-10
Yellow plastic flatbed with gray pipe load, chrome grille, stacks and windows, black plastic base, six Whizzwheels.
1. Red chassis-cab.
177-A Chemco Tanker 75mm 1983-Close $8-10
Light blue plastic tank, chrome fillers, hoses, grille, stacks and windows, black plastic base, six Whizzwheels.
1. Dark blue chassis-cab, Corgi Chemco labels on tank.
178-A Container Truck 74mm 1983-Close $8-10
Cream plastic container on light green flatbed, chrome grille, stacks and windows, black plastic base, six Whizzwheels.
1. Green chassis-cab, yellow and black Corgi labels on container.
179-A Chevrolet Corvette 72mm 1983-Close $8-10
Clear roof and windows, red interior, black dash and engine, opening hood, red taillights, black plastic base, Whizzwheels.
1. White body.
180-A Pontiac Firebird 75mm 1983-Close $8-10
Plastic spoiler, grille and interior, clear windows, black plastic base, Whizzwheels.
1. Red body, black seats & spoiler.
2. Black body, tan seats & spoiler.
3. Black body, white seats, tan spoiler. (Known lot where factory used-up excess spoiler moldings.)
4. Black body, white seats & spoiler.
5. Black body, black seats & spoiler.
6. Black body, black seats & spoiler, red area between headlamps.
181-A Mercedes-Benz 300SL 72mm 1983-Close $8-10
Opening gullwing doors, white interior, clear windows, chrome plastic base and bumpers, Whizzwheels.
1. Red body.
182-A 4x4 Renegade Jeep ?mm 1983-Close $8-10
Clear windshield, red interior, black base, Whizzwheels and spare, other details not known.
1. Yellow body?
183-A Renegade Jeep with Hood 66mm 1983-Close $8-10
White plastic hood, interior and base, Whizzwheels, other details not known.
1. Black body?
184-A Range Rover 74mm 1983-Close $8-10
Clear windshield, tan interior, black plastic grille and base, Whizzwheels.
1. Maroon body.
185-A Baja Off Road Van 69mm 1983-Close $8-10
Same casting as 91-B, black diecast base, Whizzwheels, other details not known.
1. Yellow body with red and black trim?
190-A Buick Regal Arabian Police Car 75mm 1983-Close $20-30
Same casting as 68-A, light gray interior, grille and bumpers, clear windows, red roof light, black plastic base, Whizzwheels.
1. White body, black Arabic labels. Arabian issue.
191-A Leyland Arabian Pepsi-Cola Truck 73mm 1983-Close $20-30
Clear windows, no interior, black plastic base, Whizzwheels.
1. White body, red-white-blue-light blue Pepsi logo with Arabic lettering. Arabian issue.
192-A Mercedes-Benz Arabian Ambulance 74mm 1983-Close $20-30
Same casting as 1-E, blue windows and dome light, no interior, black plastic base, Whizzwheels.
1. White body, red crescent, Ambulance and Arabic lettering, Arabian issue.
193-A Chubb Airport Crash Tender 74mm 1983-Close $20-30
Same casting as 123-A, blue windows, cream interior, panels and nozzle, black plastic base, six Whizzwheels.
1. Red body, black trim and white Arabic lettering labels. Arabian issue.
194-A Mercedes-Benz 240D Arabian Taxi 75mm 1983-Close $20-30
Clear windows, white interior, black plastic base and tow hook, Whizzwheels.
1. Red body, white Arabic lettering labels. Arabian issue.
195-A Leyland Arabian Bottle Truck 73mm 1983-Close $20-30
Clear windows, no interior, black plastic base, Whizzwheels.
1. White body, orange and green Arabic logo on white labels. Arabian issue.
196-A Police Tactical Force Van 69mm 1983-Close $8-10
Same casting as 91-B, opaque black windows, unpainted diecast base, Whizzwheels.
1. White body, black and red labels.
200-A Pencil Eater Rover 3500 77mm? 1983-Close $15-20
Pencil sharpener based on 8-D Rover 3500.
1. Details not known.
201-A Leyland Schat Bottle Truck 73mm 1983-Close $20-30
Arabian issue.
1. Details not known.
202-A Leyland 7-Up Bottle Truck 73mm 1983-Close $20-30
Arabian issue.
1. Details not known.
203-A Fiat X1/9 72mm 1983-Close $8-10
Same casting as 86-A, red interior and grille, black base, Whizzwheels.
1. Orange body?
204-A Renault 5 Turbo 68mm 1983-Close $8-10
Same casting as 102-A, clear windows, chrome mirrors, red interior, grille, bumpers and lower body stripe, black plastic base, vent and tow hook, Whizzwheels.
1. Blue body.
205-A Porsche Carrera 911 73mm 1983-Close $8-10
Same casting as 80-A, yellow interior, clear windows, black plastic base, Whizzwheels.
1. Black body.
2. Metallic light green body.
3. Yellow body.
206-A Buick Regal 75mm 1983-Close $8-10
Civilian version of 68-A, chrome interior, grille and bumpers, black plastic base, Whizzwheels.
1. Bright green body.
2. Bright red body.
3. Blue body.
207-A Ford Sierra German Police Car 75mm 1983-Close $20-30
Red interior, blue windows and dome lights, light red taillights, opening doors, black plastic base, Whizzwheels.
1. White body, green hood and stripe, white Polizei lettering. German issue.
208-A Ford Sierra German Doctor's Car 75mm 1983-Close $20-30
Same casting as 207-A, blue windows and dome lights, red interior, light red taillights, opening doors, black plastic base, Whizzwheels.
1. White body, red cross and trim and black Notarzt lettering. German issue.
209-A Leyland German Mail Truck 73mm 1983-Close $20-30
Clear windows, no interior, black plastic base, Whizzwheels.
1. Dark yellow body, black lettering labels. German issue.
210-A Safari Park Matra Rancho 73mm 1983-Close $8-10
Same casting as 76-C, clear windows, white interior, black plastic base, Whizzwheels.
1. Metallic brown body, Safari labels? German issue.
211-A Ford Escort German Driving School Car 75mm 1983-Close $20-30
Same casting as 105-A, opening doors, clear windows, white interior, black plastic base, Whizzwheels.
1. Green body, white Fahrschule lettering. German issue.
212-A VW Polo Siemens Service Car 71mm 1983-Close $20-30
Same casting as 92-A, opening doors, clear windows, white interior, black plastic base and tow hook, Whizzwheels.
1. Blue body, "Siemens Wartungsdienst" lettering. German issue.
214-A Mercedes-Benz PTT Bus 74mm 1983-Close $20-30
Same casting as 15-C.
1. Probably yellow body, details not known. Swiss issue.
215-A Swiss Red Cross Car 1983-Close $20-30
Details not known.
1. Swiss issue.
216-A Chevrolet Swissair Van 68mm 1983-Close $20-30
Blue windows, no interior, black plastic base, Whizzwheels.
1. White body, brown stripes, black name, red and white flag labels, Swiss issue.

| 217-A | Leyland Ovomaltine Van | 73mm 1983-Close | $20-30 |

217-A   Leyland Ovomaltine Van   73mm 1983-Close $20-30
Details not known.
1. Swiss issue.

218-A   Leyland Swiss TV Van   73mm 1983-Close $20-30
Clear windows, no interior, blue plastic base, Whizzwheels.
1. Blue body, white "Schweizer Fernsehan" labels. Swiss issue.

219-A   Swiss Police Car   1983-Close $20-30
Details not known.
1. Swiss issue.

220-A   Ford Transit Dropside Truck   72mm 1983-Close $8-10
Same casting as 125-A; details not known.
1. Swiss issue.

221-A   Leyland Zweifel Chips Van   73mm 1983-Close $20-30
Zweifel Chips logo; details not known.
1. Swiss issue.

222-A   Chevrolet Swissair Van   68mm 1983-Close $8-10
Appears to be British issue of 216-A.
1. Presumably same as 216-A.

223-A   Safari Park Matra Rancho   73mm 1983-Close $8-10
Same casting as 210-A.
1. Tan body, black chassis, white seats, brown mud splatters, black "SAFARI" on doors, lion head & arched "SAFARI PARK" on hood.

224-A   Chevrolet Rivella Van   68mm 1983-Close $20-30
Rivella logo; details not known.
1. Swiss issue.

225-A   Chubb Airport Crash Tender   74mm 1983-Close $20-30
Same casting as 123-A; details not known.
1. Swiss issue.

226-A   Ford Transit Wrecker   72mm 1983-Close $20-30
Same casting as 103-A; details not known.
1. Swiss issue.

227-A   Swiss Mercedes-Benz Ambulance   76mm 1983-Close $20-30
Swiss issue, same casting as 1-E.
1. Details not known.

250-A   Simon Snorkel Fire Truck   76mm 1983-Close $20-30
Same casting as 29-B, yellow snorkel parts and base, clear windows, Whizzwheels.
1. Red body, Brandbil lettering on snorkel; Danish issue.

251-A   ERF Fire Tender   76mm 1983-Close $20-30
Same casting as 26-C, yellow ladder, blue windows and dome lights, black plastic headlights and base, Whizzwheels.
1. Red body, Falck labels; Danish issue.

252-A   Ford Transit Wrecker   72mm 1983-Close $20-30
Same casting as 103-A, clear windows, red plastic boom and roof bar, black plastic base and hook, Whizzwheels.
1. Red body, Falck labels; Danish issue.

253-A   Mercedes-Benz Ambulance   76mm 1983-Close $20-30
Same casting as 1-E, blue windows and dome light, black plastic base, Whizzwheels.
1. White body, red hood and window frames, Falck labels; Danish issue.

254-A   Mercedes-Benz 240D Emergency Car   76mm 1983-Close $20-30
Same casting as 59-C, clear windows, white interior, black plastic base, Whizzwheels.
1. White body, red stripe and Falck labels; Danish issue.

255-A   Chevrolet Emergency Truck   68mm 1983-Close $20-30
Opaque black windows, black plastic base, Whizzwheels.
1. White Falck labels; Danish issue.

No #   Leyland Gamleys Van   73mm 1983-Close $20-30
Opaque black windows, black plastic base, Whizzwheels.
1. Red body, Gamleys Toyshop logo on white labels; promotional.

No #   Chevrolet UniChem Van   68mm 1983-Close $20-30
Blue windows, black plastic base, Whizzwheels.
1. White body, green and black UniChem labels; promotional.

No #   Chevrolet A.A. Van   68mm 1983-Close $20-30
Logo and other details not known.
1. Yellow body.

No #   Leyland Advance Van   73mm 1983-Close $20-30
Red-black-white Advance labels, Whizzwheels, other details not known. Promotional issue.
1. White body.

No #   Chevrolet Police Van   68mm 1983-Close $20-30
Red Police labels, black windows and base, Whizzwheels, other details not known.
1. White body.

No #   Caledonian Autominologists Van   73mm 1976- 1976 $20-30
Leyland Terrier van, blue windows, black plastic base, Whizzwheels.

Baseball Cars

All 1982 Baseball Trading Cars use the 104-A Ford Mustang Cobra with white body, amber windows, yellow interior, Whizzwheels and plastic lower body-base in varying colors; the baseball team logo is on the hood.

400-A   Baltimore Orioles $10-15
1. Orange base, orange-white-black logo.
401-A   Boston Red Sox $10-15
1. Red base, red-white-blue logo.
402-A   California Angels $10-15
1. Red base, red-white-blue logo.
403-A   Chicago White Sox $10-15
1. Red base, blue-white-red logo.
404-A   Cleveland Indians $10-15
1. Blue base, red-white-blue logo.
405-A   Detroit Tigers $10-15
1. Blue base, orange-blue-white logo.
406-A   Kansas City Royals $10-15
1. Blue base, blue-white-gold logo.
407-A   Milwaukee Brewers $10-15
1. Yellow base, blue-yellow-white logo.

408-A   Minnesota Twins $10-15
1. Red base, blue-white-red logo.
409-A   New York Yankees $10-15
1. Red base, red-white-blue logo.
2. Orange base, red-white-blue logo.
410-A   Oakland Athletics $10-15
1. Red base, yellow-green-white logo.
411-A   Seattle Mariners $10-15
1. Yellow base, yellow-blue-white logo.
412-A   Texas Rangers $10-15
1. Blue base, red-white-blue logo.
413-A   Toronto Blue Jays $10-15
1. Blue base, blue-white-red logo.
414-A   Atlanta Braves $10-15
1. Red base, blue-white-red logo.
415-A   Chicago Cubs $10-15
1. Blue base, red-white-blue logo.
416-A   Cincinnati Reds $10-15
1. Red base, red-white-black logo.
417-A   Houston Astros $10-15
1.Orange base, orange-white-blue logo.
418-A   Los Angeles Dodgers $10-15
1. Red base, blue-white-red logo.
419-A   Montreal Expos $10-15
1. Red base, blue-white-red logo.
420-A   New York Mets $10-15
1. Orange base, orange-white-blue logo.
421-A   Philadelphia Phillies $10-15
1. Yellow base, brown and white logo.
422-A   Pittsburgh Pirates $10-15
1. Yellow base, gold-white-black logo.
423-A   St. Louis Cardinals $10-15
1. Red base, red-white-yellow logo.
424-A   San Diego Padres $10-15
1. Yellow base, yellow-white-brown logo.
425-A   San Francisco Giants $10-15
1. Orange base, orange and black logo.

Hockey Cars

The 1982-83 Hockey Trading Cars use either the 104-A Ford Mustang Cobra, 72-B Jaguar XJS, or 80-A Porsche Carrera; colors, windows and bases vary.

426-A   Calgary Flames $10-15
1. Details unknown.
427-A   Boston Bruins $10-15
1. Yellow Mustang, black base, yellow interior, amber windows, black-white-yellow logo.
428-A   Buffalo Sabres $10-15
1. White Jaguar, blue base, black windows, blue-white-yellow logo.
429-A   Chicago Black Hawks $10-15
1. Details unknown.
430-A   Edmonton Oilers $10-15
1. White Mustang, orange base, yellow interior, amber windows, blue-white-orange logo.
431-A   Hartford Whalers $10-15
1. White Porsche, black base, red interior, clear windows, blue and green logo.
432-A   Montreal Canadiens $10-15
1. White Mustang, red base, yellow interior, amber windows, red-white-blue logo.
433-A   New York Islanders $10-15
1. White Mustang, blue base, yellow interior, amber windows, orange-white-blue logo.
434-A   New York Rangers $10-15
1. White Porsche, black base, red interior, clear windows, red-white-blue logo.
435-A   Philadelphia Flyers $10-15
1. White Mustang, orange base, yellow interior, amber windows, orange and black logo.
436-A   Quebec Nordiques $10-15
1. White Porsche, black base, red interior, clear windows, red-white-blue logo.
437-A   Toronto Maple Leafs $10-15
1. White Mustang, blue base, yellow interior, amber windows, blue and white logo.
438-A   Vancouver Canucks $10-15
1. Yellow Jaguar, black base and windows, red and black logo.
439-A   Winnipeg Jets $10-15
1. White Porsche, black base, red interior, clear windows, red-white-blue logo.
440-A   Detroit Red Wings $10-15
1. White Mustang, black base, yellow interior, amber windows, red and white logo.
441-A   Minnesota North Stars $10-15
1. Yellow Mustang, green base, yellow interior, amber windows, green-white-yellow logo.
442-A   Pittsburgh Penguins $10-15
1. White Jaguar, black base and windows, black and yellow logo.
443-A   St. Louis Blues $10-15
1. Yellow Jaguar, blue base, black windows, blue and yellow logo.
444-A   Washington Capitols $10-15
1. White Jaguar, red base, black windows, blue and red logo.
445-A   Los Angeles Kings $10-15
1. White Jaguar, yellow base, black windows, brown and white logo.
446-A   National Hockey League $10-15
1. White Mustang, orange base, yellow interior, amber windows, orange and black logo.

1983 Baseball Cars

The numbers of the 1983 Baseball Trading Cars begin with 5 and correspond otherwise to the 1982 numbers. All models are based on the 180-A Pontiac Firebird and have a black plastic interior, base and spoiler, clear windows, and Whizzwheels. The logo is on the roof, hood, and sides of the car. An unnumbered poster showing the entire series was available as an on-pack offer. Some of the cars shown are not as actually produced.

500-A   Baltimore Orioles $10-15
1. Orange body, white-orange-black logo.

501-A Boston Red Sox $10-15
1. Red body, red-white-blue logo.
502-A California Angels $10-15
1. Dark blue body, red and white logo.
503-A Chicago White Sox $10-15
1. Red body, red-white-blue logo.
504-A Cleveland Indians $10-15
1. White body, red and white logo.
505-A Detroit Tigers $10-15
1. Orange body, orange-white-blue logo.
506-A Kansas City Royals $10-15
1. Dark blue body, yellow-white-blue logo.
507-A Milwaukee Brewers $10-15
1. Yellow body, yellow-white-blue logo.
508-A Minnesota Twins $10-15
1. Red body, red-white-blue logo.
509-A New York Yankees $10-15
1. White body, red-white-blue logo.
510-A Oakland Athletics $10-15
1. Yellow body, yellow-white-green logo.
511-A Seattle Mariners $10-15
1. Yellow body, yellow-white-blue logo.
512-A Texas Rangers $10-15
1. White body, red-white-blue logo.
513-A Toronto Blue Jays $10-15
1. Dark blue body, red-white-blue logo.
514-A Atlanta Braves $10-15
1. White body, red-white-blue logo.
515-A Chicago Bears $10-15
1. Light blue body, red-white-blue logo.
516-A Cincinnati Reds $10-15
1. Red body, red-white-black logo.
517-A Houston Astros $10-15
1. Orange body, orange-white-blue logo.
518-A Los Angeles Dodgers $10-15
1. Dark blue body, red-white-blue logo.
519-A Montreal Expos $10-15
1. White body, red-white-blue logo.
520-A New York Mets $10-15
1. Orange body, orange-white-blue logo.
521-A Philadelphia Phillies $10-15
1. White body, brown logo.
522-A Pittsburgh Pirates $10-15
1. Yellow body, black-white-yellow logo.
523-A St. Louis Cardinals $10-15
1. Red body, red-white-blue logo.
524-A San Diego Padres $10-15
1. Yellow body, brown-white-yellow logo.
525-A San Francisco Giants $10-15
1. Orange body, black and white logo.

Football Cars

The 1983 Football Collector Cars are all based on the 179-A Chevrolet Corvette and have a red interior, black plastic base, clear windows, and Whizzwheels. They are licensed by the National Football League, and each car bears the NFL emblem on its rear window. The logo is on the hood, nose, and doors of the car.

600-A Baltimore Colts $10-15
1. Dark blue body, white and blue logo.
601-A Buffalo Bills $10-15
1. Dark blue body, red-white-blue logo.
602-A Cincinnati Bengals $10-15
1. White body, orange and black logo.
603-A Cleveland Browns $10-15
1. White body, orange-white-brown logo.
604-A Denver Broncos $10-15
1. Orange body, orange-white-blue logo.
605-A Houston Oilers $10-15
1. White body, red-white-light blue logo.
606-A Kansas City Chiefs $10-15
1. White body, orange-white-gold logo.
607-A Miami Dolphins $10-15
1. Orange body, orange-white-blue logo.
608-A New England Patriots $10-15
1. Red body, red-white-black logo.
609-A New York Jets $10-15
1. White body, green and white logo.
610-A Oakland Raiders $10-15
1. Black body, silver and black logo.
611-A Pittsburgh Steelers $10-15
1. Yellow body, black and white logo.
612-A San Diego Chargers $10-15
1. Yellow body, blue-white-gold logo.
613-A Seattle Seahawks $10-15
1. White body, blue-green-silver logo.
614-A Atlanta Falcons $10-15
1. Silver body, black-white-red logo.
615-A Chicago Bears $10-15
1. White body, orange-white-black logo.
616-A Dallas Cowboys $10-15
1. Dark blue body, silver-white-blue logo.
617-A Detroit Lions $10-15
1. White body, silver-white-blue logo.
618-A Green Bay Packers $10-15
1. White body, green-white-gold logo.

619-A Los Angeles Rams $10-15
1. Yellow body, blue-white-gold logo.
620-A Minnesota Vikings $10-15
1. Yellow body, purple and white logo.
621-A New Orleans Saints $10-15
1. Black body, gold-white-black logo.
622-A New York Giants $10-15
1. White body, red-white-blue logo.
623-A Philadelphia Eagles $10-15
1. Silver body, green-white-silver logo.
624-A St. Louis Cardinals $10-15
1. Maroon body, maroon-white-black logo.
625-A San Francisco 49ers $10-15
1. Red body, gold-white-red logo.
626-A Tampa Bay Buccaneers $10-15
1. Red body, red and white logo.
627-A Washington Redskins $10-15
1. Yellow body, maroon-white-black logo.

Corgi Rockets

Corgi Rockets were produced in 1970 and 1971. Each model had a removable chassis and ran on black or chrome Whizzwheels.

901-A Auston Martin DB6 72mm 1970-1971 $25-40
Yellow interior, green windows, black Whizzwheels.
1. Gold body.
902-A Jaguar XJ6 72mm 1970-1971 $25-40
White interior, clear windows, opening trunk, black Whizzwheels.
1. Metallic green body.
903-A Mercedes-Benz 280 SL 70mm 1970-1971 $25-40
White interior, clear windows, opening doors, black Whizzwheels.
1. Metallic copper body.
904-A Porsche Carrera 6 69mm 1970-1971 $25-40
Blue windows, chrome interior and engine, opening rear, red hood label with number 19, black Whizzwheels, base same color as body.
1. Light orange body and base, red hood.
905-A The Saint's Volvo P1800 68mm 1970-1971 $100-125
Light blue interior, clear windows, blue hood label with white Saint figure, black Whizzwheels.
1. White boody, blue hood.
906-A Jensen Interceptor 74mm 1970-1971 $25-40
White interior, amber windows, black Whizzwheels.
1. Metallic red body.
907-A Cadillac Eldorado 76mm 1970-1971 $25-40
White interior, clear windows, opening hood, black Whizzwheels.
1. Metallic copper; based on 9-A casting.
2. Metallic copper and black; based on 57-A casting.
908-A Chevrolet Astro 1 73mm 1970?-1971 $25-40
Cream interior and hood triangle, clear windshield, opening rear, chrome Whizzwheels.
1. Metallic maroon and cream body.
909-A Mercedes C111 73mm 1970?-1971 $25-40
Chrome interior hood panel and engine, blue windows, opening rear hood, white lower body-base, chrome Whizzwheels.
1. Dark blue upper body.
2. Red upper body.
910-A GP Beach Buggy 59mm 1970?-1971 $25-40
Black interior, clear windshield, wire roll bar, black Whizzwheels.
1. Pinkish orange body.
2. Light green body.
911-A Marcos XP 69mm 1970?-1971 $25-40
Chrome interior and engine, amber windows, black base, chrome Whizzwheels.
1. Gold body, red rear grille and taillights.
913-A Aston Martin DBS 73mm 1970?-1971 $25-40
Opening black hood, yellow interior, clear windows, black Whizzwheels.
1. Metallic blue body, black hood.
916-A Carabo Bertone 75mm 1970?-1971 $25-40
Orange-red interior, front and rear grilles, amber windows, black front and rear body panels, dull blue lower body-base, black Whizzwheels.
1. Metallic green upper body.
917-A Pininfarina Alfa Romeo P33 73mm 1970?-1971 $25-40
Black interior, white seats and wing, black front and rear grilles. white lower body-base, clear windshield, chrome Whizzwheels.
1. Metallic dark purple upper body.
918-A Ital Design Bizzarini Manta 72mm 1970?-1971 $25-40
Cream interior, chrome engine, clear windows, black base, chrome Whizzwheels.
1. Metallic dark blue body.
919-A Todd Sweeney Stock Car 69mm 1970?-1971 $25-40
Yellow interior, orange chassis, name labels, black Whizzwheels.
1. Light purple body, red roof.
920-A Derek Fiske Stock Car 70mm 1970?-1971 $25-40
White plastic cab with red roof, yellow interior, red chassis, name labels, black Whizzwheels.
1. Silver hood.
921-A Morgan Plus 8 67mm 1970?-1971 $25-40
Black interior, clear windshield, silver headlights, unpainted grille and bumper, silver exhaust pipes, black Whizzwheels.
1. Metallic red body.
922-A Ford Capri 74mm 1970?-1971 $25-40
Cream interior, clear windows, unpainted grille, chrome Whizzwheels.
1. Metallic light blue body.
2. Lime green body, rally version; other details not known.
923-A Ford Escort 007 70mm 1970?-1971 $100-125
Red interior, clear windows, blue, white and black lettering, stripe and number 7 labels, unpainted grille and lights, chrome Whizzwheels.
1. White body, light blue stripes.

163

924-A   Mercury Cougar XR7   79mm 1970?-1971 $25-40
Yellow interior, clear windows, unpainted grille and bumpers, black hood label, chrome Whizzwheels.
1. Bright red body, black roof.
2. Bright red body, black roof, ski rack.

925-A   Ford Capri 007   74mm 1970?-1971 $100-125
Yellow interior, clear windows, number 6 stripe and checker labels, unpainted grille, bumpers and tow hook, chrome Whizzwheels.
1. White body, black trim.

926-A   Jaguar Pace Car   74mm 1970?-1971 $25-40
White interior, clear windows, light red sign on roof, two men on rear platform, emblem and lettering labels, unpainted grille and lights, chrome Whizzwheels.
1. Metallic brown body.

927-A   Ford Escort World Cup Rally Car   70mm 1970?-1971 $25-40
Red interior, clear windows, black diecast base, grille shield and bars, silver headlights, rally labels, chrome Whizzwheels.
1. White body, red trim.

928-A   Mercedes-Benz 280SL S.P.E.C.T.R.E.   70mm 1970?-1971 $100-125
Red interior, clear windows, S.P.E.C.T.R.E. and wild boar labels, unpainted grille, chrome Whizzwheels.
1. Black body.

930-A   Bertone Runabout Barchetta   64mm 1970?-1971 $25-40
Light-red interior and body stripe, amber windshield, white lower body-base, chrome Whizzwheels.
1. Metallic green upper body.

931-A   Ole Macdonald's Truck   63mm 1970?-1971 $25-40
Brown plastic interior and rear body, unpainted engine, grille, headlights and exhaust pipes, chrome Whizzwheels.
1. Yellow cab.

932-A   The Futura   75mm 1970?-1971? $25-40?
Details not known.
1. ?

933-A   Ford Holmes Wrecker   72mm 1970?-1971 $25-40
Gold diecast booms, red hooks and cradle, amber windows and dome lights, red and yellow "Auto Rescue" labels, chrome Whizzwheels.
1. White cab and boom mountings, dark blue chassis and rear body.

937-A   Mercury Cougar XR7   75mm 1970?-1971 $25-40
Yellow interior and spoiler, clear windows, unpainted grille and bumpers, chrome Whizzwheels.
1. Metallic dark olive body.

975-A   Super Stock Gift Set No. 1   1971?-1971 $100-150
Details not known.

976-A   Ford Capri and Corgi Rockets Trailer   1971?-1971 $60-80
Yellow car interior, other details not known.
1. Purple car body.

978-A   O.H.M.S.S. Gift Set   1971?-1971 $300-500
Details not known.

Corgi Rockets Accessories

1929	Pitstop Kit A	$10-25
1933	Pitstop Kit C	$10-25
1934	Autofinish	$10-25
1935	Track Connectors	$10-25
1936	Spaceleap	$10-25
1937	Autostart	$10-25
1938	Super Crossover	$10-25
1945	Track Adapters	$10-25
1951	Support Collars and Track Links	$10-25
1952	Superloop	$10-25
1953	Hairpin Tunnel/Turret Spacehanger Bend	$10-25
1954	Cloverleaf/Crossroads Kit	$10-25
1963	New Super Track	$10-25
1970	Super Booster	$10-25
1971	Hairpin Tunnel	$10-25
1976	Quickfire Start	$10-25
1977	Lap Counter	$10-25
1979	Spacehanger Bend	$10-25
1970	Super Booster	$10-25
1971	Hairpin Tunnel	$10-25
1976	Quickfire Start	$10-25
1977	Lap Counter	$10-25
1978	Pitstop and Lube Kit	$10-25
1979	Spacehanger Bend	$10-25
2051	Action Speedset	$50-100
2052	Super Autobatics Speedset	$50-100
2053	Clover Leaf Special	$50-100
2058	Super Race-abatic Speedset	$50-100
2060	Skypark Tower Garage	$50-100
2063	Tom and Jerry Crazy Chase	$50-100
2070	Alpine Ski-set	$50-100
2071	Jetspeed Circuit	$50-100
2074	Triple Loop Speedcircuit	$50-100
2075	Grand Canyon Speedcircuit	$50-100
2079	World Champion Racing Speedset	$50-100
4000	Bizzarini Manta Electra-rockets	$50-100
4002	Alfa Romeo Montreal Electra-rockets	$50-100
4200	Electro-rockets Stunt Powerset	$50-100
4203	Electro-rockets Double 8 Raceway	$50-100

Extras

The first Husky Extras, with 1200 or 1400 numbers, were added to the Husky line in 1967. In 1970, as Corgi Juniors, they were given 1000 numbers, which will be used here for the sake of continuity. The Extras remained in production through 1972. Later some models were reissued in the regular Corgi Junior series.

1201-A   James Bond Aston Martin (Husky)   73mm 1967-1969 $150-175
1001-A   James Bond Aston Martin (Corgi Jr)   73mm 1970-1972 $125-150
Blue windows, opening roof hatch, ejecting seat with passenger, interior with driver, chrome plastic base,

ejection trigger on right side of car.
1. Metallic silver gray body, brown interior, Husky base, gray plastic wheels, (1201).
2. Metallic silver gray body, brown interior, Husky base, metal wheels with tires, (1201).
3. Metallic silver gray body, red interior, base with Corgi Junior label, metal wheels with tires.
4. Metallic silver gray body, red interior, Corgi Junior base, chrome Whizzwheels.

1202-A   Batmobile (Husky)   77mm 1967-1969 $150-175
1002-A   Batmobile (Corgi Jr)   77mm 1970-1972 $125-150
Blue canopy, red interior, two figures, chrome parts, red bat labels.
1. Black body, Husky base with Batman figure, gray plastic wheels, hitch hole, (1202).
2. Black body, Corgi Junior label on base, gray plastic wheels, hitch hole.
3. Black body, new Whizzwheels base, black Whizzwheels, hitch pin.
4. Black body, Whizzwheels base, chrome Whizzwheels, hitch pin.

1203-A   Batboat on Trailer (Husky)   88mm 1968-1969 $100-125
1003-A   Batboat on Trailer (Corgi Jr)   88mm 1970-1972 $75-100
Boat with blue windshields, two figures, red fin with bat labels, gold diecast trailer.
1. Black plastic boat with Husky name, trailer with gray plastic wheels, (1203).
2. Black plastic boat with Husky name removed, trailer with gray plastic wheels, (1203).
3. Black plastic boat with Corgi Junior name, trailer with chrome Whizzwheels, hitch with hole instead of pin.

1204-A   Monkeemobile (Husky)   76mm 1968-1969 $150-200
1004-A   Monkeemobile (Corgi Jr)   76mm 1970-1972 $125-150
Yellow interior with four figures, chrome engine, white roof, yellow Monkees logo.
1. Red body, Husky base with chassis members, metal wheels with tires. Monkees decals, (1204).
2. Red body, Corgi Junior base with chassis members, metal wheels with tires, Monkees labels.
3. Red body, flat Whizzwheels base, black Whizzwheels, Monkees labels.

1205-A   The Man From U.N.C.L.E. Car (Husky)   72mm 1968-1969 $150-175
1005-A   The Man From U.N.C.L.E. Car (Corgi Jr)   72mm 1970-1970 $1000+
Chrome interior with two figures, clear windows, opening hood with rocket launcher, metal wheels with tires, lower-body-base same color as upper body.
1. Blue body and base, chrome stripe between castings, Husky base, (1205).
2. Blue body and base, chrome stripe between castings, Corgi Junior label on Husky base. (Second example needed to authenticate)
3. Blue body and base, chrome stripe between castings, Corgi Junior label on base.

1206-A   Chitty Chitty Bang Bang   76mm 1969-1969 $150-175
1006-A   Chitty Chitty Bang Bang   76mm 1970-1972 $125-150
Red interior with four figures, gold radiator and headlights, retractible yellow side wings, red front and rear wings, metallic charcoal gray fenders and base.
1. Chrome hood and windshield, copper body, gold spoked wheels, Husky base, (1206).
2. Corgi Junior label over Husky lettering on base, otherwise as type 1.
3. Whizzwheels base, yellow front and rear wings. black Whizzwheels, otherwise as type 1.

1007-A   Ironside Police Van   67mm 1971-1972 $125-150
Yellow interior and lever, clear windows, unpainted base, lifting rear door and lowering panel with figures, San Francisco Police emblem labels, Whizzwheels.
1. Blue body.

1008-A   Popeye's Paddle Wagon   70mm 1971-1972 $150-175
Chrome grille and headlights, copper boiler and stack, figures of Popeye, Olive and Swee' Pea, decals on paddle boxes, front Whizzwheels, large black rear wheels.
1. Yellow body, light blue chassis.

1010-A   James Bond Volkswagen   ?mm 1971-1973 $175-200
Yellow interior, clear windows, number 5, stripe and lettering labels, unpainted diecast base, Whizzwheels.
1. Orange body.

1011-A   James Bond Bobsleigh   73mm 1970-1972 $250-300
Gray plastic bumper, driver figure, black and yellow checker and white 007 label, silver diecast base, black Whizzwheels.
1. Yellow body.

1012-A   S.P.E.C.T.R.E Bobsleigh   73mm 1970-1972 $250-300
Same casting and components as 1011-A, black wild boar label.
1. Orange body.

1013-A   Tom's Go Cat   68mm 1971-1972 $60-80
Dark red roof and dynamite case with yellow and red labels, red steering wheel, cat figure with gun, label on front, Whizzwheels. Note: this label says "Tom's Go Cat," that of the no. 58-B reissue says "Tom's Go Cart."
1. Yellow chassis, silver hood, silver top of roof.

1014-A   Jerry's Banger   62mm 1971-1972 $60-80
Brass cannon, light blue mounting, panniers of cannonballs and gunpowder, mouse figure, unpainted diecast base, Whizzwheels.
1. Red body.
2. Silver Body?

1017-A   Ford Holmes Wrecker   93mm 1971-1972 $150-175
Apparently a revision of Corgi Rockets 933.
1. Details not known.

Husky Accessories

1550	Playmat	$25-50
1551	Service Station and Chinese Restaurant	$25-50
1552	Westminster Bank and Woolworths	$25-50
1553	Regal Cinema and Rusts Bakery	$25-50
1554	Fisherman's Inn and Family Grocer	$25-50
1561	Triangular Traffic Signs	$15-30
1562	Circular Traffic Signs	$15-30
1571	Pedestrian Figures	$15-30
1572	Workmen Figures	$15-30
1573	Garage Personnel Figures	$15-30
1574	Public Servant Figures	$15-30
1580	Husky Collector Case	$???
1585	Husky Traveler Case	$???

Husky Majors and Corgi Super Juniors

2001-A   Four Car Garage   1968-1969, 1970-1978 $25-35
Building framework, roof with skylights, four overhead doors.
Yellow framework, blue roof and doors, Husky labels.
Yellow framework, blue roof and doors, Corgi Junior labels.

2002-A Hoynor Mark II Car Transporter 119mm 1967-69, 1970-76 $30-40
Cab body and base-grille castings, semi-trailer upper and lower decks, tailgate, rear base and two unpainted hinge bar castings, yellow plastic blocks, cast-in lettering.
1. White cab, blue windows, orange upper deck, blue lower deck and tailgate, gray baseplates, white dog's head and husky name, metal wheels with tires.
2. Yellow cab, blue windows, orange upper deck, bright blue lower deck and tailgate, white cab base, blue semi base, white "Corgi Juniors" lettering, Whizzwheels.
3. Yellow cab, clear windows, orange upper deck, bright blue lower deck and tailgate, white cab base, blue semi base, white "Corgi Juniors" lettering, Whizzwheels.
4. Red cab, otherwise as type 2.

2003-A Ford Low Loader with Loadmaster Shovel 140mm 1968-69, 1970-73 $30-40
Cab body and silver gray base castings, blue windows, semi-trailer body and tailgate castings, blue sheet metal rear base, yellow 23-A Loadmaster Shovel.
1. Red cab, blue semi, metal wheels with tires, Husky base.
2. Red cab, blue semi, metal wheels with tires, Corgi Junior base.
3. Red cab, blue semi, Whizzwheels, Corgi Junior base.

2004-A Ford Removals Van 145mm 1968-69, 1970-73 $30-40
Cab body and white base castings, blue windows, semi-trailer chassis and tailgate castings, red sheet metal rear base, chrome plastic semi-trailer body with red cast-in lettering, metal wheels with tires.
1. Blue cab, red semi chassis and tailgate, "Husky Removals" logo, Husky base.
2. Blue cab, red semi-chassis and tailgate, "Corgi Removals" logo, Corgi Junior base.

2006-A Mack Esso Tanker 180mm 1970-1979 $30-40
Cab body, opening hood and metallic dark gray base castings, blue windows, silver engine, black exhaust stack, metallic dark gray semi-trailer chassis casting with white plastic tank, chrome catwalk, red-white-blue Esso and red stripe labels, Whizzwheels.
1. White cab and tank.

2007-A Ford Low Loader and Shovel Loader 140mm 1975-1978 $30-40
Same cab, base, semi-trailer and tailgate castings as 2003-A, clear windows, blue rear base casting, Whizzwheels, orange and yellow 48-B Shovel Loader.
1. Red cab, white base, blue semi-trailer (darker than 2003).

2008-A Greyhound Bus 169mm 1976-1979 $30-40
Single body casting, white interior, amber windows, black plastic base, Whizzwheels.
1. White body, red-white-blue-black Greyhound Americruiser labels.

2009-A Aerocar 150mm 1976-1978 $40-50
Car body casting, clear windows, black interior and base, red upper wing casting, yellow lower wing-twin boom-tail connector, black propeller, red and yellow stripe and white N846 labels, Whizzwheels; made in Hong Kong.
1. Yellow car.

2011-A Mack U.S. Army Tanker 180mm 1976-1978 $35-45
Same castings as 2006-A, dark olive-brown tank and catwalk, white star and U.S. Army labels, black Whizzwheels.
1. Olive drab cab and semi-trailer chassis.

2012-A Ford U.S. Army Low Loader, Armored Car 140mm 1976-1980 $35-45
same castings as 2007-A, white star labels, 83-A Commando Armored Car, black Whizzwheels.
1. Olive drab cab and semi-trailer.

2014-A Mercedes-Benz Car Transporter 215mm 1977-1979 $20-30
Cab body and chassis-fenders castings, amber windows, yellow upper deck, red lower deck and tailgate, and two unpainted hinge bar castings, black plastic cab and semi bases and tow hook, Whizzwheels, grille-headlight label, rear stripe label.
1. White cab body, red cab chassis, lower semi deck and tailgate.

2015-A Mercedes-Benz Car Transporter, Trailer 415mm 1976-1978 $30-40
Upper and lower decks, tailgate and two unpainted hinge bar castings, black plastic tongue, base and tow hook, yellow blocks, Whizzwheels, pulled by 2014-A.
1. Yellow upper deck, red lower deck and tailgate.

2017-A Scania Dump Truck 147mm 1977-1979 $15-25
Chassis-cab and black hydraulic cylinder and exhaust stack castings, plastic tipper, green windows, black plastic front base, Whizzwheels, grille label.
1. Yellow chassis-cab, red tipper.

2018-A Scania Container Truck 138mm 1977-1979 $15-25
Chassis-cab and black exhaust stack castings, plastic flatbed, white plastic container with gray top and red rear doors, blue and black Seatrain lables, black plastic cab base, amber windows, Whizzwheels, grille label.
1. Red chassis-cab, light gray flatbed.

2019-A Scania Silo Truck 144mm 1977-1979 $15-25
Chassis-cab and black exhaust stack castings, brown, tan and white bulk containers and framework, amber windows, black plastic cab base, British Grain and grille labels, Whizzwheels.
1. Orange chassis-cab.

2020-A Mercedes-Benz Refrigerator Van 207mm 1977-1979 $20-30
Cab body, chassis and semi-trailer chassis castings, amber windows, white plastic refrigerator van body with red rear doors, red-white-blue Birdseye logo, grille and rear end labels, black plastic cab base, Whizzwheels.
1. White cab, metallic blue cab and semi chassis.

2022-A Scanotron 127mm 1979-1980 $15-25
Deck casting, magnifying lens, dark green cabin with light green diecast base, dark green chassis, chrome vegetation cutter, radar screen and parts, yellow folding rake, name labels, black Whizzwheels; cabin rocks.
1. Light green deck.

2023-A Rocketron 110mm 1979-1980 $15-25
Body casting, chrome interior, amber canopy, yellow rocket gun and hubs, black treads, compass, labels.
1. Blue body.

2024-A Lasertron 110mm 1979-1980 $15-25
Body casting, yellow laser reflector, black chassis and front body, amber windshield, red antennas, labels, six-spoke wheels with knobby tires.
1. Orange body.

2025-A Swiss PTT Bus 169mm 1977-1978 $50-60
Same casting as 2008-A, white interior, amber windows, black plastic base, Whizzwheels, red-yellow-black PTT labels.
1. Yellow body, white roof.

2026-A Magnetron 106mm 1979-1980 $15-25
Body casting, yellow interior, black sliding door, amber canopies, chrome arm with black magnet, labels, six-spoke chrome wheels with knobby tires; other details not known.
1. Red body.

2027-A Mack Ryder Rentals Van ?mm 1979-???? $30-40
Same cab as 2006-A with yellow airscreen, same semi-trailer as 2020-A without refrigerator, Whizzwheels.
1. Yellow cab and semi-trailer, both with black chassis, Ryder Truck Rental logo.

2028-A Mercedes-Benz Refrigerator Truck 125mm 1977-1978 $20-30
Same cab and semi-trailer as 2020-A, amber windows, red rear doors, black plastic cab base, grille, logo and rear end labels, Whizzwheels.
1. White cab and semi-trailer, both with metallic light blue chassis, Gervais logo label on left, Danone logo label on right side of semi-trailer.

2029-A Mack Fire Pumper 143mm 1979-Close $20-30
Cab and unpainted chassis-grille-footboard castings, red dome light, chrome sirens, blue windows, red interior and rear body, yellow ladders and hose racks, black suction hose and hose reels, number 3, "Hammond Fire Dept." and control panel labels, black plastic base, four-spoke chrome wheels.
1. Red cab and rear body, white roof panel.

Muppets

2030-A Kermit's Kar 90mm 1979-1981 $25-35
Single casting chrome headlights and engine, clear windshield, red interior, green Kermit figure, black grille and running boards, white plastic wheels.
1. Yellow body; underside of body forms base, light green collar on Kermit.
2. Yellow body; underside of body forms base, body color collar on Kermit.

2031-A Fozzie Bear's Truck 90mm 1979-1981 $25-35
Body and chassis castings, black grille and headlights, chrome horn, tan Fozzie figure, blue windshield, rear bed and signboard, Muppet Show logo labels, white plastic wheels.
1. Red body, white chassis, black grill.
2. Red body, white chassis, grill color of adjacent area.

2032-A Miss Piggy's Sports Car 99mm 1979-1981 $25-35
Body and base castings, chrome grille, exhaust pipes and spare wheel, clear windshield, Miss Piggy figure, white plastic wheels.
1. Pink body, silver base, lavender dress.
2. Pink body, silver base, white dress.
3. Pink body, silver base, magenta dress.

2033-A Animal's Percussionmobile 90mm 1979-1981 $25-35
Body and chassis castings, red Animal figure, yellow stack, cymbal, drum and wheels (shaped like drums), labels.
1. Red body, black chassis, head and arms same color.
2. Red body, black chassis, head and arms different color.

Twin Packs

2501-A	Zetor Tracor (4-C), Farm Trailer (33-A)	197?-1975	$15-20
2501-B	Doubledecker Bus (81-A) & Austin Taxi (71-B)	1980-1981	$15-20
2502-A	Tractor with Blade (43-A), Tipping Trailer (8-C)	197?-1975	$15-20
2502-B	Land Rover Wrecker (31-B), Jaguar XJS (72-B)	1980-Close	$15-20
2503-A	Land Rover Pickup (16-B), Horse Trailer (38-A)	197?-1978	$15-20
2503-B	Rover Police Car (16-C) & Helicopter (98-C)	1980-Close	$15-20
2504-A	Land Rover Wrecker (31-B), Volkswagen (17-C)	197?-1976	$15-20
2504-B	Land Rover Wrecker (31-B), Jaguar E-type (39-B)	1977-1978	$15-20
2504-C	Land Rover Wrecker (31-B), AMC Pacer (62-B)	1978-1979	$15-20
2505-A	Jaguar XJ6 (39-A) & Boat Trailer (19-B)	197?-1975	$15-20
2505-B	Daily Planet Van (50-B) & Helicopter (6-D)	1979	$75-125
2506-A	Snowmobile (18-D) & Trailer	197?-1975	$15-20
2506-B	Supermobile (11-C) & Super Van (47-B)	1979-1981	$75-125
2507-A	Tom (1213-A) & Jerry (1214-A)	197?-1975	$40-60
2507-B	Tom (58-B) & Jerry (38-B)	1980-1981	$40-60
2508-A	Army Jeep (76-B) & Field Gun (96-A)	1976-1977	$15-20
2508-B	Popeye's Tugboat (67-C), Olive's Plane (79-B)	1980-1981	$40-60
2509-A	Bucket Truck (54-A), Loadmaster Shovel (23-B)	197?-1974	$15-20
2510-A	Formula 1 (22-C), Formula 5000 (27-B) Racers	1973-1978	$15-20
2511-A	Scout Car (84-A) & Army Helicopter (34-B)	1974-1978	$15-20
2512-A	Space Shuttle (5-C), Starship Liberator (44-B)	1979-1981	$75-125
2513-A	Police Range Rover (9-C), Healer Wheeler (36-B)	1973-1976	$15-20
2513-B	ERF Fire Engine (26-C), Healer Wheeler (36-B)	1977-1980	$15-20
2514-A	Skip Dumper (85-A) & Cement Mixer (20-C)	1976-1977	$15-20
2515-A	Citroen Dyane (89-A) & Boat Trailer (19-B)	1976-1980	$15-20
2516-A	Zetro Tractor (4-C) & Tipping Trailer (8-C)	1976-1978	$15-20
2518-A	Volvo Estate Car (51-B), Caravan Trailer (65-B)	1976-1976	$15-20
2518-B	Mercedes 240D (59-C), Caravan Trailer (65-B)	1977-1980	$15-20
2519-A	Batmobile (69-A) & Batboat (1003-A)	1977-Close	$75-125
2520-A	Rough Terrain Truck (13-B), Dinghy on Trailer	1977-????	$15-20
2521-A	Army Ambulance (79-A), Helicopter (40-B)	1977-????	$15-20
2521-B	James Bond Shuttle (41-B), Drax Copter (73-B)	1980-1981	$75-125
2522-A	Centurion Tank (66-A) & Armored Car (83-A)	1977-????	$15-20
2523-A	Porsche Police Car (37-B) & Helicopter (46-B)	1977-1979	$15-20
2524-A	Fire Ball (90-A) & Golden Eagle (91-A) Vans	1978-1980	$15-20
2525-A	Triumph TR7 (10-C) & Dinghy on Trailer	1979-1980	$15-20
2526-A	Dump Truck (7-C) & Shovel Loader (48-B)	1977-1980	$15-20
2527-A	Kojack's Buick (68-A) & Police Helicopter (46-B)	1978-1979	$75-125
2528-A	Starsky & Hutch Torino (45-B) & Police Car (28-C)	1978-1980	$75-125
2529-A	Bond Lotus (60-B) & Stromberg Copter (3-D)	1978-1979	$75-125
2532-A	Ford Capri (61-C) & Ford Transit Wrecker (103-A)	1981-????	$15-20
2534-A	Locomotive (108-A) & Goods Wagon (112-A)	1981-????	$15-20
2534-B	Locomotive (108-A) & Passenger Coach (111-A)	1982-Close	$15-20
2536-A	Professionals Capri (64-B) & Police Car (16-C)	1980-????	$75-125
2542-A	Enterprise (148-A) & Klingon Warship (149-A)	1982-Close	$75-125
2550-A	Matra Rancho (76-C) & Horse Box (38-A?)	1983-Close	$15-20
2551-A	Rover 3500 (8-D) & Dinghy on Trailer	1983-Close	$15-20
2553-A	Mustang Cobra (104-A) & Boat/Trailer (19-B?)	1983-Close	$15-20
2554-A	Volvo Wagon (51-B) & Caravan Trailer (65-B)	1983-Close	$15-20
2555-A	Ford Wrecker (103-A) & Jaguar XJ-S (72—B)	1983-Close	$15-20
2595-A	Rover Triplex (138-A) & Metro Datapost (135-A)	1983-Close	$15-20

Triple Packs

2601-A	Batmobile (69-A), Batboat (1003-A) & Batcopter (78-B)	1977-1978	$200-250

Gift Sets

3001-A	Garage & three vehicles (Husky)	196?-196?	$50-75
Garage 2001-A & three Husky vehicles.			
3001-B	Garage & three vehicles (Corgi Jr)	1975-Close	$35-45
Garage 2001-A & three Corgi Jr. vehicles.			
3002-A	Batmobile & Batboat (Husky)	196?-1969	$500+
Husky Batmobile 1002-A & Batboat 1003-A.			
3002-B	Batmobile & Batboat (Corgi Jr)	1970-197?	$400+
Corgi Jr Batmobile 1002-A & Batboat 1003-A.			
3002-C	Garage Centre	1982-Close	$20-30
Garage building with lift, gas pumps, accessories.			
3003-A	Car Transporter & five cars (Husky)	196?-1969	$75-100
Transporter 2002-A & five Husky cars.			
3003-B	Car Transporter & five cars (Corgi Jr)	1970-1971?	$60-80
Transporter 2002-A & five Corgi Jr cars.			
3003-C	Garage Forecourt Set	1982-Close	$25-35
Garage with gas pumps, lift, etc.			
3004-A	Garage & two cars (Husky)	196?-196?	$40-60
Garage (2001-A) & two Husky cars.			
3004-B	O.H.M.S.S. Set	1970-1971?	$1000+
James Bond 1010-A, 1011-A & 1012-A.			
3005-A	Holiday Time Set	196?-1969	$175-200
Eight Husky vehicles including non-standard Studebaker Wagonaire.			
3005-B	Leisure Time Set	1970-197?	$125-150
Eight Corgi Jr vehicles.			
3006-A	Service Station Set	196?-196?	$40-60
Building with three Husky vehicles.			
3006-B	Playmat	1983-Close	$20-30
Vinyl playmat with printed street scene.			
3007-A	Multi-Story Car Park (Husky)	1968?-1969?	$60-80
Car park building with four Husky vehicles.			
3007-B	Multi-Story Car Park (Corgi Jr)	197?-197?	$50-75
Car park building with three Corgi Jr vehicles.			
3007-C	Wild West Set	1981-Close	$40-60
Four vehicles.			
3008-A	Crime Busters Set	1967-1969	$600+
Four superhero vehicles.			
3009-A	Service Station Set	1970-1971?	$30-50
Station building, three vehicles, gas pumps.			
3011-A	Road Construction Set	1970-197?	$50-75
Flatbed 2003-A & five vehicles.			
3013-A	Emergency Rescue Set	1977-1980	$30-50
Building with three vehicles.			
3015-A	Transporter Set	1980-Close	$40-60
Transporter 2014-A & four vehicles.			
3019-A	Agricultural Set	197?-197?	$50-75
Two buildings with six vehicles.			
3019-B	Bond Octopussy Set	1983-Close	$400+
Two vehicles & jet plane.			
3020-A	Club Racing Set	197?-197?	$50-75
Seven vehicles & accessories.			
3021-A	Emergency 999 Set	197?-1974	$50-75
Six vehicles & accessories.			
3021-B	Trucking Set	1983-Close	$40-60
Five vehicles.			
3022-A	Rescue Set	197?-1977	$75-100
Building, playmat, standard Porsche Police Car, nonstandard Land Rover Range Rover Ambulance, Coast Guard Range Rover, Rough Terrain Truck and Dinghy on Trailer.			
3023-A	Transporter Set	197?-1979	$40-60
Transporter 2014-A & four vehicles.			
3024-A1	Road Construction Set	197?-1977	$50-75
Flatbed 2003-A & five vehicles.			
3024-A2	Road Construction Set	1978-1979	$50-75
Revised version of above (different cars?).			
3025-A	Transporter Set	197?-1976	$50-75
Transporter 2002-A & five vehicles.			
3026-A	Leisure Time Set	197?-197?	$75-100
Eight vehicles.			
3026-B	Emergency Set	1976-1979	$40-60
Six vehicles & accessories.			
3028-A	Grand Prix Racing Set	197?-197?	$40-60
Set includes one nonstandard vehicle.			
3029-A	Military Set	1976-1977	$40-60
Seven vehicles including nonstandard Army Land Rover Wrecker, figures.			
3030-A	James Bond "Spy Who Loved Me" Set	1976-1978	$500++
Five vehicles including nonstandard Jaws Telephone Van, Stromberg's Mercedes and Speedboat on Trailer.			
3036-A	Garage and Four Car Set	1983-Close	$30-50
2001-A & four vehicles.			
3050-A	Concorde Set	1978-????	$40-60
650 Concorde, building, non-standard Mercedes Bus, Leyland Van and Helicopter.			

3051-A	Filling Station Set	1977-1980	$30-50
Building and three vehicles.			
3052-A	Police Station Set	1977-1980	$30-50
Building and three vehicles.			
3053-A	Fire Station Set	1977-1980	$30-50
Building and three vehicles.			
3070-A	Growler Set	1975?-1976	$40-60
Six vehicles.			
3073-A	Steer Gear-Single Pack	1977-197?	$???
Details not known.			
3074-A	Steer Gear-Double Pack	1977-197?	$???
Details not known.			
3080-A	Batman Set	1980-1981	$300-500
Five vehicles.			
3081-A	Superman Set	1980-1981	$300-500
Five vehicles.			
3082-A	James Bond Set	1980-1981	$300-500
Five vehicles, including nonstandard Jaws telephone van.			
3084-A	Cartoon Characters Set	1980-1981	$200-250
Five vehicles.			
3100-A	Construction Set	1980-198?	$40-60
Seven vehicles.			
3101-A	Fire Set	1980-198?	$40-60
Six vehicles and figures.			
3103-A	Emergency Set	1980-198?	$40-60
Six vehicles, including nonstandard Chevrolet Van and VW Polo, and figures.			
3105-A	Transporter Set	1982-Close	$40-60
Transporter 2014-A and four vehicles.			
3107-A	Sports Car Set	1982-Close	$30-50
Five vehicles.			
3108-A	Flintstone's Set	1982-Close	$200-250
Five vehicles.			
3109-A	Best of British Set	1983-Close	$40-60
Seven vehicles.			
3110-A	Emergency Set	1982-Close	$30-50
Five vehicles.			
3111-A	Wild West Railroad Set	1982-Close	$30-50
Three vehicles and buildings.			
3112-A	Wild West Frontier Set	1982-Close	$30-50
Three vehicles, including nonstandard horse-drawn flat wagon, and buildings.			
3113-A	Wild West Set	1982-Close	$40-60
Five vehicles.			
3114-A	Superheroes Set	1982-Close	$125-175
Five vehicles.			
3116-A	Crimefighters Set	1982-Close	$125-175
Five vehicles.			
3118-A	Commando Set	1982-Close	$30-50
Three vehicles and buildings.			
3121-A	Super Sports Car	1983-Close	$40-60
Seven vehicles.			
3122-A	Turbochargers Set	1983-Close	$40-60
Three vehicles, pit, Dunlop bridge.			
3123-A	Truckers Set	1983-Close	$40-60
Three vehicles and buildings.			

Corgi Qualitoys

Simple, rugged, large-scale castings intended for very young age group. All models based on same pick-up truck-like casting except for trailer. Introduced in 1969 as a separate product line. Qualitoys data obtained from *The Great Book of Corgi* by Marcel R. VanCleemput.

Q701	Pick-up Truck	$10-20
Q702	Side Tipper	$10-20
Q703	Breakdown Truck	$10-20
Q704	Tower Wagon	$10-20
Q705	Horse Box	$10-20
Q706	Giraffe Transporter	$10-20
Q707	Fire Engine	$10-20
Q708	Pick-up Trailer	$10-15

Corgi Related Products

Mettoy apparently marketed other toys unrelated to the normal Corgi Toy range but still using the Corgi logo for brand recognition. Information on these items is limited, and further details from readers would be welcomed.

M5300	The Saint's Jaguar XJS Remote Control Car	1978-????	$20-40

Large plastic 1:18 scale model identical in decoration to the related Corgi model, battery operated sound control action, packaged with red plastic clicker pistol. Made in Hong Kong for Mettoy Company Ltd. by another firm.

M53??	Interstate Crime Buster Remote Control Car	1978-????	$20-40

Large plastic 1:18 scale model nearly identical in decoration to the related Corgi Buick Regal Police Car, battery operated sound control action, siren and lights, packaged with plastic clicker made to look like a police radio. Made in Hong Kong for Mettoy Company Ltd. by another firm.

3.2: The Independent Years, 1984-1990 Renumbering

This section contains the variation listing for models produced from the time of the November 1983 Mettoy receivership up to the 1990 general renumbering resulting from the Mattel buyout. Some of the information from the chaotic time surrounding the collapse of Mettoy is derived from the 1984 catalog issued by the factory. Information on released models from this period is confusing and contradictory, since the factory was also selling off excess Mettoy inventory at this time. The J Series (Juniors) listing has been separated from the main data and placed at the end to avoid confusion due to numbering conflicts with the larger series models.

NOTE: Values shown are in U.S. dollars for mint-in-mint boxed condition as of January 1997. Subtract 35-40 percent for mint unboxed, 50-60 percent for excellent, 60-70 percent for vg/chipped.

C/D/Q Series Corgi

C 2   Fire Emergency Set Jun-88 $25-35
Red Ford Transit Van "FIRE SERVICE," Red Saab 9000, Mack CF Fire Pumper.

D 4/01   Transport of the Early 50s Set Nov-89 $40-60
AEC DD Bus and Bedford B Bus

D 7/01   Royal Mail Set Jul-89 $60-70
D957/18 Morris 1000 Van "Royal Mail," D822/09 Bedford Box Van "Royal Mail Parcels"

D 9/01   Shell Twin 1910-1940 Set Aug-89 $45-48
Thorneycroft Box Van with Roof Rack "SHELL OIL & SHELL PETROL," AEC Cabover Tanker "SHELL-MEX," "YOU CAN BE SURE OF SHELL."

C 11/01   Notruf Set Jul-89 $50-65
White Ford Sierra with Red Side Stripe and Hood Stripe "POLIZEI," White Mercedes with Red Side Stripe, Red Roof Stripe and Red Panel over Windshield, Red Range Rover with Blue Roof Bar toward Rear of Roof. (Produced for Swiss Market.)

C 12/01   3 Haulers Trucks and 4 Juniors Chevy Vans Sep-89 $35-50
Orange Tipper, Yorkie Container Truck, BP Tanker, "FIRE SALVAGE" Van, "British TELECOM" Van, "PARAMEDIC" Van, "Royal Mail Parcels" Van.

D 13/01   Police Morris Minor 1000 Van Set Aug-89 $30-50
Black Morris 1000 Van with White "POLICE" Roof Sign "Gateshead Borough Police Incedent Van," White Morris 1000 Van with White "POLICE" Sign on Roof "DOG SECTION."

D 14/01   Beano/Dandy Set Oct-89 $65-70
Yellow Bedford CA Van "THE DANDY," Lt. Blue Bedford CA Van "The BEANO"

D 15/01   G.P.O. 2 pc. Gift Set Dec-89 $60-65
Morris 1000 Van and AEC Cabover Box Van

D 16/01   Rallying with Ford Set Sep-89 $50-60
Lt. Green Ford Popular Saloon, Red Ford Cortina "29," Yellow/White Ford Zodiac "21" (Similar to D709/03)

D 17/01   Shell Twin 1950-1960 Set Aug-89 $45-65
a Yellow/Red Bedford Box Van "SHELL," Orange/White Bedford Pantechnicon "the winner ... SHELL" with Tan Horse. (First Issue.)
b Yellow/Red Bedford Box Van "SHELL," Orange/White Bedford Pantechnicon "the winner ... SHELL" with Chestnut Brown Horse. (Second Issue.)

C 19   Police 2 pc. Set Jan-88 $20-30
White Ford Transit Van with Blue Outlined Red Stripe "POLICE," C110 White BMW with Blue Outlined Red Stripe "POLICE."

C 19/03   Swedish Emergency Set Jun-89 $35-50
C676/10 Ford Transit Bus "AMBULANS," Helicopter "POLIS." (Produced for the Swedish Market.)

C 19/04   Swedish Polis Set Jun-89 $35-50
C676/11 Ford Transit Bus "POLIS," C106/06 Saab 9000 "POLIS." (Produced for the Swedish Market.)

C 19/05   Poliisi Set Aug-89 $35-50
Black Saab 9000 with Blue Lightbar on Roof "POLIISI," Black Ford Transit Van with Blue Lightbar on Roof "POLIISI," (Produced for Finnish Market.)

C 19/06   Ambulanssi Set Jul-89 $35-50
Dk.Blue Saab 9000 with Blue Lightbar on Roof ""POLIISI," White Ford Transit Van with Blue/White Lightbar on Roof "AMBULANSSI." (Produced for the Finnish Market.)

C 19/07   Norwegian Ambulance/Politibil Set Feb-90 $35-50
White/Red Ford Escort Van "AMBULANSE" with Blue/White Light Bar on Roof, White Saab 9000 "POLITI" with Blue Light Bar on Roof. (Produced for Norwegian Market)

C 19/08   Swedish Ambulance Set Aug-90 $35-50
Ford Transit Van "AMBULANS," White with Red Roof, Blue/White Lightbar, & Saab 9000 "POLIS," White with Blue Fenders & Blue Lightbar on Roof. (Produced for Swedish Market)

C 19/09   Swedish Breakdown Set Aug-90 $35-50
Ford Transit Breakdown "BJARNINGS-KAREN," Red with Yellow Side Trim, & Saab 9000 "BRANDCHEF," Red with Blue Lightbar on Roof. (Produced for Swedish Market)

D 23/01   Ford Popular Van Set Aug-89 $30-45
Lt. Blue Ford Popular Van "SIGNSMITH," Dk. Blue Ford Popular Van "M. FRASER COOK LTD.," Black Ford Popular Van "LEWIS EAST LTD."

Q 24   Austin Rover Luxury Gift Set Jan-90 $50-70
Pearlescent Cherry Red Mini, includes Book.

D 26   Cameo, 4 pc Set Aug-90 $18-25
Various Liveries.

C 27   Fire Set Jan-88 $20-30
C1185 Mack Fire Pumper "HAMMOND FIRE DEPT," C106 Saab 9000 "FIRE CHIEF."

C 27/02   Swedish Fire Set Jun-89 $35-50
C1185 Mack Fire Pumper "HAMMOND FIRE DEPT," C106/06 Saab 9000 "BRANDCHEF." (Produced for the Swedish Market.)

C 30   Tower Bridge Tourist Set May-89 $18-25
Red Routemaster "STANDARD," Black Austin London Taxi with Front Door Logo.

C 31   Piccadilly Tourist Set May-89 $18-25
Red Routemaster "STANDARD," White Ford Sierra "POLICE" with Checkered Side Trim.

C 32   Beg Ben Tourist Set May-89 $28-35
Red Routemaster "STANDARD," Black Austin London Taxi with Front Door Logo, British Airways Concord.

C 34   Tower of London Tourist Set May-89 $23-28
Red Routemaster "STANDARD," British Airways Concord, Juniors London Taxi, Juniors Jaguar XJ6 Police Car.

D 35/01   RAF Battle of Britain Set Jan-90 $38-40
a Black Ford Zephyr, Gray RAF Morris 1000 Van, Gray/Black RAF Bedford OB Coach.
b Black Ford Zephyr with Zodiac Grill, Gray RAF Morris 1000 Van, Gray/Black RAF Bedford OB Coach.

D 36/01   Racing Zephyr Set, 3 pc. Mar-90 $45-55
3 Ford Zephyrs, White with Black Hood "47," Yellow "117," Dk. Green "97."

D 37/01   Double Deck Tram —Closed Top May-90 $18-25
Penny Post

C 41   Wiltshire Fire Brigade Set Jun-85 $???
Details Not Known

D 41/01   Barton's Transport Set Jul-90 $30-35
AEC DD Bus & Bedford OB Coach.

C 43   Toymaster 3 pc. Set Aug-85 $35-45
Superhaulers Volvo Articulated Truck "TOYMASTER," Mercedes 207D Van "BMX SERVICE," Ford Escort Van "Royal Mail."

D 46/01   British Railways Set Sep-90 $30-45
Bedford Box Van & Morris J Van.

D 47/01   Minnie the Minx/Bash Street Kids Set Nov-90 $28-30
"Minnie the Minx" Morris J Van & "Bash Street Kids" AEC DD Bus.

C 48/01   Porsche Kremer Racing Set Jan-88 $20-30
C567/02 Mercedes 207D "KREMER," C100/02 Porsche 956 "taka-Q."

C 49   Transport of the '30's 2 pc. Gift Set Aug-87 $35-50
Red Thorneycroft Bus "The Times," Green Model T Ford Van with White Roof "The Times."

C 50   Transport of the '30's 3 pc. Gift Set Aug-87 $40-55
3 Model T Ford Vans, Covet Garden, Billingsgate, and Smithfield Markets.

D 51/01   Greene King Set Aug-90 $35-50
AEC Tanker & AEC Open Truck with Barrels

D 52/01   Charrington's Set Aug-90 $35-50
AEC Tanker & AEC Open Truck with Barrels

D 53/01   Rally Set Aug-90 $50-70
Black Jaguar Mk II, White Ford Cortina, Red Austin Healey with White Hard Top, Pale Blue MGA.

C 54   Swiss REGA Set Dec-86 $30-45
Red Helicopter "HB-XGY," White/Orange Mercedes Bonna Ambulance "NOTRUF 144." (Produced for the Swiss Market.)

D 54/01   National Resources Light Commercial Set Aug-90 $40-45
Bedford CA Van "GAS," Ford Popular Van "Royal Mail," Morris J Van, Morris 1000 Van.

C 55   Emergency Gift Set Oct-87 $55-75
White Ford Sierra with Blue/White Lightbar on Roof "POLITI," Red Ford Wrecker with Yellow/Black Side Decoration & Blue Boom, White/Red Ford Transit Van with Blue/White Lightbar on Roof "AMBULANSE." (Produced for the Norwegian Market.)

Q 55/01   York Fair Set Aug-90 $45-50
Bedford OB Coach & Bedford Pantechnicon

C 56 (A)   Swedish 3 pc. Emergency Set Aug-87 $55-80
Ford Sierra "POLISBIL," Mercedes Bonna Ambulance, Ford Sierra "BRANDCHEFSBIL." (Produced for the Swedish Market.)

C 56 (B)   Mini Set Sep-90 $30-40
Three Mini's (1/36), Black, Red, Gold

C 57   Volvo and Caravan Set Oct-87 $18-25
Red Volvo 760 Saloon with White/Red/Blue Caravan. (Produced for the Swedish Market.)

Q 57/01   The Northern Collection Set Sep-90 $35-40
Bedford Pantechnicon "Slumberland" & Bedford OB Coach "Standerwick"

C 61   Swiss 3 pc. Fire Set Apr-87 $55-80
C1120 Fire Engine "NOTRUF 118," Red Ford Escort Van "NOTRUF 118," White Ford Sierra with Blue Roof Light, Red Side Stripe with Blue "POLIZEI," Red Stripe Front Edge of Hood with Blue "POLIZEI," Blue "01" on Roof. (Produced for the Swiss Market.)

C 62   Swiss 3 pc. Services Set Apr-87 $55-80
White/Yellow Mercedes Van "PTT," Yellow VW Golf "PTT," Red Ford Cargo Container Truck with Gray Container "Cargo Domicile." (Produced for the Swiss Market.)

C 63   French 3 pc. Intervention Set May-87 $55-80
White Mercedes Ambulance, Blue "AMBULANCE" on Sides, Blue Stripe on Roof Sides, Red Peugeot 505 with Blue Roof Light, White Text on Doors & Hood, White Renault R5 with Black Doors, Blue Roof Light, White "POLICE" on Doors. (Produced for the French Market.)

C 65   Norwegian 2 pc. Rescue Set Oct-87 $35-50
White/Red Ford Transit Van with Blue/White Lightbar on Roof "AMBULANSE," Red/White Helicopter "LN-OSH." (Produced for the Norwegian Market.)

C 67/01   Tour de France 2 pc. Set May-87 $35-50
White Renault Alpine with Tour de France Trim, White Peugeot 505 with 2 Bicycles Mounted to Trunk, "U" Trim. (Produced for the French Market.)

C 67/02   Tour de France 2 pc. Set May-87 $35-50
White Renault Alpine with Tour de France Trim, White Peugeot 505 with 2 Bicycles Mounted to Trunk, "Z" Trim. (Produced for the French Market.)

C 67/03   Tour de France 2 pc. Set May-87 $35-50
White Renault Alpine with Tour de France Trim, White Peugeot 505 with 2 Bicycles Mounted to Trunk, "La Vie Claire" Trim. (Produced for the French Market.)

D 67/01 (B)   United Dairies Set Dec-90 $40-60
AEC Box Van & AEC Tanker

C 68   Turbos — Swedish 3 pc. Emergency Set 1987? $???
Saab 9000 "POLIS," Other Vehicles "FIRE" and "AMBULANCE," Other Details Not Known. (Produced for the Swedish Market.)

C 69 Bryant & May 2 pc. Gift Set Aug-87 $30-40
Red/White Thorneycroft Box Van with Black Roof Rack "ENGLAND'S GLORY," Yellow/Red/Black Model T Ford Van with Black Roof Rack "Swan."

D 70 Falck 2 pc Set Aug-87 $35-50
C406/02 Mercedes Bonna Ambulance, C1140/02 Ford Wrecker. (Produced for the Danish Market.)

D 71/01 Model T Ford Set Aug-89 $40-60
Lt. Blue Model T Ford Tanker "Somelyte Ltd," Red Model T Ford Tanker "TEXACO," Black/Red Model T Ford Van "A-1 SAUCE," White Model T Ford Van with Black Roof Rack "????"

D 72/01 Morris Minor Van/Ford Popular Van Set Aug-89 $40-60
Yellow/Black Morris 1000 Van "Rington's Tea," Tan/Black Morris 1000 Van "Fry's," Black Ford Popular Van "Bowyers," Yellow/Black Ford Popular Van with Red Wheels "Colman's Mustard."

C 73 2 pc. Polis Set Sep-88 $35-50
White Volvo 760 Saloon "POLIS" with 2 Blue Roof Lights, "POLIS" Helicopter. (Produced for the Swedish Market.)

C 73/01 Swedish Polis Helicopter Set Jun-90 $35-50
Hughes Cayuse Helicopter "POLIS" & Volvo 760 "POLIS." C435/13 Volvo with Blue Fenders & Blue Lightbar on Roof. (Produced for Swedish Market)

D 74/01 Pickfords Set Aug-89 $120-130
Bedford Pantechnicon, Morris 1000 Van, and Ford Popular Van All Decorated "PICKFORDS."

D 75/01 3 pc. Police Set Aug-89 $40-60
White Jaguar Mk II with Small "POLICE" Sign on Roof, Lt. Blue/White Panda Morris Minor Saloon with Small "POLICE" Sign on Roof, Black Ford Zephyr with Small "POLICE" Sign on Roof.

C 76 Little/Large 2 pc. Set Mar-88 $25-35
Corgi and Juniors Volvo Rally. (Produced for the French/Scandinavian Markets.)

C 77 Little/Large 2 pc. Set Mar-88 $25-35
Corgi and Juniors Mercedes "SERVIS." (Produced for the French/Scandinavian Markets.)

C 78 Little/Large 2 pc. Set Mar-88 $25-35
Corgi and Juniors Ford Sierra "TEXACO." (Produced for the French/Scandinavian Markets.)

C 79 Little/Large 2 pc. Set Mar-88 $25-35
Corgi and Juniors Renault 5. (Produced for the French/Scandinavian Markets.)

C 80 Little/Large 2 pc. Set Mar-88 $25-35
Corgi and Juniors Ferrari. (Produced for the French/Scandinavian Markets.)

C 81 Little/Large 2 pc. Set Mar-88 $25-35
Corgi and Juniors BMW 325i. (Produced for the French/Scandinavian Markets.)

C 82 Little/Large 2 pc. Set Mar-88 $25-35
Corgi and Juniors Volvo Saloon. (Produced for the French/Scandinavian Markets.)

D 82/01 Corgi "We're on the Move" Set Dec-90 $38-40
Bedford Pantechnicon & Bedford OB Coach

C 83 Little/Large 2 pc. Set Mar-88 $25-35
Corgi SAS Coach, Juniors Mercedes. (Produced for the French/Scandinavian Markets.)

C 88 WW I Military 2 pc. Gift Set Jul-88 $35-55
Olive Thorneycroft DD Bus "66" & "2nd Division," Olive Model T Ford Van "Order of St. Joan" with Red Cross in White Circle.

C 89 60 Years of Transport 3 pc. Gift Set Jul-88 $65-85
Thorneycroft Double Deck Bus "GENERAL," Bedford OB Coach "Midland," Double Deck Tram — Closed Top.

C 90 Model T Ford Van 2 pc. Set Jul-88 $25-45
Brown Model T Ford Van "Royal Laundry" with White Roof, White Model T Ford Van "Sunlight Laundry" with Black Roof.

C 91 Morris 1000 Van Triple Pack Set Oct-88 $40-40
Yellow Van "Telegraph & Argus," Dk. Green Van "Grattons," Dk. Green/Tan Van "Mitchell's Wool Fat Soap."

D 94/01 Whitbread Brewery Set Nov-90 $30-50
Bedford box van & Model T Van

C 96/01 Swedish Emergency Set Jun-89 $55-80
C110/04 BMW "LAKARE," C106/06 Saab 9000 "BRANDCHEF," C106/05 Saab 9000 "POLIS." (Produced for the Swedish Market.)

C 96/02 Swedish Emergency Set Jun-89 $55-80
C106/06 Saab 9000 "BRANDCHEF," C106/05 Saab 9000 "POLIS," Helicopter "POLIS." (Produced for the Swedish Market.)

C 100 Turbos — Porsche 956 Racer Jan-85 $10-12
a Yellow Body "7 Castrol"
b "PORSCHE 5 ESSO"
c "Coca-Cola," Other Details Not Known.

C 100/02 Turbos — Porsche 956 Racer Jan-88 $10-12
Yellow Body, "taka-Q 7."

C 100/03 Turbos — Porsche 956 Racer Jan-88 $10-12
Black Body, "BLAUPUNKT PORSCHE 1."

C 101 Turbos — Porsche 956 Racer Aug-85 $10-12
"14 CANON."

C 102 Turbos — Opel Manta 400 Jan-85 $10-12
Red Body, "43."

C 102/02 Turbos — Opel Manta 400 Jan-88 $10-12
Black Body, "Shell Manx Rally 18."

C 102/03 Turbos — Opel Manta 400 Jan-88 $10-12
Yellow Body, "TELECOM Mobile Phone 12."

C 102/04 Turbos — Opel Manta 400 Mar-90 $10-12
White Body, "Vauxhall-Opel, " " 6," and "Mobil 1" trim.

C 103 Turbos — Opel Manta 400 Jan-85 $10-12
White Body, "15."

C 104 Turbos — Toyota Corolla 1600 Jan-85 $10-12
a White Body, "LAING 16."
b White Body, "TOTAL 2."

C 105 Turbos — Toyota Corolla 1600 Jan-85 $10-12
a Red Body, "Dunlop 8."
b Orange Body, "TOTAL 5."

C 106 Turbos — Saab 9000 Jan-85 $10-12
a Standard Saloon, No Graphics. (Produced for the Swedish Market.)
b White Body, Swedish Flag on Doors "3."

C 106/01 Turbos — Saab 9000 Jan-88 $10-12
Red Body, "Fly Virgin."

C 106/03 Turbos — Saab 9000 Jan-88 $10-12
Black Body, "Mobil 7."

C 106/09 Turbos — Saab 9000 Mar-90 $10-12
White, "FEDERAL EXPRESS SYSTEMLINE," and "4" trim.

C 106/13 Turbos — Saab 9000 Sep-90 $18-20
Brandweer, "Alarm 06-11," produced for Dutch market.

C 106/99 a. Turbos — Saab 9000 Polis 1987? $18-20
White Body with Blue/Yellow Stripes "POLIS," Used in Set C68. (Produced for the Swedish Market. No Item Number, C106/99 Used for List Organization Only)

C 106/99 b. Turbos — Saab 9000 Polis/Poliisi 1987? $18-20
Dark Blue Body, "POLIS" on One Side, "POLIISI" on Other, Part of Set C19/06. (Produced for the Finnish Market. No Item Number, C106/99 Used for List Organization Only.)

C 106/99 c Turbos — Saab 9000 Fire Chief 1987? $10-12
Red Body, "FIRE CHIEF" & Crest on Hood, Red/White Checkered Stripe on Sides, Part of Set C27. (No Item Number, C106/99 Used for List Organization Only.)

C 107 Turbos — Saab 9000 Jan-85 $10-12
Red Body, "41."

C 108 Turbos — Chevrolet Camaro Racer Jan-85 $10-12
Red Body, Yellow Flames "52."

C 109 Turbos — Chevrolet Camaro Racer Jan-85 $10-12
White Body, Red/Blue Graphics, "NCT 84."

C 110 Turbos — BMW 635 Jan-85 $10-12
a White Body, Opposite Corners Black, "6."
b White Body, Black/Gray Stripes, "BMW 25."

C 110/02 Turbos — BMW 635 Jan-88 $10-12
White Body, "MOTUL 2."

C 110/03 Turbos — BMW 635 Jan-88 $10-12
White Body, "WARSTEINER 46."

C 110/?? Turbos — BMW 635 Jan-88 $10-12
White Body, Blue Edged Red Side Stripe with White "POLICE" on Doors. Blue "POLICE" on Hood.

C 110/07 Turbos — BMW 635 Feb-90 $10-12
Red

C 111 Turbos — BMW 635 Jan-85 $10-12
a White/Blue Body, "18."
b White Body, Blue/Red/Yellow Stripes, "ARCUS AIR 8 PIRELLI."

C 139/02 Turbos — Porsche 911 Jan-88 $10-12
Orange Body, "Jagermeister 24."

C 139/04 Turbos — Porsche 911 Oct-87 $10-12
a Yellow Body, "Denver 91."
b White Body, "Denver 91." (British Home Stores.)
c Red Body, "Denver 91."

C 139/08 Turbos — Porsche 911 Jul-89 $18-20
Rijkspolitie, (Produced for the Dutch Market.)

C 144/01 Turbos — Jaguar XJR9 Racer Jan-89 $10-12
Castrol 66

C 150/02? Turbos — Chevrolet Camaro Racer Apr-87 $18-20
Brown Body with Orange/White Stripe, White "HERSHEY'S MILK CHOCOLATE 6," Black Interior. (Part of Set C3200H. Not Available Seperately.)

C 150/03 Turbos — Chevrolet Camaro Racer Jan-90 $10-12
Red Body, Blue/White Stripes, "77."

C 150/04 Turbos — Chevrolet Camaro Racer Feb-90 $10-12
Blue, White/Black/Red Stripes, "77"

C 257 Mercedes 500 SEC "Magic Top" Jan-85 $15-18
White Body with Black Side Pinstripes on Lower Sides, Multi-piece Retractable Hard Top.

C 258 Toyota Supra 2.8L Jan-85 $15-18
a Gold Upper Body, Black Lower Body.
b Silver Upper Body, Black Lower Body.

C 258/01 Toyota Supra 2.8L Mar-87 $15-18
Black Upper Body, Gray Lower Body, Thin Red Divider Stripe at Belt Line.

C 266 Spiderbike Apr-84 $25-30
Spiderman with Motorcycle. (Continuation of Mettoy Era 266.)

C 271 James Bond Aston Martin DB5. Apr-84 $25-30
Silver Body, Automatic Features. (Continuation of Mettoy Era 271.)

C 271/01 James Bond Aston Martin DB5. Oct-88 $25-30
Silver Body, Automatic Features. (Same as Mettoy C271 Except for Base Text.)

C 279 Rolls Royce Corniche Apr-84 $15-18
a Dk. Red Body. (Continuation of Mettoy Era 279, which was Various Colors Including Dk. Blue.)
b Dk. Green Body.
c Silver Upper Body & Front, Black Below Belt Line.

C 279/01 Rolls Royce Corniche Mar-87 $15-18
Silver Upper Body & Front, Black Below Belt Line.

C 279/03 Rolls-Royce Corniche Jan-90 $15-18
Gold

C 292 Starsky & Hutch Ford Torino Feb-86 $30-40
Red Body with White Basket Handle Stripe. (Special Re-run of Mettoy Issue Produced for the French Market.)

C 299 Ford Sierra Saloon Apr-84 $15-18
a Silver Body. (Continuation of Mettoy Era 299 which was Various Colors Including Metallic Blue.)
b Red Body, White Side Stripe Below Doors.
c Blue Body, White/Red/Yellow Graphics "Industrial Control Services."

C 299/01 Ford Sierra Saloon Mar-87 $15-18
White Body, Blue/Red Racing Trim, "26" & "Lindsay Cars."

C 299/03 Ford Sierra Saloon Jan-88 $15-18
Black Body, "TEXACO," "7."

C 299/04 Ford Sierra Saloon Jan-90 $15-18
Pink, "Mr. Tomkinson Carpets"

C 299/07 Ford Sierra Saloon Feb-86 $15-18
a White Body, Black Hood, 4 Doors & Hatch, White "Polis" on Hood & Doors, Round Roof Light. (Produced for the Swedish Market.)
b White Body, Black Hood, 2 Front Doors & Hatch, White "Polis" on Hood & Doors, Round Roof Light. (Produced for the Swedish Market.)
c White Body, Blue/Yellow Side Stripes, Blue "Polis" on Hood & Doors, Round Blue Roof Light. (Produced for the Swedish Market.)

C 310 Porsche 924 Turbo Apr-84 $15-18
a Black Body, Gold Trim "PORSCHE 924." (Continuation of Mettoy Era 310.)
b Red Body, Black Trim, British Home Stores Packaging.

C 317 Peugeot 505 Politi Dec-86 $25-30
White/Black Body, Blue Roof Light, "POLITI." (Produced for the Norwegian Market.)

C 318 Jaguar XJS **Jun-86** **$15-18**
Green Body with White Side Stripe, Motul "JAGUAR 12."
C 318/01 Jaguar XJS **Mar-87** **$15-18**
Black Upper Body, Gray Lower Body, Thin Red Divider Stripe at Belt Line.
C 318/03 Jaguar XJS **Feb-88** **$15-18**
Silver
C 318/08 Jaguar XJS **Jan-90** **$15-18**
Med. Blue
C 320/01 Jaguar XJS Police **Jan-87** **$15-18**
White Body, Blue/Silver Lightbar on Roof, Red Stripe on Sides and hood with White "POLICE" & Blue Edges.
C 325/01 Jaguar XJR9 Racer **Sep-88** **$20-25**
Castrol 60, (Service Station Offer)
Q 330/01 Mini **Jul-89** **$20-25**
Metallic Brown, "1959-1989," 30th Anniversary Mini (Produced for Austin Rover)
C 330/02 Mini **Oct-89** **$15-18**
(1/36) White/Pink, "Rose"
C 330/03 Mini **Oct-89** **$15-18**
(1/36) White/Blue, "Sky"
C 330/04 Mini **Oct-89** **$15-18**
(1/36) Red/White, "Flame"
C 330/05 Mini **Oct-89** **$15-18**
(1/36) Black/White, "Racing"
C 330/10 Mini **Aug-90** **$15-18**
(1/36) Black, "After Eight"
Q 330/15 Mini **Jan-91** **$20-25**
(1/36) Black body, White roof, "Curry's Electrical Stores"
C 339 Rover Police **Apr-84** **$15-18**
a White Body, Triangular Roof Sign with Blue Light "POLICE" & "POLICE STOP," Red Side Stripe with Crest, Blue "POLICE" on White lable on Hood, Red "POLICE" on White lable on Hatch. (Continuation of Mettoy Era 339.)
b White Body, Triangular Roof Sign with Blue Light "POLICE" & "POLICE STOP," Blue Edged Red Side Stripe with Blue "POLICE" on Doors, Blue "POLICE" on White Lable on Hood, Red "POLICE" on White Lable on Hatch.
C 339/01 Rover Police **Jan-88** **$15-18**
White Body, Triangular Roof Sign with Blue Light "POLICE," Blue Edged Red Side Stripe with Simplified Crest, "POLICE" Printed on Hood & Hatch.
C 346 Citroen 2CV Charleston **Apr-84** **$15-18**
Maroon/Black Body. (Continuation of Mettoy Era 346.)
C 346/01 Citroen 2CV Dolly **Mar-87** **$15-18**
White Body, Red Top, Red Front & Rear Fenders Extending onto Rear Doors.
C 350 Toyota Celica Supra **Jan-85** **$15-18**
White/Red Body, "14."
C 351 Ford Sierra Pace Car **Jun-85** **$15-18**
White Body, Green/Yellow Stripes, Red/White/Blue Lightbar on Roof, Shield on Hood.
C 352 BMW 325i Saloon **Aug-86** **$15-18**
White Body, Black "BMW 325iX."
C 353 BMW 325i Saloon **Jul-86** **$15-18**
Red Body.
C 353/01 BMW 325i Saloon **Jan-88** **$15-18**
Red Body. (Same as C353.)
C 353/02 BMW 325i Saloon **May-87** **$25-30**
White with Red Doors, Hood &Trunk Lid, 2 Blue Roof Lights, Red Cross Logo & Whiet "NOTARZT" on Hood & Doors. (Produced for the German Market.)
C 353/04 BMW 325i Saloon **Jan-88** **$15-18**
White Body, "Castrol"
C 353/09 BMW 325i Saloon **Jan-90** **$15-18**
Black
C 354 BMW 325i Racing **Jul-86** **$15-18**
White Body, "Marcel Favraud 33."
C 356 Ford Sierra Diplomatic Protection Car **Jun-85** **$25-30**
Red Body, 2 Spotlights Beside Round Blue Roof Light, Crest on Doors, No Other Markings.
C 357 Ford Sierra Brandchefsbil **Sep-86** **$25-30**
Red Body, White "BRANDCHEFBIL" on Hood, "47" on Roof, 2 Spotlights Beside Round Blue Roof Light, Crest on Doors. (Also Used in C56.) (Produced for the Swedish Market.)
C 358 Ford Sierra Police **Feb-86** **$15-18**
White Body, Blue/White Lightbar on Roof, Checkered Side Stripe, Blue "POLICE" on Hood.
C 358/01 Ford Sierra Police **Jan-87** **$15-18**
White Body, Blue/White Lightbar on Roof, Checkered Side Stripe, Blue "POLICE" on Hood. (Jan '87 Renumbering of C358.)
C 358/02 Ford Sierra Politi **Oct-87** **$25-30**
a White Body, Blue Roof Light, Red/Blue Stripes, "POLITI," "POLITIBIL." (Produced for the Norwegian Market)
b White Body, Blue/White Lightbar on Roof, Red/Blue Stripes, "POLITI, " " POLITIBIL." (Produced for the Norwegian Market)
C 358/03 Ford Sierra Rijkspolitie **Oct-87** **$25-30**
White Body, Blue/White Lightbar on Roof, Red Stripe across Front of Hood, Red Chevrons and Dashes on Doors, Blue Shield on Front Doors. (Produced for the Dutch Market.)
C 358/04 Ford Sierra Legebil **Jan-88** **$25-30**
White Body, Black Hood & Bumpers, Red Side Stripe, 2 Blue Roof Lights, Silver Spotlight, "LEGE" on Rear Doors. (Produced for the Norwegian Market.)
C 361/01 Volvo 760 Polis **Oct-87** **$25-30**
a White Body, Blue Light on Center of Roof, "POLIS" on Hood and Doors. (Produced for the Swedish Market.)
b White Body, 2 Blue Roof Lights, "POLIS." (Produced for the Swedish Market.)
C 361/02 Volvo Politi/Politibil **May-88** **$25-30**
White Body, Blue/White Roof Lightbar, "POLITI" & "47:11." (Produced for the Danish Market.)
C 373/02 Peugeot 505 Pompiers **Feb-87** **$25-30**
Red Body with Blue Roof Light, White "SAPEURS POMPIERS" on Doors & Hood, Crest on Hood. (Produced for the French Market.)
C 373/03 Peugeot 505 Politi **1987?** **$25-30**
White Body, Black Hood & Doors, "Politi." (Produced for the Norwegian Market.)
C 378 Ferrari 308 GTS **Apr-84** **$15-18**
Red Body, No Graphics. (Continuation of Mettoy Era 378.)
C 378/01 Ferrari 308 GTS **Jan-85** **$15-18**
Red Body, Green/White/Red Hood Stripe with Black Logo, White "Ferrari" on Doors. (/01 Added to # January '87.)
C 378/02 Ferrari 308 GTS **1989?** **$15-18**
Red Body, Other Details Not Known.
C 380 BMW M1 — BASF **Apr-84** **$15-18**
Red Body, Concentric White Circle Decorations, "BASF 80." (Continuation of Mettoy Era 380)
C 382 Lotus Elite 2.2 **Apr-84** **$15-18**
Dk. Blue Body, Silver Trim. (Continuation of Mettoy Era 382.)
C 384 Renault 11 **Apr-84** **$15-18**
Red Body with Black Below Beltline, Black Chassis. (Continuation of Mettoy Era 384.)
C 384/02 Renault 11 Police **1987?** **$25-30**
White Upper Body, Black Lower Body, Hood, Doors & Hatch, "POLICE" on Doors, Reversed "POLICE" on Hood, Blue Roof Light. (Produced for the French Market.)
C 385 Mercedes 190 **Apr-84** **$15-18**
Silver Body. (New Style Body Similar to C386 But Without Spoiler or Wheel Flairs.)
C 386/01 Mercedes 2.3/16 Saloon **May-87** **$15-18**
Black Body.
C 386/02 Mercedes 2.3/16 Saloon **May-87** **$15-18**
White with Blue/Red Stripes, "17 SERVIS."
C 386/03 Mercedes Polizei **Jul-87** **$25-30**
White with Green Doors, Hood & Trunk Lid, 2 Blue Roof Lights, White "POLIZEI" on Doors & Hood. (Produced for the German Market.)
C 386/04 Mercedes 2.3/16 Rally **Jan-88** **$15-18**
White Body, "BURLINGTON AIR EXPRESS," "17."
C 386/06 Mercedes 2.3/16 Saloon **Jan-89** **$15-18**
Metalic Dk. Blue
C 386/08 Mercedes 2.3/16 Saloon **Jan-90** **$15-18**
Maroon
C 388 Mercedes 190 Taxi **Jan-85** **$15-18**
Tan Body, White Taxi Roof Sign, Black "TAXI" on Front Doors.
C 388/02 Mercedes 190 Taxi **May-88** **$20-25**
White Body & Taxi Roof Sign, Green Side Stripe & "TAXI." (Produced for the Danish Market.)
C 388/03 Mercedes 190 Taxi **Sep-88** **$20-25**
Taxi, (Produced for the Dutch Market.)
C 399 Peugeot 205 T16 Rally **Jan-85** **$15-18**
a White Body, "Shell 105."
b "PARIS 6," Monti Carlo Rally.
C 399/02 Peugeot 205 T16 Rally **Jan-87** **$15-18**
Green Body, "22 benetton"
C 399/05 Peugeot 205 T16 Rally **Jan-88** **$15-18**
Yellow Body, "2"
C 399/06 Peugeot 205 T16 Rally **Nov-89** **$20-25**
Red/White Body, "NORTH RACING," (Produced for Finnish Market)
C 402 BMW M1 **Jan-85** **$15-18**
White/Red Body, "Castrol 101."
C 404 Rover Sterling 3.5 Racing **Jan-85** **$15-18**
a Red Body, Diagonal White/Yellow Stripes on Rear Quarter, "Mirror 13 ESSO."
b Red/White Body, "1 ROVER," "TEXACO."
C 406/02 Mercedes Bonna Ambulance **Jul-87** **$25-30**
White Body, Red Stripe Above Belt on Sides & Side of Roof, Red "FALCK" Over Windshield. (Produced for the Danish Market.)
C 406/03 Mercedes Bonna Ambulance **Feb-88** **$25-30**
White Body, Blue Stripe Side of Roof, Blue "AMBULANCE" & Cross on Sides, Blue Medical Symbol on Hood. (Produced for the French Market. Re-run.)
C 406/08 Mercedes Bonna Ambulance **Oct-87** **$25-30**
White Body, Red Stripe Above Beltline on Sides and on Sides of Roof, "AMBULANCE" in Rectangle above Windshield, Blue Medical Symbol Between Side Windows. (Produced for the Dutch Market.)
C 406/09 Mercedes Bonna Ambulance **Jun-89** **$25-30**
a White with Red Side and Roof Stripes, Red Panel over Windshield, (Produced for the Swiss Market.)
b White with Red Side and Roof Stripes, No Red Panel over Windshield, (Produced for the Swiss Market.)
C 409 Allis Chalmers Fork Lift Truck **Apr-84** **$15-18**
Yellow Body, Driver with Blue Uniform, White Tank, 2 Tan Skids with Red Bins. (Continuation of Mettoy Era 409.)
C 412 Mercedes Police **1986?** **$25-30**
a Black/White Body "POLICE," Other Details Not Known. (Produced for the French Market.)
b Green/White Body "POLIZEI," Other Details Not Known. (Produced for the German Market.)
C 420 BMW M1 **Apr-84** **$15-18**
a White Body, Diagonal Red/Lt. Blue/Dk. Blue Stripe from Front Corner Over Roof, "BMW M1 11."
b White Body, Diagonal Red/Blue Stripe from Front Corner Over Roof, "ESSO 17."
C 422 Renault 5 Turbo **Apr-84** **$15-18**
a Dk. Blue Body, White Roof & Bumpers, "elf 25."
b Dk. Blue Body, White Roof & Bumpers, "elf 18."
C 422/01 Renault 5 Turbo **Feb-88** **$15-18**
Dk. Blue Body, White Roof & Bumpers, "elf 18." (Produced for the French Market, Re-run.)
C 423 Ford Escort **Apr-84** **$15-18**
a White/Dk. Blue/Lt. Blue Diagonally Striped Body, "69 Brooklyn."
b White Body, "TOTAL 84."
C 424 Ford Mustang **Apr-84** **$15-18**
Black Body, Yellow/Orange/Red Striping, "77."
C 425 London Taxi **Apr-84** **$15-18**
Black Body, Red/White Telephone Logo on Doors. (Continuation of Mettoy Era 425 which Did Not Have Door Logo.)
C 425/01 London Taxi — Radio Cab **Jan-87** **$15-18**
Black Body, Yellow/White Logo on Doors.
C 426 Rover 3500 Sterling — Hepolite **Apr-84** **$15-18**
Yellow Body, Red Stripe Over Hood & Below Belt Line on Sides, "4 Hepolite Glacier."
C 428 Renault 5 Police **1985?** **$25-30**
a White Body, Black Doors & Hood, "POLICE" Lables, Gray Base, with Antenna. (Produced for the French Market. Possibly a Mettoy Era Product.)
b White Body, Black Doors & Hood, "POLICE" Tampo Printed. Black Base, with out Antenna. (Produced for the French Market. Possibly a Mettoy Era Product.)
C 430 Porsche 924 Polizei **1985?** **$25-30**
Green/White Body "POLIZEI," Other Details Not Known. (Produced for the German Market.)
C 430/03 Porsche 924 Police **1985?** **$25-30**
Black/White Body "POLICE," Other Details Not Known. (Produced for the French Market.)
C 435 Volvo 760 GL Turbo Saloon **Jan-86** **$15-18**
a Dk. Silver Body

b Lt. Silver Body
c Bronze Body.
d Red Body. (Part of set C57. Produced for the Swedish Market.)

C 435/01 Volvo 760 GL Turbo Saloon   Jul-87 $15-18
Black Body.

C 435/02 Volvo 760 GL Turbo Saloon   Jul-87 $15-18
White Body, "21," "Gillanders Motors."

C 435/05 Volvo 760 GL Turbo Saloon   Jan-88 $15-18
Maroon Body. (Produced for the Swedish Market.)

C 435/06 Volvo 760 GL Turbo Saloon   May-88 $20-25
Blue/Red Body, White Roof Sign "TAXI." (Produced for the Danish Market.)

C 435/07 Volvo 760 GL Turbo Saloon   Nov-89 $15-18
Metallic Pale Blue

C 435/12 Volvo 760 GL Turbo Saloon   Jan-90 $15-18
Dk. Green

C 435/13 Volvo 760 GL Turbo Saloon   Jun-90 $25-30
"POLIS," White with Blue Fenders & Blue Lightbar on Roof. (Produced for Swedish Market)

C 438/01 Rover 800 (Sterling) Saloon   May-87 $15-18
White Body, Blue/White Lightbar on Roof, Red with Black/White Checkered Side Stripe, Red "POLICE" on Hood.

C 438/03 Rover 800 (Sterling) Saloon   Jun-89 $15-18
West Mercia "POLICE," Blue/White Roof Lightbar, Orange/Blue Diagonally Striped Side Trim.

C 439/01 Rover 800 (Sterling) Saloon   Jan-87   N/A
NOT PRODUCED, Number Changed to 438 When Released.

C 440/01 Porsche 944   Jul-88 $15-18
Red

C 440/02 Porsche 944 Rally   Jul-88 $15-18
White Body, "944 PORSCHE," "2"

C 440/03 Porsche 944   Jan-89 $15-18
Black

C 440/06? Porsche 944   Jan-90 $15-18
Red

C 440/06? Porsche 944 Rally   Apr-90 $15-18
White Body, "Pirelli 44," "B F Goodrich" trim.

C 441/01 Porsche 944 Racer   Jun-88 $15-18
"944 PORSCHE, " "2"

C 447 Jeep Renegade 4x4 — Open Top   Apr-84 $15-18
a Dk. Blue Body, White Chassis, Interior & Wheels, Spare on Side, Striped Trim "8." (Continuation of Mettoy Era 447.)
b Brown Body, White Chassis, Interior & Wheels, Yellow Graphics, Spare on Rear.

C 448 Jeep Renegade 4x4 —Closed Top   Apr-84 $15-18
Yellow Body, Red Top, White Wheels, Red Chassis & Interior, Striped Trim "8." (Continuation of Mettoy Era 448.)

C 451 Ford Sierra Taxi   Jun-86 $25-30
a Beige Body, Red/White Roof Sign. (Produced for the German Market.)
b Beige Body, Black/White Roof Sign. (Produced for the German Market.)

C 452 Opel Senator Polizei   1984? $25-30
a Green/White Body "POLIZEI," No Number on Roof, Other Details Not Known. (Produced for the German Market.)
b Green/White Body "POLIZEI," "452" on Roof, Other Details Not Known. (Produced for the German Market.)
c Green/White Body "POLIZEI," "17" on Roof, Other Details Not Known. (Produced for the German market.)

C 453 Ford Escort RS 1600i   Apr-84 $15-18
White Body, Black Trunk Lid & Hood Graphics, Black Side Stripe "ESCORT." (Variant of Mettoy Era 334.)

C 454 Ford Sierra Polizei   Jun-89 $25-30
a White with Red Side and Hood Stripe, Blue "POLIZEI" and "01," Blue Roof Light, Red Interior, Blue Tinted Windows, Label Sheet with "POLICE" & "POLICIA." (1st Issue, Produced for the Swiss Market.)
b White with Red Side and Hood Stripe, Blue "POLIZEI" and "01," Blue Roof Light, Black Interior, Clear Windows, Label Sheet with "POLICE" & "POLICIA." (2nd Issue, Produced for the Swiss Market.)

C 456 Ford Sierra Polizei   Aug-86 $25-45
a White Body, Green Doors Hood & Trunk Lid, "POLIZEI," Round Blue Roof Light, "456" on Roof, Red Interior. (Produced for the German Market.)
b White Body, Green Doors Hood & Trunk Lid, "POLIZEI," Round Blue Roof Light, "456" on Roof, Tan Interior. (Produced for the German Market.)

C 457 Matra Rancho   Apr-84 $15-18
Green Body with Black Trim. (Continuation of Mettoy 457, which was Red.)

C 457/02 Matra Rancho   Mar-88 $25-30
Red Body with Black Trim, "SAPEURS POMPIERS," "18." (Produced for the French Market.)

C 461 Routemaster Bus   Jul-86 $25-45
Red, "Corgi Mannheim Visit 1986" on Side Panels, Union Jack Eyebrow Panels.

C 469 (A) Routemaster Bus   Apr-84 $15-18
Red, "BTA Welcome to Britain," "14" with Green Eyebrow Panels. (Continuation of Mettoy Era 469 Except with New Eyebrow Panels.)

C 469 (B) Routemaster Bus   Jan-85 $15-25
Red, "BTA Welcome to Britain," "24 SPECIAL" Union Jack Eyebrow Panels.

C 469 (C) Routemaster Bus, Open Top   Jul-85 $25-45
Red, "BTA Welcome to Britain," "24 SPECIAL" Union Jack Eyebrow Panels.

C 469 (D) Routemaster Bus   Sep-86 $15-25
Red, "The LONDON STANDARD" on Side Panels, Union Jack Eyebrow Panels.

C 469/08 Routemaster Bus   Mar-89 $25-45
London Transport, "JACOB'S Cream Crackers," "St. PAUL'S."

C 469/15 Routemaster Bus   Jan-88 $15-25
Red, "The LONDON STANDARD" on Side Panels, "ROUTE 15" Eyebrow Panels.

C 469/18 Routemaster Bus   Nov-89 $25-45
Corning Glass

C 473 Routemaster Bus   Jul-85 $25-45
Red Body, London Transport Logo, "GOT TO GO TO GAMLEY'S."

C 476 Routemaster Bus   Apr-84 $25-45
Yellow Body, " British TELECOM ... Dial a date tonight."

C 477 Routemaster Bus   Apr-84 $25-45
Dk. Blue Upper/Lt. Blue Lower Body, Red Wheel Hubs, "International Direct Dialing" "The Buzby Bus."

C 481 Routemaster Bus   Apr-84 $25-45
White Upper/Blue Lower Body, "BRITISH EUROPEAN AIRWAYS."

C 482 Routemaster Bus   Apr-84 $25-45
Yellow Upper/Green Lower Body, Yellow Wheel Hubs, "Say 'the Leeds' and you're smiling," (Catalog Description: George Shillibeer's Routemaster.)

C 483 Routemaster Bus   Apr-84 $25-45
Dk. Orange Roof/Yellow Upper/Dk. Orange Lower Body, "SHOP LINKER," "Buy almost anything in London on the bus."

C 488 Routemaster Bus   Apr-84 $25-45
a Red Body, "The NEW Corgi Company," "29 MARCH 1984," "SOUTH WALES." (Celebration Model of Formation of Corgi Toys Ltd.)
b Yellow Body, "The NEW Corgi Company," "29 MARCH 1984," "SOUTH WALES." (Celebration Model of Formation of Corgi Toys Ltd.)
c Green Body, "The NEW Corgi Company," "29 MARCH 1984," "SOUTH WALES." (Celebration Model of Formation of Corgi Toys Ltd.)

C 489 VW Polo Polizei   1984? $25-45
Green & White Body "POLIZEI," Other Details Not Known. (Possibly a Mettoy Product.)

C 495 Mazda 4x4 Pick-up   Apr-84 $15-18
a Blue Body, Black Chassis, White Wheels, White Roof Panel, "Corgi Cruiser." (Continuation of Mettoy Era 495)
b White Body, Black Chassis, White Wheels, Blue Lower Sides "Surfrider" with Orange & Green Stripe Over Blue.

C 496 Ford Escort Van   Apr-84 $15-18
a Red Body "Royal Mail," Rear Bumpers Part of Base.
b Red Body "Royal Mail," Rear Bumpers Part of Body.

C 496/01 Ford Escort Van   Jan-87 $15-18
Red Body "Royal Mail," Rear Bumpers Part of Body. (1987 Renumbering of C496.)

C 496/02 Ford Escort Van   Jan-88 $15-18
White Body, Blue/White Lightbar Toward Rear of Roof, Blue Outlined Red Side Stripe, Blue "POLICE" on Sides and Hood, Rear Bumper Part of Body. (1987 Renumbering of C621.)

C 496/03 Ford Escort Van   Jan-87 $15-18
Blue/White Body "Gas," Rear Bumpers Part of Body. (1987 Renumbering of C498.)

C 496/04 Ford Escort Van   Jan-87 $15-18
Dk. Blue/Silver Body with Thin Red Stripe "BRITISH AIRWAYS," Rear Bumper Part of Body.

C 496/05 Ford Escort Van   Jun-86 $25-45
Red Body, Rear Bumper Part of Body, Round Blue Roof Light, "Notruf 118," Labels on Doors "Berufsfeurwehr Bern." (Part of Set C61.), (Produced for the Swiss Market.)

C 496/09 Ford Escort Van   Jan-88 $15-18
a Yellow Body, Black Ladder on Roof, Rear Bumper Part of Base, "British TELECOM," (Re-introduction.)
b British Telecom, Black Ladder on Roof, Non-opening Rear Doors.
c British Telecom, Yellow Ladder on Roof, Non-opening Rear Doors.

C 496/15 Ford Escort Van   Jun-86 $25-45
White Body, Dk. Blue Below Belt Line, Gold Stripe, Rear Bumper Part of Body, Hoover Logo on Hood & Upper Side Panels, White Crest on Lower Doors, "HOOVER SERVICE."

C 496/16 Ford Escort Van   Jul-88 $25-45
BBC

C 496/17 Ford Escort Van   Oct-88 $25-45
"On the road with Carlson," with Ford Logo on Doors.

C 496/18 Ford Escort Van   Nov-88 $15-18
a British Gas, Opening Rear Doors.
b British Gas, Fixed Rear Doors.

C 496/19 Ford Escort Van   1989? $25-45
"British TELECOM," Other Details Not Known.

C 496/20 Ford Escort Van   Apr-89 $25-45
Unigate Fresh Milk, Fixed Rear Doors.

C 496/24 Ford Escort Van   Jul-90 $35-55
PTT Telecom, Produced for the Dutch Market.

C 496/99 Ford Escort Van   Apr-84 $25-45
White Body, Rear Bumper Part of Base, 4 Red Triangles, Black "gti" (Code 2, White Models Supplied by Corgi During/After Reorganization of Company.)

C 497 Ford Escort Van   Oct-83 $15-18
Radio Rentals, White Body, Rear Bumpers Part of Base.

C 498 Ford Escort Van   Apr-84 $15-18
a Blue/White Body "Gas," Rear Bumpers Part of Base.
b Blue/White Body "Gas," Rear Bumpers Part of Body. (Renumbered C496/03 Jan. 1987.)
c Blue/White Body "Gas," Rear Bumpers Part of Body, Fitted WITH Tow Hook. (Part of Set C3.), (Renumbered C496/03 Jan. 1987.)

C 499 Ford Escort Van   Apr-84 $15-18
a Yellow Body "British TELECOM," Rear Bumper Part of Base, Black Ladder on Roof.
b Yellow Body, "British TELECOM," Rear Bumper Part of Base, Black Ladder on Roof, Fitted WITH Tow Hook. (Part of Set C17.)

C 501 Range Rover   Apr-84 $15-18
Blue Body.

K 502 Hyper Kinetic Racing Circuit   Jul-90 $???
no data available

C 503 Ford Escort Van   Apr-84 $15-18
White Body, Yellow/Red/Black Side Stripe with Large Tire Graphics "DUNLOP," Rear Bumper Part of Base.

C 503/07 Ford Escort Van   Apr-84 $25-30
Orange Body with Black "TELE," Rear Bumper Part of Base. (Produced for the Swedish Market.)

K 503 Supertrack Racing System   Jul-90 $???
no data available

C 504 Ford Escort Van   Jun-85 $25-45
Dk. Green Body "John Lewis Partnership," Rear Bumper Part of Base.

K 504 Flashback Game   Jul-90 $???
no data available

C 507 Range Rover — Paris Match VSD   Apr-84 $15-18
White Body, Spectrum Striping Over Hood and Roof Extending Down Sides, "vsd."

C 512 Ford Escort Van   Jun-85 $25-45
Yellow Body "BOLTON EVENING NEWS," Rear Bumper Part of Base.

C 514 Ford Escort Van   Jun-85 $25-45
a Oxford Blue Body "DIGBY'S TOYSTORE," Rear Bumper Part of Base.
b Cambridge Blue Body "DIGBY'S TOYSTORE," Rear Bumper Part of Base.
c Cambridge Blue Body with "CHUBB HOME PROTECTION," Rear Bumper Part of Base.

C 515 Ford Escort Van Jun-85 $25-45
Red/White/Blue Body "N.E.C.," Flags on Rear Doors, Rear Bumper Part of Base.
C 516 Mercedes 207D Van Jan-85 $15-18
a White Body, Yellow Side Stripe, Cycle Graphic with Black "BMX SERVICE."
b White Arrow ?, Details Not Known.
C 521 AEC Bus 1984? $25-45
WhiteLable Northern
C 522 Range Rover 1985? $25-45?
"STIMOROL," Other Details Not Known.
C 522/02 Range Rover Apr-88 $25-45?
Maroon, 40th Anniversary Logo on Hood.
C 524 Routemaster Bus 1985? $25-45?
"Stevenson's," Other Details Not Known.
C 528 Routemaster Bus, Open Top 1985? $25-45?
"Hamley's," Other Details Not Known.
C 529 Routemaster Bus 1985? $25-45
"Grahm Ward Calendar," Other Details Not Known.
C 530 Routemaster Bus 1985? $25-45
"Yorkshire Post," Other Details Not Known.
C 532 Ford Escort Van Jan-85 $15-18
a Yellow Body, Black Outlined White Side Stripe, Black "AA Service," Yellow Lightbar Mounted Forward on Roof, Rear Bumper Part of Base.
b Yellow Body, Black Outlined White Side Stripe, Black "AA Service," Yellow Lightbar Mounted Forward on Roof, Rear Bumper Part of Body. (Part of C20 Set.)
c Yellow Body, Black Outlined White Side Stripe, Black "AA Service," Yellow Lightbar Mounted Toward Rear on Roof, Rear Bumper Part of Body, Tow Hook. (Part of C14 Set.)
C 534 Ford Escort Van Jan-86 $15-18
White Body, Red Side Stripe Below Belt Line, "Pizza SERVICE," Rear Bumper Part of Base.
C 535 Mercedes 207D Van 1985? $25-45
"Athlon," Other Details Not Known.
C 537 Ford Escort Van Jan-85 $15-18
a White Body "R.A.C.," Amber Lightbar on Roof, Rear Bumper Part of Base.
b White Body "R.A.C.," Amber Lightbar on Roof, Rear Bumper Part of Body.
c White Body "R.A.C. Service," Blue Lightbar on Roof, Rear Bumper Part of Body, Tow Hook. (Part of C13 Set.)
d White Body "R.A.C. Service," Blue Lightbar on Roof, Rear Bumper Part of Body. (Part of C21 Set.)
C 539 Mercedes 207D Van Jan-85 $25-45
White Body, Gold Side Stripe, "group 4 Security Services."
C 541 Ford Sierra Polisbil Apr-86 $25-45
White Body, Black Doors, Hood & Trunk Lid, "POLITI" or "POLISBIL." (Produced for the Norwegian/Danish Markets.)
C 541/02 Ford Sierra Feuerwehr Mar-88 $25-45
Red Body, 2 Blue Roof Lights & Silver Center Spot Light, White "NOTRUF 112" on Doors, White "N" on Roof Over Windshield. (Produced for the German Market.)
C 542 Mercedes Bonna Ambulance Jan-89 $25-45
White Body with Red from Beltline Down, Red Stripe on Side of Roof, White "AMBULANSE" and "RODE KORS HJELPEKORPS" on Sides, Red "AMBULANSE" Added over Windshield. (Produced for the Norwegian Market.)
C 543 Ford Escort Van Jun-85 $25-45
Lt. Blue Body "TELE," Rear Bumper Part of Base. (Produced for the Norwegian Market.)
C 548 Mercedes 207D Van Jul-85 $25-45
Securitas
C 549 Ford Escort Van Aug-85 $25-45
Beige/Brown Body "Hotpoint," Rear Bumper Part of Base.
C 554 Mercedes 207D Van Aug-86 $25-45
PTT. (Produced for the Swiss Market.)
C 557 Ford Escort Van Jan-86 $20-30
Yellow Body with Black "FIRE SALVAGE," Blue Lightbar on Roof, Rear Bumper Part of Base. (Also Found in Set C6.)
C 558 Routemaster Bus, Open Top Jul-85 $25-45
Southern Vectis, "Radio Victory."
C 559 Ford Escort Van May-85 $25-45
Silver Body "Jago Automotive," Rear Bumper Part of Base.
C 560 Ford Escort Van Jan-86 $25-45
Red Body with "WILTSHIRE FIRE SERVICE" Labels, Black Ladder on Roof, Rear Bumper Part of Base.
C 561 Ford Escort Van Jun-85 $25-45
White Body "WAITROSE," Rear Bumper Part of Base.
C 562 Ford Escort Van Aug-85 $25-45
a White Body "Gamley's," Bear on Hood, Rear Bumper Part of Base.
b Red Body, "Gamley's" Labels, Rear Bumper Part of Base.
c White Body, "Gamley's" Labels (Code 2 by Gamley's), Rear Bumper Part of Base. (Surplus Stock from Mettoy.)
C 563 Ford Escort Van Dec-85 $25-45
Blue Body "McVities," Rear Bumper Part of Base.
C 564 Ford Escort Van Aug-86 $35-55
White Body "Televerket," Orange Side Stripe with Blue Door Logo. (Produced for the Swedish Market.)
C 567 Routemaster Bus **Not Produced** N/A
Not Produced, Was to be Lincoln City.
C 567 Routemaster Bus Nov-85 $25-45
White Body, London Transport, "See More London."
C 568 Mercedes 207D Van Mar-86 $20-30
Black Body with Black Roof Rack, Red/Blue/White Side Stripe, White "BFGoodrich."
C 570 Routemaster Bus Jul-85 $25-45
Bus Collectors Society
C 571 Routemaster Bus Jul-85 $25-45
Bi-Centenary Times, (Maroon)
C 572 Routemaster Bus Jul-85 $25-45
Bi-Centenary Times, (Blue)
C 574 Routemaster Bus Jun-85 $25-45
Red/White Body, "Blackpool Tramway Centenary."
C 575 Mercedes 207D Van 1985? $???
"Hertz," Other Details Not Known.
C 576 Mercedes 207D Van Mar-86 $18-20
White Body with Blue Area Below Belt Line, Red Roof, "PEPSI."
C 576/02 Mercedes 207D Van Jan-87 $18-20
White Body, Black Roof Rack with Silver & Red Racing Parts, "PORSCHE KREMER RACING."
C 576/03 Mercedes 207D Van Jan-87 $25-45
Green/Black Body, "Parceline."
C 576/04 Mercedes 207D Van Feb-87 $35-55
"FALCK." (Produced for the Danish Market.)
C 576/05 Mercedes 207D Van Jun-87 $35-55
Bahlsen. (Produced for the German Market.)
C 576/06 Mercedes 207D Van Jan-88 $35-55
Red Body, Blue Roof Light, "18," "SAPEURS POMPIERS," "AMBULANCE DE REANIMATION." (Produced for the French Market.)
C 576/07 Mercedes 207D Van May-87 $35-55
White Body, Red "LEKER OB HOBBY" Logo & Stripe. (Produced for the Norwegian Market.)
C 576/08? Mercedes 207D Van 1988? $35-55
"PTT," Other Details Not Known.
C 576/09 Mercedes 207D Van Jan-88 $18-20
White/Orange Body, "TNT Overnite." (Known with 2 wheel types.)
C 576/10 Mercedes 207D Van Aug-89 $25-45
C R Smith Double Glazing
Q 576/11 Mercedes 207D Van Nov-90 $25-45
Donald Murray Paper
C 577 Ford Escort Van Aug-85 $25-45
a White/Sky Blue Body "Plessey," Round Oval Crest with 3 Stars, Rear Bumper Part of Base.
b White/Sky Blue Body "Plessey," Round Oval Crest with 3 Feathers, Rear Bumper Part of Base.
C 578 Ford Escort Van Sep-85 $25-45
Black Body "Beatties," Rear Bumper Part of Base.
C 580 Routemaster Bus Sep-85 $25-45
Blue Body, "Guide Dogs for the Blind."
C 583 Routemaster Bus Aug-85 $25-45
Yellow/Black Body, "Manchester Evening News."
C 584 Ford Escort Van Aug-85 $25-45
Yellow/Black Body "Manchester Evening News," Rear Bumper Part of Base.
C 588 Mercedes 207D Van Sep-85 $25-45
Curtis Holt
C 589 Routemaster Bus Sep-85 $25-45
Red Body, London Transport Logo, "Autospares."
C 590 Routemaster Bus, Open Top Sep-85 $25-45
Hatfield Lions "MEDIC ALERT," Mauve/Yellow Body.
C 591 Routemaster Bus Sep-85 $25-45
Hatfield Lions "MEDIC ALERT," Mauve/Yellow Body.
C 595/04 AEC DD Bus Apr-88 $25-45
Glasgow Corporation
C 596 Routemaster Bus Jan-86 $25-45
London Transport Circle Logo, "Harrod's."
C 597 Range Rover Feb-86 $18-25
a White Body, Blue/White Lightbar toward Rear of Roof, Red Side Stripe "AMBULANCE" Over Black Chevrons, Red Cross & Red Rectangle "AMBULANCE" on Hood.
b White Body, Blue/White Lightbar toward Rear of Roof, Brown Side Stripe "AMBULANCE" Over Black Chevrons, Red Cross & Red Rectangle "AMBULANCE" on Hood.
C 597/03 Range Rover May-89 $18-25
White Body, Blue/White Lightbar toward Rear of Roof, Checkered Side Trim, "POLICE" in Blue Rectangle on Hood.
C 597/05 Range Rover Jun-89 $35-55
Red with Blue Lightbar toward Rear of Roof, "FEURWEHR 118." (Produced for the Swiss Market.)
C 597/06 Range Rover Jul-89 $35-55
White Body with Red Stripe on Hood and Roof, Blue Roof Light, "SOS 101," (Produced for the Belgian Market.)
C 597/99 Range Rover 1987? $35-55
White Body, Red Hood, Red Side Stripe, "POLIZEI," 1 Blue & 1 Amber Roof Light. (Part of Set C1412, Produced for the Swiss Market.)
C 598 Range Rover Mar-86 $18-25
White Body, Blue/White Lightbar toward Rear of Roof, Checkered Side Trim, "POLICE" in Blue Rectangle on Hood.
C 599 AEC DD Bus Feb-86 $25-45
London Transport, "WISK."
C 599/01 AEC DD Bus Jan-87 $25-45
Eastbourne Corporation — "WOODHAMS"
C 599/02 AEC DD Bus Feb-87 $25-45
Nottingham City Transport — "TRUSTEE SAVINGS BANK"
C 599/03 AEC DD Bus May-87 $25-45
Huntley & Palmers
C 599/04 AEC DD Bus 1988? $25-45
Glasgow Corporation ... "Crown Wallpapers."
C 599/05 AEC DD Bus Dec-88 $25-45
Rhondda, "PREMIUM SAVINGS BONDS."
D 599/06 AEC DD Bus Jan-89 $25-45
Morecambe & Heysham
D 599/07 AEC DD Bus Aug-89 $25-45
Bradford Corporation
D 599/09 AEC DD Bus Feb-90 $25-45
Western (Paisley)
D 599/10 AEC DD Bus Aug-90 $25-45
Brighton & Hove
D 599/11 AEC DD Bus Aug-90 $25-45
Dublin
D 599/12 AEC DD Bus Nov-90 $25-45
RAF "Wings for Victory"
Q 599/13 AEC DD Bus Sep-90 $25-45
Halifax
Q 599/99 AEC DD Bus, Open Top Jan-91 $25-45
White/Red Body, Red Interior, "Beatties ..."
C 600 Ford Escort Apr-84 $15-18
a Red Body. (1984 Transitional Number for C334.)
b Red Body, White Twin Side Stripe.

C 601　Fiat X1/9　Apr-84　$15-18
a Blue Body. (1984 Transitional Number for C314.)
b Silver Body, Red Stripe on Lower Side.
c Red Body.

C 602　Mini　Apr-84　$15-18
a Silver Body. (1984 Transitional Number for C330.)
b Orange Body, Red Side Stripe "CITY."

C 603　VW Polo　Apr-84　$15-18
a Cream Body. (1984 Transitional Number for C309.)
b White Body, Blue Twin Side Stripe.
c "PTT," Other Details Not Known

C 604　Renault 5　Apr-84　$15-18
a Dk. Blue Body. (1984 Transitional Number for C294.)
b Black Body, Red Side Stripe.

C 605　Mini Metro　Apr-84　$15-18
a Red Body. (1984 Transitional Number for C275.)
b Off Tan Body, Black Lower Sides with Red "TURBO."
c Blue Body.

C 611　Ford Escort Datapost Rally #66　Apr-84　$15-18
a Red Body "Datapost Rally 66," Black Interior, LH or RH Drive.
b Red Body "Datapost Rally 66," Tan Interior, LH or RH Drive.

C 612　Ford Escort Datapost Rally #77　Apr-84　$15-18
a Red Body "Datapost Rally 77," Black Interior, LH or RH Drive.
b Red Body "Datapost Rally 77," Tan Interior, LH or RH Drive.

C 613　Austin Mini Metro Datapost Rally #66　Apr-84　$15-18
Red Body "Datapost Rally #66."

C 614　Austin Mini Metro Datapost Rally #77　Apr-84　$15-18
Red Body "Datapost Rally #77."

C 615　Austin Mini Metro Van Royal Mail　Apr-84　$20-22
Red Body "Royal Mail," Rear Windows Painted Red.

C 616　General Motors Van "Royal Mail Parcels"　Apr-84　$15-18
Red Body "Royal Mail Parcels."

C 617　Land Rover　Apr-84　$15-18
Red Body "Royal Mail Parcels."

C 618　Superhaulers — Volvo Articulated Truck　Oct-85　$12-20
Red Body "Royal Mail Parcels."

C 619　Land Rover　Mar-86　$15-18
Tan Body with Simulated Mud Splatter, Black Roof Rack with Silver & Red Equipment, Black Diagonal "Safari" on Doors.

C 619/02　Land Rover　Mar-88　$25-30
Red Body, White Roof, "SAPEURS POMPIERS," "18." (Produced for the French Market.)

Q 619/03　Land Rover　May-90　$15-18
NORWEB

C 621　Ford Escort Van　Apr-86　$15-18
a White Body, Blue/White Lightbar on Roof, Blue Outlined Red Stripe on Sides, Large Blue "POLICE" Label on Hood, Rear Bumper Part of Base.
b White Body, Blue/White Lightbar on Roof, Blue Outlined Red Stripe on Sides, Medium Blue "POLICE" Label on Hood, Rear Bumper Part of Base.
c White Body, Blue/White Lightbar on Roof, Blue Outlined Red Stripe on Sides, Medium Blue "POLICE" Label on Hood, Rear Bumper Part of Body.
d White Body, Blue/White Lightbar on Roof, Blue Outlined Red Stripe on Sides, Blue "POLICE" Tampo on Hood, Rear Bumper Part of Body.

C 625/02　Routemaster Bus, Open Top　Jul-90　$25-45
London Transport, "Sightseeing"

C 626　Ford Escort Van　Mar-86　$25-45
Lt. Blue Body "Chubb Fire Cover," Rear Bumper Part of Base.

C 627　Routemaster Bus　Mar-86　$25-45
Edinburgh Corporation, "MODEL MOTORING."

C 628　Routemaster Bus　Feb-86　$25-45
Red Body, "POLIO PLUS"

C 630　Mercedes 207D Van　Aug-86　$25-45
Blue Arrow

C 631　Mercedes 207D Van　Jun-86　$25-45
Kay's

C 632　Ford Escort Van　Jun-86　$25-45
White Body "Kay's," Rear Bumper Part of Body.

C 633　Routemaster Bus　May-86　$25-45
Blue Body, "Hospital Radio."

C 634　AEC DD Bus　Aug-86　$25-45
Maples

C 638　Routemaster Bus　Jun-86　$25-45
Weetabix

C 640　Mini Metro　Jun-86　$20-30
Kay's

C 643　AEC DD Bus　Oct-86　$25-45
Newcastle Amber Ale

C 647　Buck Rogers Starfighter　Apr-84　$60-70
White Body, 2 Figures. (Continuation of Mettoy Era 647.)

C 648　NASA Space Shuttle　Apr-84　$18-20
White/Black Body, Red/Gold/Silver Satellite. (Continuation of Mettoy Era 648.)

C 650　Concord　Apr-84　$18-20
British Airways.

C 650/01　Concord　Jan-88　$18-20
British Airways.

C 656/01　Ford Transit Van　Aug-87　$15-18
White Body, Blue/Red Side Stripe, Blue/White Lightbar Toward Front of Roof, "RAC RESCUE SERVICE."

C 656/02　Ford Transit Van　Jul-87　$15-18
Royal Mail Datapost

C 656/03　Ford Transit Van　Jul-87　$15-18
White Body, Red Cross and Stripe on Sides Red/White Lightbar on Roof, "ambulance" on Sides and over Windshield, Reversed "ambulance" on Hood.

C 656/04　Ford Transit Van　Jul-87　$15-18
White Body, Blue/Black/Red Diagonal Stripes, "TRANSIT," Ford logo, "Shell," "Goodyear" on Sides.

C 656/05　Ford Transit Van　Aug-87　$15-18
Yellow Body, White/Black Side Stripe, Red/White Lightbar Toward Rear of Roof, "AA Service."

C 656/07　Ford Transit Van　Oct-87　$30-50
Yellow Body, Danish Post Office Markings. (Produced for the Danish Market.)

C 656/08　Ford Transit Van　Oct-87　$30-50
Dark Blue Body, Blue Lightbar on Roof "POLISI," Thin White Side Stripe with "POLIS." (Produced for the Finnish Market.)

C 656/12　Ford Transit Van　Mar-88　$30-50
Orange Body, "Ktas." (Produced for the Danish Market.)

C 656/13　Ford Transit Van　Mar-88　$30-50
White Body, Blue/White Roof Lightbar, "FALCK." (Produced for the Danish Market.)

C 656/16　Ford Transit Van　Mar-88　$30-50
Yellow Body, "DBP," "Schreib mal wieder." (Produced for the German Market.)

C 656/18　Ford Transit Van　Jun-88　$30-50
Red Body, "FALCK," " SERVICE VOGN." (Produced for the Danish Market.)

C 656/21　Ford Transit Van　Jan-89　$25-45
Lynx

C 656/28　Ford Transit Van　Apr-90　$25-45
"NOTTINGHAMSHIRE AMBULANCE SERVICE," White, 2 Red Roof Lights Mounted Diagonally

Q 656/29　Ford Transit Van　Feb-90　$15-18
Center Parcs, Elveden Forest Holiday Village

Q 656/30　Ford Transit Van　Feb-90　$15-18
Center Parcs, Sherwood Forest Holiday Village

Q 656/31　Ford Transit Van　Mar-90　$25-45
UniChem

Q 656/33　Ford Transit Van　Aug-90　$25-45
MacDougall Rose

C 674/01　Ford Transit Breakdown　May-88　$15-18
a AA Service, "Relay" Labels.
b AA Service, "Rescue" Labels

C 674/02　Ford Transit Breakdown　Jun-88　$15-18
RAC Rescue Service

C 674/04　Ford Transit Breakdown　Aug-88　$25-30
Bargningskaren, (Produced for the Swedish Market.)

C 675/01　Metrobus　Aug-88　$20-35
West Midland Travel Timesaver

C 675/02　Metrobus　Sep-88　$30-35
Reading Transport GOLDLINE.

C 675/03　Metrobus　Oct-88　$20-35
West Midland Travel

C 675/04　Metrobus　Sep-88　$22-25
Beatties, London Transport

C 675/05　Metrobus　1988?　$22-25
Beeline/Sanfords, Other Details Not Known.

C 675/06　Metrobus　Apr-89　$20-35
FastLinK, White Upper Body, Red Lower Body

C 675/07　Metrobus　Dec-88　$30-35
Hitachi, Black Body, (1988 Christmas Special)

Q 675/09　Metrobus　Nov-89　$20-35
Newcastle Busways

C 675/10　Metrobus　Nov-89　$20-35
a Beatties, Black Doors.
b Beatties, Yellow Doors.

Q 675/12　Metrobus　Nov-89　$20-35
Maidstone and District

Q 675/13　Metrobus　Nov-89　$20-35
East Kent

C 675/14　Metrobus　Feb-90　$20-35
G.M. Buses

Q 675/15　Metrobus　Mar-90　$20-35
Go-Ahead Northern, "National Garden Festival, Gateshead 1990."

C 675/16　Metrobus　Nov-90　$20-35
Bluebird

C 676/01　Ford Transit Bus　May-88　$15-30
Scottish Midland Bluebird

C 676/02　Ford Transit Bus　Jun-88　$15-30
South Wales Transport City Mini

C 676/03　Ford Transit Bus　Jul-88　$15-30
Badgerline Mini Link

C 676/04　Ford Transit Bus　Aug-88　$30-50
White Body, "FALCK SYGETRANSPORT." (Produced for the Danish Market.)

C 676/05　Ford Transit Bus　Nov-88　$15-30
Royal Mail Post Bus, Red Body, Yellow Roof.

C 676/06　Ford Transit Bus　Oct-89　$15-30
Chaserider Mini Bus

C 676/07　Ford Transit Bus　Apr-89　$15-30
British Airways

C 676/08　Ford Transit Bus　1989?　$15-30
British Airways — Club Group

C 676/09　Ford Transit Bus　1989?　$15-30
National Welsh

C 676/10　Ford Transit Bus　1989?　$30-50
Ambulans (Produced for the Swedish Market.)

C 676/11　Ford Transit Bus　1989?　$30-50
Polis (Produced for the Swedish Market.)

C 676/12　Ford Transit Bus　Apr-90　$15-30
Oxford City Nipper

C 700/01　Jaguar Mk.II Saloon　Nov-88　$15-18
Red

C 700/02　Jaguar Mk.II Saloon　1988　$15-18
Silver

C 700/03　Jaguar Mk.II Saloon　Dec-88　$15-18
Black, (1988 Christmas Special)

D 700/04　Jaguar Mk II Saloon　Mar-89　$15-18
Beige, (Photo Looks Like Silver in CCC Magazine.)

D 700/05　Jaguar Mk II Saloon　Mar-89　$15-18
Green

D 700/06 Jaguar Mk II Saloon Metallic Blue	Aug-89	$15-18
D 700/07 Jaguar Mk II Saloon Metallic Grey	Oct-89	$15-18
D 700/08 Jaguar Mk II Saloon Silver Blue	Feb-90	$15-18
D 700/09 Jaguar Mk II Saloon Willow Green	May-90	$15-18
D 700/10 Jaguar Mk.II Saloon Opalescent Maroon body	Nov-90	$15-18
D 701/01 Ford Popular Saloon Lt. Blue	1989?	$15-18
D 701/03 Ford Popular Saloon Black	Jan-89	$15-18
D 701/05 Ford Popular Saloon Fawn (Tan)	Jul-89	$15-18
D 701/07 Ford Popular Saloon Pale Green	Nov-89	$15-18
D 701/08 Ford Popular Saloon Grey	Jan-90	$15-18
D 701/09 Ford Popular Saloon Whinchester Blue	Apr-90	$15-18
C 702/01 Morris Minor Saloon BSM, Black Body with "L" Plates on Ends.	Nov-88	$15-18
C 702/02 Morris Minor Saloon Black	Nov-88	$15-18
D 702/04 Morris Minor Saloon Lilac	Jan-89	$15-18
D 702/05 Morris Minor Saloon Maroon	Jan-89	$15-18
D 702/06 Morris Minor Saloon Almond Green	Jan-90	$15-18
D 702/07 Morris Minor Saloon Ivory	Jan-90	$15-18
D 702/08 Morris Minor Saloon Clipper Blue	Apr-90	$15-18
D 702/09 Morris Minor Saloon Sage Green	Dec-90	$15-18
C 703/01 Morris Minor Police	Jul-88	$15-18

a Lt. Blue from Base of Windshield Forward and from B-Pillar to Rear, White Center, Large "POLICE" Sign on Roof, Black "POLICE" in Yellow Rectangle on Sides. (May Be Pre-Production Model.)
b Lt. Blue with White Doors, Black "POLICE" on Doors, Small White "POLICE" Sign on Roof, Thick Vent Window Post.
c Lt. Blue with White Doors, Black "POLICE" on Doors, Small White "POLICE" Sign on Roof, Thin Vent Window Post.

C 706/01 Jaguar Mk.II Police	Nov-88	$15-18
White Body, Black Beveled "POLICE" Sign with Blue Light on Roof.		
D 708/01 Ford Cortina	May-89	$15-18
White Body, Olive Green Side Trim Stripe.		
D 708/02 Ford Cortina Maroon	Jun-89	$15-18
D 708/03 Ford Cortina Monaco Red	Nov-89	$15-18
D 708/04 Ford Cortina Aqua Blue	Nov-89	$15-18
D 708/06 Ford Cortina	Jan-90	$15-18
White, "POLICE" in Blue Rectangle on Doors, Small "POLICE" Sign on Roof.		
D 708/07 Ford Cortina Black	Feb-90	$15-18
D 708/08 Ford Cortina Spruce Green	May-90	$15-18
D 708/09 Ford Cortina	Nov-90	$15-18
White body, black hood, green side stripe, black seats.		
D 709/01 Ford Zodiac Maroon/Grey	Apr-89	$15-18
D 709/02 Ford Zodiac Dk. Blue/Lt. Blue	Apr-89	$15-18
D 709/03 Ford Zodiac Yellow/White	Sep-89	$15-18
D 709/04 Ford Zodiac Red/White	Dec-89	$15-18
D 709/05 Ford Zodiac Black/Blue	Mar-90	$15-18
D 709/06 Ford Zodiac Black/Blue	Mar-90	$15-18
D 709/07 Ford Zodiac	Jun-90	$15-18
a Linden Green/Lime		
b Linden Green/Yellow (Known Production Error.)		
D 709/08 Ford Zodiac Ermine White/Gray	Nov-90	$15-18
D 710/01 Ford Zephyr Black	Jun-89	$15-18
D 710/02 Ford Zephyr Dk. Blue	Jun-89	$15-18
D 710/03 Ford Zephyr Monaco Red	Sep-89	$15-18
D 710/04 Ford Zephyr Regency Grey	Dec-89	$15-18
D 710/06 Ford Zephyr Maroon (Shown in CCC Magazine as Red)	Mar-90	$15-18
D 710/07 Ford Zephyr Pompadour Blue	Jun-90	$15-18
D 710/12 Ford Zephyr Linden Green	Dec-90	$15-18

D 711/02 Saab 96 Blue	Sep-90	$15-18
D 712/01 Saab 96 Rally Red, "283" & "Rallye Monte-Carlo"	Dec-90	$15-18
D 730/08 MGA, Hard Top Silver Body, Black Top	Apr-90	$20-22
D 731/01 MGA, Top Down British Racing Green	Mar-90	$20-22
D 732/01 MGA, Top Up Red Body, Black Top	May-90	$20-22
D 733/01 Austin Healey, Hard Top P.O. Red, "2" on Doors	Jul-90	$20-22
D 734/01 Austin Healey, Top Down Lt. Met. Blue	Jun-90	$20-22
D 735/01 Austin Healey, Top Up Pacific Green, Gray Top	Aug-90	$20-22
D 736/01 Triumph TR3a, Hard Top P.O. Red, Black Top	Aug-90	$20-22
D 737/01 Triumph TR3a, Top Down Pale Blue	Jul-90	$20-22
D 738/01 Triumph TR3a, Top Up Primrose Yellow	Sep-90	$20-22
D 739/01 Ferrari 250 GTO Red, "151" Rally Decorations	Nov-90	$15-18
D 740/01 Ferrari 250 GTO Red, (Road Version)	Sep-90	$15-18
D 741/01 Porsche 356, Top Up Red	Nov-90	$15-18
D 742/01 Porsche 356, Top Down White	Dec-90	$15-18
Q 750/02 Cameo — Model T Ford Van Royal Mail	Aug-90	$4-6
Q 752/02 Cameo — Bedford Bus Heinz	Aug-90	$4-6
Q 753/05 Cameo — AEC Box Van Stabilo	Aug-90	$4-6
Q 754/03 Cameo — Morris Tanker Cornish Cream	Aug-90	$4-6
C 769 Plaxton Coach	Apr-84	$20-25
a Rapide NATIONAL EXPRESS, White Body.		
b Rapide NATIONAL EXPRESS, Silver Gray Body.		
C 769/01 Plaxton Coach Club Cantabrica	Jan-87	$20-25
C 769/04 Plaxton Coach SAS FLYBUSSEN. (Produced for the Norwegian Market.)	Aug-87	$25-40
C 769/05 Plaxton Coach Global	Mar-88	$20-25
C 769/06 Plaxton Coach Pohjolan Lijkenne, (Produced for the Finnish Market.)	Nov-88	$25-40
C 769/07 Plaxton Coach Scottish Citylink	Nov-90	$18-20
C 769/08 Plaxton Coach Bluebird Express	Nov-90	$20-25
C 770 Plaxton Coach Silver Gray Body "Holiday Tours."	Jun-85	$20-25
C 771 Plaxton Coach Air France. (Produced for the French Market.)	Jun-85	$20-25
C 772 Plaxton Coach SAS	May-86	$20-25
C 773 Plaxton Coach Greenline.	Jun-85	$20-25
C 774 Plaxton Coach Railair Link	Jun-85	$20-25
C 775 Plaxton Coach	Dec-85	$20-25
a Oxford Citylink		
b Citylink Oxford		
C 776 Plaxton Coach Skills	Dec-85	$20-25
C 777 Plaxton Coach Taylors	Jul-85	$20-25
C 791 Plaxton Coach PTT Reisebus. (Produced for the Swiss Market.)	Dec-85	$60-65
C 792 Plaxton Coach Gatwick Flightline	Mar-86	$20-25
C 793 Plaxton Coach Instasun Express.	Mar-86	$20-25
C 799 Compressor	1984?	$30-40
"GAS," Possibly the Compressor Trailer Portion of Mettoy Era Corgitronics C1107 but without Sound. Details Not Known.		
C 803 1952 Jaguar XK120, Top Up	Apr-84	$20-22
Red Body with Fender Skirts, Black Top, No Graphics. (Continuation of Mettoy Era 803.)		
C 804 1952 Jaguar XK120, Top Down	Apr-84	$20-22
a White Body with out Fender Skirts, Black Hood Strap, "414" on Doors. (Continuation of Mettoy Era 804.)		
b Ivory Body with out Fender Skirts, Black Hood Strap, "414" on Doors.		
c Ivory Body with Fender Skirts, Black Hood Strap, "414" on Doors.		
C 805 1954 Mercedes 300S, Top Up	Apr-84	$20-22
a Lt. Gray Body, Black Top. (Continuation of Mettoy Era 805 which was Red With a Tan Top.)		
b White Body, Black Top.		
c Red Body, Other Details Not Known.		
d Tan/Beige Body, Zinc Base Introduced.		
C 805/01 1954 Mercedes 300S, Top Up Blue Body.	Mar-87	$20-22
C 806 1954 Mercedes 300S, Top Down	Apr-84	$20-22
a Dk. Gray Body. (Continuation of Mettoy Era 806 which was Black.)		

b Blue Body.
c Black/Silver, Zinc Base Introdrced.
C 806/01 1954 Mercedes 300S, Top Down — Mar-87 — $20-22
Red Body.
C 810 1957 Ford Thunderbird — Apr-84 — $20-22
a Cream Body, Red Below Belt Line, White Wall Wheels. (Continuation of Mettoy 810 which was Various Colors Including Yellow.)
b Red Body, White Side Fins, White Wall Wheels.
C 810/02 1957 Ford Thunderbird — Jun-88 — $20-22
Black Body, White Striped Fin, White Wall Tires, Red/White Seats.
C 811 1954 Mercedes 300 SL Gullwing Coupe — Apr-84 — $20-22
Silver Body. (Continuation of Mettoy Era 811.)
C 811/01 1954 Mercedes 300 SL Gullwing Coupe — Jan-87 — $20-22
Silver Body. (1987 Renumbering of C811.)
C 812 1953 MG TF, Top Down — Apr-84 — $20-22
a Yellow (?) Body, Full Windshield.
b Black Body, Full Windshield.
c Green Body, Full Windshield.
C 813 1953 MG TF, Top Up — Apr-84 — $20-22
Red Body, Black Top.
C 814 1952 Rolls Royce Silver Dawn, Top Down — Apr-84 — $20-22
Red/Black Body.
C 814 1952 Rolls Royce Silver Dawn, Top Down — Apr-86 — $20-22
Tan/White Body, Zinc Base Introduced.
C 814/01 1952 Rolls Royce Silver Dawn, Top Down — 1987? — $20-22
Silver/Black Body.
C 815 1954 Bentley 'R' Type, Top Up — Apr-84 — $20-22
a Bronze Body, Black Top.
b Black Body, Tan Top.
c Lt. Blue/Dk. Blue, Black Top, Zinc Base Introduced.
C 815/01 1954 Bentley 'R' Type, Top Up — 1987? — $20-22
Tan/White Body.
C 816 1952 Jaguar XK120, Top Down — Jun-86 — $20-22
Red Body, Green Circle with "56."
C 819 1952 Jaguar XK120, Top Down — Apr-84 — $20-22
a White Body with out Fender Skirts, Either "7" or "414" on Sides. (Catalog Data Conflicts. Possibly a Repackaging of C804.)
b White Body with Fender Skirts, Black Top, Black "7" on Doors.
C 820 Thorneycroft Open Truck with Canvas Cover — Jan-85 — $18-30
a Dark Brown Body "East Anglian Fruit Co," with Planks.
b Dark Brown Body "East Anglian Fruit Co," with out Planks.
C 821 Thorneycroft Box Van — Jan-86 — $18-30
a Green Body "Castrol," Green Roof, Black Hood.
b Green Body "Castrol," Black Roof, Black Hood.
c Green Body "Castrol," Green Roof, Green Hood.
d Green Body "Castrol," Black Roof, Green Hood.
C 821/01 Thorneycroft Box Van — Jan-88 — $18-30
Buhrmann Tettrode "HEIDELBERGER DRUKAUTOMAAT." (Produced for the Dutch Market.)
C 822/01 Bedford Box Van — Jun-88 — $18-30
Persil
D 822/02 Bedford Box Van — Nov-88 — $18-30
Tate & Lyle
C 822/03 Bedford Box Van — Sep-88 — $18-30
Gillette
D 822/04 Bedford Box Van — Mar-89 — $18-30
a Carter Paterson and Pickfords, "SOLIDOX," Body Color Roof.
b Carter Paterson and Pickfords, "SOLIDOX," Red Roof.
C 822/05 Bedford Box Van — Mar-89 — $18-30
Miller's.
D 822/07 Bedford Box Van — Aug-89 — $18-30
Cadbury
D 822/08 Bedford Box Van — Dec-89 — $18-30
Maltesers
D 822/09 Bedford Box Van — Jul-89 — $18-30
Royal Mail. (Part of D7/01 Set.)
D 822/10 Bedford Box Van — Mar-90 — $18-30
Terry's of York
D 822/11 Bedford Box Van — Aug-90 — $16-18
LNER Express Parcels Service
D 822/12 Bedford Box Van — Nov-90 — $28-30
Toymaster
D 822/13 Bedford Box Van — 1990? — $18-30
a British Railways, Ads Forward on Sides, Logo on Front of Box.
b British Railways, Ads Forward on Sides, No Logo on Front of Box.
c British Railways, Ads Rearward on Sides, Logo on Front of Box.
d British Railways, Ads Rearward on Sides, Logo on Front of Box, Small Print Behind Cab instead of at Rear of Sides.
C 823 Renault Open Truck — Jan-85 — $18-30
a Brown Cab & Rear Body, Black Hood & Fenders, Cross Symbol on Cab Sides.
b "J. GOULARD," Other Details Not Known.
C 824 Renault Box Van — 1985? — $18-30
Patisserie Marcel Gardet, Paris
C 824/02 Renault Box Van — May-88 — $18-30
Herloin
C 824/03 Renault Box Van — Aug-88 — $18-30
The' Lipton
C 824/12 Renault Box Van — 1989? — $20-22
Valognes
C 825 1957 Chevrolet Bel Air — Jan-85 — $20-22
Red Body, White Roof & Side Trim.
C 825/01 1957 Chevrolet Bel Air — Mar-87 — $20-22
Black Body, White Roof & Side Trim.
C 825/02 1957 Chevrolet Bel Air — Jun-88 — $20-22
Med. Blue Body, White Roof & Side Trim.
C 827 Thorneycroft Open Truck with Canvas Cover — Jul-85 — $18-30
a Dark Brown Body, Tan Cover, "GWR Express Cartage Service."
b Dark Brown Body, Tan Cover, GWR Logo on Cab Sides.
C 828 Thorneycroft Box Van — Jul-85 — $18-30
Blue Body "Gamley's."
C 830 Thorneycroft Box Van — May-85 — $18-30
Tan Body, White Roof, "Jacob's."
C 831 Thorneycroft Box Van — Jun-85 — $18-30
Huntley & Palmer
C 832 Thorneycroft Box Van — Jan-86 — $30-50
a "Corgi Collector Club 1st Anniversary," Address Stacked Vertically.
b "Corgi Collector Club 1st Anniversary," Address Spread Horizontally.
C 833 Thorneycroft Box Van — Jan-85 — $18-30
Green Body "MacFarlane-Lang."
C 834 Thorneycroft Box Van — Jul-85 — $18-30
Blue Body "Lyons Swiss Roll."
C 836 Thorneycroft Open Truck with Canvas Cover — Dec-85 — $18-30
Maroon Body "LMS Express Traffic Services"
C 837 Thorneycroft Open Truck with Canvas Cover — Oct-85 — $18-30
Green Body "S R Express Parcels Services."
C 838 Thorneycroft Open Truck with Canvas Cover — Aug-85 — $18-30
Blue Body "LNER Express Parcels Service."
C 839 Thorneycroft Box Van — Jun-85 — $18-30
Blue Body "Nurdin & Peacock."
C 840 Thorneycroft Box Van — Sep-85 — $18-30
Red/Beige Body "Allenbury's Foods."
C 841 Thorneycroft Box Van — Nov-85 — $18-30
a Beige/Green Body "Peek Freans" with Windshield.
b Beige/Green Body "Peek Freans" with out Windshield.
C 842 Thorneycroft Box Van — Aug-85 — $18-30
Green/Black Body "Carter Paterson," "Schweppes Seltzer Water."
C 843 Thorneycroft Box Van — Aug-85 — $18-30
Dk. Brown Body "Eddershaws."
C 845 Thorneycroft Box Van — Jun-85 — $18-30
a Silver Body "Duckham's Oils," Spoked Wheels.
b Silver Body "Duckham's Oils," Disk Wheels.
C 846 Thorneycroft Box Van — Aug-85 — $18-30
Lt. Green Body "Ind Coope & Allsopps."
C 847 Thorneycroft Box Van — Oct-85 — $18-30
Beige/Gray Body "James Keiller."
C 848 Thorneycroft Box Van — Oct-85 — $18-30
Black Body "News of the World."
C 853 Thorneycroft Box Van — Sep-85 — $18-30
Beige/Red Body "M.A.Rapport."
C 854 Thorneycroft Box Van — Jun-85 — $18-30
White Body "Lincolnshire Ambulance."
C 855 Thorneycroft Box Van — Jun-85 — $18-30
Red Body "Lincolnshire Fire."
C 856 Thorneycroft Box Van — Jun-85 — $18-30
Dk. Blue Body "Lincolnshire Police."
C 858 Thorneycroft DD Bus — Jul-86 — $20-25
a General — "SANDEMAN," Top Rail with 4 Supports.
b General — "SANDEMAN," Top Rail with 8 Supports.
C 858/01 Thorneycroft DD Bus — Jan-87 — $18-30
General — "NATIONAL MOTOR MUSEUM"
C 858/02 Thorneycroft DD Bus — Mar-87 — $18-30
Douglas Corporation Tramways — "CHARLIE CHAPLIN'S ..."
C 858/03 Thorneycroft DD Bus — May-87 — $18-30
Cambrian, "WALTER'S PALM TOFFEE."
C 858/04 Thorneycroft DD Bus — Jun-87 — $18-30
Vanguard, "IDRIS."
C 858/06 Thorneycroft DD Bus — Feb-88 — $18-30
L&NWR
C 858/07 Thorneycroft DD Bus — May-88 — $18-30
General, "OAKEY'S KNIFE POLISH"
C 858/09 Thorneycroft DD Bus — 1988? — $18-30
"Baxters" (From Set C89/01).
C 858/10 Thorneycroft DD Bus — 1988? — $18-30
General, "Schweppes Tonic Water"
C 858/11 Thorneycroft DD Bus — Dec-88 — $18-30
Great Eastern Railway, (1988 Christmas Special)
C 859 Thorneycroft Box Van — Apr-86 — $30-40
Yellow Body, Red Hood, Roof Rack, Roof & Chassis, "THORLEY'S FOOD for CATTLE."
C 859/01 Thorneycroft Box Van — Jan-87 — $30-40
Blue Body & Roof Rack, Red Roof & Fenders, "SCOTT'S EMPIRE BREAD."
C 859/02 Thorneycroft Box Van — Feb-87 — $30-40
Chivers & Sons Ltd.
C 859/03 Thorneycroft Box Van — Feb-87 — $65-75
Red/Black Body "Arnott's Biscuits." (Produced for the Austrailian Market.)
C 859/04 Thorneycroft Box Van — Jun-87 — $55-65
a Lt. Blue/Black Body "Goodyear Wingfoot Express," Brown Cowl Framing. (Produced for the U.S. Market.)
b Lt. Blue/Black Body "Goodyear Wingfoot Express," Gray Cowl Framing. (Produced for the U.S. Market. Rerun.)
C 859/05 Thorneycroft Box Van — Aug-87 — $18-30
Green Body "Grattan Warehouses Ltd."
C 859/05 Thorneycroft Box Van — Sep-88 — $18-30
Batchelor's Peas
C 859/06 Thorneycroft Box Van — Jun-87 — $18-30
Maroon Body "Kay's." (Part of Set C68.)
C 859/?? Thorneycroft Box Van — Jun-87 — $18-30
Red/White Body "Bryant & May." (Part of Set C69.)
C 859/07 Thorneycroft Box Van — Dec-88 — $18-30
Leda Salt

C 859/08 Thorneycroft Box Van		Apr-88	$18-30
Volvolutum			
C 859/09 Thorneycroft Box Van		Jun-88	$18-30
ASDA			
C 859/10 Thorneycroft Box Van		1988?	$18-30
Batchelor's Peas			
C 859/11 Thorneycroft Box Van		Dec-88	$18-30
Lea & Perrins, (1988 Christmas Special, Shown Incorrectly as Bedford in Corgi Collector Magazine #26.)			
Q 859/13 Thorneycroft Box Van		Jul-89	$18-30
McDougall's			
D 859/16 Thorneycroft Box Van		Jul-90	$18-30
ASDA 25th Birthday			
C 860 1912 40/50 hp Rolls-Royce Silver Ghost		Jan-86	$25-28
Silver Body & Window Frames, Black Fenders, Chromed Radiator & Coach Lights, Gold Headlights with out Jewels, Black Seats, Silver Wheels.			
C 860/02 1912 40/50 hp Rolls-Royce Silver Ghost		Jan-87	$25-28
Black Body & Fenders, Brown Window Frames, Chromed Radiator & Coach Lights, Gold Headlights with out Jewels, White Seats, Gold Wheels with White Tires.			
C 860/03 1912 40/50 hp Rolls-Royce Silver Ghost		1987?	$25-28
Maroon Body, Other Details Not Known.			
C 861 1927 3-litre Bentley		Jan-86	$25-28
Green Body.			
C 861/02 1927 3-litre Bentley		Jan-87	$25-28
Red Body.			
C 861/03 1927 3-litre Bentley		Jan-87	$25-28
Black Body.			
C 862 1910 Renault 12/16		Jan-86	$25-28
Yellow Body, Black Top, Black Fenders.			
C 862/02 1910 Renault 12/16		Jan-87	$25-28
Brown Body, White Top, Black Fenders.			
C 862/03 1910 Renault 12/16		Jan-87	$25-28
Blue Body, White Top, Black Fenders.			
C 863 1915 Model T Ford Phaeton, Top Up		Jan-86	$25-28
Black Body, Fenders & Top, Gold Radiator, Black Seats, Silver Wheels & Driveshaft.			
C 863/02 1915 Model T Ford Phaeton, Top Up		Jan-87	$25-28
Blue Body, Black Fenders & Top, Tan Seats, Gold Radiator, Silver Wheels & Driveshaft.			
C 863/03 1915 Model T Ford Phaeton, Top Up		Jan-87	$25-28
Red Body, Black Fenders & Seats, Ivory Top, Gold Radiator, Silver Wheels & Driveshaft.			
C 864 Model T Ford Tanker		Mar-86	$15-25
Green Body with Yellow Tank, "Pratt's motor spirit."			
C 864/01 Model T Ford Tanker		Mar-87	$15-25
Black Body with Silver Tank, "Staley Sales Corp."			
C 864/02 Model T Ford Tanker		Apr-87	$15-25
Green Body with Black Tank, "Rimer Bros. Ltd."			
C 864/03 Model T Ford Tanker		Jul-87	$15-25
Red, "San Francisco Fire Dept"			
C 864/04/5? Model T Ford Tanker		1988?	$15-25
"NATIONAL," Other Details Not Known.			
C 864/06 Model T Ford Tanker		Jul-88	$15-25
Olympic Gasoline			
C 865 Model T Ford Van		Feb-86	$15-25
a Lyons' Tea, White Roof.			
b Lyons' Tea, Black Roof.			
C 865/01 Model T Ford Van		Mar-87	$15-25
Brown/Red Body with Brown Roof Rack, "Needler's Chocolates"			
C 865/02 Model T Ford Van		Apr-87	$15-25
Yellow Body & Roof Rack, Black Fenders & Roof, "Drummer Dyes"			
C 865/03 Model T Ford Van		Jul-87	$15-25
Red Body, Fenders & Roof Rack, Black Roof, "Kalamazoo Fire Dept." (Produced for the U.S. Market.)			
C 865/04 Model T Ford Van		Oct-87	$15-25
White Body, Red Roof, Blue Fenders & Roof Rack, "Pepsi-Cola." (Produced for the U.S. Market.)			
C 865/05 Model T Ford Van		May-88	$15-25
Twinings			
C 865/?? Model T Ford Van		1988?	$15-25
"MAILES," Other Details Not Known.			
C 865/?? Model T Ford Van		1988?	$15-25
"TIMES," Other Details Not Known.			
C 865/?? Model T Ford Van		1988?	$15-25
"SWAN," Other Details Not Known.			
C 865/?? Model T Ford Van		1988?	$15-25
"POUPART," Other Details Not Known.			
C 865/?? Model T Ford Van		1988?	$15-25
"BENNETT," Other Details Not Known.			
C 865/11 Model T Ford Van		Sep-88	$15-25
a STEIFF, with Roof Rack, (Produced for the U.S. Market.)			
b STEIFF, with Roof Rack, (Produced for the U.S. Market, Rerun Jul-89.)			
Q 865/14 Model T Ford Van		May-90	$15-25
Blue Body, Black Fenders, NAAFI Logo.			
D 865/15 Model T Ford Van		Aug-90	$15-25
John Menzies			
C 867 Thorneycroft Open Truck with Barrels		Jun-86	$18-30
Green Body with Red Chassis "Thomas Wethered."			
C 867/01 Thorneycroft Open Truck with Barrels		Jan-87	$18-30
Brown/Beige Body "Charles Wells Ltd" — "HORN LANE BREWERY, BEDFORD."			
C 867/02 Thorneycroft Open Truck with Barrels		Feb-87	$20-22
Red/White Body "Toohey's Pilsner."			
C 867/03 Thorneycroft Open Truck with Barrels		Apr-87	$18-30
Dk. Green Body "The Swan Brewery Co. Ltd."			
C 867/04 Thorneycroft Open Truck with Barrels		Sep-88	$18-30
Green/White Body "Carlsberg."			
C 869 MGTF, Open Top with Roll Bar		Sep-86	$25-28
Blue, Small Arched Racing Windshields, Black Roll Bar, "113."			
C 869/01 MGTF, Open Top with Roll Bar		Jan-87	$25-28
Same as C869. Nenumbered in 1987.			

C 870/01 Jaguar XK120, Open Top with Roll Bar		Jan-87	$25-28
British Racing Green, "6," Small Arched Windshields, Silver Roll Bar.			
C 872 Model T Ford Tanker		Apr-86	$15-25
Dominion			
C 873 Model T Ford Van		Apr-86	$25-28
Zebra Grate Polish			
C 874 Model T Ford Van		Sep-86	$15-25
Corgi Collector Club 2nd Anniversary			
C 875 Model T Ford Van		May-86	$15-25
Schokolade Gold			
C 876 Model T Ford Van		Aug-86	$30-35
Dickins & Jones			
C 877 Model T Ford Van		Sep-86	$15-25
Red Body, Black Roof & Fenders, "Royal Mail."			
C 880 Model T Ford Tanker		Sep-86	$15-25
B.P.			
C 882 Thorneycroft Open Truck with Barrels		Aug-86	$18-30
Red Body "St. Winefred's."			
C 883 Thorneycroft Open Truck with Barrels		Oct-87	$18-30
Lt. Green Body "Taunton Cider."			
C 884 Thorneycroft DD Bus		Jul-86	$18-30
General — "Beer Is Best."			
C 885 Thorneycroft DD Bus		Sep-86	$18-30
a Thomas Tilling, Top Rail with 4 Supports.			
b Thomas Tilling, Top Rail with 8 Supports.			
C 888 Thorneycroft DD Bus		Jul-86	$18-30
Grants Morella Cherry Brandy			
D 889/01 Renault Open Truck with Barrels		Jul-89	$18-30
Stella Artois			
C 891 Morris 1000 Van		N/A	N/A
NOT PRODUCED. (Number Changed to C957/02 when Issued.)			
C 892 Morris 1000 Van		N/A	N/A
NOT PRODUCED. (Number Changed to C959 when Issued.)			
C 897/01 AEC Cabover Box Van		Sep-87	$18-30
Carter Paterson			
C 897/02 AEC Cabover Box Van		Sep-87	$18-30
John Knight Ltd./Hustler Soap			
C 897/03 AEC Cabover Box Van		Dec-87	$70-80
LMS Express Parcels Traffic			
C 897/04 AEC Cabover Box Van		Feb-88	$20-22
Duckham's Wear Cure Tablets			
C 897/05 AEC Cabover Box Van		Apr-88	$18-30
Amplion Radio			
C 897/06 AEC Cabover Box Van		May-88	$20-22
Weetabix			
C 897/07 AEC Cabover Box Van		Oct-88	$18-30
Mars			
C 897/08 AEC Cabover Box Van		Aug-88	$18-30
"His Master's Voice"			
D 897/09 AEC Cabover Box Van		Mar-89	$20-22
International Stores			
D 897/11? AEC Cabover Box Van		1989?	$18-30
"BP," Other Details Not Known. (May Be C897/10?)			
D 897/12 AEC Cabover Box Van		Jul-89	$45-48
Royal Mail			
D 897/13 AEC Cabover Box Van		Jul-89	$18-30
G.P.O. Telephones. (Part of D15/01 Set.)			
D 897/14 AEC Cabover Box Van		May-90	$18-30
GWR (Great Western Railway)			
C 902 Renault Box Van		Oct-85	$18-30
Royal Mail			
C 906/01 Mack Bulldog Box Van		Feb-87	$18-30
Green Body, White Roof, Black Roof Rack & Fenders, "MACK TRUCKS."			
C 906/02 Mack Bulldog Box Van		Mar-87	$28-30
Sunshine Biscuits			
C 906/03 Mack Bulldog Box Van		Apr-87	$18-30
White Rock			
C 906/04 Mack Bulldog Box Van		Aug-87	$18-30
Buffalo Fire Dept.Search and Rescue No. 3. with Black Roof Rack.			
C 906/05 Mack Bulldog Box Van		Mar-87	$18-30
White Body, Red Roof, Blue Hood, Fenders & Roof Rack, "Pepsi-Cola." (Produced for the U.S. Market.)			
C 906/06 Mack Bulldog Box Van		Jan-88	$18-30
Black/Yellow Body, Red Roof Rack, "STANLEY"			
C 906/07 Mack Bulldog Box Van		Mar-88	$28-30
Peerless Light Co.			
C 906/08 Mack Bulldog Box Van		Sep-88	$18-30
Bovril, Black/White/Red with Red Roof Rack			
C 906/09 Mack Bulldog Box Van		Aug-88	$18-30
Carnation			
C 906/10 Mack Bulldog Box Van		Jul-88	$20-22
Gulden's Mustard			
C 907 Thorneycroft Box Van		Jan-86	$18-30
Red/White Body "H.P.Sauce."			
C 910 Thorneycroft Box Van		Mar-86	$18-30
Black/White Body "Small & Parkes."			
C 911 Thorneycroft Box Van		Sep-86	$18-30
Green/Red Body "Persil." (Produced for the German Market.)			
C 913 Thorneycroft Box Van		Mar-86	$18-30
a Beige/Red Body "Dewar's" with Windshield.			
b Beige/Red Body "Dewar's" with out Windshield.			
C 914 Thorneycroft Box Van		Jun-86	$18-30
Green/Black Body "Lipton's Tea."			
C 915 Thorneycroft Box Van		Feb-86	$18-30
Red/Black Body "Oxo."			

C 916   Thorneycroft Box Van   1986? $18-30
"BRYANT," Other Details Not Known.
C 917   Renault Box Van   Feb-86 $18-30
Courvoisier
C 922   Renault Open Back Truck with Canvas Cover   Jan-86 $18-30
aux Galeries LaFayette
C 923   Renault Open Back Truck with Canvas Cover   Jan-86 $20-22
Field Ambulance
C 924   Thorneycroft Box Van   Sep-86 $25-28
Red/Black Body "Safeway."
C 925   Renault Box Van   Jun-86 $18-30
Gervais Danone. (Produced for the Belgian Market.)
C 926   Thorneycroft Box Van   Apr-86 $18-30
Black/White Body "Double Diamond."
C 929   Thorneycroft Box Van   Jul-86 $18-30
Green Body "Gamley's," with Roof Rack.
C 931   Thorneycroft Box Van   Jun-86 $30-35
Red/White Body "Stepney Tires."
C 932   Thorneycroft Box Van   May-86 $18-30
Yellow/Black Body "Puritan Soap."
C 933   Thorneycroft Box Van   Oct-86 $18-30
Red/Black Body "Punch," with Roof Rack.
D 944/01 VW Caravanette   Sep-90 $16-20
Red/Gray
C 945/01 AEC Cabover Tanker   Dec-87 $18-30
Flowers Best Bitter
C 945/02 AEC Cabover Tanker   Dec-87 $20-22
Gaymers Cyder
C 945/03 AEC Cabover Tanker   Jan-88 $18-30
Carless Petrol
C 945/04 AEC Cabover Tanker   Jun-88 $20-22
Duckham's
C 945/05 AEC Cabover Tanker   Nov-88 $18-20
Somerlite
D 945/06 AEC Cabover Tanker   Jan-89 $18-20
Redline-Glico
D 945/07? AEC Cabover Tanker   1989? $18-30
BP
D 945/08 AEC Cabover Tanker   Dec-90 $18-30
Red, White roof, "Mobilgas"
C 949/01 Bedford OB Coach   Jul-87 $45-50
a Norfolk, Dull Yellow Stripe, Smaller Destination Wording. (First Pooduction Run.)
b Norfolk, Brighter Yellow Stripe, Larger Destination Wording. (Second Pooduction Run.)
c Norfolk, Green Stripe, Larger Destination Wording. (Second Pooduction Run.)
C 949/02 Bedford OB Coach   Jul-87 $80-90
a Royal Blue, Blue Line Along Bottom. (First Production Run.)
b Royal Blue, No Blue Line Along Bottom. (Second Production Run.)
C 949/03 Bedford OB Coach   Aug-87 $50-60
Bluebird
C 949/04 Bedford OB Coach   Sep-87 $30-32
Grey Cars
C 949/05 Bedford OB Coach   Feb-88 $35-40
Crosville
C 949/06 Bedford OB Coach   Dec-87 $170-180
Southdown
C 949/07 Bedford OB Coach   Jun-88 $35-40
Eastern Counties
C 949/08 Bedford OB Coach   Dec-88 $40-45
South Midland
C 949/09 Bedford OB Coach   Oct-88 $30-32
Premier Travel
C 949/10 Bedford OB Coach   Jun-05 $25-45
Highland (Part of Mail Order Set C89.)
C 949/11 Bedford OB Coach   Nov-88 $30-32
East Yorkshire
D 949/12 Bedford OB Coach   Jan-89 $30-32
Classic
D 949/13 Bedforj OB Coach   Jun-89 $35-40
Hampshire & Sussex
D 949/14 Bedford OB Coach   Jun-89 $30-32
Wallace Arnold
D 949/15 Bedford OB Coach   Sep-89 $70-80
MacBraynes
D 949/16 Bedford OB Coach   Jun-05 $25-45
Hants and Dorset (Part of Transport of the 50s Set D4/01.)
D 949/17 Bedford OB Coach   Jan-90 $25-45
Greenslades
D 949/18 Bedford OB Coach   Jun-90 $20-25
Devon General
Q 949/19 Bedford OB Coach   Jan-90 $30-35
Southern Vectics
D 949/20 Bedford OB Coach   Jun-05 $25-45
RAF (Part of RAF Set D35/01.)
D 949/21 Bedford OB Coach   N/A   N/A
Yorkshire Traction (Not Produced, Re# D949/26.)
Q 949/22 Bedford OB Coach   Jun-90 $25-45
Boultons of Shropshire
D 949/23 Bedford OB Coach   Aug-90 $22-25
Howards of Whitby
D 949/24 Bedford OB Coach   Aug-90 $28-30
Southern National
D 949/25 Bedford OB Coach   Nov-90 $20-22
Eastern National
D 949/26 Bedford OB Coach   Aug-90 $25-28
West Yorkshire

D 949/27 Bedford OB Coach   Aug-90 $25-28
British Rail, Meadstead Destination Sign.
D 949/28 Bedford OB Coach   Aug-90 $25-45
York Fair (Part of Set Q55/01, produced for the U.S. Market.)
Q 949/30 Bedford OB Coach   Nov-90 $28-30
Western National
Q 949/31 Bedford OB Coach   Dec-90 $22-25
British Railways, Bristol Destination Sign.
C 953/01 Bedford Pantechnicon   Oct-87 $70-80
Pickfords
C 953/02 Bedford Pantechnicon   Oct-87 $85-95
Waring & Gillow Ltd.
C 953/03 Bedford Pantechnicon   Jan-88 $70-80
Frasers
C 953/04 Bedford Pantechnicon   Jan-88 $45-48
Steinway & Sons.
C 953/05 Bedford Pantechnicon   Mar-88 $22-25
Griff. Fender
C 953/06 Bedford Pantechnicon   Jul-88 $22-25
Duckham's
D 953/07 Bedford Pantechnicon   Nov-88 $45-48
Camp Hopson
Q 953/08 Bedford Pantechnicon   1989? $45-48
a Restmor (Never Produced.)
b Michael Gerson
D 953/09 Bedford Pantechnicon   Jan-89 $30-32
Stylo
D 953/10 Bedford Pantechnicon   Jun-89 $45-48
Weetabix
D 953/12 Bedford Pantechnicon   Oct-89 $45-48
Bishops Removals
D 953/13 Bedford Pantechnicon   Feb-90 $30-32
Wylie & Lockhead
D 953/14 Bedford Pantechnicon   Sep-90 $22-25
Arthur Batty Removals
Q 953/15 Bedford Pantechnicon   Aug-90 $25-45
York Fair. (Part of Set Q55/01.)
Q 953/16 Bedford Pantechnicon   Nov-90 $22-25
Lee Brothers
D 953/18 Bedford Pantechnicon   (See Notes) (See Notes)
Blackpool Tower Circus (Released as 97081)
D 953/19 Bedford Pantechnicon   (See Notes) (See Notes)
Brewer & Turnbull (Released as 97083)
D 953/20 Bedford Pantechnicon   Dec-90 $25-45
Corgi On the Move. (Part of Set D82/01.)
C 957   Morris 1000 Van   Sep-86 $15-30
Royal Mail. (Made in Portugal.)
C 957/01 Morris 1000 Van   Oct-87 $15-30
Royal Mail. (Made in G.B., Number Changed from C957 Jan '87.)
C 957/02 Morris 1000 Van   Oct-87 $15-30
Gas, (Originally announced as C891.)
C 957/03 Morris 1000 Van   Jan-88 $15-30
a Yellow/Blue Body, "CORGI Collector Club," "'87" on Left Side, "'88" on Right Side, "JAN 88" Tags, Standard Wheel Hubcaps. (Corgi Collector Club Membership Premium.)
b Yellow/Blue Body, "CORGI Collector Club," "'87" on Left Side, "'88" on Right Side, "JAN 88" Tags, Mini "Spat Type" Hubcaps. (Corgi Collector Club Membership Premium.)
C 957/04 Morris 1000 Van   Mar-88 $15-30
Castrol
D 957/05 Morris 1000 Van   Jul-89 $15-30
Yellow Body, Diagonal Roof Sign, "MICHELIN"
C 957/06 Morris 1000 Van   Jul-88 $15-30
Foyles for Books, Red Body, White Diagonal Roof Sign.
C 957/07 Morris 1000 Van   Oct-88 $15-30
MacFisheries
D 957/11 Morris 1000 Van   Jan-89 $15-30
Appleyard Nuffield, Pale Green with Diagonal Roof Sign.
D 957/12 Morris 1000 Van   Apr-89 $15-30
D. Morgan
D 957/13 Morris 1000 Van   Aug-89 $15-30
Kimberly-Clark
D 957/18 Morris 1000 Van   Jul-89 $15-30
Royal Mail, Same as D957/01 Except "Ilfracombe" Postmark. (Part of D7/01 Set.)
Q 957/20 Morris 1000 Van   Dec-89 $18-20
Guernsey Post Office
D 957/21 Morris 1000 Van   Feb-90 $15-30
7-Up, White, Diagonal Roof Sign
D 957/22 Morris 1000 Van   Apr-90 $15-30
Bishop's Removals
D 957/23 Morris 1000 Van   1990? $15-30
A. Dunn & Son
Q 957/24 Morris 1000 Van   ???-90 $40-65
British Association of Toy Retailers 40th Anniversary 1950-1990.
D 957/26 Morris 1000 Van   May-90 $25-40
NAMAC (Dutch National Diecast Collectors Club), Diagonal roof sign. UK Base. (China Base is 96843.)
C 958   Morris 1000 Van   Sep-86 $15-30
Post Office Telephones, Black Ladder on Roof. (Made in Portugal.)
C 958/01 Morris 1000 Van   Oct-87 $15-30
Post Office Telephones, Black Ladder on Roof. (Made in G.B., Number Changed from C958 Jan '87.)
D 958/02 Morris 1000 Van   Jul-89 $15-30
Post Office Telephones, Black Ladder on Roof. (Reissue of D958/01 for use in D15/01 Set.)
C 959   Morris 1000 Van   Oct-87 $15-30
Smith's Crisps, Diagonal Sign on Roof. (Originally announced as C89?.)
C 965   Model T Ford Van   Nov-86 $30-50
75th Anniversary of Ford. Gold Side Lettering. (Produced for Ford.)

C 966	Model T Ford Van	Nov-86	$15-30

a 75th Anniversary of Ford. White Side Lettering. (Publicly Released Version.)
b 75th Anniversary of Ford. White Side Lettering, White Outlined Side Window. (Publicly Released Version.)

C 968	Thorneycroft Box Van	Dec-86	$35-50

Dk. Blue Body "Radio Steiner Bern." (Produced for the Swiss Market.)

C 975	Thorneycroft DD Bus	Nov-86	$18-35

City, "Allenburys Pastilles"

D 980/01	Ford Popular Van	Jan-89	$15-30

S. A. Peacock

D 980/02	Ford Popular Van	Mar-89	$15-30

Fullers

D 980/03	Ford Popular Van	Apr-89	$15-30

Luton Motor Company

D 980/04	Ford Popular Van	Nov-88	$15-30

Corgi Collector Club '89

D 980/08	Ford Popular Van	Sep-89	$15-30

C. Pearson Quality Carpets

D 980/12	Ford Popular Van	Nov-89	$15-30

D. Sheldon

D 980/13	Ford Popular Van	Jan-90	$15-30

"LIMA FURNATURE LIMITED"

D 980/14	Ford Popular Van	Mar-90	$15-30

Cambrian Factory Ltd.

D 980/15	Ford Popular Van	May-90	$15-30

Abbeycolor

D 980/16	Ford Popular Van	Jul-90	$15-30

Royal Mail

D 981/01	Bedford CA Van	May-89	$15-30

Pickfords Heavy Haulage Ltd.

D 981/02	Bedford CA Van	Oct-89	$15-30

Cambrian News

D 981/03	Bedford CA Van	Oct-89	$15-30

a Yellow Body, Black Roof, Nose & Rear Wheel Skirts, "ROAD (AA) SERVICE." (Shown with out Roof Sign, May be Prototype.)
b Yellow Body, Black Roof, Nose & Rear Wheel Skirts, "ROAD (AA) SERVICE."

D 981/04	Bedford CA Van	Nov-89	$15-30

Express Dairy

D 981/08	Bedford CA Van	Jan-90	$15-30

Yellow Body, Dk. Blue Roof, Nose & Rear Wheel Skirts, "CORGI COLLECTOR CLUB 1990." (Same Masking as AA Van.)

D 981/09	Bedford CA Van	Nov-90	$15-30

"Evening News," Diagonal Roof Sign

D 981/10	Bedford CA Van	Aug-90	$15-30

Evening Standard

D 981/11	Bedford CA Van	Nov-90	$15-30

The Star, Red body, black diagonal roof sign "CLIFF MICHELMORE ..." "THE STAR" & "TEST MATCH LATEST" on sides.

D 982/01	Bedford Dormobile	Jun-89	$15-30

Lt. Blue/Cream

D 982/02	Bedford Dormobile	Dec-89	$15-30

Red/Cream

D 982/03	Bedford Dormobile	Mar-90	$15-30

Green/Cream

D 982/04	Bedford Dormobile	Nov-90	$15-30

Brown upper body, cream lower body.

D 983/01	Morris J Van	Apr-90	$15-30

Post Office Telephones

D 983/02	Morris J Van	May-90	$15-30

Royal Mail

D 983/04	Morris J Van	Sep-90	$15-18

Black, Metropolitan Police

D 983/05	Morris J Van	Nov-90	$15-30

Wall's Ice Cream

D 985/01	VW Van	Nov-90	$15-18

Dove blue body, white bumpers & seats.

D 987/11	AEC Cabover Box Van	May-89	$18-30

John Barker & Comp'y Ltd.

D 987/14	AEC Cabover Box Van	1989?	$18-30

G.W.R.

C 990/01	Single Deck Tram —Closed Top	Jul-88	$18-30

Southampton Corporation Tramways

C 990/02	Single Deck Tram —Closed Top	Oct-88	$18-30

Sheffield

D 990/03	Single Deck Tram —Closed Top	Jan-89	$18-30

Derby

D 990/04	Single Deck Tram —Closed Top	Jul-89	$18-30

Wolverhampton

D 990/05	Single Deck Tram —Closed Top	May-90	$18-30

Maidstone Corporation

D 990/06	Single Deck Tram —Closed Top	Jan-91	$18-30

Maidstone Corporation

C 991/01	Double Deck Tram — Open Top	Sep-88	$18-30

London County Council

C 991/02	Double Deck Tram — Open Top	May-88	$18-30

Blackpool

D 991/03	Double Deck Tram — Open Top	Mar-89	$18-30

Bath

D 991/04	Double Deck Tram — Open Top	Sep-89	$18-30

Bournemouth

D 991/05	Double Deck Tram — Open Top	Nov-89	$18-30

Burton & Ashby

D 991/06	Double Deck Tram — Open Top	Nov-89	$18-30

Croydon

Q 991/07	Double Deck Tram — Open Top	May-90	$18-30

National Garden Festival, Gateshead

D 991/08	Double Deck Tram — Open Top	Dec-90	$18-30

Llandudno and Colwyn Bay

C 992/01	Double Deck Tram —Closed Top	Aug-88	$18-30

Leeds Corporation

C 992/02	Double Deck Tram —Closed Top	Jun-88	$18-30

Glasgow

C 992/03	Double Deck Tram —Closed Top	Jul-88	$18-30

L.C.C.

C 992/04	Double Deck Tram —Closed Top	Jul-88	$18-30

Blackpool

C 992/05	Double Deck Tram —Closed Top	Oct-88	$18-30

Bradford

D 992/06	Double Deck Tram —Closed Top	Jan-89	$18-30

Southampton

D 992/07	Double Deck Tram —Closed Top	Aug-89	$18-30

Birmingham

D 992/08	Double Deck Tram —Closed Top	Jan-90	$18-30

London Transport

D 992/09	Double Deck Tram —Closed Top	Nov-90	$18-30

South Shields

D 993/01	Double Deck Tram — Fully Closed	Apr-89	$18-30

Portsmouth

D 993/02	Double Deck Tram — Fully Closed	Oct-89	$18-30

Dover

D 993/03	Double Deck Tram — Fully Closed	Nov-90	$18-30

Coventry

C 1000	Turbos Dealer Assortment	Jan-88	$???

24 Various Turbos Vehicles in Dealer Display Box.

C 1009	MG Maestro 1600	Apr-84	$25-30

a Yellow Body, White Side Stripe Above Belt Line, "AA Service" on Front Doors. (Continuation of Mettoy Era Corgitronics 1009 which Did Not Have Side Stripe or Graphics.)
b Red Body, Otherwise like Yellow Version with out Graphics. (Possibly a Mettoy Era Product.)
c White/Red Body Divided Diagonally on Sides, Yellow Side Graphics, White "19," Packaged in "CORGI SUPER SONICS" Window Box, Sound Maker Replaces Lights Inside Opaque Black Windows.

C 1106	Mercedes Loadlugger	Apr-84	$20-30

Yellow Cab "Corgi," Black Chassis, Silver Pivot Arms, Red Container "BIG BIN." (Continuation of Mettoy Era Corgitronics 1119, which May Have Different Graphics & Red Base.)

C 1109	Mercedes Articulated Truck with Refrigerated Trailer	Apr-84	$15-40

a Black Body & Trailer, "McVITIE'S bake a better biscuit."
b "SEALINK," Other Details Not Known.

C 1111	Superhaulers — Mercedes Articulated Truck	Jan-83	$15-40

Safeway Supermarkets. (Produced During Mettoy and Transition Era.)

C 1112	Mercedes Articulated Truck with Covered Dropside Trailer	Apr-84	$30-40

Yellow Cab with Blue Chassis, Yellow Trailer with Blue Fenders, Yellow Covers "MICHELIN." (Different Color Scheme than Mettoy Era 1109.)

C 1113	Hyster Stackatruck	Aug-87	$45-55

Yellow/Black, with "SEALINK" Container.

C 1114	Mercedes Grit Spreader	Apr-84	$25-35

Yellow Cab, Plow & Grit Body, Black Chassis, Orange Warning Light at Rear of Grit Body.

C 1116	Refuse Truck	Apr-84	$25-35

Orange Cab, Silver Trash Body, CITY SANITATION." (Continuation of Mettoy Era 1116.)

C 1116/02	Refuse Truck	Jan-88	$25-35

Blue Cab, White Trash Body, "BOROUGH COUNCIL REFUSE SERVICE."

C 1117	Street Sweeper	Apr-84	$25-35

a Yellow Cab & Body, Black Chassis, Diagonal Red/White Stripes "FAUN," Tan Figure. (Continuation of Mettoy Era 1117.)
b Orange Cab & Body, Black Chassis, Diagonal Red/White Stripes "FAUN," Tan Figure.

C 1117/02	Street Sweeper	Jan-88	$25-35

Red Cab, White Body, Black Chassis, Diagonal Red/White Stripes, Tan Figure.

C 1120	Dennis Ariel Ladder Fire Engine	Apr-84	$55-65

a Red Body, Yellow Extending Ladder (Same as on 1143), Yellow Outriggers, Crest on Doors.
b Red Body, White Extending Ladder, (Color?) Outriggers, Crest on Doors.

C 1122	Mercedes Cement Mixer	Apr-84	$25-35

a Orange Cab & Mixer Body, Black Chassis, Diagonal Black Stripes on Mixer Barrel.
b Orange Cab & Mixer Body, White Barrel, Black Chassis, Diagonal Black Stripes on Mixer Barrel.

C 1123	Scania Silo Truck	Apr-84	$10-15

Red Body, White Air Dam & Ladders, "Kohler." (1984 Transitional Number for C1134.)

C 1124	Scania Container Truck	1984?	$10-15

"DANZAS," Other Details Not Known.

C 1128	Mercedes Tipper Truck	Apr-84	$25-35

a Yellow Cab, Black Chassis, Red Tipper Body.
b Black Cab, Chassis & Tipper Body, White "Tarmac."

C 1129	Superhaulers — Mercedes Articulated Truck	Apr-84	$15-40

Corgi, Black Trailer, Other Details Not Known.

C 1129	Superhaulers — Mercedes Articulated Truck	Apr-84	$35-50

ASG, with Blue Cab. (Continuation of Mettoy Era 1129, Produced for the Swedish Market.)

C 1129	Superhaulers — Mercedes Articulated Truck	Apr-84	$35-50

ASG, with out Blue Cab. (Produced for the Swedish Market.)

C 1130	Superhaulers — Mercedes Fuel Tanker	Apr-84	$15-40

Yellow Cab with Red Chassis, Yellow Tank & Tank Chassis "Shell." (Shown in 1984 and 1985 Catalogs as C1141.)

C 1131	Superhaulers — Mercedes Articulated Truck	Oct-83	$15-40

Christian Salvesen

C 1137	Superhaulers — Mercedes Articulated Truck	Apr-84	$35-50

Souks Supermarket. (Produced for the Saudi Market.)

C 1139	Superhaulers — Mercedes Articulated Truck	Apr-84	$15-40

a Halls Bacon.
b Halls Bacon Reversed Labels.

C 1140/01	Ford Wrecker	Jan-87	$20-35

a White Body, Blue Crane, Yellow/Silver Lightbar on Roof, Black/Yellow/White Checkered Stripe on Sides with "POLICE RESCUE."
b White Body, Orange Crane, Yellow/Silver Lightbar on Roof, Black/Yellow/White Checkered Stripe on Sides with "POLICE RESCUE."

C 1140/02 Ford Wrecker Jul-87 $35-50
Red Body & Crane, Yellow/Silver Lightbar on Roof, Yellow "FALCK" and Falcon Logo on Sides. (Produced for the Danish Market.)

C 1140/?? Ford Wrecker 1984? $???
Yellow Body, Other Details Not Known.

C 1140/?? Ford Wrecker 1987? $???
"VIKING," Other Details Not Known.

C 1141 Superhaulers — Mercedes Fuel Tanker Apr-84 $15-40
Yellow Cab with Red 2 Axle Chassis, Yellow Tank & Tank Chassis "Shell."

C 1143/02 American LaFrance Aerial Ladder Truck Dec-90 $60-90
Limited Edition, Red, Red Wheels, Silver Ladders, Gold "F.D." & trim.

C 1144 Superhaulers — Mercedes Articulated Truck Apr-84 $15-40
a Red Cab with out Air Dam, Black Chassis, Red Trailer with Yellow "Royal Mail Parcels."
b Red Cab with Air Dam, Black Chassis, Red Trailer with Yellow "Royal Mail Parcels."

C 1145 Superhaulers — Mercedes Articulated Truck Apr-84 $15-40
Yellow Cab with Red Air Dam, Red 2 Axle Chassis, Blue Trailer with "MILK CHOCOLATE YORKIE." (Same Trailer Decoration as Used on C1002 Through Mettoy Closure. C1002 Used Scammell Casting.)

C 1146 Superhaulers — Mercedes Articulated Truck Oct-83 $15-40
Dunlop

C 1151 Scania Silo Truck Apr-84 $10-15
White Body, Red Air Dam & Ladders, "Spiller's."

C 1153 Scania Tipper Truck Apr-84 $10-15
a Yellow Body & Tipper, "WIMPEY" on Cab Doors. (1984 Transitional Number for C1133.)
b Yellow Body & Tipper, "LAING" on Dump Body.

C 1166 Superhaulers — Mercedes Fuel Tanker Apr-84 $15-40
a Tan Cab with Black Chassis, Tan Tank "GUINNESS."
b Aria Dairy (Produced for the Swedish Market.)

C 1167 Superhaulers — Mercedes Fuel Tanker Apr-84 $15-40
a Yellow Cab with Blue Chassis, Yellow Tank with Blue Chassis & Side Panels "DUCKHAMS."
b Corgi Chemco, Other Details Not Known.
c 7-Up. (Not Released)

C 1168 Superhaulers — GMC Bus Apr-84 $18-20
a White Body with Red Roof, Black Chassis, Blue Center Panel "EUROEXPRESS."
b White Body with Red Around Forward Side Windows, Black Chassis, Blue Center Panel "EUROEXPRESS."

C 1175 Superhaulers — Mercedes Articulated Truck Apr-84 $15-40
a Black Cab with Yellow Air Dam "ZANUSSI," Yellow Chassis, Black Trailer with Yellow A/C Unit & "ZANUSSI...."
b Ti Raleigh, Other Details Not Known.

C 1176 Superhaulers — Scammell Articulated Truck Apr-84 $15-40
Yellow Cab & Air Dam "Weetabix," Red 2 Axle Chassis, Yellow Trailer & A/C Unit "Weetabix."

C 1177 Superhaulers — Scammell Articulated Truck Oct-83 $15-40
a Ti Raleigh, 2 Axle Cab.
b Weetabix.
c Yellow Cab with Air Dam "NORMANS," Red 2 Axle Chassis, Yellow Trailer "NORMANS FAMILY WAREHOUSE."

C 1178 Superhaulers — Mercedes Articulated Truck Oct-83 $15-40
Maynards Wine Gums.

C 1180 Superhaulers — Mercedes Fuel Tanker 1984? $15-40
a White (?) Cab with "ATLANTIC" Logo on Doors, Blue (?) Trailer with White Side Label "ATLANTIC."

C 1180 Superhaulers — Scammell Articulated Truck Apr-84 $15-40
b White Cab with Red Air Dam, Orange Single Axle Truck Chassis, White Trailer with White A/C Unit, Red Side Panels, Black Trailer Chassis. (Possibly Issued to Use Left-over Factory Parts.)

C 1181 Scania Container Truck 1984? $???
"GRINGOIRE," Other Details Not Known.

C 1182 Scania Container Truck Apr-84 $10-15
a Red Cab & Flatbed, White Chassis & Air Dam, Red Container "HONDA."
b Dk. Blue Cab & Chassis, Yellow Box & Air Dam, "SUZUKI" & Logo.

C 1183 Scania Box Truck Apr-84 $10-15
White Cab & Chassis, Blue Air Dam & Box, "adidas."

C 1185 Mack CF Fire Pumper Apr-84 $14-16
a Red Body with White Roof Panel, Blue Light & Silver Horns on Roof, Yellow Ladders, "HAMMOND FIRE DEPT."
b Red Body with White Roof Panel, Amber Light & Silver Horns on Roof, Black Ladders, "HAMMOND FIRE DEPT."
c Red Body with White Roof Panel, Amber Light & Silver Horns on Roof, Yellow Ladders, "HAMMOND FIRE DEPT."

C 1186 Superhaulers — Scammell Articulated Truck Apr-84 $15-40
Dk. Blue Single Axle Cab with White Air Dam, Black 2 Axle Chassis, Dk. Blue Trailer "McVITIE'S...."

C 1188 Superhaulers — Scammell Articulated Truck Jul-85 $15-40
Royal Mail, 2 Axle Chassis.

C 1189 Superhaulers — Scammell Fuel Tanker Jul-85 $15-40
Yellow Cab & Tank "Duckhams," Dk. Blue 2 Axle Chassis.

C 1190 Ford Cargo Box Van Apr-86 $20-30
Red Body, Black Chassis, "EVER READY."

C 1190/01 Ford Cargo Box Van Feb-87 $35-50
Red Body, Black Chassis, "Arnott's Biscuits." (Produced for the Australian Market.)

C 1190/?? Ford Cargo Box Van 1986? $20-30
"GAS," Other Details Not Known.

K 1190/?? Ford Cargo Box Van Jul-85 $20-30
Dk Blue Cab & Chassis, White Box "Thorntons Family Confections."

C 1191 Ford Cargo Articulated Container Truck Jan-85 $30-40
White Cab, Dk. Blue Chassis & Flatbed Trailer Bed, White Trailer Wheels, 2 Dk. Blue Containers "Ford cares about quality."

C 1192 Ford Cargo Box Van Jul-85 $20-30
a Green Cab & Box, Black Chassis, "Lucas."
b White Body, Black Chassis, "PEPSI."
c "DOMIZIL," Other Details Not Known.

C 1193 Superhaulers — Volvo Car Transporter Apr-85 $15-40
Red Cab, Chassis & Lower Trailer, Silver Cab Roof "GLOBETROTTER" & Upper Trailer Deck. (Renumbered 1222 in 1986.)

C 1194 Superhaulers — Volvo Articulated Truck Apr-85 $15-40
Red Cab & Trailer, "Lee Cooper."

C 1196 Superhaulers — Volvo Articulated Truck Apr-85 $15-40
White Cab, Black Chassis, White Trailer "Hotpoint."

C 1197 Superhaulers — Volvo Articulated Truck Apr-85 $15-40
Yellow Cab, Dk. Blue Chassis & Trailer "ASG."

C 1201 Scania Container Truck 1984? $???
"INJEGODS," Other Details Not Known.

C 1203 Mercedes Box Van Jul-85 $20-30
Hemglass

C 1205 Superhaulers — Volvo Articulated Truck Jul-85 $15-40
Ballantynes, with Flat Bed Trailer.

C 1206 Superhaulers — Volvo Articulated Truck Jul-85 $15-40
Hillards

C 1207 Superhaulers — Volvo Articulated Truck Sep-85 $15-40
a "British Home Stores," Dark Blue Cab & Chassis, White Trailer.
b "British Home Stores," Dark Blue Cab with White Roof, Dark Blue Chassis, White Trailer.

C 1211 Superhaulers — Volvo Articulated Truck May-86 $15-40
Rileys Crisps

C 1212 Superhaulers — Volvo Articulated Truck Apr-86 $15-40
Orange Cab & Chassis, White/Orange Trailer, "TNT OVERNITE PARCELS EXPRESS."

C 1217 Superhaulers — Volvo Articulated Truck Jul-85 $15-40
Kay's

C 1220/01 Superhaulers — Scammell Flatbed Truck with Crates Jan-88 $15-40
Red/Black, Yellow Crates with Black Diagonal "EXPORT."

C 1221 Superhaulers — Volvo Flatbed Truck with Crates Jan-86 $15-40
Details Not Known.

C 1221/01 Superhaulers — Volvo Flatbed Truck with Crates Jan-88 $15-40
Red with Silver Roof "GLOBETROTTER," Black Trailer Deck with Red Chassis, Yellow Crates with Black Diagonal "EXPORT," Barrel Skid, Sack Skid.

C 1222 Superhaulers — Volvo Car Transporter Apr-86 $15-40
Red Cab, Chassis & Lower Trailer, Silver Cab Roof with Horns, "GLOBETROTTER" & Upper Trailer Deck.

C 1222/02 Superhaulers — Volvo Car Transporter Jan-88 $15-40
Blue Cab, Chassis & Lower Trailer, Silver Cab Roof "GLOBETROTTER" & Upper Trailer Deck.

C 1222/03 Superhaulers — Volvo Car Transporter with 3 Cars Sep-88 $40-65
Blue Cab, Chassis & Lower Trailer, Silver Cab Roof "GLOBETROTTER" & Upper Trailer Deck, 3 Juniors Volvo 760 Saloon (Red, Silver and ???), (Produced for the Swedish Market.)

C 1222/04 Superhaulers — Volvo Car Transporter Jan-89 $15-40
Yellow Cab with Silver Roof "GLOBETROTTER," Yellow Lower Trailer with Silver Upper Hinged Deck.

C 1223 Superhaulers — GMC Coach Mar-86 $35-50
"VMEbus/68000 PHILIPS," Blue Body, (Produced for the Swiss Market.)

C 1224 Superhaulers — Volvo Articulated Truck Apr-86 $15-40
Cadbury's Flake

C 1225 Superhaulers — Volvo Articulated Truck Apr-86 $35-50
Bilspedition. (Produced for the Swedish Market.)

C 1227 Superhaulers — Volvo Articulated Truck Oct-85 $15-40
Beefeater by Leisureking Ltd.

C 1228 Ford Cargo Box Van Nov-85 $20-30
Lewis's

C 1231 Superhaulers — Volvo Articulated Truck Apr-86 $15-40
McCain Oven Chips

C 1231/01 Superhaulers — Volvo Articulated Truck Jan-87 $15-40
Weetabix

C 1231/02 Superhaulers — Volvo Articulated Truck Jan-87 $15-40
a White Cab with Red Roof "WIMPY," Silver Horns, Red Chassis, White Trailer "WIMPY" with Mr. Wimpy.
b Red Cab, Black Chassis, White Trailer "WIMPY" with Mr. Wimpy.

C 1231/05 Superhaulers — Volvo Articulated Truck Aug-87 $15-40
Woolworths

C 1231/06 Superhaulers — Volvo Articulated Truck Aug-87 $15-40
a TESCO, Silver Horns on Cab Roof.
b TESCO, Air Deflector on Cab Roof.

C 1231/13 Superhaulers — Volvo Articulated Truck Sep-87 $35-50
Gamino, (Produced for the French Market.)

C 1231/15 Superhaulers — Volvo Articulated Truck Aug-87 $15-40
Dark Blue Bab & Chassis, Chromed Horns, White Trailer "BHS."

C 1231/17 Superhaulers — Volvo Articulated Truck Feb-88 $15-40
Mars

C 1231/18 Superhaulers — Volvo Articulated Truck Dec-87 $15-40
Gateway

C 1231/19 Superhaulers — Volvo Articulated Truck Mar-88 $35-50
Black, "mmm ... Marabou Non-Stop." (Produced for the Swedish Market.)

C 1231/22 Superhaulers — Volvo Articulated Truck Sep-88 $15-40
Bright Yellow Cab with White Roof, Silver Horns. Black Chassis with Yellow Dished Wheels, Lt. Yellow Trailer, "Steiff BUTTON IN EAR" Lables (Same iable on Both Sides, Bear toward Left). (Produced for the US Market.)

C 1231/23 Superhaulers — Volvo Articulated Truck Mar-89 $35-50
Red Body, Yellow Chassis, "FRIZZY PAZZY." (Produced for the Swedish Market.)

C 1231/27 Superhaulers — Volvo Articulated Truck May-89 $35-50
SAS CARGO, (Produced for the Swedish Market.)

C 1231/29 Superhaulers — Volvo Articulated Truck Aug-89 $35-50
Intermarche', (Produced for the French Market.)

C 1231/31 Superhaulers — Volvo Articulated Truck Nov-89 $15-40
a White Cab with Horns, Black Chassis, White Trailer "SAFEWAY."
b White Cab with out Horns, Black Chassis, White Trailer "SAFEWAY."

C 1231/33 Superhaulers — Volvo Articulated Truck Apr-90 $15-40
Mars (Revised Livery)

C 1231/34 Superhaulers — Volvo Articulated Truck Apr-90 $15-40
Opal Fruits

C 1231/36 Superhaulers — Volvo Articulated Truck Jan-91 $15-40
Lo-Cost Food Stores

C 1231/37 Superhaulers — Volvo Articulated Truck Jan-91 $15-40
Freia

C 1231/99 Superhaulers — Volvo Articulated Truck Jan-87 $15-40
a Datapost. (Part of D/Post Despatch Center Set, No Catalog #, C1231/99 used for list organization only.)
b Toymaster. (Part of 3 pc. Toymaster Set Apr-85, No Catalog #, C1231/99 used for list organization only.)
c Red Cab, Chassis & Trailer, Chromed Horns, "Coca-Cola" with Shadowed Wave. (BHS Issue Only Jan-87, No Catalog #, C1231/99 used for list organization only.)
d White Arrow "Kay's Mail Order Special." (Kay's Issue Only Jan-87, No Catalog #, C1231/99 used for list organization only.)
e Kays Catalog," Small Trailer. (Kay's Issue Only Apr-85, No Catalog #, C1231/99 used for list organization only.)
f Kays Catalog," Large Trailer. (Kay's Issue Only Apr-86, No Catalog #, C1231/99 used for list organization only.)
g Tropico. (Never Produced, Prototype Exists.)
C 1232 Superhaulers — Volvo Articulated Truck Aug-86 $15-40
Bosch
C 1233 Superhaulers — Volvo Articulated Truck Aug-87 $15-40
Cadbury DAIRY MILK
C 1238 Superhaulers — Seddon Atkinson Articulated Truck 1987? $15-40
Wimpy. (Same Decorations as C1231/02.). (May have/# ?.)
C 1238/01 Superhaulers — Seddon Atkinson Articulated Truck May-87 $15-40
McCain Oven Chips, Horns on Cab Roof.
C 1238/02 Superhaulers — Seddon Atkinson Articulated Truck May-87 $15-40
Cadbury's Flake, Horns on Cab Roof.
C 1238/03 Superhaulers — Seddon Atkinson Articulated Truck Jan-88 $15-40
Securicor Express, No Horns on Cab Roof.
C 1238/04 Superhaulers — Seddon Atkinson Articulated Truck Jul-88 $15-40
RADIO 1 ROADSHOW
C 1238/05 Superhaulers — Seddon Atkinson Articulated Truck Nov-88 $15-40
Silent Night
C 1238/06 Superhaulers — Seddon Atkinson Articulated Truck Mar-89 $15-40
Royal Mail Datapost
C 1238/09 Superhaulers — Seddon Atkinson Articulated Truck Jul-89 $15-40
Cadbury's
C 1238/13 Superhaulers — Seddon Atkinson Articulated Truck Jan-90 $15-40
"Cadbury's Wispa"
Q 1238/14 Superhaulers — Seddon Atkinson Articulated Truck Mar-90 $15-40
Parcel Force
C 1238/99 Superhaulers — Seddon Atkinson Articulated Truck Jun-87 $15-40
a Datapost. (Part of Datapost Set, No Catalog #, C1238/99 used for list organization only.)
b Lynx Delivery Service, No Horns on Cab Roof. (Part of BP Set, No Catalog #, C1238/99 used for list organization only.)
C 1243 Superhaulers — Volvo Articulated Truck Jun-86 $15-40
Kay's
C 1245 Superhaulers — Volvo Articulated Truck Apr-86 $15-40
Red Cab with White Roof "FUJI," Black Chassis, Green Trailer "FUJI FILM."
C 1246 Superhaulers — Scammel Articulated Truck Apr-86 $15-40
Tan Cab, Black 3 Axle Chassis, Dk. Blue Trailer, "MILK CHOCOLATE YORKIE."
C 1246/01 Superhaulers — Scammel Articulated Truck Jan-87 $15-40
a Tan Cab, Black 3 Axle Chassis, Dk. Blue Trailer, "MILK CHOCOLATE YORKIE." (Jan. 1987 Renumbering of C1246.)
b Yellow Cab, Black Chassis, Dk. Blue Trailer, "MILK CHOCOLATE YORKIE."
C 1246/02 Superhaulers — Scammel Articulated Truck Jan-87 $15-40
Red Cab, Black Chassis, White Trailer, "Dr Pepper."
C 1246/04 Superhaulers — Scammel Articulated Truck May-87 $15-40
a Red with Black 3 Axle Chassis, White "Coke" on Doors, White "Coca-Cola" on Trailer. (Produced for the U.S. Market.)
b Red with Black 3 Axle Chassis, White "Coke" on Doors, White "Coca-Cola" and Red "TURBO RACING TEAM" on Trailer. (Produced for the U.S. Market as Part of J 3600 Only.)
C 1246/05 Superhaulers — Scammel Articulated Truck May-87 $15-40
Brown with White 3 Axle Chassis, "HERSHEY'S MILK CHOCOLATE." (Produced for the U.S. Market.)
C 1246/06 Superhaulers — Scammel Articulated Truck Sep-87 $35-50
Francois Avril, (Produced for the French Market.)
C 1246/07 Superhaulers — Scammel Articulated Truck Jan-88 $15-40
Yorkie 200gms, 3 Axle Chassis, Other Details Not Known.
C 1246/08 Superhaulers — Scammel Articulated Truck Mar-89 $15-40
FAO Schwarz, White Body & Trailer, Black Chassis.
C 1246/10 Superhaulers — Scammel Articulated Truck Sep-87 $15-40
Coca-Cola, Wave has Silver Shadow. (Produced for the U.K. Market.)
C 1246/12 Superhaulers — Scammel Articulated Truck Aug-90 $15-40
Corning Glass, Produced for the U.S. Market
C 1246/99 Superhaulers — Scammel Articulated Truck Apr-84 $15-40
a Norman's Cash & Carry, 2 Axle Chassis. (No Catalog #, C1246/99 Used for List Organization Only.)
C 1247 Superhaulers — Scammel Articulated Truck Apr-86 $15-40
BFGoodrich
C 1248 Superhaulers — Volvo Articulated Truck Dec-85 $15-40
Carters Lemonade Liner
C 1249 Ford Cargo Box Van May-86 $30-50
White's Bazaar 75th Anniversary.
C 1250/01 Superhaulers — Volvo Cylindrical Tanker May-87 $15-40
TEXACO
C 1250/02 Superhaulers — Volvo Cylindrical Tanker Jul-87 $35-50
White Body and Tank, Black Chassis, "NOROL Norsk olje." (Produced for the Norwegian Market.)
C 1250/03 Superhaulers — Volvo Cylindrical Tanker Feb-88 $15-40
Polo
C 1251/01 Superhaulers — Seddon Atkinson Cylindrical Tanker May-87 $15-40
THE BOC GROUP, Horns on Cab Roof.
C 1251/02 Superhaulers — Seddon Atkinson Cylindrical Tanker Feb-88 $15-40
Rolo, Horns on Cab Roof.
C 1264/01 Superhaulers — Seddon Atkinson Fuel Tanker Jun-87 $15-40
White Cab & Tank "BP," Gray Chassis, No Horns on Cab Roof.
C 1264/02 Superhaulers — Seddon Atkinson Fuel Tanker Feb-88 $15-40
Elf, Horns on Cab Roof.
C 1265/01 Superhaulers — Volvo Tanker Jan-88 $15-40
Red Cab with Silver Roof "TEXACO," Red Tank with Black Chassis, "TEXACO."
C 1265/02 Superhaulers — Volvo Tanker Mar-89 $15-40
White Cab and Tank Body, Gray Chassis, Red "TEXACO" and Star in Black Rectangle on Tank.
C 1265/03 Superhaulers — Volvo Tanker Jul-89 $15-40
Gulf
C 1265/04 Superhaulers — Volvo Tanker Feb-90 $35-50
Neste (Produced for Finnish Market)
C 1265/05 Superhaulers — Volvo Tanker Jan-90 $15-40
"Shell"
Q 1265/06 Superhaulers — Volvo Tanker Nov-90 $35-50
BP, Produced for BP New Zealand
C 1300/02 Haulers — MAN Container Truck Jan-90 $5-10
"RALEIGH"
T(C)1300/01 Truckers (Haulers) — MAN Container Truck Apr-89 $5-10
Yorkie, (Incorrectly shown with Kenworth Cab in Corgi Collector Magazine #28, Correct Data in #29.)
C 1301/01 Haulers — MAN Tanker May-89 $5-10
BP, White Body
C 1301/02 Haulers — MAN Tanker Aug-89 $5-10
Mobil, Tan Body
C 1302/01 Haulers — MAN Tipper May-89 $5-10
Orange Body and Tipper
C 1302/02 Haulers — MAN Tipper Aug-89 $5-10
Mustard Yellow
C 1303/01 Haulers — Ford Cargo Container Truck May-89 $5-10
Schweppes, Yellow Body, Orange Container
C 1303/02 Haulers — Ford Container Truck Aug-89 $5-10
7-Up, White Body
C 1303/02 Haulers — Ford Container Truck Jan-90 $5-10
"PEPSI"
C 1304/02 Haulers — Ford Tanker Aug-89 $5-10
Shell, Yellow Body, Silver Tank
T(C)1304/01 Truckers (Haulers) — Ford Cargo Tanker Apr-89 $5-10
Duckhams Oils
C 1305/02 Haulers — Ford Tipper Aug-89 $5-10
Red/Silver
C 1305/02 Haulers — Ford Tipper Truck Jan-90 $5-10
Red/Silver
T(C)1305/01 Truckers (Haulers) — Ford Cargo Tipper Apr-89 $5-10
Green Body, Silver Gray Tipper
C 1306/01 Haulers — Kenworth Truck Mar-90 $5-10
White, "7-Up" on Green Box Body
C 1308/01 Haulers — Kenworth Dump Truck Mar-90 $5-10
Yellow with Black Dump Body
C 1365 London Bus & Taxi Set Apr-84 $20-35
C469 Routemaster Bus & Juniors J17 London Taxi. (Continuation of Mettoy Era 1365, which had Different Destination Panels on Routemaster.)
C 1383/01 Cameos — 8 Truck Assortment Apr-90 $30-50
8 Antique Trucks in Various Liveries
C 1388 Mini Assortment Jul-90 $30-40
Mini's (1/36), Blue, Yellow, Silver, Red
C 1389 Twin Pack Assortment Nov-90 $???
Various Paired Vehicles from the Standard Product Line.
C 1412 Swiss Police Set Mar-86 $40-60
White Range Rover with Red Hood & Side Stripe, One Red & One Blue Roof Light, Blue "POLIZEI" on Doors, Red/White Helicopter "POLIZEI HB-XCU." (Produced for the Swiss Market.)
C 3200 H Hershey's Milk Chocolate Turbo Racing Team Set Apr-87 $20-30
Brown "HERSHEY'S MILK CHOCOLATE" C150 Turbos Chevrolet Camaro Racer "6" & J46 Juniors Firebird "4."
K 5055 Powerplay Alarm Flashers May-90 $???
12 Pack with 5 Different Liveries, Siren and Flashing Lights Activate by Squeezing Rear Wheels.
C ? Corgi Center Playset Jul-88 $???
Ten Different Themed Playsets. (Catalog Numbers Not Known.)
Q ? Weetabix Special Edition Collection Mar-89 $35-55
Yellow Superhaulers Container Truck, C638 Routemaster Bus, and Juniors Aston-Martin DB6, All Decorated "Weetabix." (Catalog Number Not Known.)

J Series (Juniors) Corgi

J 1 A Juniors — NASA Shuttle Apr-84 $3-5
White/Black, "NASA."
J 1 B Juniors — Ford Capri Racer Jan-88 $3-5
White Body, Blue/Yellow Stripes, "DUCKHAMS 9."
J 2 Juniors — Dump Truck Apr-84 $3-5
a Yellow Cab, Red Dump Body. (old # E7-C.)
b Yellow, Black "LAING" on Dump Body. (Jan-85)
J 2/01 Juniors — Iveco Tanker Jan-88 $3-5
Red Cab, White Tank, "Esso" Logo.
J 3 Juniors — Triumph TR7 Apr-84 $3-5
a Brown Body, "THIUMPH TR7." (old # E10-C.)
b Red/Blue Body with White Trim "8." (Jan-85)
J 4 A Juniors — Starfighter Apr-84 $3-5
White Body, Blue Canopy & Engines, Yellow Winglets. (old # E13-C.)
J 4 B Juniors — Ford Transit Van Jan-88 $3-5
White Body, "PORSCHE KREMER RACING."
J 4/01 Juniors — Ford Transit Van 1988? $3-5
White Arrow
J 4/02 Juniors — Ford Transit Van 1988? $3-5
Red Body "Fire Chief"
J 4/03 Juniors — Ford Transit Van 1988? $8-12
Red Body "Brandweer"
J 4/04 Juniors — Ford Transit Van 1988? $3-5
Kay's (Part of Set J3167/06.)
J 4/05 Juniors — Ford Transit Van 1989? $3-5
Red Body "Fire Chief"
J 4/06 Juniors — Ford Transit Van Jan-90 $3-5

Red Body, "Royal Mail Parcels." (1990 Re# of J63.)

J 4/07   Juniors — Ford Transit Van   1990? $3-5
Yellow Body "AA"

J 4/08   Juniors — Ford Transit Van   1990? $3-5
White Body with Blue Outlined Red Side Stripe "POLICE."

J 4/09   Juniors — Ford Transit Van   1990? $8-12
Red Body "Falck Redningskorp." (Produced for the German Market.)

J 4/10   Juniors — Ford Transit Van   1990? $3-5
Red Body, "Parcelforce."

J 5   Juniors — Mercedes Bus   Apr-84 $3-5
a Green Body, " Holiday Inn." (old # E15-C.)
b Yellow Body "SCHOOL BUS," Opaque Black Windows. (Found in Set E (J) 3035.)
c White Body, Blue Below Belt Line on Sides, Black "HOLIDAY TOURS." (Jan-85)

J 5/02   Juniors — Mercedes Bus   Jul-88 $3-5
SAS

J 5/03   Juniors — Mercedes Bus   Jul-88 $3-5
White Body, Air France Striping, Blue "AIR FRANCE" on Sides.

J 5/04   Juniors — Mercedes Bus   Jun-89 $8-12
Yellow Body, Clear Windows, White Interior, Red Side Stripe, Black "PTT." (Produced for the French & Swiss Markets.)

J 6   Juniors — Rover Police   Apr-84 $3-5
a White Body, Blue Lightbar on Roof, Black Outlined Red Side Stripe "POLICE." (old # E16-C.)
b White Body, Red/White/Blue Lightbar on Roof, Red Side Stripe with Black "POLICE," Red Foward Hood with Black "POLICE." (Jan-85)

J 7   Juniors — ERF Fire Engine   Apr-84 $3-5
a Red Body, Silver Access Doors, Yellow Ladder. (old # E26-C.)
b Red/Silver Body, Yellow Ladder, White "FIRE" Over Cab. (Jan-85)

J 8   Juniors — Simon Snorkel Fire Engine   Apr-84 $3-5
a Red Body, Dark Yellow Base & Booms. (old # E29-D.)
b Red Body, Light Yellow Base & Booms. (1985?)
c Red Body, White Base & Booms, Black "SNORKEL" on Upper Boom Left Side. (Jan-85)
d Red Body, White Base & Booms, Black "SNORKEL" on Upper Boom Right Side, Base Text Blanked. (1988?)

J 9 A   Juniors — Cement Mixer   Apr-84 $3-5
a Yellow Body, Orange Drum & Holder. (old # E30-D.)
b Brick Red Body, Cream Drum & Holder. (Found in Set E (J) 3035.)
c White Body with Black Side Stripes & Roof, Red Drum & Holder. (Jan-85)

J 9/01   Juniors — Iveco Container Truck   Jan-88 $3-5
Mars

J 9/02   Juniors — Iveco Container Truck   Sep-88 $3-5
Mars (Revised Side Labels)

J 9/03   Juniors — Iveco Container Truck   Sep-88 $6-8
Batchelor's Peas

R 9/09   Juniors — Iveco Container Truck   Jan-91 $6-8
"Tesco," Weetabix premium offer

J 10   Juniors — Aston Martin DB5   Apr-84 $3-5
a Maroon Body, (Actually a DB6). (old # E22-B.)
b Yellow Body with Black Side Trim" DB5." (Jan-85)

J 11 A   Juniors — Volvo Wagon   Apr-84 $3-5
White Body.

J 11 B   Juniors — Volvo Support Car (Wagon)   Jan-85 $3-5
White Body with Black Roof Rack, Red/Green Stripe "Castrol" Logo.

J 12 A   Juniors — Ford Skip Truck   Apr-84 $3-5
Red Body, White Container. (old # E54-A.)

J 12 B   Juniors — Iveco Tanker   1987? $3-5
Red Cab, White Tank "TOTAL." (Also found in Set J3097.)

J 12/01   Juniors — Iveco Tanker   Jan-88 $3-5
Green Cab, White Tank, "BP Oil."

J 12/02   Juniors — Iveco Tanker   Jul-88 $8-10
Green Cab, White Tank, "BP C'est Super." (Produced for the French Market.)

J 13 A   Juniors — Refuse Truck   Apr-84 $3-5
Orange Cab & Chassis, Gray Refuse Body. (old # E55-B.)

J 13/01   Juniors — Iveco Beverage Truck   Jan-88 $3-5
Red Cab, White Body with Blue Cases, "PEPSI."

J 13/02   Juniors — Iveco Beverage Truck   Jul-88 $8-10
Red Cab, Orange Body with Yellow Cases, "Fruite' c'est plus muscle'." (Produced for the French Market.)

J 14   Juniors — Mercedes 240D Saloon   Apr-84 $3-5
a Red Body. (old # E59-C.)
b Cream Body, Red Seats. (Found in Set E (J) 3035.)
c White Body with Black Roof Rack, Green Hood & Side Stripe, Black Circle with White "6." (Jan-85)

J 15 A   Juniors — Lotus Esprit   Apr-84 $5-8
a Yellow Body, Opaque Black Slatted Windows. (Rework of James Bond Esprit E60-B to Standard Car.)
b White Body, Red Side Stripe "TURBO," Opaque Black Slatted Windows. (Found in Set E (J) 3035.)

J 15 B   Juniors — Ford Transit Van   Feb-88 $3-5
Police

J 16 A   Juniors — Ford Capri   Apr-84 $3-5
a Silver Body, Black Segmented Side Stripe. (old # E61-C.)
b Blue Body, Gold Segmented Side Stripe. (Jan-85)

J 16/01   Juniors — BMW 325I   Jan-88 $3-5
Red Body.

J 17   Juniors — London Taxi   Apr-84 $3-5
Black Body, No Markings or Trim.

J 18 A   Juniors — Jaguar XJS   Apr-84 $3-5
a White Body, Thin Green Side Stripe with Black "JAGUAR," Leaping Jaguar Logo on Hood.
b Green Body, Thin White Side Stripe with White "JAGUAR," White Leaping Jaguar Logo and "JAGUAR" on Hood. (1985?)
c Green Body, Thin White Side Stripe, "6 JAGUAR" on Sides & Hood. (Found in Set E (J) 3035 Apr-84.)
d Green Body, Thin White Side Stripe with "6 MOTUL" on Sides & Hood. (Jan-85)
e White Body, Thin Black Side Stripe with "JAGUAR," Leaping Jaguar Logo and "JAGUAR" on Hood.

J 18 B   Juniors — Jaguar XJS Police   1986? $3-5
White Body, Opaque Blue Lightbar on Roof, Blue Outlined Red Side Stripe, Red "POLICE" on Hood & Doors, Black Interior, Black Metal Base. (Part of Set J3158 & Others.)

J 19   Juniors — Matra Rancho   Apr-84 $3-5
a Green Body, Black Chassis. (old # E76-C.)
b Blue Body, Black Chassis, 2 Yellow Surf Boards on Black Roof Rack, Red/Yellow Stripes "mistral." (Jan-85)

J 19/02   Juniors — Matra Rancho   Jul-88 $8-12

Pompiers

J 20   Juniors — London DD Bus   Apr-84 $3-5
a Red Body, Large Union Jack on Sides. (old # E81-A.)
b Red Body, "SEE MORE LONDON." (Jan-85)

J 21   Juniors — Fiat X1/9   Apr-84 $3-5
a White Body, Yellow/Red Side Stripe at Sill with Black "FIAT X1/9." (old # E86-A.)
b Orange Body, Blue Stripe Over Hood Onto Sides, White Square with Black "2." (Jan-85)
c White Body, Black Diecast Base, Black Roof, Red Interior, Yellow/Black "6 FIAT HELLER." (1987?)

J 22 A   Juniors — Petrol Tanker   Apr-84 $3-5
a White Body, Black Chassis, "BP Oil." (old # E97-B.)
b White Body, Black Chassis, Orange/White Tank Graphic "Gulf." (Jan-85)

J 22/01   Juniors — BMW 325i Racer   Jan-88 $3-5
White Body, Yellow Roof, Yellow/Green Rally Trim "56."

J 23   Juniors — Renault 5 Turbo   Apr-84 $3-5
a Blue Body, White Base, White "TURBO" on Sides. (old # E102-A.)
b Blue Body, White Base, White Roof, "elf 18." (Jan-85)
c Black Body, Red Base, White Roof, "elf 18." (Jan-88)

J 24   Juniors — Ford Wrecker Truck   Apr-84 $3-5
a White Body, Red Boom & Lightbar, Black Hook, Blue Edged Red Side Stripe, Blue "RAC" and Red "RESCUE." (old # E103-A.)
b White Body, Red Boom & Lightbar, Black Hook, Blue Edged Red Side Stripe, Blue "POLICE" on Hood, Blue "RESCUE 108." (Jan-85)

J 24/02   Juniors — Ford Wrecker Truck   Jul-88 $8-10
Europ Assistance

J 25 A   Juniors — Ford Escort   Apr-84 $3-5
a Blue Body. (old # E105-A.)
b Red Body. (Jan-85)
c Red Body, Plastic Base, White Interior, White "77" hood & Sides, Yellow "Royal Mail Datapost" on Hood, Yellow "Datapost" on Sides. (1985?)
d Red Body, Plastic Base, Black Interior, White "77" hood & Sides, Yellow "Royal Mail Datapost" on Hood, Yellow "Datapost" on Sides. (1986?)
e Red Body, Black Metal Base, Gray Interior, White "77" hood only, Yellow "Royal Mail Datapost" on Hood, Yellow "Datapost" on Sides. (1986?)
f Red Body, Black Plastic Base, Black Interior, White "66" hood & Sides, Yellow "Royal Mail Datapost" on Hood, Yellow "Datapost" on Sides. (1987?)
g Red Body, Black Plastic Base, White Interior, White "66" hood & Sides, Yellow "Royal Mail Datapost" on Hood, Yellow "Datapost" on Sides. (1987?)

J 25 B   Juniors — Renault Trafic Van   Jan-88 $6-8
White Body, "AVIS VAN RENTAL."

J 25/01   Juniors — Renault Trafic Van   Mar-89 $6-8
Consumer Gas, (Produced for the Canadian Market.)

J 26   Juniors — Austin Mini Metro   Jan-85 $3-5
a White Body with Red/Orange Graphics, Black "8."
b Red Body, Black Interior, White "66" on Hood, Yellow "Royal Mail" on Hood, Yellow "Datapost" on Sides. (1985?)
c Red Body, Black Interior, White "66" on Hood & Sides, Yellow "Datapost" on Sides. (1985?)
d Red Body, Black Interior, White "77" on Hood & Sides, Yellow "Datapost" on Sides. (1985?)

J 26/02   Juniors — Austin Mini Metro Van   1985? $3-5
Red Body, Tan Interior, Red Painted Rear Windows with Yellow "Royal Mail," Yellow Logo on Sides.

J 27   Juniors — Citroen 2CV   Apr-84 $3-5
a White Body, Flowing Blue Side Stripe. (old # E115-A.)
b Yellow Body with Black Top, Duck Graphic on Hood & Doors. (Jan-85)
c Red Body, Flowers on Front Doors. (Jan-88)

J 28   Juniors — Airport Rescue Truck   Apr-84 $3-5
Red Body, Yellow Nozzle, Black/White Segmented Side Stripe, "AIRPORT RESCUE 8." (old # E123-A.)

J 29   Juniors — Mercedes 500SL   Apr-84 $3-5
a Silver Body. (old # E124-A.)
b Red Body, Silver Below Belt Lind on Sides. (Jan-85)
c Red Body, White Seats, Black Plastic Base with Tow Hook. (1986?)

J 30 A   Juniors — Ford Dropside Truck   Apr-84 $3-5
a Bright Yellow Body, Black "Whimpey" on Doors. (old # E125-A.)
b Bright Yellow Body, Black "BTS TYRE SERVICES" on Bed Sides. (Found in Set E (J) 3035. Apr-84)
c Bright Yellow Body, Black "BTS TYRE SERVICES" on Bed Sides, Black Tire Cargo. (Jan-85)

J 30 B   Juniors — BMW M3   Jan-88 $3-5
Orange Body, "Canon 44."

J 31   Juniors — Ford Sierra Saloon   Apr-84 $3-5
a Blue Body. (old # E129-A.)
b Red Body. (Jan-85)
c Red Body, Red Interior Black Base, Yellow "Post Office" in Oval on Hood Yellow "Royal Mail" & Logo on Hood. (1986?)
d Blue Body, "ICS Shell Oils 1." (Jan-88)

J 32   Juniors — Ferrari 308 GTS   Apr-84 $3-5
a Black Body. (old # E131-A.)
b Red Body, White "Ferrari" on Sides, Ferrari Logo & Italian Flag on Hood. (Jan-85)
c Red Body. (Jan-88)

J 33   Juniors — VW Turbo   Apr-84 $3-5
a White Body, Green/Blue Side Stripes "6." (old # E92-A.)
b Yellow Body, Red Stripes & Blue "Turbo" Below Belt Line on Sides. (Jan-85)

J 34   Juniors — Rover Sterling 3500 Saloon   Apr-84 $3-5
White Body, "12 Triplex." (old # E138-A.)

J 35   Juniors — Porsche 911   Apr-84 $3-5
a Black Body, 2 Thin Gold Side Stripes. (old # E139-A.)
b White Body, Blue/Green Graphics with Red "18." (Jan-85)
c Black Body, Gold Trim with White "Shell 18." (Jan-88)
d Black Body, 2 Gold Stripes on Hood, Gold "PORSCHE" on Lower Doors, Black Metal Base. (Jan-88)

J 36 A   Juniors — Ford Mustang   Apr-84 $3-5
a White Body, Blue Base, Thin Red Side Stripe with Blue Ford Logo & "MUSTANG." (old # E140-A.)
b White Body, Blue Base, Red Stripes on Hood, Blue Square with Stars on Roof, Red/Blue Stripe on Sides "MUSTANG." (Jan-85)

J 36 B   Juniors — Ferrari Testarossa   Apr-88 $3-5
Red Body.

J 37   Juniors — British Gas Van   Apr-84 $3-5
White Body, Blue Roof & Lower Sides "Gas." (old # E144-A.)

J 38   Juniors — British Telecom Van   Apr-84 $3-5

Yellow Body, "British TELECOM" with Coiled Line Logo. (old # E145-A.)

| J 39 | Juniors — Royal Mail Van | Apr-84 | $3-5 |

Red Body, Yellow "Royal Mail Datapost," "U.S. Van" or Blank Text Base, Clear, Amber, Blue or Black Windows. (All Combinations of Base & Windows Possible.)

| J 40 | Juniors — Opel Corsa/Vauxhall Nova | Apr-84 | $3-5 |

a Red Body, Black Base, Yellow "CORSA." (old # E170-A as Vauxhall Nova.)
b Yellow Body, Black Base, Thin Red Stripe on Sides at Belt Line. (Jan-85)
c White Body, Black Base, Yellow/Silver/Black Stripes, Black "OPEL" on Hood, Opel Logo on Roof. (Jan-88)

| J 41 | Juniors — Quarry Truck | Apr-84 | $3-5 |

Yellow Cab, Orange Dump Body. (old # E174-A.)

| J 42 | Juniors — Pipe Truck | Apr-84 | $3-5 |

a Green Cab, Yellow Flat Bed, Gray Pipes. (old # E175-A.)
b Green Cab, White Flat Bed, Gray Pipes. (Found in Set E (J) 3035.)

| J 43 | Juniors — Tanker Truck | Apr-84 | $3-5 |

Yellow Cab, White/Red Tank with Red "SHELL." (old # E177-A.)

| J 44 | Juniors — Container Truck | Apr-84 | $3-5 |

Red, "Coca-Cola." (old # E178-A.)

| J 45 | Juniors — Chevrolet Corvette | Apr-84 | $3-5 |

a White Body, Black Underlined Red Side Stripe "CHEVY 84." (old # E179-A.)
b White Body, Red/Blue Stripes, Chevrolet Logo on Hood, " 'VETTE85." (Jan-85)

| J 46 | Juniors — Pontiac Firebird | Apr-84 (Standard) | $3-5 |
| | | (With Advertising) | $5-8 |

a White Body, Blue Pinstripes "Yankees" (Repackaged Baseball Cars.) (old # 180-A & 500-525-A.)
b Black Body, Seats, Spoiler, Black Diecast Base. (1985?)
c Black Body with Red Panel Between Headlight Doors, Seats, Spoiler, Black Diecast Base. (Possibly U.S. Market Only. Jan-85)
d Blue Body, Silver Stars on Sides, Silver/White/Red "Schweppes" Logo on Roof, White "Soft Drinks" with Silver Stars on Hood, Black Seats, Spoiler, Black Diecast Base. (1987?)
e White Body with Red Hood, White "12" on Hood, Red "Coca-Cola 12" on Sides, Black Seats, Spoiler, Black Diecast Base. (Part of Set C3700C & Others, Not Available Separately. Apr-87)
f Brown Body with Orange/White Stripe, White "HERSHEY'S MILK CHOCOLATE 4," Black Seats, Spoiler, Black Diecast Base. (Part of Set C3200H, Not Available Separately. Apr-87)

| J 46/01 | Juniors — Pontiac Firebird | Jan-88 | $3-5 |

Silver Bidy with Thin Red Side Stripe, Black Seats, Spoiler, Black Diecast Base.

| J 46/02 | Juniors — Pontiac Firebird | Jan-88 | $3-5 |

Yellow Body with Black Stripes "Fire Bird" (sic.) & White "11," Black Seats, Spoiler, Black Diecast Base.

| J 47 A | Juniors — '54 Mercedes 300SL | Apr-84 | $3-5 |

Red Body. (old # E181-A.)

| J 47 B | Juniors — Volvo 760 | Jan-88 | $8-12 |

White Body, Blue Lightbar on Roof, "POLIS."

| J 47/01 | Juniors — Volvo 760 | Feb-88 | $3-5 |
Police

| J 48 A | Juniors — Jeep, Open Top, No Roll Bar | Apr-84 | $3-5 |

Red Body.

| J 48 B | Juniors — Jeep, Closed Top | Jan-85 | $3-5 |

a White Body, Black Top, Red/Yellow Side Graphics, Black/Yellow Hood Graphics.
b Shell 50. (Feb-88)

| J 48/02 | Juniors — Jeep, Closed Top | Jul-88 | $8-12 |
Pompiers

| J 49 A | Juniors — Jeep, Open Top with Roll Bar | Apr-84 | $3-5 |

a White Body, Red Roll Bar.
b Black Body, Red Roll Bar, White Seats. (Jan-85)

| J 49 B | Juniors — Jeep, Closed Top | Feb-88 | $3-5 |
Military USA

| J 50 A | Juniors — Range Rover, Open Top | Apr-84 | $3-5 |

a Brown Body, Tan Stripe & "RANGE ROVER."
b Black Body, Red/Orange Stripe. (Jan-85)

| J 50 B | Juniors — BMW M3 | Jan-88 | $3-5 |

White Body, "PIONEER 11."

| J 51 | Juniors — Swissair Van | Apr-84 | $3-5 |

White Body with Black Lower Sides, "swissair" with Red/White Logo. (old # E216-A.)

| J 51/01 | Juniors — Ford Transit Van | Jan-87 | $3-5 |

Yellow Body, White Side Stripe with Black Edge, "AA" & "Service" on Sides.

| J 51/02 | Juniors — Ford Transit Van | Jan-87 | $6-8 |

Batchelors, Other Details Not Known.

| J 52 | Juniors — Refuse Truck | Jan-85 | $3-5 |

a Orange Body, Black/White Shield.
b Orange Body, Black "NBC." (Aug-85)

| J 52/02 | Juniors — Refuse Truck | Jan-88 | $8-12 |

Green Body, "Proprete' de Paris."

| J 53 | Juniors — Iveco Container Truck | Aug-85 | $6-8 |

a Yellow Body with Blue Stripes "Fyffes."
b White Body, "IVECO PARTS." (Jan-88)

| J 53/02 | Juniors — Iveco Container Truck | Jun-89 | $8-12 |

Cargo Domizil, (Produced for the Swiss Market.)

| J 53/04 | Juniors — Iveco Container Truck | Jul-90 | $8-12 |

Van Gend & Loos, Produced for the Dutch Market.

| J 54 | Juniors — Renault Trafic Van | Jan-85 | $6-12 |

a White Body, Red Stripe, "AVIS TRUCK RENTAL."
b White Body, Black/Orange Stripes, "RENAULT Parts and Service." (Jan-88)
c Yellow Body, "LOCTITE." (Jan-88)

| J 54/02 | Juniors — Renault Trafic Van | Jul-88 | $8-12 |

Yellow Body, Clear Windows, Black Interior, Blue "LA POSTE." (Produced for the French Market.)

| J 54/03 | Juniors — Renault Trafic Van | Jul-88 | $8-12 |
Aeroport de Paris

| J 54/04 | Juniors — Renault Trafic Van | Jan-89 | $8-12 |

Red Body, Clear Windows, Black Interior, White "ptt post." (Produced for the Dutch Market.)

| J 54/15 | Juniors — Renault Trafic Van | Jul-90 | $8-12 |
PTT Telecom, Produced for the Dutch Market.

| J 55 | Juniors — Renault Trafic Bus | Jan-85 | $3-5 |

a Blue Body, "Grand Hotel."
b White Body with Green Stripe, "Holiday Inn." (Jan-88)

| J 55/02 | Juniors — Renault Trafic Bus | Jul-88 | $8-12 |
Gendarmerie

| J 56 | Juniors — Ford Escort Rally | Jan-85 | $3-5 |

White Body "84."

| J 57 | Juniors — Zakspeed Capri | Jan-88 | $3-5 |

Black Body, Gold/Red Trim, "52."

| J 58 | Juniors — Ford Sierra Pace Car | Jan-85 | $3-5 |

White Body, Red/White/Blue Lightbar on Roof, Black/Yellow Checkered Graphics.

| J 59 | Juniors — Range Rover Rescue | Jan-85 | $3-5 |

Red Body with Flat Roof, Black Roof Rack, Yellow Cross & Side Stripe with Black "MOUNTAIN RESCUE."

| J 60 | Juniors — Buick Police | Apr-84 | $3-5 |

a White Center Body, Black Ends, Transparent Amber Lightbar on Roof, "POLICE" in Black area on doors. Low Rear Suspension. (Continuation of Mettoy Era E150, Which Had an Offset Round Red Roof Light and "POLICE" Side Lables.)
b White Center Body, Black Ends, Opaque Amber Lightbar on Roof, "POLICE" in Black area on doors, High Rear Suspension. (1986?)
c White Center Body, Black Ends, Opaque Blue Lightbar on Roof, "POLICE" in Black area on doors, High Rear Suspension. (Known in At Least 2 Wheel Patterns. Jan-88)

| J 60/?? | Juniors — Buick Regal Sedan | 1986? | $3-5 |

a White Body, Chromed Interior, High Rear Axle, Generic Red/Yellow Corgi Card with out Number or Model Name. (May Actually Have Different Catalog Number Not Presently Known.)
b Black Body with Gold Striping on Hood, Roof & Trunk Lid, Chromed Interior, High Rear Axle. (May Actually Have Different Catalog Number Not Presently Known. 1987?)

| J 61 | Juniors — U.S. Van | Jan-85 | $3-5 |

Black Body with 2 Red Side Stripes. (Continuation of Mettoy Era E-185.)

| J 62 | Juniors — Mini Shop | Jan-85 | $3-5 |

White Body, Blue Roof, Red Stripe Below Belt Line. (Continuation of Mettoy Era E98.)

| J 63 | Juniors — Ford Transit Van, Royal Mail Parcels | 1985? | $3-5 |

a Red Body, Yellow "Royal Mail Parcels" on Sides, Silver Headlights, "Corgi" Text on Base.
b Red Body, Yellow "Royal Mail Parcels" on Sides, Red Headlights, Corgi Text on Base. (1986?)
c Red Body, Yellow "Royal Mail Parcels" on Sides, Red Headlights, Blank Base. (1987?, Re# J4/06 in 1990.)

| J 65 | Juniors — Land Rover Royal Mail | 1985? | $3-5 |

a Red Body, Black Interior, Yellow "Royal Mail" & Logo, "Corgi" Text on Base.
b Red Body, Black Interior, Yellow "Royal Mail" & Logo, Blank Base. (1987?)

| J 66 | Juniors — Land Rover Police | Jan-88 | $3-5 |

White Body, Blue Edged Red Stripe on Sides with White "POLICE," Blue "POLICE" on Upper Sides.

| J 69 | Juniors — Porsche 911 Polizei | Jan-88 | $3-5 |

White Body, Green Doors & Hood with White "POLIZEI."

| J 73 | Juniors — Ford Escort XR3 | Jan-88 | $3-5 |

Red Body.

| J 74 | Juniors — Land Rover | Feb-88 | $3-5 |

White Body, "Safari Rally 65."

| J 77 | Juniors — Ferrari Testarossa | May-88 | $3-5 |

White Body.

| J 79 | Juniors — Mercedes 300TE Ambulance | Jan-88 | $3-5 |

White Body, Blue Lightbar on Roof, Red Stripe "AMBULANCE" on Sides, Red Cross "AMBULANCE" on Hood.

| J 80 | Juniors — Mini Metro | Jun-86 | $10-15 |

White Body. (Austin Rover Promotional.)

| J 81 | Juniors — Buick Police NYPD | Feb-88 | $3-5 |

Lt. Blue Body, Blue Lightbar on Roof, Black/White Checkered Side Stripe, "NYPD," "POLICE."

| J 81/02 | Juniors — Buick Fire Chief | 1990? | $3-5 |

Red/White Body "FIRE CHIEF" with Stars, Opaque Blue Lightbar on Roof, Black Interior, High Rear Axle, Plastic "CHINA" Base.

| J 82 | Juniors — Volvo 760 Ambulance | Jan-87 | $3-5 |

White Body, Red Cross on Hood, Red "AMBULANCE" on Sides.

| J 83 | Juniors — Volvo 760 Racer | Jan-87 | $3-5 |

White Body, "21 Gillanders MOTORS."

| J 84 | Juniors — Volvo 760 Saloon | Jan-88 | $3-5 |

White Body, Thin Black Trim Stripe on Sides.

| J 85 | Juniors — Porsche 935 Racer | Jan-88 | $3-5 |

White Body, Black/Orange/Yellow Hood Stripe, "NUMERO RESERVE philippe salvet 41."

| J 86 | Juniors — Porsche 935 Racer | Jan-88 | $3-5 |

Blue Body, Yellow Stripes, "Lucas 74."

| J 87 | Juniors — Porsche 935 | Jan-88 | $3-5 |

Red Body.

| J 89 | Juniors — Mercedes Benz 2.3/16 Rally | Jan-88 | $3-5 |

White Body, Thin Red/Blue Stripe, Blue "SERVIS 17."

| J 90 | Juniors — Mercedes Benz 2.3/16 Saloon | Jan-88 | $3-5 |

Red Body.

| J 91 | Juniors — Jaguar XJ6 Police | Jan-88 | $3-5 |

White Body, Blue Lightbar on Roof, Blue Edged Yellow Side Stripe with Blue "POLICE," Blue "POLICE" on Hood.

| J 92 | Juniors — Jaguar XJ6 Saloon | Jan-88 | $3-5 |

Dk. Green Body, Leaping Jaguar Logo on Hood.

| J 93 | Juniors — Jaguar XJ6 Saloon | Jan-88 | $3-5 |

Silver with Black Side Stripe.

| J 94 | Juniors — Mercedes 230 TE Wagon | Mar-88 | $3-5 |
Red

| J 95 | Juniors — Mercedes 230 TE Taxi | Apr-88 | $3-5 |

Grayish Green, Black "TAXI" on Doors.

| J 96 | Juniors — Helicopter | 1986? | $3-5 |

Red Body, Black Rotor Blades & Base. (Also Used in Royal Mail Sets.)

| J 97 | Juniors — Land Rover ONE TEN | Jan-88 | $3-5 |

Red Body, Black Interior, Diagonal White Side Stripes, White "FIRE SALVAGE" with Black/White Crest.

| J 98 | Juniors — Porsche Targa | Mar-88 | $3-5 |

Red Body.

| J 99 | Juniors — Porsche Targa Turbo | Mar-88 | $3-5 |

White Body, Black "TURBO" on Sides.

| J 102 | Juniors — Chevy Van | Apr-86 | $3-5 |

White Body, "Wimpy."

| J 110 | Juniors — Renault Trafic Van | Aug-87 | $15-20 |

Yellow Body, Green "Crayola" on Sides. (Packaged with 64 Crayons)

| J 158 | Juniors — Datapost Twin Set | 1985? | $10-12 |

Juniors Royal Mail J63 Ford Transit Van & J65 Land Rover.

| J 160/01 | Juniors — Great Britain Themed Card | Jun-89 | $10-12 |

Juniors Metrobus "SEE MORE LONDON," London Taxi.

J 167/01 Juniors — Mercedes Ambulance Jun-89 $8-10
White Body, Red Stripe and Cross on Sides, Red Stripe on Front and Sides of Roof. (Produced for the Swiss Market.)

B 176 Juniors — Porsche 911 Turbo Sep-85 $15-20
Orange Body, "Crush" Logo on Hood in Arabic. (Produced for the Market in Oman.)

B 177 Juniors — Jaguar XJS 1984? $15-20
Silver Body, "7 Up" Logo on Hood in Arabic. (Produced for the Market in Oman.)

B 178 Juniors — Aston Martin DB5 1984? $15-20
Yellow Body, "Sun Top" Logo on Hood in Arabic. (Produced for the Market in Oman.)

B 179 Juniors — Rover Sterling 3500 1984? $15-20
White/Blue Body, "RC Cola" Logo on Hood in Arabic. (Produced for the Market in Oman.)

J 200 Juniors — Matra Rancho & Horsebox Apr-84 $8-10
a Red Range Rover or Matra Rancho, Green Horse Trailer. (old# E2550), (Catalog photo & description do not match.)
b Green Matra Rancho with Black Base, Green Horsebox Trailer. (Jan-85)

J 201 Juniors — Ford Sierra & Dinghy Apr-84 $8-10
a Yellow Ford Sierra, Black/Yellow Plastic Dinghy on Black Trailer. (old# E2551)
b Red Ford Sierra, Black/Orange Plastic Dinghy on Black Trailer. (Jan-85)

J 202 A Juniors — Ford Mustang & Powerboat Apr-84 $8-10
Red Mustang with Black Chassis, Red/White Boat with Black Outboard Motor, White Trailer. (old# E2553)

J 202 B Juniors — Mercedes & Powerboat Jan-85 $8-10
Red Mercedes with Silver Sides Below Belt Line, Red/White Boat with Black Outboard Motor, White Trailer.

J 203 Juniors — Volvo & Caravan Apr-84 $8-10
a White Volvo Wagon, White Caravan with Blue Door. (old# E2554)
b Ivory Volvo Wagon, Ivory Caravan with Red Door. (Jan-85)

J 204 A Juniors — Ford Wrecker & Jaguar Apr-84 $8-10
White Ford Wrecker "24 hour service," Red Jaguar XJS. (old# E2555)

J 204 B Juniors — Ford Wrecker & Triumph TR7 Jan-85 $8-10
White Ford Wrecker with Blue Outlined Red Stripe "POLICE," "RESCUE," Red Triumph TR7.

J 205 Juniors — Container Truck & Trailer Apr-84 $8-10
Black Truck with Yellow Container "DUNLOP," Matching Unnumbered Trailer.

J 206 Juniors — Tanker Truck & Trailer Apr-84 $8-10
a Red Truck with White Tank "TOTAL," Matching Unnumbered Trailer.
b Yellow Truck with White Tank "Shell," Matching Unnumbered Trailer. (Jan-85)

J 207 Juniors — Pipe Truck & Trailer Apr-84 $8-10
a Red Truck with White Flatbed & Gray Pipes, Matching Unnumbered Trailer.
b Red Truck with Yellow Flatbed & Gray Pipes, Matching Unnumbered Trailer. (Jan-85)

J 219/01 Juniors — Ford Sierra Jun-89 $8-10
Whitr Body, 2 Blue Roof Lights, Red Stripe on Sides and Hood, Blue "POLIZEI" and "OW 21." (Produced for the Swiss Market.)

J 239 Juniors — Datapost Twin Pack 1987? $8-10
Juniors Royal Mail J63 Ford Transit Van & J65 Land Rover.

J 240 Juniors — Police 2 pc. Set May-87 $8-10
White Jaguar XJ6 with Blue Lightbar on Roof, Blue/Yellow Side Stripe "POLICE," White Land Rover with Red/Blue Side Stripe, White "POLICE" in Stripe, Blue "POLICE" on Upper Side.

A 2411 Juniors Display Rack with 144 Juniors Vehicles Jan-88 $???
144 Juniors in One-sided Display Rack.

A 2412 Juniors Display Rack with 192 Juniors Vehicles Jan-88 $???
192 Juniors in One-sided Display Rack.

A 2473 Juniors Display Carousel with 192 Juniors Vehicles Jan-88 $???
192 Juniors in 4-sided Display Carosel.

A 2474 Juniors Display Carousel with 384 Juniors Vehicles Jan-88 $???
384 Juniors in 4-sided Display Carosel.

A 2487 Corgi/Turbos/Juniors/Display Carosel Jan-88 $???
192 Juniors, 20 Turbos, 32 Corgis in 4-sided Display Carosel.

J 2883 Juniors 3 pc. Datapost Set 1988? $13-15
Juniors Royal Mail J63 Ford Transit Van, J65 Land Rover, J96 Helicopter.

J 2885/01 Juniors 3 pc. Great Britain Themed Card Jun-89 $13-15
Juniors Metrobus "SEE MORE LONDON," London Taxi, White Jaguar XJ6 "POLICE."

J 2897/01 Juniors 4 pc. Teddy Bear Themed Card Jun-89 $13-15
Juniors Land Rover, Ford Transit Van, Ford Sierra, and Helicopter All Decorated "Royal Mail"

J 2903 Juniors 4 pc. Teddy Bear Themed Card 1988? $13-15
Juniors Land Rover, Ford Transit Van, Ford Sierra, and Helicopter All Decorated "Royal Mail"

J 2905/01 Juniors 4 pc. Teddy Bear Themed Card Jun-89 $13-15
Juniors Metrobus "SEE MORE LONDON," London Taxi, White Jaguar XJ6 "POLICE," and Red Ford Transit Van "Royal Mail."

J 2909 Juniors 32 Vehicle Dealer Assortment Jan-88 $60-80
32 Juniors Vehicles in Dealer Display Box.

J 2910 Juniors 32 Vehicle Dealer Assortment Jan-88 $60-80
32 Juniors Vehicles in Dealer Display Box.

J 3001 Juniors — Garage with 3 Cars Apr-84 $18-20
Plastic 4 Bay Garage with Juniors Ford Mustang, Mercedes 240D, Jaguar XJS. (Continuation of Mettoy Era E3001, Using Leftover Stock Vehicles.)

J 3006 Juniors — Playmat Apr-84 $15-20
Polyester Fabric, 36" x24," Printed Roadways & Buildings. (Continuation of Mettoy Era E3006.)

J 3014 Juniors 6 pc. Emergency Squad Set Apr-84 $20-25
Juniors Airport Fire Tender, Blue Helicopter, Ford Transit Breakdown, Mercedes Ambulance, ERF Fire Tender, Buick Police Car.

J 3015 Juniors — Off Road Set Apr-84 $$30-35
8 Juniors Vehicles Using Leftover Stock Mettoy Era Vehicles.

J 3019 Juniors — James Bond "Octopussy" Set Apr-84 $300+
Maroon Range Rover (Top Down), Gray Trailer, White Mini Airplane. (Continuation of Mettoy Era E3019, Trailer May Also Be Tan.)

J 3035 Juniors 12 pc. Bumper Set Apr-84 $40-66
12 Juniors Vehicles, Some May Be in Non-standard Finishes or Using Leftover Mettoy Era Stock.

J 3036 Juniors — Garage with 4 Cars Apr-84 $20-35
Plastic 4 Bay Garage with Juniors Ford Capri, Citroen 2CV, Ford Escort, Matra Rancho. (Continuation of Mettoy Era E3036, Using Leftover Stock Vehicles.)

J 3045 Juniors — Mars 4 pc. Gift Set Sep-88 $15-20
Red Renault Trafic "Maltesers," Black Iveco Box Truck "Mars," White Iveco Box Van "Bounty," Yellow Chevy Van "Opal Fruits."

J 3097 Juniors — Garage with 3 Vehicles Jan-88 $15-25
L-Shaped Plastic Service Station, J12 "TOTAL," J4 "AA," J66 "POLICE."

J 3109 Juniors 7 pc. Best of British Set Apr-84 $20-30
7 British Juniors Vehicles Usually Including London Taxi & London Bus. (Continuation of Mettoy Era E3109 Using Leftover Stock Vehicles.)

J 3121 Juniors 7 pc. Super Sports Cars Set Apr-84 $20-30
7 Juniors Vehicles in Rally Trim. (Continuation of Mettoy Era E3121 Using Leftover Stock Vehicles.)

J 3124 Juniors Car Transporter with 4 Cars Apr-84 $25-35
White/Blue Superhaulers Car Transporter with Single Axle Mercedes Truck, 4 Juniors Cars. (Continuation of Mettoy Era E3105 Using Different Cars.)

J 3125 Juniors 5 pc. Airport Set Apr-84 $20-35
Concord "BRITISH AIRWAYS," Juniors BP Tanker, Airport Fire Tender, Chevy Van "Swissair," Helicopter.

J 3125/01 Juniors 5 pc. Airport Set Jan-88 $20-35
Concord "BRITISH AIRWAYS," Juniors DD Bus, Juniors London Taxi, Renault Trafic "Grand Hotel," Ford Transit Van "AA."

J 3126 Juniors 7 pc. Holiday Set Apr-84 $20-30
Juniors Mercedes-Benz 500 SL, Caravan Trailer, Ford Transit Breakdown, Jaguar XJS, Range Rover (Top Down) with Horsebox, Corgi Plaxton Coach.

J 3128 Juniors 13 pc. Motorway Services Set Apr-84 $60-80
10 Juniors Vehicles (Some May Be in Non-standard Finishes), Superhaulers Mercedes Articulated Truck "YORKIE," GMC Bus "EUROEXPRESS," Mercedes Articulated Tanker "DUCKHAMS."

J 3136/01 Juniors 6 pc. Emergency Set Jun-89 $18-25
Juniors Yellow Ford Transit Van "AA," White Ford Transit Van with Red Stripe "POLICE," Red Land Rover "FIRE SALVAGE," Red Simon Snorkel with White Boom "SNORKEL," White Tow Truck with Red Stripe "RESCUE," Jaguar XJ6 "POLICE"

J 3138/01 Juniors 6 pc. Great Britain Set Jun-89 $18-25
Juniors White Land Rover "POLICE," London Taxi, Metrobus "SEE MORE LONDON," White Jaguar XJ6 "POLICE," Red Ford Transit Van "Royal Mail," Yellow Ford Transit Van "AA."

J 3141/01 Juniors Delivery Service 4 pc. Set Jan-89 $12-16
Juniors Royal Mail J25 Ford Escort (2X), J26 Austin Mini Metro (2X).

J 3141/02 Juniors Delivery Service 3 pc. Set 1989? $8-12
Juniors Royal Mail J25 Ford Escort, J26 Austin Mini Metro, J39 U.S.Van.

J 3155 Carry Car with 1 Juniors Vehicle Jan-88 $15-40
Red

J 3155/03 Carry Car with 1 Juniors Vehicle Jul-89 $25-50
Yellow, (Produced for Mothercare Stores)

J 3156 Carry Car with 5 Juniors Vehicles Jan-86 $30-50
Red

J 3156/01 Carry Car with 5 Juniors Vehicles Jan-88 $30-50
(Same as J3156, Models Updated.)

J 3158 Juniors 3 pc. London Scene Themed Card 1986? $8-12
Juniors Metrobus "SEE MORE LONDON," London Taxi, White Jaguar XJ6 "POLICE."

J 3161/01 Advent Calender Jan-88 $3-5
NOT A VEHICLE

J 3167/02 Juniors Superhaulers 6 pc. Set Jan-88 $30-40
C1231/02 "WIMPY," C1238/03 "SECURICOR EXPRESS," J97/?? "Royal Mail," J4 "KREMER," JJ25 "AVIS," J24 "POLICE."

J 3167/06 Kays Delivery Set Jul-89 $20-30
Superhaulers Volvo Container Truck "Kays," Juniors Ford Transit Van "Kays"

J 3168/03 Juniors Transporter Set with 6 Cars Jan-88 $35-45
C1222 Red/Silver Car Transporter, Matcking Car Transporter Trailer with Tandem Bogie Wheels, J23 "elf," J32 Red, J91 "POLICE," J83 "Gillanders," J90 Red, J93 "JAGUAR."

J 3169/02 Juniors Bumper Set with 10 Vehicles Jan-88 $30-40
J73 Red, J4 "AA," J66 "POLICE," J93 "JAGUAR," J50 "PIONEER," J18 Silver, J30 "Canon," J65 "Royal Mail," J4 "KREMER," J84 Silver.

J 3170/02 Juniors Jumbo Set with 20 Vehicles Jan-88 $60-80
J65 "Royal Mail," J19 "mistral," J46 "Schweppes," J54 "RENAULT," J32 Red, J49 Olive with Tan Roof & Red Cross Symbol, J27 Yellow, J73 "Duckhams," J4 "KREMER," J93 Green Body, J17 Taxi, J86 "74," etc.

J 3171 Juniors — Transporter Set with 3 Cars Jan-88 $20-30
C1222 Red/Silver Car Transporter, J83 "Gillanders," J30 "Canon," J73 "36."

J 3179 Juniors Postman Xmas Card Set 1987? $20-30
Juniors Royal Mail J39 U.S.Van, J63 Ford Transit Van, J65 Land Rover, J96 Helicopter.

J 3184 Juniors Datapost Despatch Center 1986? $30-45
Royal Mail Superhaulers (2X), Juniors Royal Mail J39 U.S.Van, J63 Ford Transit Van, J65 Land Rover, J96 Helicopter.

J 3186 Juniors Datapost Gift Set 1986? $20-30
Royal Mail Superhauler, Juniors Royal Mail J63 Ford Transit Van, J 65 Land Rover, J96 Helicopter.

J 3200 H Hershey's Milk Chocolate Turbo Racing Team Set Apr-87 $20-30
Brown "HERSHEY'S MILK CHOCOLATE" C150 Turbos Chevrolet Camaro Racer "6" & J46 Juniors Firebird "4."

J 3214 Juniors, Parcelforce Set Sep-90 $???
Details Not Known.

J 3215 Juniors, Transporter Set Sep-90 $35-45
Red/Silver Auto Transporter, Red/Silver Tandem Auto Transporter Trailer, 6 Cars

J 3216 Juniors, City Life Set Sep-90 $40-50
4 Cars, 3 Trucks, 2 Haulers.

J 3217 Juniors, Rally Sport Jumbo Set Sep-90 $60-80
12 Cars in Rally Trim, 2 Trucks, 2 Haulers.

J 3219 Juniors, Airport Set Sep-90 $30-45
Concord, London Taxi, 2 Trucks, 1 Hauler

J 3500 Coca-Cola 4 pc.Truck Set Apr-87 $30-50
Red Superhaulers Scammel Articulated Truck, Red Juniors Iveco Box Van, Red Juniors Iveco Beverage Truck with White Beverage Rack Carrying Red Cases, Red Juniors Renault Trafic Van, All Decorated "Coca-Cola." (Produced for the U.S. Market.)

J 3600 Coca-Cola 4 pc. Racing Set Apr-87 $30-50
Red Superhaulers Scammel Articulated Truck "TURBO RACING TEAM," Red Juniors Custom Van, Red Juniors Corvette with White Hood "7," White Juniors Firebird with Red Hood "12," All Decorated "Coca-Cola." (Produced for the U.S. Market.)

J 3700 Juniors — Coca Cola Race Team Car & Transporter May-87 $25-45
Red Scammel with White 3 Axle Chassis & "Coca-Cola" on Doors, Red Single Deck Trailer with White Chassis, White/Red Juniors Firebird "Coca-Cola 12" (3 Wheel Types), Tan Plastic Crate with Red "Coca-Cola RACING TEAM." (Produced for the U.S. Market.)

3.3: The Mattel Years: 1990 Renumbering—1995 Management Buyout

This section contains the variations listing for models produced from the time of the 1990 general renumbering resulting from the Mattel buyout to the 1995 management buyout. Note that items produced during this time would be considered Mattel products. Some are known to carry both the Corgi "Skidding Car" or "Dog Profile" logo and the Mattel "Buzzsaw" logo on the box. However, Corgi was always maintained as a separate entity within the corporation. A bit of crossover did occur between the former Juniors line and Mattel's Hot Wheels, but these will be described individually. Auto-City (Juniors and Haulers) items released by Mattel as Hot Wheels after the 1995 corporate split, if known, are also listed at the end of this section.

NOTE: Values shown are in U.S. dollars for mint-in-mint boxed condition as of January 1997. Subtract 35-40 percent for mint unboxed, 50-60 percent for excellent, 60-70 percent for vg/chipped.

90011 **Auto-City (Juniors) — Ford Transit Van Royal Mail** **1991?** **$1.25-1.50**

90012 **Auto-City (Juniors) — Ford Transit Van AA with Light** **1994?** **$1.25-1.50**

90013 **Auto-City (Juniors) — Ford Transit Van Police** **Jan-91** **$1.25-1.50**

90015 **Auto-City (Juniors) — Ford Transit Van, RAC** **Jan-91** **$1.25-1.50**

90018 **Auto-City (Juniors) — Ford Transit Van Het Belgische Rode Kruis** **Mar-91** **$3-5**

90030 **Auto-City (Juniors) — ERF Fire Engine** **1991?** **$1.25-1.50**
Red Body with Silver Sides, White "FIRE SERVICE 999" on Sides over Windows, Black Plastic Base, Blue Windows, Yellow Removable Ladder, 8-Div Wheels.

90035 **Auto-City (Juniors) — Simon Snorkel, Fire** **1991?** **$1.25-1.50**
Red Body with White Cab Roof, Silver Deck & Trim, Yellow Plastic Base & Boom, Blue Windows, Black "FIRE DEPT 07" on Cab Roof, Black "SIMON SNORKEL" on Boom, 4-Div Wheels.

90036? **Auto-City (Juniors) — Simon Snorkel Utility Service** **1994?** **$1.25-1.50**
Orange Body with Green Roof & Deck, Green Plastic Base & Boom, Blue Windows, White "S-24" on Roof and Sides, 4-Div Wheels.

90040 **Auto-City (Juniors) — Iveco Container Truck, Wispa** **Jan-91** **$1.25-1.50**

90042 **Auto-City (Juniors) — Iveco Container Truck, Mars** **1994?** **$1.25-1.50**
Dk. Brown Cab/Chassis, Dk. Brown Box with "Mars" Labels, Black Plastic Base & Interior, Clear Windows, 8-Div Wheels.

90044 **Auto-City (Juniors) — Iveco Container Truck, The Sweater Shop** **Dec-93** **$3-5**

90045 **Auto-City (Juniors) — Iveco Soda Truck Pepsi** **1994?** **$1.25-1.50**

90065 **Auto-City (Juniors) — Iveco Tanker Truck Shell** **Jan-91** **$1.25-1.50**
Yellow with White Cab/Chassis, Gray Tank with "Shell" & Stripes, Black Plastic Chassis & Interior, Clear Windows, 8-Div Wheels.

90076 **Auto-City (Juniors) — BMW 325i** **Jan-91** **$1.25-1.50**
Metallic Blue

90085 **Auto-City (Juniors) — London Taxi, Black** **1991?** **$1.25-1.50**
Black Body, Plated Base, Red Interior.

90086 **Auto-City (Juniors) — London Taxi, Cutty Sark Whisky** **May-92** **$3-5**
Yellow Body with Black Roof, Plated Base, Red Interior, "Cutty Sark Scots Whisky" Logo on Hood & Doors, 4-Div Wheels.

90089 **Auto-City (Juniors) — London Taxi, Hamley's** **Jul-94** **$3-5**

90110 **Auto-City (Juniors) — London Bus Eve. Standard** **1991?** **$3-5**

90111 **Auto-City (Juniors) — London Bus Hamley's** **Jul-94** **$3-5**

90127 **Auto-City (Juniors) — Ford Transit Wrecker, BP** **1994?** **$1.25-1.50**
Green Body with White Lower Sides & Yellow Stripe, "BP" Logos on Hood & Behind Doors, Yellow Boom & Lightbar, Black Hook, Black Plastic Base, Clear Windows, 8-Div Wheels.

90135 **Auto-City (Juniors) — Team Castrol Toyota Celica** **Jan-94** **$1.25-1.50**

90160 **Auto-City (Juniors) — Ford Sierra Tasman Blue** **Jan-91** **$1.25-1.50**

90260a **Auto-City (Juniors) — Custom Van Team Racing 15** **1994?** **$1.25-1.50**
(No Logo) White Body with Blue Sides, Gray Plastic Base, Smoked Windows, "15" & "TEAM RACING" Logos, 8-Div Wheels.

90260b **Auto-City (Juniors) — Custom Van Team Racing 15** **1995?** **$3-5**
(Hot Wheels Logo)

90270 **Auto-City (Juniors) — Formula 1 Ferrari** **1994?** **$1.25-1.50**
Red Body, Black Diecast Base, Black Plastic Driver, Ferrari Logo, "28," "FIAT," "PIONEER," & "WEBER" Logos, 5-Spoke Wheels.

90317 **Auto-City (Juniors) — Fuji Racing Car** **Aug-92** **$1.25-1.50**

90320 **Auto-City (Juniors) — Iveco Garbage Truck** **1994?** **$1.25-1.50**
Orange Cab/Chassis with Green Roof, Orange Garbage Body, Black Plastic Chassis & Interior, White "A-10" on Cab Roof, Recycle Symbols on Body Sides, Clear Windows, 8-Div Wheels.

90360 **Auto-City (Juniors) — US Custom Van** **Jan-91** **$1.25-1.50**

90361 **Auto-City (Juniors) — US Custom Van Fuji Film** **Aug-92** **$1.25-1.50**

90371 **Auto-City (Juniors) — Land Rover HM Coastguard** **Jan-91** **$1.25-1.50**

90390 **Auto City (Juniors) — Mercedes Ambulance** **1994?** **$1.25-1.50**
White Body with Orange Sash over Hood, Sides & up to Top Rear Corners, Blue Windows, Black Base, Blue "AMBULANCE DIAL 999" and Medical Symbols, 8-Div Wheels.

90420 **Auto City (Juniors) — Buick Police** **1994?** **$1.25-1.50**
Black/White Body, Opaque Blue Lightbar, Black Plastic Base, Vacuum Plated Interior & Bumpers, Clear Windows, Orange Dot with Black "P.D.9" & "POLICE" on Roof, Black "POLICE" & Shield on Doors, Silver "POLICE" & "911" on Rear, Silver Shield on Hood, 8-Div Wheels.

90430 **Auto-City (Juniors) — Volvo 760, Green** **Jan-91** **$1.25-1.50**
Green Body

90440 **Auto-City (Juniors) — Porsche 935 Red/Black** **1994?** **$1.25-1.50**
Orange Body, Vacuum Plated Interior, Clear Windows, Black Plastic Base, Deep Blue/White Graphics, "PORSCHE" on Hood, "935" on Doors, 4-Div Wheels.

90460 **Auto-City (Juniors) — Mercedes 2.3/16 Racer** **Jan-91** **$1.25-1.50**

90470 **Auto-City (Juniors) — Jaguar XJ40, Police** **1991?** **$1.25-1.50**
White Body with Yellow Lower Sides, Black Checkered Pattern Dividing Colors, Dark Blue Windows, Opaque Blue Roof Light, Black "POLICE" & Shield on Hood, "POLICE" on Trunk Lid, 4-Div Wheels.

90471 **Auto-City (Juniors) — Jaguar XJ40, Gold** **Jan-91** **$1.25-1.50**

90505 **Auto City (Juniors) — Rescue Helicopter** **1994?** **$1.25-1.50**
Turquoise/White Body with "R" Logo, Clear Windows, Yellow Plastic Base & Blades. (Base still has 007 in recessed area from earlier James Bond Drax Helicopter usage.)

90541 **Auto-City (Juniors) — Ford Mustang** **Jan-91** **$1.25-1.50**

90550a **Auto-City (Juniors) — BMW 850i, Black** **Apr-91** **$1.25-1.50**

90550b **Auto-City (Juniors) — BMW 850i** **1994?** **$1.25-1.50**
White Body with Small BMW Logo on Hood, Black Interior, Black Plastic Base, 4-Div Wheels.

90560 **Auto-City (Juniors) — Ferrari 348TB** **Apr-91** **$1.25-1.50**
Red Body with Crest on Hood, Black Plastic Base, Tan Seats, Clear Windows, 4-Div Wheels.

90570 **Auto-City (Juniors) — Mercedes 500SL** **Jan-91** **$1.25-1.50**
Day-Glow Pink Body, Crest on Hood, Black Pinstripe on Sides, Black Diecast Base, Gray Interior, Clear Windshield with Black Edge Trim, 4-Div Wheels.

90571 **Auto-City (Juniors) — Mercedes 500SL** **1994?** **$1.25-1.50**
Day-Glow Yellow Body, Silver Crest on Hood, Black Pinstripe on Sides, Black Diecast Base, Gray Interior, Clear Windshield with Black Edge Trim, 4-Div Wheels.

90580 **Auto-City (Juniors) — Jaguar XJR9 Works Team** **Jan-91** **$1.25-1.50**
Metallic Purple Body, Blue Rear Spoiler, Black Plastic Base & Interior, Clear Windows, White "6 JAGUAR" & Gold Trim, 8-Div Wheels.

90800	**Auto-City (Juniors) — Emergency Set, 24 pcs**	**Jan-91**	**$25-30**
90820	**Auto-City (Juniors) — Race Rally Set, 24 pcs**	**Jan-91**	**$25-30**
90840	**Auto-City (Juniors) — City Scene Set, 24 pcs**	**Jan-91**	**$25-30**
90880	**Auto-City (Juniors) — USA Set, 24 pcs**	**Jan-91**	**$25-30**
90940	**Themed Twin Pack Assortment, (6 Variants)**	**Aug-94**	**$15-18**
90941	**Themed Triple Pack Assortment (4 Variants)**	**Aug-94**	**$12-15**
91000	**Auto-City (Haulers) — MAN Container Truck, Perrier**	**Jan-91**	**$2-3**
91010	**Auto-City (Haulers) — Ford Cargo Container Truck, Cadbury's**	**Jan-91**	**$2-3**
91040	**Auto-City (Haulers) — MAN Open Back Tipper**	**Jan-91**	**$2-3**
91081	**Auto-City (Haulers) — Ford Cargo Container Truck, Cadbury's**	**Mar-92**	**$2-3**
91160	**Auto-City (Haulers) — Kenworth Container Truck, Pepsi**	**Jan-91**	**$2-3**
91200	**Auto-City (Haulers) — Kenworth Open Back Tipper**	**Jan-91**	**$2-3**
91300	**Superhaulers — Volvo Container Truck Orangina**	**Jan-91**	**$10-12**
91301	**Superhaulers — Volvo Container Truck Snickers**	**Jan-91**	**$10-12**
91302	**Superhaulers — Volvo Container Truck Mars**	**Mar-92**	**$10-12**
91310	**Superhaulers — Volvo Container Truck HulaHoops**	**1994?**	**$10-12**
91340	**Superhaulers — Volvo Tanker, Shell**	**Jan-91**	**$10-12**
91341	**Superhaulers — Volvo Tanker, BP**	**Jan-91**	**$10-12**
91346	**Superhaulers — Volvo Tanker, Gulf**	**Nov-93**	**$10-12**
91350	**Superhauler — Volvo Container Truck Eddie Stobart Ltd.**	**Oct-92**	**$10-12**
91351	**Superhaulers — Volvo Container Truck Eddie Stobart Ltd.**	**1994?**	**$10-12**
91352	**Auto-City (Juniors) — Ford Transit Van Eddie Stobart Ltd.**	**1994?**	**$2-3**
91353	**Auto-City (Haulers) — Ford Cargo Container Truck, Eddie Stobart Ltd.**	**1994?**	**$3-5**
91356	**Gift Set — Eddie Stobart Ltd.**	**1994?**	**$18-20**
91380	**Superhaulers — Volvo Car Transporter**	**1991?**	**$10-12**
91385	**Race Transporter, Valvoline/Mark Martin**	**May-93**	**$25-30**
91388	**Race Transporter, Quaker State/Brett Bodine**	**Jun-93**	**$25-30**
91389	**Race Transporter, Texaco Havoline Davey Allison**	**Aug-94**	**$25-30**
91391	**Race Transporter, Citgo/Morgan Shepherd**	**Aug-94**	**$25-30**
91420	**Superhaulers — Seddon Atkinson Container Truck, Perrier**	**Jan-91**	**$10-12**
91500	**Superhaulers — Scammell Container Truck 7-Up**	**Jan-91**	**$10-12**
91500	**Superhaulers — Scammell Container Truck 7-Up**	**Jan-95**	**$10-12**
91501	**Superhaulers — Scammell Container Truck FAO Schwarz, White**	**Mar-91**	**$15-20**
91510	**Superhaulers — Scammell Container Truck FAO Schwarz, Black**	**Jul-92**	**$15-20**
91610	**Ford Escort Van, AA**	**Feb-94**	**$12-15**
91612	**Ford Escort Van, Royal Mail**	**????**	**$12-15**
91620	**Ford Escort Van, Gas**	**Jul-92**	**$12-15**
91644	**Ford Transit Van, AA**	**Feb-94**	**$12-15**
91657	**Ford Transit Van, Het Belgische Rode Kruis**	**Mar-91**	**$20-25**
91700	**Metrobus — Gold Rider**	**Jun-93**	**$15-18**
91701	**Metrobus — Midland Fox**	**Jun-93**	**$15-18**
91702	**Metrobus — Airbus**	**Aug-93**	**$15-18**
91704	**AEC Open Top Regent DD Bus Atlantic Park**	**Jan-93**	**$20-22**
91705	**Metrobus — Atlantic Park**	**Jan-93**	**$15-18**
91706	**Metrobus — Northern Superliner**	**Mar-94**	**$15-18**
91710	**Metrobus — Kowloon-Canton Railway Corp.**	**Jan-95**	**$15-18**
91722	**Ford Transit Van — City Link**	**Feb-96**	**$10-12**
91760	**London Double Decker Bus, red**	**1991?**	**$10-12**
91765	**Routemaster Bus, Open Top Crossville Happy Dragon**	**Jul-92**	**$15-18**
91766	**Routemaster Bus, Open Top London Coaches**	**Apr-93**	**$15-18**
91770	**Double Decker Bus, Open Top, Guernsey**	**????**	**$15-18**
91775	**Mercedes Bonna Ambulance St. Bartholomew's Hospital**	**Jan-91**	**$12-15**
91777	**Mercedes Bonna Ambulance "Ambulans SDL951"**	**May-92**	**$15-20**
91795	**Ford Transit Bus, Oxford City Nipper**	**????**	**$12-15**
91810	**London Taxi, Computer Cab, black**	**1991?**	**$7-10**
91812	**London Taxi, Financial Times**	**Sep-92**	**$15-20**
91814	**London Taxi, Evening Standard, White**	**Jul-94**	**$15-20**
91820	**Ford Transit Wrecker, AA**	**1994?**	**$13-15**
91835	**Concord, British Airways**	**????**	**$10-12**
91839	**Metrobus, Badgerline**	**Nov-94**	**$13-15**
91842	**Metrobus, Strathtay**	**1994?**	**$13-15**
91843	**Metrobus, Cardiff Bus**	**Oct-94**	**$13-15**
91844	**Metrobus, Nottingham City Transport**	**1994?**	**$13-15**

091846	Metrobus, Crosville	Nov-91	$13-15
91847	Metrobus, East Kent	Dec-91	$13-15
91848	Metrobus, Yorkshire Rider/Yorkshire Evening Post	Jan-93	$13-15
91849	Metrobus, Yorkshire Rider/Enviornment	Jun-92	$13-15
91850	Metrobus, Reading	Jul-92	$13-15
91851	Metrobus, West Midlands Travel	May-92	$25-28
91852	Metrobus, Stevensons	Sep-92	$15-18
91853	Metrobus, Bradford	Oct-92	$13-15
91854	Metrobus, Halifax	Oct-92	$13-15
91855	Metrobus, W. Yorkshire	Oct-92	$13-15
91856	Metrobus, Sunderland	Oct-92	$13-15
91857	Metrobus, Newcastle	Oct-92	$13-15
91858	Metrobus, Leeds	Jan-93	$13-15
91859	Metrobus, York YWP	Jan-93	$13-15
91860	Metrobus, Huddersfield Tramways	Jan-93	$13-15
91861	Metrobus, Todmorden	Jan-93	$13-15
91862	Metrobus, Bradford	Jan-93	$13-15
91863	Metrobus, Huddersfield	Jan-93	$13-15
91864	Metrobus, Grey Green	Jan-93	$13-15
91870	Ford Sierra Sapphire, Police	????	$13-15
91880	Range Rover, Police	????	$13-15
91890	Ford Sierra & Caravan Trailer Set	Jan-96	$20-22
91905	Plaxton Bus, Nottingham	Mar-91	$12-14
91909	Plaxton Bus, Finnair	Oct-92	$12-14
91911	Plaxton Bus, Applebys	Nov-91	$12-14
91912	Plaxton Bus, East Kent	Dec-91	$12-14
91913	Plaxton Bus, Voyager	May-92	$12-14
91914	Plaxton Bus, Gatwick/Heathrow Speedlink	Jun-92	$12-14
91915	Plaxton Bus, Tellus Midland Red (Biggest Little Auto Show)	Sep-92	$18-20
91916	Plaxton Bus, East Yorkshire	Oct-92	$12-14
91917	Plaxton Bus, Highwayman	Nov-93	$12-14
91918	Plaxton Bus, Southend	Jun-94	$12-14
91919	Plaxton Bus, Shearings	Apr-94	$12-14
91922	Plaxton Bus, H/Hempstead	????	$12-14
91922	Plaxton Bus, Harrow	????	$12-14
91935	Land Rover, H.M. Coastguard	1992?	$10-12
92030	Ford Sierra, Metropolitan Police	????	$10-12
92445	Auto-City (Juniors) — City Set	Aug-91	$???
92451	AA Gift Set	1994?	$18-20
92452	Mounted Police Set	1994?	$18-20
92460	Auto-City (Juniors) — Race Set	Aug-91	$10-12
92475	Auto-City (Juniors) — Emergency Set	Aug-91	$10-12
92610	Auto-City (Juniors) — Parcelforce Set	Aug-91	$10-12
92625	Auto-City (Juniors) — Transporter Set	Aug-91	$10-12
92661	Hamley's 2 pc. Set	Aug-94	$5-8
92721	Hamley's 3 pc. Set	Aug-94	$10-12
92978	Ferrari 355, "Goldeneye"	Aug-95	$25-28
93080	Auto-City Super Electronic Garage	Mar-92	$40-60
93135	Auto City — Ferry Port Playset	Jun-94	$???
93171	Auto-City (Haulers) — Haulers Assortment 3 x 8 Vehicles.	Jan-95	$40-50
93176	Auto-City (Haulers) — Kenworth Dump Truck, Wolf	Jan-95	$2-3
93176	Auto-City (Haulers) — Kenworth Box Truck, 7-Up	Jan-95	$2-3
93176	Auto-City (Haulers) — Kenworth Box Truck, Pepsi	Jan-95	$2-3
93176	Auto-City (Haulers) — Kenworth Box Truck, Texaco	Jan-95	$2-3
93176	Auto-City (Haulers) — Kenworth Box Truck, Ferrari	Jan-95	$2-3
93176	Auto-City (Haulers) — Ford Cargo Truck, Mars	Jan-95	$2-3
93176	Auto-City (Haulers) — Ford Cargo Truck, Dairlea Cheese	Jan-95	$2-3
93176	Auto-City (Haulers) — M.A.N. Truck Hula Hoops	Jan-95	$2-3
93176	Auto-City (Haulers) — M.A.N. Truck Robinson's Drinks	Jan-95	$2-3
93177	Auto-City Assortment — 6 ea. of 24 Vehicles	1994?	$150-175
93179	Auto-City (Juniors) — Mercedes 2.3 Taxi	1994?	$1.25-1.50

Yellow Body with Black Doors & Hood, Black Roof Sign "TAXI," Black Plastic Base & Interior, "TAXI" over Triangle on Hood & Doors, Clear Windows, 4-Div Wheels.

93180	Space Patrol Playset	Jun-94	$???
93181	Auto-City (Juniors) — Mercedes Bus, Hertz	1994?	$1.25-1.50
93182	Auto-City (Juniors) — Miniatures Assortment, 144 Vehicles	1995?	$200-250
93183	Refuse Truck, White/Green Department of Sanitation	Jan-95	$15-18
93184	Mercedes Bonna Ambulance	Jan-95	$10-12
93185	Jet Ranger Helicopter — Sheriff's Dept.	1994?	$10-12
93186	Jeep Golden Eagle	1991?	$10-12
93187	Street Sweeper, Yellow Public Works Dept.	Jan-95	$15-18
93200	Auto-City (Juniors) — 10pc Set (Hot Wheels Box)	1996?	$13-15
93230	Auto-City (Juniors) — 6pc Set "Hot Wheels Team Racing"	1994?	$20-25
93231	Auto-City (Juniors) — 6pc Rescue Service Set with Figures	1994?	$13-15
93233	Auto-City (Juniors) — 6pc Construction Set with Figures	1994?	$13-15
93234	Auto-City (Juniors) — Ford Transit Van, BP	1994?	$1.25-1.50

Green Body with White Lower Sides & Yellow Divider Stripe, "BP" on Hood & Sides, Black Plastic Base & Interior, Clear Windows, 4-Div Wheels.

93235	Auto-City (Juniors) — Tipper Truck, Wolf	1994?	$1.25-1.50

Yellow Body with Red "WOLF" on Roof, Gray Plastic Tipper Body with Yellow "5 WOLF" on Sides, Yellow Rear Gate, Clear Windows, Black Plastic Base, 8-Div Wheels.

93236	Auto-City (Juniors) — S.W.A.T. Vehicle	1994?	$1.25-1.50

Black Body with White Roof, Gray Plastic Base, Smoked Windows, Silver "SWAT" and Shield on Sides, Orange Dots with Black "N.Y.P.D." & "60" on Roof, 8-Div Wheels.

93237	Auto-City (Juniors) — Jeep Rescue 4x4	1994?	$1.25-1.50

Turquoise/White Body with "R" Logo & "RESCUE," Yellow Seats & Grill Guard, Black Plastic Base & Roll Cage, Off-Road 4-Crown Wheels.

93416	Auto-City (Juniors) — German Police Set	Jan-95	$13-15
93417a	Auto-City (Juniors) — Roadworks Set	Jan-95	$13-15
93417b	Auto-City (Hot Wheels) — 3pc Set "Hot Wheels Team Racing"	Jan-96	$5-10

Hot Rod Custom Van with Gray Base, Jaguar XJR & F1 Racer with Black Base, all with Dk. Blue Bodies, White Trim, "Hot Wheels" and "1" Logos, Oversize Race Driver Figure, Traffic Sign, 4 Traffic Cones, Hot Wheels Auto-City Card.

93425	Auto-City (Juniors) — 6 pc. Themed Sets	Jan-95	$13-15
93500	Model Brum (From BBC TV Series)	Jul-94	$20-25

93715	Mini Set (1/36), 3 pc, for Woolworths	Sep-91	$35-40
93717	Mini Set (1/36), 3 pc, for Woolworths	Not Produced	N/A
93735	Mini Set (1/36), 3 pc, Dk. Green/White/Red	????	$35-40
94005	Super Mini's 6 pc. Set with Emblems (All 6)	Mar-92	$70-75
94030	Rolls-Royce Corniche, Silver	Mar-91	$10-12
94045	Ferrari 308 GTs, Red	Mar-91	$10-12
94060	James Bond Aston Marsin DB6, Silver	????	$32-35
94090	Ford Sierra, Dk. Blue	Mar-91	$10-12
94106	BMW 525, Blue	????	$10-12
94120	Mercedes 2.3/16 Saloon, White	Mar-91	$10-12
94140	Mini Cooper, Monte-Carlo Red/White #37	Aug-92	$10-12
94141a	Mini Cooper, Green/White (Chrome Grill)	Aug-92	$10-12
94141b	Mini Cooper, Green/White (Black Grill)	Aug-92	$18-20
94150	Porsche 944 Coupe, Red	????	$10-12
94160	Renault 5 Turbo, Orange/Black/Red #8	????	$15-18
94171	The Italian Job Minis	????	$45-50
94180	Peugeot 205 T16, Red	Mar-91	$15-18
94182	Peugeot 205 T16, White	1992?	$15-18
94183	Peugeot 205 T16, Racing Red	1992?	$15-18
94220	Turbos, Ferrari 348TB, Red	Apr-91	$10-12
94360	Turbos, BMW 850i, Gold	Apr-91	$10-12
94510	Electronics Assortment 3x Porsche, 3x Mercedes	Mar-92	$30-50
94540	Auto-City (Juniors) — Porsche 911 Targa	1994?	$1.25-1.50

Metallic Gray Body with Porsche Crest on Hood, Clear Windows, Black Plastic Base & Interior, 4-Div Wheels.

94640	Super Electronic Lamborghini Diablo	Jun-94	$20-22
94660	Super Trucks Fire Engine	1994?	$22-25
94665	Super Trucks Mobile Crane	1994?	$22-25
95007	Race Aces Assortment with Driver Mercedes-Benz 2.3	May-93	$18-20
95007	Race Aces Asstmt with Driver — Porsche 944	May-93	$18-20
95007	Race Aces Asstmt with Driver — Jaguar XJS	May-93	$18-20
95007	Race Aces Asstmt with Driver — Peugeot 205	May-93	$18-20
95007	Race Aces Asstmt with Driver — Ford Sierra	May-93	$18-20
95007	Race Aces Asstmt with Driver — BMW 525	May-93	$18-20
95100	MGF Hard Top, White (1/18)	????	$32-35
95101	MGF Hard Top, Flame Red, (1/18)	????	$32-35
95102	MGF Roadster, British Racing Green, (1/18)	????	$32-35
95103	MGB Roadster, Tartan Red, (1/18)	????	$32-35
95104	MGB Roadster, Old English White, (1/18)	????	$32-35
95105	MGF Roadster, Metallic Charcoal, (1/18)	????	$42-45
95106	MGB Roadster, British Racing Green, (1/18)	????	$42-45
95330	Jaguar XJR9, Castrol	Jan-91	$10-12
95400	Kit — Bus Garage	1994?	$15-18
95480	OOC — Bus Garage	1994?	$15-18
95607	1957 Chevrolet, Turquoise/White	????	$18-20
96011	Mr. Bean's Mini	Jan-95	$15-18
96012	Ford Sierra Cosworth, "Spender"	May-95	$15-18
96040	Jaguar XK120, Top Down, White	Jan-91	$15-18
96041	Jaguar XK120, Top Down, B R Green	Apr-91	$15-18
96042	Jaguar E Type, Top Up, Cream	Sep-91	$15-18
96043	Jaguar E Type, Top Down, Black	Oct-91	$15-18
96044	Jaguar XK120, Top Up, Black, Tan Top	Nov-91	$15-18
96060	Jaguar XK120, Top Up, Black, White Top	Apr-91	$15-18
96080	Jaguar E Type, Top Down, Red	Jun-91	$15-18
96081	Jaguar E Type, Top Down, Primrose Yellow	Mar-92	$15-18
96082	Jaguar E Type, Ken Baker Rally, Silver	Jul-92	$15-18
96140	MGA Hardtop, Red	Jun-91	$15-18
96146	Mercedes 300SL Roadster, Top Up, Silver	Aug-93	$15-18
96180	MGA, Top Up, White, Gray Top	Jan-91	$15-18
96200	Austin Healey 3000, Hardtop, Aqua/White	Apr-91	$15-18
96220	Austin Healey 3000, Top Dn., Lt. Blue/Ivory	Jan-91	$15-18
96240	Austin Healey 3000, Top Dn. with Tonneau, Ivory	Jul-91	$15-18
96300	Triumph TR3a, Top Up, Red	Apr-91	$15-18
96320	Ferrari 250 GTO Sports, Red	Jan-91	$15-18
96360	Porsche 356, Top Down, Blue	Jan-91	$15-18
96410	Mercedes-Benz 300SL, Top Down, Red	Mar-93	$15-18
96411	Mercedes-Benz 300SL, Top Down, Gray	Dec-93	$15-18
96415	Mercedes-Benz 300SL, Top Up, Ivory	Mar-93	$15-18
96416	Mercedes-Benz 300SL, Top Up, Silver	Aug-93	$15-18
96445	30th Anniversary James Bond Aston Martin DB5	Oct-93	$35-40
96481	Ford Popular, Sage Green	Feb-94	$13-15
96501	Ford Cortina, Blue	Feb-94	$13-15
96502	Ford Cortina Rally, Donnington	Aug-95	$13-15
96504	Ford Cortina, Corgi Rally	????	$13-15
96560	Jaguar Mk II Saloon, Metallic Blue	????	$15-18
96570	1957 Chevy, (50 Millionth Chevrolet)	Jun-92	$18-20
	Bronze/White		
96571	1957 Chevy, Lt. Blue/White	Sep-92	$18-20
96596	Mini Van, Surrey	????	$15-18
96655	James Bond Aston Martin, Silver, 1/43	Aug-95	$32-35
96656	James Bond Aston Martin, Gold Plated, 1/43	Aug-95	$45-48
96657	James Bond Aston Martin, Silver, 1/36	Aug-95	$20-22
96660	Saab Rally, Erik Carlsson	????	$15-18
96662	Saab Rally, P. Moss	Nov-91	$15-18
96680	Jaguar MK II, Sterling Moss	????	$15-18
96682	Jaguar MK II, Inspector Morse	May-93	$18-20
96683	Jaguar MK II, Old English White	Feb-94	$15-18
96685	Jaguar MK II, Staffordshire Police	????	$15-18
96685	Jaguar Police Car, Staffordshire	????	$15-18
96721	Ford Zephyr Rallye, Anne Hall	Jan-92	$15-18
96740	Morris Minor Saloon, Rally #121	????	$15-18
96741	Morris Minor Saloon, Himalayan Rally	Dec-91	$15-18
96742	Morris Minor Saloon London to Peking Rally	Jun-93	$15-18
96744	Morris Minor Saloon, Panda Police	Feb-94	$15-18
96745	Morris Minor Saloon, Black	Feb-94	$15-18

No.	Description	Date	Price
96746	Morris Minor Saloon Rally, Red	Feb-94	$15-18
96750	Morris Minor Convertible, Top Up	Apr-94	$15-18
Snowberry White			
96751	Morris Minor Convertible, Top Down, Blue	Mar-94	$15-18
96752	Morris Minor Convertible, Top Up	May-94	$15-18
Porcelain Green			
96753	Morris Minor Convertible, Top Down	May-94	$15-18
Frilford Gray			
96754	Morris Minor Convertible, Top ?, Yellow	????	$15-18
96755	Morris Minor Convertible, Top Up, Taupe	Oct-94	$15-18
96756	Morris 1000 Van, "Bristol Omnibus"	Mar-95	$15-18
96757	Morris Minor Convertible, Blue, "Lovejoy"	Mar-95	$15-18
96758	Morris Minor, Lt. Blue, "Some Mother's...."	Mar-95	$15-18
96759	Morris Minor, Merthyr Tydfil	Jan-95	$15-18
96760	Ford Cortina Rally, Sir John Whitmore	Jun-91	$15-18
96763	Ford Cortina Rally, Roger Clark	Feb-92	$15-18
96764	Ford Cortina Rally, John Clark	Jan-92	$15-18
96765	Morris Minor Convertible, Top Down	Jan-95	$15-18
Almond Green			
96766	Morris Minor Convertible, Top Up, Turquoise	Jan-95	$15-18
96775	Morris Minor Convertible, Top Up, White	????	$15-18
96837	Morris 1000 Van, Maidstone	Nov-94	$15-18
96839	Morris 1000 Van, Royal Mail	Aug-94	$15-18
96840	Morris 1000 Van, Bristol Water	Jul-91	$15-18
96842	Morris 1000 Van, Post Office Telephones	Jul-91	$15-18
96843	Morris 1000 Van, NAMAC	1991?	$20-22
Similar to Q957/21			
96844	Morris 1000 Van, A. Dunn & Son	Jul-91	$15-18
96845	Morris 1000 Van, Bishop's Removals	Jul-91	$15-18
96846	Morris 1000 Van, Tiger	Jun-92	$15-18
96847	Morris 1000 Van, Colman's Mustard	Feb-93	$15-18
96848	Morris 1000 Van, Bird's Custard	Jan-94	$15-18
96849	Morris 1000 Van, AA	Jan-94	$15-18
96850	Morris Minor Pick-Up, "Wimpey"	Apr-94	$15-18
96851	Morris Minor Pick-up, London Bk.	Oct-94	$15-18
96852	Morris Minor Pick-up, Gaydon	1994	$20-22
96854	Morris Minor Pick-Up, "Morris Motors"	Mar-95	$15-18
96855	Morris Van, Wiltshire Police	????	$15-18
96860	Ford Popular Van, Eastbourne Motors	Jun-91	$13-15
96863	Ford Popular Van, Sunlight Soap	Mar-93	$13-15
96865	Ford Popular Van, The Beezer	May-92	$13-15
96866	Ford Popular Van, Gas	Jan-94	$13-15
96870	Morris Minor Traveler, Dk. Green	Apr-94	$20-22
96871	Morris Minor Traveler, Black	Aug-94	$15-18
96872a	Morris Minor Traveler, Corgi Collector Club	Apr-94	$15-18
96872b	Morris Minor Traveler, Corgi Collector Club	Apr-94	$20-25
Without date			
96873	Morris Minor Traveler, Edinburgh Police	Jan-95	$15-18
96874	Morris Minor Traveler, White	Jan-95	$15-18
96880	Jaguar Mk II Rally, Stirling Moss	Jul-91	$15-18
96881	Jaguar Mk II Rally, John Coombs	Jan-92	$15-18
96886	Morris J Van, Family Assurance	Jun-94	$15-18
96887	Morris J Van, Topper	Oct-92	$15-18
96888	Morris J Van, Southdown	Nov-95	$15-18
96890	Morris J Van, Corgi Collector Club 1991	????	$20-22
96891	Morris J Van, Morris Service	Jan-93	$15-18
96892	Morris J Van, Bovril	Feb-94	$15-18
96893	Morris J Van, Royal Mail	Dec-93	$15-18
96894	Morris J Van, Post Office Telephones	Jan-94	$15-18
96895	Morris J Van, Birmingham	Mar-95	$15-18
96900	Bedford CA Van, Manchester Evening News	Aug-91	$15-18
96903	Bedford CA Van, AA Roadservice	????	$15-18
96904	Bedford CA Van, RAC	Jan-94	$15-18
96905	Booking Van, Chipperfields	Mar-95	$30-35
96906	Bedford CA Van, Blackburn with Roof Ladder	Jun-95	$15-18
96920	Bedford Dormobile, Police	Aug-91	$15-18
96923	Bedford Dormobile, St. John's Ambulance	Jan-94	$15-18
96940	VW Caravanette, Red/Gray	????	$15-18
96941	VW Caravanette, Olive/Ivory	Jan-91	$15-18
96950	Mini Van, Royal Mail	May-94	$15-18
96951	Mini Van, Police	Apr-94	$15-18
96952	Mini Van, RAC	????	$15-18
96953	Mini Van, AA Road Service	????	$15-18
96955	Mini Van, Collector Club 1994 Collector Club 10th Anniversary	Jan-94	$15-18
96956	Mini Van, Surrey Police	Jan-95	$15-18
96960	VW Van, Bosch Auto Electric	May-91	$15-18
96961	VW Van, Captain Condor	Aug-92	$15-18
96965	VW Van, Corgi Collector Club 1992	Jan-92	$15-18
96978	Thorneycroft Bus, General	????	$20-22
96980	AEC DD Bus, Stevenson's	Jul-91	$20-22
96982	AEC Regent Bus, Rochdale	Jul-92	$28-30
96985	Thorneycroft Bus, East Surrey	May-92	$20-22
96986	Thorneycroft Bus, Brighton & Hove	Mar-93	$20-22
96988	Thorneycroft Bus, Beamish	Nov-93	$20-22
96989	Thorneycroft Bus, General	????	$20-22
96990	AEC Bus Set, AEC Regal Bus AEC Regent II Bus	Nov-91	$30-35
96991	Thorneycroft Bus, Sheffield	????	$20-22
96992	Thorneycroft Bus, Norfolk Bus	????	$20-22
96993	Thorneycroft Bus, Yellow Bus	????	$20-22
96994	Thorneycroft Bus, South Wales	????	$20-22
96995	Ian Allen Anneversary Set, Bus & Van	Jun-92	$18-20
96996	Thorneycroft Bus, Tilling, Thomas Tilbury	????	$20-22
97001	AEC Regent Bus, PMT	Apr-96	$28-30
97002	AEC Regent Bus, Sheffield	May-93	$28-30
97003	AEC Regent Bus, West Bridgeford	Jul-93	$28-30
97018	AEC Regal IV Bus, Dundee	Jul-95	$28-30
97020	AEC Regal Bus, Wye Valley Motors	Apr-94	$28-30
97021	AEC Regal Bus, MacBraynes	Oct-94	$35-38
97022	Living Van, Chipperfields	May-95	$35-38
97040	VW Camper, Green/White	Jul-91	$25-28
97049	Yellowstone Park 2 PC. Set Model T Phaeton & Tanker	Aug-94	$30-35
97050	AEC Regent Bus Set	Oct-93	$30-35
97051	Invictaway Set	Nov-93	$45-50
97052	Devon General Bus Set	Jun-94	$45-50
97053	Bus Set, Seagull/Regal, York Bros.	Feb-94	$32-35
97055	OOC — Thames Valley 2 pc. set	Nov-94	$28-30
97056	OOC — Crosville 2 pc. set	Nov-94	$28-30
97057	OOC — Southdown Motor Services Set	Jul-95	$28-30
97061	Coventry Bus Set, AEC & Bedford	Sep-91	$30-35
97062	AEC DD Bus, Oxford	Jan-92	$20-22
97063	Yelloway Bus Gift Set AEC Regal/Bedford OB	Nov-91	$45-50
97064	Blackpool Set, 3 Busses	Sep-93	$55-60
97065	Stagecoach Set	Oct-93	$45-50
97068	Routemasters in Exile, North	Feb-94	$30-35
97069	The Whittles Set	Dec-93	$35-38
97070	Bus Set, Regal/Bedford, Silver Service	Feb-92	$35-38
97071	Devon Bus Set, 2 AEC Busses	Mar-92	$30-35
97072	Provincial Bus Set AEC DD & AEC Single Deck	May-92	$30-32
97074	Routemasters in Exile, South	May-94	$30-35
97075	South Wales Bus Set Bedford OB & AEC Regal	Jul-92	$40-42
97076	Alexander & Sons Bus Set	????	$35-40
97077	East Lancashire Bus Set	????	$35-40
97078	Corkills Bedford OB Bus Set	Feb-93	$32-35
97079	Premier 70th Anniversary Set	Aug-93	$38-40
97080	Bedford Pantechnicon, John Julian	Jan-91	$20-22
97081	Bedford Pantechnicon Van, Blackpool Circus (Was D953/18)	Jan-91	$28-30
97082	Bedford Pantechnicon Van, Pickfords	Apr-91	$30-32
97083	Bedford Pantechnicon Van Brewer & Turnbull (Was D953/19)	Jan-91	$28-30
97084	Bedford Pantechnicon Van, Grattan	Oct-91	$22-25
97085	Bedford Pantechnicon Van, Slumberland	Dec-91	$20-22
97086	Bedford Pantechnicon Van, Freeborns	Sep-92	$22-25
97087	Bedford Pantechnicon Van, Barnados	????	$20-22
97088	Bedford Pantechnicon Van, White & Co.	Feb-93	$22-25
97089	Bedford Pantechnicon Van, Mason's	Apr-93	$22-25
97091	Bedford Pantechnicon Van G.H. Lucking & Sons	Aug-93	$20-22
97092	Bedford Pantechnicon Van Chipperfields, B Smee	Apr-95	$25-30
97093a	Bedford Pantechnicon, Happy Birthday (Personalized)	Dec-94	$20-22
97093b	Bedford Pantechnicon, Corgi Heritage Centre (250 Made)	Jun-96	$35-40
97095	OOC — Lancashire Holiday Set	????	$30-32
97096	OOC — Capital & Highlands Set	Nov-95	$30-32
97097	OOC — Bridges & Spires Set	Nov-95	$30-32
97100	Bedford OB Coach, Isle of Man	Jan-91	$22-25
97101	Bedford OB Coach, Scilly Isles	Aug-91	$18-20
97103	Bedford OB Coach, Skills	Apr-91	$20-22
97104	Bedford OB Coach, Bronte	Oct-91	$20-22
97105	Bedford OB Coach, Felix Coaches	Jul-92	$20-22
97106	Bedford OB Coach, Fred Bibby	Sep-92	$22-25
97107	Bedford OB Coach, Murgatroyd	Sep-92	$20-22
97109	Bedford OB Coach, Whittaker Tours	May-93	$22-25
97111	Bedford OB Coach, Meredith	Sep-93	$20-22
97113	Bedford OB Coach, Warburtons	Jul-93	$20-22
97115	Bedford OB Coach, Seagull	May-95	$25-28
97120	Bedford Box Van, LMS	Mar-91	$18-20
97123	Bedford Box Van, NSPCC	Dec-91	$20-22
97124	Bedford Box Van, Youngsters Toy Shop	Mar-93	$20-22
97125	Bedford Box Van, GPO	Apr-93	$20-22
97126	Bedford Box Van, National Coal Board	Jun-93	$20-22
97130	OOC — AEC Reliance, Oxford	Sep-94	$15-18
97133	Bedford OB Coach, Wartons	Jul-91	$20-22
97140	AEC Cabover Truck, Southern Railway	Mar-91	$38-40
97150	Thorneycroft Van, Royal Castles	Oct-92	$20-22
97151	Thorneycroft Van, Sandringham	Oct-92	$20-22
97152	Thorneycroft Van, Windsor Castle	Oct-92	$20-22
97153	Thorneycroft Van, Holyrood House	Oct-92	$20-22
97154	Thorneycroft Van, Kensington Palace	Oct-92	$20-22
97155	Thorneycroft Van, Balmoral	Oct-92	$20-22
97161	AEC Cabover Tanker, Mobil	????	$38-40
97162	Atkinson Ell. Tanker, Pollack	Jun-95	$38-40
97170	Burlingham Seagull Coach, Seagull Coaches	Jun-93	$25-28
97171	Burlingham Seagull Coach, Neath & Cardiff	Jul-93	$35-40
97172	Burlingham Seagull Coach, Stratford Blue	???-93	$65-70
97173	Burlingham Seagull Coach, Ribble	Oct-93	$42-45
97174	Burlingham Seagull Bus, Yelloway	Dec-93	$42-45
97175	Daimler CW Bus, West Bromwich	Apr-94	$22-25
97176	Burlingham Seagull Bus, King Alfred	Jul-94	$22-25
97177	Burlingham Seagull Bus, N. Roadways	Nov-94	$25-28
97178	Burlingham Seagull Bus, Coliseum	Mar-95	$25-28
97179	Burlingham Seagull Bus, Banfields	????	$22-25
97180	AEC Regal Bus, Grey-Green	Aug-91	$22-25
97181	AEC Regal Bus, Timpsons	Aug-91	$22-25
97184	AEC Regal Bus, Sheffield	Dec-91	$22-25
97185	AEC Regal Bus, West Riding	Sep-92	$22-25
97186	AEC Regal Bus, Gray Cars	Feb-92	$22-25
97187	AEC Regal Bus, Hansons	May-92	$22-25
97189	AEC Regal Bus, Oxford	Oct-91	$22-25
97190	AEC Regal Bus, Ledgard	Oct-91	$22-25
97191	AEC Regal Bus, Rosslyn Motors	Dec-91	$22-25
97192	Leyland Tiger Bus, Ribble	Jul-92	$22-25
97193	AEC Regal Bus, Carneys	Sep-92	$22-25
97195	Bedford Pantechnicon, Howell's	Feb-92	$22-25

97196	AEC Regal Bus, Stanley Field	Apr-93	$25-28
97197	AEC Regal Bus, Western Welsh	Jan-93	$22-25
97198	Guy Arab Bus, Southdown	Oct-92	$55-60
97199	Guy Arab Bus, Birkenhead	???-92	$30-35
97200	BRS Parcels Services Set Bedford Box Van & Morris J Van	Oct-91	$45-48
97201	Guy Arab Bus, Birmingham City Transport	Feb-93	$22-25
97202	Guy Arab Bus, Maidstone & District	Mar-93	$22-25
97203	Guy Arab Bus, London Transport	????	$22-25
97204	Guy Arab Bus, Coventry	Sep-93	$22-25
97205	Guy Arab Bus, Bournemouth	Oct-93	$22-25
97206	Guy Arab Bus, Northern General	Nov-93	$22-25
97210	Leyland Tiger Bus, Maypole Coaches	Feb-93	$25-28
97211	Leyland Tiger Bus, Bartons	Apr-93	$25-28
97212	Leyland Tiger Bus, Ellen Smith	Oct-93	$25-28
97213	Leyland Tiger Bus, Red & White	Jan-94	$25-28
97214	Leyland Tiger Bus, Skills — 75th	????	$25-28
97216	Leyland Tiger Bus, The Delaine	????	$25-28
97230	Leyland Atlantean Bus, Ribble "Gay Hostess"	Apr-94	$30-35
97231	Leyland Atlantean Bus, Hull	Sep-94	$30-35
97232	Leyland Atlantic Bus, Wallasey	Mar-95	$42-45
97233	Open Top Atlantic Bus, Devon General	May-95	$35-38
97240	Open Top Tram, Lowestoft	Jan-91	$18-20
97241	Open Top Tram, Southern Metropolitan	Jan-91	$18-20
97260	Closed Tram, Birkenhead	Jun-91	$18-20
97261	Closed Tram, South Shields	Apr-91	$18-20
97262	FullyClosed Tram, Blackpool	Jul-93	$18-20
97263	Closed Single Deck Tram, Ashton-Under-Lyne	May-94	$18-20
97264	Fully Closed Tram, Cardiff	May-94	$18-20
97265	Fully Closed Tram, Belfast	May-94	$18-20
97266	Open Top Tram, Paisley	May-94	$18-20
97267	Closed Tram, Grimsby	May-94	$18-20
97268	Closed Tram, L.C.C.	May-94	$18-20
97269	Open Top Tram, Plymouth	May-94	$18-20
97270	Closed Tram, Bolton Corp., "ACDO"	Aug-94	$18-20
97273	Closed Tram, Blackpool	????	$18-20
97281	Closed Tram, City of Coventry	????	$18-20
97285	FullyClosed Tram, Leicester	Mar-92	$18-20
97286	FullyClosed Tram, Sunderland	Mar-92	$18-20
97287	FullyClosed Tram, Nottingham	May-93	$18-20
97288	FullyClosed Tram, Sheffield	Mar-92	$18-20
97290	Open Top Tram, Hull	Mar-92	$18-20
97291	Open Top Tram, South Shields	Mar-92	$18-20
97293	FullyClosed Tram, Newcastle	May-93	$18-20
97294	FullyClosed Tram, Birmingham	May-93	$18-20
97295	Open Top Double Deck Tram, Sheffield	Nov-93	$18-20
97296	FullyClosed Tram, Liverpool	Nov-93	$18-20
97300	Bedford Articulated Lorry, Billy Smarts	Sep-93	$25-28
97301	Bedford Articulated Lorry, London Brick	Sep-94	$25-28
97303	Bedford Articulated Truck, Chipperfields	Nov-94	$35-40
97309	Foden, BRS	????	$35-40
97310	Guy Arab Bus, Southampton City	Jan-94	$30-40
97311	Guy Arab Bus, Midland Red	Sep-94	$30-40
97312	Guy Arab Bus, Wolverhampton (Guy Motors 80th Anniversary)	Nov-94	$30-40
97313	Guy Arab Bus, Paisley	Oct-94	$30-40
97314	Guy Arab Bus, Oxford	Jun-95	$30-40
97315	Guy Arab Bus, London Wartime	Sep-95	$30-40
97316	Karrier W Trolleybus, Ipswich	Nov-95	$42-44
97317	Foden, Scottish & Newcastle	Aug-95	$45-48
97318	Scammell Scarab, Webster's Brewing	Aug-95	$25-28
97319	ERF Tanker, Bass Ale	Aug-95	$45-48
97320	American LaFrance Ladder, Open Cab, Red	Mar-91	$40-42
97321	American LaFrance Ladder, Closed Cab Centerville	Feb-92	$40-42
97322	American LaFrance Pumper, Closed Cab Ext. Bmpr., Chicago	Apr-93	$25-28
97323	American LaFrance Pumper, Closed Cab Carnegie	Jun-93	$25-28
97324	American LaFrance Aerial Ladder Truck Open Cab, Orlando	Nov-93	$40-42
97325	American LaFrance Pumper, Closed Cab Ext.Bmpr, Denver	Dec-93	$25-28
97326	American LaFrance Pumper, Open Cab Orlando	Apr-94	$25-28
97327	Atkinson 8 Wheel, Eddie Stobart	Sep-95	$32-35
97328	AEC Tanker, Major Oil, "BP"	Nov-95	$45-48
97329	Bedford O Articulated, B.R.S.	Sep-95	$25-28
97331	American LaFrance Gift Set Scottsdale & South River	Oct-92	$65-70
97334	Atkinson 8 Wheel Truck, Lucozade	Jul-95	$45-48
97335	Scammell Scarab, Eskimo Frozen Foods	Sep-95	$25-28
97336	Daimler CW Bus, Glasgow	Oct-95	$35-38
97337	Mini Van, Esso's Fawley Refinery	Nov-95	$15-18
97338	Surtees, Mike Hammond	1994?	$13-15
97339	Mini Van, Fire Service	1994?	$15-18
97340	Burlingham Seagull Bus, Trent	Nov-95	$20-22
97341	Atlantean Bus, Maidstone	Sep-95	$35-38
97342	Burlingham Seagull Coach West Coast Motor Service Co. Ltd.	Sep-95	$25-28
97343	Morris Minor Traveler, Bomb Disposal	Oct-95	$15-18
97344	Morris Pickup, Blue Circle	Nov-95	$15-18
97345	Morris Minor Convertible, Top Down, Black	Nov-95	$15-18
97346	Morris Minor Pickup, Tarmac	Aug-95	$15-18
97347	Bedford OB Coach, Malta	Nov-95	$25-28
97351	AEC Ladder Truck Set	Not Produced	N/A
97352	AEC Ladder Truck, Stoke-on-Trent	Sep-93	$32-35
97353	AEC Ladder Truck, Dublin	May-94	$32-35
97355	AEC Pump Escape, Nottingham	Sep-92	$38-40
97356	AEC Pump Escape, Angus	????	$38-40
97357	AEC Pump Escape, Hertfordshire	May-93	$30-32
97358	AEC Pump Escape, Cleveland (UK)	Oct-93	$35-38
97359	AEC Water Tender Truck, Dublin	Jan-94	$32-35
97360	AEC Pump Escape, Rotherham	1994?	$30-32
97361	AEC Ladder Truck, New Zealand	Sep-95	$38-40
97363	Tiger Cub Bus, Edinburgh	Nov-95	$20-22
97364	Tiger Cub Bus, North Western	Jul-95	$20-22
97365	Double Deck Tram, Open Top, Blackpool	Sep-95	$20-22
97366	Atkinson 8 Wheel T/T, Tennant	Nov-95	$58-60
97367	Scammel Highwayman Tanker, Pointer	Sep-95	$45-48
97368	Scammel Highwayman Crane, Pickfords	Oct-95	$28-30
97369	AEC Truck/Trailer, Eddie Stobart	Jul-95	$42-45
97370	AEC Flatbed, Federation Ales	Jul-95	$25-28
97371	Bedford O Van, Cameron Ale	Sep-95	$25-28
97372	Atkinson Tanker, Mackeson	Jul-95	$45-48
97373	Hesketh 308/Ford Cosworth V8, James Hunt	Sep-95	$15-18
97374	Surtees TS9/Ford Cosworth V8, John Surtees	Sep-95	$15-18
97375	Shadow DNI/Ford Cosworth V8, Jackie Oliver	Sep-95	$15-18
97376	Ferrari 312B, Mario Andretti	Sep-95	$15-18
97377	Lotus 72D/Ford Cosworth V8, Emerson Fittipaldi	Sep-95	$15-18
97378	Surtees TS9B/Ford Cosworth V8, Mike Hailwood	Sep-95	$15-18
97385	AEC Ladder Truck, Cardiff	Oct-93	$35-38
97386	AEC Ladder Truck, Bristol	Mar-93	$32-35
97387	American LaFrance Aerial Ladder Truck, Closed Cab, Denver	Nov-94	$40-42
97389	1957 Chevy, Chicago Fire Chief	Aug-94	$18-20
97391	AEC Pumper Set	Not Produced	N/A
97392	Simon Snorkel, West Glamorgan	Oct-94	$42-45
97393	American LaFrance Pumper, Closed Cab, Ext. Bmpr., Wayne	Aug-94	$25-28
97395	American LaFrance Pumper, Open Cab, Vero Beach	Jan-95	$25-28
97396	57 Chevy, California Highway Patrol	Jan-95	$18-20
97397	57 Chevy, Fire Chief, Pensacola	Nov-95	$18-20
97398	American La France Aerial Ladder Tk, Open Cab, Jersey City	Apr-95	$40-42
97399	Simon Snorkel, Cleveland, U.K.	Aug-95	$42-45
97400	Cameo Assortment 5 pc Set	Apr-91	$25-28
97403	Cameo Assortment 8 pc. Set,	Mar-92	$40-42
97405	Cameo Assortment, 6 pc. Set, Fina	May-92	$30-32
97408	Cameo Assortment, 8 pc. Set, Cars	Mar-92	$40-42
97411BE	Cameo — Brit. European Air Bus	????	$4-6
97411BO	Cameo — Brit. Overseas Air Bus	????	$4-6
97411CH	Cameo — Charrington Truck	????	$4-6
97411EP	Cameo — Elf Petroleum Tanker	????	$4-6
97411FB	Cameo — Fyffes Bananas Truck	????	$4-6
97411FL	Cameo — Flowers Bitters Truck	????	$4-6
97411GC	Cameo — Gaymers Cyder Truck	????	$4-6
97411JL	Cameo — Joseph Lucas Truck	????	$4-6
97412CD	Cameo — Citroen 2CV "Dolly"	????	$4-6
97412MC	Cameo — Mini Cooper	????	$4-6
97412MM	Cameo — Morris Minor	????	$4-6
97412VW	Cameo — Volkswagen	????	$4-6
97426	Cameo 3 pc. Set, Co-op/Cadbury's	May-92	$15-18
97427	Cadbury's "Sixties" Cameo Collection	Mar-93	$15-18
97445	Royal Cameo Collection, QEII & Prince Phillip	????	$12-15
97450	Mack B Pumper, Chicago	????	$30-32
97451	Mack CF Pumper, Berwick	????	$30-32
97461	Cameo — Model T Van Welsh Garden Festival		
97462	Cameo — Model T Van, Dulux	Jul-92	$4-6
97463	Cameo — Model T Van, Kleen-e-ze	Jul-92	$4-6
97465	Cameo — Model T Van, Princes Spreads	Mar-93	$4-6
97466	Cameo — Model T Van, Johnnie Walker	Jul-93	$4-6
97469	Cameo — Model T Van, Victrola	Aug-94	$4-6
97470	Cameo — Model T Van, Chupa Chups	Aug-91	$4-6
97476	Cameo — Mini, Safeguard	Nov-93	$4-6
97541	Morris 1000 Van Royal Mail/Post Office Set, 3 Vans	Dec-93	$50-60
97635	GMC TD4502 Bus, Los Angeles Motor Coach	Nov-95	$35-45
97680	Jaguar E Type 2 pc Set,	Jul-91	$22-25
	Gray Top Down and Red Top Up		
97681	Stirling's Choice Set, Austin Healey 3000 & Jaguar XK120	Nov-91	$22-25
97690	Ferrari 3 pc Set, Olive, Tan, Dk. Blue	Oct-91	$32-35
97695	The Abingdon Collection, 3 pcs.	Aug-92	$32-35
97697	Leicester & Rutland Police Set	Nov-93	$28-30
97698	Metropoliton Police Set	Sep-93	$28-30
97700	Jaguar 3 pc Set, XK120, E-Type, Mk'l	Jul-91	$32-35
97701	Jaguar E Type Racing Set, 2 pc.	Sep-91	$22-25
97702	Jaguar Set, XK120, XKE, Mk II	May-92	$22-25
97706	Jaguar XK120 Set, First Time Out	Nov-93	$25-28
97708	Tour de France Set	Nov-93	$30-35
97709	Alpine Rally Set	Dec-93	$25-28
97712	Monte-Carlo Mini-Cooper Set, '64, '65, '67	Oct-92	$45-50
97714	D-Day 50 Years Set	Jun-94	$30-35
97721	Durham Police Set, Jaguar & Mini	Feb-94	$25-28
97722	S. Glamorgan Police Set	Apr-94	$28-30
97730	Austin Healey Set, 3 Cars	May-92	$35-38
97735	The Cumbrian Set, Morris J & Bedford O	Jul-92	$30-35
97740	The Times 2 pc Set, Morris 1000 Van & Bedford CA Van	Jul-91	$25-28
97741	Jersey Island Transport Set 2 Bedford OB Coaches	Jan-91	$35-38
97742	John Smith's 2 pc Set, Thorneycroft Barrel Truck & Tanker	Apr-91	$30-35
97743	United Daries Set	????	$22-25
97746	Toymaster Gift Set, 2 pc, Bedford Van/Morris 1000 Van	Nov-95	$22-25
97747	Webster's Brewery Set, Thorneycroft Barrel Truck & Tanker	Oct-91	$40-45
97749	British Rail Gift Set, 2 pc,	Jan-92	$40-45
97750	East Kent Gift Set, Bedford Bus/AEC Regal Bus	Dec-91	$35-40
97751	Bass 2 pc. Set, Thorneycroft Barrel Truck & Model T Van	Oct-92	$35-40
97752	Ruddles 2pc. Set, Bedford Box Van & Thorneycroft Barrel Truck	Sep-92	$40-45
97753	Terrys 2 pc. Set, Thorneycroft Box Van & Model T Van	Sep-92	$35-40
97754	LMS 2 pc, Thorneycroft Van & COE Box Van	Jan-93	$40-45
97755	Whitbread 2pc.Set, AEC Tanker & Thorneycroft Barrel Truck	Jul-92	$40-45
97765	Strathblair Bus Set, Bedford OB/Morris Van	????	$35-40
97770	Mini Van, Hamleys	Sep-95	$15-18
97771	Mini Van, Cavendish Woodhouse	Sep-95	$15-18
97772	Mini Van, Burberrys	Sep-95	$15-18

97780	Jaguar Through the Years Set	????	$32-35
97781	Tate & Lyle Set, Foden & Bedford Trucks	????	$40-45
97793	Terrys of York Set, 2 Vans	????	$35-38
97800	Reading, Sunbeam W. Trolleybus	Feb-94	$32-35
97801	Sunbeam Trolley Bus, Maidstone	Jan-94	$40-45
97802	Metrobus, Cleveland Transit	Feb-96	$13-15
97803	Metrobus, Kingston upon Hull City Transport	Feb-96	$13-15
97810	Leyland Tiger Cub, Leicester	Sep-95	$22-25
97811	OOC — Weymann Trolleybus, Notts & Derby Traction Co.	Sep-95	$15-18
97813	OOC — B.U.T. Trolleybus, Brighton Corp.	Apr-95	$13-15
97814	OOC — AEC Regent II, London Transport	Sep-95	$13-15
97820	Daimler CW Bus, West Bromwich	Mar-94	$25-28
97821	Daimler Duple Coach, Swan	Mar-94	$22-25
97822	Daimler CW Bus, Derby Corp.	May-94	$28-30
97823	Daimler Duple Coach, Blue Bus	May-94	$22-25
97824	Daimler Fleet Bus, Birmingham	Jul-94	$30-35
97825	Daimler Duple Coach, Burwell & Districts	Dec-94	$20-22
97826	Daimler Fleetline Bus, Manchester	Oct-94	$20-22
97827	Daimler CW Bus, Sheffield	Aug-94	$28-30
97828a	Daimler Fleetline, Rochdale	Apr-95	$30-35
97828b	Daimler Fleetline, Corgi Heritage Center (Qty: 500)	Jul-95	$50-60
97829	Daimler CW Utility Bus, Douglas	Jun-95	$30-35
97830	Daimler Duple Bus, Scout	Mar-95	$30-35
97831	Royal Mail 2 pc Set, Cameo	Nov-94	$15-18
97832	Pickfords 2 pc Set, Cameo	Nov-94	$15-18
97833	Railway 4 pc Set, Cameo	Nov-94	$28-30
97835	OOC — Leyland Leopard, Ribble	Oct-94	$13-15
97836	OOC — Leyland PS1/ECW, East Yorkshire	Jan-95	$15-18
97837	OOC — Leyland PDIA/ECW, North Western Road Car Co. Ltd.	Sep-95	$15-18
97838	OOC — Leyland PS1/ECW, Birch Bros.	Jul-95	$15-18
97839	OOC — Leyland PDIA/ECW Eastern Counties	Apr-95	$15-18
97840	Scammell Hiwayman Tanker, Shell/BP	Jul-95	$45-48
97850	OOC — Bristol-L, Merthyr	May-94	$13-15
97851	OOC — Bristol-K, Hants	May-94	$13-15
97852	OOC — Bristol-L, Maidstone	Dec-94	$13-15
97853	OOC — Bristol-K, Bristol Omnibus Co.	Dec-94	$13-15
97854	OOC — Bristol-K, Western National	Nov-94	$13-15
97855	OOC — Bristol-L, United Auto	Jul-94	$13-15
97856	OOC — Bristol-K, West Yorkshire	Aug-94	$13-15
97857	OOC — Bristol K, London	Dec-94	$13-15
97858	OOC — Bristol K6B/ECW Caledonian Omnibus	Jul-95	$15-18
97859	OOC — Bristol K, Bristol Tramways	Feb-95	$15-18
97860	OOC — Bristol L, Bath Tramways	Nov-95	$15-18
97867	OOC — Bristol K, North Western Road Car	Mar-95	$15-18
97868	OOC — Bristol L, Eastern Counties	Jul-95	$15-18
97869	OOC — Bristol L5G/ECW, Lincolnshire Road Car	Jul-95	$15-18
97870	OOC — Karrier W. Trolley, Newcastle	Oct-94	$40-42
97871	OOC — Karrier W Trolley, Bradford	Apr-95	$40-42
97875	OOC — Bristol Bus, Cardiff 75th Anniversary	????	$15-18
97885	Highwayman, Caravan & Trailer, Chipperfields	May-95	$50-60
97886	Highwayman with Crane, Chipperfields	Dec-94	$35-45
97887	Bedford with Horse Trailer, Chipperfields	Aug-95	$50-60
97888	Foden Pole Truck with Caravan, Chipperfields's	Aug-95	$60-70
97889	AEC Truck & Trailer, Chipperfields	Sep-95	$50-60
97891	AEC Truck & Trailer, Billy Smart's Circus	Dec-92	$50-60
97892	AEC Truck & Trailer, S. Houseman	Feb-93	$40-45
97893	AEC Truck & Trailer, J. Ayers	Dec-92	$40-45
97894	AEC Mercury, Pickfords	Nov-93	$45-48
97895	AEC Flatbed Truck with 2 Trailers, BRS	Feb-94	$45-48
97896	AEC 8 Wheel Pole Truck, Chipperfields	Feb-95	$50-60
97897	Scammell Highwayman & Trailers Billy Smart's Circus	Jan-96	$50-60
97898	AEC 8-Wheel Pole Truck, Chipperfields	????	$50-60
97900	OOC — BET Federation, Devon General	Jun-94	$15-18
97901	OOC — Leyland Leopard, Midland Red	????	$15-18
97902	OOC — AEC Reliance Potteries Motor Traction	Apr-95	$15-18
97903	OOC — Leyland Leopard, Londonderry	Aug-95	$15-18
97904	OOC — AEC Reliance, Leicester	Nov-95	$15-18
97905	OOC — Leyland Leopard, Safeway Serv.	Nov-95	$13-15
97906	OOC — Highlands Set	1994?	$18-20
97907	OOC — Bridges and Spires Set	1994?	$18-20
97910	Scammell Scarab, Railfreight Grey	Jan-94	$13-15
97911	Scammell Scarab, British Railways	Jul-93	$13-15
97912	Scammell Scarab, Royal Mail	Dec-93	$13-15
97913	Scammell Scarab, Rail Freight	????	$25-28
97914	Scammell Scarab, BRS Parcels	Nov-94	$28-30
97915	Highwayman & 2 Trailers, Chipperfields	Oct-94	$50-60
97916	Scammell Scarab, Corgi	????	$30-35
97917	Scammell Scarab, Watneys	Jan-95	$25-28
97920	Hiwayman with 2 Trailers, R. Edwards	Jun-94	$45-48
97930	ERF Tanker, Blue Circle Cement	Apr-94	$45-48
97931	AEC Flatbed Truck, Greenall Whitley	Oct-94	$45-48
97932	AEC Tanker, North Eastern Gas Board	????	$40-45
97940	ERF 8 Wheel Truck, Eddie Stobart	Aug-94	$45-48
97941	OOC — Leyland PD2/MCW Orion, St. Helens	Jul-95	$15-18
97942	ERF Flatbed with Barrels, Flowers	????	$42-45
97943	OOC — AEC Regent, Douglas Corp Trans.	Apr-95	$15-18
97944	OOC — Leyland PD2/MCW Orion, Newcastle	Feb-95	$15-18
97945	OOC — Leyland PD2/MCW Orion Ribble Motor Services Ltd.	Oct-95	$15-18
97950	Foden Tanker, Guinness	May-93	$45-48
97951	Foden Tanker, Milk Marketing Board	Aug-93	$45-48
97952	Foden Tanker, Hovis	Oct-93	$45-48
97955	Foden, Moore Ltd., "Guinness"	May-94	$45-48
97956	Foden 8 Wheel Truck, Pickfords	Oct-94	$45-48
97957	ERF 8 Wheel Truck, Chipperfields	Jan-95	$50-60

97965	OOC — Lancashire Set	1994?	$18-20
97970	Foden Elliptical Tanker, Regent	Mar-94	$45-48
97971	Foden 8 Wheel Rigid, Robson	????	$45-48
97975	Scammel H'wman & 2 Trlrs, Chipperfields	????	$45-48
97980	ERF Elliptical Tanker, ESSO	????	$45-48
98100	Volvo Container Truck, Swift Service	Nov-93	$10-12
98101	Volvo Container Truck, Amtrak	Nov-93	$10-12
98102	Volvo Container Truck, U.T.C.	Dec-93	$10-12
98103	Volvo Container Truck, P&O Ferrymasters	Dec-93	$10-12
98104a	Morris 1000 Van, Royal Mail	Jun-93	$15-18
98104b	Morris 1000 Van, Royal Mail (with Xmas Ad)	????	$15-18
98105	Bedford CA Van, AA	1994?	$15-18
98106	Bedford CA Van, Police	????	$15-18
98108	Ford Popular Van, Royal Mail	1994?	$13-15
98109	Ford Popular Van, Royal Mail	????	$13-15
98120	Jaguar E Type, Top Up, B.R. Green	Apr-93	$13-15
98121	Jaguar E Type, Top Down, Lt. Met. Blue	????	$13-15
98122	Porsche 356, Top Up, black	Apr-93	$13-15
98123	Porsche 356, Top Down, Silver	Apr-93	$13-15
98124	Ferrari 250 GT, red	Apr-93	$13-15
98130	Ford Cortina, White with Olive Stripe	Mar-93	$15-18
98131	Jaguar Mk.II Saloon, Silver Blue	Mar-93	$15-18
98132	Ford Popular Saloon, Black	Mar-93	$18-20
98136	Mini Cooper, Green/White	Mar-93	$15-18
98137	Mini Cooper, Wickerwork	Oct-93	$15-18
98138	Mini Cooper, Brit. Green	Feb-94	$15-18
98139	Mini Cooper, red/white	Feb-94	$15-18
98141	Mini Cooper, Liverpool Police	????	$15-18
98150	Open Top Tram, Lowestoft	Jul-93	$15-18
98151	Open Top Tram, South Metropolitan	Jul-93	$15-18
98152	Closed Top Tram, Glasgow	Jul-93	$15-18
98153	Closed Top Tram, London Transport	Jul-93	$15-18
98154	FullyClosed Tram, Dover	Jul-93	$15-18
98161	AEC Regal Bus, Eastern Counties	Jun-93	$22-25
98162	AEC Regal Bus, Wallace Arnold	Jul-93	$30-32
98163	Bedford OB Coach, Grey Green	Apr-93	$20-22
98164	Bedford OB Coach, Edinburgh	Jun-93	$20-22
98165	Ford Cortina, London Transport	Sep-95	$13-15
98304	Superhauler — Volvo Container, Christian Salvesen	Feb-94	$10-12
98305	Superhauler — Volvo Container Truck, Excel	Feb-94	$10-12
98306	Superhauler — Volvo Container Truck, Dodds	Apr-94	$10-12
98307	Superhauler — Volvo Container Truck, Lynx	Apr-94	$10-12
98365	Open Top Tram, Blackpool	????	$15-18
98380	John Force 2 pc. Funny Car Set, Castrol GTX	1995	$32-35
98381	Race Transporter with Funny Car, Mooneyes/Christian Salvesen	1995	$32-35
98382	Race Transporter with Funny Car, Kendall/Chuck Etchells	1995	$32-35
98383x	Race Transporter with Funny Car, Fruit of the Loom/? (Not Produced)		N/A
98383	Race Transporter with Funny Car, In-Out, Burger/Mark Oswald	1995	$32-35
98384	Race Transporter with Dragster, Am. Int'l, Airways/Scott Kalitta	1995	$32-35
98385	Race Transporter with Funny Car, Western Auto/Al Hoffman	1995	$32-35
98399	Race Transporter, Mello Yello/Kyle Petty	1994	$25-30
98400	Race Transporter, Maxwell House/Bobby Labonte	Aug-94	$25-30
98401	Race Transporter, Motorcraft/Lake Speed	Aug-94	$25-30
98404	Race Transporter, Raybestos/Jeff Burton	Aug-94	$25-30
98405	Race Transporter, DuPont/Jeff Gordon	1994	$25-30
98407	Race Transporter, Family Channel/Ted Musgrave	1994	$25-30
98408	Race Transporter, Kellogg's/Terry Labonte	1994	$25-30
98421	MCI 102DL3, Demo Bus	Aug-94	$40-50
98422	MCI 102DL3, Peter Pan Trailways	Aug-95	$40-50
98427	MCI 102DL3, Peter Pan Birthday	Aug-94	$40-50
98431	MCI 102DL3, Peter Pan Birthday (Bank)	Sep-94	$40-50
98432	MCI 102DL3, Demo Bus (Bank)	Sep-94	$40-50
98433	MCI 102DL3, Peter Pan Trailways (Bank)	Sep-94	$40-50
98449	White Tanker, The Petrol Corp.	Mar-95	$28-30
98450	Mack B Series Pumper, Chicago	Aug-95	$28-30
98451	Mack CF Pumper, Berwick	Oct-95	$25-28
98452	White Tanker, Volunteer Fire Department	Apr-95	$28-30
98453	Mack B Truck, Breyer 45th Anniversary	Apr-95	$32-35
98454	Mack B Truck, Wilton Farm Dairy	Jun-95	$32-35
98455	White Open Truck with Canvas Cover, P.P.R.	Sep-95	$32-35
98456	White Open Truck with Sacks, Scheiwe's Coal	Aug-95	$32-35
98457	White Open Truck with Soda Cases White Rock Club Soda	Aug-95	$30-32
98458	White Open Truck with Barrels, Jacob Ruppert's Beer	May-95	$30-32
98459	White Open Truck with Beer Cases Triple XXX Root Beer	Apr-95	$32-35
98460	Yellow 743, New York World's Fair	Aug-94	$22-25
98461	Yellow 743, Greyhound "Battle of Britain"	Aug-94	$22-25
98462	Yellow 743, Greyhound, "Chicago"	Aug-94	$22-25
98464	Yellow 743, Burlington Trailways	Aug-94	$22-25
98465	Yellow 743, Burlington Trailways "Pin Stripe"	Aug-94	$22-25
98467	Yellow 743, Public Service of New Jersey	Mar-95	$22-25
98468	Yellow 743, Champlain with Billboards	Aug-94	$28-30
98469	Yellow 743, Greyhound Lines	????	$28-30
98470	Yellow 743, Greyhound "Silverside"	Mar-95	$28-30
98471	Yellow 743, Greyhound "Battle of Britain"	????	$28-30
98472	Yellow 743, Greyhound "The W.A.C. Needs You"	Apr-95	$32-35
98473	Yellow 743, Greyhound "Join The WAVES"	Apr-95	$32-35
98475	VW Caravan, Fire Marshall	Nov-95	$20-22
98480	Mack Bulldog Van, Greyhound Express	1994	$15-18
98481	Mack Bulldog Van, Goodyear Wingfoot Express	Aug-94	$15-18
98484	Mack CF Pumper, Chicago	Aug-94	$25-28
98485	Mack CF Pumper, Neptune	????	$25-28
98486	Mack B Pumper, Paxtonia	Mar-95	$28-30
98510	Race Transporter with Dragster, Pennzoil/Eddie Hill	1995	$32-35
98511	Race Transporter with Dragster, Valvoline/Joe Amato	Aug-94	$32-35

98512	Race Transporter with Dragster, Budweiser/Kenny Bernstein	1994	$32-35
98513	Race Transporter with Dragster, McDonald's/Cory Mac	1995	$32-35
98514	Race Transporter with Dragster, La Victoria/Mike Dunn	1994	$32-35
98515	Race Transporter with Dragster, Castrol Syntec/Pat Austin	1995	$32-35
98517	Race Transporter with Dragster, Mopar/Tommy Johnson Jr.	1995	$32-35
98518	Race Transporter, Oldsmobile/Warren Johnson	Aug-94	$25-30
98519	Race Transporter, Super Clean/Larry Morgan	Aug-94	$25-30
98520	Race Transporter, Motorcraft/Bob Glidden	Aug-94	$25-30
98521	Race Transporter, Slick 50/Rickie Smith	Aug-94	$25-30
98524	Race Transporter, Mopar/Darrell Alderman	1995	$25-30
98525	Race Transporter, Winn Dixie/Mark Martin	1994	$25-30
98529	Race Transporter, FAO Schwarz	1995	$25-30
98600	GMC TD4502 Bus, Pacific Greyhound Lines	Nov-95	$35-45
98601	GMC TD4502 Bus, Pacific Electric	????	$35-45
98602	GMC TD4505 Bus, Greyhound Lines	Nov-95	$35-45
98603	GMC TD4506 Bus, Detroit D.S.R.	Nov-95	$35-45
98604	GMC TD4705 Bus, Fifth Avenue Coach Co.	Nov-95	$35-45
98650	MCI 102DL3, California Charter	????	$40-50
98651	MCI 102DL3, Thrasher Brothers The Barons	????	$40-50
98652	MCI 102DL3, P.C.S.T. Sea World	Nov-95	$40-50
98653	MCI 102DL3, P.C.S.T. Sea World (Bank)	????	$40-50
98751	Chitty Chitty Bang Bang (Reissue)	????	$100-120
98754	Bedford CA Van, Adventure	Dec-91	$25-30
98755	Ford Popular Van, Hotspur	Nov-91	$13-15
98756	Morris Minor Van, The Rover	Dec-91	$25-30
98757	VW Van, Skipper	Jan-92	$25-30
98758	Morris 1000 Van, The Wizard	Feb-92	$25-30
98759	The Dandy-Desperate Dan-Korky the Cat Set	Jan-92	$50-60
98960	The Beano, Morris J & Morris 1000 Vans	May-92	$55-65
98965	Dan Dare Eagle Set, VW Van & Bedford CA Van	May-92	$55-65
98970	X-Men Set, Morris J Van & Bedford CA Van	Sep-92	$50-60
98972	Spiderman Set	Sep-92	$50-60
98973	Captain America Set, VW Van & Ford Popular Van	Oct-92	$50-60
99054	Triumph TR3A, Top Up, Cream	????	$15-18
99076	Bently 3 Litre, Pewter (Civil Service Motoring Association)	1991?	$80-100
99104	Metrobus, Graham Ward	Jan-91	$13-15
99105	British Railways Set, 2 pcs (D46/1)	????	$32-35
99106	Bash Street Kids Set, 2 pcs (D47/1)	????	$32-35
99107	Bedford Dormobile, Brown/Cream	????	$15-18
99119	Bedford Bus, Eastern-National	????	$20-22
99140	Morris J Van, Pickfords	????	$15-18
99725	Whitbread Cameo 10 pc. Set	Jul-94	$60-70
99726	Cameo Chocolates 10 pc. Set	Jul-94	$60-70
99728	D-Day Cameo 10 pc. Set	Jul-94	$60-70
99801	Morris J Van, Walls Ice Cream	????	$15-18
?	Mini Checkmate (1/36)	????	$10-12
?	Mini Cooper (1/36)	????	$10-12
?	Mini Designer (1/36)	????	$10-12
?	Mini Neon (1/36)	????	$10-12
?	Morris 1000 Van, Corgi Classics 3rd Motor Show	Jun-94	$15-30
?	OOC — Leyland Leopard, Midland Red	Jun-94	$15-30
?	Scammell Scarab with Covered Trailer	Nov-94	$20-25

Club 10th Anniversary

?	Chipperfieldss 1995 Calender (Not A Model)	Dec-94	$15-18
?	Race Transporter, Kodak/ (?)	1995?	$25-35?
?	Jaguar XK120, Chrome Plate on Black Base	Apr-95	$20-40
?	Corgi 6 pc. Police Collection with Wood Base	Apr-95	$100-125
?	Corgi 7 pc. British Van Collection, Wood Base	May-95	$100-125
?	Corgi 7 pc. European Sports Car Collection Wood Base	May-95	$100-125
?	Burlingham Seagull, Banhields Coaches (Model Collector)	May-95	$25-30
?	Mini-Cooper (1:36), "Issigonis"	Jul-95	$10-12
?	Cameo — Mini, Filofax	Jul-95	$3-5
?	Cameo — Morris Open Truck, HSS	Jul-95	$3-5
?	MGF Top Down — MG Press Drive 95	1995	$80-100

Hot Wheels Made From Former Corgi Auto-City (Juniors) Dies

Early 1996 models considered Auto-City range vehicles in separate Hot Wheels range, baseplate text revised while in production replacing "Corgi" with "Hot Wheels" logo. Late 1996 and onward considered regular Hot Wheels range, models redecorated and fitted with Hot Wheels style wheels and sold intermixed with existing Hot Wheels models, heavily used in limited edition releases.

15111	Hot Wheels Auto-City Action Squad Set Rescue Station	1996	CURRENT

Fold-out Action Scene, White/Yellow Helicopter, Orange/Blue Jeep 4x4, Figure & Loose Accessories.

15113	Hot Wheels Auto-City Action Squad Set Skip Loader	1996	CURRENT

Fold-out Action Scene, Yellow/Silver Skip Loader (former E85-A), Figure & Loose Accessories.

15114	Hot Wheels Auto-City Action Squad Set Fire Station	1996	CURRENT

Fold-out Action Scene, Snorkel Fire Engine (former 90035), Figure & Loose Accessories.

15115	Hot Wheels Auto-City Action Squad Set Helicopter Squad	1996	CURRENT

Fold-out Action Scene, White/Yellow Helicopter, Figure & Loose Accessories.

15116	Hot Wheels Auto-City Action Squad Set F1 Racer Pit	1996	CURRENT

Fold-out Action Scene, Red F1 Racer, Figure & Loose Accessories.

?????	Hot Wheels — Porsche 911 Targa	1996	CURRENT

Details not yet known.

16247-0910	Holiday Hot Wheels — Porsche 911 Targa	1996	CURRENT

Red Vacuum Plated Body, HW Dished 5-Spoke Wheels with Green Spokes, Green Interior, Santa Figure Driving, Blue & Green Presents on Spoiler, "Happy Holidays '96" Trim, Clear/Green Case in Special Turntable Card.

16249-0910	Holiday Hot Wheels — Porsche 911 Targa	1996	CURRENT

Green Vacuum Plated Body, HW Dished 5-Spoke Wheels with Red Spokes, Red Interior, Santa Figure Driving, Red Santa's Sack on Spoiler, "Happy Holidays '96" Trim, Clear/Red Case in Special Turntable Card.

16301	Hot Wheels — Mercedes 500SL, #49.!	1996	CURRENT

Metallic Gray Body, Black Base, Red Interior, Black Trimmed Windshield with HW Logo in Bottom Right Corner, HW Dished 5-Spoke Wheels with Silver Spokes, Silver Grill, Red Taillamps.

?????	Hot Wheels — Gold Series III 16 Car Set	1996	CURRENT

All Former Corgi Vehicles, Black Bodies with Gold Wheel Centers, London Taxi has FAO Schwarz Logo on Sides. (FAO Schwarz Exclusive)

?????	Hot Wheels — 1957 T-Bird	1996	CURRENT

Numerous uses in sets in various colors, full details not yet known.

3.4: Corgi Classics Ltd.—New Independence
1995 Management Buyout-Present

This section contains the known or announced variations listing for models produced from the time of the January 1, 1996, new numbering system implementation onward to the publication date. Models produced by Corgi Classics Ltd. are presented here. Note that the Auto-City product line remained with Mattel at the time of the management buyout. Models from the Auto-City line are to be produced by Mattel as "Hot Wheels," although any variations known to have been issued will be listed in the previous section under each model's former number.

Detail Cars, which are marketed by Corgi Classics Ltd. in the British market, are actually produced by another firm and are not included in this section.

01801 Jaguar Mk II Saloon — "BUSTER" — Feb-96 CURRENT
Red Body, Chromed Wire Wheels.

01802 Jaguar Mk II — "INSPECTOR MORSE" — NOT ISSUED N/A
Planned 6/96 Reissue of earlier version.

02401 Austin Healey, Top Up — Primrose/Black — Jan-96 CURRENT
Primrose Yellow/Black Body, Black Top, Chromed Wire Wheels, Side Window Frames, Windshield Wipers, etc.

02501 Austin Healey, Top Down — Jan-96 CURRENT
Ivory/Black Body, Chromed Luggage Rack, Wire Wheels, Windshield Wipers, etc.

02601 Ferrari 250 GTO — Yellow — Mar-96 CURRENT
Yellow Body, Wire Wheels, Chromed Windshield Wipers & Trim Pieces.

02701 Jaguar E Type, Top Down — Mar-96 CURRENT
Opalescent Dark Green Body, Black Boot Cover, Chromed Wire Wheels, Rear View Mirrors, Windshield Wipers, etc.

02801 Jaguar E Type, Top Up — Mar-96 CURRENT
Black Body, Tan Top, Chromed Wire Wheels, Rear View Mirrors, Windshield Wipers, etc.

02901 Jaguar XK 120, Top Up — Jan-96 CURRENT
British Racing Green Body with Fender Skirts, Body Color Wheels with Chromed Hubcaps, Chromed Rear View Mirrors, etc.

03001 Jaguar XK 120, Top Down — Jan-96 CURRENT
Gunmetal Gray Body with Fender Skirts, Lt. Gray Top, Body Color Wheels with Chromed Hubcaps, Chromed Rear View Mirrors, etc.

03201 MGA, Top Up — Iris Blue — Jan-96 CURRENT
Iris Blue Body, Dk. Blue Top (Shown as Removable Hardtop in Catalog), Chromed Wire Wheels, Rear View Mirrors, Windshield Wipers, etc.

03301 MGA, Top Down — Orient Red — Jan-96 CURRENT
Red Body, Chromed Wire Wheels, Rear View Mirrors, Windshield Wipers, etc.

03401 Mercedes-Benz 300 SL Roadster, Top Down — Mar-96 CURRENT
Pearl Green Body, Silver Wheels with Yellow Hubcaps, Chromed Trim, Rear View Mirrors, Windshield Wipers, etc.

03501 Mercedes-Benz 300 SL Roadster, Top Up — Mar-96 CURRENT
Black Body & Top, Silver Wheels with Red Hubcaps, Chromed Trim, Rear View Mirrors, Windshield Wipers, etc.

03701 Porsche 356, Top Up — White — Mar-96 CURRENT
White Body, Black Top, Chromed "Porsche" Wheels, Windshield Wipers, Rear View Mirrors, Door Handles, & Engine Grill.

03801 Porsche 356, Top Down — Red — Mar-96 CURRENT
Red Body, Black Boot Cover, Chromed "Porsche" Wheels, Windshield Wipers, Rear View Mirrors, Door Handles, & Engine Grill.

04001 Triumph TR3a, Top Up — Sebring White — Jan-96 CURRENT
White Body, Black Top, Chromed Wire Wheels, Luggage Rack, Rear View Mirrors, Windshield Wipers, etc.

04101 Triumph TR3a, Top Down — Black — Jan-96 CURRENT
Black Body, Tan Boot Cover, Chromed Wire Wheels, Rear View Mirrors, Windshield Wipers, etc.

04401 Mini — Viking Express — Apr-96 CURRENT
White Body, Blue Base, "VIKING EXPRESS 197," Other Rally Graphics. (1/36)

04402 Mini — Corgi Classics — May-96 CURRENT
White Body, Blue Base, Blue Rally Headlamps, "Corgi Classics 193," Other Rally Graphics. (1/36)

04403 Mr. Bean's Mini — Aug-96 CURRENT
Identical to Mattel Era 96011.

04404 Mini — Gislaved — Oct-96 CURRENT
White Body, Blue Base, Blue Rally Headlamps, "Swedish Rally 102," Other Rally Graphics. (1/36)

04405 Mini — 1996 Network Q RAC Rally — Oct-96 CURRENT
Yellow Body, Blue Base & Roof, Blue Rally Headlamps, "140," Other Rally Graphics. (1/36)

04406 Mini — Dron 1996 Monte Carlo Rally — Oct-96 CURRENT
Red Body & Base, Red Rally Headlamps, White Roof, "113," Other Rally Graphics. (1/36)

04407 Mini — Crellin/Hopkirk 1994 Monte Carlo Rally — ???-97 CURRENT
??? Body & Base, ???

04408 Mini — Byson/Bird 1996 Monte Carlo Rally — Jan-97 CURRENT
Red Body & Base, White Roof, "111," Other Rally Graphics. (1/36)

04409 Mini — Equinox — Jan-97 CURRENT
Purple Body & Base, Silver Pinstripe & Small Equinox Graphics. (1/36)

05601 Bedford CA Van — Kodak — Aug-96 CURRENT
Yellow Body "Kodak CAMERAS & FILMS," Red Wheels. (Golden Oldies Limited Edition.)

05602 Bedford CA Van — Ovaltine — Jun-96 CURRENT
Lt. Blue Body "OVALTINE." (Golden Oldies Limited Edition.)

06201 Morris J Van — Cydrax — Jul-96 CURRENT
Green Body with Black Fenders "CYDRAX," Green Wheels. (Golden Oldies Limited Edition.)

06202 Morris J Van — OXO — Oct-96 CURRENT
Blue Body with Black Fenders "BEEFY OXO," Blue Wheels. (Golden Oldies Limited Edition.)

06501 Morris 1000 Van — Shell/BP — Jun-96 CURRENT
Green/Red Body "SHELL," Red Wheels. (Golden Oldies Limited Edition.)

06502 Morris 1000 Van — Nestle's — Sep-96 CURRENT
Red Body "NESTLE'S," Yellow Wheels. (Golden Oldies Limited Edition.)

06601 Morris 1000 Advance Publicity Van — Carter's — Jul-96 CURRENT
Red & Yellow Body, Red Sign on Cab Roof, 2 Red Lights & Merry-Go-Round Horse on Rear Roof, Red Wheels

07101 Corgi Collector Club Land Rover — 1996 — Aug-96 CURRENT
Green Body & Wheels, "CCC 96" Registration Tags, Corgi Logo & "1996" on Hood. (Produced from Modified Mettoy Era C438 Dies.)

09701 ERF 8 Wheel Rigid Truck with Load — ERF — Sep-96 CURRENT
Gray Cab with Black Roof, Black Fenders, Red Wheels & Chassis, Tan Plastic Tarp on Grey Flatbed Body "E.R.F. PARTS DEPT."

09801 ERF Flatbed with Barrels & Chains, John Smith's — Mar-96 CURRENT
Green Cab & Flatbed, Black Chassis, Tan Crates, Brown Barrels.

09802 ERF Flatbed with Chains — Corgi Classics Ltd. — Mar-96 CURRENT
Yellow Body, Lt. Blue Fenders & Chassis, Yellow Wheels, Box Load with Various Corgi Logo's, "CORGI CLASSICS LIMITED AUGUST 1995." (Limited to Collector Club Mail Orders.)

09901 ERF Dodgem Truck & Box Trailer — Pat Collins — Apr-96 CURRENT
Green/White Body, Red Chassis, Dodgem Cars in Truck.

10101 ERF 5V 8 Wheel Rigid Dropside Lorry — ???-97 CURRENT
Details Not Available at Time of Publication

12401 Foden Flatbed with Barrels & Chains Fremlins — May-96 CURRENT
Black Cab & Flatbed, Red Chassis & Wheels, Tan Crates, Brown Barrels, "FREMLINS TRADITIONAL BEERS & ALES."

12501 Foden 4 Wheel Flatbed Truck — Blue Circle Cement — Feb-96 CURRENT
Yellow Cab & Flatbed, Black Chassis, Silver Flatbed Deck, Blue Wheels, "BLUE CIRCLE PORTLAND CEMENT."

12601 Foden 8 Wheel Closed Pole Truck, Silcock's — Feb-96 CURRENT
Brown Upper Cab & Box Body, Red Lower Cab & Chassis, Red Wheels, White Box Roof.

12801 Foden FG Artic & Long Platform, Edward Beck & Son Ltd. — Feb-97 CURRENT
Yellow Cab with Roof Sign, Black Chassis & Fenders, Red Wheels, Yellow Flatbed Trailer with Black Fenders & Red Wheels.

13501 Foden S21 Artic & Low Loader, GC Munton — ???-97 CURRENT
Details Not Available at Time of Publication

13701 Foden S21 Tanker, Arrow — ???-97 CURRENT
Details Not Available at Time of Publication

15101 Scammell Scarab, Express Dairy — Aug-96 CURRENT
Dark Blue/Cream Cab, Dark Blue Chassis & Trailer, Gray Crates with White Milk Bottles, "EXPRESS DAIRY."

15201 Scammell Scarab, M & B — Apr-96 CURRENT
Yellow Cab "M & B No. 301," Blue Chassis, Yellow Dropside Trailer "It's Marvellous Beer," Brown Barrels.

15202 Scammell Scarab with Barrel Load, Bulmer's Cider — Jul-96 CURRENT
Green Body, White Cab Roof, Red Chassis & Wheels, Black Barrels.

15901 Scammell Highwayman Generator Truck with Closed Pole Trailer & Dodgem Trailer, Anderton & Rowlands — Nov-96 CURRENT
Brown Cab & Trailer Bodies, Red Front Fenders, Wheels, Chassis & Trailer Chassis.

16101 Scammell Highwayman Crane Truck, Crow — May-96 CURRENT
Red Cab, Wheels Crane Body & Chassis, Black Front Fenders.

16301 Scammell Highwayman & Tanker Trailer, Guiness — Apr-96 CURRENT
Dk. Blue, Red Wheels, "Guinness."

16302 Scammell Highwayman & Tanker Trailer, Esso — Feb-96 CURRENT
Red Cab with Small "Esso" on Roof, Red Chassis & Wheels, Red Tank with Black Fittings "Esso."

16303 Scammell Highwayman & Tanker Trailer, Ever Ready — ???-97 CURRENT
Blue Cab, Tank & Wheels, White Cab Roof, Black Chassis, "EVER READY BATTERIES for life!."

16401 Scammell Highwayman & 33 FT. Trailer, Siddle C. Cook Ltd. — Apr-96 CURRENT
Red Cab, Chassis, Wheels & Flatbed Trailer, Black Fenders on Truck & Trailer, "SIDDLE C. COOK LTD." & "103."

16501 Scammell Highwayman Ballast Truck with Closed Pole Trailer & Caravan — Carters — Jan-96 CURRENT
Red/Black/White Truck "CARTERS No.1," Red/Yellow/White Trailers.

16502 Scammell Highwayman Ballast Truck with Closed Pole Trailer & Caravan — Pat Collins Fair — Jul-96 CURRENT
Red Truck & Pole Trailer Chassis, White Upper & Green Lower Trailers

16601 Scammell Highwayman Ballast Truck & Covered Land Rover Set- Pickfords — Jan-97 CURRENT
Dark Blue Ballast Truck with Black Fenders & Chassis and Red Wheels, Dark Blue Covered Land Rover w. White Roof and Red Wheels, Yellow Roof Light & 2 Chromed Spot Lights on Roof of Land Rover, "PICKFORDS" on Both Vehicles.

16701 Scammell Highwayman Artic & Low Loader, Wreckin' — Apr-97 CURRENT
Details Not Available at Time of Publication

16901 Scammell Highwayman Ballast & Low Loader — Hallett Siberman — ???-97 CURRENT
Details Not Available at Time of Publication

17501 Scammell Constructor — Siddle Cook — ???-97 CURRENT
Details Not Available at Time of Publication

17601 Scammell Constructor & 24 Wheel Low Loader — Hill of Botley — ???-97 CURRENT
Details Not Available at Time of Publication

17602 Scammell Constructor & 24 Wheel Low Loader — Sunter Bros. Ltd. — ???-97 CURRENT
Details Not Available at Time of Publication

17701 2 Scammell Constructor & 24 Wheel Low Loader — Pickfords — ???-97 CURRENT
Details Not Available at Time of Publication

18301 Bedford Pantechnicon — Watts Bros — Jun-96 CURRENT
Maroon/Ivory Body & Box, "WATTS BROS of BEVERLEY Yorks...."

18302 Bedford Pantechnicon — "Moving Story" — Apr-96 CURRENT
Green/White/Red Cab & Van Body, "ELITE INTERNATIONAL STORAGE AND REMOVALS."

18401 Bedford O Articulated Truck with Covered Dropside Trailer — British Rail Jan-96 CURRENT
Brown Cab with Cream Roof, Brown/Black Chassis, Brown Trailer & Cover "BRITISH RAILWAYS... door to door."

19201 Bedford S Emergency Tender May-96 CURRENT
Red Body with White Lower Stripe, Single Blue Light on Cab Roof, "CAMBRIDGESHIRE FIRE AND RESCUE SERVICE."

19301 Bedford S Van — Lyons Aug-96 CURRENT
Dk. Blue Body "LYONS SWISS ROLLS," Lt. Blue Wheels. (Golden Oldies Limited Edition.)

19302 Bedford S Van — Weetabix May-96 CURRENT
Yellow Body "Weetabix." (Golden Oldies Limited Edition.)

19303 Bedford S Van — Spratts Oct-96 CURRENT
Red Cab & Wheels, Red/White Body "SPRATTS." (Golden Oldies Limited Edition.)

19401 Bedford S Sack Truck — Ken Thomas Ltd. Oct-96 CURRENT
Dark Green Body, Red Chassis & Wheels, Tan Load Cover.

19601 Bedford S Bottle Truck — Bass Worthington Sep-96 CURRENT
Blue Cab, Chassis & Bed, White Cab Roof, Red Wheels, Brown Crates, "Bass Worthington."

19702 Bedford S Canvas Back Truck, Joshua Tetley Sep-96 CURRENT
Dark Blue All Over, "TETLEY'S" and Logo on Canopy.

19901 Bedford S Articulated Flatbed Truck — BRS Jan-97 CURRENT
Red Cab, Chassis, Wheels, & Flatbed Trailer, Black Fenders Including Trailer, Gray Load Cover, Red Roof Sign "BRITISH ROAD SERVICES."

20001 Bedford S Dropside Lorry — W&J Riding ???-97 CURRENT
Details Not Available at Time of Publication

20201 Bedford S Elliptical Tanker — Esso ???-97 CURRENT
Details Not Available at Time of Publication

20901 AEC Flatbed with Barrels & Chains — Truman's Aug-96 CURRENT
Black Body & Chassis, White Cab Roof, Red Wheels, "TRUMAN'S," Tan Crates, Brown Barrels.

21201 AEC Box Van — Mackintosh's Apr-96 CURRENT
Red Cab with White Roof, Black Chassis, Red Wheels, Red Box with White Roof "Mackintosh's Quality Street."

21301 AEC Articulated Truck — Ferrymasters May-96 CURRENT
White/Yellow Cab "FERRYMASTERS," Black Chassis, Yellow Wheels, White/Yellow Trailer "FERRYMASTERS THE INTERNATIONAL HAULIERS."

21401 AEC Refrigerated Articulated Truck, Wall's Mar-96 CURRENT
Lt. Blue Cab, Black Chassis & Wheels, Cream/Lt. Blue Trailer "Wall's ICE CREAM."

21402 AEC Refrigerated Articulated Truck, Daniel Stewart Jun-96 CURRENT
Maroon Cab with White Roof "DANIEL STEWART," Black Chassis, White Trailer with Maroon Stripe & A/C Unit.

21701 AEC 8 WheelClosed Pole Truck with Open Pole Trailer Dec-96 CURRENT
Brown Cab, Chassis & Box, White Roof, Red Wheels, Red & Brown Trailer

21901 Leyland Emergency Tender — St. Helen's Feb-96 CURRENT
White Body with Red Stripes, Silver Ladders, "ST. HELENS CB FIRE SERVICE."

22001 AEC Turntable Ladder Truck, West Yorkshire Fire Brigade Jan-97 CURRENT
Red & Silver Body, Red Wheels, Red/White Checkered Pattern on Doors, "WEST YORKSHIRE" in White Rectangle on Sides.

22101 Leyland Ergomatic & 33ft. Trailer — BRS Oct-96 CURRENT
Red Cab, Trailer & Wheels, Black Chassis, "BRITISH ROAD SERVICES."

23001 Ford Transcontinental with Box Trailer ???-97 CURRENT
Details Not Available at Time of Publication

24201 Leyland Elliptical Tanker, McKelvie & Co. Ltd. Jul-96 CURRENT
Brown Cab & Tank, Red Chassis & Wheels.

24202 Leyland Elliptical Tanker — Power ???-97 CURRENT
Details Not Available at Time of Publication

24301 Leyland Cylindrical Tanker, Wm. Younger & Co. Ltd. May-96 CURRENT
Dk. Blue Cab, Red Chassis, Dk. Blue/White/Red Tank "Get Younger Every Day."

24302 Leyland Cylindrical Tanker, Double Diamond Jul-96 CURRENT
Details Not Available at Time of Publication

24401 Leyland 8 Wheel Flatbed Truck — Codona's Pleasure Fairs Oct-96 CURRENT
Brown Cab & Flatbed, Black Chassis, Red Wheels.

24501 Leyland 8 Wheel Flatbed Truck with Covered Load — J&A Smith of Maddiston Mar-96 CURRENT
Dk. Brown/Cream Cab "SMITH FOR SERVICE...." Black Chassis, Dk. Brown Flatbed & Wheels, Brown Load Cover.

24601 Leyland 8 Wheel Platform Lorry & Trailer Feb-97 CURRENT
Red Cab & Flatbed Bodies "BRITISH ROAD SERVICES," Black Fenders, Black Barrel Load.

24701 Leyland Beaver Box Trailer — Michelin Sep-96 CURRENT
Yellow Cab, Black Chassis, Yellow Wheels, Silver Trailer with White Michelin Figure on Front.

24801 Leyland 8 Wheel Dodgem Truck with Caravan — Silcock's Jun-96 CURRENT
Brown Cab, White Chassis & Wheels, Brown & White Box Body & Trailer, Multi-color Dodgem Cars.

25101 Leyland 4 Wheel Rigid Truck & Container Aug-96 CURRENT
Dark Blue Cab, White Container & Bed, Red Wheels, "BRITISH ROAD SERVICES MEAT HAULAGE."

25102 Leyland Beaver 4 Wheel Rigid Truck & Container, Eddie Stobart Jan-97 CURRENT
Dark Green Cab with White Roof, Dark Green Flatbed Body, Red Chassis, Fenders & Wheels, Dark Green Container with White Roof "Eddie Stobart Ltd. Express Haulage."

25301 Leyland Lorry with Reels Feb-97 CURRENT
Dk. Blue/Powder Blue Cab "HOLT LANE TRANSPORT," Dk Blue Flat Bed Body, Red Chassis & Wheels, Black Reels "BICC."

27201 Atkinson Elliptical Tanker — Fina Fuel Oils Jan-96 CURRENT
Lt. Blue Cab & Chassis, Dk. Blue Tank "FINA FUEL OILS."

27301 Atkinson Cylindrical Tanker Nov-96 CURRENT
Red Cab with Black Roof, Black Chassis with Red Wheels, Plated Tank "BULWARK."

27501 Atkinson 8 Wheel Flatbed Truck with Crate Load — Aaron Henshall Jan-97 CURRENT
Medium Blue Cab & Flatbed, Dk. Blue Fenders, Red Chassis & Wheels, "AARON HENSHALL" Markings, 4 Crates Marked "FRAGILE."

27601 Atkinson 8 Wheel Flatbed Truck with Load Cover, F.B. Atkins May-96 CURRENT
Brown Bab with White Roof, Red Chassis & Wheels, Brown Flatbeds, Gray Covers "F. B. ATKINS. Haulage Contractor."

27602 Atkinson 8-Wheel Flatbed Truck with Load Cover, Billy Crow & Sons Mar-96 CURRENT
Lt. Blue/Red Cab "CROW'S," Red Chassis & Wheels, Black Fenders, Lt. Blue Flatbeds, Gray Covers.

27701 Atkinson Articulated Horsebox — Whitbread Mar-96 CURRENT
Brown Cab with White Roof & Black Chassis, Brown Trailer with White Roof "WHITBREAD."

27801 Atkinson Open Pole Truck Anderton & Rowland's Sep-96 CURRENT
Brown Cab & Box, Red Chassis & Wheels, White Roof.

27901 Atkinson Articulated Tanker, Vaux Breweries Ltd. Aug-96 CURRENT
Red Truck & Tank, Black Trailer Chassis, Red Wheels, "Vauxbeers"

28001 Atkinson Artic with Covered Trailer — Sutton's ???-97 CURRENT
Details Not Available at Time of Publication

30201 Thames Trader Dropside, R.A. Kembery & Sons Sep-96 CURRENT
Brown Body, Black Chassis.

30301 Thames Trader — Slumberland Sep-96 CURRENT
Red Body "Slumberland." (Golden Oldies Limited Edition.)

30302 Thames Trader — Ever Ready May-96 CURRENT
Blue Body "Ever Ready," Red Wheels. (Golden Oldies Limited Edition.)

30303 Thames Trader — Heinz Jul-96 CURRENT
Red Cab & Fenders, Yellow Body & Wheels "HEINZ 57 VARIETIES." (Golden Oldies Limited Edition.)

30304 Thames Trader Box Van — Robson's Feb-97 CURRENT
Red/White/Black Cab, Black Chassis & Wheels, Red/White Box "ROBSON'S CARLISLE, LONDON & GLASGOW SERVICE."

30401 Thames Trader Elliptical Tanker — Gulf ???-97 CURRENT
Details Not Available at Time of Publication

31001 Shap Fell Set — (Leyland & Atkinson) BRS Dec-96 CURRENT
Leyland Articulated Flatbed & Load and Atkinson 8 Wheel Rigid Flatbed Truck, both Red with Black Chassis, Red Wheels.

31002 Benzole Set — Foden FG Tanker & Morris J Van Jan-97 CURRENT
Both Trucks Yellow with Black Fenders, Black "NATIONAL BENZOLE MIXTURE" on Sides.

31003 AEC Ergomatic Artic & Scammell H'wayman Crane, Chris Miller ???-97 CURRENT
Details Not Available at Time of Publication

31004 Scammell Highwayman Artic & Bedford Artic, Wynn's ???-97 CURRENT
Details Not Available at Time of Publication

31005 Bedford S Artic & Land Rover — Shell ???-97 CURRENT
Details Not Available at Time of Publication

31006 Thames Trader Tipper & Morris 1000 Van, Wynn's ???-97 CURRENT
Details Not Available at Time of Publication

31601 Accessory Log Load Nov-96 CURRENT
Load to Fit Open Trucks or Trailers. (Does Not Include Vehicle)

31602 Accessory Cement Load Nov-96 CURRENT
Load to Fit Open Trucks or Trailers. (Does Not Include Vehicle)

31701 Eddie Stobart Set — 2 Vehicles Jan-97 CURRENT
Foden FG 8 Wheel Flatbed and Minivan, Both Decorated for "EDDIE STOBART LTD."

31702 Fairground Set — 2 Vehicles Jan-97 CURRENT
Red/Yellow ERF 4 Wheel Box Van & Circus Caravan Trailer, Yellow/White VW Van with Diagonal Roof Sign, "SADDLER'S FAMOUS FUNFAIR."

31703 "Signature" Chipperfields's Set — 4 Vehicles Nov-96 CURRENT
ERF Fire Engine, Red Ford Thames Trader Box Van, Red/White Land Rover Pick-Up, Yellow/Blue Morris 1000 Pick-Up.

31801 Road Transport Goods Depot Kit E. Stobart May-96 CURRENT
Peaked Roof Depot Building in Kit Form.

31802 Road Transport Goods Depot Kit — BRS May-96 CURRENT
Peaked Roof Depot Building in Kit Form.

33001 Routemaster Around Britain Set of 4 Jul-96 CURRENT
London Transport, Bournemouth, McGills of Barrhead, Delaine Coaches Ltd.

33201 AEC Regal Coach — Finglands Jul-96 CURRENT
Tan/Brown Body, Brown Wheels, Purple Uniformed Team on Roof, Poster on Grill.

33501 Leyland Atlantean Open Top Bus, Guide Friday May-96 CURRENT
Dk. Green/Ivory Body, "THE BRIGHTON TOUR."

33801 Bedford OB Coach — Titfield Thunderbolt Jan-97 CURRENT
Ivory Body with Blue Roof & Fenders, Blue Wheels.

34101 Burlingham Seagull Coach, Ribblesdale Batty-Holt Feb-96 CURRENT
Silver/Blue Body, Figures of Team on Roof, "BURNLEY F.C." Destination Sign, "BURNLEY FOOTBALL CLUB LEAGUE CHAMPIONS" Signs.

34701 Karrier W Trolleybus, Nottingham City Transport Mar-96 CURRENT
Dark Green Body, Cream Trim, "43 TRENT BRIDGE" Destination Signs, "DAYBROOK ARE QUALITY CLEANERS" Panels.

34702 Sunbeam Trolleybus — Ashton Under Lyme Jan-97 CURRENT
Dark Blue Body, Cream Trim, "MANCHESTER" Destination Signs.

34801 Leyland Olympian Bus — Western Welsh Jan-96 CURRENT
Red Body, "CARMARTHEN" Destination Sign, "YOU'LL BE TWICE THE MAN ON WORTHINGTON" Side Panels.

34901 Leyland Royal Tiger Bus, Manchester Corp. Jan-97 CURRENT
Red Body with Cream Window Stripe Outlined in Black Red Wheels with Whitewall Tires, " CITY CIRCLE B" Destination Sign, "CITY CIRCLE BUS SERVICE" on White Side Panels Protruding over Windows.

35001 AEC Routemaster Bus, RM5 London Transport Mar-96 CURRENT
Red Body, "8 OLD FORD" Destination Signs, "ROUTEMASTER TRY OUT YOUR NEW LONDON BUS" Panels.

35002 AEC Routemaster Bus, RM664, London Transport Jun-96 CURRENT
Silver Body, "207 HAYES STN" Destination Signs, "DAILY EXPRESS" Panels.

35003 AEC Routemaster Bus — Shillibeer Aug-96 CURRENT
Green/Cream Body, "69 WALTHAMSTOWN GARAGE" Destination Sign, "1812...." Side Panels.

35004 AEC Routemaster Bus, RM1933, London Transport Feb-97 CURRENT
Red/White/Silver Body, "24 PIMLICO" Destination Signs, "ZETTERS" Side Panels.

35201 Daimler CW Utility Bus — Green Line Apr-96 CURRENT
Red Roof, Green/White Body, "GREEN LINE 722" Destination Signs.

36601 Double Deck Tram, Open Top — Wallasey Mar-96 CURRENT
Yellow/Ivory Body, "VIA RAKE LANE" Destination Signs, "BROWN & POLSON'S" Panels.

36602 Double Deck Tram, Open Top — Leicester Mar-96 CURRENT
Dk.Blue/Ivory Body, "AYLESTONE" Destination Signs, "BUBBLY" Panels.

36603 Double Deck Tram, Open Top, Closed Ends, West Hartlepool May-96 CURRENT
Lt. Green/White Body, "SEATON" Destination Signs, "THE NORTHERN DAILY MAIL" Panels.

36701 Double Deck Tram, Fully Closed, London Transport Mar-96 CURRENT
Red/White/Gray Body, "HIGHBURY" Destination Signs, "BUY Walter's "Palm" Toffee" Panels.

36702 Double Deck Tram, Fully Closed — Dundee Mar-96 CURRENT
Gray/Ivory/Green Body, "LOCHEE" Destination Signs, "Weston's QUALITY BISCUITS" Panels.

36801 Double Deck Tram, Closed Top — Glasgow Mar-96 CURRENT
Gray/Maroon/Ivory/Orange Body, "ELDERSLIE" Destination Signs, "SAY C-W-S AND SAVE" Side Panels.

36802 Double Deck Tram, Closed Top — Leeds   Mar-96   CURRENT
Dk.Blue/White Body, "Yorkshire Relish" Panels.
36901 Single Deck Tram, Closed Top — Blackpool   Jan-97   CURRENT
Dark Green Body with Ivory Window Stripe, "FLEETWOOD" Destination Sign, "FLEETWOOD TO BLACKPOOL" Lower Side Panels.
40101 OOC — Weymann Trollybus, Maidstone Corporation   Feb-96   CURRENT
Brown/Cream Body, Brown Wheels, "BARMING FOUNTAIN INN" Destination sign, "W. J. ODDS Ltd. TIMBER" Side Panels.
40102 OOC — Park Royal Trolleybus, Hastings Tramways   Jul-96   CURRENT
Dark Green/Cream Body, "SILVERHILL 6" Destination Sign, "LONGLEY'S" Side Panels.
40201 OOC — Leyland Leopard — Midland Red   Feb-96   CURRENT
Red Body & Wheels, Black Roof, "SHREWSBURY X96" Destination Sign.
40202 OOC — AEC Reliance, British European Airways   Jun-96   CURRENT
Details Not Available at Time of Publication
40203 OOC — BET Federation — East Kent   Feb-97   CURRENT
Red/White Body, Red Wheels, ??? Destination Sign.
40301 OOC — Burlingham Seagull Coach, Wallace Arnold   Mar-96   CURRENT
Cream Body, Red Wheels, "SWITZERLAND" Destination Sign.
40302 OOC — Burlingham Seagull Coach — P.M.T   Sep-96   CURRENT
Cream/Red Body, "LONDON" Destination Sign.
40303 OOC — Burlingham Seagull Coach, Silver Star   ???-96   CURRENT
Silver Body, "MANCHESTER LIVERPOOL" Destination Sign.
40401 OOC — AEC Regent II — Kingston upon, Hull City Transport   Mar-96   CURRENT
Dk. Blue Body with White Trim, Dk. Blue Wheels, "22 COTTINGHAM RD" Destination Signs, "There's SUNSHINE in OUTSPAN" Side Panels."
40402 OOC — AEC Regent II, Newcastle Corporation   May-96   CURRENT
Details Not Available at Time of Publication
40403 OOC — AEC Regent II — Eastbourne Corp.   Aug-96   CURRENT
Dark Blue/Cream/White Body, "LANGNEY" Destination Sign, "BARKERS" Side Panels.
40404? OOC AEC Regent II, Brighton, Hove & District   Jul-96   CURRENT
Red/Tan Body, Red Wheels, "DYKE ROAD 52" Destination Sign, "TAMPLIN'S" Side Panels. (OOC Mystery Tour Mystery Bus.)
40501 OOC — Bristol L — London Transport   Feb-96   CURRENT
Green/Cream Body, Green Wheels, "32e THE COLLEGE" Destination Sign, "Horby Bond" Advertisement over Side Windows.
40601 OOC — Leyland PS1 — Western Welsh   Mar-96   CURRENT
Red Body with Cream Stripes, Black Wheels, "PENARTH" Destination Sign.
40602 OOC — Leyland PS1, Isle of Man Road Services   Jan-97   CURRENT
Red Body with Black Outlined Cream Stripe, Red Wheels, "PORT ERIN" Destination Sign.
40701 OOC — Bristol K — United Counties   Mar-96   CURRENT
Green/Ivory Body, Black Wheels, "WOOTTON 104 KEMPSTON" Destination Signs, "DU LUX DU-LITE" Side Panels.
40801 OOC — Leyland PD1 — Hants & Dorset Motor Services   Jun-96   CURRENT
Dark Green Body with Cream Stripe, "SOUTHAMPTON 47" Destination Sign, "TIZER" Side Panels.
40802 OOC — Leyland PD1 — Crosville   Sep-96   CURRENT
Green Body with Cream Stripes, "LLANDUONO 409" Destination Sign, "CROSVILLE LUXURY COACHES" Side Panels.
40901 OOC — Leyland PD2 Chesterfield Transport   Feb-96   CURRENT
Green/Cream Body, Green Wheels, "HOLYMOORSIDE 26" Destination Sign.
40902 OOC — Leyland PD2 (BMMO) A1 Service   Aug-96   CURRENT
Blue/White Body, Red Fenders, Wheels & Stripes, "KILMARNOCK" Destination Sign.
40903 OOC — Leyland PD2 (BMMO) Lytham St. Annes   Jan-97   CURRENT
Blue/White Body, Blue Wheels, "11A BLACKPOOL" Destination Sign.
41001 OOC — AEC Regent V Aberdeen Corp.   Mar-96   CURRENT
Cream/Green Body, Green Wheels, "GARTHDEE 1" Destination Signs, "McEWAN'S EXPORT" Side Panels.
41002 OOC — AEC Regent V Hebble Motor Services   Jul-96   CURRENT
Red Body & Wheels, Black Fenders, "HALIFAX 7" Destination Signs, "it's better...." Side Panels.
41101 OOC — Leyland PD2 Manchester Corp.   Mar-96   CURRENT
Red/White Body, Red Wheels, "1 LIMITED STOP GATLEY" Destination Signs.
41201 OOC — Leyland PD2 — Cardiff Corporation   Jun-96   CURRENT
Details Not Available at Time of Publication
41601 OOC — Guy Breakdown Wagon Bournemouth Corp.   Jul-96   CURRENT
Yellow Body, Black Fenders, Wheels & Crane.
42101 OOC — AEC Tower Wagon — Brighton   Oct-96   CURRENT
Red/Yellow Body, Red Tower & Wheels.
42301 OOC — Bristol Tower Wagon — Maidstone & District   May-96   CURRENT
Cream/Dk. Green Body and Tower, Dk. Green Wheels.
42501 OOC — Bedford OB Coach with Quarter Lights, Royal Blue   Sep-96   CURRENT
Cream Body, Dk. Blue Roof, Fenders & Wheels.
42502 OOC — Bedford OB Coach with Quarter, Lights, Trossachs   Nov-96   CURRENT
White Body, Red Roof, Hood Top & Fenders, White Wheels.
42601 OOC — Bedford OB Coach — Macbrayne   Oct-96   CURRENT
Red/Cream/Green Body, Black Fenders, Red Wheels.
42602 OOC — Bedford OB Coach, Mountain Goat   Dec-96   CURRENT
White Body, Green Fenders, Wheels & Side Stripe.
42701 OOC — Van-Hoolalizee Coach — Shearings   Oct-96   CURRENT
Blue Body, Orange "SHEARINGS."
42702 OOC — Van-Hoolalizee Coach, National Express   Nov-96   CURRENT
White Body, Red/Blue "RAPIDE NATIONAL EXPRESS."
42801 OOC — Dennis Dart Kingfisher Huddersfield Flagship   Jan-97   CURRENT
White Body, Red/Yellow/Blue Banner on Side "FLAGSHIP," "X37 HALIFAX" Destination Sign.
42902 OOC — Optare Delta Coach — Northumbria   Nov-96   CURRENT
Red/White/Gray Body, "NORTHUMBRIA."
43002 OOC — Leyland Olympian — Crossville   Dec-96   CURRENT
Green/White/Blue Body, Red Dragon Head "COASTLINER," "CROSVILLE WALES."
44901 Bus Station Kit   Jul-96   CURRENT
Plastic Bus Station Model
45001 OOC — Dorset Delights Set   Mar-96   CURRENT
Yellow Bournemouth Weymann Trolleybus, Red/Cream Wilts & Dorset Bristol L Bus, Cardboard Bus Station.
45002 OOC — Varsity Set   Apr-96   CURRENT
Burlingham Seagull & BET Federation.
45003 OOC — Devon Cream Set — Devon General   Jul-96   CURRENT
AEC Regent V "VISIT AQUALAND," AEC Breakdown Wagon

45201 MGB Roadster, Top Up — Primrose Yellow   Aug-96   CURRENT
(1:18 Scale) Primrose Yellow Body, Black Soft Top Up.
45400 Bus Garage Kit   Jul-96   CURRENT
Details Not Available at Time of Publication
46601 MGF Top Down — Amaranth   Aug-96   CURRENT
(1:18 Scale) Midnight Purple Body, Top Down.
50601 Mack AC Bulldog Box Van- The Katy   Aug-96   CURRENT
Red/Gray/White Body with Red Roof Rack, Red Chassis with Black Wheels, "M-K-T," "The Katy, DALLAS TEXAS, SERVES THE SOUTH WELL."
51201 1957 Chevrolet Fire Chief Car — Centerville   Jun-96   CURRENT
Red Body, White Roof, Silver Side Spear, Single Small Red Light on Roof.
51301 1957 Chevrolet Sheriff's Car — San Diego   Feb-96   CURRENT
Green Body with White Doors & Roof, Siren & 2 Spotlights on Roof.
51302 1957 Chevrolet Sheriff's Car — Lionel City   Oct-96   CURRENT
Black Body with White Doors & Roof, Siren & 2 Spotlights on Roof.
51701 American LaFrance Pumper — Staten Island   Apr-96   CURRENT
Red/White Body, Yellow/White Stripes, Closed Crew Cab, Std Front Bumper, Red/White Lightbar on Cab Roof.
51801 American LaFrance Aerial Ladder Truck Lionel City   Oct-96   CURRENT
Red Body, Closed Red/White/Blue Crew Cab, Std Front Bumper, Gray Ladders, Red/White Lightbar, Open Tiller, "LIONEL CITY FIRE DEPT."
51901 American LaFrance Aerial Ladder Truck   Jun-96   CURRENT
Red Body, Closed Crew Cab, Std Front Bumper, Gray Ladders, Red/White Lightbar, EnClosed Tiller, "BOSTON FIRE DEPT. 20."
52001 Mack CF Series Pumper — Jersey City   Mar-96   CURRENT
Yellow Body, Round Red Light on Cab Roof.
52002 Mack CF Series Pumper   May-96   CURRENT
Red/White/Blue Body, Red/White Lightbar on Roof, "LIONEL CITY FIRE CO."
52301 Mack B Series Semi with Box Trailer   Aug-96   CURRENT
Dk. Green Cab & Trailer, Black Chassis, Yellow Edged Orange Stripe, "Great Northern."
52501 Mack B Series Box Van   Aug-96   CURRENT
Dk. Blue Cab, Blue Box with Dk. Blue Roof "New York Central System," Blue Wheels.
52503 Mack B Series Box Van   Nov-96   CURRENT
Blue Cab with "L" Logo on Doors, Orange Wheels, Orange Box with Cream Roof & Blue Stripe "LIONEL CITY EXPRESS CO. MOVING STORAGE PACKING."
52601 Mack B Series Pumper, Open Cab   May-96   CURRENT
Red Body, "MALVERN FIRE COMPANY."
52602 Mack B Series Pumper, ? Cab   Jul-96   CURRENT
Red Open Cab Body, "Gettysburg Fire Dept."
52701 Mack B Series Ariel Ladder Truck, Closed Cab Chicago   May-96   CURRENT
Red Body & Trailer, Black Cab Roof, Gray Ladders, "CHICAGO FIRE DEPT. 38."
52801 Mack B Series Semi with Covered Trailer   Aug-96   CURRENT
Green Cab, Trailer & Covers "RAILWAY EXPRESS AGENCY," Black Chassis & Wheels, "R.E.X. 2095."
53901 Yellow Coach 743 Bus — Union Pacific   Feb-96   CURRENT
Blue/White Body, "CHICAGO AND NORTHWESTERN STAGES" on Left Side, "UNION PACIFIC STAGES" on Right Side, "OMAHA" Destination Sign, "1007."
53902 Yellow Coach 743 Bus — Lionel Bus Lines   Mar-96   CURRENT
Red/Dk. Blue Body, "LIONEL CITY" Destination Sign, "148."
54001 GM 4506 Bus — Surface Transportation Sys.   Feb-96   CURRENT
Cream/Maroon/Silver Body, 3 Small Lights Over Windshield, Narrow Bumper, "GM COACH" Destination Sign, "1197."
54002 GM 4506 Bus — Madison Avenue Coach Co.   Mar-96   CURRENT
Cream/Green/Green Body, 3 Large Lights Over Windshield, Wide Bumper, "4th & Madison Av" Destination Sign, "1707."
54003 GM 4505 Bus — St. Louis   Mar-96   CURRENT
White/Cream/Red Body, No Detail Over Windshield, Wide Bumper, "99 RUSSELL" Destination Sign, "4796."
54004 GM 4507 Bus — New York   Apr-96   CURRENT
Green/Gray Body, Vent Grill over Windshield, Wide Bumper, "SPECIAL" Destination Sign, "2203."
54005 GM 4502 Bus — Public Service   May-96   CURRENT
Silver/Cream/Red Body, No Detail Over Windshield, Wide Bumper, "61 NORTH BERGEN" Destination Sign.
54006 GM 4502 Bus — Wabash Railway   Aug-96   CURRENT
Dk. Blue Body, Red Edged White Stripe "WABASH RAILWAY," No Detail Over Windshield, Wide Bumper, "CREW" Destination Sign.
54007 GM 4502 Bus — Lionel Bus Lines   Apr-96   CURRENT
Cream/Dk.Blue/Orange Body, 3 Large Lights Over Windshield, "LIONEL CITY" Destination Sign.
54101 GM 4509 Bus — Greyhound Lines   May-96   CURRENT
Dk. Blue/White Body, Vent Grill over Windshield, Wide Bumper, "CHICAGO" Destination Sign, "K1468."
54102 GM 4509 Bus — Red Arrow Lines   Jun-96   CURRENT
Silver/Cream/Red Body, 3 Large Lights Over Windshield, Large Bumper, "SPRINGFIELD" Destination Sign.
54103 GM 4507 Bus — Lionel City Coach Co.   Oct-96   CURRENT
Blue/Orange/Cream Body, Vent Grill Over Windshield, Large Bumper, "CHESTERFIELD" Destination Sign.
54301 GM 5301 Bus — New York Bus   Nov-96   CURRENT
Blue/White/Silver Body, White Wheels, A/C Unit, "MANHATTAN EXPRESS" Destination sign, "New York Bus Service" on Sides.
54302 GM 5301 Bus — Lionel City Transit   Nov-96   CURRENT
Blue/Ivory/Orange/Silver Body, Orange Wheels, A/C Unit, "NEW YORK" Destination Sign, "Lionel City Transit" on Sides.
54401 GM 5301 Bus — Lionel City Bus Services   Jun-96   CURRENT
Red/White/Blue Body, No A/C Unit, No Center Exit Door, "LIONEL CITY" Destination Sign, "148."
54402 GM 5301 Bus — Greyhound   Aug-96   CURRENT
Blue/Silver/Silver Body, Silver Wheels, No A/C Unit, No Center Exit Door, "PALO ALTO" Destination Sign, "9651."
54501 GM 5301 Bus — San Diego   Nov-96   CURRENT
Blue/White Silver Body, White Wheels, No A/C Unit, "3 MISSION HILLS" Destination Sign, "Entertainment" Side Panels.
54502 GM 5301 Bus — Pennsylvania   Dec-96   CURRENT
Brown Body, Silver Wheels, No A/C Unit, ?? Center Exit Door. "PITTSBURG" Destination Sign.
54601 GM 5301 Bus — D.C. Transit   Oct-96   CURRENT
Green/Silver/White Body, A/C Unit, Center Exit Door, "G8 PRINCE GEORGE'S HOSPITAL"

Destination Sign, "5700."

54602   GM 5301 Bus — Chicago Transit Authority   **Aug-96   CURRENT**
Green/Yellow/Silver/White Body, A/C Unit, Center Exit Door, ??? Destination Sign, "CTA," "ROCKY V" Side Panels.

56901   Cameos — Chipperfieldss 10 pc. Set   **Jul-96   CURRENT**
Ten Cameo Series Trucks in Chipperfieldss Red/Light Blue/White Livery.

57601   Range Rover — Police   **Apr-96   CURRENT**
White Body, Yellow/Blue Checkered Side Decoration, Blue "POLICE" on Rear Fenders, Reversed Blue "POLICE" on Hood, Blue/White Lightbar on Roof Toward Rear.

57701   Porsche 944 — Police   **Apr-96   CURRENT**
White Body, Yellow/Red/Blue Side Stripe "POLICE," ? on Roof.

57801   BMW Saloon — Hampshire Police   **Apr-96   CURRENT**
White Body, Blue Outlined Red Side Stripe "POLICE," Blue/White Lightbar on Roof.

57901   Land Rover — U.N.   **Apr-96   CURRENT**
White Body, "MILITARY POLICE 534" on Sides.

58101   Ford Transit Van — Wiseman Dairies   **Feb-96   CURRENT**
Black/White "Cow" Pattern on Body, Oval Green "wiseman Dairies" Loge on Hood and Sides, "FRESH MILK DAILY" on Sides.

59901   Concord — British Airways   **May-96   CURRENT**
White Body, "British Airways."

60001   Mounted Police Gift Set   **May-96   CURRENT**
White 1:36 Land Rover & Horsebox, Outlined Red Side Stripe on Both with Shield & Black "POLICE," Brown Horse with Mount.

?????   Corgi Roadshow Vehicle   **Aug-96   CURRENT**
Ford Aeromax Racing Transporter Casting, Yellow/Blue Body, "Corgi Classics Roadshow"

?????   Shell Racing Transporter Vehicle   **Nov-96   CURRENT**
Kenworth Racing Transporter Casting, Black/White Body, "Shell" Racing Decorations on Each Side of Trailer, One Side for Indy Racing, Other for Busch Car Racing, Christmas Promotion at Shell Stations Marketed with 3 1:64 Racers from Another Manufacturer.

?????   OOC — Leyland (?) DD Bus, Kowloon Motor Bus Co.   **Jan-97   CURRENT**
Red Body with White Roof, Crest on Upper Sides (Ltd. Edition: 5000)

Section 4
Appendices

British/U.S. Glossary of Terms

British Term:	American Term:
Artic	Semi, Tractor-trailer
Bonnet	Hood
Boot	Trunk Lid, Deck Lid
Box Van	Delivery Truck
Breakdown Truck	Tow Truck, Wrecker
Estate Car	Station Wagon
Hood	Convertible Top
Horsebox	Horse Trailer
Lorry	Large Truck
Milk Float	Milk Truck
Overriders	Bumper Guards
Petrol	Gasoline
Refuse Wagon	Garbage Truck
Saloon	Sedan
Tipper	Dump Truck
Tram	Trolley Car, Street Car
Transfer	Decal
Tyres	Tires
Windscreen	Windshield
Wing Windows	Vent Windows

Diecast Model Hobby Glossary of Terms

Variation: Model based upon the same casting or model number as another, but with easily recognizable or significant differences.

Sub-variation: Model outwardly similar to another, but with some minor difference.

Original: As-produced by the original manufacturer.

Restored: Modified to resemble the as-produced condition by means of repair, replacement of parts, and/or exterior finish.

Mint (M): Condition exactly as-produced without wear, soil, corrosion, oxidation, scrapes, chips, cracks, or scuffs.

Near-Mint (NM): Mint except for minor soil or minor oxidation as would occur through exposure to air or careful handling over time.

Excellent (E): Condition just below Mint at which models may have minor scuffing, edge wear, or fading, but without chips, cracks, scratches, or damage.

Very Good (VG): Condition below Excellent at which models may have some chips, scratches, or corrosion, but without damage or missing parts and with most of the original finish remaining.

Chipped (CH): Additional suffix to condition used by some vendors identifying a model of a higher condition except for one obvious blemish or chip in the finish.

Boxed (B): Suffix to condition signifying inclusion of the original box. The box is considered to be in Excellent condition unless otherwise specified.

Card: Packaging in which a model is surrounded on 5 sides by a clear vacuum formed plastic "bubble" and sealed to a flat cardboard backing card.

Crimping: A process by which two very tight fitting objects are forced together by applying pressure.

Peening: A process by which an object's shape is changed by repeated impact.

Vacuum Forming: A process by which a heated flat sheet of plastic is drawn down over a shaped "form" by applying a vacuum.

Stamping: A process by which sheet metal is bent and cut to shape by force between two "dies."

Die Casting: A process by which an object is formed from molten metal which is injected under pressure into the cavity of a 'die set' and cooled.

Injection Molding: A process similar to Die Casting except molten plastic is injected into a "mold."

Deflashing: A process by which excess material is removed from an object by tumbling in an abrasive material.

Tampo Printing: A process by which ink or paint may be transferred from a flat plate to an irregularly shaped object by means of a soft pad.

Mask Spraying: A process by which sprayed paint is prevented from coating some part of a surface, being blocked by a reusable 'mask'.

Silk Screening: A process by which ink or paint is applied to a surface by being forced through the weave of a specially prepared silk screen which acts as a mask for the pattern to be applied.

Vacuum Plating: A process by which a reflective metallic coating is applied to a surface by being sprayed into a chamber under vacuum.

Flocking: A process by which a surface is sprayed with an adhesive then pressure coated with loose fibers giving a "fuzzy" texture.

Decal (Transfer): A decoration printed on a transparent media which is soaked from a backing paper with water and applied to a surface, being held in place by a clear water-soluble adhesive.

Label (Sticker): A decoration printed onto a paper or plastic sheet which has an adhesive backing and is cut to shape. It is peeled from a waxed carrier sheet and applied to the dry surface of an object.

Flash: Excess material from a die casting or molding process formed by molten material entering the cracks between parts of the die or mold.

Corgi Timeline

1934 —Mettoy Co. Ltd. founded in Northampton.

1938 —First stamped metal toys produced in-house by company.

1941 —Toy production stops as production is converted to defense contracts.

1945 —Toy production resumes. Plastic toys and stamped steel toys manufac tured.

1948 —Swansea factory leased.

1950 —Mettoy's First Die Cast Vehicles produced, lasting until 1952.

1952 —Company headquarters moved to Swansea except for design and devel opment.

1955 —Promotional CWS Soft Drink Truck Produced, only Pre-Corgi model to be later incorporated into Corgi range (with addition of windows and color change.

1956 —Corgi Toys introduced, first diecast toys on market with windows. Most had standard and mechanical (friction motor) versions.

1957 —Corgi Majors introduced with introduction of 1101 Carrimore Car Trans porter. Corgi Gift Sets introduced with GS1

1957 —"Castoys" reintroduced lasting through 1959, overlapping Corgi Produc tion. (Note: Windows were fitted to late Castoys!)

1959 —"Glideamatic" spring suspension and vacuum formed interior introduced on 222 Renault Floride, later retrofit to others.

1959 —Last Corgi with friction motor produced.

1960 —Chipperfield Circus models introduced.

1960 —Opening hood introduced on 218 Aston Martin DB4. Model also had early cast wheels.

1961 —Shaped wheels, vacuum-plated parts, "jeweled" headlights, opening trunk, removable spare tire, and self-centering steering introduced on 224 Bentley Continental. Shaped spun aluminum wheels phased into production on most models.

1961—Corgi Kits introduced.

1961 —Vacuum plated "Trophy" models first produced without Corgi name for Marks & Spencer.

1962 —Battery powered flashing lights introduced on 437 Cadillac Ambulance.

1963 —"Trans-O-Light" light tubes introduced on 441 VW Toblerone Van.

1963—Retractable headlamps introduced on 310 Chevrolet Corvette Stingray.

1963—Opening doors and tipping front seats introduced on 241 Ghia L6.4.

1963 —Lines Bros. (maker of rival Spot-On Toys) takes over Meccano (maker of arch-rival Dinky Toys). Spot-On Toys phased-out.

1964 —Corgi Classics introduced.

1964 —Husky Toys introduced as a private brand produced for Woolworth by Mettoy.

1964 —Operating windshield wipers introduced on 247 Mercedes Benz 600 Pull man.

1965 —First Character Car, James Bond Aston Martin, introduced.

1965 —Musical Chimes fitted to 474 Musical Walls Ice Cream Van.

1965—Roof operated steering and mud flaps introduced on 256

Volkswagen 1200 in East African Safari trim.

1966 —Batmobile and Man from UNCLE car introduced.

1967 —Backlit simulated television and flock sprayed "carpet" introduced on 262 Lincoln Continental Executive Limousine.

1967 —Green Hornet car introduced.

1968—Take-Off-Wheels introduced on 341 Mini-Marcos GT 850. Reworked models previously issued with standard wheels include Rover 2000 and Oldsmobile Toronado.

1968 —Extending aerial ladder introduced on 1143 American LaFrance Aerial Rescue truck.

1968 —Chitty-Chitty-Bang-Bang introduced.

1968 —Mattel Inc. launches Hot Wheels line of die-cast toy cars and radically changes the toy car market with their low-friction wheels and track sets. Other brands see an instant sales drop and scramble to revise their products to compete.

1969 —Fire destroys warehouse at Swansea factory. Production record, and much stock lost.

1969 —Whizzwheels introduced on 344 Ferrari 206 Dino Sport. Initial wheels used wide soft plastic tires on metal wheels with Nylon hubs. All-plastic Wizzwheels introduced the following year. Most existing models would be retrofitted or discontinued.

1969 —Corgi Rockets released to combat Hot Wheels. Track sets available for a short time until potential litigation from Mattel over patent rights forces their removal from sale. Rockets cars withdrawn when Whizzwheels fitted to Juniors.

1969 —Qualitoys line of rugged toys for younger children introduced.

1970 —Husky Toys renamed Corgi Juniors and mass marketed. Some Husky model numbers reduced by 50 to compact number series.

1971 —Track sets for larger Corgi models released briefly, then withdrawn due to potential Mattel litigation over patent rights..

1972 —Formula 1 cars introduced

1972 —Corgi Aircraft introduced, produced in Hong Kong.

1972 —Tekno (diecast toy rival from Denmark) closes.

1973 —Larger 1/36 scale introduced on 323 Ferrari Daytona.

1973 —Corgi Tanks introduced on 901 British Centurion Mk III Tank.

1974—1/18 scale introduced on 190 John Player Special Lotus.

1974 —Water squirter introduced on 1103 Pathfinder Airport Crash Truck.

1978 —St. Michael range of rebadged Corgi Toys introduced by Marks & Spen cer, most with different graphics than used on existing Corgi models.

November 30, 1979—Meccano Ltd. (maker of arch-rival Dinky Toys) closes.

1981 —Corgitronics introduced. First attempt to incorporate microchip sound de vices into diecast toys. Corgitronics not continued after failure of Mettoy. (Toys were ahead of their time. Market for toy cars with sound had not yet developed.)

1982 —Lesney (maker of rival Matchbox Toys) calls in receivers. Matchbox prod uct line bought by Universal Toys and production moved to the Far East.

1982 —Corgi Classics reintroduced with 801 1957 Ford Thunderbird.

April 1983—*Lledo (new rival) formed from parts of the bankrupt Lesney assets and begins production of diecast models targeted to adults.*

October 31, 1983—*Mettoy Co. Ltd. calls in receivers.*

March 29, 1984—*Corgi Toys Ltd. formed to continue the production of Corgi Toys. Rights for Dragon computer sold to third party company. Other Mettoy prod ucts not continued.*

1984—*Corgi Junior Product line Renumbered from E series to J series.*

1984—*Corgi Collector Club formed to create closer link between collectors and Corgi Toys Ltd.*

1985—*Corgi Classics commercial vehicles introduced with Thorneycroft Van*

1986—*Thirtieth anniversary of the introduction of Corgi Toys.*

1986—*Corgi Toys Ltd. voted British Toy Company of the Year by the National Association of Toy Retailers.*

1987—*Dinky Toys reintroduced as a nostalgia product line by Universal Match box, directly in competition with Corgi Classics and Lledo Days-Gone mod els.*

December 18, 1989—*Mattel Inc. purchases Corgi Toys Ltd.*

1990—*All Corgi products introduced or in production renumbered into Mattel- compatible system.*

1990—*First Corgi Classics vehicles made in China are introduced. (Some Jun iors made in the Far East as far back as the Mettoy Era.)*

January, 1991—*Swansea factory and offices closed; Corgi moves to Mattel UK Headquarters in Leicester.*

1991—*Chitty-Chitty-Bang-Bang reissued.*

1992—*Tyco Toys Inc. purchases rival Universal Matchbox.*

1994—*New Chipperfields Circus Series introduced. New series based on actual Chipperfields vehicles, not reissues of 1960s toys.*

1994—*Original Omnibus Co. line of 1:76 scale model busses introduced. OOC models directly in competition with models produced by Exclusive First Edi tions (new rival in 1:76 scale segment of the market.)*

1995—*Corgi Heritage Center opened to house factory museum collection.*

August 7, 1995—*Corgi Classics Ltd. formed from management buyout from Mattel. Auto-City line (former Corgi Junior and Haulers lines) remains with Mattel and becomes the Hot Wheels Auto-City line.*

1996—*Fortieth anniversary of the introduction of Corgi Toys.*

1996—*New numbering scheme introduced for new models, grouping models using the same castings together.*

1996—*Golden Oldies Limited Edition models and Corgi Classic of the Month Club introduced.*

1996—*Lledo (rival of Corgi Classics) launches separate "Vanguards" range of highly detailed scale vintage vehicles to compete directly with the Corgi Classics range, which itself is steadily improving the level of detail on the models introduced.*

1996—*Former junior-size Corgi vehicles begin appearing in Hot Wheels pack aging outside of the United States, including some old stock models which are still marked "Corgi" on the base.*

1996—*Corgi reenters the 1/18 scale market with MGF and MGB models.*

1996—*Corgi Classics Ltd. purchases some of the assets of Bassett Lowke Ltd., which had ceased production prior to the transaction.*

Bibliography

Corgi Toys catalogs, Husky Toys catalogs, and Corgi Juniors catalogs: The Mettoy Company Ltd. (PLC), 1960-1983.

Corgi Toys catalogs and Corgi Classics catalogs. Corgi Toys Ltd., 1984-1989.

Corgi Toys, Corgi Classics, Corgi American Classics, and Corgi, The Original Omnibus Company catalogs, and Corgi Racing Collectibles catalogs: Corgi Sales, Mattel UK Ltd, 1990-1995.

Corgi Classics Catalog, The Original Omnibus Catalog, and *The Golden Oldies Collection Catalog.* Corgi Classics Ltd., 1995-1996.

Pownall, Susan, Ed., *Corgi Collector Magazine,* Issues 7-85. Corgi Collector Club.

Bailey, Roger, Ed., *Classic Toys Magazine,* Vol. 2, Issues 10 and 11. Classic Toys Ltd.

West, Richard, Ed., *Model Collector Magazine,* Vol. 10, Issues 2-10. Link House Magazines Ltd.

Hammel, Tom, Ed. or Bunte, Jim, Ed., *Collecting Toys Magazine,* Vol. 1, Issue 1 through Vol. 4, Issue 4. Kalmbach Publishing Co.

Korbeck, Sharon, Ed. or Hammel, Tom, Ed., *Toy Collector and Price Guide Magazine:* Vol. 5, Issue 3, Vol. 7, Issues 1 and 2. Krause Publications.

Korbeck, Sharon, Ed., *Toy Shop Magazine,* Vol. 9, Issues 6-17. Krause Publications.

Mack, Charles, Ed., *Matchbox U.S.A. Magazine:* Vol. 7, Issue 4. Matchbox U.S.A.

Van Cleemput, Marcel R., *The Great Book of Corgi.* New Cavendish Books, 1989.

Force, Edward, *Corgi Toys.* Schiffer Publishing Ltd., 1984 (Revised 1991).

Richardson, Mike & Sue, *The Hornby Companion Series Vol. 4— Dinky Toys & Modelled Miniatures.* New Cavindish Books, 1981.

Wieland, James and Force, Edward, *Corgi Toys —The Ones With Windows.* Motorbooks International, 1981.

Wieland, James and Force, Edward, *Tootsietoys — World's First Diecast Models.* Motorbooks International, 1980.

Parker, Bob, *The Complete Book of Hot Wheels.* Schiffer Publishing Ltd., 1995.

Stoneback, Bruce and Diane, *Matchbox Toys.* Chartwell Books Inc., 1993.

Case, Roger and Korbeck, Sharon, Ed., *Toys and Prices—1996 Third Edition.* Krause Publications, 1996.

Huxford, Sharon and Bob, Ed., *Schroeder's Collectable Toys Antique to Modern Price Guide.* Collector Books Division, Schroeder Publishing Co. Inc., 1996.

O'Brien, Richard, Ed., *Collecting Toys No. 7-A Collector's Identification and Value Guide.* Books Americana Inc., 1995.

O'Brien, Richard, Ed., *Collecting Toy Cars and Trucks—Identification and Value Guide.* Books Americana Inc., 1994.

The Encyclopedia of Corgi Toys contains all of the information known to the author as of the publication date. There are certain to be some additional variations which have not been included. If a model which isn't *exactly* described in the variation listings is found, please photocopy, fill out and mail this form to the address below. (One report for each model.) Please be as descriptive as possible (i.e.: "metallic royal blue," not "dark blue"). Attach sketches if they are helpful in explaining the model. Your data may then be incorporated into future revisions of *The Encyclopedia of Corgi Toys.* Thank you for your help.

Bill Manzke

Corgi/Husky/Corgi Junior Variation Report Form

YOUR NAME AND ADDRESS: (optional)

Description of Model

(CIRCLE ONE): Corgi, Husky, Corgi Jr., Rockets, Other:

NUMBER: (If known)

DOES MODEL HAVE A BOX? (Yes/No) If Yes, list copyright date (on bottom?). Describe box:

DESCRIBE WORDING/NUMBERS ON BASE OF MODEL:

PRIMARY BODY COLOR:

2ND BODY COLOR:

BASE COLOR AND TYPE:

INTERIOR COLOR:

COLOR OR TINT OF WINDOWS:

COLOR OF GRILL/BUMPERS/ETC.:

DESCRIBE LABELS/DECALS/PRINTING:

WHEEL TYPE: Smooth, Shaped, Wire, Cast (fine fins), Cast (heavy spokes), Other:

AXLE TYPE: Crimped to wheels, peened ends with wheels free, Whizzwheels, other:

TIRE TYPE: Smooth ("Rubber"),Tread ("Plastic"), Wide with tread ("Thick Plastic"), Other:

Operating Features

FIGURES/LOOSE PARTS: (included with model)

PRESENT CONDITION OF MODEL:

WAS MODEL PART OF A SET? (Yes/No) If yes, please describe:

COULD MODEL BE FACTORY GOOF? (Yes/No) **PRE-PRODUCTION:** (Yes/No)

ARE YOU MODEL'S ORIGINAL OWNER? (Yes/No)

ARE YOU UNCERTAIN OF THE AUTHENTICITY OF ANY PART OF MODEL: (Yes/No)

DESCRIBE ANYTHING ELSE UNUSUAL ABOUT MODEL WHICH IS NOT STATED ABOVE: (Use the back of this form if necessary).

Mail completed report form to:

CORGI TOY VARIATION REPORTS
c/o Schiffer Publishing Ltd.
77 Lower Valley Rd.,
Atglen, PA 19310-9717

If you prefer e-mail, contact:

manzke.madhouse@mci2000.com

You will receive an acknowledgement by mail.